Lecture Notes of the Institute for Computer Sciences, Social Informatics and Telecommunications Engineering 603

The LNICST series publishes ICST's conferences, symposia and workshops.

LNICST reports state-of-the-art results in areas related to the scope of the Institute.

The type of material published includes

- Proceedings (published in time for the respective event)
- Other edited monographs (such as project reports or invited volumes)

LNICST topics span the following areas:

- General Computer Science
- E-Economy
- E-Medicine
- Knowledge Management
- Multimedia
- Operations, Management and Policy
- Social Informatics
- Systems

Angel A. Juan · José-Luis Guisado-Lizar ·
María-José Morón-Fernández ·
Elena Perez-Bernabeu
Editors

Simulation Tools and Techniques

16th EAI International Conference, SIMUtools 2024
Bratislava, Slovakia, December 9–10, 2024
Proceedings

Springer

Editors
Angel A. Juan
Universitat Politècnica de València
Valencia, Spain

José-Luis Guisado-Lizar
Universidad de Sevilla
Seville, Spain

María-José Morón-Fernández
Universidad de Sevilla
Seville, Spain

Elena Perez-Bernabeu
Universitat Politècnica de València
Valencia, Spain

ISSN 1867-8211 ISSN 1867-822X (electronic)
Lecture Notes of the Institute for Computer Sciences, Social Informatics and Telecommunications Engineering
ISBN 978-3-031-87344-7 ISBN 978-3-031-87345-4 (eBook)
https://doi.org/10.1007/978-3-031-87345-4

This Springer imprint is published by the registered company Springer Nature Switzerland AG
The registered company address is: Gewerbestrasse 11, 6330 Cham, Switzerland

Preface

We are delighted to introduce the proceedings of the 16th edition of the European Alliance for Innovation (EAI) International Conference on Simulation Tools and Techniques (SIMUtools 2024). This conference brought together researchers, developers, and practitioners from around the world who are leveraging and developing research work in the fields of systems modeling and simulation, including modeling techniques, simulation software, combination of artificial intelligence and simulation, application of high-performance computing to simulation, simulation performance, and applications to a wide variety of fields, including for example wildfire risk, water infrastructures, road traffic, electric vehicles, logistics, medical sciences, and communication networks. The conference was dedicated to fostering interdisciplinary collaborative research in these areas and its application domains.

SIMUtools 2024 was hosted at the Crowne Plaza Bratislava Hotel in Bratislava (Slovakia) on 9th and 10th December 2024. The technical program consisted of 26 full papers in oral presentation sessions at the main conference track, authored by scientists from a large variety of countries from Europe, America, and Asia. These papers were selected from 63 submissions. Each submission was reviewed following a single-blind process with a minimum of 3 reviews per paper. Aside from the high-quality technical paper presentations, the technical program also featured three keynote speeches. The first one, entitled "The Difficulty of Adjusting Difficulty in Proof-of-Work Blockchains" was given by William Knottenbelt, from Imperial College London, UK. The second one, entitled "Simulation Modeling in the Digital Twin Era" was given by Stephan Onggo, from the University of Southampton, UK. And the third one, entitled "Facilitating Resilience during an African Swine Fever Outbreak in the Austrian Pork Supply Chain through Hybrid Simulation Modelling" was given by Patrick Hirsch, from BOKU University, Austria.

Coordination with the Steering Committee Members, Imrich Chlamtac, Gabriel Wainer, Angel A. Juan, José-Luis Guisado-Lizar, José Luis Sevillano Ramos, and Helen D. Karatza, was essential for the success of the conference. We sincerely appreciate their constant support and guidance. It was also a great pleasure to work with such an excellent Conference Manager, Veronika Kissova, and Organizing Committee team, formed by Angel A. Juan, José-Luis Guisado-Lizar, Gabriel Wainer, María-José Morón-Fernández, Elena Perez-Bernabeu, Dagmar Cagáňová, David Ragel Díaz-Jara, Xabier A. Martin, Betsaida Alexandre Barajas, Celia Osorio, Patricia Carracedo, Veronika Tsertsvadze, Daniel Cagigas Muñiz, Javier Panadero, Agustín Riscos-Núñez, and Veronika Kissova, for their hard work in organizing and supporting the conference. In particular, we are grateful to the Technical Program Committee, and to the Reviewers, who completed the peer-review process for the technical papers and helped to put together a high-quality technical program. We are also grateful to all the authors who trusted us and submitted their papers to the SIMUtools 2024 conference.

We strongly believe that the SIMUtools conference provides a good forum for all researchers, developers, and practitioners to discuss all science and technology aspects that are relevant to simulation tools and techniques. We also expect that future SIMU-tools conferences will be as successful and stimulating as indicated by the contributions presented in this volume.

December 2024

Angel A. Juan
José-Luis Guisado-Lizar
Gabriel Wainer

Organization

Steering Committee

Imrich Chlamtac	University of Trento, Italy
Gabriel Wainer	Carleton University, Canada
Angel A. Juan	Universitat Politècnica de València, Spain
José-Luis Guisado-Lizar	University of Seville, Spain
José Luis Sevillano Ramos	University of Seville, Spain
Helen D. Karatza	Aristotle University of Thessaloniki, Greece

Organizing Committee

General Chair

Angel A. Juan	Universitat Politècnica de València, Spain

General Co-chairs

José-Luis Guisado-Lizar	University of Seville, Spain
Gabriel Wainer	Carleton University, Canada

TPC Chairs

Angel A. Juan	Universitat Politècnica de València, Spain
José-Luis Guisado-Lizar	University of Seville, Spain

TPC Co-chairs

María-José Morón- Fernández	University of Seville, Spain
Elena Perez-Bernabeu	Universitat Politècnica de València, Spain
Dagmar Cagáňová	Newton University, Czechia

Web Chairs

David Ragel Díaz-Jara	University of Seville, Spain
Xabier A. Martin	Universitat Politècnica de València, Spain

Publicity and Social Media Chairs

Betsaida Alexandre Barajas	University of Seville, Spain
Celia Osorio	Universitat Politècnica de València, Spain

Workshops Chair

Patricia Carracedo	Universitat Politècnica de València, Spain

Sponsorship and Exhibits Chair

Veronika Tsertsvadze	Universitat Politècnica de València, Spain

Publications Chairs

Daniel Cagigas Muñiz	University of Seville, Spain
Javier Panadero	Universitat Autònoma de Barcelona, Spain

Posters and PhD Track Chair

Agustín Riscos-Núñez	University of Seville, Spain

Conference Manager and Local Chair

Veronika Kissova	EAI – European Alliance for Innovation n.o., Slovakia

Technical Program Committee

Abdurrahman Alshareef	King Saud University, Saudi Arabia
Agustín Riscos-Núñez	University of Seville, Spain
Angel A. Juan	Universitat Politècnica de València, Spain
Betsaida Alexandre Barajas	University of Seville, Spain
Daniel Cagigas Muñiz	University of Seville, Spain
David Ragel Díaz-Jara	University of Seville, Spain
Elena Cerezuela Escudero	University of Seville, Spain
Elena Perez-Bernabeu	Universitat Politècnica de València, Spain
Fernando Díaz del Río	University of Seville, Spain
Francesco Quaglia	Università di Roma Tor Vergata, Italy
Javier Panadero	Autonomous University of Barcelona, Spain

José-Luis Guisado-Lizar	University of Seville, Spain
Lei Shi	South East Technological University, Ireland
Linbo Luo	Xidian University, China
Maria Blas	INGAR CONICET – Universidad Tecnológica Nacional, Argentina
María-José Morón-Fernández	University of Seville, Spain
Moritz Schweppenhäuser	Fraunhofer Institute FOKUS, Germany
Patricia Carracedo	Universitat Politècnica de València, Spain
Samuel Kounev	University of Würzburg, Germany
Srikanth B. Yoginath	Oak Ridge National Laboratory, USA
Xiao Song	Beijing University, China

Contents

Simulation Tools and Methods

Sim-Learnheuristics: A Tool for Decision Making Under Stochastic and Dynamic Conditions

Angel A. Juan[1,3](✉), Majsa Ammouriova[2], Veronika Tsertsvadze[1], and Celia Osorio[1]

[1] Universitat Politècnica de València, Alcoy 03801, Spain
[2] German Jordanian University, Amman 11180, Jordan
maysa.ammouri@gju.edu.jo
[3] Euncet Business School, Terrassa 08225, Spain
ajuanp@gmail.com

Abstract. Complex decision-making processes, especially those associated with NP-hard optimization problems, become even more challenging when faced with uncertainty and dynamic conditions. Traditional approaches like simulation and heuristics provide effective but limited solutions, often unable to adapt to changing environments. In this paper, we introduce sim-learnheuristics, a methodological tool combining simulation, metaheuristics, and machine learning. Sim-learnheuristics employ simulation models to model uncertainty, metaheuristic algorithms to efficiently explore the solution space, and machine learning methods to guide and adapt the heuristic process based on evolving conditions. We describe the methodology, provide pseudo-code, and discuss the main parts of an implementation that illustrates the adaptability of this approach. A review of related work is included, showing the potential of sim-learnheuristics to improve decision making in real-life scenarios under dynamic and stochastic conditions.

Keywords: Simulation · Metaheuristics · Machine Learning

1 Introduction

Given that real-life scenarios are subject to dynamic and uncertainty conditions, both machine learning (ML) and simulation techniques are frequently employed for decision making across various sectors such as manufacturing, logistics, transportation, healthcare, finance, smart cities, sustainable transportation, and telecommunications [3]. Stochastic uncertainty is represented using either theoretical or empirical probability distributions [14]. A logical model of the

Supported by the Investigo Program (INVEST/2023/304), Horizon Europe (HORIZON-MISS-2021-CIT-02-01-101096405), and the Spanish Ministry of Science and Innovation (PID2022-138860NB-I00 and RED2022-134703-T).

A. A. Juan et al. (Eds.): SIMUtools 2024, LNICST 603, pp. 3–12, 2025.
https://doi.org/10.1007/978-3-031-87345-4_1

system is built, and simulations are run to evaluate the system performance under different scenarios, each representing a possible configuration of the system [8]. Similarly, machine learning models are frequently employed to predict the behavior of complex processes [5].

However, ML methods or simulation models alone lack the ability to optimize complex systems, as they do not provide the tools to efficiently explore the vast solution spaces typical of complex decision-making processes that can be modeled as combinatorial optimization problems [2]. For this reason, complex decision making under dynamic and stochastic scenarios requires combining simulation with ML and an optimization engine [9]. Examples include determining the best distribution plan in a vehicle routing problem (VRP) with dynamic travel times and random demands [12], optimizing a scheduling plan in a flow shop with dynamic processing times and random machine failures [13], or configuring assets in a portfolio optimization problem with a dynamic budget and stochastic returns [10]. The optimization problems underlying these decision-making processes are usually NP-hard in nature, which means that metaheuristics are required to provide high-quality solutions within reasonable timeframes [7].

Simheuristics are designed to solve large-scale, NP-hard combinatorial optimization problems that include stochastic elements, such as probabilistic constraints or stochastic objective functions [2]. During the last decade, simheuristics have become a popular method for addressing stochastic optimization problems [6]. However, real-world decision making often involves not only randomness but also dynamic factors that change over time or fluctuate based on environmental conditions. For example, travel times can vary due to traffic or weather conditions, customer demands may adjust based on external influences or the order of deliveries, machine processing times can change depending on the machine's fatigue level, and resource availability may shift due to real-time variables. In such situations. To account for these dynamic factors, ML models, especially learnheuristics [1], can be quite effective. Combining learnheuristics with simheuristics, known as sim-learnheuristics, can significantly enhance the ability of simheuristics to handle dynamic elements. The ML component improves predictions of dynamic inputs, feeding them into the simheuristic algorithm. This integration enables better forecasting of how variables will change, resulting in more adaptive and robust solutions. Thus, sim-learnheuristics, the integration of simulation models with ML methods and metaheuristic algorithms, is an effective way to support real-world decision making under uncertainty and dynamic conditions.

This paper provides an overview of sim-learheuristics, including key concepts, recent applications, and ongoing research directions. The rest of the manuscript is structured as follows: Sect. 2 discusses the dynamic and stochastic optimization problems that can be addressed with simlearnheuristics. Section 3 explains the core methodology. Section 4 reviews some recent papers that illustrate the use of this hybrid tool. Section 5 summarizes computational results of the aforementioned papers. Finally, Sect. 6 concludes the paper.

2 Stochastic and Dynamic Problems

Many combinatorial optimization problems in industries such as transportation, logistics, manufacturing, energy, and finance are still often modeled using deterministic and static approaches. However, deterministic models fail to account for the inherent uncertainty and dynamism found in real-world decision making, such as fluctuating travel or processing times, random or dynamic customer demands, etc. Part of the reason for this is the increased complexity that dynamic and stochastic inputs or constraints introduce into the modeling and solving process. As a result, numerous studies focus on finding optimal solutions to deterministic versions of these problems rather than high-quality solutions that incorporate dynamic and stochastic elements. This approach often leads to solutions that are optimal for a model that does not fully represent the real-world conditions. When such deterministic solutions are applied in practice, they frequently prove to be suboptimal.

Sim-learnheuristic algorithms aim to bridge this gap by incorporating stochastic and dynamic elements into the solution-building process. Typically, the stochastic and dynamic optimization models used will have to optimize an objective function:

$$f(s) = E[\Phi(s, X)] \tag{1}$$

subject to:

$$Pr\Big(g_i(s, X) \leq l_i(X)\Big) \leq t_i \qquad \forall i \in I \tag{2}$$

$$Pr\Big(g_j(s, X) > l_j(X)\Big) \leq t_j \qquad \forall j \in J \tag{3}$$

$$g_k(s) \leq t_k \qquad \forall k \in K \tag{4}$$

$$s \in S \tag{5}$$

In Eq. (1), s represents a candidate solution (a configuration of decision variables), and S is the space of all possible solutions (Eq. (5)). The function $\Phi(s, X)$ in Eq. (1) is a function which value depends on s and on vector X composed of both random variables and dynamic inputs. Usually, the expected value of $\Phi(s, X)$ is the goal to be optimized. For example, the function might represent the travel time in the VRP that is affected by routes (s) and unexpected delays on these routes.

Equations (2) and (3) define probabilistic constraints. For instance, the probability that the number of serviced customers in solution s, $g_i(s, X)$, falls below a certain threshold $l_i(X)$ is less than a user-defined limit t_i (Eq. (2)). Likewise, the probability that a time delay in solution s, $g_j(s, X)$, exceeds an upper limit $l_j(X)$ is constrained by a predefined threshold t_j (Eq. (3)). Functions $g_i(s, X)$ and $g_j(s, X)$ depend on solution s and variable X. Equation (4) refers to standard deterministic constraints that are common in combinatorial optimization problems that have no probabilistic component.

3 Sim-Learnheuristics Methodology

When addressing a deterministic optimization problem, it is often assumed that optimal or near-optimal solutions will still perform well when moderate uncertainty or dynamism is introduced. For example, in a VRP, a routing plan that performs near-optimally under deterministic conditions is expected to continue performing effectively even if some travel times exhibit slight variations. Similarly, in a deterministic flow-shop problem, job configurations that guarantee a low makespan will likely provide a reasonably good makespan even when job processing times suffer from moderate variability.

For any solution configuration s in a deterministic optimization problem with objective function $f(s)$, its value under deterministic conditions is $determ(s) = f(s)$, while its expected value under stochastic and dynamic conditions is $stoch - dyn(s) = E[f(s)]$. Under moderate uncertainty, it is reasonable to expect a strong positive correlation between $determ(s)$ and $stoch - dyn(s)$, meaning that high-performing solutions for the deterministic case are also likely to perform well on average in the stochastic and dynamic case. However, this correlation does not necessarily imply that the best deterministic solution will also be the best under stochastic and dynamic conditions. For instance, solution s_1 might outperform solution s_2 in the deterministic scenario, yet s_2 could excel over s_1 in the stochastic and dynamic case. In the VRP example, this could occur if s_2 provides a more balanced route distribution, making it more resilient to moderate fluctuations in travel times or customer demands without causing excessive delays or route failures.

Figure 1 shows the logic behind the sim-learnheuristic approach. The process begins by simplifying a stochastic and dynamic optimization problem into its deterministic version, where all random variables and dynamic inputs are replaced with their expected or estimated values. A metaheuristic algorithm is then used to explore the solution space, generating increasingly better solutions for the deterministic version of the problem. Once a promising solution is identified by the metaheuristic, it is evaluated by the simulation and ML modules to assess its performance under stochastic and dynamic conditions. Given that simulations can be computationally intensive, it is often beneficial to limit the number of runs for each evaluation to avoid slowing down the metaheuristic's convergence toward near-optimal solutions.

To illustrate this evaluation process using a sim-learnheuristic approach, we present an example that demonstrates how the program would choose between a simulation and a ML method based on the node type in a Team Orienteering Problem (TOP) (Listing 1). The code assumes deterministic rewards for each node while incorporating random and dynamic travel times (costs). This design takes into account that routes exceeding the maximum allowed cost may lead to the loss of accumulated rewards.

As explained in [2], the simulation feedback can also be employed to better guide the searching process carried out by the metaheuristics. This feedback can even be further processed by a ML component in order to better identify promising solutions or to create a surrogate model of the simulation component

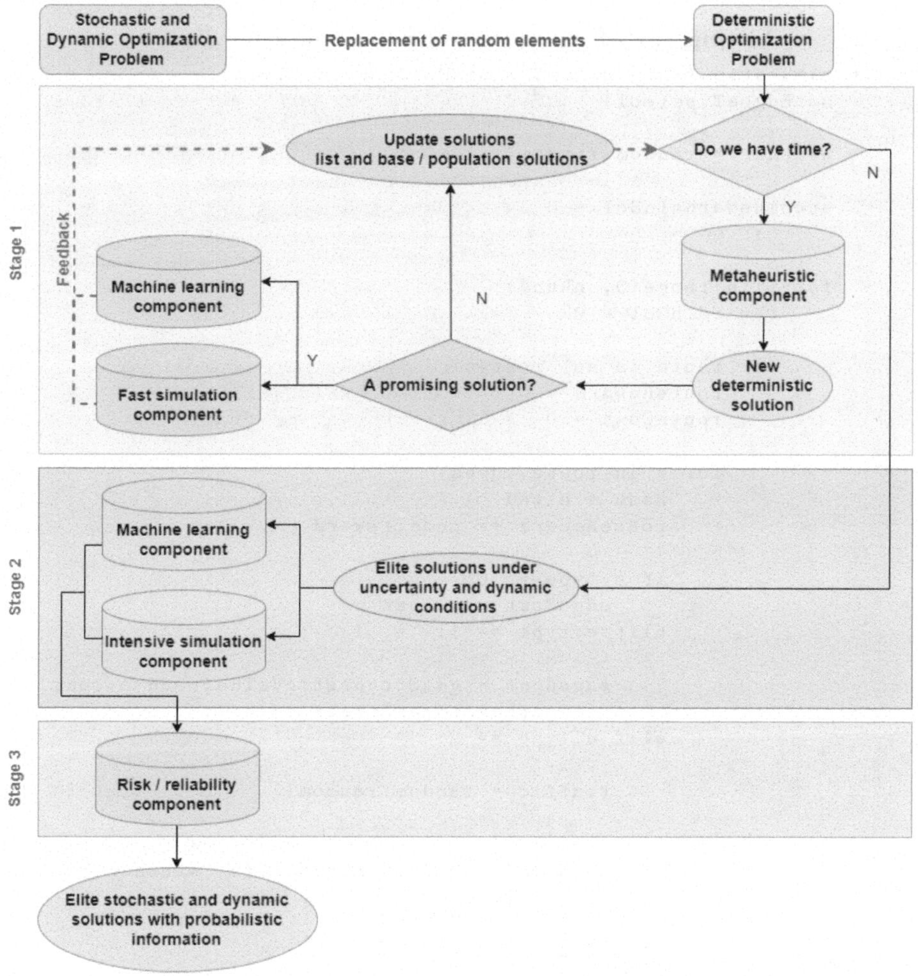

Fig. 1. The logic behind sim-learnheuristics.

that saves computational time. At the end of this first stage, a shortlist of elite solutions is generated. Each of these solutions is expected to perform well under uncertainty and dynamic conditions based on initial estimates. To improve the precision of these estimates, a more detailed simulation is run for each elite solution. Finally, the results from these simulations can be used to conduct a risk or reliability analysis on the elite solutions, providing valuable probabilistic insights that enhance the decision-making process by detailing the stochastic behavior of each elite solution.

Listing 1. Python code for evaluating routes in a TOP.

```
def simulation(sol, nRuns, routeMaxCost, varLevel):
    setEdgesType(sol)  # Set the type of each edge (det/stoch/
        dyn) for experiments
    weather = random.random()  # Daily weather adversity level,
        a random value between 0 (low) and 1 (high)
    accumRewardsInSol = 0  # Accumulated solution rewards after
        multiple runs

    for i in range(0, nRuns):
        rewardInSol = 0  # Solution reward for this run

        for route in sol.routes:
            routeReward = 0  # Route reward for this run
            routeCost = 0  # Time- or distance-based cost

            for e in route.edges:
                node = e.end  # End node of the edge
                routeReward += node.reward

                if e.type == 0:
                    edgeCost = e.cost
                elif e.type == 1:  # Edge e has a stochastic
                    travel time
                    edgeCost = getStochasticValue(mean=e.cost,
                        varLevel=varLevel)
                elif e.type == 2:  # Edge e has a dynamic travel
                     time depending on weather and traffic
                    traffic = random.random()  # Edge traffic
                        adversity level, between 0 (low) and 1 (
                        high)
                    edgeCost = getDynamicValue(e, weather,
                        traffic)

                routeCost += edgeCost

            if routeCost > routeMaxCost:  # Violates constraint
                on max cost
                routeReward = 0  # Penalty for violating the max
                     time allowed per route

            rewardInSol += routeReward

        accumRewardsInSol += rewardInSol

    sol.reward_sim = accumRewardsInSol / nRuns  # Average reward
        across runs
```

4 Related Work

Authors in [11] present a sim-learnheuristic method specifically designed for the TOP in the context of unmanned aerial vehicles. Unlike earlier research that focused on deterministic or stochastic versions of the problem, their approach tackles a more complex scenario incorporating deterministic, stochastic, and dynamic factors. The problem becomes particularly challenging due to uncertain travel times, which are influenced by dynamic factors such as weather and traffic. To solve this problem, the authors propose a sim-learnheuristic approach that integrates a biased-randomized heuristic multi-start (BR-MS), Monte Carlo simulation (MCS) and a multiple regression model. In their research, the problem is reformulated in its deterministic version, and all variables are substituted with their expected or most likely values to eliminate uncertainty [11]. This problem is then solved using BR-MS to generate multiple high-quality solutions. These deterministic solutions are evaluated with a limited number of MCS runs, where random variables and dynamic factors are assigned values based on probability distributions or ML models, and constraints are tested under uncertain conditions. Following this evaluation, a subset of top-performing solutions undergoes a more extensive examination with a greater number of MCS runs. The solutions are then ranked, considering not only their expected values but also measures such as variance and reliability. The innovative aspect of [11] is their ability to generate new solutions by using a biased-randomized version of the savings-based heuristic to introduce randomness.

Similarly, Authors in [4] investigate a dynamic and stochastic version of the capacitated dispersion problem (CDP). For addressing the dynamic variant of CDP, the authors propose a sim-learn heuristic algorithm. This approach integrates metaheuristics, simulation, and ML to manage the complexity of the problem effectively. The metaheuristic component is designed to address the deterministic variant of the problem through a dual-phase strategy. In the initial phase, a constructive heuristic is employed to generate candidate solutions tailored to the specific instance being analyzed. This is executed in a classic multi-start pattern, allowing the generation of multiple diverse solutions. The following phase uses a BR-MS, which refines these solutions, potentially improving their quality and optimizing the overall results. Then, [4] incorporate a simulation component in order to address the stochastic nature of the CDP. By iterating through several possible outcomes, the simulation captures real-world uncertainties, ensuring that the proposed solutions are robust against fluctuations in demand and capacity. Furthermore, the ML component applied uses a logistic regression model to predict the likelihood of a facility's capacity meeting the required demand. This predictive element enables dynamic adjustments to the allocation of resources, ensuring that the solution remains responsive to new data as it becomes available.

Table 1 provides an overview of the methodologies, ML components, simulation approaches, and heuristic techniques used in the reviewed works, highlighting the distinctive strategies each sim-learnheuristic approach brings to decision-making.

Table 1. Comparison of sim-learn heuristic approaches in related work.

Publication	[4]	[11]
Problem	TOP	CDP
ML Component	Multiple regression model for uncertainty	Logistic regression to predict demand fulfillment
Simulation Component	Monte Carlo simulation for solution evaluation	Iterative simulation for solution validation
Heuristic Component	BR-MS	Constructive heuristic and BR-MS refinement

5 Computational Results

This section provides an overview of two recent articles, which demonstrate the efficiency of sim-learnheuristics in addressing well-known NP-hard, large-scale stochastic and dynamic optimization problems. Table 2 reports the obtained results for a set of problems solved using sim-learnheuristics. This table shows the value associated with the best solution to the deterministic and static version of the problem (OBD), the expected value associated with the OBD solution when this solution is run under a stochastic and dynamic scenario (OBD-H), and the OBH value, which indicates the expected value using our sim-learnheuristic approach.

Table 2. Summary of sim-learnheuristics results.

Publication	Problem	Type of problem	Framework	OBD	OBD-H	OBH
[11]	Team Orienteering Problem (TOP)	Max.	Sim-Learn	352.47	209.73	233.10
[4]	Capacited Dispersion Problem (CDP)	MaxMin.	Sim-Learn	71.50	31.90	61.70

Figure 2 presents a graphical representation of the results from Table 2, where the vertical axis shows the percentage gap between OBD-H and OBH with respect to OBD (baseline at 0% gap). The results show that, for the two problems considered, the solutions provided by the sim-learnheuristic approach (OBH) outperform those of the deterministic version when the latter is applied under uncertainty and dynamic conditions (OBD-H). This indicates that optimal or near-optimal solutions for deterministic versions of optimization problems will typically become sub-optimal solutions when applied in stochastic and dynamic scenarios.

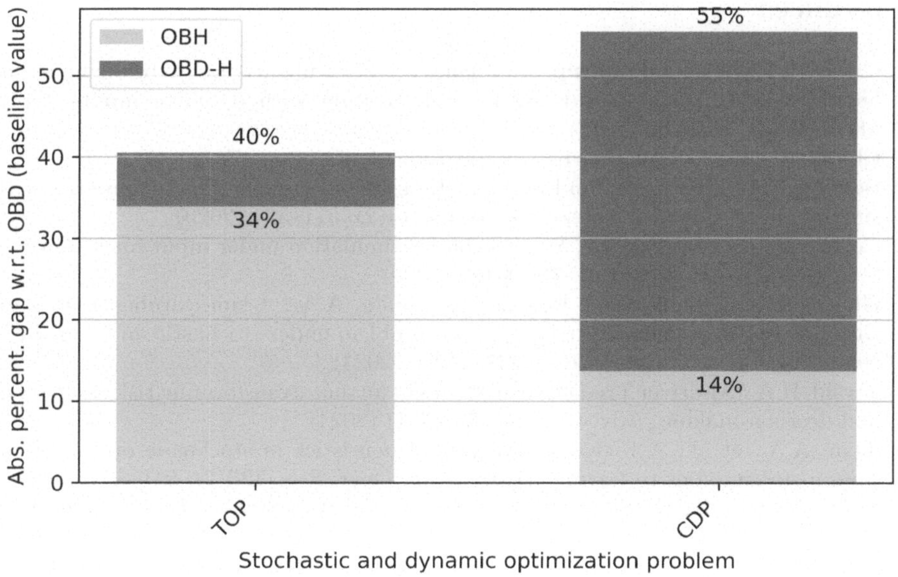

Fig. 2. Gaps of OBD-H and OBH solutions with respect to OBD solution (baseline at 0% gap).

6 Conclusions

This paper has introduced sim-learnheuristics as a simulation-based tool that can be employed to support complex decision-making processes like those involving stochastic and dynamic conditions. While pure simulation models are effective at capturing randomness, they lack the capability to optimize complex systems. Similarly, while pure simulation-optimization tools can handle the random inputs and probabilistic constraints frequently encountered in practice, they lack the capability to consider dynamic inputs. Hence, the coordinated contribution of ML is also required. As industries such as transportation, logistics, supply chain management, telecommunications, energy, and finance become more intricate and large-scale, these emerging sim-learnheuristics methods might become increasingly crucial for managing dynamism and uncertainty.

There are various ways to embed simulation and ML into a metaheuristic framework, and this paper has outlined our approach to it. For computational reasons, it is key to find a balance in allocating computing resources between the simulation, the ML and the optimization components. Also, simulation and ML outcomes should be employed to guide the metaheuristic search more effectively. This is an emerging hybrid methodology with many open research lines, including different designs for combining simulation, ML, and metaheuristics, as well as many potential applications in different industries and business.

References

1. Calvet, L., Armas, J.d., Masip, D., Juan, A.A.: Learnheuristics: hybridizing metaheuristics with machine learning for optimization with dynamic inputs. Open Math. **15**(1), 261–280 (2017)
2. Chica, M., Juan, A.A., Bayliss, C., Cordón, O., Kelton, W.D.: Why simheuristics? benefits, limitations, and best practices when combining metaheuristics with simulation. SORT-Stat. Oper. Res. Trans. **44**(2), 311–334 (2020)
3. Corlu, C.G., Akcay, A., Xie, W.: Stochastic simulation under input uncertainty: a review. Oper. Res. Perspect. **7**, 100162 (2020)
4. Ghorbani, E., Gomez, J.F., Panadero, J., Juan, A.A.: A sim-learnheuristic algorithm for solving a capacitated dispersion problem under stochastic and non-static conditions. AIMS Math. **9**(9), 24247–24270 (2024)
5. Javaid, H.A.: Ai-driven predictive analytics in finance: transforming risk assessment and decision-making. Adv. Comput. Sci. **7**(1) (2024)
6. Juan, A.A., et al.: A review of the role of heuristics in stochastic optimisation: from metaheuristics to learnheuristics. Ann. Oper. Res. **320**(2), 831–861 (2023)
7. Martí, R., Sevaux, M., Sörensen, K.: 50 years of metaheuristics. Eur. J. Oper. Res. (2024)
8. Nelson, B.: Foundations and Methods of Stochastic Simulation. Springer, Heidelberg (2021)
9. Ordu, M., Demir, E., Tofallis, C., Gunal, M.M.: A novel healthcare resource allocation decision support tool: a forecasting-simulation-optimization approach. J. Oper. Res. Soc. **72**(3), 485–500 (2021)
10. Panadero, J., Doering, J., Kizys, R., Juan, A.A., Fito, A.: A variable neighborhood search simheuristic for project portfolio selection under uncertainty. J. Heurist. **26**, 353–375 (2020)
11. Peyman, M., Martin, X.A., Panadero, J., Juan, A.A.: A sim-learnheuristic for the team orienteering problem: applications to unmanned aerial vehicles. Algorithms **17**(5), 200 (2024)
12. Rios, B., Xavier, E.C., Miyazawa, F.K., Amorim, P., Curcio, E., Santos, M.J.: Recent dynamic vehicle routing problems: a survey. Comput. Ind. Eng. **160**, 107604 (2021)
13. Schumacher, C., Buchholz, P., Fiedler, K., Gorecki, N.: Local search and tabu search algorithms for machine scheduling of a hybrid flow shop under uncertainty. In: 2020 Winter Simulation Conference (WSC), pp. 1456–1467 (2020)
14. Zakaria, A., Ismail, F.B., Lipu, M.H., Hannan, M.A.: Uncertainty models for stochastic optimization in renewable energy applications. Renew. Energy **145**, 1543–1571 (2020)

The Role of Interfaces in Modelling

Tristan Caulfield(✉), Marius-Constantin Ilau, and Manuela Bujorianu

University College London, London, UK
{t.caulfield,marius-constantin.ilau.18,l.bujorianu}@ucl.ac.uk

Abstract. Modelling is often used as a tool to help with design, analysis, and management of systems. With systems growing in complexity, with diverse components and interconnections with other systems, modelling approaches can benefit from an understanding of interfaces—both how they can be represented in models, and how they be used between models. In this work we discuss this dual view of interfaces, and develop a set of four elements of interfaces that modelling approaches should be able to capture: functionality, specification, policy, and environment. We then look at how this view of interfaces can be implemented, using an extension to an existing modelling framework as an example.

Keywords: Modelling · Interfaces · Systems

1 Introduction

The systems we design, build, use, and rely upon are becoming increasingly sophisticated, complex, and intertwined with other systems. To understand how systems behave or perform it is becoming necessary to consider and reason about interactions with other systems and the wider ecosystem, which can be considered as a composition of interlinked heterogeneous socio-technical systems.

The idea of *interface* is common across many disciplines from engineering to natural and social sciences. Different disciplines define interface in different ways, but, broadly speaking, this concept is used to describe where and how the interactions between systems, entities, or objects take place.

In this paper, we argue that the concept of interface is important for modelling and reasoning tools that support the design, testing, analysis, and management of systems and ecosystems.

One approach to handling the complexity of modern systems is to think in terms of interactions between components (e.g. systems, sub-systems, agents, objects, and so on), rather than of the whole system. There are several advantages to this approach. Reasoning at this level can lead to a complexity reduction in the analysis of systems, and systems—and indeed models of the systems—can be constructed component-by-component and then composed together.

Interfaces define or capture the interactions between components. This is true for systems and also models of systems, and leads us to consider that interfaces

A. A. Juan et al. (Eds.): SIMUtools 2024, LNICST 603, pp. 13–26, 2025.
https://doi.org/10.1007/978-3-031-87345-4_2

may have a dual purpose in models: first, models can capture an interface that is present in a target system—a model *of* an interface—and, second, interfaces can exist *between models*, facilitating model construction and analysis. An interface in a model may in fact serve both purposes, where the boundaries of component models match those of the target system. We argue that this dual-purpose view of interfaces is beneficial for modelling, particularly for the heterogenous and socio-technical ecosystems of today.

Our views on interfaces and modelling have evolved as we have worked to implement a useful and general form of interfaces into a modelling framework [20] that we have been developing. To do this we needed to understand the role of interfaces in systems, and determine the aspects and properties of interfaces that modelling tools should be able to capture. We believe that other modelling approaches and tools can benefit from this view of interfaces. For this reason, we present a broad, high-level view of ideas about interfaces in this paper, and only focus on our specific implementation as an example.

In Sect. 2, we begin with a discussion around the definition of interface, look at the role of interfaces in systems, and then look at the use of interfaces in models and the potential benefits that arise. The potential range of interfaces present in systems is vast, particularly in heterogenous, socio-technical systems which integrate many different types of components. In Sect. 3, we develop a set of fundamental elements, or attributes, of interfaces which an implementation of interface in a modelling framework should be able to capture in order to be able to represent the wide range of interfaces. Section 4 provides a sketch of how this view of interfaces was implemented in the SysModels [20] modelling package, and we conclude in Sect. 5.

2 Interfaces

We begin this section by exploring definitions of interface and their importance for thinking about systems. We then look at the role of interfaces in models, followed by interfaces between models.

In the introduction, we wrote that interfaces describe where and how the interactions between systems, entities, or objects take place. Dictionary definitions are aligned with this. For example, the Oxford Pocket Dictionary of Current English:

n.

1. a point where two systems, subjects, organizations, etc., meet and interact: *the interface between accountancy and the law.*
   - chiefly Physics: a surface forming a common boundary between two portions of matter or space, e.g., between two immiscible liquids: *the surface tension of a liquid at its air/liquid interface*
2. Computing: a device or program enabling a user to communicate with a computer.
   - a device or program for connecting two items of hardware or software so that they can be operated jointly or communicate with each other

v. [intr.] (interface with)
1. interact with (another system, person, organization, etc.): *his goal is to get people interfacing with each other*
2. Computing: connect with (another computer or piece of equipment) by an interface.

And Merriam-Webster:

1. a: the place at which independent and often unrelated systems meet and act on or communicate with each other
   b: the means by which interaction or communication is achieved at an interface
2. a surface forming a common boundary of two bodies, spaces, or phases

From these dictionary definitions, we see that interfaces represent a point of interaction between two different systems or conceptual environments, including interfaces between systems, between objects, between computer software or hardware, between people and computers, and more. We also see that interfaces also describe or establish boundaries for systems.

Interfaces can be both intentionally designed and also perceived or defined in existing systems. For example, the surface where two physical objects touch can be considered an interface: energy, whether heat or physical force, is transferred from one to the other. If the two objects are gears, for example, the teeth of the gears form a physical interface *designed* to transfer kinetic energy; if the objects are two rocks, randomly found touching in nature, their shared surface can also be understood as an interface. Designed interfaces are common in created systems, but interfaces can also be perceived when a system is studied. For example, looking at an organization, two internal business groups may communicate through particular employees. This mode of working may have evolved over time without specific intent, but when looking at the system, a boundary can be perceived between the two groups and the employees can be seen as the interface between them—in a sense, the 'integrative devices' of Lawrence & Lorsch [18] can be thought of as interfaces.

Designed interfaces are extremely common in man-made systems. For example, in digital systems: application programming interfaces, or APIs, specify how software components interact. A program uses an API to access the operating system functionality, and remote APIs can be used by client software to interact with servers over a network. Network interfaces allow devices to connect to a network to transmit and receive data. User interfaces allow humans to interact with software and hardware systems. But designed interfaces do not have to be only technical in nature: the door into an office building is an interface between the outside and inside, for example.

These definitions and examples already show that 'interface' can be used to represent a broad range of interactions and, naturally, the functionality, structure, or behaviour of interfaces changes depending on the interaction. We can easily imagine a system that incorporates many of the above interface examples at the same time: an organization whose employees use devices that access a network to perform various business functions. The heterogeneous systems and ecosystems that we wish to be able to model may contain many different types of interaction between many different types of components; we want to develop an approach to modelling interfaces that can capture all of these various types of interaction.

2.1 Systems and Interfaces

In this section, we discuss the importance of interfaces for the design, analysis, and management of systems. Returning to the idea of a dual purpose of interfaces in models, this section focuses on the first: models *of* interfaces (Fig. 1).

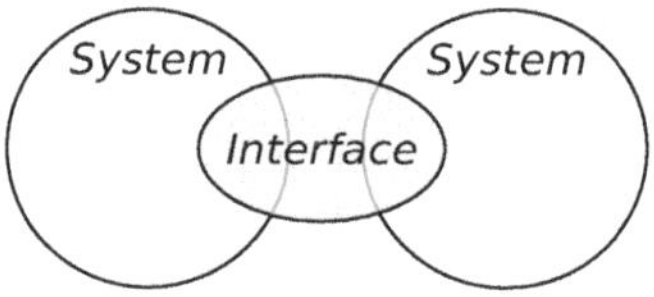

Fig. 1. An interface between two real-world systems.

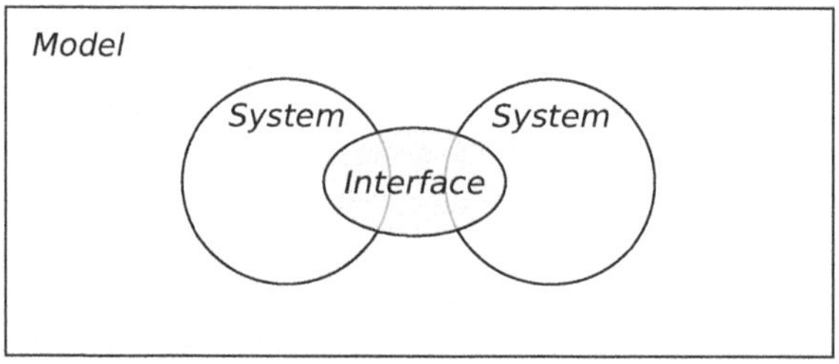

Fig. 2. A model of two real-world systems and the interface between them.

Systems tend to become more complex over time—both existing systems as they evolve, and newly-constructed systems that are more complex than their predecessors. There are many reasons for this, starting with technological advances that need integration procedures to interact with pre-existing systems or even lead to large architectural changes, new research paradigms re-defining the notion of system and the criteria for what constitutes quality when related to system design, and the inclusion of social elements within the concept of system.

Systems affect the daily lives of their users, stakeholders and developers and generate new phenomena that need to be understood and analysed in order to ensure correct (and good) design, operation, and outcomes. Modelling is often used as a tool to support system design, analysis, and management and, because of the increasing complexity of systems, we require ways of modelling more complex types of interaction between system components which may greatly differ in epistemics, ontologies, or simply means of construction.

For understanding to be possible and for the analysis to be consistent, the supporting tools used in the modelling act must be abstract and generic enough to be able to capture the potentially diverse range of system components, yet structured and with the capability to treat them in a similar manner for the sake of consistency. This is true for both system components and the interfaces between them.

Systems evolve through three approaches: additive development, which involves incorporating new sub-components alongside existing ones; integrative development in which the system is connected directly with other systems; and, transformative processes which require the modification or update of existing sub-components. Interfaces play a crucial role in all three methods, not only serving as links or connectors between components or subsystems, but also providing operations to make that connection meaningful. This can mean physical connection, the transfer of force or energy, or the flow of information from one system to another.

Delving deeper into the role aspects, interfaces have been historically known for playing a significant role in the dynamics and the hierarchical structure of complex systems. They influence how changes or perturbations propagate throughout the system and represent therefore an obvious location choice for observing such processes. Because of that, the concept of interface becomes central for defining properties such as adaptability, reconfiguration, resilience, and dynamic nature of complex systems.

Furthermore, reasoning at the level of interfaces can lead to a complexity reduction in the analysis of systems because observation of system behaviour at its interfaces provides a method of verification that does not require detailed observation of individual sub-components. This does not mean that internal aspects of system components are not being taken into account, but rather that the behaviour of such components can be verified from their interactions with other components.

Using the interface abstraction also encourages the analyst, designer, or modeller to think about the interaction between sub-components from the very start, reducing the risk of over-focusing on a singular component. Interfaces are necessary for thinking about the interactions between different subsystems, components, as well as the environment surrounding the ecosystem.

Tools, processes, and methodologies aimed at the design and analysis of modern systems and ecosystems need to take account of interfaces in a way that works at all scales.

2.2 Interfaces in Models

In the previous subsection, we discussed how the notion of interface provides a series of benefits in better understanding the complex nature of heterogeneous systems. In this section we will look at the second part of the dual role of interfaces in models: interfaces *between* models.

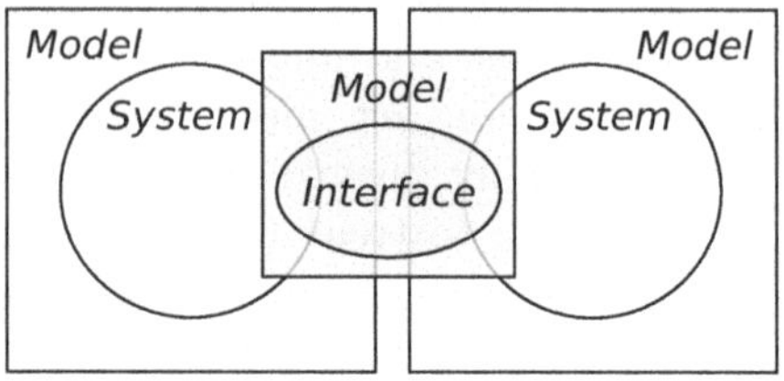

Fig. 3. A model of an interface acting as an interface between two models of systems.

Designing a (heterogeneous) system inherently implies constructing (at least) a conceptual model of it, and therefore the interfaces of that system are captured in such a model. This is like the example depicted in Fig. 2. Beyond just capturing 'real-world' interfaces in models, we argue that modelling approaches can also benefit from incorporating a notion of interface between models. This view is shown in Fig. 3.

Using interfaces this way in modelling allows for the integration and interoperability of different components or subsystems within a model. Much like real-world systems, a model of a system can benefit from the ability to develop parts of it independently and later integrate them. In this way, interfaces play much the same role in both real-world systems and system models—they define how two systems or components interact and what is required for them to be interoperable. The enable the construction of a larger model or ecosystem model through the composition of smaller component models.

Following from this, interfaces support modularity in models. Models with well-defined interfaces are modular, meaning they can be divided into distinct components that can be verified and changed independently. This supports the concept of substitution, where one version of a component in a model may be substituted for another to explore the changes in system behaviour, and refinement, where the fidelity or level of abstraction of a model component may be increased or decreased, without making changes to any other model components. This improves the adaptability of models to changing requirements or environments. Interfaces between models also provide abstraction by concealing the inner structure of components, allowing only essential functionalities to be used for interactions with other components.

Beyond the advantages in terms of model development, construction, and refinement, the use of interfaces between models allows us to move towards new approaches for reasoning about models. Interfaces define the interactions between components, allowing reasoning about each component's behavior locally, without considering the entire system. Compositional (or modular) reasoning involves breaking down a complex ecosystem into smaller, more manageable components, and to determine local properties of these components that guarantee desired properties of the global system.

This view of interfaces also allows us to consider local reasoning [10], where properties of the system can be verified by considering only a small part of the system while disregarding the rest that is not important for the property that has to be checked. The main benefit of this lies in the ability to analyze the properties of a particular component in a model's decomposition without the necessity to consider other components, except in relation to their interfaces or connection points with that specific component. A precise, formal description of these properties can be found in [11].

In modeling, an explicit use of interface between models—as opposed to just modelling interfaces—acts as a boundary or abstraction that defines the interaction between different components or systems within a larger model. The purpose of such an interface representation is to encapsulate the essential characteristics and behaviors of the components involved, allowing for modularization, abstraction, and the associated substitution and refinement, as well as enabling reasoning about the model at the level of the interface.

3 Fundamental Elements of Interfaces

In the previous section, we looked at the definition of interface, and discussed why interfaces are valuable for the design, management, and analysis of systems, and how models can be built of systems with interfaces between components (Fig. 2). We then saw how the use of interface between models (Fig. 3) provides a number of benefits. These dual views can overlap when the interface between models is a model of the real-world interface.

However, we have yet to address what we want to capture when we model an interface. Naturally, this is heavily dependent on the modelling task. However, as noted earlier, modern, heterogeneous systems may contain interactions between many different types of components, and the interfaces that mediate these interactions may vary significantly in purpose and function. If we desire a consistent approach to modelling a range of interfaces, we need to first understand what aspects of interfaces may be important from a modelling perspective. From there, we can create a modelling approach that is capable of capturing these elements in a consistent way.

In this section we define and describe the fundamental elements, or properties, of interfaces that a modelling approach must support if it is to be able to capture the wide range of different interfaces present in the heterogeneous socio-technical systems and ecosystem we describe above.

We propose four fundamental elements:

- Functionality—what an interface does,
- Specification—how an interface achieves the functionality,
- Policy—which places restrictions on interface behavior, and
- Environment—the external influences on interface behavior.

We expand on these brief definitions and explain their inclusion below.

We do not specify *how* each of these elements should be captured in a model, but we argue that it should be possible to somehow represent each of them. Different approaches to modelling can provide different means to incorporate each of the elements. And, naturally, the level of detail present for each element depends on the purpose of the model—the level of abstraction should be suitable to the modelling task. We will give an example of how these elements can be captured in a modelling approach in Sect. 4.

We have deduced these elements from definitions and examples, and thus we can not say that a modelling approach that supports these four elements is capable of representing *all* interfaces, but we will show that they can be used to represent a wide range of examples.

It is worth noting that not all interfaces require all of the elements. For instance, our previous example of two rocks touching clearly has no policy associated with it. However, many interfaces do have aspects of policy which one may want to capture in a model and therefore it is one of our fundamental elements.

3.1 Functionality

The first fundamental element is functionality which represents what an interface *does*. For each of these elements we will first discuss how it relates to interfaces in the real world and then how that translates to what the element captures in a model.

The functionality element of an interface represents the set of designed and accounted for operations, and their outcomes, available to be performed at interface level. As we have seen from the definitions and examples before, interfaces are designed to enable (or used to identify) interaction between systems or components. This interaction is the functionality of the interface.

In designed interfaces, the goal or purpose of the interface is directly related to its functionality. For example, a network API is designed to enable remote clients to interact with a server; the functionality is, at a high level: receiving requests from the clients, invoking the appropriate functionality on the server, and then responding to the client. For identified interfaces, such as our example of two rocks, there is no specific design intent, and functionality refers to the observed interaction—the transfer of energy between the objects through their points of contact (the interface).

The functionality element refers to *what* an interface does, so it is clear why a modelling approach must support this. While models are approximations or abstractions of a system, they still seek to represent the behaviour of the system at a level appropriate for the modelling purpose, and this behaviour includes the interactions enabled or described by interfaces.

As a running example through all four fundamental elements, consider a model of a simple wireless network at a high level of abstraction. The interface we are concerned with is the wireless interface from a device to the router. The functionality of this interface is to transfer messages between the device and the router.

3.2 Specification

The second fundamental element is specification. By this we mean a detailed description of how the functionality is achieved both at the level of structure and behaviour. There might be a number of ways to achieve equivalent functionality; specification refers to *how* the functionality is achieved.

The specification of an interface defines the purpose of the interface and its intended use within the system or applications and can include requirements, characteristics, and behavior such that the interface meets its purpose.

In contrast to functionality, the extent to which specification needs to be captured in a model is extremely dependent on the modelling purpose. It is likely that in many cases functionality alone is sufficient, but specification, or the effects of specification, can be important to capture in some circumstances.

Returning to the wireless network example, specification here might refer to the protocols used, the transmission rate, and so on. These might not be directly relevant for a model, unless a high degree of fidelity is required, but the effects of these might be important to capture: they affect the time it takes for a message to be transferred from the device to the router.

3.3 Policy

The third fundamental element of interfaces is policy, which captures constraints that influence the specification and functionality of an interface both statically and dynamically. A key observation is that there are two 'types' of policy: static and dynamic.

Static refers to constraints that affect the design or implementation of an interface. For example, a fire door, which is an interface between a building and outside, is subject to size requirements, materials requirements, etc., according to the local fire code. Static policy is typically reflected in the specification and functionality of the interface. So, much like specification, when modelling this, we need to capture the relevant effects of these policies in the model of the interface. For example, we might need to capture the maximum flow rate of people through the door (based on its size) but not the material it is constructed from. Similarly, for models being used in the design of new systems, the relevant effects of any static policy must be incorporated.

Dynamic policy refers to constraints on the operation of an interface as it is used that reflect decisions about how the interface can or should be used. In models of an interface, this is often captured more explicitly than static policy, which tends to be incorporated in fixed ways into specification and functionality. Dynamic policy, by contrast, can potentially be violated.

For example, a policy might give a weight limit for a bridge (an interface between the road networks on two sides of a river). Engineers adjusting traffic light patterns in one of the road systems might cause excess numbers of vehicles to cross the bridge in a short time frame, exceeding the weight limit. For models of interfaces, we want to be able to check, validate, or verify these dynamic policies. A modelling approach should be able to capture both aspects of policy.

In our wireless network example, static policy could refer to the maximum transmission power of devices as allowed by local regulation, which would get incorporated into specification and would affect the maximum usable range of the interface. Dynamic policy could refer to rate limits set by the network administrator; these could be violated if a device sends too many messages.

3.4 Environment

Our final fundamental element, the environment, represents an abstraction collectively encompassing all the external entities and processes that can directly or indirectly influence the interface's performance.

In the case of modelling, there is usually a difference between the level of detail of the model and environment; the purpose of the process of conceptualising an environment is to produce the smallest possible representation of external factors, without including elements that are not relevant for the specific model.

In our wireless networking example, the environment could capture the interference or noise from other nearby networks which causes delays or loss of messages.

3.5 Discussion

We feel that these four fundamental elements represent the main aspects of interfaces that a modeller may want to capture in a model. These evolved over time through repeated discussions, exploration of examples, and reflection on the definition of interface. We believe they are sufficiently general to model a wide range of interfaces, and specific enough to enable those developing modelling approaches or tools to implement methods to capture each of the elements.

Not all of the fundamental elements need be present in every model of an interface. Some elements might be missing from the original real-world system, such as policy in our earlier example of the heat transfer between two rocks touching. Or some elements might not be important enough or relevant enough for the modelling task—as with modelling in general, what is included depends on the level of abstraction and the purpose of the model.

4 Use in Modelling

In this section, we seek to illustrate how the concept of interface above, including the four elements, can be implemented and used in a modelling framework, SysModels [20]. We will give a brief background of the modelling approach, describe our early implementation of interfaces, and discuss the changes made to implement this new view of interfaces. We keep the discussion at a high level; details of the mathematical foundations of the approach and implementation details are available in many of the references below.

This approach use a set of concepts based on ideas from distributed systems. These concepts are processes, locations, resources, and environment. Despite their origins in the distributed systems world, these concepts are general enough to be applied to model any type of system. Very briefly, resources can be used to represent physical, digital, or conceptual things; for example, an object, some data, or a right-of-way at an intersection. Resources exist in locations, which represent physical, virtual, or conceptual places. Processes manipulate these resources: creating, removing, and moving them in and between locations. These three concepts combine to produce a representation of a system, which sits inside an environment, which is an abstraction of events from outside of the system that interact with it.

The distributed systems metaphor offers a number of advantages. First, generality: this conceptualization offers a set of ideas applicable for modeling virtually any type of system. Second, scale-freeness: the concepts can be used for constructing representations at any level of abstraction—a location could be an area in computer memory, a room, an office building, an entire city, for example. And third, recognizability: these concepts are familiar across a wide range of disciplines, which is beneficial when expertise from non-modellers is required for modelling a system.

The basic concepts that form the distributed systems metaphor have been used to construct executable frameworks for practical model construction. The earliest implementation attempted was Dahl & Nygaard's Simula [16], which was an Algol simulation framework that mainly focused on the notion of processes. Further implementations such as Birtwistle's Demos [7,8] but without an explicit characterization of the nature of systems such as that provided by the distributed systems metaphor, and without explicit conceptualizations of locations, environments, or interfaces. The authors have continued to develop the conceptualisation in a series of works such as [1,13–15], and consider applications in, for example [3,4,12,19]. A previous implementation of these ideas, Gnosis [13], has been used in significant commercial applications [2,5,6] derived from an industry-based research project [17]. The Julia `SysModels` package [20], which we refer to here, is an improved, more modern implementation of these ideas.

4.1 Evolution of Interface Implementation

As our understanding of interface has changed, so has the implementation in the SysModels package. The initial implementation of interfaces was aimed solely at enabling composition of models. Interfaces, as used then, identified locations where a model could be composed with another model—essentially a location shared between two models—and located actions, that allow processes to cross model boundaries. Figure 4 depicts this implementation: two models can be composed together at the shared locations defined in their interfaces.

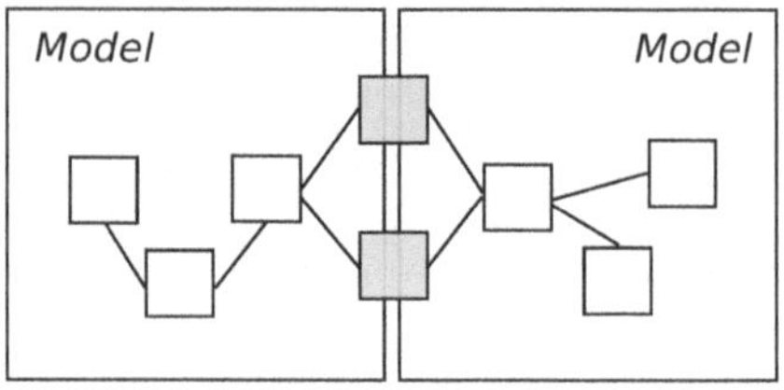

Fig. 4. Previous SysModels implementation of interface. Interfaces were shared locations where models can be composed together along with located actions that define how processes cross model boundaries.

This is sufficient to allow for composition and substitution but not enough for the more sophisticated conception of interface we developed above. The observation that real-world interfaces often have structure and function initiated the search for a better understanding of how to represent interfaces, and lead directly to this work.

As discussed above, different modelling approaches will require different ways to implement interfaces that capture that the four fundamental elements. In this case, the solution was to consider interfaces as models, with their own locations, resources, processes, and environment. This is what is shown in Fig. 3: the interface between the two system models is a model itself.

We termed such interfaces as Interface Models. Standard models are now termed Basic Models, and the previous idea of interface was retained as a Basic Interface, used to compose Basic Models with Interface Models.

As Interface Models are now models, complete with location, resource, process, and environment, they can directly capture the functionality, specification, and environment elements. Functionality is implemented using processes, locations, and resources; specification can determine the parameters of the functionality, or even how it is implemented; and, the interface environment can be captured using the model environment.

The remaining fundamental element, policy, requires additional support—dynamic policy, in particular. Static policy is reflected in functionality and specification so has no additional requirements. However, dynamic policy refers to policy constraints that may be violated, which implies that they need to be checked dynamically as the model executes. Interface Models extend Basic Models with a set of formulae which can contain policy statements. For example, statements like "there should not be more than 10 car resources in this bridge location" can be encoded as an Interface Model formula. As the model executes, the statements are checked against the state of the model to see if policy is violated.

Details of how Interface Models and dynamic model checking are implemented in the framework and in the mathematical foundations are given in [9].

With this, Interface Models are capable of capturing all four of the fundamental elements. Because Interface Models use the same distributed systems concepts as Basic Models they are also scale-free and general in terms of what they can capture, allowing for the construction of models of a diverse range of components with a consistent treatment of interface between them.

5 Conclusion

In this work we have advocated for a view of interfaces in modelling that recognises the value of being able to capture interfaces *in* models—and thus capture interactions between system components—and to use interfaces *between* models, to facilitate model construction and analysis.

We proposed a set of four fundamental elements of interface that highlight important aspects of interfaces that may help modelling approaches represent a large range of interfaces in a consistent way. We also described how we adapted an existing modelling framework, SysModels, so it can capture all four elements in its representation of interface. This framework uses a distributed systems metaphor, which can express ideas around interface very naturally, but we believe that other modelling approaches will also be able to adopt this view of interfaces.

As systems continue to evolve and diverse systems become increasingly interconnected, the need for robust and flexible modeling approaches will only intensify. Our hope is that this work will contribute to a deeper understanding of the role of interfaces in systems modeling, ultimately leading to improved design, analysis, and management of systems.

References

1. Anderson, G., Pym, D.: A calculus and logic of bunched resources and processes. Theor. Comput. Sci. **614**, 63–96 (2016)
2. Baldwin, A., et al.: Economic methods and decision making by security professionals. In: Schneier, B. (ed.) Economics of Information Security and Privacy III, pp. 213–238. Springer, New York (2013). https://doi.org/10.1007/978-1-4614-1981-5_10
3. Baldwin, A., Caulfield, T., Ilau, M.-C., Pym, D.: Modelling organizational recovery. In: Jiang, D., Song, H. (eds.) SIMUtools 2021. LNICST, vol. 424, pp. 284–314. Springer, Cham (2022). https://doi.org/10.1007/978-3-030-97124-3_23
4. Beautement, A., et al.: Modelling the human and technological costs and benefits of usb memory stick security. In: Managing Information Risk and the Economics of Security, pp. 141–163 (2009)
5. Beres, Y., Griffin, J., Shiu, S., Heitman, M., Markle, D., Ventura, P.: Analysing the performance of security solutions to reduce vulnerability exposure window. In: 2008 Annual Computer Security Applications Conference (ACSAC), pp. 33–42 (2008)
6. Beresnevichiene, Y., Pym, D., Shiu, S.: Decision support for systems security investment. In: 2010 IEEE/IFIP Network Operations and Management Symposium Workshops, pp. 118–125 (2010)
7. Birtwistle, G.: Demos—discrete event modelling on Simula. Macmillan (1979)
8. Birtwistle, G.: Demos implementation guide and reference manual. Technical Report 81/70/22, University of Calgary (1981)

9. Bujorianu, M., Caulfield, T., Ilau, M.C., Pym, D.: Interfaces in ecosystems: concepts, form, and implementation. In: Submitted to SimuTools 2024 (2024)
10. Calcagno, C., O'Hearn, P.W., Yang, H.: Local action and abstract separation logic. In: 22nd Annual IEEE Symposium on Logic in Computer Science (LICS 2007), pp. 366–378 (2007)
11. Caulfield, T., Ilau, M.-C., Pym, D.: Engineering ecosystem models: semantics and pragmatics. In: Jiang, D., Song, H. (eds.) SIMUtools 2021. LNICST, vol. 424, pp. 236–258. Springer, Cham (2022). https://doi.org/10.1007/978-3-030-97124-3_21
12. Caulfield, T., Pym, D., Williams, J.: Compositional security modelling: structure, economics, and behaviour. Lect. Notes Comput. Sci. **8533**, 233–245 (2014)
13. Collinson, M., Monahan, B., Pym, D.: A Discipline of Math. Systems Modelling. College Publns. (2012)
14. Collinson, M., Pym, D.: Algebra and logic for resource-based systems modelling. Math. Struct. Comput. Sci. **19**, 959–1027 (2009)
15. Collinson, M., Monahan, B., Pym, D.: Semantics for structured systems modelling and simulation. In: Proceedings of Simutools 2010. ACM Digital Library (2010). ISBN 78-963-9799-87-5
16. Dahl, O.-J., Nygaard, K.: Simula: an algol-based simulation language. Commun. ACM **9**(9), 671–678 (1966)
17. Hewlett-Packard Laboratories. Security Analytics. https://www.hpl.hp.com/news/2011/oct-dec/security_analytics.html. Accessed 10 May 2021
18. Lawrence, P.R., Lorsch, J.W.: Differentiation and integration in complex organizations. Admin. Sci. Q. 1–47 (1967)
19. Pym, D., Shiu, S.: Security analytics: bringing science to security management. IISP Pulse **4**(Summer), 12–13 (2010)
20. Caulfield, T.: SysModels. https://github.com/tristanc/SysModels. Accessed 22 Mar 2023

Interfaces in Ecosystems: Concepts, Form, and Implementation

Manuela Bujorianu[1], Tristan Caulfield[1(✉)], Marius-Constantin Ilau[1], and David Pym[1,2,3]

[1] Department of Computer Science, University College London, London, UK
{l.bujorianu,t.caulfield,marius-constantin.ilau.18,d.pym}@ucl.ac.uk, david.pym@sas.ac.uk

[2] Department of Philosophy, University College London, London, UK

[3] Institute of Philosophy, University of London, London, UK

Abstract. The world we inhabit is constantly increasing in complexity and with this comes a need for new ways of understanding and thinking that can manage this complexity. A key part of managing this complexity involves constructing models of ecosystems of systems and reasoning about their properties. One approach to modelling systems has been based on a process-algebraic formulation of an abstract view of distributed systems. Here, building on this view, we concentrate on modelling ecosystems of systems by developing a rather general concept of interface between systems. Interfaces between models describe how they can be composed together to construct a model of an ecosystem. By introducing the idea of local reasoning, building on work in program analysis and verification, we develop tools for analysing the behaviour and performance of ecosystem models in an efficient way.

Keywords: Ecosystems · Interfaces · Modelling

1 Introduction

The concept of a distributed system is a basic one in informatics, deriving from core ideas in the theory of computer systems. Traditionally, this would mean a collection of computing components which appear as a singular, coherent entity, can communicate and have the same notion of time. In the context of ecosystems of systems—now pervasive in our world—this serves as a starting point for a consistent modelling theory explicitly considering heterogeneity. The argument is as follows: to deal with the variety of existing systems and their increasing complexity from a modelling perspective, a decomposition to a set of basic concepts must be constructed; this set of concepts has to be general enough to allow for modelling ecosystems, but at the same time be simple enough not to alter or over-complicate the model meaning. We abstract this set of concepts from the notion of distributed system and construct what we call, by generalization, the *distributed systems metaphor*.

A. A. Juan et al. (Eds.): SIMUtools 2024, LNICST 603, pp. 27–47, 2025.
https://doi.org/10.1007/978-3-031-87345-4_3

For the practical purposes of simulation modelling—see, for example, [50] for a survey of the overall ideas—the executions of models can be captured, for instance, by the dynamics of the many forms of process algebra. Examples include [3,11,13–16,23,24,33] and many more, including those, described in various previous Simutools papers [11,13,16] that are intended to support implementations of the 'distributed systems metaphor'—in which a system is modelled in terms of its *locations*, *resources*, and *processes*, relative to its *environment*—as described in [3,11,13–16]. The history of this work can be traced to Birtwistle's 'Demos: Discrete Event Modelling on Simula' [9]. These approaches can be implemented by tools such as those described in languages such as Gnosis [14,16] and Julia [8,27]. In particular, the modelling approach based on the 'distributed systems metaphor', is conveniently captured in Julia using the 'SysModels' package that is available at [10]. A more abstract view may be found in [19] (in these proceedings).

The distributed systems metaphor notwithstanding, there are very many—far too numerous to discuss here—informal definitions of systems discussed across many disciplines. However, following [19], we can identify a common core of these definitions, all supported by the distributed systems metaphor and its implementations, that will serve as a starting point for our work:

> A system is something whose behaviour is reflected in the behaviour of its components.

This definition is deceptively simple: it identifies, at least implicitly, not only *behaviour* and *components*, but also *composition* (necessarily, of components) and so (again, necessarily) *interfaces* between components. This definition amounts to an abstraction and generalization of the characterization of systems that is provided by the distributed systems metaphor (e.g., [11,12]).

In this paper, we work towards constructing a framework and discipline for model engineering that will provide—in a scale-free form, applicable across the scope of the distributed systems metaphor—the tools and approaches required for building models of large, complicated ecosystems. We start from building basic models using the distributed systems paradigm before introducing a general concept of interface and discussing how such models can be composed using these. Beyond the structural requirements for model composition, we also introduce the idea of dynamic model checking, to verify that the behaviour of composed models is correct with respect to the requirements of their interfaces.

To understand the role of dynamic model checking, it is perhaps helpful to compare with the idea of run-time verification from computer science. The main difference between runtime verification and the approach presented in this paper can be observed by understanding the nature of the object of inquiry: the former interacts with a system, whereas the latter interacts with a system representation. Runtime verification is a procedure applied at the level of a software system, usually based on a different set of abstractions than those used in the system's design and development. In other words, it is an external procedure that is used for monitoring properties of system states directly. Although they have similar goals, dynamic model checking, as a procedure, operates at a different conceptual layer, serving as a verification tool for model properties that have already been abstracted or inferred from a system. Thus, in run-time verification, the abstraction is implicit and mainly focused on the definition of properties, whereas in dynamic model checking, the abstraction and inference processes used for designing and constructing the model and the definition of model properties are underlined by the same explicit distributed systems metaphor. The benefits are twofold: firstly, conceptual consistency across model design, construction, and verification is required to limit possible errors in translating the model properties to system properties; secondly, this implies a higher degree of generality for dynamic model checking.

In Sect. 2, we discuss our use of distributed systems as a metaphor for ecosystems of systems. We discuss how to model distributed systems at the level of abstraction of the metaphor, including giving a presentation that is adapted to the needs of implementation, and explain how to associate a rich logical language with such models. In Sect. 3, we explain how to model the compositional structure of ecosystem models using a rather general notion of interface for the implementation-adapted presentation version of models together some logical specification of required properties and policies. Then, in Sect. 4, we explain how our theory of composition and local reasoning can be used to support reasoning about the behaviour of composite models. Particularly, we show that our notion of locality includes meaning explicitly and is not solely grounded on model state: to reason about the property of a sub-model locally implies using only the relevant and meaningful information, even if the model state contains more than that. In Sect. 5, we explain how to establish a theory of local reasoning (in the sense of Separation Logic [26,43]) for our interface-mediated theory of composition and discuss how it supports a substitution operation for models. Appendices A and B sketch the underlying process-theoretic and logical theory.

Related work, including [1,2,48,49] among others, also addresses the concept of interface, but lacks the close structural integration with logic and does not address the ideas around local reasoning. Milner's work on bigraphs considers interfaces in an abstract setting (e.g., [36]), and has been related to logical work (e.g., [17]), but again local reasoning is not considered. We give a more complete account of related work on interfaces in Appendix C, which explains how our very general, yet ecosystem-motivated, notion of interface captures a wide range of the notions of interface that are in the literature on systems and modelling.

2 The Distributed Systems Metaphor

We use the distributed systems metaphor to describe ecosystems. We begin, in this section, with how the metaphor describes individual systems. Our modelling approach for ecosystems is then component-based. Ecosystems are thought of as systems of systems, or systems with different components, which interact, collaborate, inter-operate to achieve coherent goals.

In moving from modelling systems to ecosystems of systems, it is therefore necessary to define interfaces that enable interactions between component systems. Such interfaces will be the focus of this paper and are developed and analysed in subsequent sections.

For now, beginning with the motivation of capturing individual systems, there are three key ingredients upon which we draw:

- *Location.* Distributed systems naturally have a concept of location and distinct locations may be connected to one another. This is the system's underlying structure or architecture. In the setting of computer systems, components are present at different locations and connected by a network. In the more general view, locations can be physical (e.g., a room, a container), logical (e.g., an address in computer memory), or abstract (e.g., the location where a semaphore exists).
- *Resource.* Resources exist at locations and are manipulated by processes as they execute. Examples of resources include units of data (and information), physical entities, and other derived notions.
- *Process.* Processes execute and manipulate resources—such as consuming, creating, and moving them between locations—as they execute and deliver the required system behaviour.

These concepts can be used to build a representation of a system's structure and operation, but there is one more concept required: the environment in which the system operates.

- *Environment.* Environments capture the world outside of, and its interaction with, the system of interest.

Throughout this paper we illustrate its ideas and approach with a recurring example of supply chains—classically, the sequence of processes involved in the production and distribution of a commodity, but now also encompassing information supply—with our basic conception of the structure of supply chains being essentially that of [21]. In this view, can be seen to be a quite generic notion of system. The supply chain example will be used in more detail in subsequent sections. For now, we focus on more generic issues.

Figure 1 illustrates the general set-up that we seek to analyse. Here the idea is that two supply chains, the input chain and the output chain, are connected by an interface. From one point of view, each of the input and output chains is itself an ecosystem of component systems, respectively C_is and D_js. From another, each of the input and output ecosystems can be seen as a single distributed system. Either way, the range of architectures of supply chains—encompassing forms of serial and parallel composition—can be described in the ways given in [21]. This illustrates that the distinction between what constitutes the component systems and what constitutes is a design decision that should be driven by an understanding of the purpose of the system.

From the ecosystem perspective, each of the component systems (i.e., the Cs and Ds) resides at a location. These locations are connected by the routes

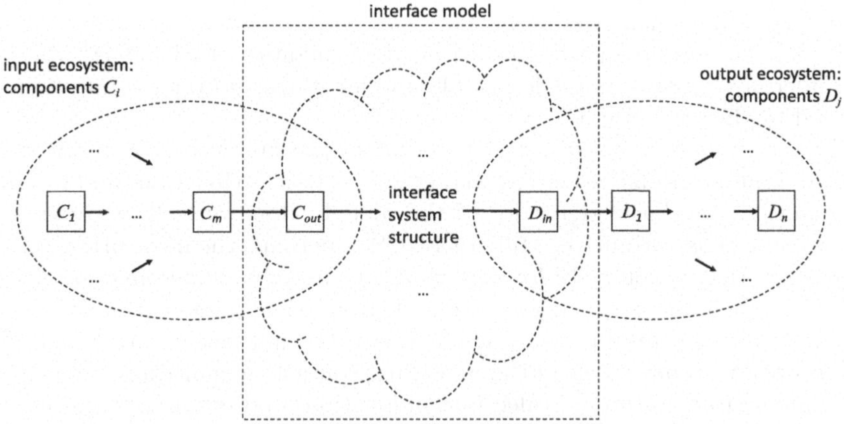

Fig. 1. A composition of supply chains.

along which the commodities supplied to and from the components are moved. Of particular importance in this view is the role of the interface, which may in general itself be modelled as system in the same way as the components. In order for the input and output ecosystems to be composed, two key conditions must be satisfied: first, each of the input and output ecosystems must have an appropriate architecture of locations—that is, their graphs must 'match' with the interface mode at C_{out} and D_{in}—and their modification functions (that is, the signatures of the models) must be consistent; second, there must be satisfaction of a range of logically expressible properties—for example, that, at a given point in the execution, sufficient quantities of a given resource are available at a specified location or that all of a given collection of supplying components have completed their required supply tasks.

Checking the properties of large complex systems for compatibility is, in general, an expensive, perhaps intractable, task. In this paper, as described in subsequent sections, we propose a theory and implementation of local reasoning in which we check, dynamically, the properties that are required to ensure that composition through given interfaces works as intended. In practice, this will capture most of the possible sources of error and, in particular, support checking that the substitution of one component for another preserves the required functionality of the ecosystem.

2.1 The Mathematics of Modelling Distributed Systems

The formal mathematical framework that captures the distributed systems metaphor for modelling systems is presented in Appendices A and B. In Appendix A, we given a calculus of processes in which location-resource-process states co-evolve as actions occur. This is written as $L, R, E \xrightarrow{a} L', R', E'$, which the action a evolves the state L, R, E—read as the process state E evolving at location L relative to resources R at location L—to a new state L', R', E'. The three components are defined separately. The pure process part is essentially Milner's SCCS [31], the resource part is based on the semantics of BI [39,41], the logic that underpins Separation Logic [26,43], and locations and their connections are captured by directed graphs.

These components naturally fit together in the presence of a 'modification function' from locations, resources, and (basic) actions to locations and resources that describes the basic signature of the model. Moreover, all of these structures are in a sense primitive: Milner's SCCS is perhaps the most primitive process algebra that is complete for describing recursively enumerable graphs and employs a synchronous concurrent product, from which, under modest assumptions, asynchronous products can be recovered (but not vice versa) [31,44]. This latter property is convenient in the modelling context: semantically, we can consider a model to be given by collections of locations and resources together with a modification function that specifies the actions that are available to construct processes [3,14,15].

Associated with the calculus of processes is a substructural logic, described in Appendix B, that has natural interpretation as a logic of resources (and also locations) in the sense of BI [39,41] and Separation Logic [26,43]. Properties ϕ of states L, R, E are described by a semantic judgement of the form $L, R, E \models \phi$ and natural notions of process equivalence and logical equivalence coincide (see Appendix B). These correspondences lead to a natural and conceptually simple modelling framework.

In the basic presentation of the mathematical set-up, we can suppress the concept of location, though not of course in the implemented models described in Sect. 2.2. Technically, locations are handled in essentially the same way as resources, and suppressing them simplifies the presentation of the basic theory. The framework we sketch in Appendices A and B has been developed in detail in [3,12,14,15].

2.2 Implementing Models of Distributed Systems

As we have discussed, an ecosystem is thought of as a system of systems that brings together a collection of systems in order to achieve and overall goal. The composite supply chain, as in Fig. 1, Each constituent system may have its own policies, objectives, and resources while coordinating within the whole ecosystem and adapting to accomplish the overall goals.

The description of models sketched above, in Sect. 2, lies at a wholly semantic level and is not formulated with the needs of implementation foremost. Our implementations—in Julia [27] and building on an earlier bespoke tool called Gnosis [14,16], using the SysModels package [46]—are based on the more specific formulation of *basic models*, building on the ideas presented in [12], which we now sketch and which are the basis of our implementation work.

A basic model is intended to capture the simplest convenient representation of a model of a single system using the distributed systems metaphor. Each basic model encapsulates the primitives we have discussed above—locations, resources, processes, and environment. In Sect. 3, we give an account of interaction between models through a notion of interface formulated at a similar level of abstraction.

Basic Model. A basic model is a representation of a single system that corresponds to the semantic definition discussed above, but which specifies locations as directed graphs, with vertices labelled by resources, and which identifies the actions and processes that are available.

Formally, a basic model is a tuple $M = \langle \mathcal{G}(\mathcal{V}[\mathcal{R}], \mathcal{E}), \mathcal{A} \rangle$, where $\mathcal{G}(\mathcal{V}[\mathcal{R}], \mathcal{E})$ is a directed graph with vertices $\mathcal{V}$, labelled with resources $\mathcal{R}$, and edges $\mathcal{E}$, and $\mathcal{A}$ is a set of actions specified by a modification function μ—given by $\mu : (a, \mathcal{V}, \mathcal{R}) \mapsto (\mathcal{V}', \mathcal{R}')$, the action a evolves the process E to E', $\mathcal{R}$ to $\mathcal{R}'$, and $\mathcal{V}$ to $\mathcal{V}'$—as defined in Appendix A.

It is this specification that is used as the basis of the Julia implementation. Locations are specified as objects with links to other location objects—forming a (directed) graph. These locations can contain resources, which are specified using Julia types. Processes are implemented as Julia functions, which provides a natural way of expressing sequences of actions (such as moving resources, or waiting for some duration, and so on).

A scheduler coordinates the execution of these processes. Models are executed on a single thread, but in a way that simulates parallel execution of processes. Events—parts of processes to be executed—are stored in a queue, ordered by time; the scheduler dequeues the first event and executes it. For example, a process that is currently executing at time t can pause its execution for 30 s. It gets paused and added to the queue to resume execution at time $t + 30$, and the scheduler begins executing the next item from the queue. In [14,16], the scheduler for Gnosis is given a semantics in terms of the calculus of locations, resources, and processes discussed above. The scheduler implemented in Julia could be given a very similar semantics.

The implementation also handles contention for resources. Processes must claim resources before they use them, and can release them after. Only one process can claim a particular resource at a time. If a desired resource is not available (because it has already been claimed, or because it is not present) a process will wait until the resources become available, so forming an implicit queue for resources.

The implementation of these concepts provides a useful tool for building executable models of systems. In the next sections, we explore how the concepts and implementation can be augmented to capture interactions between systems, which forms the basis for modelling ecosystems.

3 Interfaces and Composition

To begin thinking about how systems interact, we first need a concept that captures where and how these interactions happen. In this section, we introduce the *basic interface* and then extend our definition of basic model with this concept.

It is helpful to first revisit the concept of environment. Systems do not exist in isolation; they interact with the world—other systems—around them. However, we do not always want to explicitly model all of these adjacent systems. Instead, we use the concept of an environment, which models external events that have an effect on the system. When these events occur, associated actions inside a model are executed.

In the distributed systems paradigm, model-model interaction can happen in two ways. First, akin to environment-model interaction, one model can initiate an action in another model. Second, models might share locations and interact by manipulating resources in these shared locations. The combination of both of these is also possible: one model may move a resource into a shared location and initiate an action, for example.

Basic Interfaces. A *basic interface*, which describes the locations and actions involved in such interactions, is defined as follows: $I = \langle \mathcal{G}(\mathcal{V}_I[\mathcal{R}_I], \mathcal{E}_I), \mathcal{A}_I \rangle$, where $\mathcal{G}(\mathcal{V}_I[\mathcal{R}_I], \mathcal{E}_I)$ is a directed graph with vertices $\mathcal{V}_I$, labelled with resources $\mathcal{R}_I$, and edges $\mathcal{E}_I$, and $\mathcal{A}_I$ is a set of actions specified by a modification function.

Model. The locations and actions in a basic interface lack purpose unless associated with a model. A *model* is given by a tuple $M = \langle \mathcal{G}(\mathcal{V}[\mathcal{R}], \mathcal{E}), \mathcal{A}, \mathcal{I} \rangle$, where $\langle \mathcal{G}(\mathcal{V}[\mathcal{R}], \mathcal{E}), \mathcal{A} \rangle$ is a basic model, and $\mathcal{I}$ is a set of basic interfaces such that $\mathcal{G}(\mathcal{V}_I[\mathcal{R}_I], \mathcal{E}_I)$ is sub-labelled graph of $\mathcal{G}(\mathcal{V}[\mathcal{R}], \mathcal{E})$ (that is, it is a subgraph and all the resources labelling each vertex in the interface also label the same vertex in the model) and $\mathcal{A}_I \subseteq \mathcal{A}$.

Environment. We can now (informally) define an *environment* of a model. It associates to some or all of the actions in a model's basic interfaces a probability distribution. In an implementation of this framework, actions that are associated with probability distributions are initiated by sampling the distribution.

Composition of Models. A model as defined above can have multiple basic interfaces, each defining parts of the model—locations and actions—through which it can interact with other models. The *composition* operation joins two models using a specified basic interface from each one.

Let $M_1 = \langle \mathcal{G}(\mathcal{V}_1[\mathcal{R}_1], \mathcal{E}_1), \mathcal{A}_1, \mathcal{I}_1 \rangle$ and $M_2 = \langle \mathcal{G}(\mathcal{V}_2[\mathcal{R}_2], \mathcal{E}_2), \mathcal{A}_2, \mathcal{I}_2 \rangle$ be two models whose sets of actions have consistent modification functions (i.e., that agree on actions present in both). Consider two basic interfaces

$$I_1 = \langle \mathcal{G}(\mathcal{V}_{I_1}[\mathcal{R}_{I_1}], \mathcal{E}_{I_1}), \mathcal{A}_{I_1} \rangle \text{ and } I_2 = \langle \mathcal{G}(\mathcal{V}_{I_2}[\mathcal{R}_{I_2}], \mathcal{E}_{I_2}), \mathcal{A}_{I_2} \rangle$$

and suppose that at least one of $\mathcal{V}_{I_1} \cap \mathcal{V}_{I_2} \neq \emptyset$ and $\mathcal{A}_{I_1} \cap \mathcal{A}_{I_2} \neq \emptyset$. The composition $M_1 \circ_{I_1, I_2} M_2$, where $I_1 \in \mathcal{I}_1$ and $I_2 \in \mathcal{I}_2$, is defined pleasingly simply as follows:

$$M_1 \circ_{I_1, I_2} M_2 = \langle \mathcal{G}(\mathcal{V}_1 \oplus \mathcal{V}_2[\mathcal{R}_1 \oplus \mathcal{R}_2], \mathcal{E}_1 \oplus \mathcal{E}_2), \mathcal{A}_1 \oplus \mathcal{A}_2, \mathcal{I}_1 \oplus \mathcal{I}_2 \rangle$$

where $\mathcal{V}_1 \oplus \mathcal{V}_2 = \mathcal{V}_1 \cup \mathcal{V}_2$, $\mathcal{E}_1 \oplus \mathcal{E}_2 = \mathcal{E}_1 \cup \mathcal{E}_2$, $\mathcal{A}_1 \oplus \mathcal{A}_2 = \mathcal{A}_1 \cup \mathcal{A}_2$, $\mathcal{I}_1 \cup \mathcal{I}_2$, and for each $v \in \mathcal{V}_1 \oplus \mathcal{V}_2$,

$$v[\mathcal{R}_1 \oplus \mathcal{R}_2] = \begin{cases} v[\mathcal{R}_1] & = \text{ if } v \in \mathcal{V}_1 \wedge v \notin \mathcal{V}_2 \\ v[\mathcal{R}_2] & = \text{ if } v \in \mathcal{V}_2 \wedge v \notin \mathcal{V}_1 \\ v[\mathcal{R}_1 \cup \mathcal{R}_2] & = \text{ otherwise} \end{cases}$$

In this definition, it might be expected that the interfaces used to form a composition would not be available for further compositions, so that we should then have $\mathcal{I}_1 \cup \mathcal{I}_2 \backslash \{I_1, I_2\}$ above. However, such a requirement is not needed and its absence provides a more general and practically more realistic model of the concept of interface. The requirement that at least one of $\mathcal{V}_{I_1} \cap \mathcal{V}_{I_2} \neq \emptyset$ and $\mathcal{A}_{I_1} \cap \mathcal{A}_{I_2} \neq \emptyset$ ensures that we are actually achieving composition. If both intersections are empty, then the two models are necessarily executing independently of each other.

The following basic properties are easy to establish:

Proposition 1 (Composition Soundness). *If M_1 and M_2 are models as above, then so is $M_1 \circ_{I_1,I_2} M_2$.*

Proposition 2 (Commutativity). *If M_1 and M_2 are models as above, then $M_1 \circ_{I_1,I_2} M_2 = M_2 \circ_{I_2,I_1} M_1$.*

Proposition 3 (Associativity). *Consider the compositions $(M \circ_{I_1,I_2} N) \circ_{I_3,I_4} P$ and $M \circ_{J_1.J_2} (N \circ_{J_3,J_4} P)$ of models M, N, and P using interfaces I_is and J_js, for $1 \leq i, j \leq 4$. Then*

$$(M \circ_{I_1,I_2} N) \circ_{I_3,I_4} P = M \circ_{J_1.J_2} (N \circ_{J_3,J_4} P)$$

provided, for $1 \leq k \leq 4$, $I_k = J_k$.

When two models are composed using their basic interfaces it follows, by construction, that their basic architectures fit together. This, however, is not enough for their composition necessarily to function as intended. Each model has a collection of functions that it is intended to be able to perform and a collection of properties that can be expected of it and, whenever it is composed with another model, it is necessary to specify which of these must be preserved.

The simplest away to achieve this is to associate with each model a logical formula, using the logical language of Appendix B, that expresses the functionality and properties that must be preserved.

With this last step, we at last have a viable notion of interface. This notion substantially generalizes and makes cleaner that given in [12].

Interface Model. An interface model is a pair $I = \langle M, \phi \rangle$, where M is a model, and ϕ is a set of formulae (in the language of logic described in Appendix B) that describe properties of the model that must be preserved under composition. We identify a set of formulae with the conjunction ($\wedge$) of its elements as necessary. We refer to these formulae as *interface formulae.*

Note that the notion of an interface model strictly generalizes that of a model: simply take the interface model $\langle M, \{\top\} \rangle$, which places no constraint on M.

When two interface models are composed, it is necessary that their basic structure (that is, their basic actions do the same things at the same places) and the properties that they each require to be preserved under composition be consistent. These requirements are captured by the notion of admissibility,

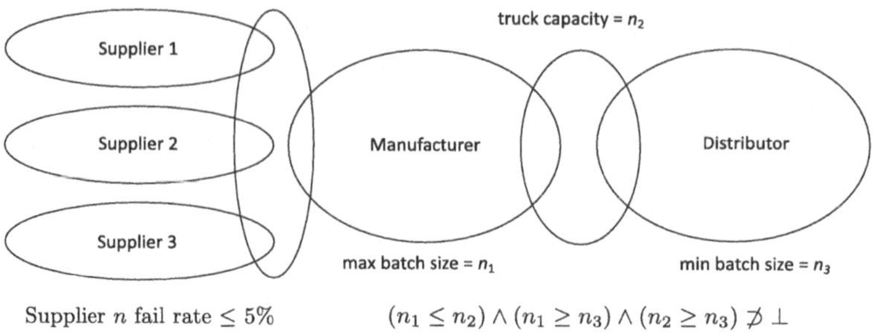

Fig. 2. Composition of Supply Chains: Structure and Logical Conditions.

which requires that their modification functions (signatures) and their interface formulae be consistent.

Admissibility. Let $\langle M_1, \phi_1 \rangle$ and $\langle M_2, \phi_2 \rangle$ be interface models such that M_1 and M_2 have consistent modification functions (i.e., that agree on actions present in both). Let $M_1 \circ M_2$ denote a composition of M_1 and M_2 using some choice of interfaces. Then the composition of $\langle M_1, \phi_1 \rangle$ and $\langle M_2, \phi_2 \rangle$, denoted $\langle M_1, \phi_1 \rangle \circ \langle M_2, \phi_2 \rangle := \langle M_1 \circ M_2, \phi_1 \wedge \phi_2 \rangle$, is admissible if $\phi_1 \wedge \phi_2 \not\supset \bot$.

A simple example of this is illustrated in Fig. 2 in which the composition of the suppliers, the manufacturer, and the distributor is supported bu interfaces that match the architecture and in which the necessary conditions are all consistent.

Proposition 4 (Composition Soundness). *If* $\langle M_1, \phi_1 \rangle$ *and* $\langle M_2, \phi_2 \rangle$ *are interface models, then so is their composition* $\langle M_1, \phi_1 \rangle \circ \langle M_2, \phi_2 \rangle$.

Proposition 5 (Commutativity and Associativity). *Commutativity of composition of interface model follows as for models. Associativity of composition of interface models* $\langle M_1, \phi_1 \rangle$, $\langle M_2, \phi_2 \rangle$, *and* $\langle M_3, \phi_3 \rangle$ *holds as for models provided also* $\phi_1 \wedge \phi_2 \wedge \phi_3 \not\supset \bot$.

The notion of composition established in this section determines the conditions under which, in a model of an ecosystem, one component model may be replaced by another of the same component system. The concept of substitution is developed in Sect. 5.

4 Dynamic Model Checking

We have built up a picture of how ecosystem models can be constructed, building on the concepts of basic model and basic interface to define composition of models, finishing with the definition of interface models, which associate logical formulae with models. These formulae express the required functionality and properties of models that must must be preserved, particularly when models are composed. This is important for a variety of purposes. For example, it allows the modeller to ensure: that model behaviour matches the real-world behaviour of the system being modelled; that the composition of models is correct and matches specification and behaves as intended; and, that changes in model parameters or substitution of models still satisfy requirements. We propose *dynamic model checking* as a method of verifying these formulae during the execution of implemented models. This is different from the usual notion of model checking (e.g., [4,20]): dynamic model checking verifies a model during the circumstances of a particular execution of a model, rather than under all possible circumstances; it is localized in space and time—it checks properties only in a small region of the model, at the interfaces, at specific times during execution.

If there are stochastic elements in the model, the results of dynamic model checking may change depending on what happens during the execution of a model. Repeated executions of the model are required to reach a desired level of confidence that model is correct with respect to the specified formulae.

To implement dynamic model checking using the Julia SysModels package [27,46], we need a way to express resources, locations, process execution, and formulae, together with the ability to evaluate formulae as the model executes. This follows the pattern introduced in Sect. 2.2:

- resources residing at locations are represented in the code of an implemented model as a vector of resource objects, declared as Julia types, inside a location object, with links to other objects;
- process evolution, through occurrences of sequences of actions, is represented using Julia functions;
- *then* interface formulae are represented as Julia functions that return booleans, based on the state of processes and the presence of resources in locations.

We illustrate this using the simple supply-chain example shown in Fig. 2. In this scenario, a number of suppliers supply goods to a manufacturer, which transforms them into finished goods and transfers them to a distributor. For this example, we consider two properties that we want to verify using dynamic model checking. The first is the failure rate of the goods from the suppliers, and the second is the compatibility between the manufacturer's and distributor's batch sizes and the capacity of the trucks that is used to move the finished goods between them.

The manufacturer requires a failure rate of less than 5% from the suppliers. We can express this in the logical language described in Appendix B as $\phi = (\text{Fail(Supplier n)} \leq 5\%)$, for each Supplier 1, 2, 3. This needs to be translated into a statement in the Julia language to work with the implementation:

```
state(proc_goods, 'receiving') &&
length(at(loc_input, r-> r isa FaultyGood)) /
length(at(loc_input, r-> r isa InputGood))
< 0.05
```

Formulae are implemented as functions that return true/false; they check the state of processes using the `state` function and can inspect resources at locations using `at`. Processes use a pair of functions `set_state` and `reset_state` to declare when they enter and leave a particular state—essentially giving a label to an action or sequence of actions for reference by formulae. The `at` function can specify a filter, used to select only certain types of resource or resources with specific properties from a location.

This example is checking whether the `proc_goods` process is in a particular state ('receiving') and whether the ratio of faulty goods to correct goods in location `loc_input` is less than 5%, using `at` to select `FaultyGood` resources and then all `InputGood` resources. The `length` function is built into Julia and returns the size of the vector.

For efficiency, formulae are only evaluated when relevant locations or process states are updated. Here, formulae are evaluated only when resources are added or removed at `loc_input`, or when the state of the process is updated to 'receiving'. We can write formulae to check that batch sizes are correct,

```
state(distrib_proc, 'receiving') &&
length(at(loc_distributor, r->r isa FinishedGood)) >=
distrib_min_size
```

and also that truck capacity is not exceeded,

```
state(truck_proc, 'collecting') &&
length(at(loc_output, r->r isa FinishedGood)) <=
truck_max_size
```

These formulae are associated with an interface model in the code. The first formula above is associated with the manufacturer model, the second with the distributor model, and the final with the trucking model. All the models are composed to form one model.

Although the scenario, models, and formulae in this example are fairly trivial, they demonstrate how all of the concepts we have discussed in this paper come together to enable the construction and the checking of composition in ecosystem models. Because models are built using resource, location, and process, the relatively simple `state` and `at` used in the construction of formulae can be used to build up complex expressions about the state of a model. Future work will increase the expressiveness of the implemented logic; for example, referring to a history of states.

5 Model Management: Substitution and Local Reasoning

In this section, we discuss how substitution and local reasoning, two tools which support the management of the modelling process, are enabled with the approach presented above. The practice of modelling is active: as models of ecosystems are developed, it is natural that the function and specification of their component models may evolve. If one component model is replaced withe another, we must ensure that the resulting model still satisfies the requirements for it to interact with the other models in the ecosystem.

For example, consider the supply chain depicted in Fig. 2. Suppose Supplier 2 ceases to trade and must be replaced by a different supplier. We can substitute a model of the new supplier. The conditions for the Manufacturer remain the same, and we can verify that the modified supply chain, including the new supplier, continues to satisfy the structural requirements, as specified by the modification function, and the logical condition on the fail rate.

It can be seen that the formulation of the concepts of interface and dynamic model checking presented here support this requirement for substitution. Indeed, dynamic model checking can be seen as delivering a form of local reasoning, as has been very successfully employed in program analysis and verification [26,29,43], but at the level of general ecosystem models.

6 Conclusion: Towards Model Engineering

In this paper, we have presented an approach to modelling ecosystems based on concepts from distributed systems. We have developed the notion of a basic model, expanded it with basic interfaces to define a model, and and subsequently to an interface model, which has associated formulae that characterize the requirements of composition. We have then described how these formulae can be evaluated as a model executes, in order to verify properties of the model, through dynamic model checking.

This approach enables the composition of models in such a way that properties essential for the composition to function properly can be verified locally at the interfaces between components, while avoiding the need to verify the correctness of components while doing so. This supports more robust construction of large ecosystem models at limited computational cost. It also provides support for useful modelling tools such as substitution and principles of local reasoning that go beyond the basic requirements of composition. We view this work as early progress towards a rigorous discipline of model engineering.

A A Calculus of Locations, Resources, and Processes

Our starting points are Milner's synchronous calculus of communicating systems, SCCS [32]—perhaps the most basic of process calculi, the collection of which includes also CCS [31], CSP [24], Meije [44], and their derivatives, as well as the π-calculus [34], bigraphs [36] and their derivatives—and the resource semantics of bunched logic [18,39,41,42].

Our presentation here follows Chap. 2 of [14]. We start with the following:

- A monoid of actions, Act, with a composition ab of elements a and b and unit 1;

- The following grammar of process terms, E, where $a \in \mathsf{Act}$ and X denotes a process variable:

$$E ::= 0 \mid a \mid a : E \mid \sum_{i \in I} E_i \mid E \times E \mid X \mid fix_i X.\mathsf{E} \mid (\nu R).E \mid \ldots$$

Most of the cases here, such as 0, action, action prefix, sum, concurrent product, and recursion, will seem quite familiar. The last one, however, which we call hiding, is available because we integrate the notions of resource and process. Its meaning is discussed below; it replaces and generalizes restriction. The expression $fix_i X.\mathsf{E}$, where E is a tuple of processes, means $(fix X.\mathsf{E})_i$, the ith component of the tuple $(fix X.\mathsf{E})$ over an indexing set I. The unsubscripted form $fix X.\mathsf{E}$ stands for the family over i of $fix_i X.\mathsf{E}$ s. As Milner ([32], for example) explains, the case in which the indexing set has just one element is sufficient for finite processes.

Mathematically, the notion of resource—which covers examples such as space, memory, and money—is based on (ordered, partial, commutative) monoids (e.g., the non-negative integers with zero, addition, and less-than-or-equals): each type of resource is based on a basic set of resource elements, resource elements can be combined, and resource elements can be compared. Although, for brevity, we describe the set-up here for resource-process states, R, E, everything we describe here can be set up for location-resource-process pairs, L, R, E, though there are some delicate issues that are beyond the scope of this short paper; see [3,14,15].

Formally, we consider pre-ordered, partial commutative monoids of resources, $(\mathbf{R}, \circ, e, \sqsubseteq)$, where $\mathbf{R}$ is the carrier set of resource elements, $\circ$ is a partial monoid composition, with unit e, and $\sqsubseteq$ is a pre-order on $\mathbf{R}$. The basic idea is that resources, R, and processes, E, co-evolve, $R, E \xrightarrow{a} R', E'$, according to the specification of a partial 'modification function', $\mu : (a, R) \mapsto R'$, that determines how an action a evolves R to R' and E to E'.

Modification functions can be seen as the signature of model, specifying the basic evolutions of states via basic actions from which the overall evolution of a model is constructed. In the presence of locations, L, modifications have the form $\mu : (a, L, R) \mapsto (L', R')$, a evolves E to E', R to R', and L to L'.

The base case of the operational semantics, presented in Plotkin's SOS style [40], is given by Action prefix and Concurrent composition, $\times$, exploits the monoid composition, $\circ$, on resources,

$$\frac{}{R, a : E \xrightarrow{a} R', E'} \quad \mu(a, R) = R' \quad \text{Action}$$

$$\frac{R, E \xrightarrow{a} R', E' \quad S, F \xrightarrow{b} S', F'}{R \circ S, E \times F \xrightarrow{ab} R' \circ S', E' \times F'} \quad \text{Concurrent}$$

This (rather general [32,44]) notion of composition at the level of process does not explain the engineering concept of the composition of models, with its requisite notions of interface and substitution, that we discuss in the sequel.

A modification function is required to satisfy some basic coherence conditions (in certain circumstances, additional structure may be required [3]): for all actions a and b and all resources R and S, and where $\simeq$ is Kleene equality: $\mu(1, R) = R$, where 1 is the unit action, and if $\mu(a, R)$, $\mu(b, S)$, and $R \circ S$ are defined, then $\mu(ab, R \circ S) \simeq \mu(a, R) \circ \mu(b, S)$.

Sums, Recursion, and Hiding are formulated in familiar ways:

$$\frac{R, E_i \xrightarrow{a} R', E'}{R, \sum_{i \in I} E_i \xrightarrow{a} R', E'}\ \text{Sum} \qquad \frac{R, E_i[fixX.\mathsf{E}/X] \xrightarrow{a} R', E'}{R, fix_i X.\mathsf{E} \xrightarrow{a} R', E'}\ \text{Recursion}$$

$$\frac{R \circ S, E \xrightarrow{a} R' \circ S', E'}{R, (\nu S)E \xrightarrow{(\nu S)a} R', (\nu S')E'}\ \text{Hiding}$$

In Recursion, I is an indexing set and E_i is the ith component of a tuple of processes, and substitution is capture-avoiding. In Hiding, the resource S becomes bound to the process E. This construction replaces, and generalizes, the restriction operation of calculi such as SCCS.

The notion of equality between location-resource processes is given by the idea of bisimulation (see [32,33], for example. Specifically, bisimulation equivalence can be defined as follows: two process states $\mathcal{S}$ and $\mathcal{T}$ are bisimilar, written $\mathcal{S} \approx \mathcal{T}$, if $\approx$ is the largest relation on process states that is closed under the following conditions:

- if $\mathcal{S} \xrightarrow{a} \mathcal{S}'$, then there is an evolution $\mathcal{T} \xrightarrow{a} \mathcal{T}'$ such that $\mathcal{S}' \approx \mathcal{T}'$
- if $\mathcal{T} \xrightarrow{a} \mathcal{T}'$, then there is an evolution $\mathcal{S} \xrightarrow{a} \mathcal{S}'$ such that $\mathcal{S}' \approx \mathcal{T}'$.

For this notion of (strong) bisimulation, two bisimilar processes have the same set of traces/behaviours. Again, this definition of bisimulation can readily be adapted to states L, R, E, though, again, there are some delicate issues that are beyond the scope of this paper; see [3,14,15].

B A Modal Logic

Here we follow Chap. 3 of [14]. Process calculi such as SCCS, CCS, and others come along with associated modal logics [5,22,33,45]. Similarly, the calculus sketched here has associated modal logic [3,14,15]. The basic logical judgement is of the form $R, E \models \phi$, read as 'relative to the available resources R, the process E has property ϕ'. For our purposes, we work with the following language:

$$\begin{aligned} \phi := \mathrm{p} \mid \neg\phi \mid \top \mid \bot \mid \phi \wedge \phi \mid \phi \vee \phi \mid \phi \supset \phi \mid \langle a \rangle \phi \mid [a]\phi \\ \mid I \mid \phi * \phi \mid \phi \mathrel{-\!\!*} \phi \mid \langle a \rangle_\nu \phi \mid [a]_\nu \phi \end{aligned}$$

Building on the ideas of the bunched logic BI (e.g., [18,39,41,42]), which is the basis of Separation Logic [26,43], this logic has, the usual classical connectives, $\top$, $\wedge$, $\rightarrow$, $\bot$, $\vee$ that are defined, in the usual way, by semantic clauses of a satisfaction relation, where $\mathcal{V}$ is an interpretation of propositional letters, beginning

$$R, E \models \mathrm{p} \ \text{ iff } (R, E) \in \mathcal{V}(\mathrm{p})$$

and proceeding as

$$R, E \models \phi \wedge \psi \text{ iff } R, E \models \phi \qquad R, E \models \psi$$

and so on. Note that an intuitionistic version is also possible. The logic also has a separating conjunction, $*$, with unit I, defined by

$$\begin{array}{rl} R, E \models \phi * \psi & \text{iff there are } S,\ T \text{ and } F, G \text{ s.t. } S \circ T \sqsubseteq R,\ F \times G \approx E, \\ & \text{and } S, F \models \phi \text{ and } T, E \models \psi \end{array}$$

where $\approx$ is bisimulation as sketched above, together with a corresponding separating implication, $-\!\!*$. Note that the truth condition for $*$—called a 'separating conjunction', since its conjuncts use separate resources—requires the combination of resources from the truth conditions for its component formulae.

The relationship between truth and action is captured by the clauses of the satisfaction relation for the (additive) modalities, given essentially as follows (recall that $R' = \mu(a, R)$):

$$\begin{array}{l} R, E \models \langle a \rangle \phi \text{ iff there exists } E' \text{ s.t. } R, E \xrightarrow{a} R', E' \text{ and } R', E' \models \phi \\ R, E \models [a]\phi \text{ iff for all } E' \text{ s.t. } R, E \xrightarrow{a} R', E',\ R', E' \models \phi \end{array}$$

Similarly, in addition to the usual quantifiers and modalities, this logic has the separating modalities, $\langle a \rangle_\nu \phi$ and $[a]_\nu \phi$, as developed in [3,14,15].

Predicate versions of this logic—of the kind required for this paper—are also available, allowing quantification over both actions and terms. The details require some care, and will reported elsewhere, but the basic idea is that quantification over action variables taking values in Act and term variables taking values in a specified domain $\mathcal{D}$, as part in general of a model $\mathcal{M}$ defined in a standard way, is understand as for states S as

$$\begin{array}{lll} \mathcal{S} \models_{\mathcal{M},\rho} \exists \alpha.\phi & \text{iff} & \text{there exists } a \in \mathsf{Act} \text{ such that } \mathcal{S} \models_{\mathcal{M},\rho[\alpha:=a]} \phi \\ \mathcal{S} \models_{\mathcal{M},\rho} \forall \alpha.\phi & \text{iff} & \text{for all } a \in \mathsf{Act},\ \mathcal{S} \models_{\mathcal{M},\rho[\alpha:=a]} \phi \\ \mathcal{S} \models_{\mathcal{M},\rho} \exists z.\phi & \text{iff} & \text{there exists } d \in \mathcal{D} \text{ such that } \mathcal{S} \models_{\mathcal{M},\rho[z:=d]} \phi \\ \mathcal{S} \models_{\mathcal{M},\rho} \forall z.\phi & \text{iff} & \text{for all } d \in \mathcal{D},\ \mathcal{S} \models_{\mathcal{M},\rho[z:=d]} \phi \end{array}$$

where ρ assigns values in Act and $\mathcal{D}$ and $\models_{\mathcal{M},\rho}$ denotes satisfaction in a model $\mathcal{M}$ in the usual way. We elide the detail of the connection to the implemented models discussed in this paper.

The basic connection between the process calculus and the logic is given by a form of van Benthem-Hennessy-Milner theorem that relates process equivalence, as given by bisimulation, and logical equivalence (e.g., [3,5,14,15,22,33,45]). Essentially—though some care must be taken [3,14], either restricting the logic or employing a slightly different semantics—for image-finite processes E and F and any R,

$$R, E \approx R, F \quad \text{iff} \quad R, E \equiv_{\text{MBI}} R,\ \text{F}$$

Specifically, this holds for the basic monoidal theory of resources, as described above, only for some (large) fragments of the logic [14,15], but, with a slightly different theory of resource—essentially, using two monoidal operations—as described in [3], it holds for the full logic with states R, E and S, F (and hence L, R, E and M, S, F). This generalization is slightly mis-stated in [11].

Logics based on the language of MBI have proved valuable in program analysis—see the Infer tool [29]—partly by virtue of their deployment of local reasoning, based on the connective $*$.

C Definitions of Interfaces in the Literature

In this appendix we briefly discuss how interface concepts from the systems and modelling literature relate to our ideas on interface presented in this paper.

Interface Automata. The first formal interface theory was proposed by de Alfaro and Henzinger in [1]. There, an interface theory comprises an interface algebra together with a component algebra to differentiate the interface specifications from component implementations. An interface is represented by an input/output automaton, which is an automaton whose transitions are labelled with input or output actions. The main requirement in this setting is that connection is properly accomplished in the sense that for every output one interacting component produces, the other component is ready to receive it.

This approach corresponds to the case when the models have only basic interfaces. Our interface models extend this type of interaction, allowing for some possible transformations of the model outputs before being received by another model.

Modal I/O Automata for Interface. A modal transition system (MTS) [28] associates with each state transition, a classification/modality—may or must—expressing transition behaviours that (i) necessarily occur (must modality), (ii) possibly occur (may modality), and (iii) not possibly occur (absence of a transition). Modal I/O Automata for Interface is an approach that uses combinations of Interface Automata (IA) and Modal Transition Systems (MTS), through the labelling of may and must modalities with input/output features.

The modal I/O Automaton model can be thought of as a particular case of our interface model in which we express the may and must modalities using appropriate logical formulae.

Relational Interfaces. The theory of relational interfaces [47] specifies interfaces as relations between inputs and outputs. This interface theory includes explicit notions of environments and the compatibility of the interface with the environment.

Relational interfaces can be thought of as a particular case of our interface models in which there is no internal structure, and the logical formulae model the relationships between inputs and outputs.

Contract Theories. Contract theories [6,7,30] are specializations of interface models in the sense that they obey to the concept of separation of concerns. They separate the assumption specification from the guarantees specification. The first use of the concept of contract [30] specifies preconditions and postconditions as state predicates for the methods of a class, and invariants for the class itself. The precondition expresses requirements that any operation has to satisfy if it is to be correct; the postcondition expresses properties that are ensured after the execution of the operation. In [6], the notion of a contract for a component is built as a pair of assertions, which express its assumptions and promises. The assertions talk about the entire component behaviour. Then, a contract is an assertion on the component behaviors (the promise) subject to certain assumptions.

The contract model can be seen as a special example of our interface model with no internal structure where the contract (assume-guarantee) assertions are special logical formulae about the ecosystem components.

Interfaces in Concurrent Kleene Algebra. Concurrent Kleene algebra (CKA) [25] has been defined as an algebraic framework to reason about concurrent programs. CKA basic ingredients are events, which are occurrences of certain primitive actions. A set of events is called a trace and represents a program or a specification. A trace defines a graph with events as nodes and arrows corresponding to dependences like causal or temporal succession and the like. The basic idea of the interface model [38] is to consider subgraphs, called graphlets, of that overall graph as events of their own. The sets of incoming and outgoing arrows of a graphlet constitute its input/output interface.

In this case, the interface model defined as a graphlet can be directly related to our model of basic interface. Note that, in our approach, we consider not only the incoming and outgoing arrows, but also the internal structure of the subgraph that models the basic interface.

Bigraphs. Bigraphs [35–37] represent a formalism designed for modelling agents, their spatial arrangement, and their inter-connections. The formalism for describing a bigraph can be done either as a graph or an algebraic form. A bigraph is modelled as the superposition of a graph (the link graph) and a set of trees (the place graph). In the graphical description, the nodes encode agents or other entities. The spatial configuration is described by node nesting. The vertices have associated controls that form a signature. As well, the nodes have an arity (i.e., the number of ports for a given node to which link-graph edges may connect). A bigraph may have associated with it one or more regions (or roots) which describe adjacent parts of the system. In the bigraph structure, we have also *sites*. Nodes, sites and roots are the places of a bigraph.

Formally, a bigraph is defined as:

$$F = (\mathbf{V}, \mathbf{E}, ctrl, prnt, link) : \langle k, X \rangle \rightarrow \langle m, Y \rangle$$

thought of as a superposition of a place graph $F_P = (\mathbf{V}, ctrl, prnt) : k \rightarrow m$ and a link graph $F_L = (\mathbf{V}, \mathbf{E}, ctrl, link) : X \rightarrow Y$

A bigraph has two faces: an outer and an inner interface. Each of these interfaces is a pair containing a face for the place graph and a face for the link graph. For a place graph, a face is a natural number. In this framework we treat a natural number as the set of numbers that are strictly smaller; that is, $n = \{0, 1, \ldots, n-1\}$.

For a link graph, a face is set of labels—that is, those attached to the unconnected edges. A bigraph can have inner names and outer names, which define the bigraph interfaces.

A bigraph is able to interact with its external environment through its interfaces. When the interfaces of two bigraphs are matching, we can define their composition.

Because a bigraph is built as the superposition of two graphs (link graph and place graph), the corresponding interfaces can also be thought of as a superposition of the interfaces associated with the component graphs. Even though the component graph interfaces are different objects, the essence of their definition is the same: input/output variables. Therefore, we can link these interfaces with our basic interfaces.

References

1. de Alfaro, L., Henzinger, T.A.: Interface automata. In: Proceedings of the 8th European Software Engineering Conference Held Jointly with 9th ACM SIGSOFT International Symposium on Foundations of Software Engineering, Association for Computing Machinery, New York (2001). https://doi.org/10.1145/503209.503226
2. de Alfaro, L., Henzinger, T.A.: Interface theories for component- based design. In: Henzinger, T.A., Kirsch, C.M. (eds.) Embedded Software. LNCS, pp. 148–165. Springer, Heidelberg (2001)
3. Anderson, G., Pym, D.: A calculus and logic of bunched resources and processes. Theoret. Comput. Sci. **614**, 63–96 (2016)
4. Baier, C., Katoen, J.-P.: Principles of Model Checking. MIT Press, Cambridge (2008)
5. van Benthem, J.: Logical Dynamics of Information and Interaction. Cambridge University Press, Cambridge (2011)
6. Benveniste, A., Caillaud, B., Ferrari, A., Mangeruca, L., Passerone, R., Sofronis, C.: Multiple viewpoint contract-based specification and design. In: de Boer, F.S., Bonsangue, M.M., Graf, S., de Roever, W.-P. (eds.) Formal Methods for Components and Objects. LNCS, pp. 200–225. Springer, Heidelberg (2008)
7. Benveniste, A., et al.: Contracts for system design. Found. Trends® Electron. Des. Automation **12**(2–3), 124–400 (2018). https://doi.org/10.1561/1000000053.
8. Bezanson, J., Karpinski, S., Shah, V.B., Edelman, A.: Julia: a fast dynamic language for technical computing. arXiv:1209.5145 (2012)
9. Birtwistle, G.: Demos - Discrete Event Modelling on Simula. Macmillan, New York (1979)
10. Caulfield, T.: SysModels Julia package. https://github.com/tristanc/SysModels. Accessed 10 May 2021
11. Caulfield, T., Ilau, M.-C., Pym, D.: Engineering ecosystem models: semantics and pragmatics. In: International Conference on Simulation Tools and Techniques, pp. 236–258. Springer (2022)
12. Caulfield, T., Pym, D.: Modelling and simulating systems security policy. In: Proceedings of SimuTools (2015)

13. Caulfield, T., Pym, D.: Modelling and simulating systems security policy. EAI Endorsed Trans. Secur. Saf. **3**(8), e3–e3 (2016). (Proc. Simutools 2016, Prague)
14. Collinson, M., Monahan, B., Pym, D.: A Discipline of Mathematical Systems Modelling. College Publications, Madrid (2012)
15. Collinson, M., Pym, D.: Algebra and logic for resource-based systems modelling. Math. Struct. Comput. Sci. **19**, 959–1027 (2009)
16. Collinson, M., Monahan, B., Pym, D.: Semantics for structured systems modelling and simulation. In: Proceedings of Simutools 2010. ACM Digital Library (2010). ISBN 78-963-9799-87-5
17. Conforti, G., Macedonio, D., Sassone, V.: Spatial logics for bigraphs. In: Caires, L., Italiano, G.F., Monteiro, L., Palamidessi, C., Yung, M. (eds.) ICALP 2005. LNCS, vol. 3580, pp. 766–778. Springer, Heidelberg (2005). https://doi.org/10.1007/11523468_62
18. Galmiche, D., Méry, D., Pym, D.: The semantics of BI and resource tableaux. Math. Struct. Comput. Sci. **15**, 1033–1088 (2005)
19. Galmiche, D., Lang, T., Pym, D.: Minimalistic system modelling: behaviours, interfaces, and local reasoning. In: Proceedings of 16th EAI International Conference on Simulation Tools and Techniques (SIMUtools), Springer, Heidelberg. Preprint: https://arxiv.org/abs/24010.16109 (2024)
20. Goudsmid, O., Grumberg, O., Sheinvald, S.: Compositional model checking for multi-properties. In: Henglein, F., Shoham, S., Vizel, Y. (eds.) VMCAI 2021. LNCS, vol. 12597, pp. 55–80. Springer, Cham (2021). https://doi.org/10.1007/978-3-030-67067-2_4
21. Håkansson, H., Persson, G.: Supply chain management: the logic of supply chains and networks. Int. J. Logistics Manage. **15**(1), 11–26 (2004). https://doi.org/10.1108/09574090410700202
22. Hennessy, M., Plotkin, G.: On observing nondeterminism and concurrency. In: Proceedings of the 7th ICALP, Lecture Notes in Computer Science, vol. 85, pp. 299–309. Springer, Cham (1980)
23. Hillston, J.: A Compositional Approach to Performance Modelling. Cambridge University Press, Cambridge (1996)
24. Hoare, C.: Communicating Sequential Processes. Prentice-Hall International, London (1985)
25. Hoare, T., Möller, B., Struth, G., Wehrman, I.: Concurrent kleene algebra and its foundations. J. Logic Algebraic Program. **80**(6) (2011). https://doi.org/10.1016/j.jlap.2011.04.005
26. Ishtiaq, S.S., O'Hearn, P.: BI as an assertion language for mutable data structures. In: Proceedings of POPL. ACM SIGPLAN Notices, vol. 36, no. 3, pp. 14–26 (2001). https://doi.org/10.1145/373243.375719
27. Julia: The Julia Programming Language. http://julialang.org. Accessed 22 Mar 2023
28. Larsen, K.G., Nyman, U., Wąsowski, A.: Modal I/O automata for interface and product line theories. In: De Nicola, R. (ed.) ESOP 2007. LNCS, vol. 4421, pp. 64–79. Springer, Heidelberg (2007). https://doi.org/10.1007/978-3-540-71316-6_6
29. Meta: Open-sourcing Facebook Infer. https://engineering.fb.com/2015/06/11/developer-tools/. Accessed 22 Mar 2023
30. Meyer, B.: Applying "design by contract.". Computer **25**(10), 40–51 (1992). https://doi.org/10.1109/2.161279
31. Milner, R. (ed.): A Calculus of Communicating Systems. LNCS, vol. 92. Springer, Heidelberg (1980). https://doi.org/10.1007/3-540-10235-3

32. Milner, R.: Calculi for synchrony and asynchrony. Theor. Comput. Sci. **25**(3), 267–310 (1983)
33. Milner, R.: Communication and Concurrency. Prentice-Hall, Hoboken (1989)
34. Milner, R.: Communicating and Mobile Systems: the π-Calculus. Cambridge University Press, Cambridge (1999)
35. Milner, R.: Bigraphs and their algebra. Electron. Notes Theor. Comput. Sci. **209**, 5–19 (2008)
36. Milner, R.: Bigraphs as a model for mobile interaction. In: Corradini, A., Ehrig, H., Kreowski, H.-J., Rozenberg, G. (eds.) ICGT 2002. LNCS, vol. 2505, pp. 8–13. Springer, Heidelberg (2002). https://doi.org/10.1007/3-540-45832-8_3
37. Milner, R.: The Space and Motion of Communicating Agents. Cambridge University Press, Cambridge (2009). https://doi.org/10.1017/CBO9780511626661
38. Möller, B., Hoare, T.: Exploring an interface model for CKA. In: Hinze, R., Voigtländer, J. (eds.) MPC 2015. LNCS, vol. 9129, pp. 1–29. Springer, Cham (2015). https://doi.org/10.1007/978-3-319-19797-5_1
39. O'Hearn, P.W., Pym, D.J.: The logic of bunched implications. Bull. Symb. Log. **5**(2), 215–244 (1999)
40. Plotkin, G.D.: A structural approach to operational semantics. Technical report DAIMI FN-19, Computer Science Dept., Aarhus University, Aarhus, Denmark (1981)
41. Pym, D.: Resource semantics: logic as a modelling technology. ACM SIGLOG News **6**(2), 5–41 (2019). https://doi.org/10.1145/3326938.3326940
42. Pym, D.J., O'Hearn, P.W., Yang, H.: Possible worlds and resources: the semantics of BI. Theor. Comput. Sci. **315**(1), 257–305 (2004)
43. Reynolds, J.C.: Separation logic: a logic for shared mutable data structures. In: Proceedings of LICS 2002, pp. 55–74. IEEE Computer Society (2002)
44. de Simone, R.: Higher-level synchronising devices in Meije-SCCS. TCS **37**, 245–267 (1985)
45. Stirling, C.: Modal and Temporal Properties of Processes. Springer, New York (2001)
46. Caulfield, T.: SysModels. https://github.com/tristanc/SysModels. Accessed 22 Mar 2023
47. Tripakis, S., Lickly, B., Henzinger, T., Lee, E.: A theory of synchronous relational interfaces. ACM Trans. Program. Lang. Syst. **33**(4), 1–41 (2011)
48. Tripakis, S.: Compositionality in the science of system design. Proc. IEEE **104**(5), 960–972 (2016). https://doi.org/10.1109/JPROC.2015.2510366
49. Tripakis, S., Lickly, B., Henzinger, T., Lee, E.: A theory of synchronous relational interfaces. ACM Trans. Program. Lang. Syst. **33**(4, Article 14), 1–41 (2011). https://doi.org/10.1145/1985342.1985345
50. Ören, T., Zeigler, B.P., Tolk, A.: Body of Knowledge for Modeling and Simulation: A Handbook by the Society for Modeling and Simulation International (Simulation Foundations, Methods and Applications), Springer (2023)

Minimalistic System Modelling: Behaviours, Interfaces, and Local Reasoning

Didier Galmiche[1], Timo Lang[2], and David Pym[2,3](✉)

[1] Université de Lorraine, CNRS, LORIA, Nancy, France
didier.galmiche@loria.fr
[2] University College London, London, UK
timo.lang@ucl.ac.uk
[3] Institute of Philosophy, University of London, London, UK
d.pym@ucl.ac.uk, david.pym@sas.ac.uk

Abstract. The infrastructure upon which the functioning of society depends is composed of complex ecosystems of systems. Consequently, we must reason about the properties of such ecosystems, which requires that we construct models of them. There are very many approaches to systems modelling, typically building on complex structural and dynamic frameworks. For example, there are simulation modelling tools based on a theoretical treatment of a 'distributed systems metaphor' for system modelling. These tools are based on the concepts of location, resource, and process. They are well developed and have proved valuable in a range of settings. Arguably, however, the foundations of modelling technologies remain underdeveloped. Our purpose here is to explore a foundational modelling framework based on minimal assumptions, starting from a primitive notion of behaviour, and to show that such an approach allows the recovery of the key ideas, including a generalized CAP theorem, required for effective modelling of and reasoning about ecosystems of systems. We establish a logic of behaviours and use it to express local reasoning principles for the compositional structure of systems.

Keywords: System Modelling · Behaviour · Logic · The CAP Theorem · Local Reasoning

1 Introduction

The aim of this paper is to propose and study an extremely simple but general framework for modelling *distributed systems*, seen as a metaphor for ecosystems of systems. We stress that what we describe is a foundational conceptual framework for constructing models, not a specific model.

There is a good deal of work on systems modelling in the literature, much of it—such as [28] and [3,13,16–18], for example—deriving from process algebra. Some of this work, such as [12,13], considers composition of models via notions

A. A. Juan et al. (Eds.): SIMUtools 2024, LNICST 603, pp. 48–71, 2025.
https://doi.org/10.1007/978-3-031-87345-4_4

of interface. Other work, such as [23], derives from the world of management science and organizational theory. Other approaches are based more immediately on notions of composition and interface and their dynamics. For example, interface automata [1,2], relational interfaces [42], and bigraphs, [35,36]. Our approach differs from all of these (and others) in its desire to employ minimal assumptions about structure and dynamics, beginning with a very primitive notion of behaviour. Our aim is to explore the (arguably underdeveloped) *foundations* of system modelling, not to replace existing frameworks and tools.

For the practical purposes of simulation modelling—see, for example, [43] for a survey of the overall ideas—behaviour can be captured, for example, by the dynamics of the many forms of process algebra. Examples include [3,12, 15–18,28,29,34] and many more, including those, described in various previous Simutools papers [12,15,18] that are intended to support implementations of the 'distributed systems metaphor'—in which a system is modelled in terms of its *locations*, *resources*, and *processes*, relative to its *environment*—as described in [3,12,15–18]. The history of this work can be traced to Birtwistle's 'Demos: Discrete Event Modelling on Simula' [7].

These approaches can be implemented by tools such as those described in languages such as Gnosis [16,18] and Julia [6,31]. In particular, the modelling approach based on the 'distributed systems metaphor', is conveniently captured in Julia using the 'SysModels' package that is available from GitHub [14].

Indeed, the distributed systems metaphor notwithstanding, there are very many—far too numerous to discuss here—informal definitions of systems discussed across many disciplines. However, we can identify a common core of these definitions, all supported by the distributed systems metaphor and its implementations, that will serve as a starting point for our work:

> A system is something whose behaviour is reflected in the behaviour of its components.

This definition is deceptively simple: it identifies, at least implicitly, not only *behaviour* and *components*, but also *composition* (necessarily, of components) and so (again, necessarily) *interfaces* between components. This definition amounts to an abstraction and generalization of the characterization of systems that is provided by the distributed systems metaphor (e.g., [12,13]).

In our framework, then, the notion of a 'behaviour' will be a primitive. The standard model of a behaviour is a trace (finite or infinite), but we do not have to subscribe to this interpretation. Indeed, our primitive notion of behaviour requires not even a commitment to that degree of structure, although traces will be an important example. The architectural aspect of a system, namely its component subsystems, will be considered a priori knowledge.

We will see that from this simple starting point—that is, a primitive notion of behaviour—a rather expressive theory emerges. In Sect. 2, we introduce the main notions of our modelling approach. Essentially, we define what we consider to be a 'system', and this will built on a primitive notion of *behaviour*. After defining the crucial notion of an *implementation* between systems, we then derive further well-known concepts from system modelling; in particular, *interfaces* and *composition.*

A thorough epistemological investigation of our choices of primitives is beyond the scope of this paper. However, we believe it is evident that we have identified a credible minimalistic position.

In Sect. 3, by way of demonstrating the relevance of our approach, we use our framework to establish an abstract statement of the famous CAP theorem [10, 27]. Brewer's original conjecture [9] is expressed rather generally. It concerns three key properties of distributed systems. We suppose a system with multiple, connected components that is intended to deliver a specified service. Informally:

- *(C)onsistency*: all the system's clients see the same data at the same time, irrespective of the component of the system to which they connect;
- *(A)vailability*: every request for the service that is sent to the system receives a response that is not the 'error' response;
- *(P)artition-tolerance*: the system continues to deliver the service even if there are failures of the connections between its components.

Brewer stated that these three guarantees cannot be satisfied simultaneously in a distributed system. Gilbert and Lynch gave a formal formulation and proof [26] in a set-up that is quite concrete. Specifically, they give a formal statement of Brewer's conjecture for an account of the CAP properties in 'web services'. In our framework, we are able to establish the CAP theorem in a conceptually quite general way. However, we show, in Appendix A, that Gilbert and Lynch's formulation can be recovered from ours.

In Sect. 4, we introduce a primitive logic of behaviours in which formulae are satisfied relative to 'behaviours as worlds'. We consider the basic classical propositional connectives and modal operators, so obtaining a syntactic variant of **S5**. We establish the equivalence of behavioural equivalence and logical equivalence (see, for example, [5, 8, 41]). We discuss local reasoning principles (in the sense, for example, of [37]) for the composition of systems. Finally, in Sect. 5, we discuss a range of directions for future research, including *time* (Sect. 5.1) and *tableaux proof systems* for the logic (Sect. 5.2).

2 The Basic Theory

Any formal model of a distributed system, including system models constructed through the 'distributed systems metaphor' mentioned above, must capture the following two key points:

- **The topology of the system:** How do the components of the system sit together?
- **The dynamics of the system:** How does the system as a whole and its components behave?

Of these two, modelling the topology is unproblematic: We can usually take some graph-like structure, where edges denote potential communication channels between the parts of a system.

Modelling the dynamics of a system is a more subtle issue. It is usually not feasible to give a full realistic description of a system's behaviour; therefore one works with abstractions. The choice of abstraction is then dependent on the intended application. Some common formalizations of behaviour include *state sets*, (finite or infinite) *traces* and possibly stochastic extensions thereof.

We seek a common abstraction of these formalizations. To this end, it is useful to contemplate the relation between the topological and the dynamical aspect of a distributed system. We can always observe the following *reflection principle*:

> The global behaviour of a system is reflected in the local behaviour of its components.

This principle connects the topological and dynamical aspects of a system by expressing a functional relationship between global and local behaviours, manifesting in various ways. For example, the global behaviour of an input/output system might be modelled by the trace $\langle read(x), write(y), write(y'), read(x')\rangle$ of interactions; at the component responsible for reading the inputs, this global behaviour will be reflected as $\langle read(x), read(x')\rangle$. Cyberphysical systems might have complex behaviours, including a measuring of temperature, and one simple component that only records whether the system is overheated; then the global behaviour of the system is reflected by one of the behaviours $overheat = 0$ or $overheat = 1$.

The above reflection principle forms the core of our modelling approach. It then turns out that we can leave the question what behaviours 'really are' largely open. What matters is only the relation between global and local behaviours, as mediated by the reflection function.

2.1 Systems and Implementations

We assume a given collection $\mathbb{C}$ of *basic components* that will form the building blocks of our distributed systems. Each $c \in \mathbb{C}$ comes equipped with a set $\mathrm{Beh}(c)$, whose elements we call *behaviours*. For nonempty $C \subseteq \mathbb{C}$ we call $\mathrm{Beh}(C) := \Pi_{c\in C}\mathrm{Beh}(c)$ a *set of* C-snapshots.

Definition 1 (system).

- *A* system *is a function whose codomain is a set of snapshots.*
- *If* $f : B \to \mathrm{Beh}(C)$ *is a system, we call the elements of* $\mathrm{Beh}(f) := B$ *and* $\mathrm{Comp}(f) := C$ *the* behaviours of f *and the* components of f, *respectively.*

We think of a system as a set B of high-level descriptions of system behaviours together with a translation f into concrete component behaviours. In this way the definition of a system proposed here is not a fully semantic definition: We do allow, e.g., that $f(b_1) = f(b_2)$ for *different* $b_1, b_2 \in B$. Such behaviours then differ only by their high-level description, not by any observable factors component behaviour. The motiviation for allowing syntactic elements is that it facilitates the modelling of a system.

On the other hand, a fully semantic view of systems could be obtained by requiring f to be injective. In this case, a system can be identified with a (labelled) subset of $\mathrm{Beh}(C)$.

Example 1. Consider two components $c, d \in \mathbb{C}$ with $\mathrm{Beh}(c) = \{x\}^*$ and $\mathrm{Beh}(d) = \{y, z\}^*$. Then every $S \subseteq \{x, y, z\}^*$ can be seen as the behaviours of a system f with $\mathrm{Comp}(f) = \{c, d\}$ where f projects on substrings, e.g. $f(xxyxzzxy) = (xxxx, yzzy)$. Note that this f is not injective, as we have $f(xxyxzzxy) = f(xxxxyzzy)$.

Before coming to our second crucial definition, we introduce some notational conventions. If $f : B \to \mathrm{Beh}(C)$ and $D \subseteq C$, we denote $f_D : B \to \mathrm{Beh}(D)$ the composition of f with the obvious projection function $\mathrm{Beh}(C) \to \mathrm{Beh}(D)$. If D is a singleton $\{d\}$ we write f_d instead of $f_{\{d\}}$. In Example 1 we have $f_d(xxyxzzxy) = yzzy$. It will be useful to view sets of components as systems; for this, we identify $C \subseteq \mathbb{C}$ with the identity function $\mathrm{Beh}(C) \to \mathrm{Beh}(C)$.

Definition 2 (implementation). *Let f, g be systems with* $\mathrm{Comp}(g) \subseteq \mathrm{Comp}(f)$. *An* implementation *of g in f is a function $\sigma : \mathrm{Beh}(f) \to \mathrm{Beh}(g)$ such that $f_{\mathrm{Comp}(g)} = g \circ \sigma$.*

In other words, $\sigma : \mathrm{Beh}(f) \to \mathrm{Beh}(g)$ is an implementation if the following diagram commutes:

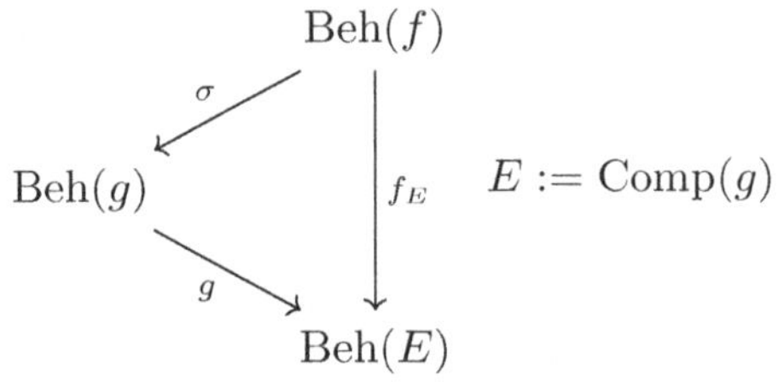

In this case we write $f \overset{\sigma}{\Longrightarrow} g$ and say that f *implements* g *(via* σ*)*, or that g is a *subsystem* of f. If f implements g, then the local behaviour of f at $c \in \mathrm{Comp}(g)$ can always be explained in terms of the behaviour of g. We say that σ *realizes* $y \in \mathrm{Beh}(g)$ if there is an $x \in \mathrm{Beh}(f)$ such that $\sigma(x) = y$.

As a simple example of Definition 2, systems implement their components: For $C \subseteq \mathrm{Comp}(f)$ we have $f \overset{f_C}{\Longrightarrow} C$ because $f_C = id_C \circ f_C$. Here we have used the identification of C with the system id_C as described above.

It should be stressed that $f \overset{\sigma}{\Longrightarrow} g$ does *not* mean that f is in control of g. While σ denotes a relation between the behaviours of f and g, this relation is not necessarily causation. In fact, our model does not have an explicit notion of causation, say via input and output polarities (inputs react, outputs act). On the other hand, such notions can be derived from the set-up, for example:

Definition 3. *If* $f \overset{\sigma}{\Longrightarrow} g$ *and* σ *is* surjective, *then* σ *is called an* input implementation. $E \subseteq \mathrm{Comp}(f)$ *is an* input of f *if* f_E *is an input implementation.*

The intuition is the following: if σ is surjective, then every behaviour of g is realized by σ. Thus g is not constrained as a subsystem of f, and we can think of f as merely 'observing' the behaviour of g and possibly reacting to it.

We end this section with a simple yet fundamental example that illustrates how a basic communication channel between two systems can be modelled in our framework. A general treatment of the composition of systems follows in the next section.

Example 2 (message passing). Let Σ be an alphabet, and let c be a 'communication component' with $\mathrm{Beh}(c) = \Sigma^*$; that is, behaviours are finite Σ-strings. Now for some arbitrary set $G \neq \emptyset$ of additional behaviours, let g be a system with $\mathrm{Beh}(g) \subseteq G \times \{send(s) \mid s \in \Sigma^*\}$ that implements c via $g_c(g, send(s)) = s$. Furthermore let f be another system with $\mathrm{Beh}(f) \subseteq F \times \{receive(s) \mid s \in \Sigma^*\}$ that implements c via $f_c(f, receive(s)) = s$ and where $F \cap G = \emptyset$, and assume moreover that c is an input of f: for all $s \in \Sigma^*$, there exists $x \in f$ such that $(x, receive(s)) \in \mathrm{Beh}(f)$.

We now construct a system h that allows message passing from g to f. For this let $\mathrm{Comp}(h) = \mathrm{Comp}(f) \cup \mathrm{Comp}(g)$ and let $\mathrm{Beh}(h)$ contain those triples $(y, transmit(s), x)$ such that $(y, send(s)) \in \mathrm{Beh}(g)$ and $(x, reveice(s)) \in \mathrm{Beh}(f)$. Then h implements both f and g, and it stipulates that the messages that g sends are those that f receives.

We conclude this section by introduction a notion of *system equivalence*.

Definition 4. f *and* g *are equivalent, written* $f \equiv g$, *if* $f \Longrightarrow g$ *and* $g \Longrightarrow f$.

2.2 Compositions

Definition 5 (environment and composition). *An* environment for for g_1 and g_2 *is any system* f *implementing both* g_1 *and* g_2. *An environment* f *is a* composition *if* $\mathrm{Comp}(f) = \mathrm{Comp}(g_1) \cup \mathrm{Comp}(g_2)$.

We write $g_1 \overset{\sigma_1}{\Longleftarrow} f \overset{\sigma_2}{\Longrightarrow} g_2$ to denote a system f implementing both g_1 and g_2.

Definition 6 (interface). $\mathsf{Int}(g_1, g_2) := \mathrm{Comp}(g_1) \cap \mathrm{Comp}(g_2)$ *is called the* interface *of* g_1 *and* g_2.

If $g_1 \overset{\sigma_1}{\Longleftarrow} f \overset{\sigma_2}{\Longrightarrow} g_2$ and $I := \mathsf{Int}(g_1, g_2)$ we have the following commutative diagram, assuming $I \neq \emptyset$:

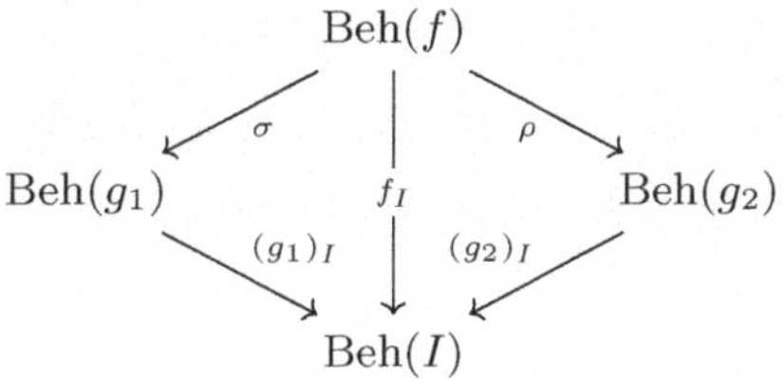

Call $(y_1, y_2) \in \mathrm{Beh}(g_1) \times \mathrm{Beh}(g_2)$ *compatible* if $I = \emptyset$ or $(g_1)_I(y_1) = (g_2)_I(y_2)$. One is often interested in compositions which are 'derived' from the systems g_1 and g_2; such compositions impose only those restrictions on its subsystems that are necessary to compose them. This is captured in the next definition.

Definition 7 (free composition). *A composition* $g_1 \overset{\sigma_1}{\Longleftarrow} f \overset{\sigma_2}{\Longrightarrow} g_2$ *is called* free *if for every compatible pair* $(y_1, y_2) \in \mathrm{Beh}(g_1) \times \mathrm{Beh}(g_2)$ *there exists* $x \in \mathrm{Beh}(f)$ *such that* $\sigma_1(x) = y_1$ *and* $\sigma_2(x) = y_2$.

For example, the system h from Example 2 is a free composition. Given two systems f, g, there is a canonical free composition of f and g whose behaviours are exactly the compatible pairs and which has projections as implementation functions. We denote this composition by $f \otimes g$; it is essentially the category-theoretic *pullback* of the maps $(g_1)_I$ and $(g_2)_I$.[1]

Definition 8 (canonical free composition). *Let* f, g *be two systems. Let* $I := \mathsf{Int}(f, g)$. $f \otimes g$ *is the composition of* f *and* g *whose behaviour set is* $\{(x, y) \in \mathrm{Beh}(f) \times \mathrm{Beh}(g) \mid I = \emptyset \vee f_I(x) = g_I(y)\}$, *whose function is given by*

$$(f \otimes g)_c(x, y) = \begin{cases} f_c(x) & \text{if } c \in \mathrm{Comp}(f) \\ g_c(y) & \text{if } c \in \mathrm{Comp}(g) \setminus \mathrm{Comp}(f) \end{cases}$$

Note that if $c \in \mathsf{Int}(f, g)$, then $(f \otimes g)_c(x, y) = f_c(x) = g_c(y)$ by compatibility.

We say that f is *runnable* if $\mathrm{Beh}(f) \neq \emptyset$ (or equivalently, $f \neq \emptyset$). The existence of at least one compatible pair is the minimal requirement for runnable compositions:

Lemma 1. *If* $\mathsf{Int}(f, g) \neq \emptyset$, *a runnable composition of* f *and* g *exists iff there is a compatible pair.*

Proof. If some compatible pair exists, then $f \otimes g$ as described in Definition 8 above is runnable. Conversely, let $f \overset{\sigma}{\Longleftarrow} h \overset{\rho}{\Longrightarrow} g$ be any runnable composition of f, g and pick $z \in \mathrm{Beh}(h)$. Let $x = \sigma(z)$, $y = \rho(z)$, and $I = \mathsf{Int}(f, g)$. Then, by the properties of implementations, we can show that (x, y) is a compatible pair: $f_I(x) = f_I(\sigma(z)) = h_I(z) = g_I(\rho(z)) = g_I(y)$.

We can show that 'directed' compositions are always runnable:

Lemma 2. *Assume that* g *is runnable. If* $\mathsf{Int}(f, g) = \mathrm{Comp}(e)$ *and the system* e *is an input of* f *(see Definition 3), then there is a runnable composition of* f *and* g.

Proof. Let $f \overset{\rho}{\Longrightarrow} e$ be an input implementation and $g \overset{\sigma}{\Longrightarrow} e$ any implementation. Since g is runnable, there exists $y \in \mathrm{Beh}(g)$, and as e is an input component we can find $x \in \mathrm{Beh}(f)$ such that $\rho(x) = \sigma(y)$. For $I := \mathrm{Comp}(e)$ we consequently have $f_I(x) = e(\rho(x)) = e(\sigma(y)) = g_I(y)$ and so (x, y) is a compatible pair. Thus f and g are composable by Lemma 1.

[1] Pullbacks as models of synchronization also appear in [4].

Example 3. Let f, g be systems with $\mathrm{Beh}(f) \subseteq \{a,b,c\}^*$ and $\mathrm{Beh}(g) \subseteq \{b,c,d\}^*$, both closed under inital segments (think traces of actions), and let $\mathsf{Int}(f,g) = \{e\}$ where $\mathrm{Beh}(e) = \{b,c\}^*$. Assuming that f and g implement e via the obvious projections, $\mathrm{Beh}(f \otimes g)$ consists of pairs $(s_1, s_2) \in \{a,b,c\}^* \times \{b,c,d\}^*$ whose restriction to the common actions $\{b,c\}$ coincides. For example, if $x = \langle a,b,b,c,a,b\rangle \in \mathrm{Beh}(f)$ and $y = \langle b,d,b,c,d,b\rangle \in \mathrm{Beh}(g)$ then $(x,y) \in \mathrm{Beh}(f \otimes g)$, as their restriction to $\{b,c\}$ coincides in the trace $\langle b,b,c,b\rangle$. We can interpret this as a partially asynchronuous computation:

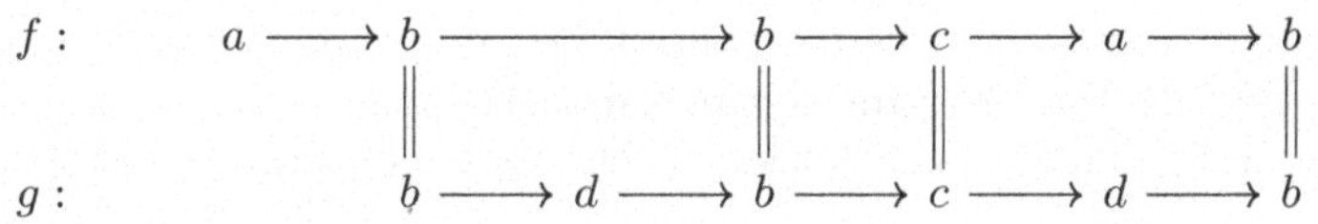

Example 4 (heaps). Take as basic components a set L of *locations*, with $\mathrm{Beh}(l) = \mathbb{N}$ for $l \in L$. For $L_0 \subseteq^{fin} L$, $S(L_0)$ is the system whose behaviours are the L_0-based *heaplets*, i.e. functions $h : L_0 \to \mathbb{N}$. S_0 implements every $l \in L_0$ via the function $h \mapsto h(l)$. An L_0-stream is the system whose behaviours are sequences σ of commands $l := n$ where $l \in L_0$ and $n \in \mathbb{N}$. It implements S_0 via the function that sends σ to the the heaplet h where $h(l)$ is the value n of the last command $l := n$ in σ. Let L_0 be the disjoint union of L_1 and L_2. Then every L_0-stream is the free composition of an L_1-stream and an L_2-stream.

In Example 3, nothing is said about the temporal relation between actions outside the interface, and so we have a model of 'true' asynchronicity. On the other hand, if $f \overset{\sigma}{\Longleftarrow} h \overset{\rho}{\Longrightarrow} g$ is any free composition, then one can show that h factors through $\mathrm{Beh}(f \otimes g)$ via a *surjective* map:

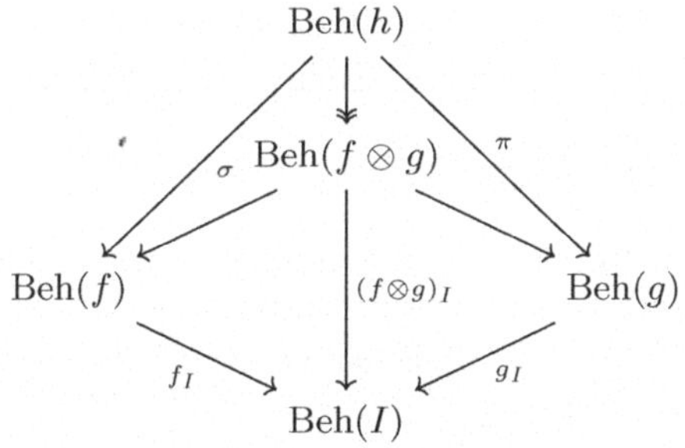

Intuitively, this means that in any free composition h, $\mathrm{Beh}(h)$ extends $\mathrm{Beh}(f \otimes g)$ with some extra information. This can be seen as the information about how a pair (x,y) of compatible behaviours is combined together: is it sequential, synchronous, or asynchronous?

Example 5. Let f and g be as in Example 3. Let h be a system whose behaviours are all elements of $\{a,b,c,d\}^*$ whose restriction to actions in $\{a,b,c\}$ and $\{b,c,d\}$

lies in Beh(f) and Beh(g), respectively. h is a free composition of f and g via the obvious projection maps. Assuming again that $x = \langle a, b, b, c, a, b \rangle \in$ Beh(f) and that $y = \langle b, d, b, c, d, b \rangle \in$ Beh(g) we now have, for example, that $\langle a, b, d, b, c, a, d, b \rangle \in$ Beh(h). Thus h 'linearizes' the behaviours x and y.

3 Implementation Guarantees and the CAP Theorem

The aim of this section is to prove a formal version of the Brewer's CAP theorem. Recall that the CAP theorem states that the three guarantees of *consistency, availability* and *partition-tolerance* cannot be simultanously satisfied in a distributed system (cf. the introduction to this article).

We start by formalizing the notion of an *implementation guarantee*:

Definition 9 (implementation guarantee). *An* implementation guarantee *for a system g is a set $\mathcal{X} \subseteq \mathcal{P}(\mathrm{Beh}(g))$. The implementation $f \overset{\sigma}{\Longrightarrow} g$ satisfies $\mathcal{X}$, written $\sigma \models \mathcal{X}$, if $\{\sigma(x) \mid x \in \mathrm{Beh}(f)\} \in \mathcal{X}$.*

Definition 10 (consistency). *For $C \subseteq \mathrm{Beh}(g)$, the implementation guarantee $\{X \subseteq \mathrm{Beh}(g) \mid X \subseteq C\}$ is called C-*consistency guarantee.

Simply put, an implementation guarantee satisfies C-consistency if it only realizes behaviours in C. To avoid trivial solutions to consistency, one also needs to consider guarantees that sufficiently many behaviours are realized. We formula such *availability guarantees* relative to a binary relation $R \subseteq \mathrm{Beh}(g)^2$. Henceforth $R(x, \bullet) := \{y \mid xRy\}$ and $dom(R) := \{x \mid R(x, \bullet) \neq \emptyset\}$.

Definition 11 (availability). *For a binary relation R on Beh(g), the implementation guarantees*

$$\{X \subseteq \mathrm{Beh}(g) \mid \forall x \in X(x \in \mathrm{dom}(R) \textit{ implies } \exists y \in X \cap R(x, \bullet)\}$$
$$\{X \subseteq \mathrm{Beh}(g) \mid \forall x \in X(R(x, \bullet) \subseteq X)\}$$

are called weak *and* strong R-availability, *respectively.*

More directly, if an implementation realizes some behaviour $x \in \mathrm{dom}(R)$, then weak (resp. strong) R-availability states that it must also realize some (resp. all) $y \in R(x, \bullet)$. Strong availability corresponds to the *input-enabledness* condition used in I/O-automata [33].

Definition 12 (partition-tolerance). *Let $f \overset{\sigma_1}{\Longrightarrow} g_1$ and $f \overset{\sigma_2}{\Longrightarrow} g_2$. The implementation guarantee*

$$\{X \subseteq \mathrm{Beh}(f) \mid \forall x_1, x_2 \in X \exists x \in X \sigma_1(x) = \sigma_1(x_1), \sigma_2(x) = \sigma_2(x_2)\}$$

is called (σ_1, σ_2)-partition-tolerance.

Partition-tolerance states that every pair $\sigma_1(x_1)$ and $\sigma_2(x_2)$ of realized behaviours of g_1 and g_2, where possibly $x_1 \neq x_2$, can also be *jointly* realized by some single behaviour x. In other words, implemented behaviours in g_1 never restrict implemented behaviours in g_2 and vice versa. This means that no communication (that is, 'message passing') between the components g_1 and g_2 is necessary to run the system (neither has to wait for the other).

The final definition needed to state the CAP theorem is that of entanglement. We think here of a situation where a system has two subsystems, comes with a consistency guarantee, and there are two relations modelling different ways of evolving the system. Entanglement then denotes that, for every initial behaviour and evolution to an intermediate behaviour via the first relation, there is a further evolution into a 'problematic' behaviour via the second relation such that the following holds:

> Whenever two behaviours look like the problematic behaviour from the perspective of the first subsystem, but look like the behaviour of the initial and intermediate behaviour from the perspective of the second subsystem, then at least one of them fails consistency.

Definition 13 (entanglement). *Let* $f \overset{\sigma_1}{\Longrightarrow} g_1$ *and* $f \overset{\sigma_2}{\Longrightarrow} g_2$ *and* $C \subseteq \mathrm{Beh}(f)$. *Two relations* $R, S \subseteq \mathrm{Beh}(f)^2$ *of behaviours are* C-entangled over (σ_1, σ_2) *if they satisfy the condition*

$$\begin{aligned} \forall w \in \mathrm{Beh}(f) \exists x \in R(w, \bullet) \cap dom(S) \forall v \in S(x, \bullet) \forall y, z \in \mathrm{Beh}(f) : \\ \sigma_1(y) = \sigma_1(z) = \sigma_1(v) \wedge \sigma_2(y) = \sigma_2(w) \wedge \sigma_2(z) = \sigma_2(x) \\ \Rightarrow y \notin C \vee z \notin C \end{aligned} \qquad (*)$$

which is illustrated by the following picture:

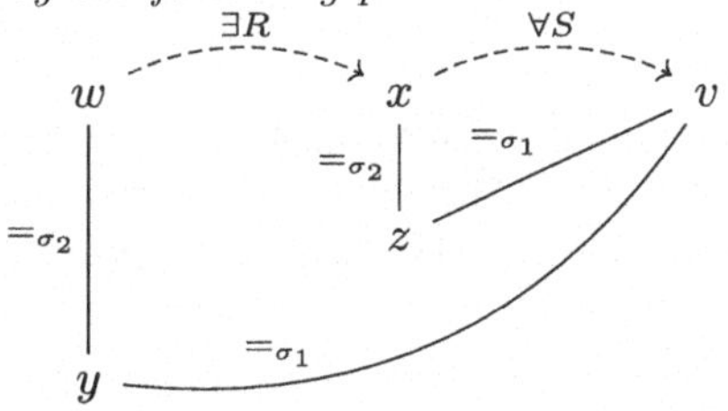

We now state and prove a formalized version of the CAP theorem.

Theorem 1 (generalized CAP theorem). *Let* $f \overset{\sigma_1}{\Longrightarrow} g_1$ *and* $f \overset{\sigma_2}{\Longrightarrow} g_2$. *Let* $C \subseteq \mathrm{Beh}(f)$ *and assume that* $R, S \subseteq \mathrm{Beh}(f)^2$ *are* C*-entangled over* (σ_1, σ_2).

Then every runnable implementation of f *must violate at least one of the following guarantees:*

- C*-consistency*
- *strong* R*-availability and weak* S*-availability*
- (σ_1, σ_2)*-partition-tolerance*

Proof. Let $h \stackrel{\sigma}{\Longrightarrow} f$ be any implementation of f, and assume that it satisfies (2) and (3). We show that $\sigma \not\models C$-consistency. Let $w \in \mathrm{Beh}(f)$ be any behaviour realized by σ, and pick x as in the entanglement condition. By strong R-availability, σ realizes x. By weak S-availability and the fact that $x \in dom(S)$, σ also realizes some $v \in S(x, \bullet)$. By (σ_1, σ_2)-partion-tolerance σ also realizes behaviours y, z such that $\sigma_1(y) = \sigma_1(z) = \sigma_1(v)$ and $\sigma_2(y) = \sigma_2(w)$, $\sigma_2(z) = \sigma_2(x)$. But then by entanglement, σ realizes a behaviour that is not in C, violating C-consistency.

Of course, the usual formulation of the CAP theorem (cf. [27]) does not involve a complicated entanglement condition. This is because it deals with a concretely given set of implementation guarantees. Our formulation on the other hand starts from arbitrary guarantees derived from the sets C, R, and S, none of which needs to be a 'read' or 'write' guarantee as in [27]. The entanglement condition is a logical abstraction of the relation between read and write guarantees in CAP that allows the proof to go through. To verify that Theorem 1 is indeed a generalization of CAP, we show in Appendix A how to recover a standard form of the CAP theorem from it. This also shows in detail how a more traditional process-based view of systems can be modelled in our behaviour-based view.

4 Logic and Local Reasoning Principles

We now describe a simple logic of systems, and use this logic to state some local reasoning principles.

Our logic is one of system behaviours, asserting properties of behaviours through a satisfaction relation between systems and formulae of the form

$$f, \mathcal{V}, x \models \phi$$

where f is a system, x is a behaviour of f, and $\mathcal{V}$ is a valuation. This relation will be defined formally below.

The idea of such a logic is related to logics of state in the sense of van Benthem-Bergstra and Hennessy-Milner (commonly known as 'Hennessy-Milner' theorems)—see, for example, [5,34,41]—in which a process with state E is judged to satisfy a property ϕ, denoted $E \models \phi$. In this setting, 'action modalities' such as $[a]\phi$, where a denotes a basic action, play a key role in connecting the processes and the logic:

$$E \models [a]\phi \text{ iff for all evolutions } E \xrightarrow{a} E',\ E' \models \phi$$

The key result in such a setting is that bisimulation equivalence of processes is equivalent to their logical equivalence.

In our setting, we establish what may be understood as a corresponding result between systems with equivalent behaviours and their logical properties. Our result does not, however, require the presence of action modalities. Behaviours are a basic component of models and the formula $\Box\phi$ simply characterizes all of the behaviours of the system. This is explained formally in Sect. 4.2.

We employ also structural connectives to characterize the compositional structure of systems and, through a key concept of *interface*, how the behaviour of one component of a system affects a component to which it is connected. We introduce 'local reasoning' principles, borrowing the name from Separation Logic [30, 37, 39], to characterize these ideas. Connectives of this kind are also present in logics of state for processes; see, for example, [3, 16, 17, 19]).

4.1 The Elementary Logic

For every basic component $c \in \mathbb{C}$, we assume a set $Var(c)$ of variables. All of these sets are assumed to be disjoint. A *valuation* is a function $\mathcal{V}$ mapping each $p \in Var(c)$ to a subset of $\text{Beh}(c)$.

For $C \subseteq \mathbb{C}$, the *elementary* C*-logic* $\mathcal{L}(C)$ is built from variables in $\bigcup_{c \in C} V(c)$ and the boolean connectives $\wedge$ and $\neg$. It is interpreted over triples $(f, \mathcal{V}, x)$ where f is a system with $\text{Comp}(f) \supseteq C$ and $x \in \text{Beh}(f)$ using the following clauses:

$$
\begin{aligned}
f, \mathcal{V}, x \models p &:\iff f_c(x) \in \mathcal{V}(p) \qquad\qquad (p \in Var(c)) \\
f, \mathcal{V}, x \models \varphi \wedge \psi &:\iff f, \mathcal{V}, x \models \varphi \text{ and } f, \mathcal{V}, x \models \psi \\
f, \mathcal{V}, x \models \neg\varphi &:\iff f, \mathcal{V}, x \not\models \varphi
\end{aligned}
$$

We write $f, \mathcal{V} \models \varphi$ if $f, \mathcal{V}, x \models \varphi$ for all $x \in \text{Beh}(f)$. As usual, we can define further boolean connectives $\varphi \vee \psi := \neg(\neg\varphi \wedge \neg\psi)$ and $\varphi \to \psi := \neg\varphi \vee \psi$. We let $\mathcal{L} := \mathcal{L}(\mathbb{C})$ and $\mathcal{L}(f) := \mathcal{L}(\text{Comp}(f))$.

For example, for $p \in Var(c)$ and $q \in Var(d)$ we have $f, \mathcal{V} \models p \to q$ iff $f_d(x) \in \mathcal{V}(q)$ whenever $f_c(x) \in \mathcal{V}(p)$. That is, if some behaviour of f locally satisfies p at the component c, then it locally satisfies q at d.

Lemma 3 (absoluteness). *Let* $f \overset{\sigma}{\Longrightarrow} g$ *and* $\alpha \in \mathcal{L}(g)$*. Then, for all* $x \in \text{Beh}(f)$*,*

$$
f, \mathcal{V}, x \models \alpha \iff g, \mathcal{V}, \sigma(x) \models \alpha
$$

Proof. By induction on α. We only show the case $\alpha = p_c$, which uses the properties of implementations:

$$
f, \mathcal{V}, x \models p_c \iff f_c(x) \in \mathcal{V}(p_c) \iff g_c(\sigma(x)) \in \mathcal{V}(p_c) \iff g, \mathcal{V}, \sigma(x) \models p_c
$$

As a corollary, we can observe that $g, \mathcal{V} \models \alpha$ implies $f, \mathcal{V} \models \alpha$ whenever $f \overset{\sigma}{\Longrightarrow} g$ and $\alpha \in \mathcal{L}(g)$. Thus properties of g that are expressible in $\mathcal{L}(g)$ are inherited by any system implementing g.

We can state a first simple local reasoning principle: In order to prove that a system satisfies some $\mathcal{L}$-property β, it suffices to find subsystems g and h of f and a property α such that g enforces that α is true at the interface of f and g, and h satisfies β whenever it satisfies α at its interface.

Theorem 2 (Local reasoning I). *Let* $g \overset{\sigma}{\Longleftarrow} f \overset{\pi}{\Longrightarrow} h$ *and* $I = \mathsf{Int}(f, g) \neq \emptyset$*. The rule*

$$
\frac{g, \mathcal{V} \models \alpha \quad h, \mathcal{V} \models \alpha \to \beta}{f, \mathcal{V} \models \beta}
$$

is admissible for all $\alpha \in \mathcal{L}(I)$ *and* $\beta \in \mathcal{L}(h)$*.*

Proof. Let $x \in \text{Beh}(f)$. By assumption, $g, \mathcal{V}, \sigma(x) \models \alpha$. As g implements the interface I (seen as a system), Lemma 3 implies $I, \mathcal{V}, g_I(\sigma(x)) \models \alpha$. Furthermore, $g_I(\sigma(x)) = h_I(\pi(x))$, so we have $I, \mathcal{V}, h_I(\pi(x)) \models \alpha$. Another application of Lemma 3 yields $h, \mathcal{V}, \pi(x) \models \alpha$. By assumption we have $h, \mathcal{V}, \pi(x) \models \alpha \to \beta$ and so $h, \mathcal{V}, \pi(x) \models \beta$ follows. Thus, by yet another application of Lemma 3, $f, \mathcal{V}, x \models \beta$ as desired.

Note that this theorem applies in particular to $f = g \otimes h$ (see Definition 8).

Example 6. Consider two components c and d with $\text{Beh}(c) = \text{Beh}(d) = \mathbb{Q}$. Let g be a system implementing c and having $d \notin \text{Comp}(g)$. We think of g as a system that, among other things, records the temperature in Celsius in its component c. Moreover let h be a converter from Celsius to Fahrenheit, modelled as follows: $\text{Comp}(h) = \{c, d\}$, $h = id : \text{Beh}(h) \to \text{Beh}(c) \times \text{Beh}(d)$ where $\text{Beh}(h) = \{(x, y) \in \mathbb{Q} \mid y = x * 1.8 + 32\}$. Let $p_c \in V(c)$ and $p_d \in V(d)$ be variables with $\mathcal{V}(p_c) = [0, 10]$ and $\mathcal{V}(p_d) = [32, 50]$. Assume we know that $g \models p_c$, that is, only temperatures between 0 and 10 degree Celsius are measured by g. Then we can formally derive that $g \otimes h$ only records temperatures between 32° and 50° Fahrenheit:

$$\frac{g, \mathcal{V} \models p_c \quad h, \mathcal{V} \models p_c \to p_d}{g \otimes h, \mathcal{V} \models p_d}$$

4.2 Adding a Universal Modality

A standard extension $\mathcal{L}(C) \subseteq \mathcal{L}(C)^{\Box}$ adds a universal modal operator $\Box$ to the language, subject to the following clause for satisfaction:

$$f, \mathcal{V}, x \models \Box\varphi :\iff f, \mathcal{V}, y \models \varphi \text{ for all } y \in \text{Beh}(f)$$

$\Box\varphi$ therefore denotes a property φ that holds for *all* behaviours $x \in \text{Beh}(f)$. This corresponds to the standard clause for $\Box$ in modal logic in the case that the accessibility relation is universal; that is, in which each element is related to every other element. We therefore obtain a syntactic variant of the well-known modal logic **S5**.

In the setting or process algebras, such as those discussed above that provide bases for simulation modelling, it is more natural to work with action modalities/formulae such as $[a]\phi$, as discussed above, in which the action a refers to an evolution of process state. In our setting, the simple modality refers directly to behaviours. In both cases, however, van Benthem-Bergstra-Hennessy-Milner equivalence theorems can be obtained—see Theorem 6.

In the presence of the modal operator $\Box$, Lemma 3 fails, but some variants of it remain provable. Call a formula in $\mathcal{L}^{\Box}$ *positive* (resp. *negative*) if no $\Box$ appears in the scope of an odd (resp. even) number of $\neg$'s. By a simple induction we can show the following:

Lemma 4 (directed absoluteness). *Assume* $f \overset{\sigma}{\Longrightarrow} g$. *Then for all* $x \in \mathrm{Beh}(f)$,

$$
\begin{aligned}
&g, \mathcal{V}, \sigma(x) \models \alpha \text{ implies } f, \mathcal{V}, x \models \alpha \quad \text{for positive } \alpha \in \mathcal{L}(g)^{\Box} \\
\text{and} \quad &f, \mathcal{V}, x \models \alpha \text{ implies } g, \mathcal{V}, \sigma(x) \models \alpha \quad \text{for negative } \alpha \in \mathcal{L}(g)^{\Box}.
\end{aligned}
$$

By tracking the absoluteness properties used in the proof of Theorem 2, we can generalize slightly:

Theorem 3 (Local reasoning II). *Let* $g \overset{\sigma}{\Longleftarrow} f \overset{\pi}{\Longrightarrow} h$ *and* $I = \mathsf{Int}(f, g) \neq \emptyset$. *The rule*

$$\frac{g, \mathcal{V} \models \alpha \quad h, \mathcal{V} \models \alpha \to \beta}{f, \mathcal{V} \models \beta}$$

is admissible for all $\alpha \in \mathcal{L}(I)$ *and positive* $\beta \in \mathcal{L}(h)^{\Box}$.

The next local reasoning principle makes use of the notion of an input (Definition 3).

Theorem 4 (Local reasoning III). *Assume* $I = \mathsf{Int}(f, g) \neq \emptyset$ *is an input to* g. *The rule*

$$\frac{f, \mathcal{V} \not\models \alpha \quad g, \mathcal{V} \models \neg\alpha \to \neg\beta}{f \otimes g, \mathcal{V} \not\models \beta}$$

is admissible for all $\alpha \in \mathcal{L}(I)$ *and negative* $\beta \in \mathcal{L}(g)^{\Box}$.

Proof. Pick some $x \in \mathrm{Beh}(f)$ such that $f, \mathcal{V}, x \models \neg\alpha$. By absoluteness, we have $I, \mathcal{V}, f_I(x) \models \neg\alpha$. Since I is an input to g, we can find $y \in \mathrm{Beh}(g)$ such that $g_I(y) = f_I(x)$. Again by absoluteness we obtain $g, \mathcal{V}, y \models \neg\alpha$ and hence $g, \mathcal{V}, y \models \neg\beta$. As $\neg\beta$ is positive it follows that $f \otimes g, \mathcal{V}, (x, y) \models \neg\beta$.

Thus to show that some negative β fails in $f \otimes g$ where the interface is an input to g, it suffices to show that f fails some property α at the interface and that this failure causes the failure of β in g. This needs not be true if f is not an input, as then the behaviour failing α might not be realized in $f \otimes g$.

For systems with a trivial interface we can show the following:

Theorem 5. *The rule*

$$\frac{h, \mathcal{V} \models \beta}{g \otimes h, \mathcal{V} \models \beta}$$

is admissible for all $\beta \in \mathcal{L}(h)^{\Box}$ *given that* $\mathsf{Int}(g, h) = \emptyset$.

Proof. It suffices to prove by induction over $\delta \in \mathcal{L}(h)^{\Box}$ that

$$g \otimes h, \mathcal{V}, (x, y) \models \delta \iff h, \mathcal{V}, y \models \delta$$

This follows from the fact that $\mathrm{Beh}(g \otimes h) = \mathrm{Beh}(g) \times \mathrm{Beh}(h)$ whenever $\mathsf{Int}(g, h) = \emptyset$. We illustrate one step of the induction:

$$\begin{aligned} g \otimes h, \mathcal{V}, (x, y) \models \Box\delta' &\iff \forall x' \in \mathrm{Beh}(g) \forall y' \in \mathrm{Beh}(h).\ g \otimes h, \mathcal{V}, (x', y') \models \delta' \\ &\overset{IH}{\iff} \forall x' \in \mathrm{Beh}(g) \forall y' \in \mathrm{Beh}(h).\ h, \mathcal{V}, y' \models \delta' \\ &\iff \forall y' \in \mathrm{Beh}(h).\ h, \mathcal{V}, y' \models \delta' \\ &\iff h, \mathcal{V}, y \models \Box\delta' \end{aligned}$$

Remark: If β encodes a Hoare triple, then the above is a frame rule (cf. [30]).

Finally, we state a Hennessy-Milner Theorem (see, e.g., Theorem 2.24 in [8]) for our logic. The usual reference to bisimulations can be avoided here as we are working with the simple modal logic **S5**; instead, we use the notion of a *type*.

Definition 14. *For a system f with* $\mathrm{Comp}(f) = C$ *and* $x \in \mathrm{Beh}(f)$ *we define* $\mathsf{tp}(x) := \{p \in V(C) \mid f, x \models p\}$. *Moreover, we define* $\mathsf{tps}(f) := \{\mathsf{tp}(x) \mid x \in \mathrm{Beh}(f)\}$.

Theorem 6. *Let f, g be two systems with* $\mathrm{Comp}(f) = \mathrm{Comp}(g) =: C$, *and assume $V(C)$ is finite.*[2] *For any* $(x, y) \in \mathrm{Beh}(f) \times \mathrm{Beh}(g)$, *the following are equivalent:*

1. $f, x \models \varphi \iff g, y \models \varphi$, *for all* $\varphi \in \mathcal{L}(C)$, *and*
2. $\mathsf{tp}(x) = \mathsf{tp}(y)$.

The following are also equivalent:

1. $f, x \models \varphi \iff g, y \models \varphi$, *for all* $\varphi \in \mathcal{L}(C)^{\Box}$, *and*
2. $\mathsf{tp}(x) = \mathsf{tp}(y)$ *and* $\mathsf{tps}(f) = \mathsf{tps}(g)$.

Proof. We show only the second equivalence. For (1)⇒(2), we argue as follows: Let $D := \mathsf{tp}(x)$, and define $\varphi_D := \bigwedge\{p \mid p \in D\} \wedge \bigwedge\{\neg p \mid p \in V(C) \setminus D\}$. Then $f, x \models \varphi_D$ and so $g, y \models \varphi_D$ by assumption, which in turn implies $\mathsf{tp}(y) = \mathsf{tp}(x) = D$. Now let $D \in \mathsf{tps}(f)$, say $D = \mathsf{tp}(x')$ for some $x' \in \mathrm{Beh}(f)$. Then $f, x \models \neg\Box\neg\varphi_D$, and so by assumption $g, y \models \neg\Box\neg\varphi_D$. It follows that for some $y' \in \mathrm{Beh}(g)$, $g, y' \models \varphi_D$ and so $\mathsf{tp}(y') = D$, which implies $D \in \mathsf{tps}(g)$. Hence $\mathsf{tps}(f) \subseteq \mathsf{tps}(g)$, and by a symmetric argument we get $\mathsf{tps}(g) \subseteq \mathsf{tps}(f)$.

(2)⇒(1) is achieved by induction on φ; we only consider the case that $\varphi = \Box\psi$. Assume towards a contradiction that $f, x \models \Box\psi$ and $g, y \not\models \Box\psi$. The latter means that $g, y' \not\models \psi$ for some $y' \in \mathrm{Beh}(g)$. By assumption, there is an $x' \in \mathrm{Beh}(f)$ such that $\mathsf{tp}(x') = \mathsf{tp}(y')$. Then by the induction hypothesis, $f, x' \not\models \psi$, contradicting $f, x \models \Box\psi$. Conversely, if $f, x \not\models \Box\psi$, then $f, x' \not\models \psi$ for some $x' \in \mathrm{Beh}(f)$. Pick $y' \in \mathrm{Beh}(g)$ with $\mathsf{tp}(y') = \mathsf{tp}(x')$; by the induction hypothesis, $g, y' \not\models \psi$ and so $g, y \not\models \Box\psi$ follows.

[2] For simplicity we here use this condition stronger than *image-finiteness* that appears in Hennessy-Milner theorems in modal logic, see, for example, [41].

4.3 Adding Structural Connectives

We have discussed extensively the sense in which systems consist of components, connected by interfaces. We have also established an elementary logic of system behaviours and, while we have considered some basic notions of local reasoning, we have not yet given a logical characterization of the compositional structure of systems.

To this send, we now consider two 'structural' connectives that are closely related to the multiplicative conjunction found in relevance and bunched logics. In particular, their use to characterize system structure resembles the use of such connectives in the family of 'separation logics' and related ideas [20,30,38,39].

We define the following ternary relation between system–behaviour pairs, which syntactically overloads the $\otimes$-operator from Definition 8:

$$\begin{aligned}
`(f,x) = (f_1,x_1) \otimes (f_2,x_2)' :\Longleftrightarrow\ & f \equiv f_1 \otimes f_2 \text{ and } \forall i \in \{1,2\} \\
& \forall c \in \mathrm{Comp}(f_i) : f_c(x) = (f_i)_c(x_i) \\
`(f,x) = (f_1,x_1) \overrightarrow{\otimes} (f_2,x_2)' :\Longleftrightarrow\ & (f,x) = (f_1,x_1) \otimes (f_2,x_2) \text{ and} \\
& \mathsf{Int}(f_1,f_2) \text{ is an input to } f_2
\end{aligned}$$

The first clause uses the equivalence notion $\equiv$ from Definition 4.

We can now define a logic $\mathcal{L}^*(C)$ that extends $\mathcal{L}(C)$ with binary operators $*$ and $\overrightarrow{*}$, which are interpreted as follows:

$$\begin{aligned}
f,\mathcal{V},x \models \varphi * \psi \iff\ & (f,x) = (f_1,x_1) \otimes (f_2,x_2) \text{ for some} \\
& f_1,\mathcal{V},x_1 \models \varphi \text{ and } f_2,\mathcal{V},x_2 \models \psi \\
f,\mathcal{V},x \models \varphi \overrightarrow{*} \psi \iff\ & (f,x) = (f_1,x_1) \overrightarrow{\otimes} (f_2,x_2) \text{ for some} \\
& f_1,\mathcal{V},x_1 \models \varphi \text{ and } f_2,\mathcal{V},x_2 \models \psi
\end{aligned}$$

Evidently, $*$ and $\overrightarrow{*}$ are multiplicative conjunctions. The first characterizes a simple (ordered) decomposition of a system into two components. The second also does this, but, in addition, identifies the interface that supports the output of the first component to be the input to the second.

Theorem 7 (local-global). *The following is a theorem for all positive φ in $\mathcal{L}^{\Box}$:*

$$\varphi * \top \to \varphi$$

That is, if a positive formula φ holds in a part of the system, then it holds in the whole system.

Proof. Assume $f,\mathcal{V},x \models \varphi * \top$, and let $(f_1,x_1),(f_2,x_2)$ be system-behaviour pairs as in the satisfaction clause for $*$. Thus $f_1,\mathcal{V},x_1 \models \varphi$. As f implements f_1 via an implementation σ that satisfies $\sigma(x) = x_1$ and φ is positive, it follows from Lemma 4 that $f,\mathcal{V},x \models \varphi$.

Theorem 8 (global-local). *The following is a theorem for all negative φ in $\mathcal{L}^{\Box}$:*

$$\varphi \to (\psi * \psi' \to (\psi \wedge \varphi) * \psi')$$

That is, if a negative formula φ holds globally and some formula ψ holds locally, then φ holds at that location as well.

Proof. Assume both φ and $\psi * \psi'$ hold in a system. Clearly we must have at least $(\psi \wedge \varphi) * \psi'$ or $(\psi \wedge \neg\varphi) * \psi'$ in the same system, so it suffices to show that $(\psi \wedge \neg\varphi) * \psi'$ cannot be the case. Indeed, as $\neg\varphi$ is positive we have $(\neg\varphi) * \top \rightarrow \neg\varphi$, or equivalently $\varphi \rightarrow \neg(\neg\varphi * \top)$, from Theorem 7. As we assume φ this implies $\neg(\neg\varphi * \top)$, which is stronger than the required $\neg((\psi \wedge \neg\varphi) * \psi')$.

Just as in linear, bunched, and relevance logics, the multiplicative conjunction $*$ gives rise to another connective $-\!\!*$ called the 'magic wand':

$$f, \mathcal{V}, x \models \varphi -\!\!* \psi \iff f \otimes g, \mathcal{V}, (x, y) \models \psi \quad \text{whenever } g, \mathcal{V}, y \models \varphi$$

Using $-\!\!*$, a system f can reason about its place inside a larger structure $f \otimes g$. More specifically, $f, \mathcal{V}, x$ satisfies $\varphi -\!\!* \psi$ if, whenever 'plugged into' a system satisfying φ, the combined system satisfies ψ. Using $\vec{\otimes}$ instead of $\otimes$ in the clause above defines a 'directed magic wand', which then specifies properties of combined systems where f acts as an input.

We mention one further variant of a multiplicative conjunction. Defining

$$\text{`}(f, x) = (f_1, x_1) \otimes_d (f_2, x_2)\text{'} :\iff (f, x) = (f_1, x_1) \otimes (f_2, x_2) \text{ and } \mathsf{Int}(f_1, f_2) = \emptyset$$

we introduce $*_d$ via the clause

$$f, \mathcal{V}, x \models \varphi *_d \psi \iff (f, x) = (f_1, x_1) \otimes_d (f_2, x_2) \text{ for some } f_1, x_1, \mathcal{V} \models \varphi \text{ and } f_2, x_2, \mathcal{V} \models \psi$$

This—very restrictive—conjunction corresponds exactly to the multiplicative conjunction of Separation Logic [30,39], where it is stipulated that the heap is split into disjoint parts. In our context, this means that the two subsystems f_1 and f_2 have no components in common.

We leave a more systematic study of these structural connectives to further work. In particular, we would like to explore extensions of the Hennessy-Milner theorem (Theorem 6) for $*$ and $\vec{*}$.

5 Discussion and Conclusion

We have established a minimalistic, behaviour-based framework for systems modelling. We have shown that it encompasses key ideas from systems theory and have given a logical analysis that supports reasoning about compositional structure. In particular, it can be shown that the framework can be used to give a semantics to the modelling tools based on the distributed systems metaphor, as discussed in Sect. 1, though the details of this are beyond our present scope.

This includes the approach to interfaces, composition, and local reasoning as described, for example, in [12,13,15].

We have also shown that even a rather concrete property of distributed system—namely the CAP theorem—is witnessed in the framework.

In Sect. 4, we have laid out a minimal logical theory that, in addition to having the standard classical connectives, is sufficient to characterize basic system evolution (through a modality) and compositional structure (through multiplicative conjunctions). The latter come in two versions, $*$ and $\vec{*}$, conveying whether a system can be split into subsystems satisfying certain properties, or extended to a larger system. These structural connectives, which are similar to those considered in logics for process algebras (for example, [3,17–19]) and Separation Logic (for example, [30,37]).

5.1 Time

In this section, we briefly sketch how to introduce an explicit notion of time into our set-up. There are several ways of achieving this. The obvious one would be to abandon the principle that behaviours are 'unstructured' sets, instead imposing that they carrier a partial order $<$ which is interpreted as a 'happens before' relation. In the trace model, we could then state for example that $\langle a, b\rangle < \langle a, b, c\rangle$; that is, the behaviour $\langle a, b, c\rangle$ is a *continuation* of the behaviour $\langle a, b\rangle$.

It turns out, by adopting a different philosophy, that such a modification of the framework is not necessary. Instead of treating time as something inherent to a system, we think of it as being *observed* from outside the system. Thus in order to introduce time to a system f, we should look at a larger system that includes an *observer* of f.

Definition 15. *A* timed implementation for f *is a composition of f with some basic component c, where f is an input and $c \notin \mathrm{Comp}(f)$ is a basic component whose behaviour set is a partial order.*

Here we think of $\mathrm{Beh}(c)$ as some form of bookkeeping of the behaviours of f: For $t, t' \in \mathrm{Beh}(c)$, $t < t'$ means that c may experience t before t'. Incompatible behaviours denote observations in different histories of the observer.

Let the timed implementation be given as $f \overset{\sigma}{\Longleftarrow} h \overset{\rho}{\Longrightarrow} c$. We can then import this ordering of events into the behaviours x, y of f by setting $x \leq y$ if whenever $\sigma(v) = x$ and $\sigma(w) = y$ for some behaviours $v, w \in \mathrm{Beh}(h)$, then we have $\rho(v) \leq \rho(w)$. Thus $x \leq y$ holds if y can only be observed by c after x. $\leq$-minimal elements in $\mathrm{Beh}(f)$ can be identified with initial states of f.

5.2 Tableaux Systems

A substantial and theoretically important development—beyond our present scope—would be to provide a proof system for the logic, together with associated meta-theoretical results. One approach would be to develop a labelled tableaux system, similar to those developed for other logics involving mixes of classical and substructural connectives and modalities (see, e.g., [24,32,38]).

We discuss how such a system of labelled tableaux can be developed from standard knowledge about tableaux (rules, branchs, closure) [22,40] and from previous works on labelled tableaux for BI logic and some extensions [24,25,32]. The main questions concern the definition of labels, of labelled formulas, of sets of label constraints, in such a way one can define closure conditions for a tableaux branch and also what is a tableaux proof for the given logic. As the labels and constraints have to capture the semantics of the logic then the main challenge in our setting is to use the structure of the logic's models—here our system models—to determine a system of labels to be used to express the constraints one has to assert or to check when tableaux rules are applied.

The set-up of the logic presented in Sect. 4 is more complicated than previously studied logical set-ups, and providing a labelled tableaux system for our new logic presents more challenges. It is necessary and non-trivial to identify an appropriate algebra of labels that captures the semantics specified by the satisfaction relation

$$f, \mathcal{V}, x \models \phi$$

as defined in Sect. 4, where f is a system, $\mathcal{V}$ is a valuation, and $x \in \mathrm{Beh}(f)$. Unpacking this, we can see some of the challenges. Recall that, for every basic component $c \in \mathbb{C}$, we assume a set $Var(c)$ of variables, and a *valuation* is a function $\mathcal{V}$ mapping each $p \in Var(c)$ to a subset of $\mathrm{Beh}(c)$.

The tableaux rules for the $\wedge$ and $\vee$ connectives can have the following form:

$$\frac{(\mathbb{T}(\phi \wedge \psi), l)}{\begin{array}{c}(\mathbb{T}(\phi), l)\\(\mathbb{T}(\psi), l)\end{array}}\ \mathbb{T}\wedge \qquad \frac{(\mathbb{F}(\phi \wedge \psi), l)}{(\mathbb{F}(\phi), l) \mid (\mathbb{F}(\psi), l)}\ \mathbb{F}\wedge$$

$$\frac{(\mathbb{T}(\phi \vee \psi), l)}{(\mathbb{T}(\phi), l) \mid (\mathbb{T}(\psi), l)}\ \mathbb{T}\vee \qquad \frac{(\mathbb{F}(\phi \vee \psi), l)}{\begin{array}{c}(\mathbb{F}(\phi), l)\\(\mathbb{F}(\psi), l)\end{array}}\ \mathbb{F}\vee$$

Note that there is no change of label l when rules are applied. If we look at the semantics for these connectives we can propose to have l being of the form (f, x).

Structural connectives, such as our $*$ and $\overrightarrow{*}$, typically refer to labels that correspond to components of decomposition of the systems that support the conjunctions $\phi * \psi$ and $\phi \overrightarrow{*} \psi$ in Sect. 4.3. Tableaux systems have been given for various versions of BI (e.g., [20,24,25]) dealing with the connectives $*$ and $-\!\!*$. In that setting, the multiplicative conjunction, $*$, can have the following rules:

$$\frac{\langle \mathbb{T}(\phi * \psi), l\rangle}{\begin{array}{c}\langle \mathbb{T}(\phi), l_1\rangle\\ \langle \mathbb{T}(\phi), l_2\rangle\end{array}}\ S(l, l_1, l_2)\ \mathbb{T}* \quad \text{and} \quad \frac{\langle \mathbb{F}(\phi * \psi), l\rangle}{\langle \mathbb{F}(\phi), l_1\rangle \mid \langle \mathbb{F}(\psi), l_2\rangle}\ R(l, l_1, l_2)\ \mathbb{F}*$$

Here the rule $\mathbb{T}*$ introduces new labels l_1 and l_2 and the label constraint (or assertion) $S(l, l_1, l_2)$ that is satisfied and the rule $\mathbb{F}*$ can be applied only if there exist l_1 and l_2 among the existing labels that satisfy the label constraint (or requirement) $R(l, l_1, l_2)$ from a specific closure of the set of assertions. The labels, their composition (with and operator $\bullet$) and the label constraints allows us to capture the relational semantics of $*$ (see [20,21,25]).

In order to consider $*$ in our logic, we can propose that $l = (f, x)$, $l_1 = (f_1, x_1)$ and $l_2 = (f_2, x_2)$, and $S(l, l_1, l_2)$ and $R(l, l_1, l_2)$ of the form $l = l_1 \bullet l_2$. The conditions on the f_is in the definition of $*$ are essential local and then we can expect to find a way to express the constraints and to reason on their satisfaction and resolution.

The interface-mediated $\overrightarrow{*}$ rule requires that the labelling algebra maintain dependencies across different branches of the tableau as specified by the condition that '$\mathsf{Int}(f_1, f_2)$ is an input to f_2'. This is a relatively complex and delicate development of the underlying approach to defining tableaux systems, which we defer to another occasion.

Finally modalities, such as our $\Box$, typically require a relationship on labels that corresponds to an accessibility relation on worlds. In our case, accessibility is generated by behaviours.

$$\frac{\langle \mathbb{T}(\Box\phi), l\rangle}{\langle \mathbb{T}(\phi), m\rangle}\ S(l,m)\quad \mathbb{T}\Box \qquad \text{and} \qquad \frac{\langle \mathbb{F}(\Box\phi), l\rangle}{\langle \mathbb{F}(\phi), m\rangle}\ R(l,m)\quad \mathbb{F}\Box$$

Here, if we look the semantics of our logic, we could consider $l = (f, x)$ and $m = (f, y)$ with, respectively, the assertion $S(l, m)$ and the requirement $R(l, m)$ expressing a relation between x and y that corresponds to the accessibility relation associated to our $\Box$.

All these points illustrate that the definitions of labels and label constraints, and their treatment and resolution during a tableau construction, require a deeper analysis and a relatively complex and delicate development in order to propose a tableaux calculus that will be proved sound and complete. Such questions will be explored in future work.

5.3 Other

Other future work might include systematic approaches to extensions of the theory, while staying true to the minimalistic spirit in which the present work has been carried out. For example, two general notions, which have not been discussed, are *abstraction* and *refinement* of systems [11] together with *substitution* (see, for example, [12]) of models. The theory needed to support these ideas will necessarily require an extension of our Hennessy-Milner theorem (Theorem 6) to include the structural connectives. The development of such a theory is a substantial project for further work.

Other theoretical work might include the incorporation of causality concepts (and associated notions) into the minimalistic framework. Again, this is further work.

More applied work might consider the integration stochastic behaviours, execution and simulations, and model-checking, so providing the basis for the framework to account for—that is, give semantics for—a wide range of system modelling approaches.

Acknowledgements. This work has been partially supported by the UK EPSRC research grants EP/S013008/1 and EP/R006865/1. The authors are grateful to Tristan Caulfield for helpful discussions of the systems background to the ideas presented.

A Proof of Recovering a Standard Form of the CAP Theorem

We start with an informal presentation and proof of CAP. Consider the situation where there are two replicated copies of a database. User 1 and 2 interact with their respective copy of the database by overwriting the dataset, or by requesting to read the current value of the data. In this scenario, the CAP guarantees can be formulated as follows:

- *consistency*: Any read returns the content of the latest write (by either user) at time of the submission of the read request, or any later write.
- *availability*: Any read and write requests are eventually performed.
- *partition-tolerance*: The system tolerates arbitrary message loss between the two databases.

A semi-formal proof that these guarantees cannot be satisfied simultaneously runs as follows: the current value of the database, and assume the connection between the two copies of the database breaks down. Now imagine user 2 writing the data $\chi' \neq \chi$ on the database, followed by user 1 requesting to read the data. By the availability and partition-tolerance requirements, the system must eventually return an answer χ'' to user 1. Clearly, if $\chi'' \neq \chi'$ then consistency is violated as the return value is outdated. So assume $\chi'' = \chi'$. But now, as the first copy of the database has lost its connection to the second one, it cannot distinguish between the situation where the write of user 2 has occurred and a situation where no such write occurred. Thus, χ' will also be the return value for user 1 in case the write didn't occur, and in that situation χ' would be an outdated value thus violating consistency.

We now formalize this scenario to show that the impossibility result is an instance of Theorem 1. In fact, by writing out the proof of Theorem 1 with the formalization presented below one essentially obtains the proof in [26]. For $i = 1, 2$ consider a language Σ_i that contains for every timestamp $t \in \mathbb{Q}_0^+$ and string s one of the atoms below left, with their intended interpretation given on the right:

$$\begin{aligned} t : rd^i? & \quad \ldots \text{ at time } t\text{, user } i \text{ requests a read} \\ t : rd^i(s) & \quad \ldots \text{ at time } t\text{, user } i \text{ reads value } s \\ t : wr^i(s) & \quad \ldots \text{ at time } t\text{, user } i \text{ writes value } s \end{aligned}$$

A sequence in $(\Sigma_1 \cup \Sigma_2)^*$ is *well-formed* if its timestamps are strictly ascending. Let $\mathcal{S}$ denote the set of well-formed sequences, and let $\mathcal{S}_i := \mathcal{S} \cap \Sigma_i^*$.

We consider a composition $g_1 \overset{\sigma_1}{\Longleftarrow} f \overset{\sigma_2}{\Longrightarrow} g_2$ where the behaviour sets of g_1, g_2 and f are $\mathcal{S}_1, \mathcal{S}_2$ and $\mathcal{S}$, respectively. The implementation σ_i is the obvious projection function that removes from a sequence in $\mathcal{S}$ all actions not initiated by the user i. The *current value at* t of a sequence in $\mathcal{S}$ is the value of the latest write in it (by either user) with timestamp $\leq t$; if no such write exists, the current value equals some fixed string s_0 that we call the *initial value*. A sequence in $\mathcal{S}$ is *consistent* if whenever $t : rd^i?$ and $t' : rd^i(s)$ are a pair of actions in the sequence with $t < t'$ and no read by i in between, then s coincides with the current value at some timestamp $\geq t$ and $\leq t'$. Let C be the set of all consistent sequences.

Define two binary relations on $\mathcal{S}$. R relates any sequence to the same sequence appended with $t : wr^2(s)$, for some string s (and sufficiently large t). S relates a sequence to the same sequence appended with $t : rd^1?$, a finite string of actions by user 2, and a final $t' : rd^1(s)$, for some string s. So, if an implementation of f satisfies strong R-availability, it allows user 2 to write anything at any time. If it satisfies weak S-satisfiability, it allows user 1 to send a request anytime and wait until it is answered.

So, clearly C-consistency, strong R-, and weak S-availability are are required guarantees in the CAP scenario. We will now show that these are incompatible with (σ_1, σ_2)-partition-tolerance. By Theorem 1, it suffices to demonstrate the entanglement condition. Indeed, let $w \in \mathcal{L}$ and let $x \in R(w, \bullet)$ an extension of w with $t : wr^2(s)$ where s is neither s_0 nor the value of any write in w. Now consider any $v \in S(x, \bullet)$. Such v is of the form $v = w \frown \langle t : wr^2(s), t' : rd^1?, \ldots, t'' : rd^1(s') \rangle$, where the dotted part contains only actions by user 2. Let $y, z \in \mathcal{L}$ satisfy $\sigma_1(y) = \sigma_1(z) = \sigma_1(v)$, $\sigma_2(y) = \sigma_2(w)$ and $\sigma_2(z) = \sigma_2(x)$. Therefore, $y = w \frown \langle t' : rd^1?, t'' : rd^1(s') \rangle$ and $z = w \frown \langle t : wr^2(s), t' : rd^1?, t'' : rd^1(s') \rangle$. We have to show $y \notin C$ or $z \notin C$. Let us assume $z \in C$. Then $s' = s$. Since, by construction, s is neither s_0 nor the value of any write in w, it follows that $y \notin C$. This demonstrates the entanglement condition.

References

1. de Alfaro, L., Henzinger, T.: Interface automata. In: ESEC/FSE 2001, pp. 109–120. ACM (2001)
2. de Alfaro, L., Henzinger, T.A.: Interface theories for component-based design. In: Henzinger, T.A., Kirsch, C.M. (eds.) EMSOFT 2001. LNCS, vol. 2211, pp. 148–165. Springer, Heidelberg (2001). https://doi.org/10.1007/3-540-45449-7_11
3. Anderson, G., Pym, D.: A calculus and logic of bunched resources and processes. Theor. Comput. Sci. **614**, 63–96 (2016)
4. Bednarczyk, M.A., Bernardinello, L., Caillaud, B., Pawłowski, W., Pomello, L.: Modular system development with pullbacks. In: van der Aalst, W., Best, E. (eds.) ICATPN 2003. LNCS, vol. 2679, pp. 140–160. Springer, Heidelberg (2003). https://doi.org/10.1007/3-540-44919-1_12
5. van Benthem, J., Bergstra, J.: Logic of transition systems. J. Logic Lang. Inform. **3**, 247–283 (1994)
6. Bezanson, J., Karpinski, S., Shah, V.B., Edelman, A.: Julia: a fast dynamic language for technical computing (2012). arXiv:1209.5145
7. Birtwistle, G.: Demos—Discrete Event Modelling on Simula. Macmillan (1979)

8. Blackburn, P., de Rijke, M., Venema, Y.: Modal Logic. Cambridge University Press, Cambridge (2001)
9. Brewer, E.: Towards robust distributed systems (abstract). In: Proceedings of the Nineteenth Annual ACM Symposium on Principles of Distributed Computing, PODC 2000, p. 7. Association for Computing Machinery, New York (2000). https://doi.org/10.1145/343477.343502
10. Brewer, E.: CAP twelve years later: how the 'rules' have changed. Computer **45**(2), 23–29 (2012). https://doi.org/10.1109/MC.2012.37
11. Butler, M.J.: Mastering system analysis and design through abstraction and refinement (2013). University of Southampton eprints. https://eprints.soton.ac.uk/349769/1/Butler.pdf. Accessed 22 Mar 2023
12. Caulfield, T., Ilau, M.C., Pym, D.: Engineering ecosystem models: semantics and pragmatics. In: International Conference on Simulation Tools and Techniques, pp. 236–258. Springer, Cham (2022)
13. Caulfield, T., Pym, D.: Modelling and simulating systems security policy. In: Proceedings of the SimuTools (2015)
14. Caulfield, T.: SysModels Julia Package. https://github.com/tristanc/SysModels. Accessed 20 Sept 2024
15. Caulfield, T., Pym, D.: Modelling and simulating systems security policy. EAI Endorsed Trans. Security Saf. (Proc. Simutools 2016, Prague) **3**(8), e3 (2016)
16. Collinson, M., Monahan, B., Pym, D.: A Discipline of Mathematical Systems Modelling. College Publications, London (2012)
17. Collinson, M., Pym, D.: Algebra and logic for resource-based systems modelling. Math. Struct. Comput. Sci. **19**, 959–1027 (2009). https://doi.org/10.1017/S0960129509990077
18. Collinson, M., Monahan, B., Pym, D.: Semantics for structured systems modelling and simulation. In: Proceedings of the Simutools 2010. ACM Digital Library (2010). ISBN 78-963-9799-87-5
19. Dam, M.: Relevance logic and concurrent computation. Ph.D. thesis, University of Edinburgh (1989)
20. Docherty, S.: Bunched logics: a uniform approach. Ph.D. thesis, University College London (2019)
21. Docherty, S., Pym, D.: Modular tableaux calculi for separation theories. In: Baier, C., Dal Lago, U. (eds.) FoSSaCS 2018. LNCS, vol. 10803, pp. 441–458. Springer, Cham (2018). https://doi.org/10.1007/978-3-319-89366-2_24
22. Fitting, M.: First-order Logic and Automated Theorem Proving. Texts and Monographs in Computer Science. Springer, Cham (1990)
23. Forrester, J.: Counterintuitive behavior of social systems. Technol. Rev. **73**(3), 52–68 (1971)
24. Galmiche, D., Kimmel, P., Pym, D.: A substructural epistemic resource logic: theory and modelling applications. J. Logic Comput. **29**(8), 1251–1287 (2020). https://doi.org/10.1093/logcom/exz024
25. Galmiche, D., Méry, D., Pym, D.: The semantics of BI and resource tableaux. Math. Struct. Comput. Sci. **15**(6), 1033–1088 (2005). https://doi.org/10.1017/S0960129505004858
26. Gilbert, S., Lynch, N.: Brewer's conjecture and the feasibility of consistent, available, partition-tolerant web services. ACM SIGACT News **33**(2), 51–59 (2002). https://doi.org/10.1145/564585.564601
27. Gilbert, S., Lynch, N.: Perspectives on the CAP Theorem. IEEE Comput. **45**, 30–36 (2012). https://doi.org/10.1109/MC.2011.389

28. Hillston, J.: A Compositional Approach to Performance Modelling. Cambridge University Press, Cambridge (1996)
29. Hoare, C.: Communicating Sequential Processes. Prentice-Hall Inc., USA (1985)
30. Ishtiaq, S., O'Hearn, P.W.: Bi as an assertion language for mutable data structures. In: Proceedings of the 28th ACM SIGPLAN-SIGACT Symposium on Principles of Programming Languages, POPL 2001, pp. 14–26. Association for Computing Machinery (2001). https://doi.org/10.1145/360204.375719
31. Julia. http://julialang.org
32. Larchey-Wendling, D.: The formal strong completeness of partial monoidal Boolean BI. J. Logic Comput. **26**(2), 605–640 (2014). https://doi.org/10.1093/logcom/exu031
33. Lynch, N., Tuttle, M.: An introduction to input/output automata. Laboratory for Computer Science, Massachusetts Institute of Technology (1988)
34. Milner, R.: Communication and Concurrency. Prentice-Hall Inc., USA (1989)
35. Milner, R.: Bigraphs as a model for mobile interaction. In: Corradini, A., Ehrig, H., Kreowski, H.-J., Rozenberg, G. (eds.) ICGT 2002. LNCS, vol. 2505, pp. 8–13. Springer, Heidelberg (2002). https://doi.org/10.1007/3-540-45832-8_3
36. Milner, R.: Bigraphs and their algebra. Electron. Notes Theor. Comput. Sci. **209**, 5–19 (2008)
37. O'Hearn, P.: Separation logic. Commun. ACM **62**(2), 86–95 (2019)
38. Pym, D.J.: Resource semantics: logic as a modelling technology. ACM SIGLOG News **6**(2), 5–41 (2019). https://doi.org/10.1145/3326938.3326940
39. Reynolds, J.C.: Separation logic: a logic for shared mutable data structures. In: Proceedings of the 17th Annual IEEE Symposium on Logic in Computer Science, LICS 2002, pp. 55–74. IEEE Computer Society, USA (2002)
40. Smullyan, R.M.: First-Order Logic. Dover (1968)
41. Stirling, C.: Modal and Temporal Properties of Processes. Springer, Cham (2001)
42. Tripakis, S., Lickly, B., Henzinger, T., Lee, E.: A theory of synchronous relational interfaces. ACM Trans. Program. Lang. Syst. **33**(4), 1–41 (2011)
43. Ören, T., Zeigler, B.P., Tolk, A. (eds.): Body of Knowledge for Modeling and Simulation: A Handbook by the Society for Modeling and Simulation International (Simulation Foundations, Methods and Applications). Springer, Cham (2023)

Traffic Simulations

Integrating Simulation and AI for Optimal Electric Vehicle Charging Infrastructure: Achievements and Future Directions

José-Luis Guisado-Lizar[1,2,3(✉)], David Ragel-Díaz-Jara[1,3], Antonio Navas-Orozco[1,3], José Morera-Figueroa[1,3], Fernando Diaz-del-Rio[1,2,3], María José Morón-Fernández[1,2,3], E. Cerezuela-Escudero[1,2,3], Miguel Cardenas-Montes[4], and Gabriel Jiménez-Moreno[1,2,3]

[1] Department of Computer Architecture and Technology, Universidad de Sevilla, Avenida Reina Mercedes s/n, 41012 Sevilla, Spain
jlguisado@us.es
[2] I3US Research Institute, Universidad de Sevilla, Seville, Spain
[3] SCORE Lab, Universidad de Sevilla, Seville, Spain
[4] CIEMAT, Centro Inv. Energéticas Medioambientales y Tecnológicas, Madrid, Spain
https://grupo.us.es/sanevec/en/

Abstract. Electric vehicles (EVs) are the most prominent technology for reducing road transport emissions. Their rapid adoption necessitates efficient deployment of charging infrastructure. This study presents works in progress in an innovative approach integrating simulation and artificial intelligence (AI) to optimize EV charging station placement. We develop a microscopic traffic simulation model combining cellular automata and agent-based techniques to capture the dynamic interactions between vehicles, charging stations, and urban environments. Genetic algorithms and neural networks are employed to navigate the complex solution space and identify optimal configurations. The model considers multiple factors including traffic patterns, air quality, grid impacts, and urban mobility. The objective of this holistic approach is to improve charging infrastructure planning, leading to reduced congestion, lower emissions, and enhanced urban mobility. We discuss achievements to date and outline future research directions.

Keywords: Electric Vehicle Charging · Infrastructure Optimization · Cellular Automata · Agent-Based Modeling · Traffic · Sustainable Transportation · Air Quality · Modeling · Simulation

---

This work is part of the projects SANEVEC TED2021-130825B-I00, and SAINEVRA (PID2023-151065OB-I00), funded by Ministerio de Ciencia, Innovación y Universidades (MICIU), Agencia Estatal de Investigación (AEI) of Spain, MCIN/AEI/ 10.13039/501100011033, and by the European Union NextGenerationEU/PRTR.

A. A. Juan et al. (Eds.): SIMUtools 2024, LNICST 603, pp. 75–87, 2025.
https://doi.org/10.1007/978-3-031-87345-4_5

1 Introduction

The climate crisis driven by greenhouse gas emissions is one of the most pressing challenges facing humanity on a global scale today. It poses serious threats to ecosystems, societies, economies, and even physical security due to increasing extreme weather events. As a result, there is an urgent need for action to reduce greenhouse gas emissions. A major contributor to these emissions is the transport sector, which accounted for about a quarter of the total CO_2 emissions of the European Union in 2019, with 72% of that coming from road transport [10]. Consequently, decarbonizing the transport sector by adopting clean technologies is essential to achieving key climate and environmental goals. Currently, electric vehicles (EVs) are the most prominent technology for reducing road transport emissions. Across Europe, for instance, electric mobility is anticipated to represent around 55% of all transportation by 2030, considering all types of vehicles, according to the existing policies scenario outlined by the International Energy Agency [15].

To support the transition to EVs, a robust public charging infrastructure will be essential. Projections for 2030 suggest that hundreds of thousands of public charging stations (CSs) will be required, marking a significant increase from a decade ago. As an example, in Spain, the National Integrated Energy and Climate Plan 2021–2030 [13] has set targets for the electrification of road transport by 2030 of 5 million electric vehicles, including cars, vans, motorbikes and buses. To reach this target, it is necessary to deploy an appropriate public charging infrastructure, which has been estimated for 2030 at around 250,000 public charging points, according to a study by the consultancy firm Everis, while in 2019 there were slightly less than 8,000 charging points [11].

Determining the optimal locations and sizes of public CSs in both urban and intercity areas is a critical and complex task influenced by several interconnected factors. These factors include traffic patterns, air quality and carbon footprint of traffic (especially if a substantial fraction of vehicles still use combustion engines), queue times at CSs, travel times between origin and destination considering varying traffic conditions and the detours required to reach CSs, the characteristics and operation of the power grid, the construction costs of new CSs relative to their proximity to power grid infrastructure, and the variability of charging fees.

In addition, vehicle traffic is a classic example of a complex system consisting of many interacting components that give rise to emergent properties at the global level, which are difficult to predict in advance except by simulation. One emergent property of traffic is the occurrence of traffic jams, and the location of CSs can alter their patterns, as some of the authors of this work have recently demonstrated [12]. These patterns, in turn, shape pollution levels and the carbon footprint of traffic, further impacting the optimal positioning of CSs.

Therefore, determining the optimal location of CSs must consider the feedback loops and synergies among all the aforementioned interdependent variables. Simulation is essential for accurately predicting the behavior of such a complex system, as it captures the emergent properties that could otherwise be overlooked through excessively simplified models. Besides, artificial intelligence (AI) optimization algorithms, such as genetic algorithms, simulated annealing, reinforcement learning, particle swarm, or ant colony optimization, can play a critical role in optimizing this process by efficiently navigating the vast solution space to find an effective and robust solution.

In this paper, we present research on integrating simulation and AI to optimize EV charging infrastructure, conducted as part of the SANEVEC project ("A simulation approach to determine the deployment of an urban network of electric vehicle charging stations for environmental and social benefits", https://grupo.us.es/sanevec/en). This project is funded by the Ministry of Science, Innovation, and Universities of Spain, together with the NextGenerationEU program of the European Union. Additionally, we outline future directions to be explored in the upcoming SAINEVRA project ("Simulation and artificial intelligence holistic approach for nationwide charging station deployment to solve electric vehicle range anxiety"), which has been accepted for funding by the Ministry of Science, Innovation, and Universities of Spain, and is set to commence in late 2024.

The rest of this paper is structured as follows: Sect. 2 reviews the state of the art, providing an overview of relevant research in this field. Section 3 details the methodology employed in this work, including the simulation models and AI algorithms used for optimization. In Sect. 4, we present and discuss the results obtained from our study. Finally, Sect. 5 concludes the paper, highlighting key findings and outlining future challenges and directions for further research in this area.

2 State of the Art

Most research on determining the optimal configuration of CSs has overlooked the feedback loops between the interdependent variables critical to this problem. Instead, it has largely relied on static approaches that focus on evenly distributing resources based on historical traffic data, while considering only one or two of these variables. However, some previous studies began to explore specific methodological aspects of this problem. Recent works of Jordán et al. [16] and Martí et al. [18] employ a genetic algorithm to calculate the most suitable locations for EV CSs in an interurban environment. The first one considers population, traffic density, social network activity, distance to the nearest station, and percentage of uncovered area for the fitness function of the genetic algorithm. The second one considers shortest routes to possible target destinations (calculated by using Dijkstra's algorithm with Contraction Hierarchies) and population density, traffic density, and social network activity for the fitness function. They open a very promising approach, but it can not be an effective methodology for the real world because they do not employ simulation to take into account the dynamic effects of traffic congestion, and they do not consider the building costs of each CS (and its possibly necessary power line to the nearest substation) in its candidate location, occupation of the different CSs and their effects on travel

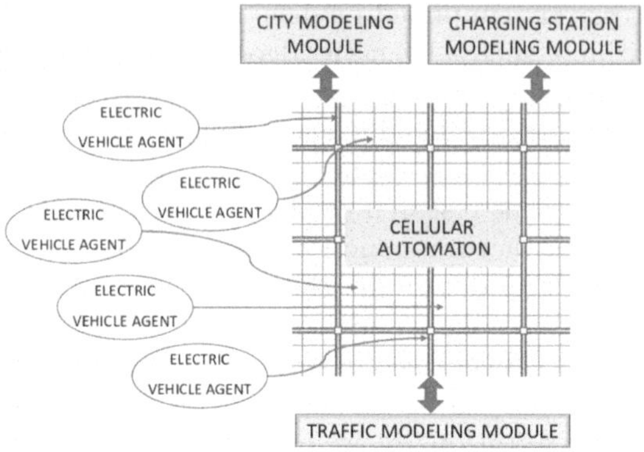

Fig. 1. The simulation model is based on a cellular automaton that represents city roads. EVs and ICEVs are agents that occupy one cell, and in the next time step can move to another nearby cell. CSs are also agents located in a road cell.

times, or the carbon footprint due to traffic in the highway network. All of these criteria will be considered in the SAINEVRA project.

Moreover, lengthy charging durations and uncertainty regarding outlet availability are key issues contributing to consumer reluctance to use public CSs [7]. These challenges are largely due to the absence of efficient management systems capable of monitoring the entire network of public CSs. Such systems are essential for providing accurate information on the availability and occupancy of charging outlets, as well as estimating potential wait times for EVs seeking to charge. Addressing these issues is critical for improving the usability and appeal of public EV charging facilities. Modeling traffic is an essential ingredient for that.

Traffic simulation models can be microscopic, mesoscopic and macroscopic. Microscopic models simulate individual vehicles, macroscopic models describe the traffic at a high level of aggregation as flow (number of vehicles per hour that pass a certain point), and mesoscopic models are at an intermediate level of detail, for instance describing the individual vehicles, but not their interactions [5]. Two types of microscopic models have been used to model traffic: cellular automata (CA) and agent-based models (ABM). CA are a class of mathematical systems with spatial and temporal discrete character, that evolve based on local interactions and synchronous parallel updates in time [17]. Since the seminal contributions of K. Nagel and M. Schreckenberg [20], followed by the work of B. Chopard [9], these methods have been effectively applied in the simulation of vehicular traffic. For instance, they have been successfully used to model traffic in a highway network in a German state [19]. In relation to EVs, Xiang et al. [27] have employed a CA model to study the electricity demand of a CS for different traffic flows, but with a model of very limited extent, which only includes one road, one intersection and one CS. ABMs simulate the actions and interactions of a set of autonomous elements called agents. Viswanathan et al. [26] used an

ABM model to investigate the optimal allocation of CSs in a city, although in that model vehicles had fixed routes (based on daily traffic data) from an origin to a destination, so it lacks realism. Zhai et al. [30] employ a hybrid CA-ABM mesoscopic simulation model, with cells of 1 km, to calculate the CS demand over a 54-node power distribution system and a 25-node traffic network. Chen et al. [6] employ a macroscopic model to investigate the optimal deployment of CSs and charging lanes along a singular road.

Members of the SANEVEC project have used a hybrid CA-ABM microscopic model to simulate the behavior of individual vehicles, including EVs and internal combustion engine vehicles (ICEVs), and also the operation of CSs, demonstrating that the layout of urban charging stations can profoundly change the traffic patterns in a city, which are an emergent property of traffic as a complex system [12]. Subsequent advances have already been made within the SANEVEC project [1]. The same type of model was later used to optimize EV routing strategies to CSs in urban environments [8]. Although microscopic traffic models can be computationally demanding, project members improved runtime efficiency through optimized memory management and enhanced thread parallelism, achieving performance far beyond simpler codes [22].

Another recent promising approach for traffic modeling involves the use of AI machine learning techniques, particularly neural network models such as long short-term memory, gated recurrent units, stacked autoencoders, and deep reinforcement learning. These models have demonstrated potential for accurately predicting road traffic patterns by capturing the dynamic, temporal dependencies inherent in traffic data, as noted in recent studies [23,28]. However, there is not much research on the training of machine learning models using microscopic traffic simulators that contemplate many different traffic patterns. Some preliminary works on this approach are [2,29]. In contrast, in the field of computational fluid dynamics and meteorology, this approach has been widely used [25]. Going further, feedback between a traffic simulation model and a neural network can be addressed to improve both tools.

3 Methodology

3.1 Simulation Model

To simulate traffic patterns in a real city, taking into account both ICEVs and EVs, as well as the impact of CS locations, we employ a hybrid microscopic model. This model combines cellular automata and agent-based models to capture the complex interactions among vehicles, the electric grid, air pollution, and overall urban mobility [21], and is represented in Fig. 1.

- Cellular Automata (CA): In our system, the CA component is responsible for simulating the dynamic properties of traffic flow across a city, including congestion patterns, road usage, and the temporal evolution of traffic density. These properties are continuously updated in parallel to reflect changes as vehicles move and interact within the road network.

- Agent-Based Models (ABMs): ABMs represent individual agents—in this case, vehicles and CSs—as autonomous decision-makers. Each car is treated as an agent with specific characteristics, such as destination, fuel type (ICEV or EV), and battery level (for EVs). The agents make decisions based on their current state. For example, EV agents decide when and where to charge based on their battery level, proximity to CSs, and traffic conditions. ABMs are crucial for capturing the stochastic and heterogeneous nature of vehicle behavior, particularly as EVs choose CS locations and adapt to changing urban conditions.

3.2 Optimization Approach

We integrate AI optimization algorithms to identify the optimal or near-optimal configuration of CS locations and sizes. Specifically, we utilize a combination of genetic algorithms and neural networks:

- Genetic Algorithm (GA): The GA is employed to explore the vast solution space of potential CS placements and sizes. The algorithm iterates through generations, evolving candidate solutions by applying crossover, mutation, and selection processes. The objective is to improve key performance indicators (KPIs), such as traffic congestion, air pollution, and urban mobility efficiency, by optimizing the placement and sizing of CSs in response to changing urban patterns.
- Neural Networks (NNs): Neural networks will be used to predict and evaluate the outcomes of different CS configurations on urban variables such as traffic flow, air quality, and electric grid usage. NNs are trained on simulation data generated by the CA-ABM model to provide quick and accurate predictions, which allow the GA to make informed decisions during optimization.

3.3 Feedback and Synergies

The proposed system captures the complex feedback loops and synergies between traffic patterns, CS locations, air quality, and electric grid load. For instance, some CSs can attract traffic of many EVs willing to charge, leading to traffic jams in the vicinity, which reduce the air quality in the area if many ICEVs are also involved. A high occupation of some CSs can also lead to a high electric grid load. Unlike traditional static models, our simulation dynamically adjusts vehicle routes, traffic jams, and congestion levels based on the evolving placement of CSs. This holistic approach enables a more realistic representation of how CS infrastructure influences urban traffic flow, with direct consequences for air pollution, carbon footprint, and noise levels.

3.4 Urban Mobility and Environmental Impact

The model aims to improve urban mobility by recommending specific configurations of CS placements and charger quantities. These configurations minimize traffic congestion, resulting in:

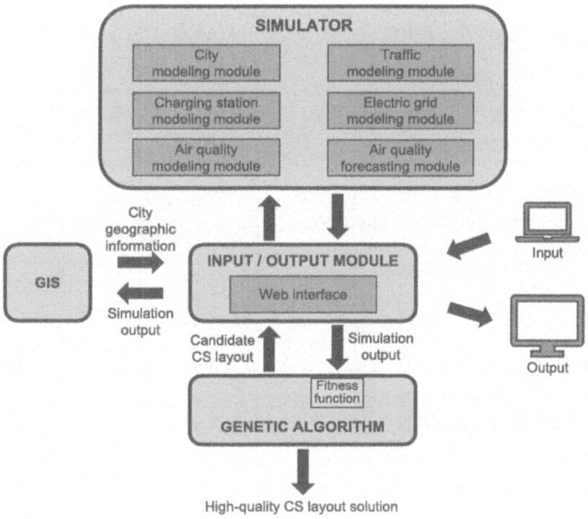

Fig. 2. Schematic view of the framework that is being developed in the SANEVEC project.

- Reduced urban transport times, as optimized CS locations prevent traffic bottlenecks and minimize detours.
- Lower air pollution and carbon footprint, by reducing traffic jams where both EVs and ICEVs are involved, and by encouraging EV adoption through optimized charging accessibility.
- Decreased noise pollution, as smoother traffic flow reduces the time spent in high-traffic areas.

3.5 Air Quality Modeling

We have performed several simulated experiments on a rectangular synthetic city consisting on squared cells that accumulate pollution unless they are part of a building. We modeled the emission of different pollutants due to EV and ICEV (Petrol and Diesel) traffic, including exhaust pollutants such as CO_2 and non-exhaust pollutants such as PM_{10}, using the tabulated data from [14] and [24].

Additionally, we have developed a mathematical model, based on [3], to take wind, atmospheric loss, and diffusion into account in the evolution of the pollution level of the experiments. After fixing values for the parameters that model these phenomena, a linear transformation of the pollution level matrix is performed for each of them (in that particular order, by convention) every time step.

Using high-performance computing (HPC) and parallelization techniques, several thousand combinations of different parameters were simulated in our synthetic city to analyze their individual and correlated effects in the city pollution.

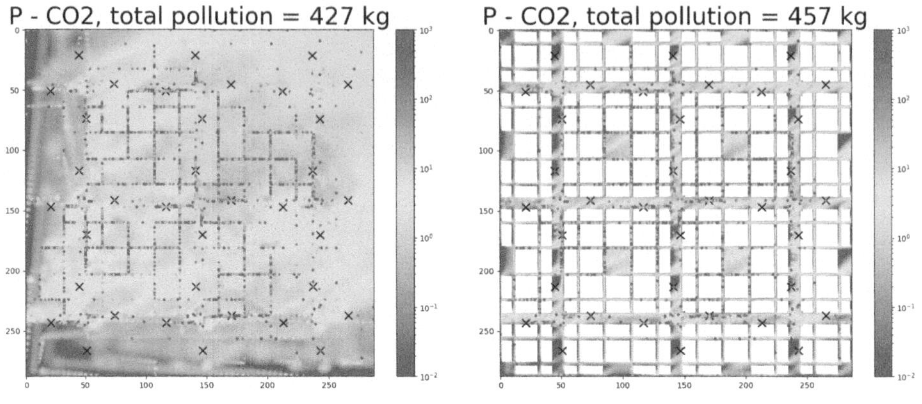

(a) Without buildings. (b) With buildings.

Fig. 3. Map of CO2 pollution levels after 1 h of simulation for the synthetic city in logarithmic scale, from 10^{-2} g to 10^3 g per cell. Total pollution level is displayed at the top. The black crosses are the 36 small CSs. The magenta, blue and cyan dots are EVs, Petrol ICEVs and Diesel ICEVs, respectively. The experiment considers the same random seed with 15% of the cells occupied by cars, 35% of which are EVs, and half of the remaining cars are Diesel (the rest are Petrol), and a wind vector of $\mathbf{w} = (5, 3)$ km/h, where the first component represents the wind speed in the x-direction (east-west) and the second component represents the wind speed in the y-direction (north-south). The effect of the presence of buildings is displayed.

3.6 The Framework

Within the SANEVEC project, we are developing a framework for the optimal determination of the location of EV CSs in a city, the structure of which is shown in Fig. 2. It has four main components: the simulator, the GA module, the Geographic Information System (GIS) module and the input/output module. The simulator is the core component and is further divided into 6 modules, as shown in the figure. The current version of the framework, including source code, is publicly available at: https://github.com/sanevec/pysimtravel3.

4 Results

We have successfully developed an initial version of the simulator, in which a mixture of EVs and ICEVs navigate through a synthetic city. Using it, we are currently evaluating the effects of different simulation parameters, related to traffic, wind, and other factors, employing the modeling techniques indicated in Sect. 3. In Fig. 3 we have presented two simulated scenarios: one that includes buildings and the other that does not. As we can observe, the effects of the wind on pollution affect as expected, that is, the absence of buildings facilitates the ability of the wind to disperse the pollution more effectively and to carry it away from the city, demonstrating the foreseeable patterns of wind behavior.

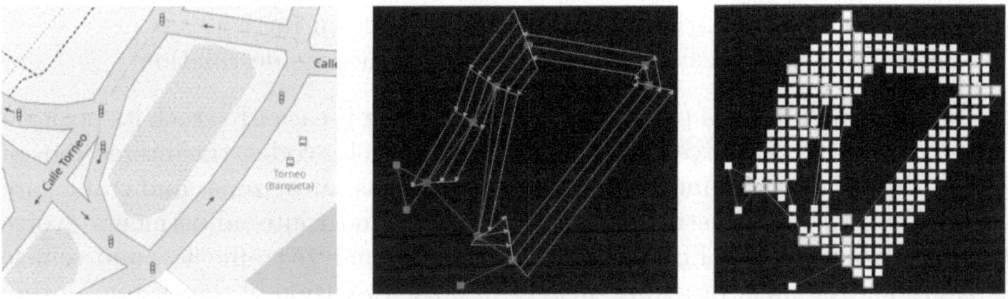

(a) (b) (c)

Fig. 4. Steps of the procedure followed for generating a CA grid from real-city data. (a) Map of the Seville city portion extracted from the OpenStreetMap GIS. (b) Lane graph generated from the geographical data, with vertices and lanes identified. (c) Grid representation used for CA simulation, showing lane structures with cells highlighted.

In addition, in order to build a simulator that reproduces the structure of a real city, we first extracted geographical data from the Geographic Information System OpenStreetMap. The procedure is shown in Fig. 4. The street map, courtesy of OpenStreetMap, represents a well-known and complex node in the city of Seville (Spain). The objective of this process is to transition from the street map to a grid format suitable for simulation using a CA. This transformation involves several stages, including the conversion of the street map into a lane graph and finally into a grid representation. The street map is represented as a graph, with its vertices and edges, shown in blue on the lane graph. Lanes are colored in green. Certain edges contain information regarding the number of lanes; however, in some cases these data are incomplete and must be inferred. For example, in the lower area of the lane graph representation, one of the edges lacks complete information about the number of lanes. In this case, a conservative approach is taken by representing at least one lane. To transition from the lane graph to the grid and enable simulation in a CA, the Bresenham algorithm [4] is applied. When drawing parallel lines, small gaps may appear that are filled in and represented in red. In this case, a white cell indicates that there is no bifurcation at the end of the street.

The vehicle movement algorithm is inspired by the Nagel-Schreckenberg model [20], where each vehicle attempts to move at the maximum road speed but adjusts its speed based on the vehicle ahead. However, a vehicle can overtake another one if there is space available in the cells of the adjacent lanes. In Fig. 5, we observe the progression of vehicle movement through the portion of the city of Seville shown in Fig. 4, with snapshots taken at 4 consecutive time steps. The color coding used is as follows:

- **Purple**: vehicle position.
- **Red**: safety zone behind a vehicle, where no other vehicle can enter.
- **Orange**: cell recently passed by a vehicle; any vehicle entering must reduce the speed accordingly.

- **Yellow**: cell passed earlier; vehicles must slow down further.
- **Green**: the vehicle occupying this cell has reached its destination.

The blue oval highlights a particular vehicle, making it easier to track its position as it navigates the city streets. As indicated by the color codes, the interactions of vehicles with their surrounding environment, such as safety zones and traffic, are represented visually, illustrating how congestion and route adjustments evolve dynamically over time. This visual sequence helps analyze traffic flow and vehicle distribution over time, providing insight into the evolution of the system during the simulation.

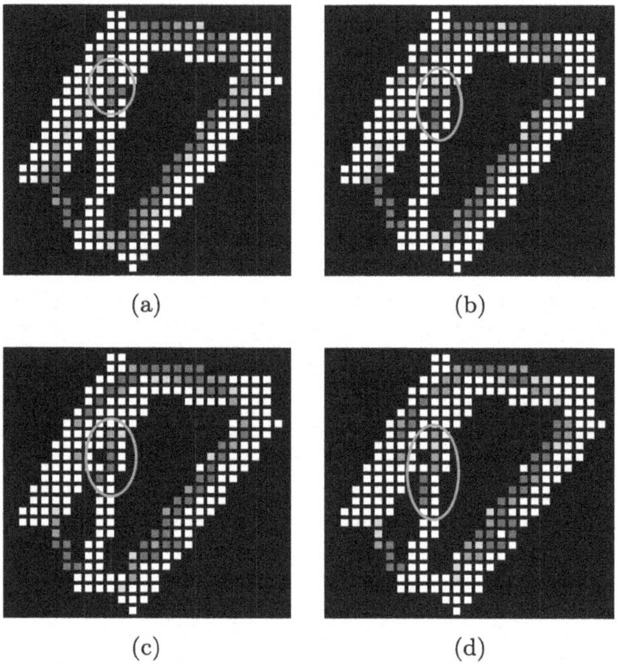

Fig. 5. Sequence of simulation snapshots showing the movement of vehicles through the portion of the city of Seville shown in Fig. 6. Subfigures (a) to (d) differ in one time step each. To help understand the figure, the blue oval highlights the position of a particular vehicle through the simulated sequence. The color codes are indicated in the text of the paper.

The final structure of a large portion of a real city (a neighbourhood of Seville, Spain) is shown in Fig. 6, displaying the distribution of one-directional lanes. The lanes are populated by CA cells, which serve as the pathways for vehicle agents to navigate through the neighborhood. This structure forms the basis for simulating traffic patterns and vehicle behavior in a real-world urban environment.

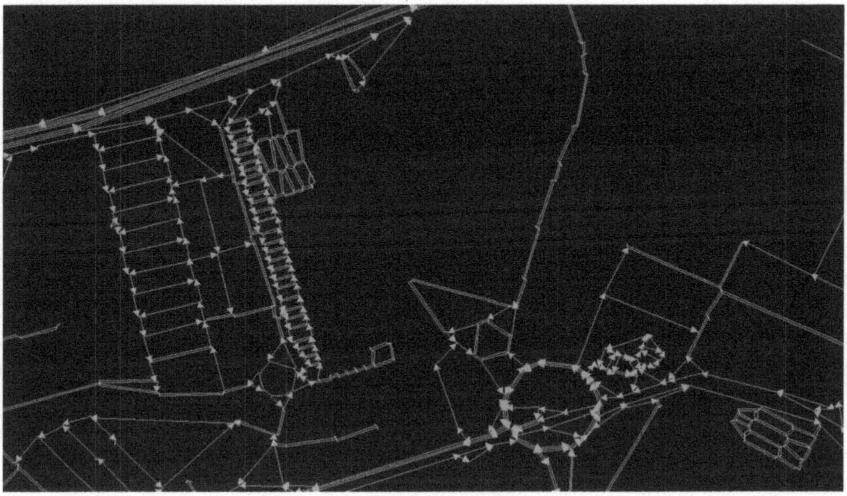

Fig. 6. Large portion of a real city (Seville, Spain) with one-directional lane distribution, extracted from the OpenStreetMap GIS. Each lane is populated by CA cells in which the vehicle agents navigate.

5 Conclusions and Future Challenges

In this work, we have presented research on the integration of simulation and artificial intelligence techniques to optimize the deployment of the EV charging infrastructure. Our hybrid cellular automata and agent-based model, coupled with genetic algorithms and neural networks, provides a comprehensive framework to capture the complex dynamics of urban traffic, EV charging behavior, and environmental effects.

In addition to introducing the concept ideas, we have presented preliminary results that include achievements such as simulations of the air pollution produced by the simulation with a mixture of EVs and ICEVs (Petrol and Diesel), studied with and without buildings. We have also presented the procedure to generate a CA grid from real-city data obtained from the OpenStreetMap GIS, and to simulate traffic of vehicles on that grid.

Future work will focus on refining the model parameters, validating the model against real-world data, exploring its applicability in diverse urban contexts, and expanding the scope to address nationwide charging networks. Our objective with this research is to contribute to the development of sustainable transportation systems and support the transition to electric mobility.

References

1. A simulation approach to determine the deployment of an urban network of electric vehicle charging stations for environmental and social benefits. SANEVEC TED-2021 1800583003 (2021), research project funded by the Ministerio de Ciencia e Innovación (MCIN), Agencia Estatal de Investigación (AEI) of Spain, and by the European Union NextGenerationEU/PRTR (2021)

2. Abduljabbar, R., et al.: Development and evaluation of bidirectional lstm freeway traffic forecasting models using simulation data. Sci. Rep. **11** (2021). https://doi.org/10.1038/s41598-021-03282-z
3. Benjavanich, S., Ursani, Z., Corne, D.: Forecasting the flow of urban pollution with cellular automata. In: 2017 Sustainable Internet and ICT for Sustainability (SustainIT), pp. 1–6 (2017). https://doi.org/10.23919/SustainIT.2017.8379801
4. Bresenham, J.E.: Algorithm for computer control of a digital plotter. IBM Syst. J. **4**(1), 25–30 (1965). https://doi.org/10.1147/sj.41.0025
5. Burghout, W.: Mesoscopic simulation models for short-term prediction (2005). https://www.researchgate.net/publication/255654806, pREDIKT project report CTR2005
6. Chen, Z., Liu, W., Yin, Y.: Deployment of stationary and dynamic charging infrastructure for electric vehicles along traffic corridors. Transport. Res. Part C: Emerg. Technol. **77**, 185–206 (2017). https://doi.org/10.1016/j.trc.2017.01.021
7. Council, E.V.: Electric vehicle consumer behavior (2021). https://www.fuelsinstitute.org/Research/Reports/EVConsumer-Behavior/EV-Consumer-Behavior-Report.pdf, fuels Institute Report
8. Diaz-Jara, R., et al.: Integrating efficient routes with station monitoring for electric vehicles in urban environments: simulation and analysis. In: Proceedings of the 15th EAI International Conference on Simulation Tools (SIMUtools 2023), Seville, Spain (2023)
9. Dupuis, A., Chopard, B.: Parallel simulation of traffic in Geneva using cellular automata, pp. 89–107. Nova Science, USA (2001)
10. European Environment Agency: Decarbonising road transport - the role of vehicles, fuels and transport demand (2022). https://www.eea.europa.eu/publications/transport-and-environment-report-2021/at_download/file, eEA Report No 2/2022
11. Everis, Transport & Environment: Estudio sobre el despliegue de la infraestructura de carga del vehículo eléctrico en España (Enero 2021). https://ecodes.org/images/que-hacemos/01.Cambio_Climatico/Incidencia_politicas/Movilidad/2021_02_Estudio_sobre_el_.pdf
12. García-Suárez, A., Guisado-Lizar, J.L., Diaz-Del-rio, F., Jiménez-Morales, F.: A cellular automata agent-based hybrid simulation tool to analyze the deployment of electric vehicle charging stations. Sustainability **13**(10), 5421 (2021). https://doi.org/10.3390/su13105421
13. Gobierno de España: Plan Nacional Integrado de Energía y Clima 2021–2030 (Enero 2020). https://www.miteco.gob.es/images/es/pnieccompleto_tcm30-508410.pdf
14. Int Panis, L., Broekx, S., Liu, R.: Modelling instantaneous traffic emission and the influence of traffic speed limits. Sci. Total Environ. **371**(1), 270–285 (2006). https://doi.org/10.1016/j.scitotenv.2006.08.017
15. International Energy Agency: Global EV Outlook 2023 (2023). https://www.iea.org/reports/global-ev-outlook-2023
16. Jordán, J., Martí, P., Palanca, J., Julian, V., Botti, V.: Interurban charging station network: an evolutionary approach. Neurocomputing **529**, 214–221 (2023). https://doi.org/10.1016/j.neucom.2023.01.068
17. Kroc, J., Jiménez-Morales, F., Guisado-Lizar, J., Lemos, M., Tkac, J.: Building efficient computational cellular automata models of complex systems: background, applications, results, software and pathologies. Adv. Complex Syst. **22**(5) (2019). https://doi.org/10.1142/S0219525919500139

18. Martí, P., Llopis, J., Julian, V., Novais, P., Jordán, J.: Validating state-wide charging station network through agent-based simulation. In: PAAMS 2023, Communications in Computer and Information Science, vol. 1838. Springer, Cham (2023). https://doi.org/10.1007/978-3-031-37593-4_13
19. Mazur, F., Chrobok, R., Hafstein, S.F., Pottmeier, A., Schreckenberg, M.: Future of traffic information: online simulation of a large scale freeway network. In: Proceedings of IADIS International Conference WWW/INTERNET 2004, pp. 665–672 (2004). https://www.researchgate.net/publication/220969356
20. Nagel, K., Schreckenberg, M.: A cellular automaton model for freeway traffic. J. Phys. I **2**, 2221–2229 (1992). https://doi.org/10.1051/jp1:1992277
21. Ragel-Díaz-Jara, D., et al.: Integrating efficient routes with station monitoring for electric vehicles in urban environments: Simulation and analysis. In: Simulation Tools and Techniques: 15th EAI International Conference, SIMUtools 2023, Seville, Spain, 14–15 December 2023, Proceedings. Springer, Cham (2024). https://link.springer.com/book/9783031575228
22. del Rio, F.D., et al.: Comparing the efficiency of traffic simulations using cellular automata. In: Proceedings of the 15th EAI International Conference on Simulation Tools and Techniques (SIMUtools 2023), Seville, Spain (2023)
23. Sroczyński, A., et al.: Road traffic can be predicted by machine learning equally effectively as by complex microscopic model. Sci. Rep. **13**, 14523 (2023). https://doi.org/10.1038/s41598-023-41902-y
24. Timmers, V.R., Achten, P.A.: Non-exhaust PM emissions from electric vehicles. Atmos. Environ. **134**, 10–17 (2016). https://doi.org/10.1016/j.atmosenv.2016.03.017. https://www.sciencedirect.com/science/article/pii/S135223101630187X
25. Vinuesa, R., Brunton, S., et al.: The transformative potential of machine learning for experiments in fluid mechanics. Nat. Rev. Phys. **5**, 536–545 (2023). https://doi.org/10.1038/s42254-023-00622-y
26. Viswanathan, V., Zehe, D., Ivanchev, J., Pelzer, D., Knoll, A., Aydt, H.: Simulation-assisted exploration of charging infrastructure requirements for electric vehicles in urban environments. J. Comput. Sci. **12**, 1–10 (2016). https://doi.org/10.1016/j.jocs.2015.10.012
27. Xiang, Y., Liu, Z., Liu, J., Liu, Y., Gu, C.: Integrated traffic-power simulation framework for electric vehicle charging stations based on cellular automaton. J. Mod. Power Syst. Clean Energy **6**(4), 816–820 (2018). https://doi.org/10.1007/s40565-018-0379-3
28. Xiao, Y., Liu, J., Wu, J., Ansari, N.: Leveraging deep reinforcement learning for traffic engineering: a survey. IEEE Commun. Surv. Tutor. **23**(4), 2064–2097 (2021). https://doi.org/10.1109/COMST.2021.3102580
29. Yang, H., Li, X., Qiang, W., Zhao, Y., Zhang, W., Tang, C.: A network traffic forecasting method based on SA optimized ARIMA-BP neural network. Comput. Netw. **193**, 108102 (2021). https://doi.org/10.1016/j.comnet.2021.108102
30. Zhai, Z., Su, S., Liu, R., Yang, C., Liu, C.: Agent-cellular automata model for the dynamic fluctuation of EV traffic and charging demands based on machine learning algorithm. Neural Comput. Appl. **31**, 4639–4652 (2019). https://doi.org/10.1007/s00521-018-3841-2

Integrating Fast Electric Vehicle Charging and Charge-Site Power-Limiting in SUMO

Filip Lukic[1], Maria S. Forkaliuk[2], and Gerald Franzl[1](✉)

[1] Department for Integrated Sensor Systems, University for Continuing Education Krems, Wiener Neustadt, Austria
https://www.donau-uni.ac.at/diss

[2] Department of Automation and Intelligent Information Technologies, Vinnytsia National Technical University, Vinnytsia, Ukraine
https://aiit.vntu.edu.ua/

Abstract. Fast charging of electric vehicles is important for drivers who cannot charge overnight or while at work, and obviously along highways. Latter is the topic of the R&D project that triggered the presented adoption of SUMO to realistically simulate fast and smart charging. Fast charging is characterised by a state-of-charge related charging power decline, which is added to the existing charging station model and executed using TraCI. Smart charging limits the total power drawn from the electric grid, i.e., dynamically limits the sum drawn by the charging points that constitute a charging site, and is implemented by grouping charging points and regularly adjusting the individually provided power. First, the implementation and required code extensions to realize these features in SUMO are presented in detail. Second, simulation results based on a finite multi-server queueing model show the practical effects of fast and smart charging at highway charging sites.

Keywords: Electric Vehicle Charging · Fast Charging · Smart Charging · Dynamic Charging Power · Power Limiting · Power Demand Histogram

1 Introduction

The increasing share of electric vehicles (EVs) on the roads also raises the demand to re-charge en route. Most charging occurs while the vehicle is parked for extended times, i.e., overnight or while the driver is at work [1]. These charging events are well served by AC chargers [2]. Only occasionally travel EVs

The work presented has been conducted in the course of the national R&D project *eAlloc* funded by the Austrian Climate and Energy Fund (KLIEN) in the 3rd call of the *Zero Emission Mobility* program, administered by the Austrian Research Promotion Agency (FFG) under project No 885026.

A. A. Juan et al. (Eds.): SIMUtools 2024, LNICST 603, pp. 88–104, 2025.
https://doi.org/10.1007/978-3-031-87345-4_6

distances that exceed the range of the battery, which causes the demand to re-charge every 200 to 400 km [3]. Fast DC charging is required to re-charge 40 to 80 kWh in 30 to 60 min, in particular along highways [4].

Eclipse SUMO (Simulation of Urban MObility) [5] can be used to simulate any traffic scenario and is based on modelling both, vehicles and roads as detailed as possible, to achieve a maximally realistic model of real world scenarios. When the project *eAlloc* started [6], only a simple AC charging station was available in SUMO. In this paper, we enhance the charging station and the electric vehicle modules with the features required to model fast DC charging [7] and smart charging [8].

First, we show how to generate and insert charging sites consisting of any number of charging points, each attached to a traffic lane that allows EVs to approach and connect to an individual charging point and offer space to wait for the re-charging. Next, we address how to model and implement fast DC charging considering the limitations introduced by (a) the EV charger electronics, (b) the fast charging performance that decreases with the battery's state of charge (SoC), (c) the charging point, and (d) the smart charging mechanism that prevents an overload of the grid access and might beyond that also support renewable electricity supply [9,10]. Finally, we present an example on how to determine the impact of smart charging on the re-charging performance.

Section 2 addresses the import and adjustment of a real street network, and the generation and insertion of DC charging sites. The developed fast DC charging model is presented in Sect. 3, introducing the different limitations and their dynamic adjustment during simulation runs. Smart charging, the limitation introduced across entire charging sites, is introduced and explained in Sect. 4. The exemplary result presented in Sect. 5 shows how the added features work. Section 6 concludes the paper by showing how to evaluate the smart charging impact on a site's charging performance. Section 7 summarises the presented work and provides an outlook on what can be achieved with the introduced features.

2 Composition of a Street Network File

To evaluate the fast and smart re-charging of electric vehicles (EVs) along highways in SUMO, we need a street network with adjacent charging sites that provide a feasible number of fast DC charging points. To cover distances that require re-charging en route, a relatively large street network is required. As an example, we use the highway network of Austria, including the connecting section across Bavaria.

2.1 Extracting the Highway Network from Public Map Data

To import the highway infrastructure only, we apply the following tool chain: *Geofabrik* → *Osmosis* → *netconvert* → *NetEdit*. *Geofabrik* [11] provides map sections in the *OpenStreetMap*(OSM) [12] format, which include the complete map data of the regions downloaded. *Osmosis* [13] is used to extract the highways into a new OSM file, which than is converted into a SUMO network file using *netconvert* [14]. To add missed highway sections, necessary inter-connecting roads, and to fix possible import and conversion glitches, the *NetEdit* tool [15] comes in handy. In the end, we get a street network as shown in Fig. 1.

Fig. 1. Austrian highway network ready for being used in SUMO.

2.2 Composing and Inserting DC Charging Sites

Charging sites are modelled as a multi-lane road, where each lane hosts a charging station that provides exactly one charging point, as shown by the example in Table 1. The number of charging points per site, their individual static power limit and the supported plug types are specified in a human-readable and editable comma-separated values (CSV) file, where each line represents one charging point, as shown in Table 1.

Table 1. Charging site configuration using a CSV table

	$P_{\max}^{\mathrm{CP}}$	plug type
	150000	CCS2
	100000	CCS1
	115000	CHAdeMO
	122000	CCS2
	135000	CCS2

The numbers shown in the SUMO graphical user interface (GUI) next to the charging points is the power $P_{\mathrm{ch}}^{\mathrm{EV}}(t)$ currently drawn by the connected EV, or the static power limit $P_{\max}^{\mathrm{CP}}$ of the charging site, when no EV is connected.

Where slip roads from and to the highway connect petrol station, we place such an EV charging site in between the open endpoints, as shown by the example in Table 2. Charging sites in close vicinity to a highway, accessible only by leaving the highway, are placed in between the nearest slip roads to and from the highway, again connecting the open slip road ends. To consider the time needed to actually reach these, we add the average time to travel there to the start charging delay Δt, which in case of highway connected sites only covers the time needed to plug in and get the authorisation to charge (approx. 1 minute).

Table 2. Site location CSV table to insert charging sites

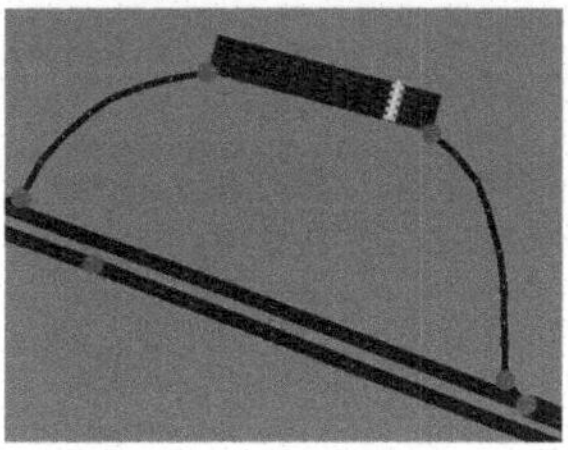

from node	to node	design CSV	Δt	$P_{\max}^{\mathrm{CS}}$
2134185703	970593884	testCS1.csv	5	300000
413910991	413910995	testCS2.csv	1	500000
370147908	370147959	testCS3.csv	1	900000
369658340	368997193	testCS1.csv	9	250000
⋮	⋮	⋮	⋮	⋮
1276708788	1276708798	testCS3.csv	1	750000
9079992763	9079992764	testCS2.csv	1	600000
1732051581	639607892	testCS2.csv	3	500000

The insertion into the SUMO map file is performed by a Python script, which generates charging sites as specified in the charging site design CSV file (Table 1), and connects it to the open slip road ends, i.e., the map-node-IDs in the net.xml file, as specified in the site location CSV file (Table 2). This CSV file also specifies the start charging delay Δt and the static power limit of the entire charging site $P_{\max}^{\mathrm{CS}}$ (group power). Latter is used in Sect. 4 to implement *smart charging*. Whereas the site location CSV file is unique and covers all charging sites, any number of site design CSV files can by created and reused as needed.

3 Dynamic EV Charging

The charging station object found in SUMO covers charging with constant power. Fast DC charging is, however, dynamically limited by the EV's battery state and the EV's integrated charging control. Using *Traffic Control Interface* (TraCI) [16,17], which is installed with SUMO, the power output of charging points can be dynamically adjusted while the simulation is running, i.e., while an EV is charged.

The following changes need to be made in the SUMO source code to enable dynamic charging power adjustment:

1. Add to `src/libsumo/ChargingStation.cpp`:

```
void ChargingStation::setPower(const std::string& stopID, double power) {
    MSStoppingPlace* sp = getChargingStation(stopID);
    MSChargingStation* cs = dynamic_cast<MSChargingStation*>(sp);
    cs->setChargingPower(power);
}
```

2. Add to **src/microsim/trigger/MSChargingStation.cpp**:

```
void MSChargingStation::setChargingPower(double power) {
    if (power >= 0) { myChargingPower = power; }
}
```

3. Add to **src/libsumo/TraCIConstants.h**:

```
TRACI_CONST int VAR_POWER = 0xfe;
```

4. Add to **tools/traci/constants.py**

```
VAR_POWER = 0xfe
```

5. Add to **tools/traci/_chargingstation.py**:

```
def setPower(self, stopID, power):
    self._setCmd(tc.VAR_POWER, stopID, "d", power)
```

6. Change the code to check for the constant **VAR_POWER** and add a new case in **src/traci-server/TraCIServerAPI_ChargingStation.cpp**:

```
if (variable != libsumo::VAR_PARAMETER && variable != libsumo::VAR_POWER){
...
...
...
case libsumo::VAR_POWER: {
    double power = 0;
    if (!server.readTypeCheckingDouble(inputStorage, power)) {
        return
        ↪   server.writeErrorStatusCmd(libsumo::CMD_SET_CHARGINGSTATION_VARIABLE,"Setting
        ↪   power requires a double.", outputStorage);
    }
    libsumo::ChargingStation::setPower(id, power);
    break;
}
```

Note that only the definition is shown in detail, not the declaration of functions. Once the source code changes are made, the SUMO project needs to be built anew (re-compiled), so the changes become integrated and applied.

3.1 Dynamic Power Output Integration

To use the introduced dynamic adjustment option, the existing charging station objects need an attribute that limits the current power output: A dynamic parameter named *allowedPowerOutput* is added to each charging point, adding the following node to the XML file,

```
<chargingStation id="cs_0" lane="T0_0" startPos="15" endPos="20" friendlyPos="true"
↪   power="150000">
    <param key="allowedPowerOutput" value="150000"/>
</chargingStation>
```

where *id*, *lane*, *startPos*, *endPos*, *friendlyPos*, and *power*, specify the static parameters of a charging point, and the *param key* `allowedPowerOutput` introduces the dynamically adjustable power limiting *value*.

3.2 Charging Curve Integration

The actual charging power is dynamically adjusted by the EV's charging electronic to prevent the battery from harm. In particular to prevent it from overtemperature and over-voltage, by decreasing the charging power in the course of the charging process. To cover this dynamic behaviour, a user-defined EV type needs to include the dynamic parameter `"allowedPowerIntake"` to retrieve this attribute during simulation runs.

```
<vType id="Unknown_1" minGap="2.5" maxSpeed="41.66" emissionClass="Energy/default"
↪   color="blue" accel="1" decel="1" sigma="0">
    <param key="has.battery.device" value="true"/>
    <param key="airDragCoefficient" value="0.6"/>
    <param key="constantPowerIntake" value="160"/>
    <param key="frontSurfaceArea" value="3"/>
    <param key="internalMomentOfInertia" value="0.01"/>
    <param key="maximumBatteryCapacity" value="70000"/>
    <param key="maximumPower" value="100000"/>
    <param key="propulsionEfficiency" value="0.9"/>
    <param key="radialDragCoefficient" value="0.5"/>
    <param key="recuperationEfficiency" value="0.9"/>
    <param key="rollDragCoefficient" value="0.01"/>
    <param key="stoppingTreshold" value="0.1"/>
    <param key="vehicleMass" value="1615"/>
    <param key="allowedPowerIntake" value="120000"/>
</vType>
```

The above example of a customised EV model (defined in XML) includes many dynamic parameters to realistically model an EV. Most of these attributes are introduced and explained in detail in [18,19], and all these remain unchanged.

3.3 Charging Power Calculation

To determine how much power an EV connected to a charging point gets per simulation tick, three things need to be present:

- $P^{\text{CP}}_{\text{max}}$ being the allowed power output of the charging point
- $P^{\text{EV}}_{\text{max}}$ being the maximum power intake of the EV's charging port
- $P^{\text{SoC}}_{\text{max}}$ being the charging curve that limits the power intake

The allowed power output of the charging point and the maximum power intake of the vehicle can be obtained via TraCI. The SoC-dependent power intake of the EV is calculated by applying the empirically derived charging power decline

$$P^{\text{SoC}}_{\text{max}} = 1.1 * BatterySize * \frac{110 - SoC}{33} \tag{1}$$

where *BatterySize* is the usable battery capacity of the EV in Wh and *SoC* is the currently reached SoC in % [0..100] of the usable battery capacity.

Figure 2 depicts the three power-limiting factors. The actual power intake during a simulation tick is the minimum of the three factors, represented by the red curve.

This momentary charging power is dynamically set as the power output of the charging station object. The energy charged $E_{ch}^{EV}(\text{tick}_i)$ is the duration of a simulation tick multiplied by the dynamically set output power.

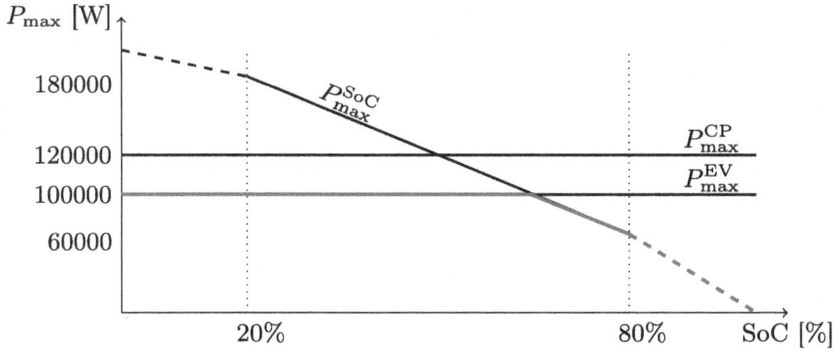

Fig. 2. Approximated DC charging curve. (Color figure online)

To actually achieve the above-specified charging behavior using TraCI, the code shown below is implemented to calculate and accurately set the power output of every occupied charging point in each simulation tick.

```
csId = traci.vehicle.getParameter(vehId,"device.battery.chargingStationId")
actualBattery =
↪   float(traci.vehicle.getParameter(vehId,"device.battery.actualBatteryCapacity"))
maxBattery = float(traci.vehicle.getParameter(vehId,"device.battery.maximumBatteryCapacity"))
maxPsoc = 1.1 * maxBattery * (110 - 100 * actualBattery/maxBattery) / 33
maxPcp = float(traci.chargingstation.getParameter(csId,"allowedPowerOutput"))
maxPev =
↪   float(traci.vehicletype.getParameter(traci.vehicle.getTypeID(vehId),"allowedPowerIntake"))
traci.chargingstation.setPower(csId,min(maxPsoc, maxPcp, maxPev))
```

Using the connected vehicle's ID (**vehId**), the charging point ID (**csId**), the current charging state *actualBattery*, and the battery capacity *maxBattery* are retrieved to determine the three power limits P_{max}^{SoC}, P_{max}^{CP}, and P_{max}^{EV}. The minimum of them is set as the current charging power of the charging point identified by `csID`.

For the charging site power limitation presented next, the above-determined charging power becomes the desired power P_{des}^{CP}. The actual charging power P_{adj}^{CP} can be curtailed, i.e., $P_{adj}^{CP} \leq P_{des}^{CP}$.

4 Smart Charging Sites

To implement *smart charging*, i.e., site power demand limitation, the charging points of a charging site need to be grouped. Dynamic parameters come in handy and are added to match the criteria for the charge site power limitation. The script that inserts charging sites into the street network also groups the charging points by automatically setting the dynamic `group` parameter to the line number in the location CSV file (Table 2). The resultant XML charging point definition

```
<chargingStation id="cs_0" lane="T0_0" startPos="15" endPos="20" friendlyPos="true"
↪   power="150000">
    <param key="group" value="0"/>
    <param key="chargingPort" value="CCS2"/>
    <param key="allowedPowerOutput" value="150000"/>
    <param key="groupPower" value="200000"/>
    <param key="chargeDelay" value="5"/>
</chargingStation>
```

contains now the `"group"` *value*, which specifies to which charging site the respective charging point belongs, the `"groupPower"` *value* that limits the total power $P_{\max}^{\mathrm{CS}}$ that a group may use to charge EVs, and the `"chargeDelay"` *value* to specify the Δt before actual charging begins, as detailed in Sect. 2.2. The other dynamic parameters are those introduced in Sect. 3.2. In addition, is the `aliquotPowerAdjustment` parameter added to the Python code shown at the end of Sect. 3.3.

Every *chargingStation* object (charging point) is also a *stop* object in SUMO. Therefore, the simulation domain functions in TraCI that check whether a vehicle stops or leaves a *stop*, are used to identify and list occupied charging points, as shown below.

```
for veh in traci.simulation.getStopStartingVehiclesIDList():
    csId = traci.vehicle.getParameter(veh, "device.battery.chargingStationId")
    if (csId != "NULL"):
        vehList.append(veh)
        traci.chargingstation.setParameter(csId, "desiredPower", 0)
        traci.chargingstation.setParameter(csId, "aliquotPowerAdjustment", 1)
for veh in traci.simulation.getStopEndingVehiclesIDList():
    vehList.remove(veh)
```

First, the `getStopStartingVehiclesIDList()` function is used to iterate through all vehicles that entered a *stop*. Vehicles that stopped at a stop with set *device.battery.chargingStationId*, which identifies it as a charging point, become added to `vehList`, and the dynamic parameters `"aliquotPowerAdjustment"` and `"desiredPower"` of the *chargingStation* object become initialised. Second, the `getStopEndingVehiclesIDList()` function is used to remove from `vehList` all vehicles that left a *stop* in the current time step. Note that trying to remove an object that is not in the list causes no error. In the end, `vehList` contains now all vehicles that currently stop at a charging point. The `aliquotPowerAdjustment` parameter can now be calculated using the following method:

```
def calculateAliquotPowerAdjustments(vehList):
    csDict = {}
    for veh in vehList:
        csId = traci.vehicle.getParameter(veh, "device.battery.chargingStationId")
        group = traci.chargingstation.getParameter(csId, "group")
        if group in csDict: csDict[group] += [csId]
            else: csDict[group] = [csId]
    for key in csDict:
        csGroup = csDict[key]
        maxPower = int(traci.chargingstation.getParameter(csGroup[0], "groupPower"))
        sumDesired = 0
```

```
for csId in csGroup:
    desired = traci.chargingstation.getParameter(csId, "desiredPower")
    sumDesired += float(desired)
factor = 1
if sumDesired > maxPower:
    factor = maxPower / sumDesired
for csId in csGroup:
    traci.chargingstation.setParameter(csId, "aliquotPowerAdjustment", factor)
```

First, the dictionary `csDict` is created to categorize the currently used charging points CP(i) into `csDict[group-ID]` groups. The `csDict[group-ID]` lists are than used to calculate the adjusted charging powers $P_{\text{adj}}^{\text{CP}(i)}$ according to

$$P_{\text{des}}^{\text{CS}(k)} = \sum_{\texttt{csId}(\text{CP}(i))\in\texttt{csDict}[k]} P_{\text{des}}^{\text{CP}(i)} \quad \Rightarrow \quad \Delta_{\text{pow}}^{\text{CS}(k)} = \min\left(1, \frac{P_{\text{max}}^{\text{CS}(k)}}{P_{\text{des}}^{\text{CS}(k)}}\right) \tag{2}$$

$$P_{\text{adj}}^{\text{CP}(i)} = \Delta_{\text{pow}}^{\text{CS}(k)} * P_{\text{des}}^{\text{CP}(i)} \quad \forall_{\text{CP}(i)\in\texttt{csDict}[k],k} \tag{3}$$

where $P_{\text{des}}^{\text{CP}(i)}$ is the power the CP(i) wishes to provide, k is the `group-ID` of CS(k), and $P_{\text{des}}^{\text{CS}(k)}$ is the total desired power of the charging site specified in line k in the site location CSV. Equation 2 yields the $\Delta_{\text{pow}}^{\text{CS}(k)}$ in the range [0..1] required to set the `"aliquotPowerAdjustment"` *value* of all the currently occupied charging points, which than is applied according to Eq. 3 to implement smart charging site power limitation.

The Python code introduced at the end of Sect. 3.3, which is executed in every times step of the simulation, is finally extended to multiply the already calculated desired power $P_{\text{des}}^{\text{CP}}$ by the `"aliquotPowerAdjustment"` *value* $\Delta_{\text{pow}}^{\text{CS}}$ to get the actual charging power $P_{\text{ch}}^{\text{EV}} = P_{\text{adj}}^{\text{CP}}$ with which the connected vehicle can charge its battery in the current simulation time step.

```
def setChargingStationPowers(vehList):
  for veh in vehList:
    ...
    ...
    ...
    power = min(maxPsoc, maxPcs, maxPev)
    traci.chargingstation.setParameter(csId, "desiredPower", power)
    factor = float(traci.chargingstation.getParameter(csId, "aliquotPowerAdjustment"))
    actualPower = power * factor
    traci.chargingstation.setPower(csId, actualPower)
```

To keep the computation effort reasonable, group power limits are re-evaluated every 60 s only, i.e., every 60 ticks in SUMO, while the reminder of the Phyton code remains executed in every tick. However, this up to one minute delay causes short power peaks on the grid access, which are also visible in the example presented next.

5 Resultant Dynamic Charging Power Adjustment

To show the effect of the different limitations and adjustments, we need a situation where several EVs arrive at the same charging site within a short duration of time, such that their individual charging processes overlap and cause a total charging demand that exceeds the charging site power limit, i.e., $\sum P_{\text{des}}^{\text{CP}} > P_{\text{max}}^{\text{CS}}$. Figure 3 shows such a parallel charging of four EVs over time, in particular the dynamic charging power provided by the charging points these EVs connect to. The simulation step is set to one second to clearly see the effects of the different dynamic adjustments performed.

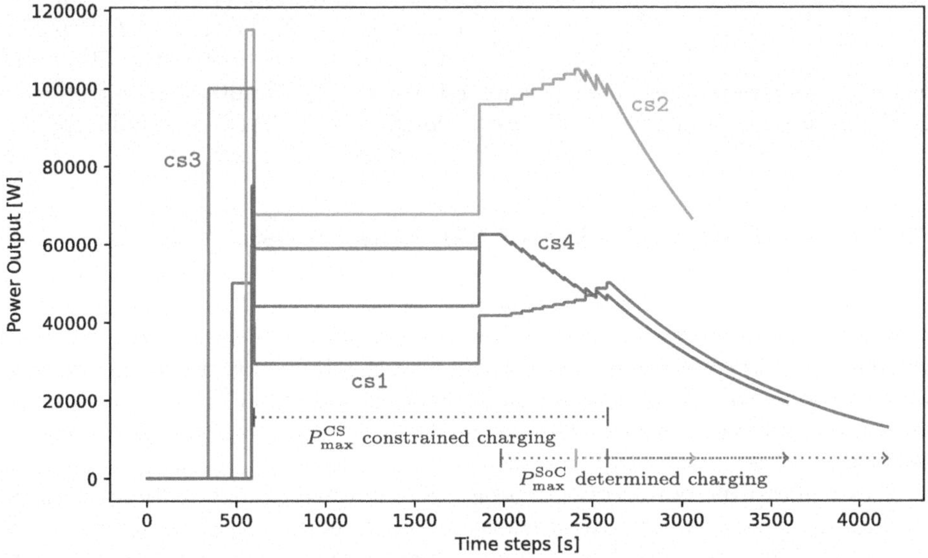

Fig. 3. Simulated charging point output of a charging site where four EVs happen to be charged in parallel and are constrained by a maximum site power of 200 kW. (Color figure online)

The charging site power limit $P_{\text{max}}^{\text{CS}}$ is set to 200 kW. The first arriving EV chooses charging at the charge point `cs3` (green line) and is limited to 100 kW, the second chooses `cs1` (blue line) and is limited to 50 kW, the third chooses `cs2` (orange line) and is limited to 115 kW, and the fourth chooses `cs4` (red line) and is limited to 75 kW.

When the 3rd EV arrives, the site limit is reached, i.e., $100 + 50 + 115 = 265 > 200$, but due to the up to 60 second delay until the group adjustment is re-evaluated, instantly no power curtailment is performed. In addition, the fourth EV also arrives within this delay, such that its initial power is also not constrained instantly. Therefore, at around 600 seconds (steps) into the simulation, we see the powers that the EVs draw without smart charging control, i.e., when no group limit is applied, here causing 340 kW in total.

Once the group power limiting is enforced beyond time step 600, the power drawn by each EV is aliquot reduced to $58.8 + 29.4 + 67.7 + 44.1 = 200$. This situation persists until the first arriving EV at `cs3` (green line) stops charging after 1500 s (25 min). At this time, the curtailment per remaining EV is relaxed to $41.7 + 95.8 + 62.5 = 200$.

At time step 2000, the *charging curve*, i.e., the SoC determined desired power of the fourth EV connected to `cs4` (red line) $P_{\max}^{\mathrm{SoC}}(\mathrm{cs4})$ begins to reduce the individual power demand to a value below the aliquot possible. In consequence, the power curtailment for the other two EVs at `cs1` and `cs2` is dynamically relaxed minute by minute, until their SoC determined limitation becomes effective at time step 2450 for `cs2` and at time step 2600 for `cs1`. Beyond latter time step, the EVs charge at their individual SoC determined limits, $P_{\max}^{\mathrm{SoC}}(\mathrm{cs2})$ and $P_{\max}^{\mathrm{SoC}}(\mathrm{cs1})$, because the sum of these declining desired powers remains below the site limit, such that no group adjustment is enforced. Hence, the minute steps introduced by the group adjustment intervals are no longer visible in the remaining power traces until the EVs stop charging and leave the charging site.

6 Stochastic Evaluation of Charging Sites

The charging service achieved by randomly arriving EVs at a charging site that implements a site-power limitation (Smart Charging) needs to be monitored at different arrival-rates to assess the impact that the limitation practically causes. This is possible with SUMO, as shown in Fig. 3, for individual EVs. If we compare the charging service of several thousand EVs, solid statistical results can be derived.

To simulate different arrival patterns, i.e., inter-arrival distributions, according arrival sequences need to provided as an input for SUMO. Generating a specific charging demand distribution is another challenge caused by the very realistic traffic simulation provided by SUMO. Therefore, a dedicated simulation tool [20] is used to specifically evaluate the stochastic properties of DC charging sites. This tool applies event based simulation and models charging sites as finite multi-server queueing system [21], where the charging points are the servers, the EVs the clients, and the queue is limited by the available parking space. The dynamic power intake (charging curve) and the site power limiting (smart charging) are the same as outlined above.

For the exemplary results shown in this section, we assume five DC charging points, each capable of providing up to 150 kW, ten waiting spaces, and a site power limit set to 300 kW. The simulated EVs all have a battery capacity of 60 kWh and a maximum charging power of 120 kW, i.e., less than the charging point limit, but if three or more EVs are charged in parallel, the sum of the individual charging demands can be beyond the site power limit, such that smart charging becomes used. The EV arrivals to the charging site occur uncorrelated, i.e., with a negative exponential distributed inter-arrival time in between successive arrivals. The charging time is Erlang_2 distributed with mean being half an hour, and the charging demand is Beta distributed with mean being 80 % of the battery capacity, i.e., 48 kWh.

6.1 Queueing Probability

With uncorrelated arrivals, some EVs will need to wait until a charging point becomes idle because all are occupied when these EVs arrive. The consequential mean waiting-time is represented by the bold red curve in Fig. 4. The service-time, shown in blue, does not depend on the arrival rate, which increases linearly along the x-axis. The sum of the two is the sojourn-time, the time an EV spends at the charging site, and that is shown in magenta.

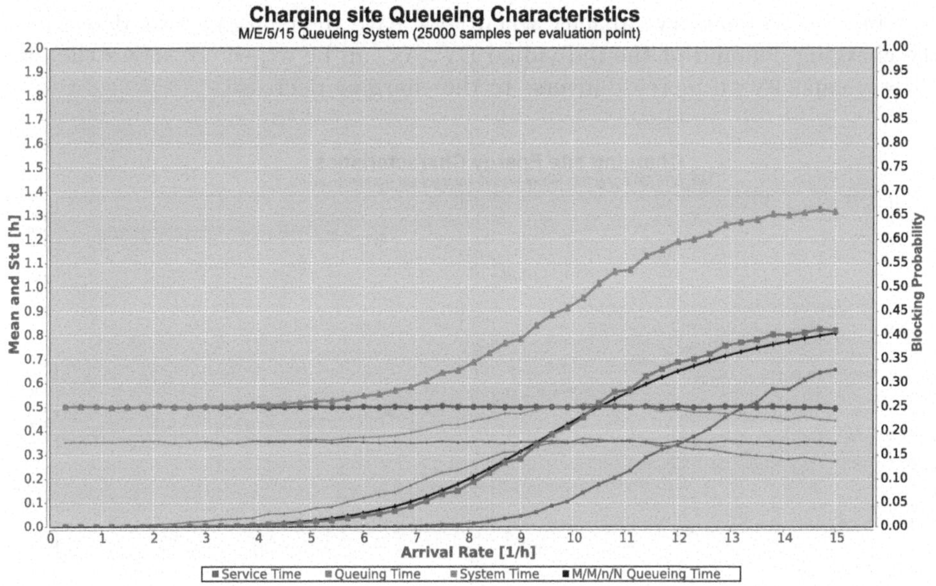

Fig. 4. Stochastic waiting-time and blocking-probability of a charging site example with 5 charging points and an average charging time of 30 min. (Color figure online)

The narrow lines in the bottom show the standard deviation of the equally coloured property, to complete the stochastic presentation of the gained results. A large standard deviation (or variance) indicates that the samples of the monitored property deviate more from the mean, such that experiencing a system behaviour close to the mean value is less likely.

Finally, the black curve close to the waiting time is the analytically calculated waiting time of the Markovian queueing system where also the service-times (charging duration) would be uncorrelated and thus, negative exponentially distributed. The purple line shows the blocking rate, i.e., the fraction of arriving EVs that are deflected to some other charging possibility because no parking space is available at the time these arrive.

6.2 Charging Performance

If the EVs currently connected to the charging points of a charging site want to draw more power than the site can provide, the provided power per charging point is aliquot curtailed, which decreases the charging speed. If the time for charging is determined when an EV arrives, as we assume here, less energy is charged. The average energy charged is shown by the bold blue curve in Fig. 5. With increased arrival rate these situations occur more often, and accordingly the average charging performance drops. The medium thick blue curves above and below show the 90 % and 10 % percentiles. These, as well as the red curve showing the idle battery capacity when EVs leave the charging site, depend on the charging demand of the individual EV. As can be expected, shows the idle battery capacity an increase inverse to the charging decrease.

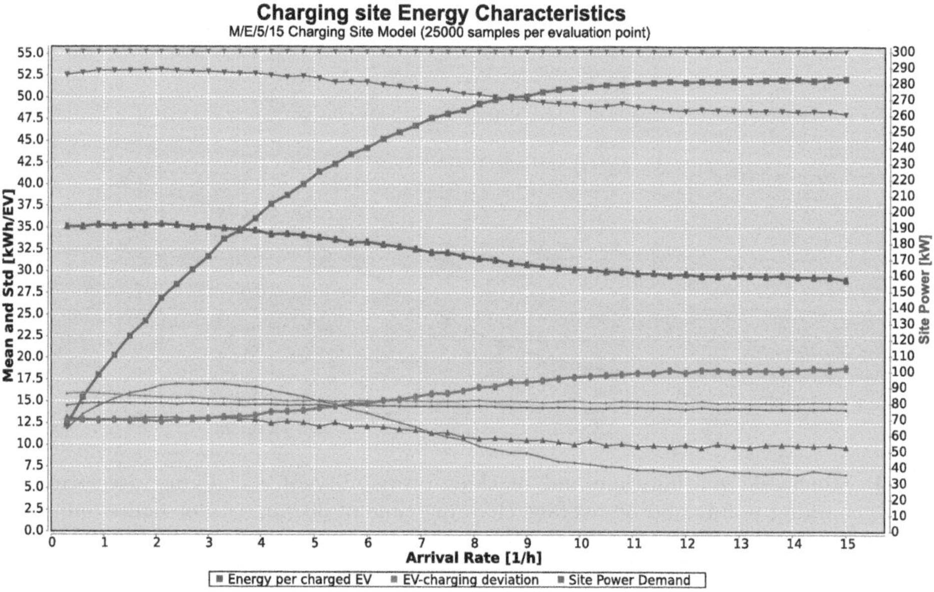

Fig. 5. Charging performance of the same charging site example. (Color figure online)

Finally, the bold purple line shows how the mean site power demand increases, and the narrow line above proves that the monitored peak power can reach the site power limit even at low arrival rates, just not so often. The narrow lines in the bottom again show the standard deviation of the different properties to complete the picture.

6.3 Site Power Demand

From Fig. 5 we can conclude that the site power limitation has no dramatic impact, especially when the mean traffic load is not too high, in particular below half the critical load (number of servers/mean service time), which for the examples is five arrivals per hour. How often the site power limitation is active depends on the arrival rate, as can be seen in the site power histogram presented in Fig. 6.

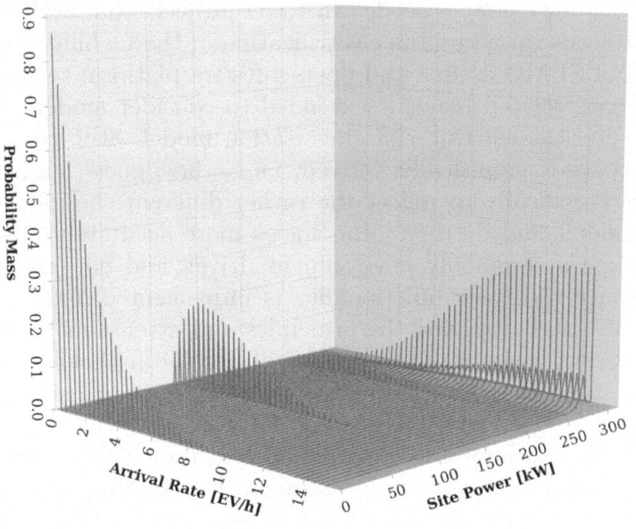

Fig. 6. Site power demand histogram, again for the same charging site example.

At very low arrival rates, the site is idle most of the time, which causes the high probability of zero power demand shown on the left edge. Next we recognise the peaks at 120 kW and less prominent at 240 kW, which result from one and two EVs charged at their maximum power rating, respectively.

On the right edge, we see the probability that the site power limit is reached, where charging power curtailment becomes active. The probability rises with the traffic load and reaches around 30 % when the site becomes overload, i.e., when the arrival rate exceeds the critical load. That the probability saturates in overload is due to the assumption that arriving EVs that find no parking-space continue to an alternative charging site.

The ripple just below the maximum power most probably results from a timing issue or slight overreaction of the limiting, but could not be confirmed yet. Still, from the simulation results it can be verified that Smart Charging (site power limiting) can effectively reduce the grid access power demand without severe impact on the charging performance. In the future, it may also be used to respond to demands from the electricity grid, e.g., to support the grid-voltage by dynamically increasing the site limit to better utilise nearby renewable sources, i.e., to mitigate the curtailment of renewable sources.

7 Summary

The presented adoptions of SUMO and usage of TraCI to handle dynamic charging power adjustments enable the simulation of fast and smart DC charging of electrical vehicles. Future traffic loads to charging sites can be simulated, and thereby the charging performance in relation to the composition of charging sites evaluated, as it is for example needed in R&D projects that address the future challenges and needs raised by the electrification of the mobility sector.

The utility of SUMO as free and open software platform to simulate traffic flows and evaluate related issues is extended to consider modern EV charging techniques beyond the existing charging station model. Still, the implemented DC charging curve is empirically derived, i.e., a first guess, and may need to be defined EV specifically to reflect the rather different charging behaviors of different EV models and battery technologies more accurately. Also the smart charging strategy is commonly environment driven and not just static power limiting. But once the basic functionality is implemented, more sophisticated usage can be evaluated applying the principles and extensions presented.

Future work in related R&D projects will use the introduced functionality to evaluate the time that EV drivers need to spend at charging sites, how to make smart DC charging effectively support the energy transition, and how to counteract waiting times by providing a sufficient number and variety of smart DC charging points. Further, it can be assumed that the site power demand does not increase linearly with the sum over the peak powers of installed charging points due to the statistical averaging over parallel charging events and due to the SoC-dependent decline of the charging power.

Smart DC charging provides the flexibility to dynamically adjust the power drawn from the local electricity grid, and thereby, it utilises volatile renewable sources better and at the same time mitigates the stress these put on the grid.

Acknowledgements. Special thanks are expressed to the research partners in the project *eAlloc* who participated in vivid discussions on fast EV charging issues and contributed ideas and concepts that all influenced the presented approach in a way.

References

1. Frendo, O., Gaertner, N., Stuckenschmidt, H.: Real-time smart charging based on precomputed schedules. IEEE Trans. Smart Grid **10**(6), 6921–6932 (2019). https://doi.org/10.1109/TSG.2019.2914274
2. Yasko, M., Balint, A., Driesen, J., Martinez, W.: Future workplace EV charging architectures: DC and AC charging choices. In: 2023 IEEE International Conference on Electrical Systems for Aircraft, Railway, Ship Propulsion and Road Vehicles & International Transportation Electrification Conference (ESARS-ITEC), pp. 1–7 (2023). https://doi.org/10.1109/ESARS-ITEC57127.2023.10114837
3. Zeillinger, K.: Von der Adria zur Ostsee – elektrisch. ÖAMTC *autotouring.at* (2022). https://www.oeamtc.at/autotouring/auto/e-auto-auf-der-langstrecke-55798787

4. Ahmadi, M., Kaleybar, H.J., Brenna, M., Castelli-Dezza, F., Carmeli, M.S.: Implementation of DC micro grid tied PV-storage based EV fast charging station. In: 2021 IEEE International Conference on Environment and Electrical Engineering and 2021 IEEE Industrial and Commercial Power Systems Europe (EEEIC/I&CPS Europe), pp. 1–6 (2021). https://doi.org/10.1109/EEEIC/ICPSEurope51590.2021.9584631
5. Lopez, P.A., et al.: Microscopic traffic simulation using SUMO. In: 2018 21st International Conference on Intelligent Transportation Systems (ITSC), pp. 2575–2582 (2018). https://doi.org/10.1109/ITSC.2018.8569938
6. eAlloc: Dynamically Optimizing the Allocation of e-cars to Charging Sites. R&D project, Austrian Climate and Energy Fund (KLIEN), 3rd Zero Emission Mobility call (2021–2025). https://projekte.ffg.at/projekt/4031006
7. Saner, C.B., Saha, J., Srinivasan, D.: A Charge curve and battery management system aware optimal charging scheduling framework for electric vehicle fast charging stations with heterogeneous customer mix. IEEE Trans. Intell. Transp. Syst. **24**(12), 14890–14902 (2023). https://doi.org/10.1109/TITS.2023.3303621
8. Wang, Q., Liu, X., Du, J., Kong, F.: Smart charging for electric vehicles: a survey from the algorithmic perspective. IEEE Commun. Surv. Tutor. **18**(2), 1500–1517 (2016). https://doi.org/10.1109/COMST.2016.2518628
9. Dubey, A., Santoso, S.: Electric vehicle charging on residential distribution systems: impacts and mitigations. IEEE Access **3**, 1871–1893 (2015). https://doi.org/10.1109/ACCESS.2015.2476996
10. Frendo, O., Gaertner, N., Stuckenschmidt, H.: Open source algorithm for smart charging of electric vehicle fleets. IEEE Trans. Ind. Inf. **17**(9), 6014–6022 (2021). https://doi.org/10.1109/TII.2020.3038144
11. Geofabrik GmbH Karlsruhe: OpenStreetMap Data Extracts. http://download.geofabrik.de/. Accessed 07 Sept 2023
12. OpenStreetMap Foundation: OpenStreetMap Foundation: OpenStreetMap® is *open data*, licensed under the Open Data Commons Open Database License (ODbL) by the OpenStreetMap Foundation (OSMF). https://www.openstreetmap.org/. Accessed 21 Sept 2024
13. Henderson, B.: Osmosis 0.49.2. https://github.com/openstreetmap/osmosis/releases/tag/0.49.2. Accessed 21 Sept 2024
14. German Aerospace Center (DLR) and others: netconvert – From 30.000 feet. https://sumo.dlr.de/docs/netconvert.html. Accessed 21 Sept 2024
15. German Aerospace Center (DLR) and others: netedit – From 30.000 feet. https://sumo.dlr.de/docs/Netedit/index.html. Accessed 21 Sept 2024
16. Wegener, A., Piórkowski, M., Raya, M., Hellbrück, H., Fischer, S., Hubaux, J.P.: TraCI: an interface for coupling road traffic and network simulators. In: Proceedings of the 11th Communications and Networking Simulation Symposium, CNS '08, pp. 155–163. Association for Computing Machinery, New York (2008). https://doi.org/10.1145/1400713.1400740
17. Wegener, A., Hellbruck, H., Wewetzer, C., Lubke, A.: VANET simulation environment with feedback loop and its application to traffic light assistance. In: 2008 IEEE Globecom Workshops, pp. 1–7 (2008). https://doi.org/10.1109/GLOCOMW.2008.ECP.67
18. German Aerospace Center (DLR) and others: Electric in Eclipse SUMO. https://sumo.dlr.de/docs/Models/Electric.html. Accessed 21 Sept 2024
19. Kurczveil, T., López, P.Á., Schnieder, E.: Implementation of an energy model and a charging infrastructure in SUMO. In: Behrisch, M., Krajzewicz, D., Weber,

M. (eds.) SUMO 2013. LNCS, vol. 8594, pp. 33–43. Springer, Heidelberg (2014). https://doi.org/10.1007/978-3-662-45079-6_3

20. Forkaliuk, M., Franzl, G., Bisikalo, O.: Evaluating fast charging of electric vehicles along motorways using finite multi-server queueing system simulation. Inf. Technol. Comput. Eng. **21**(2), 77–90 (2024). https://doi.org/10.31649/1999-9941-2024-60-2-77-90. https://itce.com.ua/en/journals/t-21-2-2024
21. Kleinrock, L.: Queueing Systems – Volume 1: Theory. Wiley-Interscience, New York ∘ Chichester ∘ Brisbane ∘ Toronto (1975). ISBN: 978-0-471-49110-1

A Simheuristic for the Stochastic Multi-Depot Traveling Facility Location Problem with Electric Vehicles

Marc Escoto[1(✉)], Angel A. Juan[1,2], Antoni Guerrero[3], and Veronica Medina[1]

[1] Universidad Politécnica de Valencia, 03801 Alcoy, Spain
{mescgom,ajuanp,vmedrid}@upv.es
[2] Euncet Business School, 08225 Terrassa, Spain
[3] Baobab Soluciones, 28003 Madrid, Spain
antoni.guerrero@baobabsoluciones.es

Abstract. This paper addresses the traveling salesman problem with multiple depots, facility location and stochastic travel times, considering electric vehicles with limited battery capacity. Due to stochastic variations in travel times, vehicles may risk running out of battery during their routes, leading to penalty costs for route failures. Given the NP-hard nature of this problem, we propose a simheuristic approach that integrates Monte Carlo simulation with a metaheuristic algorithm. This approach handles both the stochastic aspects and the optimization requirements. Results show that our simheuristic outperforms the optimal or near-optimal solutions designed for traditional deterministic scenarios when applied in stochastic settings.

Keywords: Simheuristic · Bias randomization · Simulation · Electric vehicles

1 Introduction

Optimization in logistics and transportation planning has received increasing attention in recent years, driven by the need to minimize costs and improve efficiency [4]. Among various optimization problems, routing problems, such as the traveling salesman problem (TSP) [9], the vehicle routing problem (VRP) [7] and the team orienteering problem (TOP) [8], have been extensively studied. Although the single-depot deterministic TSP and the facility location problem (FLP) have been extensively studied, less attention has been given to the multi-depot traveling facility location problem with stochastic travel times when electric vehicles are considered. Stochastic behavior has been widely studied in

The present work has been partially funded by the IA4TES project, funded by the Spanish Government, as well as by the Spanish Ministry of Science - AEI (PID2022-138860NB-I00 and RED2022-134703-T).

A. A. Juan et al. (Eds.): SIMUtools 2024, LNICST 603, pp. 105–115, 2025.
https://doi.org/10.1007/978-3-031-87345-4_7

routing problems, as it effectively captures the uncertainty present in real-world scenarios. However, as electric vehicles become increasingly common and due to their limited driving range, the impact of incorporating stochasticity becomes more significant. In particular, considering stochastic travel times can lead to routes that exceed the battery's capacity, presenting a critical limitation.

This paper addresses the multi-depot traveling facility location problem (MDTFLP) with stochastic traveling times and driving-range limitations. In this problem, multiple electric vehicles with limited driving range are employed to visit a set of locations. Each vehicle starts from a different depot, to which they return after their route is completed. In addition, travel times are stochastic, which means that sometimes routes might fail by not being able to cover the assigned locations before the associated vehicles run out of battery. In these cases, a penalty cost applies, since the route has to be repaired by sending a new battery to the vehicle. In Fig. 1, an illustrative example is presented. In this multi-depot and stochastic version of the problem, the objective is to minimize the expected value of the total distance traveled. As it will be discussed in this paper, a solution that works well in a deterministic scenario may not perform optimally when uncertainties are introduced, making it necessary to develop methods that account for stochasticity.

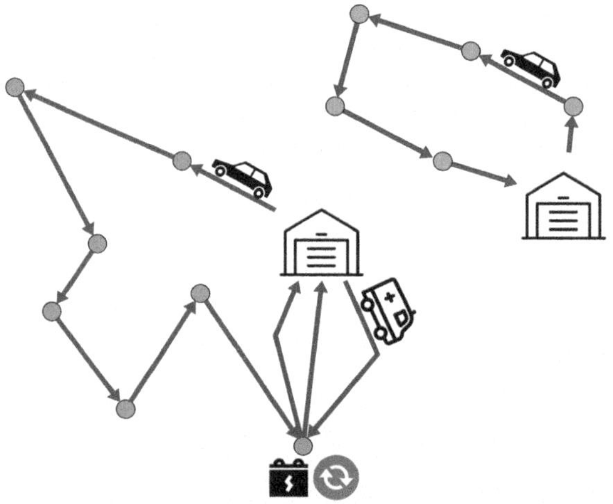

Fig. 1. An illustrative example of an instance where an emergency vehicle (in green), is used to change an original vehicle's battery (in red). (Color figure online)

In order to solve the aforementioned stochastic optimization problem, this paper proposes a simheuristic algorithm [3], which combines Monte Carlo simulation with a biased-randomized heuristic. The deterministic version of the problem serves as a baseline for comparison, while the stochastic version introduces variability in travel distances, simulating real-world scenarios where distance uncertainty affects route planning. The remaining of the paper is structured as follows: Sect. 2 reviews some related work. Section 3 provides a detailed problem definition, including a more formal description. Section 4 outlines the solving methodology, which combines Monte Carlo simulation with a biased-randomized heuristic and local search techniques, tailored for both the deterministic and stochastic cases. Section 5 presents the computational experiments and results, comparing the performance of the proposed methodology based on instances that extend the classical TSP ones to the stochastic scenario. Finally, Sect. 6 concludes the paper with a summary of findings and suggestions for future research directions.

2 Related Work

Given the concrete characteristics of the problem presented in this paper, very few papers in the literature approach a similar problem. This section presents a review of some of them. One of the first articles where a similar problem to the one presented in this paper is studied is the one written by Chan et al. [2], where a multi-depot traveling facility location problem with driving range limitations is considered. In this case, the number of depots to be selected is not fixed, vehicles have a maximum driving range and capacity, and some nodes contain multiple demands. In this paper, a savings-based algorithm is utilized to solve the problem. Burger et al. [1] tackle a similar problem, differing from the one approached in this paper in that route balancing is not required. The authors provide optimal solutions for several instances of their problem, which represents the closest available approximation to a benchmark solution.

3 Formal Modeling Details

The problem described in this paper consists of a stochastic version of the deterministic MDTFLP, which serves as a baseline in several aspects. As stated in Sect. 1, an optimal solution to the deterministic version is not guaranteed to be an optimal solution when uncertainty is introduced. In this sense, the solution generated by solving the deterministic problem is simulated in the stochastic environment to obtain an expected performance (cost) value. This new value serves as a comparison benchmark for the solutions generated by the simheuristic approach, which takes into account the uncertainty of the problem while generating solutions.

In order to model the deterministic version of the problem, we follow the formulation presented by Kara et al. [6], concretely a variation of the closed-path multi-depot and multi-vehicle TSP. In this problem, all nodes are fully connected and the distances between nodes are symmetrical, therefore, the problem is defined on a complete undirected graph $G = (V, A)$, where A is the set of arcs and V is the set of nodes. In order to represent the distances among nodes, a symmetrical cost matrix $C = (c_{ij})$ is utilized. In the case of the stochastic model, the elements of the matrix serve as a base to build the stochastic cost matrix $C' = (c'_{ij})$, in which each element c'_{ij} follows a probability distribution with an average value of c_{ij}. In this case, a lognormal probability distribution is utilized. Nodes represent either depots or customers, with $D \subseteq V$ acting as the set of depots and $V' = V \backslash D$ as the set of customer nodes. A total of m vehicles are involved, with each depot $k \in D$ having one vehicle initially located. The objective of the problem is to determine balanced routes for all vehicles, ensuring every customer is visited exactly once. Routes will be balanced according to the number of visited nodes each vehicle and thus, each vehicle visits either $\lfloor \frac{|V'|}{|D|} \rfloor$ or $\lfloor \frac{|V'|}{|D|} \rfloor + 1$ customers. The term "fixed-destination" refers to the requirement that all vehicles return to their respective depots after completing their tours. Finally, in order to convert the problem into its facility location version, all aspects made in this part regarding the set of depots should be considered as constraints, only having as an initial parameter the number of depots to be selected. This should be done in a similar way as in Chan et al. [2], where a more complex mathematical model for a similar problem is presented.

In the stochastic version, an additional constraint is introduced, which is determined by the distance traveled on the longest route of the deterministic solution. This distance serves as a maximum value for the routes generated in the stochastic problem, representing the maximum capacity of the battery and limiting the distance each traveler can cover. Instead of implementing this restriction as a hard constraint, we opt for a more realistic approach by adding a penalty cost whenever the constraint is violated. The remaining battery of the vehicle is monitored throughout the route, and whenever the stochastic distance from the vehicle's current node to the next node exceeds the maximum distance the vehicle can travel, the penalty cost is applied. This penalty is determined by twice the distance from the depot to the vehicle's current node, simulating the use of an "emergency vehicle" to deliver a new battery, allowing the vehicle to complete its route. To implement this constraint into the model, we create a new dummy variable that tracks the cumulative cost at each point of the route. Formally speaking, we introduce to the problem a maximum distance D_{max}, a variable m_i^k to represent the cumulative cost at node i on route k, and a binary variable z_i^k to indicate whether node i is the first node on route k where the cumulative cost m_i^k exceeds D_{max}. Then, we implement the following constraints:

A first constraint is implemented for the cumulative cost calculation. This constraint checks whether the maximum distance has been surpassed and resets the cumulative cost to 0 once the maximum distance is exceeded.

$$m_j^k \geq m_i^k(1 - z_i^k) + c'_{ij} \cdot x_{ijk}, \quad \forall i \in V, \quad \forall j \in V, \quad \forall k \in D.$$

$$m_k^k = 0, \quad \forall k \in D.$$

where x_{ijk} is the binary decision variable indicating whether vehicle k travels from node i to node j and c'_{ij} is the stochastic distance from i to j. Next, we introduce a constraint to activate the penalty at the corresponding node.

$$\sum_{j \in V} m_j^k \cdot x_{ij} - D_{max} \leq M \cdot z_i^k, \quad \forall i \in V, \quad \forall k \in D.$$

$$\sum_{j \in V} m_j^k \cdot x_{ij} - D_{max} \geq -M \cdot (1 - z_i^k), \quad \forall i \in V, \quad \forall k \in D.$$

where M is a large constant. The first equation forces z_i^k to be one when the maximum distance is exceeded, while the second one forces the variable to be zero when D_{max} is not exceeded.

The objective function considered for the deterministic problem is the 'min-sum' goal, which aims to minimize the total distance traveled by all vehicles. This objective can be expressed as $min \sum_{k \in D} c_{ij} \cdot x_{ijk}$, where c_{ij} represents the deterministic distance between nodes i and j. Other optimization objectives include the 'minmax' objective, which aims to minimize the distance covered by the longest route, ensuring a more balanced distribution of the workload among all vehicles. Since in this problem route balancing is already addressed and is based on a different criterion, namely the number of nodes visited, we opted for the first option. In its stochastic version, the new objective function takes into account the penalties for breaking the maximum distance constraint. Therefore, the new function can be expressed as

$$min \sum_{k \in D} c'_{ij} \cdot x_{ijk} + \sum_{i \in D, k \in D'} (c'_{ik} + c'_{ki}) \cdot z_i^k$$

4 Solving Methodology

Our approach involves using a biased-randomized heuristic for the deterministic version, as it is known to provide highly competitive solutions in relatively short computing times. This biased-randomized algorithm (BRA) is combined with a local search (LS) heuristic, which improves the solutions generated by the BRA. This combined methodology is implemented iteratively as long as the time limit permits. The flow diagram of the proposed methodology can be found in Fig. 2.

The methodology is divided into two stages. In the first stage, a pool of different solutions are generated using the BRA. Next, several promising solutions are chosen and refined to produce near-optimal results. The approach in the first stage of this problem involves generating a large number of diverse solutions to identify an optimal way to cluster the nodes. This process relies on the concept of marginal distance between a node and a depot, defined as the difference between the distance from the node to a specific depot and the distance to the nearest depot among the remaining depots. Additionally, an adaptive biased randomization technique is applied, which allows the method to explore a wider range of node combinations. To generate the solution pool, once the nodes are divided into clusters, a combination of the nearest neighbor algorithm (NN) and a fast, shallow local search is used to find a solution for the TSP within each cluster. The total cost is then calculated for each solution, and the 10 lowest-cost solutions are selected to provide greater variability for the second stage.

In the second stage, an enhancement procedure is applied to refine the selected promising solutions. This procedure iteratively uses a self-tuning, biased-randomized version of the NN, combined with a more comprehensive local search, applied to the predetermined clustering of nodes. After the enhancement procedure has been applied to all the promising solutions, the best one is selected based on the total cost. This heuristic provides near-optimal solutions for the deterministic problem, which serves as a baseline for comparing the solutions generated by the method used for the stochastic version.

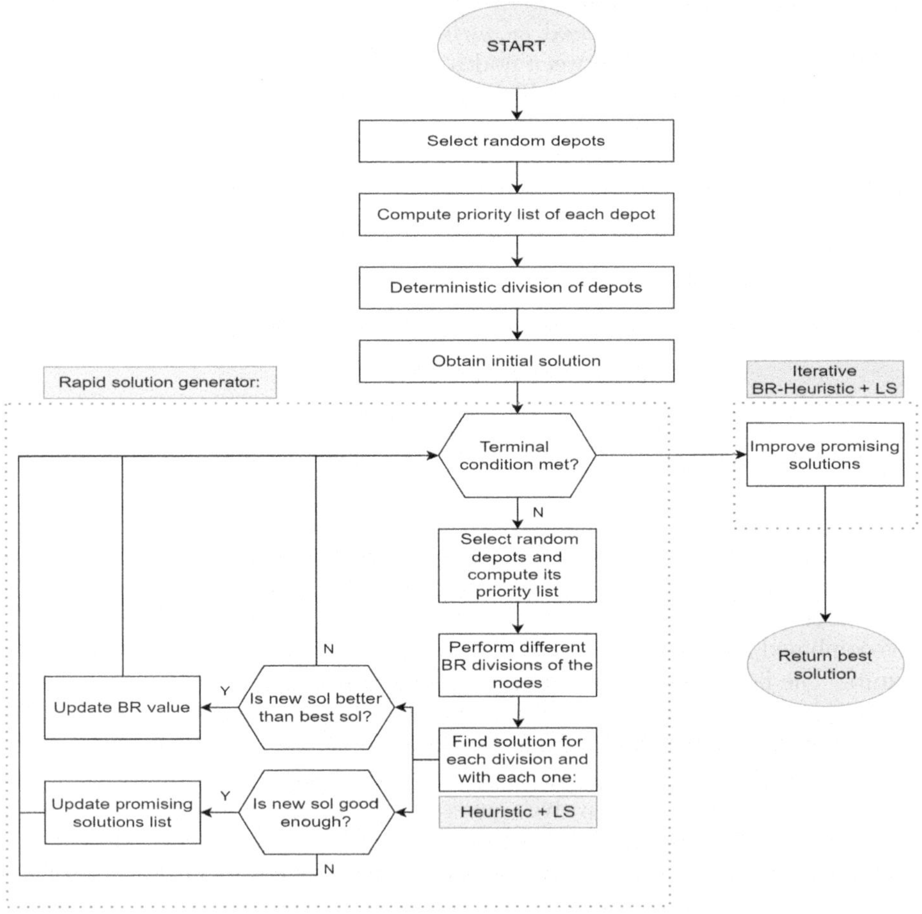

Fig. 2. Flow diagram of the method utilized to solve the deterministic version of the problem.

The methodology used to approach the stochastic version is an enhanced version of the BRA, designed to handle the uncertain nature of the problem, and is referred to as a BR-Simheuristic. The enhancement consists in introducing into the methodology a simulation process to ensure that the solution generated is not only competitive in terms of distance, but it behaves well when uncertainty is introduced into the problem. The process is introduced each time a new solution is generated, enhancing the development of the list of promising solutions. In these simulations, distances between nodes are randomly selected according to the distribution and the average distance across all simulations is then taken as the solution's distance.

5 Computational Experiments and Results

The methodology described in Sect. 4 has been implemented in Julia 1.10 and executed on a Windows 11 personal computer equipped with an $i7$-$1165G7$ CPU running at 2.80 GHz and 8 GB of RAM. To evaluate the effectiveness of our approach, we test it on seven classical TSP instances, which include problems with node counts ranging from 52 to 280. These instances are available from TSPLIB, a library provided by Heidelberg University (http://comopt.ifi.uni-heidelberg.de/software/TSPLIB95/). A maximum execution time of 100 seconds is allocated for all instances, regardless of the number of depots, with each instance evaluated using 10 different random seeds and the best result among them selected for further analysis. To simulate the solutions provided by the algorithms, a lognormal probability distribution is utilized to randomize the distances among all nodes, with a selected variance of 0.5. To compare the solutions obtained by the simheuristic with those of the simulated deterministic solutions, 1000 runs of the simulation were performed, both in the intensive simulation phase of the simheuristic as well as in the simulation of the solution obtained from the deterministic problem. Meanwhile, 100 simulation runs were conducted in the fast simulation phase.

In Tables 1 and 2, we present the results of simulating the deterministic solution in the stochastic scenario alongside those provided by the simheuristic methodology. The tables include the distance from the deterministic problem ($Det.\ distance(1)$), the total cost of simulating this solution under stochastic conditions ($Sim.\ cost(2)$), and the cost from the simheuristic solution ($SH\ cost(3)$). It also displays the route failure ratios, i.e., the ratio of the number of routes where an emergency vehicle had to be displayed to the total number of routes, for both the simulated deterministic solution ($RFR(2)$) and the simheuristic solution ($RFR(3)$), expressed as percentages. Finally, the gaps between the deterministic cost and the costs of the simulated deterministic and simheuristic solutions are shown as ($Gap(1-2)$) and ($Gap(1-3)$), respectively, calculated as $100(Sim.\ cost - Det.\ dist)/Det.\ dist$.

The results show a reduction in average stochastic costs with both 2 and 3 depots, where the gap decreases from 2.14% and 2.29% to 1.42% and 1.54% respectively. In addition, the RFR is decreased from 24.91% and 16.76% to

Table 1. Results obtained for 2 depots.

Instance	Det. dist(1)	Sim. cost(2)	RFR(2)	Gap(1–2)	SH cost(3)	RFR(3)	Gap(1–3)
berlin52	7787.63	8027.77	24.50	3.08	7914.88	32	1.63
st70	689.69	730.6	25.40	5.93	701.63	25.35	1.73
eil101	652.84	669.23	24.40	2.51	656.1	1.6	0.50
kroB100	22184.87	22435.6	26.40	1.13	22301.44	24.6	0.53
kroC100	21327.31	21965	25.35	2.99	21433.85	24.15	0.50
kroD100	21744.62	21959.62	24.80	0.99	21837.35	24.2	0.43
kroE100	22521.79	22831.36	24.45	1.37	22527.57	0	0.03
kroA100	21379.14	21582.74	23.55	0.95	21492.05	25.01	0.53
kroB200	30158.78	30391.38	25.40	0.77	31152.43	0.58	3.29
ch150	6603.62	6681.33	24.10	1.18	6686.93	8.61	1.26
tsp225	2640.8	2691.28	26.85	1.91	2685.91	24.15	1.71
a280	1766.55	1817.03	23.75	2.86	1852.91	42.23	4.89
Average:	13288.14	13481.91	24.91	**2.14**	13436.92	19.37	**1.42**

Table 2. Results obtained for 3 depots.

Instance	Det. dist(1)	Sim. cost(2)	RFR(2)	Gap(1–2)	SH cost(3)	RFR(3)	Gap(1–3)
berlin52	7981.91	8461.85	16.9	6.01	8022.01	0	0.50
st70	698.76	721.34	16.93	3.23	711.266	2.26	1.79
eil101	654.2	673.59	16.17	2.96	662.51	0	1.27
kroB100	22752.76	23287.84	16.93	2.35	22916.4	28.88	0.72
kroC100	21373.99	21594.66	17.57	1.03	22159.94	33.32	3.68
kroD100	21902.58	22093.15	16.4	0.87	22110.55	16.93	0.95
kroE100	22782.37	23325.52	16	2.38	22683.17	0	−0.44
kroA100	21433.17	21635.13	16.9	0.94	21532.57	16.56	0.46
kroB200	30292.36	30517.9	17	0.74	30750.08	28.2	1.51
ch150	6640.78	6718.13	16.93	1.16	6927.23	30.56	4.31
tsp225	2710.04	2760.59	16.5	1.87	2796.87	19.16	3.20
a280	1805.66	1876.97	16.83	3.95	1814.67	7.56	0.50
Average:	13419.05	13638.89	16.76	**2.29**	13590.61	15.29	**1.54**

19.37% and 15.29% respectively. While the average RFR decreases, there is considerable variability in the results of the simheuristic procedure. On the one hand, the RFR results from simulating the deterministic solution are as expected: the longest route tends to fail 50% of the time, which results in a RFR approximately $100/(2 * NDepots)$, as seen in Tables 1 and 2. This is because the maximum allowed distance for each route in the simulated solution is determined by the longest route in the deterministic solution. On the other hand, the RFR results from the simheuristic procedure show significant variability, indicating that the simheuristic identifies different ways to improve the deterministic solutions. From this, we can deduce that in instances where the simheuristic outperforms the deterministic approach, two main factors are responsible. The first factor is seen in solutions where the RFR is close to 0%. These solutions tend to have more balanced routes, and since no penalties are incurred, the total cost is lower than that of the simulated deterministic solution. In Fig. 3, a comparison between the solutions provided by the deterministic method and the simheuristic is shown, illustrating this phenomenon.

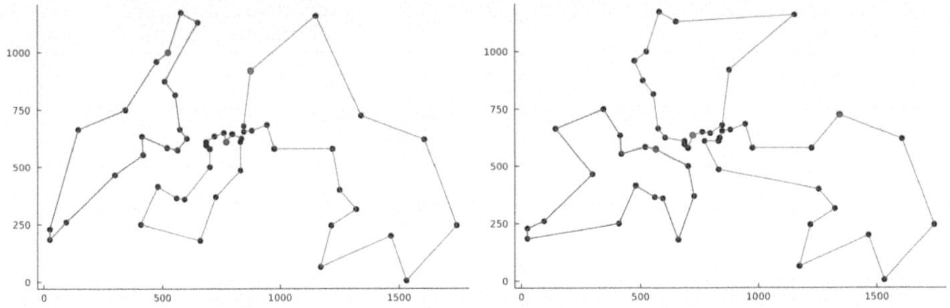

(a) Solution of the BR-Heursitic

(b) Solution of the BR-Simheuristic.

Fig. 3. A comparison between the solutions provided by the deterministic method and the simheuristic for the berlin52 instance with 3 depots.

The second factor involves the order in which nodes are visited and the selection of depots. These decisions can significantly influence total cost, as solutions with similar RFR can face lower penalty costs for route violations when compared to the deterministic solution. Additionally, it can be observed that the simheuristic approach tends to have larger gaps with larger instances. This occurs because the simulation process takes longer as the number of nodes increases, leading to slower convergence in larger instances, since the same time limit is applied to both small and large instances. Figure 4 presents a boxplot visualizing the gap between the deterministic solutions and their simulated counterparts, as well as the gap between the simheuristic results and the deterministic solutions.

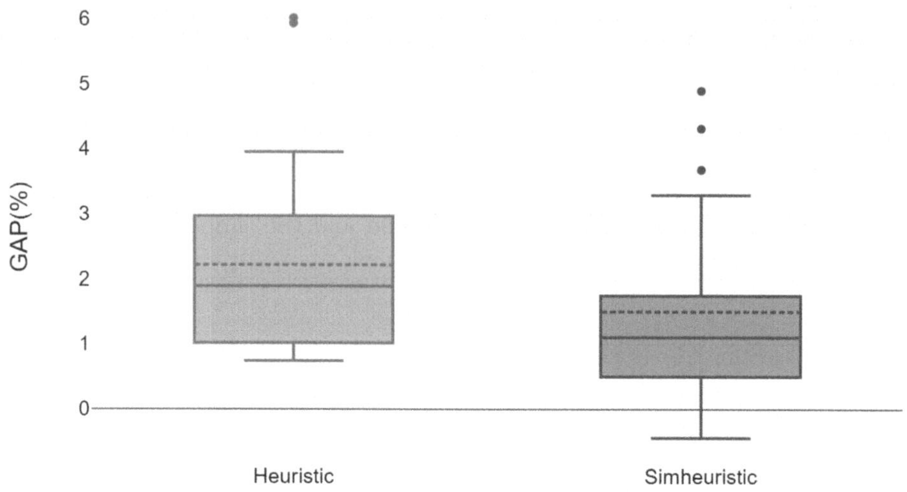

Fig. 4. A boxplot illustrating the comparison in gaps between the deterministic and the simheuristic methods.

6 Conclusions

This paper analyzes the multi-depot and multi-vehicle traveling salesman problem with stochastic distances, incorporating a soft constraint related to the maximum distance an electric vehicle can cover. Rather than treating the maximum distance as a hard constraint, when this limit is exceeded, a penalty cost is applied. This penalty represents the cost of using an emergency vehicle to deliver a new battery to the original vehicle, adding realism to the problem. Given the complexity and stochastic nature of the problem, as well as the need for fast computational times to solve such realism-imitating problems, an biased-randomized simheuristic methodology is presented. Our approach is capable of delivering high-performing solutions to the stochastic problem within short computing times. Computational experiments highlight the effectiveness of using a simheuristic compared to the simulated results of a deterministic version, emphasizing the importance of considering the stochastic nature of optimization problems in the solving methodology.

For future research, a variety of paths can be explored. Firstly, even though the simheuristic presented in this paper produces better solutions when addressing the stochastic version of a problem compared to its heuristic counterpart, the effects of combining simulation and optimization methods are often more pronounced in other types of metaheuristic procedures, such as iterated local search or variable neighborhood search [5]. These approaches allow for more effective feedback to be given to the metaheuristic, enhancing solution quality. Secondly, with the rapid evolution of artificial intelligence in recent years, particularly its use in handling dynamic scenarios, a combination of simulation, machine learning, and optimization techniques could provide a powerful methodology for addressing problems characterized by both uncertainty and dynamism. This integration would offer a robust tool set for modeling real-world problems with added realism. Lastly, other types of simulation techniques, such as fuzzy uncertainty modeling, can be explored. Fuzzy logic allows for handling vagueness and ambiguity in input data, which could further enhance the robustness of solutions in environments where uncertainty is not strictly probabilistic but more subjective or imprecise. This could open up new avenues for solving complex, real-life problems with multiple layers of uncertainty.

References

1. Burger, M., Su, Z., De Schutter, B.: A node current-based 2-index formulation for the fixed-destination multi-depot travelling salesman problem. Eur. J. Oper. Res. **265**(2), 463–477 (2018)
2. Chan, Y., Baker, S.F.: The multiple depot, multiple traveling salesmen facility-location problem: vehicle range, service frequency, and heuristic implementations. Math. Comput. Model. **41**(8–9), 1035–1053 (2005)
3. Chica, M., Juan, A.A., Bayliss, C., Cordón, O., Kelton, W.D.: Why simheuristics?: benefits, limitations, and best practices when combining metaheuristics with simulation. SORT: Stat. Oper. Res. Trans. **44**(2), 0311–334 (2020)
4. Chung, S.H.: Applications of smart technologies in logistics and transport: a review. Transport. Res. Part E: Logist. Transport. Rev. **153**, 102455 (2021)
5. Gruler, A., Quintero-Araújo, C.L., Calvet, L., Juan, A.A.: Waste collection under uncertainty: a simheuristic based on variable neighbourhood search. Eur. J. Ind. Eng. **11**(2), 228–255 (2017)
6. Kara, I., Bektas, T.: Integer linear programming formulations of multiple salesman problems and its variations. Eur. J. Oper. Res. **174**(3), 1449–1458 (2006)
7. Konstantakopoulos, G.D., Gayialis, S.P., Kechagias, E.P.: Vehicle routing problem and related algorithms for logistics distribution: a literature review and classification. Oper. Res. Int. J. **22**(3), 2033–2062 (2022)
8. Martins, L., Tordecilla, R.D., Castaneda, J., Juan, A.A., Faulin, J.: Electric vehicle routing, arc routing, and team orienteering problems in sustainable transportation. Energies **14**(16), 5131 (2021)
9. Pop, P.C., Cosma, O., Sabo, C., Sitar, C.P.: A comprehensive survey on the generalized traveling salesman problem. Eur. J. Oper. Res. **314**(3), 819–835 (2024)

Effect of Maintenance and Failure on Electrical Vehicles Charging Scheduling at an Airport

Primoz Godec(✉) and Steve McKeever

Department of Informatics and Media, Uppsala University, Uppsala, Sweden
primoz.godec@im.uu.se

Abstract. As the aviation industry works towards decreasing its carbon dioxide emissions, managing energy usage at airports is an important consideration. Our focus is on electric vehicles (EV) that add to the energy demands of an airport but can be undertaken at low peak times if the owner's return date is known. We present different greedy algorithms for EV charging scheduling . We compare their performance to the presently used immediate algorithm and before departure charging. A key novelty is that we simulate and examine the impact of charging point failure and maintenance on the performance of the algorithms. Our simulations suggest a greedy EV scheduling algorithm will reduce the energy load at peak hours and fill valleys compared to the current immediate charging approach. The load deviation scores, which measure how well the load is balanced, are 717.1 for the greedy algorithm and 730.0 for the immediate approach. However, the greedy algorithm will not lower the satisfaction of charging demand in scenarios with no charging failure.

Keywords: Vehicle charging scheduling · Electrical vehicles · Charging simulation · Charging station failure and maintenance simulation

1 Introduction

Airports are major consumers of electricity. Terminals, utility buildings, public transport, and operational vehicles all consume energy. Swedavia[1] has a goal of enabling fossil-free domestic flights and national fossil-free travel from 2030. Understanding the impact of such electrification on existing infrastructure is vital in order to ensure the needs can be met. In Sweden, electrical energy is generated primarily from hydropower (40%), followed by nuclear power (29%) and wind power (21%). Sweden aims to expand renewable capacity, including investments in solar and storage technologies, to achieve a fossil-free energy system by 2045[2].

[1] Swedavia AB is a Swedish state-owned company, which owns and operates ten of Sweden's busiest airports.

[2] https://fossilfrittsverige.se/.

A. A. Juan et al. (Eds.): SIMUtools 2024, LNICST 603, pp. 116–127, 2025.
https://doi.org/10.1007/978-3-031-87345-4_8

The electricity grid can only handle a certain load, and the costs of expansion are high. Renewable electricity generation and storage is currently limited but expected to rise in the future[3]. Currently, only a small number of electricity consuming activities at one of Sweden's major airports are amenable to optimisation. Our focus is on electric vehicle charging for passengers which is currently undertaken as soon as their car is plugged into a charger. On the assumption that the charging station knows when the car will be retrieved, strategies can be employed to reduce the grid load by charging overnight when usage is low. Overnight charging is also cost-effective since electricity prices are typically lower at night due to reduced demand. Sweden's northern latitude limits solar power's impact on pricing. Consequently, in the next decade at least, lower nighttime costs are expected to continue as demand remains low (See footnote 2).

As critical components of contemporary society, airports must manage and demonstrably optimise energy consumption, necessitating the adoption of advanced and innovative digitalisation solutions. We show, through the use of simulations based on real data, how simple optimisation strategies can reduce peak usage and adapt to both known interruptions and unforeseen charging failures[4].

This paper is structured as follows. In Sect. 2 we discuss related work in order to position our contribution. In Sect. 3 we discuss both the data and our methodology. In Sect. 4 we describe our tool while in Sect. 5 we discuss the four scenarios that we simulate. In Sect. 6 we summarise our analysis and suggest avenues of future work.

2 Related Work

Scheduling of vehicle charging has become an active field in the last ten years with the onset of affordable electric vehicles. Swedavia is increasing electricity usage at its major airports which is expected to overwhelm the electricity grid at peak hours (See footnote 4). Our work focuses on optimising grid usage of EV cars to relieve the overall load at peak times. This will be achieved by scheduling charges to hours with less load and so achieve a more even distribution of the grid.

As finding an optimal solution for a given scenario is often an NP-complete problem, researchers have developed different algorithms to optimize their objectives. Genetic algorithms (GA) are commonly used for vehicle charging scheduling [4,5,11]. They are adaptive heuristic search algorithms inspired by natural selection and genetics. They solve optimisation and search problems by maintaining a population of "individuals", evaluating their fitness, and evolving better solutions through genetic recombination and mutation. GA generate high-quality, but not always optimal, solutions. They can handle multiple objectives simultaneously, making them useful in complex scenarios. On the other hand GA

[3] https://www.swedavia.com/globalassets/ahr/2024/swedavia-annual-and-sustainability-report-2023.pdf.

[4] This project is funded by Vinnova in collaboration with Swedavia, Project number: 2023-01893.

may not converge sufficiently quickly. In contrast to other GA solutions mentioned above, Che et al. [3] propose a dual population genetic algorithm to avoid converging too early and thereby improve global optimization performance.

Another bio-inspired algorithm is particle swarm optimization (PSO), motivated by the social behaviour of birds flocking. Finding optimal solutions involves a group of particles that move through the solution space. In each step, they adjust their positions based on their own experience and the experience of neighbouring particles to converge on the best solution. PSO does not necessarily find the optimal solution but one that is usually close to the global optimal. Especially in high-dimensional space, it may be trapped at the local optimal point. PSO was used to schedule car charging by Celli et al. [2] and Yang et al. [14].

Reinforcement learning (RL) aims to maximize rewards by an agent exploring an environment through trial and error. RL can be used to solve complex problems such as charging car scheduling. However, it requires a lot of data and can be computationally complex. Wang et al. [13] use reinforcement based Q-learning for charging scheduling with an approximate Q-table to overcome the dimensionality issue of complex charging scheduling problem. Zhao & Liang [16] combine RL with a genetic algorithm. They use RL to fine-tune GA's scheduling results. Advances in deep model development enabled deep reinforcement learning to be another option for car scheduling [7,12]. In deep RL, the neural network replaces the Q-table to overcome dimensionality issues for complex problems. Aljafari et al. [1] and Park & Moon [10] propose multi-agent deep reinforcement learning where collaboration between agents can lead to more efficient problem-solving and better performance.

Scheduling can be performed using mathematical optimisation, where the problem is described as a mathematical model with a set of decision variables and a set of constraints. The problem is resolved by a solver that attempts to infer the values of decision variables. Korolko & Sahinoglu [8] and Koufakis et al. [9] defined the problem as mixed integer programming. They solved the problem using a cutting plane optimisation algorithm and a commercial CPLEX solver, respectively. Ioakimidis et al. [6] solved a linear programming problem with an interior point algorithm. The car charging scheduling problem is too complex to be solved by dynamic programming. Such problems can be estimated with approximate dynamic programming by introducing approximations and simplifying the solution space. Zhang & Li [15] proposed the car charging scheduling solution based on approximate dynamic programming.

Most related studies [1,3,5–7,9–11,13–16] focus on scheduling EV charging at public charging stations where cars are parked for a shorter period and, more commonly, during the day. These two reasons explain the need for sophisticated charging algorithms to uncover optimal usage. In contrast, the charging requirements at an airport are based on different needs where passengers leave their car to charge for many days while travelling. Thus, the charging opportunities are longer and can be scheduled overnight when the grid load is considerably less. We aim to implement a solution that shaves the grid load peaks and moves charging into the "valleys" (night). We do not require an optimal solution but one that can fulfil our goals. As a result, we implemented a simpler, computationally less complex, and faster greedy algorithm, enabling integration with other electricity usage simulations later in the project. Unlike machine learning-based black box algorithms, greedy algorithms also benefit from transparency.

3 Data and Methodology

To study the effect of the charging strategies on the airport's electricity consumption realistically, it is beneficial to perform a simulation on actual data. This section presents the data used for simulation and scheduling algorithms.

3.1 Data

We simulate the scheduling using real car charging data from the public charging station at one of Sweden's major airports. The station currently has 10 charging points. The data covers a 522-day period between 2022-12-13 and 2024-05-20, comprising 1390 charging sessions. Each session lasts from the car arriving at the station and being plugged in right until departure. For each charging session, data contain the charger ID, the start and the end of the session (the time of cars' arrival and departure), and the amount of energy charged (in kWh). Since nearly all cars are parked at the station for periods longer than required for charging, we assume that each car's data represents the energy the car needs. To simulate a more significant load to the airport grid with massive overall electricity consumption, we upscaled the existing data 10-fold to run the simulation using 100 stations and ten times as many charging sessions.

For scheduling, we assume that we do not know in advance when the car will arrive. We schedule the charging when the car is at the station. However, we do know the last available slot for charging as we expect car owners to report their anticipated departure time. For the purpose of simulation, these departure times were inferred from the actual data.

3.2 Scheduling Algorithms

We implemented four different scheduling algorithms.

An immediate scheduler represents the current charging situation. Cars start charging immediately after the arrival and charge until they are fully charged or depart. This algorithm does not consider the electricity grid load.

A greedy algorithm schedules charging individually based on cars' departure time and when electricity usage is low. It orders the charging so the car that departs earliest is scheduled first, such that each car is expected to charge in the time slot with the lowest predicted grid load at the airport. The algorithm considers only slots for each car between the scheduled time (when scheduling is performed) and departure. After one car is scheduled, its expected charging load is added to the common load, and the next is scheduled to charge. The greedy algorithm places charging into predefined time slots of length t. For the experiment in this paper, we used a time slot of 30 min.

Considering that cars typically remain at charging stations for nearly three days on average, with some parked for up to two weeks, it is advantageous for battery health to charge vehicles closer to their departure time. Since greedy and immediate algorithms do not meet this requirement, we developed two additional algorithms specifically designed to address this issue.

The before-departure scheduler is the opposite of the immediate. It will start charging the car just before departure, regardless of the grid load. *The greedy last-day scheduler* is a version of the greedy scheduler that considers only time slots 36 h (1 and a half days) before departure. Therefore, at least one whole night, when the grid load is typically lower, is available for charging.

The computational complexity of scheduling n cars is $O(n)$ for the immediate and before departure algorithm and $O(n \cdot m)$ for the greedy algorithms, where m is the number of slots available before each car's departure. With 30-min slots, the algorithm tests $d \cdot 48$ slots for each car parked d days at the station.

Figure 1 shows an example ten-day schedule generated by immediate and greedy algorithms. The schedules and grid load graph show that the greedy algorithm mainly chooses to charge during the night when the grid load is lower (blue line on the top graph). The immediate algorithm mainly increases the grid load when it is already high.

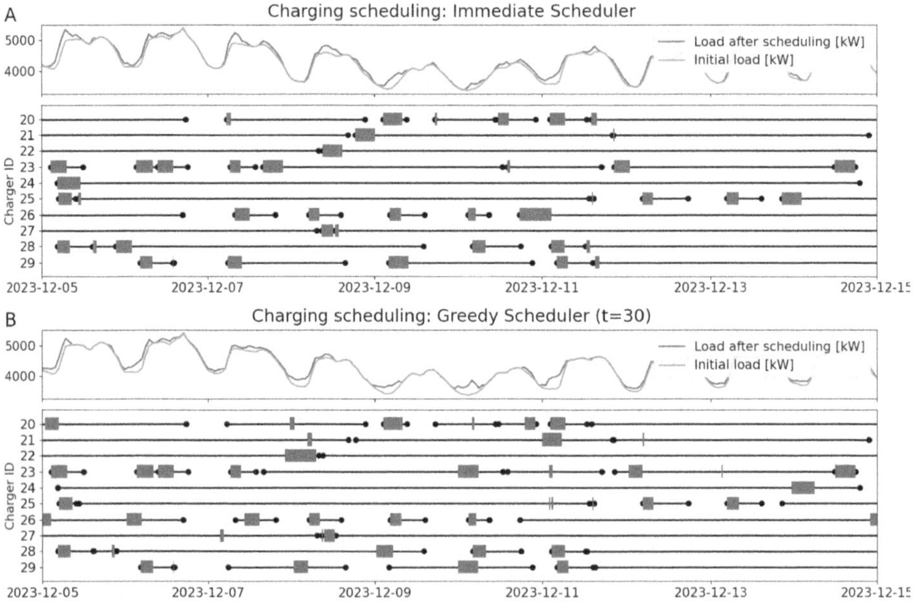

Fig. 1. An example of charging scheduling with immediate (A) and greedy (B) algorithms for ten days. The top graphs on both figures show the grid load excluding car charging (orange) and after car charging load (blue). On the bottom graphs, each row represents one of the selected charging points. Black lines mark periods when cars are parked and plugged in, while the blue bars mark the slots when cars are being charged. (Color figure online)

4 Simulation

This paper simulates the scheduling of car charging over the whole data period (2022-12-13 to 2024-05-20). Car charging (re)scheduling is run for every new car arrival since it affects the assignment of slots. In order to ensure optimal allocation, we reschedule the charging for all vehicles at the station that are not fully charged. This can lead to a car currently charging being rescheduled to a new slot. Since new cars, in our case, arrive infrequently, rescheduling causes only a few charging interruptions. Charging point failure can also cause the car currently charging not to charge according to the schedule, so rescheduling is also required after every failure of any charging point.

Charging schedules can be affected by maintenance and station failures. We define maintenance as a predicted time when charging is halted and can be planned for. Failure is unpredictable and can affect scheduled charging. Thus, rescheduling is required after a failure is fixed. We simulate different probabilities of maintenance and failures. By probability, we mean the percentage of time affected by maintenance or failure. The studied charging station has a failure probability of around 1%, according to sources from Swedavia. Since failure probability can increase with greater charging demand in the future, we simulated probabilities between 0% and 10%. Failure or maintenance periods are randomly generated, lasting 30 s to 12 h.

Figure 2 shows schedules for the same 10-day period as Fig. 1 and includes maintenance (grey stripes) and failures (red stripes). We can see how maintenance impacts the greedy scheduler. For example, in the first session on charging point 29, the charging is pushed to a less favourable time before departure. The charging time is also reduced compared to a situation without maintenance (Fig. 1-B). Failure interrupts the first session on charging point 20, so charging must continue later at a less favourable time for the grid load.

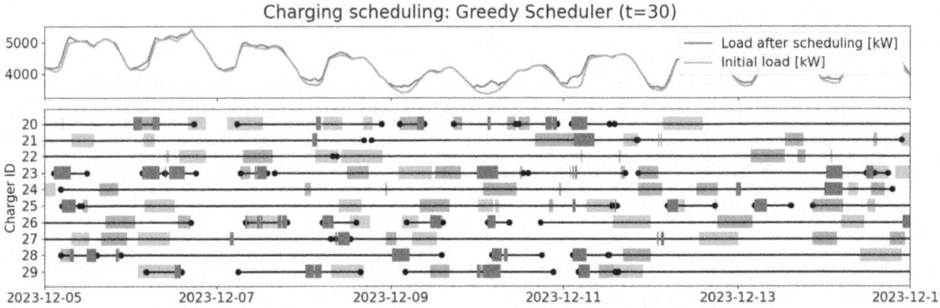

Fig. 2. An example of charging scheduling adopting a greedy algorithm with interruptions. The graph is similar to the one in Fig. 1. Additionally, it includes maintenance periods (grey) and charging failure periods (red). (Color figure online)

We measure two metrics: the impact of scheduling on grid load and user dissatisfaction with charging. The impact on grid load is calculated as the root mean square deviation of the electricity grid load from its mean value, which measures how well the charging schedule fills valleys and shaves peaks. Dissatisfaction measures average energy (in kWh) missing from fully charged cars.

5 Results

As the electrical grid can only handle a certain load, we can reduce it by scheduling charging to hours with less load (usually night hours). We compare the proposed greedy algorithm with other algorithms in Case 1. As all electrical devices need maintenance and are prone to failure, we inspect the effect of maintenance (Case 2) and failure (Case 3) on scheduling. Case 4 simulates the realistic scenario when both maintenance and failures affect charging.

5.1 Case 1: Scheduling Without Interruptions

First, we compare all scheduling algorithms described in Sect. 3.2 without any interruption (maintenance and charging point failures). As seen from the results in Table 1, the lowest impact on grid load was due to the greedy schedulers. The scheduler with shorter time slots performs slightly better due to more scheduling flexibility. The last-day greedy scheduler performs slightly worse due to a more limited selection of time slots, as it can only charge 36 h before departure.

Immediate and before-departure schedulers have a worse impact on the grid load than expected since they do not schedule based on knowledge of electricity usage. The reason that the before-departure scheduler has a slightly worse grid load impact is that cars more often depart during the day (grid peak time) and more often arrive earlier in the morning (grid load is not so high yet). It results in charging after arrival having a better impact on the grid load than that before departure. Dissatisfaction is identical for all schedulers since they can use all available time, and the car is at the station if needed. It is not 0 since some cars are not parked long enough at the station to charge fully.

Table 1. The table shows both scores and charging dissatisfaction for scheduling without interruptions. The score is the root mean square deviation of the grid load after scheduling from its average, where a lower value means a better charging strategy for the electrical grid load. Dissatisfaction measures the average energy in kWh that cars are missing from fully charged.

	Score	Dissatisfaction
Immediate Scheduler	730.034	0.046
Before-departure Scheduler	735.077	0.046
Greedy Last Day Scheduler 30	718.139	0.046
Greedy Scheduler 30-min	717.111	0.046
Greedy Scheduler 10-min	717.071	0.046

5.2 Case 2: Scheduling with Predictable Maintenance

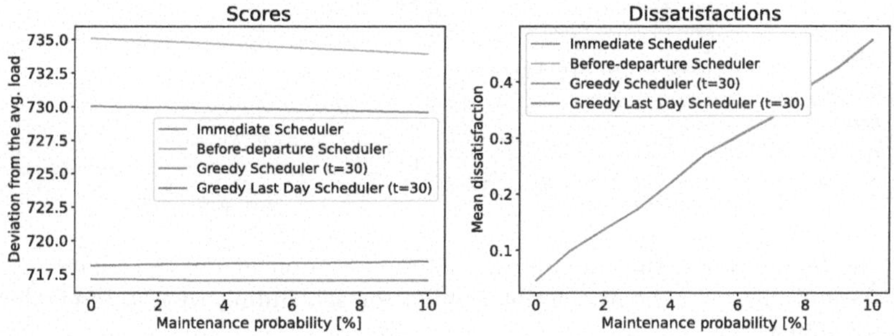

Fig. 3. The figure shows the root mean square deviation of the electricity grid load score (left) and charging dissatisfaction (right) for scheduling with different levels of maintenance probability. All algorithms have equal dissatisfaction scores since the disruption is known in advance and considered while scheduling. It results in all curves being hidden under the red curve. (Color figure online)

The second case inspects the impact of predictable maintenance on the scheduling. Since maintenance is known in advance during scheduling, the algorithm can account for it when creating the schedule. We tried different maintenance probabilities from 0% to 10%; the probability is the percentage of time that the charging point is under maintenance and unable to charge.

The results in Fig. 3 indicate that maintenance has no significant effect on the algorithms' impact on grid load. Greedy algorithms seem to find other suitable slots even when the maintenance probability is high (10%). Before-departure and immediate schedulers' scores slightly improved, because some of the charging at grid high time was moved to later or the car could not charge, causing less impact on the grid load. Dissatisfaction with higher maintenance probability increased from 0.046 to 0.477, which is expected since maintenance prevents cars parked for a shorter time from fully charging. Maintenance impacts all algorithms equally since the disruption is known in advance and is taken into account.

5.3 Case 3: Scheduling with Random Failures

We inspected the impact of unpredictable failure periods on the schedules. Failure periods are unknown in advance, so cannot be scheduled ahead of time. When failure happens, charging needs to be rescheduled. We tried different failure probabilities from 0% to 10%; the probability is the percentage of time that the charging point is under failure and unable to charge.

From the results in Fig. 4, we can observe a slight but not significant impact of failure on greedy algorithms scores, caused by the fact that charging affected by a failure must be rescheduled to another slot, which might be less optimal for grid load. Before-departure schedulers' scores improved, probably because some

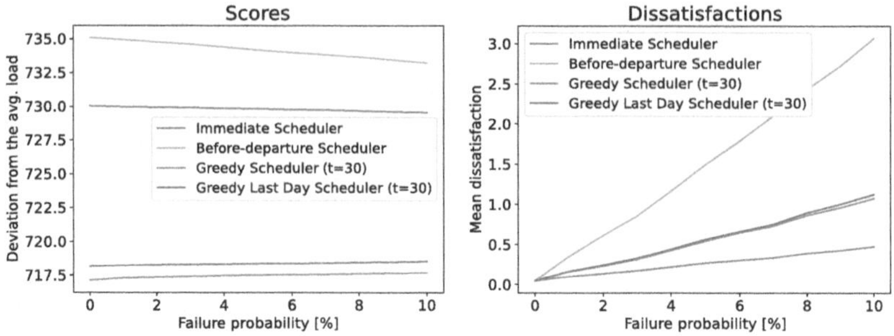

Fig. 4. The figure shows the root mean square deviation of the electricity grid load score (left) and charging dissatisfaction (right) for scheduling with different levels of failure probability.

of the charging at grid high time was moved to later or the car could not charge, causing less impact on the grid load.

Failures increase dissatisfaction but affect scheduling algorithms differently. The before-departure scheduler is the most affected, with a dissatisfaction of 3.069 when the failure probability is 10%. It schedules charging just before departure, and cars affected by failure cannot continue charging afterwards. Both greedy algorithms have a similar dissatisfaction rating, with the last-day greedy scheduler having a slightly higher value. The limitation on charging in the last 36 h leaves less space for charging after failure. As expected, the immediate algorithm has the lowest dissatisfaction since it starts to charge immediately and offers more space to fulfil cars' needs in case of failures.

5.4 Case 4: Scheduling with Maintenance and Failures

Finally, we combine both predictable maintenance (presented in Sect. 5.2) and unpredictable failures (from Sect. 5.3) in the joint experiment. We tried different combinations of maintenance and failure probabilities.

Heat maps in Fig. 5-A show the impact on the grid load at different maintenance and failure rates. It presents a similar picture to that seen in previous cases, namely that unpredictable failures affect the score more than maintenance, which can be explained by incorporating maintenance into the scheduling. The dissatisfaction score in Fig. 5-B shows a similar picture. Dissatisfaction increases faster when failure probability increases. It is most significant for the before-departure scheduler, where failure impacts dissatisfaction more, as discussed in Sect. 5.3. For the immediate scheduler, failure and maintenance have the same effect, as charging would continue immediately after maintenance or failure.

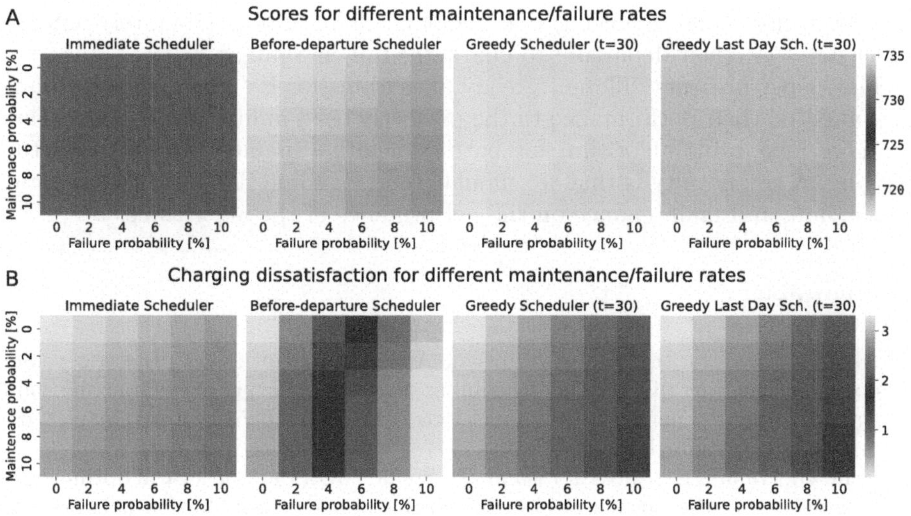

Fig. 5. A) Score – the impact of schedules by different algorithms on the grid, measured as the root mean square deviation of the grid load. B) The dissatisfaction score for each algorithm.

6 Discussion

To prepare for increasing energy demands at airports, simulations suggest a greedy EV scheduling algorithm will efficiently reduce the energy load at peak hours and fill valleys compared to the current immediate charging approach. However, the greedy algorithm will not lower the satisfaction of charging demand in scenarios with no charging failure. Introducing charging failures and scheduled maintenance has a minor impact on the greedy algorithm's performance. It still functions significantly better than the presently used immediate algorithm. We notice an increase in charging dissatisfaction with higher failure and maintenance rates, but with more realistic, lower failure rates, the increase in dissatisfaction with both the greedy and immediate algorithms is similar.

Although the proposed greedy algorithm does not provide optimal scheduling, it provides sufficient scheduling for the current scenario with a limited number of charging points and high variations between day and night loads. Moreover it is robust, fast and transparent. However, when the number of charging points and stations increases, the need to consider more sophisticated machine learning-based algorithms might arise. In anticipation of the increase in both charging points and electric vehicles – including airside vehicles, we plan to run simulations with augmented versions of our data, and greater randomness, to gauge expectant needs of one of the Sweden's major airports. Our algorithm can be improved to adopt multiple strategies depending on anticipated reliability and departure dates. Our simulation runs showed that the most dissatisfied car owners were those with charging needs when failures occurred and those parked for a very short time. Knowing this might result in users deliberately entering earlier dates for their departure to guarantee full charging.

This paper presents different greedy algorithms for EV charging scheduling. We compared their performance to the presently used immediate algorithm and the more favourable algorithm for battery health – namely, before departure charging. A key novelty is that we simulate and examine the impact of charging point failure and maintenance on the performance of the algorithms.

References

1. Aljafari, B., Jeyaraj, P.R., Kathiresan, A.C., Thanikanti, S.B.: Electric vehicle optimum charging-discharging scheduling with dynamic pricing employing multi agent deep neural network. Comput. Electr. Eng. **105**, 108555 (2023). https://doi.org/10.1016/j.compeleceng.2022.108555
2. Celli, G., Ghiani, E., Pilo, F., Pisano, G., Soma, G.G.: Particle swarm optimization for minimizing the burden of electric vehicles in active distribution networks. In: 2012 IEEE Power and Energy Society General Meeting. pp. 1–7 (2012). https://doi.org/10.1109/PESGM.2012.6345458
3. Che, S., Chen, Y., Wang, L., Xu, C.: Electric vehicle ordered charging planning based on improved dual-population genetic moth-flame optimization. Algorithms **17**(3), 110 (2024). https://doi.org/10.3390/a17030110
4. Ghofrani, M., Arabali, A., Etezadi-Amoli, M.: Electric drive vehicle to grid synergies with large scale wind resources. In: 2012 IEEE Power and Energy Society General Meeting. pp. 1–6 (2012). https://doi.org/10.1109/PESGM.2012.6345662
5. Hou, S., Jiang, C., Yang, Y., Xiao, W.: Electric vehicle charging scheduling strategy based on genetic algorithm. J. Phys: Conf. Ser. **1693**(1), 012104 (2020). https://doi.org/10.1088/1742-6596/1693/1/012104
6. Ioakimidis, C.S., Thomas, D., Rycerski, P., Genikomsakis, K.N.: Peak shaving and valley filling of power consumption profile in non-residential buildings using an electric vehicle parking lot. Energy **148**, 148–158 (2018). https://doi.org/10.1016/j.energy.2018.01.128
7. Jin, J., Xu, Y.: Optimal policy characterization enhanced actor-critic approach for electric vehicle charging scheduling in a power distribution network. IEEE Trans. Smart Grid **12**(2), 1416–1428 (2021). https://doi.org/10.1109/TSG.2020.3028470
8. Korolko, N., Sahinoglu, Z.: Robust optimization of EV charging schedules in unregulated electricity markets. IEEE Trans. Smart Grid **8**(1), 149–157 (2017). https://doi.org/10.1109/TSG.2015.2472597
9. Koufakis, A.M., Rigas, E.S., Bassiliades, N., Ramchurn, S.D.: Offline and online electric vehicle charging scheduling with V2V energy transfer. IEEE Trans. Intell. Transp. Syst. **21**(5), 2128–2138 (2020). https://doi.org/10.1109/TITS.2019.2914087
10. Park, K., Moon, I.: Multi-agent deep reinforcement learning approach for EV charging scheduling in a smart grid. Appl. Energy **328**, 120111 (2022). https://doi.org/10.1016/j.apenergy.2022.120111
11. Su, J., Lie, T.T., Zamora, R.: A rolling horizon scheduling of aggregated electric vehicles charging under the electricity exchange market. Appl. Energy **275**, 115406 (2020). https://doi.org/10.1016/j.apenergy.2020.115406

12. Wan, Z., Li, H., He, H., Prokhorov, D.: Model-free real-time EV charging scheduling based on deep reinforcement learning. IEEE Trans. Smart Grid **10**(5), 5246–5257 (2019). https://doi.org/10.1109/TSG.2018.2879572
13. Wang, S., Bi, S., Zhang, Y.A.: Reinforcement learning for real-time pricing and scheduling control in EV charging stations. IEEE Trans. Industr. Inf. **17**(2), 849–859 (2021). https://doi.org/10.1109/TII.2019.2950809
14. Yang, J., He, L., Fu, S.: An improved PSO-based charging strategy of electric vehicles in electrical distribution grid. Appl. Energy **128**, 82–92 (2014). https://doi.org/10.1016/j.apenergy.2014.04.047
15. Zhang, L., Li, Y.: Optimal management for parking-lot electric vehicle charging by two-stage approximate dynamic programming. IEEE Trans. Smart Grid **8**(4), 1722–1730 (2017). https://doi.org/10.1109/TSG.2015.2505298
16. Zhao, X., Liang, G.: Optimizing electric vehicle charging schedules and energy management in smart grids using an integrated GA-GRU-RL approach. Front. Energy Res. **11**, 1268513 (2023). https://doi.org/10.3389/fenrg.2023.1268513

Validation and Verification Techniques in Simulation Modelling for Freight Transportation

Jakub Woletz[1](✉), Christoph Kogler[2], and Pavel Maxera[1]

[1] Institute of Forensic Engineering, Brno University of Technology, Brno, Czech Republic
{jakub.woletz,pavel.maxera}@vut.cz

[2] Institute of Production Economics and Logistics, University of Natural Resources and Life Sciences, Vienna, Austria
christoph.kogler@boku.ac.at

Abstract. The credibility of simulation models for freight transportation builds on solid verification and validation processes. They are essential to ensure that simulation models accurately represent the systems they intend to mimic and produce reliable outcomes. Consequently, this paper reviews the documentation of verification and validation techniques in more than one hundred discrete event and agent-based simulation publications from the past decade to identify relevant methods and their frequency of application. Future simulation research on verification and validation approaches and helpful guidelines are needed to ensure rigorous implementation in logistical modelling.

Keywords: Logistics · Terminals · Discrete Event · Agent-Based · Simulation

1 Introduction

The complexity of operations in freight transportation necessitates consistent and efficient planning. This includes managing various modes of transport and terminal operations. Important topics are capacity utilization as well as transportation cost and emission reduction. According to Kogler [1], poorly planned transportation can also lead to critical quality loss emphasising the need for robust management strategies. Discrete simulation methods are used to model the behaviour of systems over time. Systems are represented by components such as entities, agents, attributes, state variables and a set of discrete events, each occurring at a specific point in time [2]. Strengths of discrete simulation are the ability to model complex systems with interacting components as well as providing detailed insights into the behaviour of systems [3]. However, challenges include the need for significant computational resources and extensive data collection to ensure accuracy [4]. Verification and validation are essential components in the process of simulation modelling, ensuring the reliability of models used in decision-making [5]. These processes are vital for the field of freight transportation and terminal logistics, where even

A. A. Juan et al. (Eds.): SIMUtools 2024, LNICST 603, pp. 128–135, 2025.
https://doi.org/10.1007/978-3-031-87345-4_9

minor errors in a model can lead to significant disruptions and inefficiencies. In simulation modelling, particularly in discrete event simulation and agent-based simulation, the need for further development in verification and validation is recognized [4].

Despite the recognized importance of verification and validation in ensuring the reliability of simulation models, there is limited comprehensive data on the prevalence of these practices across the literature on logistics. Consequently, the objective of this preliminary study was to identify the relevance of reported verification, validation, and credibility techniques in simulation modelling within the context of freight transportation. Specifically, this research seeks to determine how frequently these critical processes are applied in existing studies, which techniques are most used, and how rigorously they are implemented. By reviewing the relevant literature, this conference paper contributes to reveal the potential for improvement and further research in simulation modelling to enhance the robustness and reliability of simulation outcomes.

2 Verification, Validation, and Credibility

Verification involves checking that the model is correctly implemented in accordance with its conceptual design. This step is crucial to identify discrepancies between the model design and its implementation. Techniques for verification include, e.g., repeated simulation runs to ensure consistency, and structured walkthroughs, where experts systematically review the model's logic and code. In a study conducted by Asteris et al. [6], debugging was highlighted as a critical step in ensuring the accuracy of their container port infrastructure model. They employed structured walkthroughs to ensure that every component functioned as intended. Similarly, Mustafee and Bischoff [7] used repeated simulation runs to verify the consistency and reliability of their container loading models, allowing them to identify and rectify errors or inconsistencies in the simulation. Jaoua et al. [8] verified their real-time fleet management simulation through simulation with known inputs and extensive debugging. Windisch et al. [9] adopted a modular evaluation approach, where each component of the simulation model was verified individually before integrating it into the larger system. This method is particularly effective in complex models, as it allows the isolation and correction of errors at an early stage. Sun et al. [10] employed animation tracking and extreme value parameterization to verify their simulation for seaport container terminals. These techniques were instrumental in ensuring that the model performed accurately under a wide range of conditions, including extreme scenarios. Verification is about checking the correctness of the model and ensuring that the model is robust and capable of handling different inputs and conditions. This robustness is essential to increases stakeholders' confidence in the simulation results [4].

Validation is the process of determining whether a simulation model accurately represents the real system it is intended to emulate. According to Law [11], validation is critical for ensuring that the model's outputs are reliable and can be used to make informed decisions. In the context of freight transportation and terminal logistics, validation often involves comparing the simulation results with real-world data, conducting sensitivity analyses, and involving experts to assess the model's accuracy. Karttunen et al. [12] demonstrated the importance of real-world data in their study on the cost-efficiency of intermodal container supply chains. By comparing their simulation results with historical data, they were able to validate the accuracy of their model and establish confidence in its predictive capabilities. Sensitivity analysis is another powerful tool for validation. Carteni and Luca [13] used historical data comparison and sensitivity analysis to validate their planning model for container terminals. Windisch et al. [9] employed sensitivity analysis to test the robustness of their forest biomass supply chain model. By varying input parameters and observing the effects on the model's outputs, they could assess how sensitive the model was to changes in the input data. This method is particularly useful in identifying which parameters have the most significant impact on the model's results, allowing for advanced decision support. Eriksson et al. [14] applied a combination of expert judgment and real-world data comparison to validate their models of stump fuel cost. By consulting with experts, they ensured that their model was accurate and reflective of industry practices. Expert involvement is crucial in cases where real-world data is missing, or when the model reflects complex and nuanced behaviours that are difficult to capture through data. Sun et al. [10] used statistical tests alongside expert judgment to validate their simulation. This dual approach provided a robust validation process, ensuring that the simulation was statistically sound and practically applicable. The combination of these methods underscores the importance of using multiple validation techniques to enhance the reliability and applicability of simulation models.

Credibility in simulation modelling refers to the level of trust stakeholders place in the model and its results. According to Banks et al. [4], achieving credibility is crucial for ensuring that the simulation outputs are accepted by decision-makers and are used to guide real-world actions. Credibility is established, e.g., through transparency, stakeholder involvement, and detailed documentation that clearly outlines the assumptions and processes used in the model. Beaudoin et al. [15] emphasized the role of expert judgment in establishing credibility in their simulation of log yard operations. By involving industry experts in the modelling process, they were able to incorporate practical insights and ensure that the model reflected real-world conditions. This involvement enhanced the model's accuracy and increased its acceptance among stakeholders. Kogler and Rauch [16] contribute an innovative approach for bidirectional knowledge transfer through serious-game based simulation workshops. Also, visualizations and detailed process documentation are important aspects for establishing credibility. Elbert and Reinhardt [17] provide comprehensive flow diagrams and parameter tables in their study on shuttle train capacity utilization. These tools helped stakeholders to understand how the model operates and ensured that the simulation's assumptions were clear and well-founded. Visualization techniques were also used by Zamora-Cristales et al. [18] to make complex simulation outputs more accessible and understandable to non-technical stakeholders. Furthermore, stakeholder involvement is a key factor in establishing credibility. Kogler and Rauch [19] used animation views, flow diagrams, and key performance indicator cockpits for the involvement of industry and scientific experts and vivid dissemination. By engaging stakeholders early and regularly, simulation modellers ensure that the model is aligned with practical operational needs and that its results are viewed as credible.

3 Methodology

A comprehensive literature analysis revealed a research gap of a review on verification and validation in logistical simulation modelling. Therefore, a clear research methodology was development and implemented to present and discuss first findings within the scope of this conference paper. This sets the stage for the ambition to present further systematic and narrative elements and deeper analysis in the future.

The first steps of the planning process included reviewing the scientific literature in databases, monitoring critical research gaps, and finding a focus area of research that differed from reviews of the existing literature. In the following data collection phase, databases were selected, and keywords were defined to search and organise references and screen, select, and exclude articles. The literature search included the Web of Science, Scopus, and Google Scholar databases. The search query was "(simulation) AND (discrete simulation OR discrete event simulation OR agent-based simulation) AND (transport OR transportation) AND (freight OR cargo)". Furthermore, a modified search dictionary was considered that used synonyms such as freight transportation, terminal logistics, management, and discrete simulation modelling. The search included scientific literature written in English and published from 2012 to the end of 2023. Standardised keyword-based database search queries were supplemented by checking the reference lists of relevant articles.

After excluding irrelevant articles that contain search terms or their synonyms in other contexts, more than 100 articles were selected, organized, and studied in detail. Comparability between these studies is ensured by the fact that they all use simulation as their main methodological tool and focus on similar logistical systems and processes. The literature was clustered, evaluated, and categorized to build a database for statistical analysis. First preliminary results of this ongoing process are presented in this conference paper.

4 Preliminary Results

First statistical insights on verification in Fig. 1 show that 39% of the reviewed studies reported on repeated simulation runs, 29% employed structured walk-throughs, and 21% applied warm-up periods. Animation tracking and extreme value parameterization were documented in 10% and 9% of studies, respectively, while modular evaluations were mentioned in 7%. Figure 2 provides results for the validation domain, where 79% of studies used existing real-life business data, 17% employed statistical tests or confidence intervals, 13% relied on expert estimates, and 13% utilized sensitivity analysis. Only 3% of the studies reported on using literature data for validation. For establishing credibility, 49% of studies used case study data, 49% employed business process diagrams, 17% used animation and visualization, 15% involved expert or manager participation, 9% utilized state charts, and 9% provided written assumption documents (Fig. 3).

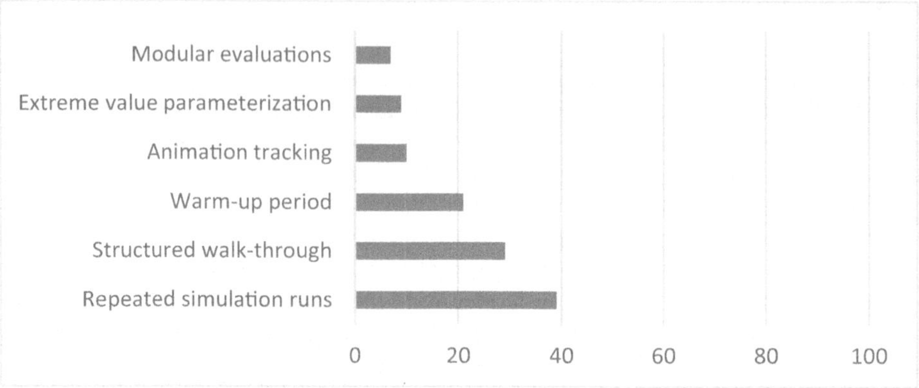

Fig. 1. The percentage of studies applying the listed verification methods

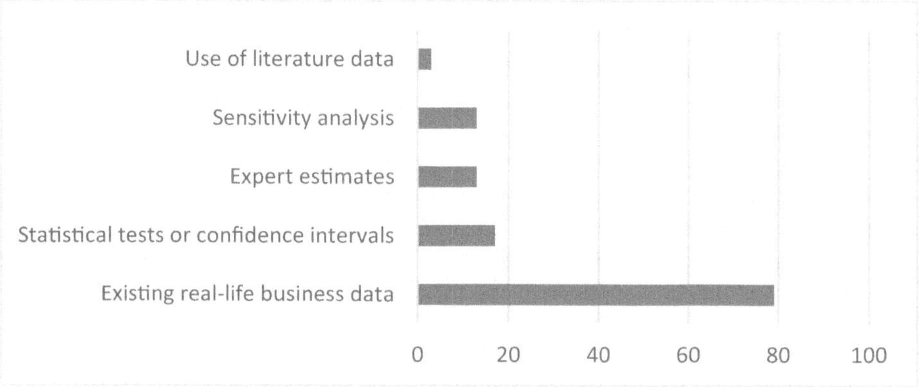

Fig. 2. The percentage of studies applying the listed validation methods

Surprisingly, a significant portion of the studies did not report on applying verification, validation, or credibility methods. By examining the data, it was found that 20% of the studies did not mention any verification techniques, 14% lacked any reported validation methods, and 10% did not address credibility. These preliminary findings indicate potentials for improvement in logistical simulation modelling, as the absence of sophisticated verification, validation, and credibility undermines the reliability and trustworthiness of the results, developed strategies, and managerial implications.

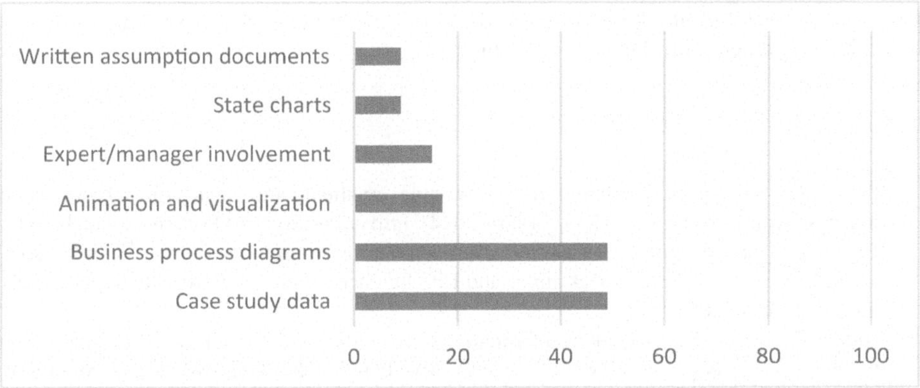

Fig. 3. The percentage of studies applying the listed methods for establishing credibility

5 Conclusion

Discrete simulation is a powerful and frequently applied method for modelling freight transportation and terminal logistics. However, its effectiveness is heavily dependent on rigorous verification, validation, and the establishment of credibility.

Among the most important verification techniques are repeated simulation runs, structured walk-throughs, and modular evaluations. Repeated simulation runs are crucial because they ensure the reliability of the model's outputs. Structured walk-throughs allow experts to systematically review the model's logic and implementation, helping to identify and correct any discrepancies early in the development process. Modular evaluations enable the verification of individual components of the model before they are integrated into the larger system, ensuring that each part functions correctly.

Real-life business data was used for validation to provide a direct comparison of the simulation results and historical data. Statistical tests and sensitivity analysis quantify the reliability of the simulation outcomes to ensure robustness of the model under varying conditions. Expert judgment was used when empirical data was insufficient or unavailable, allowing professionals to assess the model's validity based on their knowledge and experience.

Credibility is established through case study data, business process diagrams, and the involvement of stakeholders throughout the modelling process. These methods ensure that the model aligns closely with real-world operations and gains the trust of those who rely on its outputs. Animation and visualization also play a crucial role in making the model's behaviour transparent and understandable, which further enhances its credibility.

It is crucial to report on the application of verification, validation and methods for establishing credibility. Transparent documentation allows other researchers and practitioners to understand and trust the methods used, replicate the study, and build upon the existing work. Without detailed documentation and reporting, the reliability of the simulation models remains uncertain, which could lead to scepticism or misapplication of the results. Therefore, clear guidelines for applying and standards for comparable reporting on verification, validation, and credibility techniques are necessary to advance the field of logistical simulation modelling.

References

1. Kogler, C.: Transport simulation for sustainable, resilient, and quality-preserving wood logistics. Simul. Notes Eur. **34**(2), 51–60 (2024). https://doi.org/10.11128/sne.34.tn.10681
2. Kogler, C.: Decision support by discrete event simulation for the wood supply chain. Dissertation, University of Natural Resources and Life Sciences Vienna (2020). https://permalink.obvsg.at/bok/AC16139733
3. Kogler, C., Rauch, P.: Discrete event simulation of multimodal and unimodal transportation in the wood supply chain: a literature review. Silva Fennica. 52(4) (2018). https://doi.org/10.14214/sf.9984
4. Banks, J., Carson, J.S., Nelson, B.L., Nicol, D.M.: Discrete-event system simulation. 5th ed. Pearson Education, United States (2014). ISBN 978–0136062127
5. Sargent, R.G.: Verification and validation of simulation models. J. Simul. **7**(1), 12–24 (2013). https://doi.org/10.1057/jos.2012.20
6. Asteris, M., Collins, A., Jones, D.F.: Container port infrastructure in north-west Europe: policy-level modeling. J. Policy Modeling **34**(2), 312–324 (2012). https://doi.org/10.1016/j.jpolmod.2012.01.004
7. Mustafee, N., Bischoff, E.E.: Analysing trade-offs in container loading: combining load plan construction heuristics with agent-based simulation. Int. Trans. Oper. Res. **20**(4), 471–491 (2013). https://doi.org/10.1111/itor.12017
8. Jaoua, A., Riopel, D., Gamache, M.: A simulation framework for real-time fleet management in internal transport systems. Simul. Model. Pract. Theory **21**(1), 78–90 (2012). https://doi.org/10.1016/j.simpat.2011.10.003
9. Windisch, J., Röser, D., Mola-Yudego, B., Sikanen, L., Asikainen, A.: Business process mapping and discrete-event simulation of two forest biomass supply chains. Biomass Bioenerg. **56**, 370–381 (2013). https://doi.org/10.1016/j.biombioe.2013.05.022
10. Sun, Z., Lee, L.H., Chew, E.P., Tan, K.C.: MicroPort: a general simulation platform for seaport container terminals. Adv. Eng. Inform. **26**(1), 80–89 (2012). https://doi.org/10.1016/j.aei.2011.08.010
11. Law, A.M.: Simulation Modeling and Analysis, 6th edn. McGraw-Hill Education, New York (2024)
12. Karttunen, K., Väätäinen, K., Asikainen, A., Ranta, T.: The operational efficiency of waterway transport of forest chips on Finland's Lake Saimaa. Silva Fennica, 46(3) (2012). https://doi.org/10.14214/sf.49
13. Carteni, A., de Luca, S.: Tactical and strategic planning for a container terminal: Modelling issues within a discrete event simulation approach. Simul. Model. Pract. Theory **21**(1), 123–145 (2012). https://doi.org/10.1016/j.simpat.2011.10.005
14. Eriksson, A., Eliasson, L., Hansson, P.-A., Jirjis, R.: Effects of supply chain strategy on stump fuel cost: a simulation approach. Int. J. For. Res. 1–11 (2014). https://doi.org/10.1155/2014/984395
15. Beaudoin, D., Lebel, L., Soussi, M.A.: Discrete event simulation to improve log yard operations. INFOR. Inf. Syst. Oper. Res. **50**(4), 175–185 (2012). https://doi.org/10.3138/infor.50.4.175
16. Kogler, C., Rauch, P.: Game-based workshops for the wood supply chain facilitate knowledge transfer. Int. J. Simul. Model. **19**(3), 446–457 (2020). https://doi.org/10.2507/IJSIMM19-3-526

17. Elbert, R., Reinhard, D.: Increasing capacity utilization of shuttle trains in intermodal transport by investing in transshipment technologies for non-cranable semi-trailers. In: 2016 Winter Simulation Conference (WSC), pp. 2358–2369. IEEE (2016). https://doi.org/10.1109/WSC.2016.7822276
18. Zamora-Cristales, R., Boston, K., Sessions, J., Murphy, G.: Stochastic simulation and optimization of mobile chipping economics in processing and transport of forest biomass from residues. Silva Fennica **47**(5), 937 (2013)
19. Kogler, C., Rauch, P.: Lead time and quality driven transport strategies for the wood supply chain. Res. Transp. Bus. Manage. **47** (2023). https://doi.org/10.1016/j.rtbm.2023.100946

Logistics and Manufacturing

A Simulation-Optimisation Tool for Routing Drones in Realistic Conditions

Xabier A. Martin[1(✉)], Peter Keenan[2], Javier Panadero[3], Sean McGarraghy[2], and Angel A. Juan[1]

[1] Research Center on Production Management and Engineering, Universitat Politècnica de València, Alcoy, Spain
{xamarsol,ajuanp}@upv.es
[2] Centre for Business Analytics, School of Business, University College Dublin, Belfield, Ireland
{peter.keenan,sean.mcgarraghy}@ucd.ie
[3] Department of Computer Architecture and Operating Systems, Universitat Autònoma de Barcelona, Bellaterra, Spain
javier.panadero@uab.cat

Abstract. The use of drones for routing and monitoring tasks has grown significantly, with applications such as traffic surveillance and road inspections gaining prominence . These real-world scenarios often involve unpredictable factors like fluctuating service times, which add complexity to traditional routing problems. This paper introduces a simulation-optimisation framework for routing drones under realistic conditions . To efficiently solve this problem, we propose a simheuristic approach that integrates a biased-randomised iterated local search metaheuristic with Monte Carlo simulation. Our computational experiments validate the efficiency, robustness, and speed of the proposed method, providing high-quality solutions to routing challenges in uncertain environments.

Keywords: Routing drones · Simulation-optimisation · Uncertainty

1 Introduction

With the increasing use of drones for tasks such as traffic monitoring and road inspections, routing these vehicles efficiently in dynamic, real-world conditions has become a critical challenge. These operations often face uncertainties like variable service times, which add complexity to traditional routing models. To address these practical needs, it's essential to develop robust optimisation methods that can handle such unpredictability while still delivering high-quality solutions quickly. One such relevant problem is the team orienteering arc routing problem (TOARP), introduced by [4]. In the TOARP, a predetermined fleet of vehicles, initially located at a central depot, needs to navigate using some traversing arcs before returning to the central depot. Along the way, the vehicles aim to maximise their cumulative profits by visiting a set of profitable arcs, while

A. A. Juan et al. (Eds.): SIMUtools 2024, LNICST 603, pp. 139–149, 2025.
https://doi.org/10.1007/978-3-031-87345-4_10

they must visit a set of required arcs. Additionally, the vehicles must adhere to a given maximum time limit, ensuring that they reach the central depot on time or before a specified limit. Consequently, the TOARP can be regarded as a specific case of the more general time-capacitated arc routing problem in which not all arcs are required [5]. This problem is known to be NP-hard, since it is a hybridisation of the arc routing problem (ARP) and team orienteering problem (TOP), which indicates its high computational complexity in finding optimal solutions. However, its practical relevance extends beyond theoretical complexity, as it finds numerous applications in real-life logistics and transportation [11].

Uncertainty is a fundamental aspect of real-world systems, including routing problems, where inputs such as travel times are often not known in advance and fluctuate. This stochastic uncertainty presents substantial challenges in crafting efficient and cost-effective solutions to combinatorial optimisation problems. Simulation-based optimisation methods, which integrate metaheuristics with simulation, have been proposed to tackle such issues [2]. In recent years, simheuristics have gained prominence for addressing various combinatorial optimisation problems with stochastic elements [6]. This paper proposes a simheuristic algorithm to address the TOARP with random service times, where the travel times along the arcs are not fixed but vary according to probabilistic distributions. By introducing this variant, we aim to develop more robust strategies where travel times are uncertain, thus enhancing the applicability of the TOARP to real-world situations involving stochastic travel times.

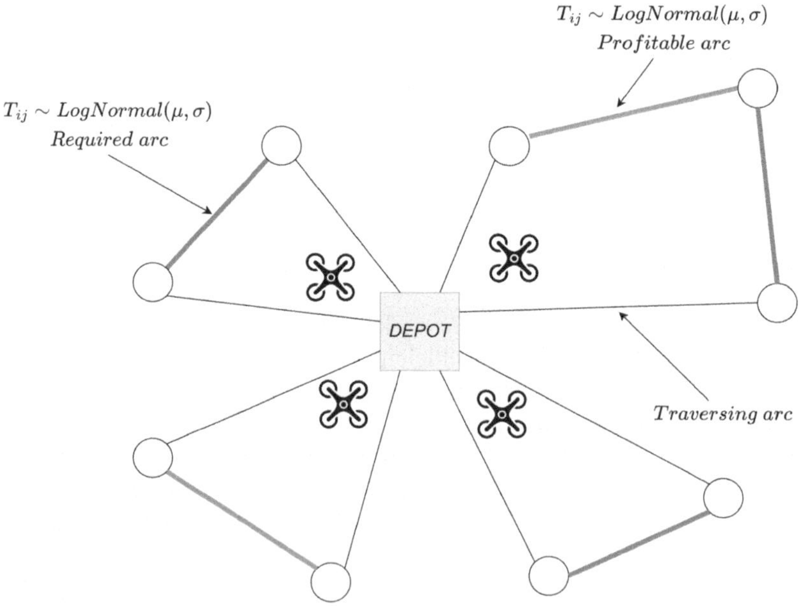

Fig. 1. Schema of a TOARP solution with random service times.

Figure 1 depicts a simple example of such a TOARP with random service times. The example contains a central depot, from which four drones depart, service the required and profitable arcs, and come back to the depot. Along their route, the drones traverse several arcs, some of which are required (red lines), others of which are profitable (blue lines), with the rest being traversing arcs used to reach the other kinds of arcs. In this example, the service times along the required or profitable arcs are not fixed but instead vary according to probabilistic distributions. These random service times introduce variability in the travel duration along these arcs, reflecting the uncertainty inherent in real-world routing scenarios.

The main contributions of this paper are as follows: (*i*) extending the TOARP to include random service times, where travel times along the arcs are modelled as stochastic variables; (*ii*) proposing a novel simheuristic algorithm that integrates simulation-based techniques with optimisations strategies to effectively tackle this extended TOARP. The simheuristic algorithm combines a biased-randomised iterated local search (ILS) metaheuristic with Monte Carlo simulation to account for the variability in service times.

The remainder of this paper is structured as follows. Section 2 offers a review of existing work on the TOARP. Section 3 proposes a biased-randomised simheuristic to solve the TOARP with random service times. Section 4 describes the computational experiments, while Sect. 5 presents the results obtained and shows the effectiveness of the proposed simheuristic algorithm. Finally, Sect. 6 summarises the main conclusions of this work and offers several research lines.

2 Related Work

[4] introduced the TOARP as an extension of the TOP by associating customers, demands, and rewards with arcs. The authors provided a comprehensive formulation and implemented a branch-and-cut algorithm for the resolution of the problem. Building on the original work on the TOARP, [3] utilised a matheuristic approach to tackle the TOARP and achieved optimal solutions for nearly all tested instances, with only one exception. [9] proposed a novel approach using column generation to address the limitations of existing branch-and-cut methods. Their approach transforms the problem from a customer-on-arc to a customer-on-vertex representation, simplifying both the branching and pricing phases and providing a more effective solution for instances where knapsack constraints heavily influence performance. Recent research has introduced variations of the TOARP to address additional challenges. [1] explore the correlated arc orienteering problem in situations where the rewards of arcs exhibit correlation, such as in road inspection tasks following a flood, where neighbouring roads are also likely to be affected. [12] introduced a robust version of the TOARP in a disaster context. This problem was transformed into a variant of the TOP on a simple graph and solved using a Lagrangian relaxation and branch-and-price framework. The approach was validated with real-world instances, demonstrating its effectiveness in handling complex routing challenges under uncertainty.

Apart from the work by [12], we did not find any other study addressing the TOARP with random service times. The inclusion of random service times adds a significant layer of complexity, making the problem more representative of real-world scenarios where travel times are uncertain. This variant is particularly relevant for applications where unpredictable factors, such as traffic conditions or varying task durations, affect the routing schedule. Incorporating stochastic elements into the TOARP allows for the development of more robust and resilient routing strategies, which are crucial for efficient decision-making in dynamic and uncertain environments.

3 Methodology

In order to solve the TOARP with random service times, we present a biased-randomised simheuristic based on the approach proposed by [7]. This approach efficiently searches for high-quality solutions and demonstrates effectiveness in finding competitive solutions for the deterministic version of the problem.

Algorithm 1 outlines the main components of the simheuristic algorithm. First, the optimisation problem is initially converted to its deterministic version, where variables are replaced by their expected or most likely values. This effectively removes the uncertainty in the problem. Thus, an initial feasible solution is generated for the deterministic TOARP using a novel savings heuristic inspired by the savings heuristic for solving the TOP [8]. This initial solution is refined through a local search procedure that applies several local search operators to find the local minimum within the current neighbourhood. Next, the initial solution is simulated with a low number of simulation runs to evaluate its expected profit under uncertainty. This initial solution serves as the starting point and is assigned as both the base solution and the best solution found so far for the ILS. Next, the ILS generates multiple high-quality solutions to the deterministic version of the problem. In particular, the base solution is destroyed and then reconstructed using two operators, a remove-insert operator and an exchange operator, to produce a new solution. This new solution is then refined through a local search procedure that employs five distinct operators to find the local minimum within the current neighbourhood. If the profit of the new solution is higher than that of the base solution, the algorithm performs a simulation with a low number of simulation runs to evaluate its expected profit under uncertainty. If the expected profit of the new solution is higher, the base solution is updated to this new solution, and if it outperforms the best-found solution, the best solution is updated accordingly. Moreover, the new solution is inserted into a pool of elite solutions, which will be further examined under uncertainty after the maximum allowed computational time is reached. To avoid local optima and enhance solution diversity, the algorithm incorporates an acceptance criterion based on a credit mechanism [10]. If the new solution's profit is worse than the base solution's, but the difference is less than the credit (the improvement achieved in the last update), the base solution is updated. Finally, once the maximum allowed computational time is reached, the algorithm evaluates all elite solutions stored in the pool by running a high number of simulation runs to refine their expected profits. The solution with the highest expected profit is returned as the final output of the simheuristic algorithm. The selection of the best solution could also take into account measures of interest beyond just the expected value, such as variance or reliability, to ensure a more robust decision-making process.

Algorithm 1. Simheuristic algorithm.

```
function SIM-TOARP(instance, maxTime, α, β, T_max)
    initSol ← GENINITSOL(instance, α, β, T_max)
    initSol ← LOCALSEARCH(initSol, T_max)
    SIMULATION(initSol, T_max, nShort)
    baseSol ← initSol
    bestSol ← initSol
    poolEliteSols ← ∅
    time ← 0
    credit ← 0
    while time ≤ maxTime do
        newSol ← PERTURBATION(baseSol, T_max)
        newSol ← LOCALSEARCH(newSol, T_max)
        Δ ← PROFIT(baseSol) − PROFIT(newSol)
        if Δ < 0 then
            SIMULATION(newSol, T_max, nShort)
            Δ ← EXPPROFIT(baseSol) − EXPPROFIT(newSol)
            if Δ < 0 then
                credit ← −Δ
                baseSol ← newSol
                if EXPPROFIT(newSol) > EXPPROFIT(bestSol) then
                    bestSol ← newSol
                    INSERT(poolEliteSols, newSol)
                end if
            end if
        end if
        if 0 < Δ ≤ credit then
            credit ← 0
            baseSol ← newSol
        end if
        time ← UPDATETIME()
    end while
    for sol ∈ poolEliteSols do
        SIMULATION(sol, T_max, nLong)
        if EXPPROFIT(sol) > EXPPROFIT(bestSol) then
            bestSol ← sol
        end if
    end for
    return bestSol
end function
```

Algorithm 2 depicts the simulation procedure, which estimates the performance of a solution under uncertainty scenarios with random service times. The procedure keeps track of the accumulated profit, initialised to zero at the start of the simulation. The simulation is then run multiple times, and in each run, the profit of the solution is computed and added to the accumulated profit. To compute the solution's profit, the procedure iterates through the routes in the solution. For each route, it calculates the route's profit and cost, both initialised to zero. Specifically, for each arc in the route, its random service time is sampled using a non-negative probability distribution, such as the Weibull or Log-Normal distributions, to account for uncertainty. The profit of the arc is added to the route's profit if the arc is profitable. After processing all arcs in the route, a penalty is applied if the expected route cost exceeds the maximum travel time, resulting in the loss of all profits collected from the visited profitable arcs. Once all simulation runs are complete, the expected profit is computed as the average accumulated profit across all runs and is assigned as the expected profit of the solution.

Algorithm 2. Simulation procedure.

```
function SIMULATION(sol, T_max, nRuns)
    sumProfit ← 0
    for i ← 1 to nRuns do
        solProfit ← 0
        for route ∈ GETROUTES(sol) do
            routeCost ← 0
            routeProfit ← 0
            for arc ∈ GETARCS(route) do
                arcCost ← GETSTOCHASTICVALUE(arc, varLevel)
                routeCost ← routeCost + arcCost
                routeProfit ← routeProfit + GETPROFIT(arc)
            end for
            if routeCost > T_max then
                routeProfit ← 0
            end if
            solProfit ← solProfit + routeProfit
        end for
        sumProfit ← sumProfit + solProfit
    end for
    expProfit ← sumProfit/nRuns
    SETEXPPROFIT(sol, expProfit)
end function
```

4 Computational Experiments

The proposed simheuristic algorithm has been implemented in Julia 1.10.2. Computational experiments have been executed on an Intel Xeon E5-2630 v4 2.20

GHz multi-core processor with 32 GB of RAM. A maximum time limit of 300 seconds has been established for each benchmark instance. For parameter settings, a brief tuning process on a random subset of instances has been conducted. Based on this tuning, the β parameter of the skewed geometric distribution has been selected from the interval $(0.1, 0.3)$, which has consistently provided excellent performance. Each instance has been run 10 times using different random number generator seeds to account for variability, and the best results from these runs have been reported.

The performance of the proposed simheuristic algorithm has been evaluated using an extended set of TOARP benchmark instances [4]. These instances, initially developed for testing deterministic algorithms, have been adapted to incorporate random service times, providing a more realistic assessment of the algorithm's effectiveness under uncertainty. These benchmark instances are publicly available at the following website, together with their optimal and best-known lower bounds: http://www.uv.es/corberan/instancias.htm. The benchmark instances consist of four sets of instances (R, G, D and T50) with 2, 3 or 4 vehicles. Three of the sets (R, G and D) have been generated from instances of the undirected Rural Postman Problem. However, T50 has been deliberately created for the TOARP. Table 1 reviews the benchmark main properties, such as the number of instances, number of nodes, number of arcs, and number of required and profitable arcs for three different p values. The p parameter controls the probability of certain arcs being required or not, so the number of required arcs increases as p increases. In this work, we focus on using the T50 instances, as they are considered the most challenging instances to solve. Given their complexity, they provide a robust measure for evaluating the performance of the simheuristic.

Table 1. Characteristics of the TOARP instances of classes.

Set	# Inst	$\|V\|$	$\|A\|$	$p = 0$		$p = 0.25$		$p = 0.5$	
				$\|A_R\|$	$\|A_P\|$	$\|A_R\|$	$\|A_P\|$	$\|A_R\|$	$\|A_P\|$
R	15	11–27	42–296	0	7–20	0–7	3–17	3–11	1–11
D	27	17–100	96–846	0	10–121	2–28	6–95	6–64	4–70
G	27	18–100	54–394	0	11–113	1–25	7–91	6–57	3–64
T50	20	50	298–300	0	54–65	-	-	23–38	24–38

The adapted instances transform the deterministic service times into random variables following a probability distribution function. Specifically, instead of assuming constant service times t_{ij} for each arc $(i, j) \in A$, we consider a more realistic scenario where service times are modelled as random variables T_{ij}. The deterministic service times t_{ij} found in the original instances are treated as the expected values of the random service times T_{ij}, which we model using a log-normal probability distribution due to its suitability for non-negative variables, such as service times. The log-normal distribution is characterised by two parameters: the location parameter, μ_{ij}, and the scale parameter, σ_{ij}, which are derived from the expected value $E[T_{ij}] = t_{ij}$ and the variance $Var[T_{ij}] = k \cdot E[T_{ij}]$. Here, k serves as a design parameter that controls the level of uncertainty in the service times. By adjusting k, we can simulate different levels of variability, ranging from low ($k = 0.25$), medium ($k = 0.5$), to high ($k = 1$) uncertainty. This extension enables us to test the robustness and effectiveness of our simheuristic algorithm across a spectrum of scenarios with varying degrees of unpredictability in service times, providing a comprehensive evaluation of its performance under realistic conditions. Lastly, a nonlinear penalty is included to handle real-world scenarios where travel times are uncertain, and it is essential to complete routes within a predefined maximum driving range $T_{\max}$. Observe that, optimal solutions for the deterministic version of the TOARP will be the same as the ones that maximise the expected profit under uncertainty with a linear objective function. However, this condition will not hold if the objective function is modified to include a nonlinear penalty to account for the uncertainty in travel times. As a result, if a route exceeds this maximum range $T_{\max}$, the collected profit from the route is set to zero. Thus, the optimal solutions for the TOARP with random travel times will no longer be the same as the optimal solutions for the deterministic TOARP with this nonlinear penalty. However, our simheuristic algorithm should obtain solutions that account for this nonlinear penalty, and outperform the optimal deterministic solution under uncertain conditions.

5 Results and Discussion

Table 2 presents the results of our simheuristic algorithm for the deterministic version of the TOARP. It groups the instances based on the number of vehicles $|K|$ and the parameter p (percentage of required edges). For each group, several key metrics are reported: the number of instances solved to optimality by the branch-and-cut algorithm proposed by [4] (# Solved), the number of optimal solutions found by our simheuristic algorithm (# Opt), and the average and maximum percentage gap between the solutions found by simheuristic and the best-known solution (BKS) obtained by the branch-and-cut algorithm (Av. and Max. Gap). Additionally, the average and maximum percentage gaps are calculated exclusively for instances where the optimal solution is available (Av. and Max. Gap*). Notice that, our simheuristic algorithm is able to consistently obtain high-quality solutions. Observe that its performance varies with the number of vehicles and the parameter p. The algorithm is particularly effective for a smaller vehicle count ($|K| = 2$), achieving more optimal solutions and lower average gaps. As the number of vehicles increases, achieving optimality becomes more challenging, and the average gaps become more noticeable. However, if we compare the average gaps calculated with respect to the optimal solutions and the branch-and-cut algorithm, the average gap is significantly lower when considering the optimal solutions. This discrepancy suggests that the upper bounds obtained through the branch-and-cut algorithm may deviate significantly from the optimal solutions.

Table 2. Computational results for the sets of instances T50.

		$p = 0$	$p = 0.5$
$\|K\| = 2$	# Solved	10	10
	# Opt	0	4
	Av. Gap	0.96	0.48
	Av. Gap∗	0.96	0.46
	Max. Gap	1.58	1.84
	Max. Gap∗	1.58	1.84
$\|K\| = 3$	# Solved	10	10
	# Opt	1	1
	Av. Gap	0.69	1.68
	Av. Gap∗	0.69	1.83
	Max. Gap	1.85	3.29
	Max. Gap∗	1.85	3.29
$\|K\| = 4$	# Solved	10	10
	# Opt	0	0
	Av. Gap	4.85	2.91
	Av. Gap∗	0.85	2.67
	Max. Gap	7.97	5.68
	Max. Gap∗	1.59	3.90

Figure 2 shows a summary of the performance of our simheuristic algorithm for the different k levels of uncertainty. The boxplot displays the different levels of uncertainty and the percentage gaps with respect to the BKS in the horizontal and vertical axes, respectively. In particular, it compares the best-found deterministic solutions reported in Table 2 (OBD), with the best-found stochastic solutions by the simheuristic algorithm (OBS). Observe that, our simheuristic algorithm obtains percentage gaps of 2.95%, 3.91%, and 5.27% when compared to the percentage gaps of 28.17%, 35.54%, and 43.72% obtained by the OBD under uncertainty. Moreover, our simheuristic algorithm consistently obtains solutions closer to the BKS, which indicates that the simheuristic solutions are not penalised and lose the collected profit. This underscores the efficiency and quality of our simheuristic algorithm in finding high-quality solutions for scenarios with uncertainty, and outperforming the best-found solutions for the deterministic versions of the problem under different uncertainty levels.

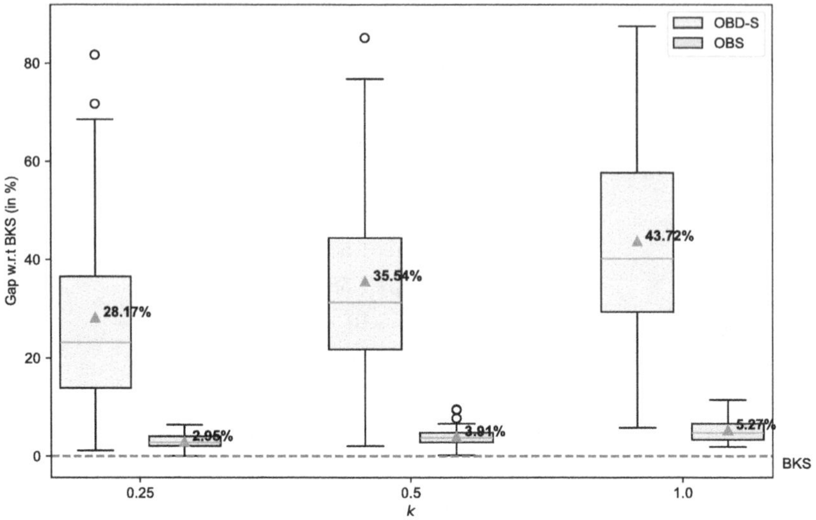

Fig. 2. Percentage gaps of our simheuristic algorithm for different k levels.

6 Conclusions

This paper presented the TOARP with random service times and proposed a biased-randomised simheuristic algorithm to solve the aforementioned problem. The solution approach combined a biased-randomised iterated local search metaheuristic that offers near-optimal solutions for the deterministic version of the problem with Monte Carlo simulation to effectively handle uncertainty in service times. The performance of the simheuristic was evaluated using adapted benchmark instances from the TOARP. The results demonstrated that our approach is capable of generating high-quality solutions under uncertainty, highlighting its robustness and competitiveness across various problem instances.

Several research lines can be explored next as follows: (*i*) introducing dynamic conditions, such as UAV battery levels or weather changes, which would necessitate the extension to a sim-learnheuristic framework; (*ii*) extending the current simheuristic approach to consider multi-objective optimisation, allowing for the simultaneous minimisation of travel times, maximisation of collected profits, and minimisation of operational costs or environmental impact.

References

1. Agarwal, S., Akella, S.: The correlated arc orienteering problem. In: International Workshop on the Algorithmic Foundations of Robotics, pp. 402–418. Springer, Cham (2022)
2. Amaran, S., Sahinidis, N.V., Sharda, B., Bury, S.J.: Simulation optimization: a review of algorithms and applications. Ann. Oper. Res. **240**(1), 351–380 (2016)

3. Archetti, C., Corberán, Á., Plana, I., Sanchis, J.M., Speranza, M.G.: A matheuristic for the team orienteering arc routing problem. Eur. J. Oper. Res. **245**(2), 392–401 (2015)
4. Archetti, C., Speranza, M.G., Corberán, Á., Sanchis, J.M., Plana, I.: The team orienteering arc routing problem. Transp. Sci. **48**(3), 442–457 (2014)
5. de Armas, J., Keenan, P., Juan, A.A., McGarraghy, S.: Solving large-scale time capacitated arc routing problems: from real-time heuristics to metaheuristics. Ann. Oper. Res. **273**(1), 135–162 (2019)
6. Juan, A.A., et al.: A review of the role of heuristics in stochastic optimisation: from metaheuristics to learnheuristics. Ann. Oper. Res. **320**(2), 831–861 (2023)
7. Martin, X.A., Keenan, P., Panadero, J., McGarraghy, S., Juan, A.A.: A biased-randomised iterated local search for the team orienteering arc routing problem allowing different origin and destination. J. Heuristics (2024). accepted
8. Panadero, J., Juan, A.A., Bayliss, C., Currie, C.: Maximising reward from a team of surveillance drones: a simheuristic approach to the stochastic team orienteering problem. Eur. J. Ind. Eng. **14**(4), 485–516 (2020)
9. Riera-Ledesma, J., Salazar-González, J.J.: Solving the team orienteering arc routing problem with a column generation approach. Eur. J. Oper. Res. **262**(1), 14–27 (2017)
10. Talbi, E.G.: Metaheuristics: From Design to Implementation, vol. 74. Wiley, Bognor Regis (2009)
11. Wang, K., Wu, Q., He, X., Hu, C., Chen, N.: Optimizing UAV traffic monitoring routes during rush hours considering spatiotemporal variation of monitoring demand. Int. J. Geogr. Inf. Sci. **36**(10), 2086–2111 (2022)
12. Zhang, G., Jia, N., Zhu, N., Adulyasak, Y., Ma, S.: Robust drone selective routing in humanitarian transportation network assessment. Eur. J. Oper. Res. **305**(1), 400–428 (2023)

AKRIMA - An Automated Adaptive System for Crisis Monitoring and Management

Annegret Janzso(✉), David Kaub, Philipp Flügger, Krzysztof Marek Graca, Veronika Kurchyna, Patrick Mertes, Nhat Tran, Jan Ole Berndt, and Ingo Timm

German Research Center for Artificial Intelligence (DFKI), Cognitive Social Simulation,Behringstr. 21, 54296 Trier, Germany
Annegret.Janzso@dfki.de

Abstract. With the increase in natural disasters due to climate change, the resilience of production companies and supply chains has moved into focus. This paper proposes AKRIMA, an automated adaptive system for crisis monitoring and management, to support companies in identifying potential issues while offering relevant reaction mechanisms during crisis scenarios. Thus, the aim is to strengthen resilience and secure supply chains. To achieve this, a focus is set on pandemics and heavy rain (flooding) scenarios. This covers contexts that heavily influence companies and relevant supply chains, although the approach can be applied to further scenarios as well. Being able to identify arising issues, adapt processes, and determining alternative courses of action in a timely manner, as well as being able to overcome these issues in the long term does not only help secure economic functions, but also allows for a resilient distribution of important goods such as basic needs and medical products. As a result, a demonstrator is set up to visualize processes and simulate scenarios and situations in combination with a detailed process analysis, allowing interested users an initial interaction with the system itself and displaying methods that AKRIMA can support.

Keywords: agent-based modelling · crisis reaction · decision-making

1 Introduction

Recent crisis scenarios, such as floods, the COVID-19 pandemic, and others, have shown that reactions to these events are often insufficient, requiring increased focus on adaptation and prevention. Especially with climate change on the rise, it is to be expected that such disasters have and will become more common [2,4]. While fighting to stabilize the climate, it is a must to adapt to new situations, deal with crises as they occur, and minimize damages by identifying issues in advance. When it comes to situations of this type, making the correct decisions is vital and can save lives, bringing a lot of pressure on decision-makers, which

A. A. Juan et al. (Eds.): SIMUtools 2024, LNICST 603, pp. 150–166, 2025.
https://doi.org/10.1007/978-3-031-87345-4_11

can cause additional stress and therefore error. Especially in already stressful situations, this is a huge issue that requires support and assistance [32].

The AKRIMA project is focused on two main scenarios, depicting different types of potential crisis situations: Pandemics and Extreme Weather Situations such as heavy rain, causing floods. In the context of pandemics, multiple countries are affected, thereby negatively influencing international supply and supply chains. This is often carried over long periods of time, as seen, for example, in the COVID-19 pandemic. In cases of extreme weather, issues are initially restricted to the direct area of impact, but when observing supply chains, this dimension widens to other regions as well, as the event causes these chains to become disturbed. Individual temporal steps are important here, from the extreme weather situation occurring over immediate damage control, to continuous damages, such as reduced harvest due to dying crops or similar issues. Aiming to support decision-making processes in crisis scenarios, the AKRIMA project sets a focus on logistic processes in critical infrastructure for the supply of basic goods. Thereby, two main goals are defined:

1. Development and creation of a simulation-based evaluation system towards reaction mechanisms during crises for businesses, as well as the evolution and optimization of these processes. This is not only relevant to support the economy, but also to ensure production and distribution of necessities such as food or medical equipment.
2. Application and further development of Artificial Intelligence (AI) methods for the automated evaluation of such mechanisms in the context of logistical processes and critical infrastructure. By offering a dynamic, preemptive, and partially automated adjustment, challenging tasks in crisis management, such as decision-making, can be supported. This support in decision-making processes is built on the proposal of adequate reactions to situations as they occur, while predicting possible developments and identifying issues.

These goals aim to support the security of relevant processes, as well as the security of the population during times of crisis. This includes the protection and rescue of people by securing access to emergency services such as firefighters or ambulances, however the main focus is the upkeep of critical infrastructure in logistical processes. Supply chains are of particular interest, as breaks within the chain cause delays, shortages, and increased prices of resources, as seen in past events [16,38]. Formalizing the effects of crisis situations and proposing possible actions to reduce effects overall strengthens logistical processes.

To support the cooperative development of further functionalities beyond the AKRIMA project as well as propose an approach to the design of adaptive monitoring systems in general, this paper presents how such a project can be structured on both a conceptual and technical level. Thus, Sect. 2 details essential knowledge and related work to provide context for the concept presented in Sect. 3 and the use-case-specific methodology used in Sect. 4. Section 5 summarizes the challenges encountered and solutions developed, along with potential directions for future advancements. Finally, Sect. 6 concludes this work by summarizing the overall contributions and impact of AKRIMA.

2 Background

This section describes different methods used within the AKRIMA project, in context with their relevance to the topic, detailing other approaches that successfully utilized specific methods in their work.

Planning in AI deals with the automatic creation of plans to achieve specific goals. The initial situation, available actions and desired target states are modeled using formal languages such as the Planning Domain Definition Language (PDDL) [1] to produce a structured and adaptive plan [14]. This method models logistical processes in a structured manner and adapts them dynamically to changing conditions. By using AI-based planning, not only can current processes be reviewed, but they can also be adjusted in a predictive and partially automated manner. This facilitates decision-making, particularly in crisis management, as processes are continuously evaluated based on the current situation and available options for action, enabling an efficient response to crisis situations and the achievement of set goals.

Agent-Based Modelling (ABM) is an established method within crisis management [7,26], as well as within planning and evaluating adaptive logistical processes [37]. ABM also finds application in the examination of the effectiveness of protective measures [3,7,23,24], for example during the COVID-19 pandemic [6,9,20]. The AScore project [28,35], on which this project builds upon, has successfully utilized ABM to facilitate decision-making and support informed decisions, making it a reasonable choice when extending the project to other crisis scenarios and applications, like logistic processes. An ABM, in the context of the AKRIMA project, models real-world entities such as individuals, workers, and resources, allowing for the simulation of interactions in crisis scenarios. Agents in the model represent people carrying out daily activities, such as commuting to work or attending school, with interactions at shared locations where events like infections can occur. This enables the evaluation of various crisis management strategies, such as hygiene measures or staggered work shifts, and helps assess their effectiveness in controlling the spread of infections or addressing the impact of physical events like flooding.

Data Farming [5,33] can be used as a basis within the project. While data mining utilizes intelligent algorithms to recognize patterns within existing large datasets, data farming explores the usage of intelligent simulation to generate meaningful data required for specific analyses [15,33]. This utilizes a simulation model that generates examples of procedures and events based on stochastic effects or systematic variation of its parameters. This is especially useful in applications in which situations must be covered that have not yet occurred in the real world [15,26]. For crisis management, this specifically allows the assessment of potential damages, which then can be systematically avoided or reduced. In 2024, heavy rainfall caused flooding in multiple parts of southern Germany, causing high material and personal damage in regions where such events have not previously occurred. Using simulations to identify flood-prone areas (e.g., [12]), such catastrophes could have been anticipated and damages minimized.

Geographic Information Systems (GIS) can be used for the digital representation and visualization of the street network. They can allow for the identification of infrastructure and buildings, as well as for geolocations of companies and supply chains. They also enable the definition of boundaries and spatial points of interest, such as hospitals, fire stations or waterways. Open Street Map[1] (OSM) data is used as a particular data source in this project. Especially in crisis scenarios, an environmental analysis of the area can determine which people, infrastructures, and delivery services and paths are most likely to be affected. By extending OSM data with census data[2], an identification of households and their according buildings is possible, which allows for the creation of a synthetic population for simulation purposes. Combining OSM and ABM is not a new approach [13], as it allows realistic paths within the simulation based on public data. It also allows for easy connections of multiple businesses and proper assessment of logistical routes, similar as shown in previous approaches within this context [21].

Crisis Management Systems are often built on structures and best practices found in previous crisis scenarios. The *Incident Command System* (ICS) builds on such best practices to assign tasks and strategies when a crisis occurs. However, a lack of contextualization may cause this process to miss important cues and therefore not lead to the best outcome of specific situations [8]. Other approaches, such as the *Supply Chain Resilience Assessment Model* (SCRAM) [31], focus directly on supply chains on a global level, by assessing links that are affected by crisis events. This allows an assessment of the supply chain resilience and points out specific areas of improvement.

The AKRIMA approach adds on to previous methodologies by integrating AI methods into simulation- and other analysis tools to investigate potential crisis outcomes as well as their impact on the supply chain. Further, it aims to highlight relevant solutions specific to the current situation and allows for the identification of weaknesses in supply chains, thus enabling decision-makers to implement necessary measures before the immediate need for action arises.

3 The AKRIMA Approach

To address the goals formulated in Sect. 1 the AKRIMA management cycle proposes an integrated process combining multiple tools and services into an overarching architecture. **Evaluation and Analysis** require tools for the assessment of the logistical routine in the supply chains, as well as the current situation

[1] https://www.openstreetmap.de/.
[2] https://www.zensus2011.de/.

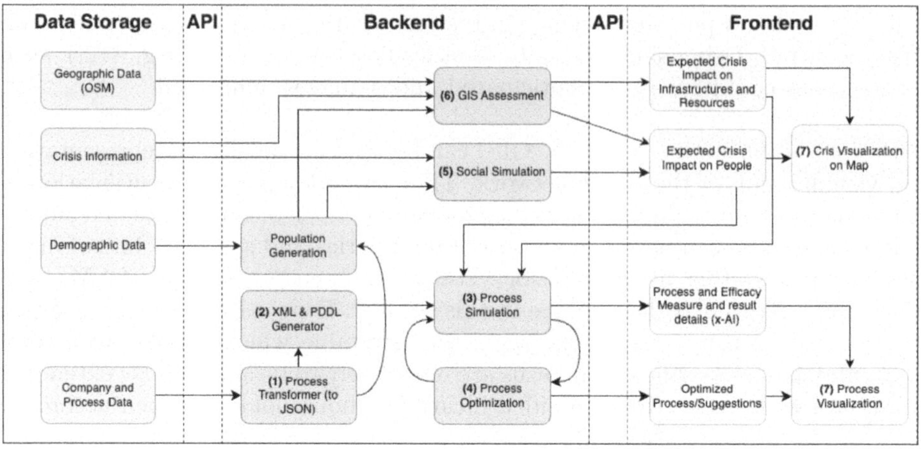

Fig. 1. AKRIMA architecture overview

within a crisis. Data needs to be recorded, aggregated and presented in a dashboard for evaluation according to various criteria and key indicators. **Simulation** investigates the strengths and weaknesses of planned or available crisis reaction mechanisms. Depending on the scenario, different methods can assess their expected impact and the efficacy of reactions available in a given situation. **Planning** aims to serve measures that are optimized based on the assessment of efficacy as suggestions. Decision-makers can then approve or adapt such suggestions. The **Implementation** of such measures includes the gathering of specific key indicators that can be reused in the **Appraisal** step to conclude the adaptive control loop. Based on that process, the following artifacts are derived, which are also displayed in Fig. 1:

1. Transformer for table-based descriptions of business and logistic processes into an object-oriented data structure
2. Generator to create BPMN XML and PDDL representations of the processes for analysis and visualization
3. Process simulation to identify the efficacy of a given process within a specific situation and / or applied reaction mechanism, i.e. measures
4. Algorithmic optimization of configurations, i.e. resource or personnel allocation for processes
5. Social Simulation to investigate infection processes during a pandemic.
6. Analysis tools for assessment of geographic and environmental impact of a crisis based on OSM
7. Back-end application with APIs, managing access and interaction of modules
8. Front-end application for visualization

The following sections describe the individual building blocks of the AKRIMA approach in more detail to further specify the individual steps mentioned above.

3.1 Process Simulation

A process analysis performed by the project partners at Technical College Wildau (TH Wildau) concludes important information and relevant data of processes within a company. Specialized parser within the AKRIMA-System use the data to create a JSON-object representation, which allows for a standardized exchange between systems, i.e., via APIs. This representation forms the baseline of all further functions within the system.

To visualize company processes, the JSON-format data created during analysis is converted into a BPMN 2.0 XML format using a specially developed XML-generator. The resulting XML data is presented as an interactive diagram in the front-end to deliver a clear and intuitive overview of the processes to the user. Additionally, the JSON-format is used to define these processes as a formal planning problem for AI-based planning, which rates the current situation through algorithmic evaluation and supports the user in best practice planning. The results of the planning component can be used to rate the processes and to portray them within the visualization component (see also Sect. 4.2). This offers users a clear overview of the current situation and supports them in making well-founded decisions, optimizing processes, and recognizing risks early on.

3.2 Social Simulation and Environment Analysis

Social simulation is used to generate insights into infection dynamics within possible infection scenarios and allows the valuation of measures available to a company. The simulation is based on a synthetic population of the region to model general infection spread but focuses on tracking the likelihood of infections or illnesses among a company's employees. The impact of local and global measures on the availability of personnel can be tested and used to configure the process analysis for further investigation. Alternatively, the insights can be used directly as a basis for informed decision-making within a crisis.

For heavy rain and flooding events, other analysis tools become necessary to assess the impact of an event. Data from OSM and sources like BFG (the German federal institute of hydrology) for historic flooding events, DWD (German weather service) for current or historic weather information and WSV (the German federal waterways and shipping administration) for water levels can be used to model historical, current or possible future events and their geographical dimensions and affected infrastructure. Combining such models with information about employees and the (synthetic) population allows for an assessment of affected people and required supply and assistance. To ensure availability of dynamic data from such APIs during times of high demand, all time series data is replicated by the project partner Aimpulse Intelligent Systems GmbH and provided via highly scalable APIs.

3.3 Logistic Resilience Score

A *Logistics Resilience Score* (LRS) is being developed to assess different conditions throughout the simulation, based on their overall resilience in crisis situations. The LRS is a key performance indicator model that plays a central role in assessing the resilience of logistics processes. Developed in collaboration with the TH Wildau, it combines a variety of key figures and indicators into a comprehensive assessment model.

Typical operational metrics, such as inventory levels or staff availability, are linked to specific indicators for crisis situations, such as 7-day incidents or information on infrastructure failures. These various parameters are incorporated into the LRS, which maps both internal factors such as process performance and external influences such as crisis developments and the resulting demand dynamics. By adapting the weights of individual indicators in the computation of LRS, the score can be customized for the specific needs and situations of different companies and organizations.

The goal of the LRS is to provide a comprehensive assessment of the current state of a company within a networked supply chain. Based on this analysis, the resilience of the logistics processes is assessed. This is done by creating simulation-based data, supported by AI-assisted data farming, to run through possible crisis scenarios and make their impact on logistics processes measurable.

To assess the resilience of logistics systems, the LRS is combined with a quality function. This specially developed function evaluates the results of the simulations and provides the LRS for optimization. This allows the strengths and weaknesses of crisis response mechanisms to be identified and targeted for improvement. This strengthens the resilience of logistics systems in the long term.

3.4 Use Cases

The following paragraphs include more detail on each of these scenarios in the AKRIMA context. Defining these scenarios includes the determination of the types of influences on logistical chains with regard to the availability of and influences towards infrastructure, actors, resources and tasks.

Pandemic. Challenges arise for company processes during pandemics due to the influence of local infection numbers and different types of safety methods on international chains of delivery, (temporary) under-staffing, companies only being able to run on reduced capacity, and more, leading to issues on local levels for the companies [29]. This causes a temporary shortage of resources, such as missing personnel and lack of materials [10]. Further, legalities such as compulsory testing at places of work bring additional processes and tasks to be organized, managed, and performed by the company. Previous work on this scenario comes from the AScore project, which introduced a simulation-based information management system for local decision-makers [34]. The insights and expertise gained from this project are now being extended to logistics and include an evaluation of reaction mechanisms. To allow this, as well as the inclusion of additional crisis scenarios, a representation of the consequences of a pandemic onto supply chains based on gathered experiences in decision support within a pandemic situation is being created.

Extreme Weather Situation. The likelihood of extreme weather situations is rising within the context of climate change, even in previously calm regions [11,27]. In Germany, especially heavy rain and flooding is of interest. People affected by a flooding event both directly and indirectly may not be available for an employer and therefore not available to sustain important processes. Additionally, important resources might be destroyed, production facilities damaged or unavailable, and transportation routes on land, such as roads or railways, but also waterways can become unusable, which forces a change of transportation mode or path for the suppliers, if they are at all available due to the situation. Due to the expected relevancy of such extreme weather situations, these scenarios are being modeled to ensure the applicability of resulting coping methods. This adds weather consequences and representation of local infrastructure to the formalization of crisis scenarios.

4 Implementation and Application

This section is focused on the practical implementations of the approach specified above. This includes the general methodology in Sect. 4.1 as well as the resulting dashboard and simulation described in Sect. 4.2.

4.1 Methodology

The software artifacts described in Sect. 3 are at the core of the AKRIMA platform, with different components connected to data storage and interactive front-end applications via APIs. Figure 1 illustrates the way the different components are interconnected. Here, three major areas of tasks covered by the back-end components are defined:

1. The **synthetic population** generation, which operates on a mix of geographic, demographic and company-specific data to portray regional populations with particular focus on employment and necessary personnel for crucial steps in the examined processes. This synthetic population is the base for both the **social simulation** and a component for
2. **GIS-based Assessments**, supported by OSM and other geographic data, as well as information specific to the current crisis and the populations affected by this. It yields information on the expected crisis impact on both infrastructure and the population, which can be visualized in the front-end. Additionally, this assessment is important for
3. the **Process Analysis**, consisting of process simulation and optimization based on company data and previous simulation results from the other components. Based on performance measures and detailed results explanations, leaning into principles of x-AI, users receive further information on suggested process optimizations and evaluation results, with the simulation and optimization components providing feedback for each other.

This interplay of components is aided by APIs connecting the different software artifacts with both the necessary data sources and the visualization components in the front-end as a crucial element for the interactive dashboard for effective decision support.

A key aspect of the implementation is resilience towards crisis situations. Resilience can be improved by widely processing, analyzing, and visualizing the given data. Visualizing information, for example, through maps or other graphical depictions, can help stakeholders to quickly gain an overview of the situation and recognize potential problems early on. The implemented map component (see Fig. 2) shows information relevant to the current situation, like alarms, water levels, and flooded areas. For planning logistic processes, it provides insights into the best mode of transport, reachability and routing to suppliers and customers, as well as points of change for transportation. Alternatively, information about the robustness of the road network or other processes to a given event can be depicted on a map based on the calculation of the Robustness of Accessibility Index (RoA) [18]. This allows a valuation of the disruption of a service like emergency services or logistic processes within a network. The results can be looked at for single samples or aggregated for districts, cities, or regions. Testing of AKRIMA has primarily focused on evaluating the resilience of traffic infrastructure and the functioning of essential services, such as fire stations and hospitals, under various regional flooding scenarios. However, the RoA and additional impacts or indicators have not yet been assessed beyond these initial infrastructure tests. Expanding resilience assessments to include further testing with additional performance indicators will be essential. The outlook section addresses potential applications and scenarios for broader resilience assessments within the AKRIMA framework (see Sect. 5).

All data is preprocessed and within the back-end and made available via a REST API to the front-end via (GEO)JSON. These reduce load on the client side and allow other authorized applications to use the analytic tools provided by the AKRIMA API. To achieve this simulation-based evaluation and evolution of mechanisms, an agent-based simulation model (ABSM) has been developed based on an existing pandemic model [28,35]. The model consists of agents, locations and infrastructure, assets and routines which are conceptualized and implemented for the given scenarios, logistic chains, and crisis reaction mechanisms. Synthetic Populations have been generated to abstract from reality. Their correctness, as well as the results, have been analyzed during pre- and post-processing of the dynamic analysis of the simulation. The synthetic population was constructed using data from established sources such as the census[3] and microcensus[4][5], providing a foundation grounded in official and widely accepted

[3] https://www.zensus2011.de/DE/Home/Aktuelles/DemografischeGrunddaten.html?nn=559100.

[4] https://www.destatis.de/DE/Themen/Arbeit/Arbeitsmarkt/Erwerbstaetigkeit/Tabellen/pendler1.html.

[5] https://www.destatis.de/DE/Themen/Branchen-Unternehmen/Unternehmen/Kleine-Unternehmen-Mittlere-Unternehmen/_inhalt.html.

demographic data. To address slight inaccuracies caused by anonymization in these datasets, statistical validation and methods like simulated annealing were applied to enhance alignment with actual demographic distributions. This approach ensures that the synthetic population is both reliable and representative for simulation purposes. Crisis scenarios are created using historical data from sources such as the Robert Koch Institute (RKI) for pandemics[6] and the Federal Waterways Authority (BfG) for flooding[7]. These datasets serve as the foundation for realistic and scalable simulations, with plans in place to incorporate external hydrological models for dynamic flooding scenarios. The use of official data ensures the accuracy and reliability of the synthetic crisis simulations. The systematic exploitation of possible developments based on hypothesis-driven simulation for Data Farming can produce real effects of simulated crisis scenarios of the past and anticipate possible impacts of events that have not yet occurred. Thereby, the agent-based simulation allows a preemptive evaluation of crisis reaction mechanisms. Overall, this implementation of relevant artifacts for simulation-based evaluation and evolution of crisis reaction mechanisms realizes the conceptual model created during analysis using AI algorithms. The defined crisis reaction mechanisms have been implemented, simulated and evaluated, before being optimized by AI-assisted evolution processes, following the process for successful execution of simulation studies by A. Law [22]. The simulation-based evaluation of crisis reaction mechanisms is ranked using the LRS to reflect the effectiveness of alternative reaction options. The evolution of mechanisms utilizes this process to automatically rank and adjust the generated options. Improving the scores thereby shows the improvement of success due to optimization.

At the time this paper is published, the LRS is still in its conceptual form but has been validated through expert interviews and workshops with crisis management and infrastructure resilience stakeholders. These engagements have refined the framework, aligning it with real-world needs. While no testing with real-world or simulated data has been conducted at this point, such testing will be considered once the model is operational.

To tackle the question of how far the crisis resilience of a company is strengthened by the AKRIMA method, the simulation of crisis scenarios and crisis reaction mechanisms for chains of delivery, as well as the resulting revelations regarding the defined goals and practical requirements for each scenario, are compared. The resulting solutions created by the simulation-based evaluation of crisis reaction mechanisms and AI-based evolution of the mechanisms are visualized in a dashboard (see also 4.2). Continuous interaction with users ensures the practicality of the solution rather than just an abstract result and allows for adjustments when necessary. Following the principles of Explainable AI (XAI), explanations of the discovered weaknesses and proposed adjustments are part of the output. This allows the AI-generated results to be generally plausible to humans. More importantly, this allows human decision-makers to better evaluate what

[6] https://github.com/robert-koch-institut.

[7] https://geoportal.bafg.de/CSWView/od.xhtml.

impacts an adjustment could actually have and whether it is reasonable. This is an important contribution to the practical applicability of AI technology in crisis management, strengthening trust and transparency in the interaction between humans and machines. The model and simulation have been structured for the systematic exploration of possible developments of crisis scenarios using known and possible crisis reaction mechanisms by following the procedure protocol of A. Law [22].

4.2 Dashboard and Simulation

The execution of a simulation study typically bases the definition of the model on empiric data to ensure the relevancy of aspects in the systems being properly transferred into the model. The aforementioned steps have therefore been followed to define and implement the model on empiric data to allow reality-near application. Using LRS as a basis for the AI-based automated evolution to assess reaction mechanisms allows comparison of individual scenarios and the effectiveness of individual crisis reaction mechanisms as well as their optimizations. Therefore, changes in goodness of different solutions or adjustments of one solution can be found and compared, which additionally judges the effectiveness of the AI-based evolution. The results gathered through execution and analysis within the diffusion can then be presented, as well as the automated evaluation via intelligent model analysis utilizing the hypothesis-driven simulation studies [25].

The developed and implemented components of the agent-based simulation are built upon the principle of the SoSAD-model [36] in the form of agents, locations, infrastructure, assets, and routines within a social simulation. This allows a requirement-based simulation of pandemic situations. Therefore, the model has been adapted to fit specified needs in terms of, i.e., modeling specific companies and strategies. In the flooding scenario, for example, a scenario-based data analysis for flooding events has been applied, which, in combination with a synthetic population and OSM data, allowed to identify people, resources, and delivery routes affected by such an event. To generate arbitrary ad-hoc synthetic populations to monitor new regions, efficient models and data structures are applied. These include, among others, nearest neighbor models like the Ball Tree, statistical approaches like Simulated Annealing [19], or libraries for working with geospatial data like Geopandas [17]. Logistical processes and crisis reaction mechanisms are formally represented using the PDDL [1]. This allows automatic AI-based planning of the execution in the simulation. The resulting simulation model collects input from data storage and can be configured with simulations specific to the situation. This process utilizes the data science framework *taipy*[8] to post process data by creating analysis pipelines for the simulation output. Further, simulation results are evaluated using intelligent model analysis based on the same principle. Pattern recognition, data correlation, and sensitivity analysis

[8] https://taipy.io/.

allow evaluating crisis reaction mechanisms based on their identifying numbers and LRS within the simulation.

The dashboard allows for direct interaction with the tools provided by the AKRIMA project, to simulate scenarios and test different approaches directly. The dashboard is included within a demonstrator, which allows interested users to test the tool for themselves as well. The system provides predefined alarms tailored to various crisis scenarios for testing and experimentation. For example, in a flooding scenario, an alarm is triggered if water levels exceed a critical threshold or when a supplier is unable to deliver promised goods. Based on these alarms, users can explore the situation in detail through multiple crisis components simultaneously, or focus on specific scenarios as needed. One core feature is the Map-View, which visually represents how different alarms are triggered by conditions such as rising flood levels (see Fig. 2). Additionally, the dashboard graphically illustrates alternative response processes (see Fig. 3), providing users with a fast understanding of each processs functionality and advantages. The pandemic dashboard gives insights into the current pandemic situation, shows sickness rates for employees, and allows for assessment of the effectiveness of measures through simulation.

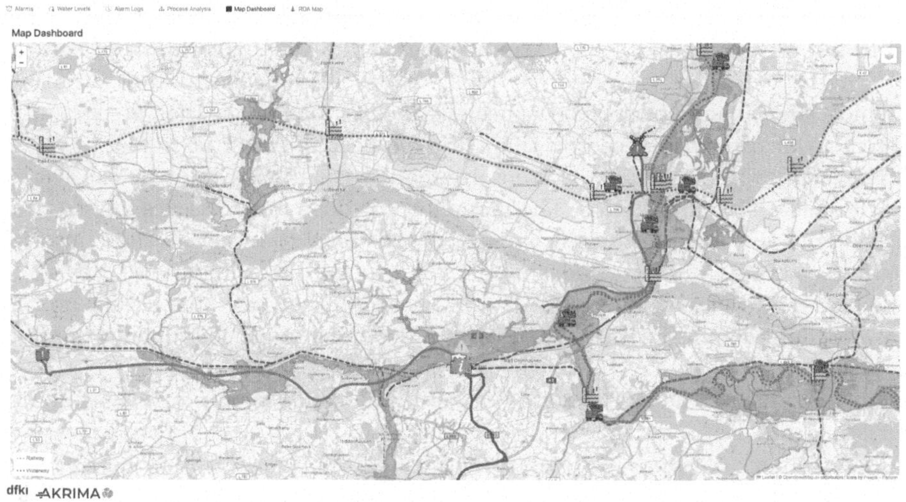

Fig. 2. Map-View with Floods and Alarms

5 Challenges and Solutions

Despite the described progress, there are some limitations that can potentially be tackled in future work. As described throughout the previous sections, AKRIMA is focused on a dynamic, preemptive and partly automated adjustment of crisis management, thereby observing in what way AI can support cognitively taxing tasks by providing decision-makers with information that is relevant to the current situation. The basis thereof is a machine-usable collection of relevant processes and reaction mechanisms to secure the resilience of supply chains. Such a formalization of impacts of crisis scenarios (as described in Sect. 3.4) and possible actions to limit effects thereof is being created with a focus on logistics.

It is important to ensure usage or development of a formal language to ensure capability with the applicable methods for later adjustments of methods compatible with AI-Assistance. Existing AI methods to systematically adjust options in action taking utilize multi-criteria optimization [30], which can be applied for crisis reaction mechanisms as well. These methods rate possible actions and possible adjustments using functions of goodness and fitness. This allows for systematic testing of options, as well as accepting or rejecting them on a situational basis, thereby learning the strategics of crisis reaction. Further, a given protocol of all changes shows causes of success, such that in combination with direct use cases within the simulation, a basis of explainability on the AI-based generated options (XAI) on crisis management is created. Efforts to formalize the effects of crises, as well as possible actions to reduce those, are a strong and important requirement. The required formal language must be compatible with the used methods to ensure the later adjustment of the AI-based methods. The artificially created data (Data Farming, see Sect. 2) for exploration of the crisis scenarios can then be evaluated. This enables the identification of situations in which mechanisms performed especially well or bad, such that a concluding judgement of resilience based on the LRS (see Sect. 3.3) can be made.

For future work, a number of steps are required to further improve the system and make it usable in practice. The manual recording of processes is impractical, especially in the case of process changes and the need to integrate these into the existing system. Computerized support for process recording could provide a remedy. The development of editors and wizards based on the existing process analysis could help users record processes independently, thus reducing the need for experts.

Looking ahead, the RoA provides a foundation that allows investigating further scenarios. Beyond the current applications, the RoA could be applied to evaluate impact of floods and other disruptive events in the road network, on

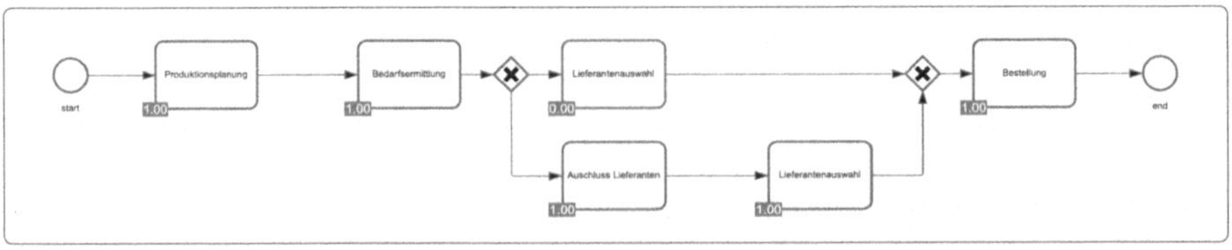

Fig. 3. Process Analysis for Explainability of Processes

transportation networks and the reachability of delivery targets. Further exhaustion due to heat exposure in cities on typical walking paths can be estimated and alternatives identified. This can be especially relevant for vulnerable groups and can support the development of climate adaptation strategies and contribute to enhancing infrastructure resilience. Integrating the RoA as an indicator of the LRS allows for a better overview of the current situation and evaluation of crisis response measures.

Connecting ARKIMA to ERP systems is also an important issue. In order to produce accurate and reliable analyses, the AKRIMA system needs access to current company data, such as stock levels and delivery intervals. The development of interfaces or connectors to ERP systems could help to keep this data up to date and reliable. This information could also support process analysis, as some of this data is also used here.

While the goal of AKRIMA is not to predict exact outcomes, the aim is to evaluate the effectiveness of different crisis response measures. As new data becomes available, the model is recalibrated to improve its accuracy, enabling it to adapt to new scenarios even with limited data. Local data can be utilized to validate the results.

Since the research demonstrator provided by AKRIMA is not a ready to use system and is not yet deployed in any real-world application, historical recovery data is currently unavailable. Currently, the system does not provide any measures to evaluate the recovery rate within- or post-crisis, but since AKRIMA can compare a simulated state or a scenario with the desired state of a process, a measure could be derived by tracking changes of this ratio, and thus enable evaluation of a recovery rate. Such data could serve as benchmarks for observing processes and tracking post-crisis recovery.

6 Conclusion

AKRIMA aims to create interfaces between ecosystems on different platforms and scenarios, allowing usage of data and services from all systems where necessary. Especially the complexity of formalized supply chains, as well as the ABSM on demand-based evaluation and evolution of crisis reaction mechanisms via data farming and optimization, make this project unique. The adaptable crisis management framework adjusts to diverse scenarios, providing tailored recommendations and monitoring tools. By integrating internal and external factors, it enables organizations to quickly assess crisis impacts and respond effectively. Decision-makers can prioritize key indicators and align strategies with their specific needs.

In this paper, the project's fundamentals have been outlined, the concept and scenarios for AKRIMA presented, described how AKRIMA has been and will be implemented and used, and finally the key features of the dashboard demonstrator showcased. It has been shown that it is possible to successfully implement a system like AKRIMA and demonstrate its potential in practice. By using the demonstrator in several workshops, presenting the system to potential users, thereby gathering valuable feedback, was possible. This feedback was crucial for the further development of AKRIMA and the reactions were very positive. The tools that have been developed have proven that they can support decision-making and help to better assess the situation. In conclusion, this paper has shown that AKRIMA is a promising system that already has received positive feedback. The limitations mentioned above provide starting points for future developments to further improve the application and efficiency of the system. Future updates can aim to expand the adaptability of the map, allowing it to dynamically adjust to the specific crisis at hand and present additional context-specific information based on the ongoing alarms. These results also pose as a great basis for future inclusion and usage within an ecosystem, including an AI-based crisis management in further projects.

Acknowledgements. This work has been conducted in the context of AKRIMA - Automatic Adaptive Crisis Monitoring and Management System, a consortium project funded from 01/2022 until 12/2024 within the "Research for civil security" program (`sifo.de`) by the German Federal Ministry of Education and Research (BMBF) under grant number 13N16251. The project is supported by the Technical College Wildau and Aimpulse Intelligent Systems GmbH.

References

1. Aeronautiques, C., et al.: Pddl— the planning domain definition language. Technical report(1998)
2. Atanga, R.A., Tankpa, V.: Climate change, flood disaster risk and food security nexus in Northern Ghana. Front. Sustain. Food Syst. **5**, 706721 (2021)
3. Axelrod, R.: Advancing the art of simulation in the social sciences. In: Simulating Social Phenomena, pp. 21–40. Springer (1997)
4. Banholzer, S., Kossin, J., Donner, S.: The impact of climate change on natural disasters. In: Zommers, Z., Singh, A. (eds.) Reducing Disaster: Early Warning Systems For Climate Change, pp. 21–49. Springer, Dordrecht (2014). https://doi.org/10.1007/978-94-017-8598-3_2
5. Barry, P., Koehler, M.: Simulation in context; using data farming for decision support. In: Proceedings of the 2004 Winter Simulation Conference, 2004, vol. 1. IEEE (2004)
6. Booth, W.: A chilling scientific paper helped upend US and UK coronavirus strategies. Wash. Post **17** (2020)
7. Bortz, M., Burger, M., Fiedler, J., Gramsch, S., Leithäuser, N., Mohring, J.: Epidemiologie-modellierung, simulation und entscheidungsunterstützung für lokale entscheidungsträger. Whitepaper, Fraunhofer-Institut für Techno-und Wirtschaftsmathematik ITWM (2020)
8. Buck, D.A., Trainor, J.E., Aguirre, B.E.: A critical evaluation of the incident command system and NIMS. J. Homel. Securi. Emerg. Manage. **3**(3) (2006). https://doi.org/10.2202/1547-7355.1252
9. Chang, S.L., Harding, N., Zachreson, C., Cliff, O.M., Prokopenko, M.: Modelling transmission and control of the COVID-19 pandemic in Australia. Nat. Commun. **11**(1), 5710 (2020)
10. Chen, X., Chong, W.F., Feng, R., Zhang, L.: Pandemic risk management: resources contingency planning and allocation. Insur. Math. Econ. **101**, 359–383 (2021)

11. Ebi, K.L., et al.: Extreme weather and climate change: population health and health system implications. Annu. Rev. Public Health **42**(1), 293–315 (2021)
12. Groth, M., Bender, S., Wübbelmann, T.: The current use and limitations of water related digital twins–a practical view on urban climate change adaptation. In: KEEP ON PLANNING FOR THE REAL WORLD. Climate Change calls for Nature-based Solutions and Smart Technologies. Proceedings of REAL CORP 2024, 29th International Conference on Urban Development, Regional Planning and Information Society, pp. 605–616. CORP–Competence Center of Urban and Regional Planning (2024)
13. Gumble, H.: Creating a raster agent-based modelling environment from volunteered geographic information. In: 29th Annual GIS Research UK Conference (GISRUK), Cardiff, Wales, UK (Online) (2021)
14. Haslum, P., Lipovetzky, N., Magazzeni, D., Muise, C.: An Introduction to the Planning Domain Definition Language. Synthesis Lectures on Artificial Intelligence and Machine Learning, Springer, Cham (2019)
15. Horne, G.E., Meyer, T.E.: Data farming: Discovering surprise. In: Proceedings of the 2004 Winter Simulation Conference, 2004, vol. 1. IEEE (2004)
16. Jagtap, S., et al.: The Russia-Ukraine conflict: its implications for the global food supply chains. Foods **11**(14), 2098 (2022)
17. Jordahl, K., et al.: geopandas/geopandas: v0.8.1 (2020). https://doi.org/10.5281/zenodo.3946761
18. Kaub, D., et al.: Shortest-path-based resilience analysis of urban road networks. In: Freitag, M., Kinra, A., Kotzab, H., Megow, N. (eds.) Dynamics in Logistics, pp. 132–143. Springer, Cham (2024). https://doi.org/10.1007/978-3-031-56826-8_10
19. Kirkpatrick, S., Gelatt, C.D., Vecchi, M.P.: Optimization by simulated annealing. Science **220**(4598), 671–680 (1983)
20. Klein, E., Lin, G., Tseng, K., Schueller, E., Kapoor, G., Laxminarayan, R.: COVID-19 for India updates. Economics, and Policy and Johns Hopkins University, USA, Center for Disease Dynamics (2020)
21. Knake-Langhorst, S., Linder, C., Mazzega, J.: Gaia-x 4 ki: Daten-und dienste-ökosystem für ki-orientierte forschung & entwicklung. ACIMobility Summit, pp. 1–10 (2021)
22. Law, A.M.: Simulation Modeling and Analysis, 5th edn. McGraw-Hill Education, New York (2013)
23. Law, A.M., Kelton, W.D., Kelton, W.D.: Simulation Modeling and Analysis, vol. 3. Mcgraw-hill, New York (2007)
24. Lee, B.Y., et al.: A computer simulation of vaccine prioritization, allocation, and rationing during the 2009 H1N1 influenza pandemic. Vaccine **28**(31), 4875–4879 (2010)
25. Lorig, F., Lebherz, D.S., Berndt, J.O., Timm, I.J.: Hypothesis-driven experiment design in computer simulation studies. In: 2017 Winter Simulation Conference (WSC), pp. 1360–1371. IEEE (2017)
26. Lorig, F., Timm, I.J.: Simulation-based data acquisition. In: Arabnia, H.R., Daimi, K., Stahlbock, R., Soviany, C., Heilig, L., Brüssau, K. (eds.) Principles of Data Science. TCSCI, pp. 1–15. Springer, Cham (2020). https://doi.org/10.1007/978-3-030-43981-1_1
27. McBean, G.: Climate change and extreme weather: a basis for action. Nat. Hazards **31**, 177–190 (2004)
28. Memmel, M., Berndt, J.O., Timm, I.: AScore-developing a cockpit for regional pandemic management in Germany with agent-based social simulation. REAL CORP **2021**, 65–75 (2021)

29. Meyer, B.H., Prescott, B., Sheng, X.S.: The impact of the COVID-19 pandemic on business expectations. Int. J. Forecast. **38**(2), 529–544 (2022)
30. Odu, G., Charles-Owaba, O.: Review of multi-criteria optimization methods-theory and applications. IOSR J. Eng. **3**(10), 01–14 (2013)
31. Pettit, T.J., Croxton, K.L., Fiksel, J.: Ensuring supply chain resilience: development and implementation of an assessment tool. J. Bus. Logist. **34**(1), 46–76 (2013)
32. Phillips-Wren, G., Adya, M.: Decision making under stress: the role of information overload, time pressure, complexity, and uncertainty. J. Decis. Syst. **29**(sup1), 213–225 (2020)
33. Sanchez, S.M., Sánchez, P.J.: Better big data via data farming experiments. In: Tolk, A., Fowler, J., Shao, G., Yücesan, E. (eds.) Advances in Modeling and Simulation. SFMA, pp. 159–179. Springer, Cham (2017). https://doi.org/10.1007/978-3-319-64182-9_9
34. Schewerda, A., Kurchyna, V., Berndt, J.O., Timm, I.J.: From research to crisis management: multiagent simulation for local governments. In: Dignum, F., Mathieu, P., Corchado, J.M., De La Prieta, F. (eds.) Advances in Practical Applications of Agents, Multi-Agent Systems, and Complex Systems Simulation. The PAAMS Collection. LNCS, pp. 507–513. Springer, Cham (2022). https://doi.org/10.1007/978-3-031-18192-4_45
35. Tapp, L., Kurchyna, V., Nogatz, F., Berndt, J.O., Timm, I.J.: School's out? Simulating schooling strategies during COVID-19. In: International Workshop on Multi-Agent Systems and Agent-Based Simulation, pp. 95–106. Springer, Cham (2022)
36. Timm, I.J., Berndt, J.O.: Kognitive sozialsimulation für das covid-19-krisenmanagement-social simulation for analysis of infectious disease control (sosad). Technical report Technical report, Deutsches Forschungszentrum für Künstliche Intelligenz (DFKI) (2020)
37. Van Heeswijk, W.J., Mes, M.R., Schutten, J., Zijm, W.: Evaluating urban logistics schemes using agent-based simulation. Transp. Sci. **54**(3), 651–675 (2020)
38. Wan, Z., Su, Y., Li, Z., Zhang, X., Zhang, Q., Chen, J.: Analysis of the impact of Suez canal blockage on the global shipping network. Ocean Coast. Manag. **245**, 106868 (2023)

ARMS: Activity-Resource Modelling Simulator

Angelo Di Iorio, Marco Ferrati(✉), and Davide Rossi

Department of Computer Science and Engineering, University of Bologna, Bologna, Italy
{angelo.diiorio,marco.ferrati2,daviderossi}@unibo.it

Abstract. Activity-based process modeling languages, such as Business Process Model and Notation (BPMN), face challenges in accurately representing manufacturing processes, limiting their effectiveness for simulation purposes. In contrast, specialized manufacturing process simulation tools typically adopt a resource-based approach which, while effective in certain aspects, often lacks robust process modeling capabilities and requires custom coding to define detailed system behaviors. Although prior research has explored extending BPMN to better support manufacturing scenarios, there is still a lack of tools that integrate both activity-centric and resource-centric approaches for comprehensive modeling and simulation.

In this work, we address this gap by proposing a novel metamodel that extends BPMN with enhanced resource capabilities. We present a process modeler that allows users to design manufacturing processes and a corresponding simulator that uses these models to generate insightful information about the process performance through simulation. The solution proposed is then validated using both made-up and real-world manufacturing scenarios.

Keywords: Manufacturing · simulation · modeling · BPMN

1 Introduction

Most available simulation proposals in the manufacturing domain, including academic prototypes and commercial products, are based on the resource-centric approach (such as FlexSim®, AnyLogic®, Arena®, Warteschlangensimulator [8]). The underlying engine for all these products uses a Discrete Event Simulation (DES) approach [6,7], where the production floor is modeled as a queuing system. In these systems, each *executor* is represented by an event queue, and routes are used to link executors, carrying parts or products. These solutions have proven capable of creating sophisticated, detailed simulations that accurately describe the dynamic evolution of the production processes. However, their use requires specific skills: they adopt non-standard modeling notations, often comprising a visual representation enriched with ad-hoc code (written in

A. A. Juan et al. (Eds.): SIMUtools 2024, LNICST 603, pp. 167–185, 2025.
https://doi.org/10.1007/978-3-031-87345-4_12

a variety of general-purpose or domain-specific languages) to describe the production process in sufficient detail. In this context, by code we do not mean simple expressions, which are almost unavoidable when modeling the behavior of a complex system (e.g., those used to implement branching decisions), but rather algorithms that influence the overall semantics of the process. Although the use of this kind of code is usually presented as reserved for intricate scenarios, it often becomes necessary to represent the complexity of most real-world manufacturing processes, which hampers the adoption of these tools by users with limited programming proficiency.

Past research has attempted to address this problem by proposing modeling solutions capable of capturing the structure of processes, even highly complex ones, without relying on coding. Most of these proposals adopt BPMN (Business Process Model and Notation) [12], the de facto standard for modeling, enacting, and simulating business processes, as a starting point, enriching it with elements suited to the specific requirements of the manufacturing domain. The core element of a BPMN model is the action, an atomic unit of work that must be executed for the process to progress. This marks a fundamental distinction from the resource-centric approaches previously discussed. To highlight this difference, we refer to the BPMN approach as an activity-centric one.

The adoption of BPMN is justified by its ability to describe complex processes without the need to resort to coding, as demonstrated by the variety of workflow patterns it supports [15]. The designers of BPMN also sought to define a language in which nearly all semantically relevant elements have a notational counterpart, ensuring that the overall semantics of the model are clearly represented in a corresponding diagram. However, this does not imply that BPMN is "superior" to other approaches; its ability to express rich semantics "just by the diagram" is due to its limited support for concerns outside the control-flow perspective [9]. As a result, the use of BPMN for modeling production processes is hindered by its limited capacity to model resources and the relationships between resources and activities.

More specifically, BPMN's metamodel includes *Resource* and *ResourceRole* classes, but their specification is deliberately vague (e.g., "[...] can be Human Resources as well as any other resource assigned to Activities during Process execution time" [12]). Resources can be associated with processes and activities, but the only semantically defined relationship between an activity and a resource role is the one in which the resource role appears as a *Performer*, i.e., the executor to which the activity is assigned.

The aim of our work is to enable analysts to create simulation models of manufacturing processes that capture as much semantics as possible from their graphical representation and from the element's properties (all of which can be edited in a modeling tool), eliminating the necessity to resort to coding for most real-world processes.

With this objective in mind, this paper presents the development of a simulator and a modeler that allow the simulation of manufacturing scenarios, modeled using a mix of activity-based and resource-based approaches, and simulated with a discrete event simulator capable of parsing those models.

The contributions of this paper are:

- an extension of BPMN able to capture most manufacturing processes with a simple and coherent notation;
- a modeler capable of modeling processes that relates activities with resource related concepts;
- a simulator which accepts the model produced by the modeler and simulate it providing insightful data regarding the process described by the model.

The rest of the paper is structured as follows. Section 2 reviews the related works, providing an overview of existing research on BPMN extension and resource-based simulation approaches in manufacturing. In Sect. 3, we describe our methodology, outlining the proposed metamodel, and the development of the process modeler and the simulator. Section 4 presents the evaluation, where we assess the effectiveness of our approach through a real world case study. Finally, Sect. 5 discusses the conclusions and future works, summarizing our results and highlighting potential directions for further research and development.

2 Related Works

The field of process modeling and simulation is vast and well-established. Various activity-centric process modelling languages and techniques are available and used in practice [19], both BPMN-based and non-BPMN-based. Notable examples based on BPMN include Scylla and BPSim. Scylla, based on the work of Pufahl, Wong, and Weske, is an extensible BPMN process simulator that supports the simulation of complex scenarios with a plugin-based architecture [14]. We considered adopting Scylla, but we realized that the plugins we needed to develop would have been too convoluted, resulting in a very complex architecture. BPSim [20], on the other hand, is a WfMC (Workflow Management Coalition) standard that integrates with BPMN to define scenarios and simulation parameters. However, it lacks the capability to model rich resource relationships, which are commonly needed in manufacturing scenarios. In manufacturing process modeling and simulation, BPMN has been employed in several studies, with extensions made to better capture the nuances of manufacturing workflows [3,5,13,21]. Despite the endeavour, they concentrate only on few aspects of the manufacturing process. Various non-BPMN-based alternatives have been considered as well. For instance, [4] compares six notations (flowchart, Petri net, DFD, Role activity diagram, BPMN, and Business use case) concluding that only Petri nets and BPMN are suited for simulation. DPMN [17] attempts to integrate BPMN with Discrete Event Simulation (DES) and in [18] the work is extended to considering resource-constrained activities. Although it focuses on the direction of mixing activity-centric with resource-centric modeling it lacks some relevant features of a manufacturing environment such as many-to-many relationships between activities and performers and the possibility to specify how products transforms during the process. As an alternative to activity-centric modeling, discrete event simulation (DES) has been often proposed for simulating manufacturing processes [1,2,10,11]. Although DES provides robust simulation capabilities, modeling manufacturing processes using this method can be challenging, as it typically requires specialized skills, such as learning a non-standard notation or relying on programming to model more complex scenarios.

The novelty of our proposal lies in its integration of a resource-centric approach within an activity-centric metamodel, effectively representing individual executors and their compatibility with specific activities. Furthermore, the metamodel accounts for product transformations throughout the process, as well as the executors' accessory requirements. Our solution provides users with both a modeler and a simulator, enabling the modeling of complex resource allocation and transformation using a BPMN extension. This approach eliminates the need for ad-hoc coding and significantly reduces the skill requirements compared to traditional resource-centric simulators.

3 Methodology

Our approach consists in complementing an existing activity-based approach which primarily addresses the control-flow perspective, namely BPMN, with additional concepts meant to capture a resource perspective able to describe elements that are pertinent to the simulation of manufacturing processes. Given our aim of conducting simulations, we designed a metamodel that allows users to express detailed information necessary for such analysis. To achieve these objectives, we have developed two complementary software components: a modeler and a simulation engine. As illustrated in Fig. 1, users interact with these components to model and simulate processes. The modeler enables users to define the process, including properties necessary for simulation. Once the process is modeled, users can generate a file that represents the designed process, which serves as input to the simulation engine. The simulator processes this input and executes the simulation. Upon completion, users can review the simulation results and derive insights from the collected data. For example they could identify bottlenecks or visualize heat-maps on the model representation.

3.1 Metamodel

The metamodel was designed from two interwoven activities: literature analysis and domain expert elicitation. Specifically, we interacted with two domain experts from a consulting firm with interviews and with sessions of participatory design [16] in which we co-modeled scenarios they proposed with BMPN, annotating all relevant concepts not addressed by the notation.

The metamodel described in this section, illustrated in Fig. 2, comprises two categories of elements: structural and dynamic, represented in the diagram with distinct colors. Structural elements (depicted in blue) define the process' elements and parameters, whereas dynamic elements (depicted in green) are runtime entities that are instantiated and altered during the simulation.

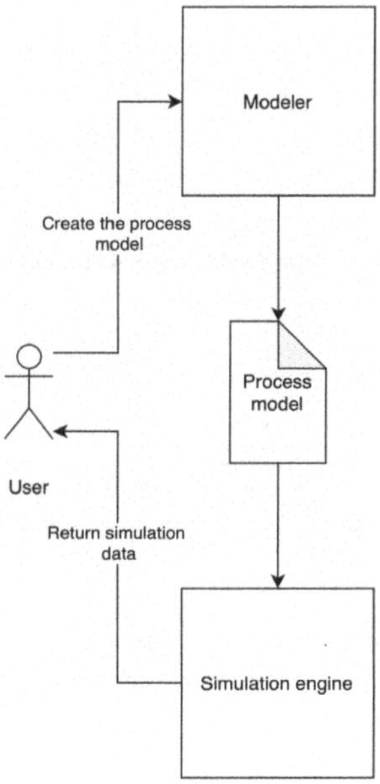

Fig. 1. System-User interaction workflow

The primary concepts are: *Activity*, *Executor*, *Product*, and *Accessory*. *Activity* represents a task within a manufacturing process; it serves as a natural starting point given the activity-centric approach we embraced. In the BPMN metamodel it can be aligned with the corresponding *Activity* entity. Activities can be grouped together and executed under some conditions (for instance, using a washing machine that can wash 15 items at the same time). Prioritization strategies are also necessary since different activities might be competing for using the same resources. The attribute *priority* was indeed introduced to address this last issues.

The *Executor* entity represents any kind of resource engaged in performing an activity. They can represent humans or production machines. *Executors* are characterized by the attribute *quantity* which specifies their number of available executors with the same characteristics. When adopting the metamodel with BPMN this entity, as explained in Sect. 1, can be aligned with *Performer*.

A *Product* is any object that undergoes processing and transformation during the manufacturing process, representing a single item moving throughout the production floor. Its life-cycle will be managed by the simulator. It is a dynamic entity of the metamodel. Therefore, it is expected to be created during the simulation.

To enable users to model the different types of products present in the manufacturing process, we introduced the *ProductFamily* entity.

Accessory represents a resource that might be necessary for an executor to effectively execute a task. These are passive elements that contribute to the pro-

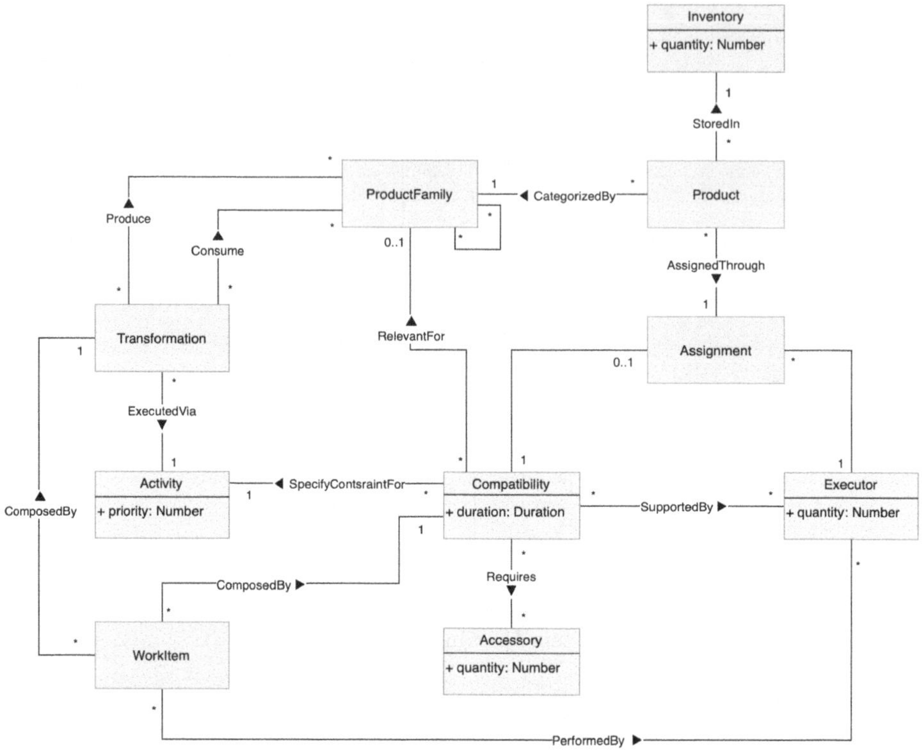

Fig. 2. Metamodel diagram

cess. The *quantity* attribute captures scenarios where there's a limited number of these resources available to executors. For example, consider a worker tasked with "Digging a hole" who requires an auxiliary resource: a shovel. The shovel is an accessory and there could be only two shovels for three workers.

A *WorkItem* is another dynamic element and it is generated upon the activation of a task, with one or more potential *Executors* identified based on compatibility criteria to carry it out. When specific *Executors* are assigned to these *WorkItems*, an *Assignment* instance is created. This assignment process can follow various policies, and it represents a well-known optimization problem. The simplest approach is an eager policy, where unassigned executors continuously search for available compatible *WorkItems*, claim them for execution, and mark them as unavailable to other compatible executors.

Finally, *Inventory* represents the quantity of available products from which an activity can draw upon. It can also model all those situations where products are stocked somewhere during the production process.

After the definition of the fundamental entities let us discuss the associations between these.

Compatibility relates *Activity*, *ProductFamily*, and *Executor*. It is very common, in fact, that a given product can only be produced by a given machine. Similarly, some operators are specialized for executing some tasks. *Compatibility* allows users to describe which executor can work on which kind of product in an activity. Moreover, it carries the information about how long the executor takes to perform the activity. Very often, in fact, the same task can be executed by different executors, but each of them takes a different time to complete that task. For instance, a modern machine could be more efficient than an older one, or their performance can be affected by external factors.

From the perspective of an activity, *Compatibility* can be thought of as a matrix. For example, Tables 1a and 1b show an example of two compatibility matrices for activities "3D-printing handle" and "3D-printing box". Each activity has columns representing the potential executors that can be assigned to that activity: Printer1 (P1), Printer2 (P2), and Printer3 (P3) for "3D-printing handle" and Printer1 (P1), Printer4 (P4), and Printer5 (P5) for "3D-printing box". In the rows we have the products that will be worked on that activities: "PLA" and "ABS". The intersection indicates which executor can work on which product for the activity: in "3D-printing handle", "PLA" can be worked by P1 and P2, and "ABS" can be worked by P2 and P3. In "3D-printing box", "PLA" can be worked by P1 and P5, while "ABS" can be worked by P1 and P4.

Table 1. Compatibility matrices

	P1	P2	P3
PLA	•	•	
ABS		•	•

(a) Compatibility matrix for activity "3D-printing handle"

	P1	P4	P5
PLA	•		•
ABS	•	•	

(b) Compatibility matrix for activity "3D-printing box"

Note also that a given activity might be performed by an executor by using one or more resources together—for instance, an operator using a washing machine and some detergents—or by different executors that work together—an assembly line with multiple operators. The association between *Compatibility* and *Accessory* captures these relations and their cardinality.

Assignment represents the history of assignments, detailing which activities and specific products each executor has worked on. For example, take the scenario described in Table 1a, the simulator can decide to assign the executor P1 to work on a product belonging to the PLA family for the activity "3D-printing handle". This decision is allowed because the compatibility between activity, executor, and product family is defined through the Compatibility entity.

It is quite common that the same executor is selected to perform different activities on the same resource in order to increase efficiency. Consider for instance some quality check activities on some products being produced: it would be better if an executor checks the same product. This is only possible when tracing the associations between activities, products and executors.

To explain how products are transformed during the process, there are two associations. There is a self-association in *ProductFamily*, and an association class (*Transformation*) between *Activity* and *ProductFamily*. The self-association in *ProductFamily* allows us to describe from which products a product comes and into which products it can transform. In addition, the auxiliary entity *Transformation* indicates in which activity a product undergoes a transformation. Since many transformations can be possible in an activity, we used many-to-many cardinality on *Consume*/*Produce*. Moreover, this entity allows us to model a batch activity. Through the *Consume* and *Produce* relationships we can model scenarios where to perform an activity we have to wait for a certain number of items to be ready.

Finally, the association *Inventory-Product* serves to designate the specific inventory where a particular product can be located and accessed. This association is between *Inventory* and *Product*, and not between *Inventory* and *ProductFamily* because we want to keep track of the specific products inside the inventory and not only the family of these products.

3.2 Model Editing

Ideally, extending BPMN with the metamodel we just discussed also entails determining notational symbols for each element of our metamodel, in line with the principle of capturing "as much semantics as possible from the diagram," which characterizes BPMN. However, this would have resulted in very convoluted diagrams, severely hampering readability and understandability. To address this, we adopted a pragmatic approach, opting to represent *Executors* notationally (using hexagon shapes), to partially depict the *Compatibility* relationship using dashed lines connecting executors and activities, and the *Inventory* entities as data storage. All other elements and relationships are rendered with specific input widget forms, tailored to each element.

3.3 Tool

Modeller The modeler is designed to extend standard BPMN to include the resource elements described before. This extension enables users to capture resource interaction within business process diagrams, ensuring that both process and their associated resources are represented. The modeler[1], shown in Fig. 3, has been implemented as a web application using two core technologies: React[2] and BPMN-js[3]. By leveraging BPMN-js, which provides a modeler for standard

[1] https://github.com/jjocram/ARMS-Editor.
[2] https://react.dev.
[3] https://bpmn.io/toolkit/bpmn-js/.

BPMN, we were able to focus on extending its capabilities to support the aforementioned resource modeling features. Specifically, our solution implements the following features:

- a BPMN extension that incorporates new elements such as: executors, new connections, inventories, compatibilities and transformations;
- a rendering mechanism to display executors and the connection between executors and activities;
- a linter enforcing validation rules for the new elements. For instance, the modeler shows errors when an executor or activity is not properly connected to other elements or when they are missing information necessary for the simulation;
- specific widgets to specify compatibilities between executors, activities, and product properties, as well as transformations from one product to another, prioritization of activities, assignment of accessories to executors, and requests for specific products amount to be produced.

The modeler allows users to download a `.bpmn` file that represents the process they want to simulate. This file follows the standard BPMN format but includes additional elements. Specifically, within the `<bpmn:extensionElements>` tag, four new elements are introduced:

- *Compatibility*: represents a compatibility between an activity and an executor. It specifies the product properties and the duration;
- *Transformation*: it is associated with an activity and specified the product properties is applies to, the updated product properties after the activity completion, the required input products and the resulting output products;
- *ProductRequest*: represent which products we want to produce during the process;
- *Accessory*: represents which and how many accessories are available in the process.

Moreover, *Executor* elements has been added to the list of elements among *Task*, *Gateway*, and *Connection*.

The following example represents the transformation in an assembling activity. Three components ("Frontal frame A", "Right stem A", and "Left stem A") from three inventories are taken as input and consumed to produce an "Assembled frame A". The quantity attribute in the *TransformationInputs* represents how many items are necessary. Figure 4 represents the widget to model this transformation.

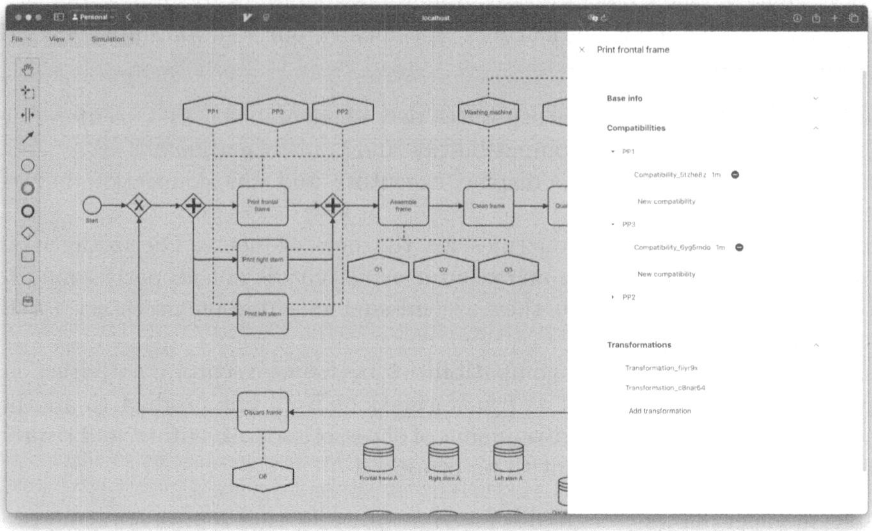

Fig. 3. Screenshot of the modeler

```
<factory:transformation id="Transformation_26c94ww" activityId="
    Activity_143dkap">
  <factory:transformationProductProperty
    key="type"
    value="A" />
  <factory:transformationInput
    id="Inventory_0wqk0gz"
    quantity="1" />
  <factory:transformationInput
    id="Inventory_0cd51gu"
    quantity="1" />
  <factory:transformationInput
    id="Inventory_0e3a21a"
    quantity="1" />
</factory:transformation>
```

Regarding how compatibilities are saved, each of them represent a connection between an activity and an executor. Moreover, they specify which product's properties are required and which accessories are needed. The compatibility matrices showed in Table 1a is represented as follow:

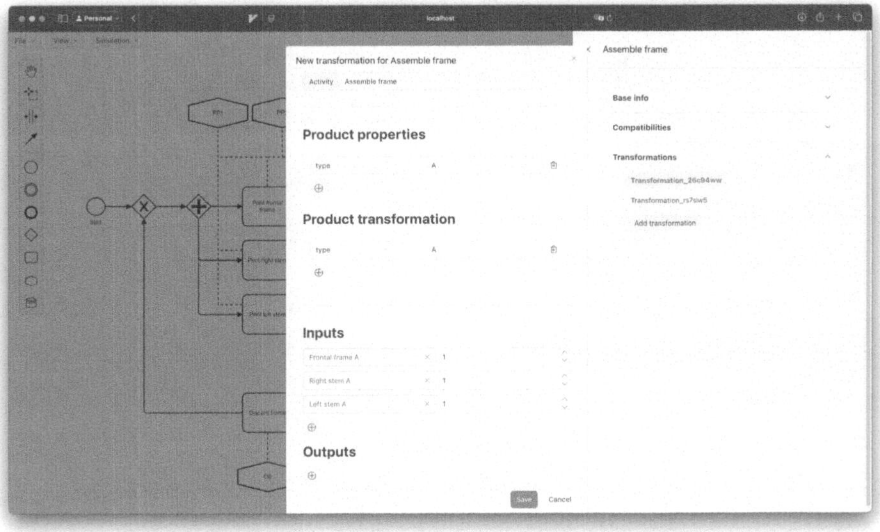

Fig. 4. Widget for modeling transformations.

```
<factory:compatibility id="Compatibility_50lyth8" time="1"
    timeUnit="m" idActivity="3D-printing handle" idExecutor="P1">
    <factory:productProperties key="type" value="PLA"/>
</factory:compatibility>

<factory:compatibility id="Compatibility_50lytr7" time="1"
    timeUnit="m" idActivity="3D-printing handle" idExecutor="P2">
    <factory:productProperties key="type" value="PLA"/>
</factory:compatibility>

<factory:compatibility id="Compatibility_50lyt5h" time="1"
    timeUnit="m" idActivity="3D-printing handle" idExecutor="P2">
    <factory:productProperties key="type" value="ABS"/>
</factory:compatibility>

<factory:compatibility id="Compatibility_50lye9h" time="1"
    timeUnit="m" idActivity="3D-printing handle" idExecutor="P3">
    <factory:productProperties key="type" value="ABS"/>
</factory:compatibility>
```

Figure 5 shows the widget to model the first compatibility.

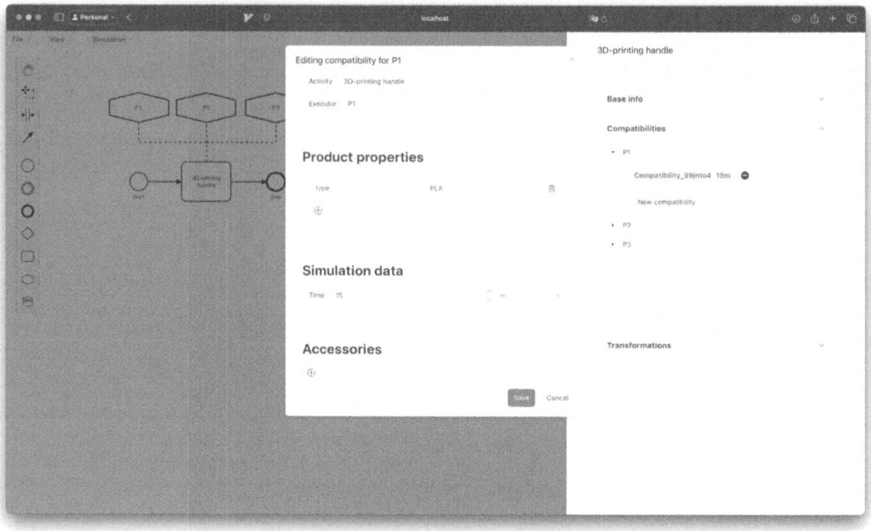

Fig. 5. Widget for modeling compatibilities.

Simulation Engine The simulation engine[4] is a discrete-event simulator built on top of Kalasim[5]. It operates based on a Petri net-inspired formalism, incorporating places and transitions. In this implementation, places hold a list of *ControlTokens*, which are moved by transitions when specific conditions are met. Each BPMN element is implemented as a class, using places and transitions to match its execution semantics. Alongside *ControlTokens*, additional places store *ProductTokens* which represent the products undergoing processing. These tokens enable tracking of product modifications throughout the process, allowing compatibility checks based on product properties rather than type alone. Furthermore, *Accessories* are also implemented as places, with the number of tokens corresponding to the quantities specified in the model. This structure supports flexible and accurate representation of dynamic processes and product variations within the simulation environment.

There are a couple of other entities which facilitate accurate representation of the model:

- *Compatibility*: this entity, embedded within an *Activity*, references an *Executor* and specifies product properties to guide selection. It also includes a list of required accessories and the task duration;
- *Transformation*: representing the *Transformation* entity in the metamodel diagram, this entity contains information on how to apply a transformation

[4] https://github.com/jjocram/ARMS-Simulation-Engine.
[5] https://www.kalasim.org.

to a *ProductToken*, as well as the required input resources and the resulting outputs allowing to model the batch size.

The simulation begins at the BPMN *StartEvent*, where the initial number of *ControlTokens* and *ProductTokens* is generated according to the *ProductRequests*. Each token is then distributed to the subsequent elements in the process. Independently, each element checks if its transition conditions are met. If so, it executes its specific logic and this cycle is repeated until all tokens reach an *EndEvent*.

Activities and executors operate with additional logic. Each activity maintains a list of compatibilities, defining which executors can process a product based on its properties. When *ControlToken* and *ProductToken* arrive at an activity, the appropriate executor is selected, and a new *WorkItem* is added to that executor's queue. A *WorkItem* represents a specific task that an executor must complete. It includes details such as the required duration, the necessary accessories, and the depletable resources needed for execution. Additionally, it specifies which resources will be produced as a result of completing the task.

Each *Executor* monitors its queue for pending work items. Upon detecting a work item, the executor retrieves the necessary tokens from the accessory places, consumes the tokens specified in the transformation's input, advances the simulation time according to the work item's duration, generates tokens for the transformation's output, and finally moves both the *ControlToken* and *ProductToken* forward in the process.

The simulation ends when no further events remain in the simulation queue, indicating that all *ControlTokens* have reached an *EndEvent*. At this stage, the simulator saves a set of simulation data, including resource utilization levels over time, resource statistics, and component utilization metrics. This data, automatically collected by Kalasim, can then be further analyzed to draw insights and conclusions about the simulated process. For example they could be used to identify bottlenecks or to plot a heat-map on top of the model representation.

4 Evaluation

To evaluate our solution, we asked for help from the domain experts to combine real-world scenarios and create a unique and more complex one. The result is a process which describes how frames for eyeglasses are produced in a manufacturing environment.

We then built a model for this scenario with our modeler, downloaded and given as input to the simulator. The scenario can be summarized as follows:

> Two types of frames for eyeglasses are manufactured on a production line. The goal is to produce 100 frames of type A and 100 frames of type B. Each frame consists of two stems (left and right) and the frontal lens mount. These components are printed on a press printer. There are three press printers in the production area (PP1, PP2, PP3). Type A stems can only be printed on PP1, while type B stems can be printed on PP1 and

PP2. The frontal frame for both types A and B can be printed with any of the three printers. Each press printer takes 1 minute to print a piece and requires the corresponding mould, with only one mould available for each piece. This means that two printers cannot print the same item at the same time. The three printers have a start-up time of 10 minutes, and it is preferable to use a printer that is already running. In addition, the printing of frontal frames has a higher priority because it is a more complex activity. An operator manually assembles the final frame. There are three operators (O1, O2, and O3) who can assemble the frames. O1 takes 1 minute, while O2 and O3 each take 2 minutes each.
Once assembled, the frames are placed in a tumbler, of which there is only one in the production area. The frames are processed in the machine for 24 hours and the machine has a capacity of 15 frames at a time.
A quality check is carried out by two operators (O4, and O5) on one item out of every 20 frames and it takes 2 minutes. If a frame is found to have some defects, it is discarded and has to be reprinted. The frames are then stored in a warehouse, waiting for the next activity.
Every Monday, a lorry arrives at the production site to collect all the frames that are ready for painting. The painting process is done off-site and takes 2 days. Once the frames are back on the production floor, they undergo another round of cleaning, and a final quality check.

Figure 6 represents the process as modeled in the modeler. Keep in mind that not every entity will be showed in the diagram. Some of them are detailed with specific widgets in the modeler when the related diagram elements are selected (as shown in Fig. 4 and Fig. 5).

After the modeling phase, we gave the model file as input to the simulation engine which performed the simulation and returned insightful data about the process. For example, we were interested in analyzing the time required to produce the final glass products. To obtain these results, we recorded the accumulation of *ProductTokens* in the end place over time. An example of the diagram showing the growth levels of the two final products is plotted in Fig. 7.

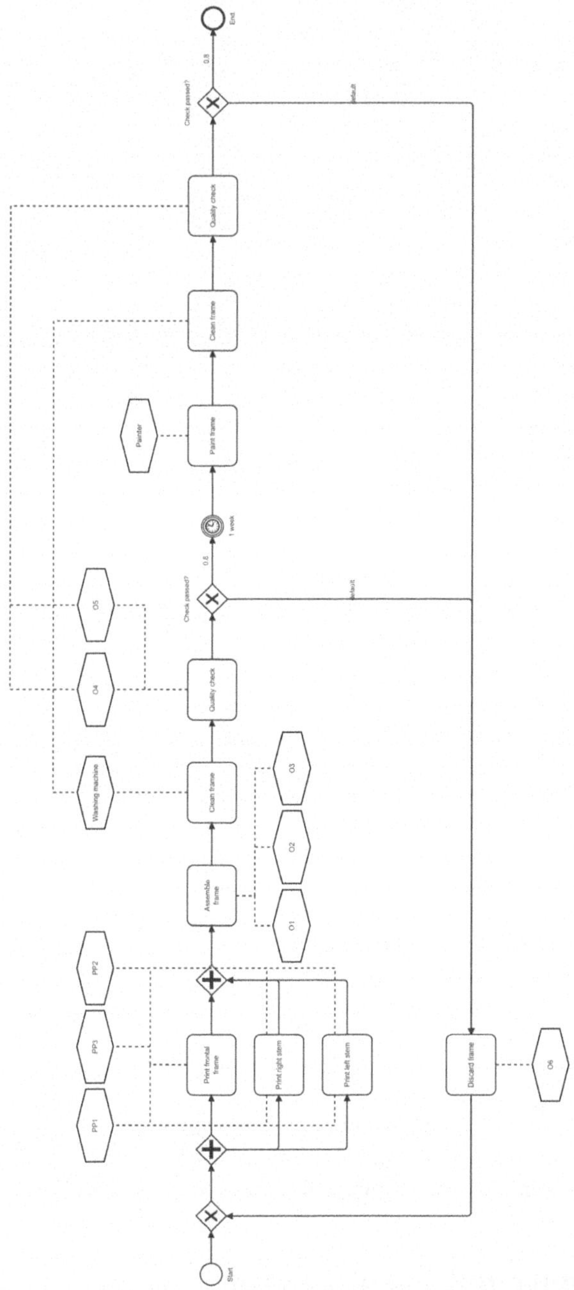

Fig. 6. Diagram representing the scenario's activities, resources, and how they are interconnected.

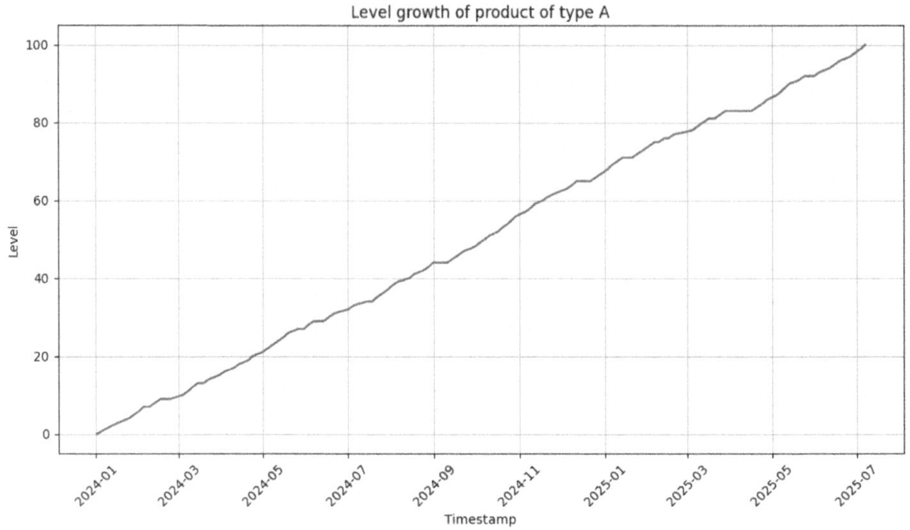

(a) Level growth of type A.

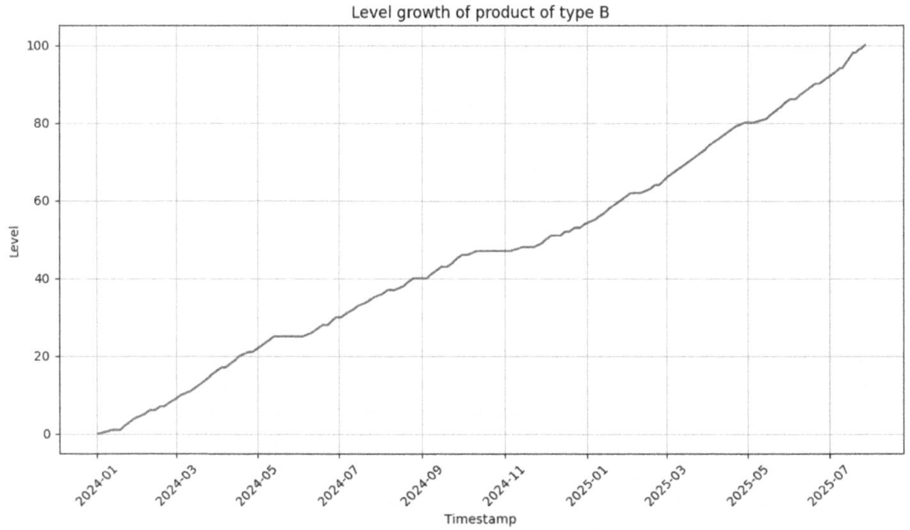

(b) Level growth of type B.

Fig. 7. Level growth of glasses of type A and B.

5 Conclusions and Future Works

The overall goal of our work is to empower individuals with limited programming skills to design manufacturing process models that can be directly translated into simulation data and used within simulation tools.

Toward this goal, we presented three interlinked components: (i) a BPMN extension to visually edit models representing manufacturing processes, (ii) a graphical modeling tool that integrates it seamlessly and export simulation data and (iii) a simulator capable of processing these data straightforwardly.

We propose to enhance BPMN diagrams with elements derived from a resource-centric approach and simulation data. Such an approach proved to facilitate the simulation analysis of even complex manufacturing processes, limiting the complexity for the final users.

It is worth highlighting the main threats to validity of our work at this stage.

First of all, the metamodel is built on top of a subset of BPMN that, for instance, does not include sub-processes, groups, and pools. This can result in issues with the modeling of large processes. We are actively working to support the full specification and we are confident that this will be possible with no major reconsideration of the current design choices.

The current validation is also limited. It is true that we built the metamodel in collaboration with domain experts and we verified it on real cases, thus ensuring that common issues are addressed and common manufacturing processes are captured but we have only performed limited simulations and we need to test the overall system on a larger scale.

Related to this point, we still have to assess the generalizability of our approach. It might be more difficult to apply it where a higher degree of detail is required, for instance to control the production floor and the interaction between machines and users. Some manufacturing processes could not satisfactorily be addressed by our approach but we expect these cases to be quite limited.

Some more work is also needed on the implementation side. First of all we are building an integrated environment, where users can run the simulation directly within the modeler. More importantly, we plan to include reporting functionalities that show the results of the simulation directly in the original diagram, for instance through heat-maps that would allow users to easily identify bottlenecks and wastes. The inclusion in the metamodel of further BPMN elements, as mentioned above, will also require us to include these in the visual modeler and possibly add panels to configure these elements and their properties.

A further improvement might also be to extend the visual modeler to control simulation parameters. This is actually not trivial, not because of implementation difficulties, but because of the risks of burdening the users' interaction and to overload the metamodel. There is also a technical counterpart to this issue: which is the best place and format to store simulation data? BPMN is well integrated with BPMSim, a standard expressly designed to include simulation parameters in BPMN, thus a very good candidate to be integrated in our system. But BPSim does not fully supports our extension so we would have to extend it as well. Again, it is a trade-off that needs a deeper analysis that we have only started at this stage.

Last but not least, we plan to explore how to support the definition of decision strategies. In the current implementation, some basic policies are hard-coded in BPMN gateways and users have no capabilities for configuring them. We plan to let users define guards based on a simple expression language or to use a set of predefined policies and predicates, but this solution requires further investigation.

Acknowledgments. We would like to express our gratitude to the NextGenerationEU for its co-funding, which made this research possible. We also extend our thanks to Bonfiglioli Consulting, an additional co-founder, for their support and collaboration. Special appreciation goes to Prof. Dr. Mathias Weske for his constructive ideas and insightful feedback throughout the metamodel definition process. Additionally, we acknowledge Roberto Mitugno for his contributions to the modeler software.

References

1. Agalianos, K., Ponis, S.T., Aretoulaki, E., Plakas, G., Efthymiou, O.: Discrete event simulation and digital twins: review and challenges for logistics. Procedia Manufact. **51**, 1636–1641 (2020). https://doi.org/10.1016/j.promfg.2020.10.228. https://www.sciencedirect.com/science/article/pii/S2351978920320990
2. Babulak, E., Wang, M.: Discrete event simulation: state of the art. Aitor Goti (Hg.): Discrete Event Simulations. Rijeka, Kroatien: Sciyo, pp. 1–9 (2010)
3. Bocciarelli, P., D'Ambrogio, A., Giglio, A., Paglia, E.: A BPMN extension for modeling cyber-physical-production-systems in the context of industry 4.0. In: Fortino, G., et al. (eds.) 14th IEEE International Conference on Networking, Sensing and Control, ICNSC 2017, Calabria, Italy, 16–18 May 2017, pp. 599–604. IEEE (2017). https://doi.org/10.1109/ICNSC.2017.8000159
4. Choudhary, R., Riaz, N.: A business process re-engineering approach to transform business process simulation to BPMN model. PLoS ONE **18**(3), 1–25 (2023). https://doi.org/10.1371/journal.pone.0277217
5. Erasmus, J., Vanderfeesten, I.T.P., Traganos, K., Grefen, P.: Using business process models for the specification of manufacturing operations. Comput. Ind. **123**, 103297 (2020). https://doi.org/10.1016/J.COMPIND.2020.103297
6. Fishman, G.S.: Discrete-event simulation: modeling, programming, and analysis, vol. 537. Springer (2001)
7. Goldsman, D., Goldsman, P.: Discrete-event simulation. In: Modeling and Simulation in the Systems Engineering Life Cycle: Core Concepts and Accompanying Lectures, pp. 103–109. Springer (2015)
8. Herzog, A.: Simulation mit dem warteschlangensimulator. Angenommen zur Veröffentlichung (2021)
9. Jablonski, S., Bussler, C.: Workflow management - modeling concepts, architecture and implementation. International Thomson (1996)
10. Mourtzis, D.: Simulation in the design and operation of manufacturing systems: state of the art and new trends. Int. J. Prod. Res. **58**(7), 1927–1949 (2020). https://doi.org/10.1080/00207543.2019.1636321
11. Mourtzis, D., Doukas, M., Bernidaki, D.: Simulation in manufacturing: review and challenges. Procedia Cirp **25**, 213–229 (2014)
12. OMG: Business process model and notation (BPMN) (2011)
13. Pufahl, L., Weske, M.: Batch activities in process modeling and execution. In: Basu, S., Pautasso, C., Zhang, L., Fu, X. (eds.) ICSOC 2013. LNCS, vol. 8274, pp. 283–297. Springer, Heidelberg (2013). https://doi.org/10.1007/978-3-642-45005-1_20

14. Pufahl, L., Wong, T.Y., Weske, M.: Design of an extensible BPMN process simulator. In: Teniente, E., Weidlich, M. (eds.) BPM 2017. LNBIP, vol. 308, pp. 782–795. Springer, Cham (2018). https://doi.org/10.1007/978-3-319-74030-0_62
15. Russell, N., van der Aalst, W., ter Hofstede, A., Edmond, D.: Workflow resource patterns: identification, representation and tool support. In: Pastor, O., Falcão e Cunha, J. (eds.) CAiSE 2005. LNCS, vol. 3520, pp. 216–232. Springer, Heidelberg (2005). https://doi.org/10.1007/11431855_16
16. Spinuzzi, C.: The methodology of participatory design. Tech. Commun. **52**(2), 163–174 (2005). https://www.ingentaconnect.com/content/stc/tc/2005/00000052/00000002/art00005
17. Wagner, G.: Information and process modeling for simulation-part i. J. Simul. Eng. **1**, 1 (2018)
18. Wagner, G.: Business process modeling and simulation with DPMN: resource-constrained activities. In: 2020 Winter Simulation Conference (WSC), pp. 45–59 (2020). https://doi.org/10.1109/WSC48552.2020.9383915
19. Weske, M.: Business Process Management - Concepts, Languages, Architectures. Third Edition. Springer (2019). https://doi.org/10.1007/978-3-662-59432-2
20. WfMC: Bpsim (2016)
21. Zor, S., Schumm, D., Leymann, F.: A proposal of BPMN extensions for the manufacturing domain. In: Proceedings of the 44th CIRP International Conference on Manufacturing Systems (2011)

Improvements to the Region-Based Petri Nets Synthesis Algorithm for Process Mining

Shengrui Peng(✉) and Helena Szczerbicka

Leibniz Universität Hannover, Welfengarten 1, 30167 Hannover, Germany
{peng,hsz}@l3s.de

Abstract. This paper tackles the computational hurdles in region-based Petri net (PN) synthesis, focusing on the time-consuming identification of minimal regions essential for accurate model construction. Given the limitations of existing algorithms in handling complex systems, we introduce an improved algorithm that integrates advanced multiset expansion techniques to enhance the generation of minimal regions significantly. This approach accelerates the computation process while maintaining the accuracy and robustness necessary for effective PN construction [5]. We contextualize our contributions by reviewing recent advancements in region-based discovery algorithms, highlighting our algorithm's improved capability to construct k-bounded PN with complex behaviors such as concurrency prevalent in process mining. Comparative analysis and empirical validation show that our algorithm outperforms existing methods in speed and scalability without sacrificing detail in process dynamics representation. This research contributes to both the theoretical framework of PN synthesis and the practical aspects of process mining tool design.

Keywords: Petri nets · Theory of region · Process mining

1 Introduction

Process mining is an interdisciplinary field focused on constructing detailed process models from *event logs* to facilitate in-depth analysis. As modern information systems generate vast data volumes, efficiently constructing process models from these datasets is challenging. Various *discovery algorithms* have been developed to tackle this issue, creating diverse models such as *transition systems* (TS), *Petri nets* (PN), and *Business Process Modeling Notation* [24]. Our study concentrates on *Petri nets* due to their robust mathematical framework and effectiveness in representing complex processes. We are particularly interested in *region-based process discovery algorithms*, known for their capability to model

Supported by Deutsche Forschungsgemeinschaft (DFG).

A. A. Juan et al. (Eds.): SIMUtools 2024, LNICST 603, pp. 186–201, 2025.
https://doi.org/10.1007/978-3-031-87345-4_13

complex behaviors such as concurrency and invisible transitions. However, these algorithms tend to perform poorly with large datasets [1].

One major obstacle in region-based approaches is the time-intensive computation of minimal regions, crucial for constructing PNs [1]. In this work, we introduce an enhanced algorithm for generating minimal regions, combined with a significantly more efficient multiset expansion algorithm. This approach accelerates the computation process while maintaining the accuracy and robustness necessary for effective PN construction. Furthermore, we compare the improved algorithm proposed in this work to the original one proposed in [5,8].

This paper is organized as follows: Sect. 2 presents a comprehensive literature review, setting the context and highlighting previous work in the field. Section 3 introduces essential foundational concepts such as labeled transition systems, Petri nets, and the theory of regions, crucial for understanding the subsequent content. Section 4 details our proposed region-based PN synthesis algorithm, elaborating on its design and functionality. In Sect. 5, we demonstrate the effectiveness of our algorithm through various numerical experiments, providing empirical evidence to support its validity. Finally, Sect. 6 concludes the paper, by summarizing the key findings and their implications in the broader context of process mining and systems modeling.

2 Literature Review

Process mining aims to derive process models, such as PN, from sets of example behaviors. [24] provides a comprehensive introduction to this research area. The primary task in this field is *process discovery*, which constructs models from event logs. Other significant tasks include *data processing* and *conformance checking*. Data processing addresses complex issues in event logs such as noise, incompleteness, and structural problems, with efforts like [15,25] focusing on object-centric event logs. Conformance checking involves evaluating how well an event log and the recorded behaviors align with a process model, either pre-defined or derived from process discovery [9].

The PN approach, originally proposed by [17], is widely used for modeling systems characterized as concurrent, asynchronous, distributed, parallel, nondeterministic, and/or stochastic. An extensive review of the Petri net approach, covering its properties, analysis, and applications, is provided in [16]. The *Petri net synthesis problem*, as described in [13], focuses on generating *elementary Petri nets* from *labeled transition systems* due to their limitations in demonstrating complex process structures such as concurrency. This approach is one of several specifications aiming to synthesize a model of a concurrent system from sequential observations. The foundational solution presented in this work leverages the *theory of regions*, introduced by [14]. An elementary PN represents a successful solution to the synthesis problem when the reachability graph is isomorphic to the given TS. [10] provided another seminal contribution to this field, focusing on the generation of a safe PN (Definition 2) from a labeled TS. Subsequently, [12] introduced a broader class of derivable labeled TS, termed the *excitation-closed transition system*. As the concept of *region* is extended by adopting the multiset notion, the region-based approach is able to generate k-bounded Petri nets [5]. [2] gives a general overview of methods and techniques for solving the *PN synthesis problem*.

The inherent link between *process discovery* and region-based *PN synthesis* is significant [6]. An iterative approach introduced in [27] gradually builds the TS, addressing computational challenges with large datasets. In [23], a two-step approach is presented, starting with the construction of a TS from event logs, followed by deriving PNs using the region-based method. An incremental approach was proposed in [19], which aims to improve the efficiency and scalability of region-based algorithms for deriving Petri nets from transition systems or event logs. However, the region-based approach, especially when extended to generate k-bounded PNs, is noted for its computational intensity [1].

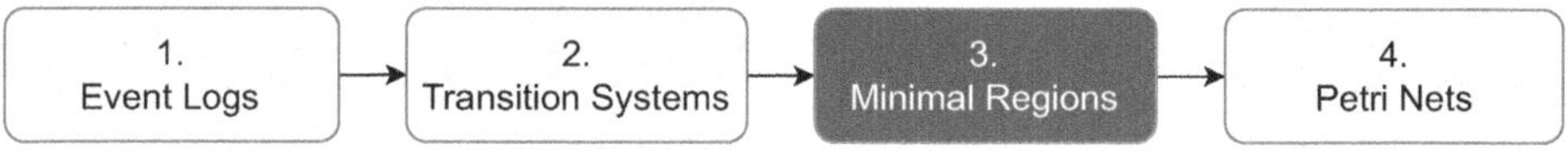

Fig. 1. Working steps of region-based process mining.

In this study, we enhance the region-based process discovery algorithm for deriving k-bounded PN from TS. Unlike approaches in [20,21] that decompose TS to keep PN construction feasible, our work aims to improve computational performance by optimizing the generation of minimal regions, i.e., the third step shown in Fig. 1.

3 Preliminaries

In this section, we explore foundational concepts vital for developing an advanced region-based PN synthesis algorithm for process mining, the main focus of this paper. Each topic is selected to offer a comprehensive theoretical background that enhances understanding of our proposed algorithm.

3.1 Transition System and Petri Nets

Theoretically, unlike finite automata that define a single initial state, TS in process mining, represented as a quadruple, can possess multiple initial states to reflect distinct trace beginnings in event logs. To simplify the scenarios, we consider TS with a single initial state. A labeled TS is defined as follows:

Definition 1 (Labeled Transition System). *A labeled transition system is a quadruple* $\mathsf{TS} = (S, E, F, s_{ini})$*, where* S *is the set of states,* E *is the set of events,* $F : S \times E \times S$ *is the set of labeled flows,* $s_{ini} \in S$ *is the initial state.*

Due to the existence of numerous extensions of PNs, the PNs defined in Definition 2 are often called *elementary Petri nets.* Figure 2 shows the graphical representation of the PN elements.

Definition 2 (Petri net [16]**).** *A Petri net (*PN*) is a 4-tuple* (P, T, W, M_0)*, where* P *is a finite set of places,* T *is a finite set of transitions,* $W \subseteq (P \times T) \cup (T \times P)$ *is the set of weighted flows,* M_0 *is the initial marking. A marking represented by the distribution of tokens in places is a state in PN. The intersection of the set of places and the set of transitions is the empty set, i.e.,* $P \cap T = \emptyset$*.*

Petri nets are called ***safe*** *when each place can hold a maximum of one token. Petri nets are called* ***pure*** *if there is no self-loop in the net.*

Definition 3 (Reachability Graph [16]**).** *Let* $\mathsf{PN} = \{P, T, W, M_0\}$ *be a Petri net, let* C *be the set of reachable states of* PN*, and let* G *be the set of reachable state transitions of* PN*. Then the graph* RG(PN) *is the* ***reachability graph*** *of* PN.

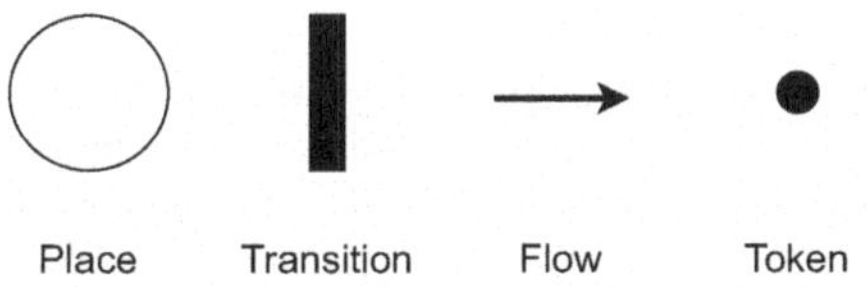

Fig. 2. PN elements

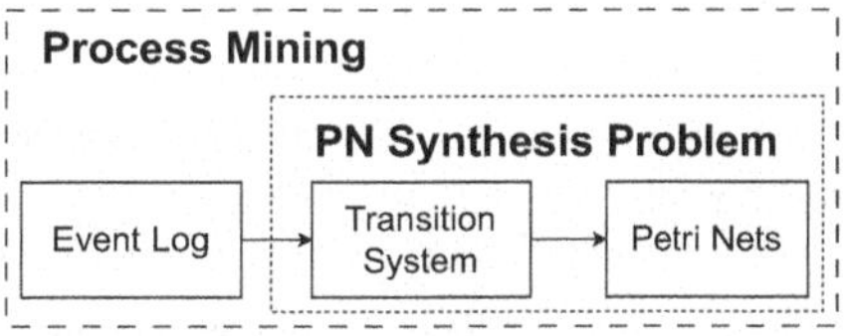

Fig. 3. Relations

3.2 PN Synthesis Problem and Process Mining Problem

Before exploring the essential concepts for constructing a PN from a TS using the *theory of regions*, it is crucial to delineate the distinctions between the *PN synthesis problem* and the *process mining problem.* Though both include the generation of PNs, their motivations and methodologies vary markedly. For a better clarification, we introduce firstly the notion of *language* w.r.t. a transition system and its *overapproximation.* Then, we draw the definition of these two core problems.

Definition 4 (Language of TS and Overapproximation [19]**).** *The* ***language*** *of a transition system, denoted by* $\mathcal{L}(\mathsf{TS})$*, is the set of transition sequences feasible from the initial state. For two transition systems* TS_1 *and* TS_2*.* TS_2 *is called an* ***overapproximation*** *of* TS_1*, when* $\mathcal{L}(\mathsf{TS}_1) \subseteq \mathcal{L}(\mathsf{TS}_2)$*.*

Definition 5 (PN Synthesis Problem). *Given an abstract state graph* $\mathcal{G}$*, such as a transition system. Construct some ("small") PN s.t.* $\mathcal{G}$ *is isomorphic to the reachability graph of PN, i.e.,* $\mathcal{G} \simeq \mathsf{RG}(\mathsf{PN})$*.*

Definition 6 (Trace and Event Log). *Given the universe of activities $\mathcal{A}$. A* ***trace*** *$\sigma = < a_1, \ldots, a_n > \in \mathcal{A}^*$ is a sequence of activities, where $\mathcal{A}^*$ is the Kleene closure of set $\mathcal{A}$. An event log is a multiset of traces, i.e., $\mathsf{L} \in \mathcal{B}(\mathcal{A}^*)$.*

Definition 7 (Process Mining Problem). *The objectives of the process mining problem can be articulated as follows [3]: given an event log L, we are searching for a preferably small finite marked PN, s.t. 1) $\mathcal{L}(\mathsf{TS}) \subset \mathcal{L}(\mathsf{PN})$; and 2) $\mathcal{L}(\mathsf{PN}) \setminus \mathcal{L}(\mathsf{TS})$ is minimal, which implies that the synthesized PN should be the tightest overapproximation over the TS.*

A key distinction between these challenges lies in their starting points. PN synthesis begins with a TS, often overlooking how these TSs are derived. Conversely, process mining starts with data [22] - specifically, *event logs* - and the initial step involves constructing an appropriate TS to support PN model generation, as illustrated in Fig. 3.

Furthermore, the objectives of PN synthesis and process mining differ markedly. PN synthesis aims to create a precise model that strictly adheres to a predefined set of behaviors, typically from theoretical environments, necessitating that the synthesized PN's reachability graph be *isomorphic* to the original TS. *Isomorphism* here implies a strong structural equivalence.

In contrast, process mining aims to discover, monitor, and optimize real processes by extracting insights from event logs. The primary goal is to generate a process model that encapsulates the behavior of the data. For us, this process model is a PN, and the data is represented by a TS. Ideally, the reachability graph of the synthesized PN should approximate the initial TS, a relationship often characterized by *bisimilarity*, indicating that both share the same *language*.

3.3 Theory of Regions

In this section, we outline the fundamental concepts of the *theory of regions*, as discussed in foundational works [10,12–14]. This theory provides a method to address challenges detailed in Sect. 3.2, particularly in constructing k-bounded PNs from a given TS. Aligned with process mining objectives, the *theory of regions* aims to derive process models from event logs, establishing a direct link between the TS and PN. It identifies *regions* in the TS, correlating them with *places* in the PN, thereby ensuring a *1-1 correspondence* between the states in the TS and the *markings* in the PN.

The integration of multisets into the *theory of regions* significantly enhances PN synthesis algorithms. This advancement not only supports the generation of safe PNs but also facilitates the development of k-bounded PNs, greatly increasing the expressiveness of PN models. Specifically, it allows for a more efficient system behavior representation, requiring fewer places to model equivalent behaviors and thus simplifying the structural complexity of the models. Importantly, this approach eliminates the need for label splitting. An example of this advancement is illustrated in Fig. 4.

Definition 8 (Multiset). *A multiset $\hat{r}$ of a set S is a mapping $\hat{r} : S \to \mathbb{N}$.*

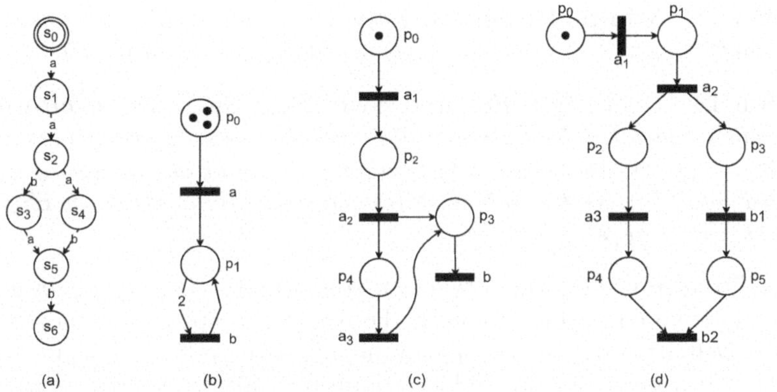

Fig. 4. PN Synthesis with different bounds [5]

Definition 9 (Support, Power, Boundedness). *The* ***support*** *of a multiset is the set of states whose multiplicity is greater than zero, i.e.,* $\mathsf{support}(\tilde{r}) = \{s \mid \tilde{r}(s) > 0\}$. *The* ***power*** *of a multiset* $\tilde{r}$ *is equal to the greatest multiplicity in* $\tilde{r}$, *denoted by* $\tilde{r}^{\diamond} = \max_{s \in S} \tilde{r}(s)$. *A multiset* $\tilde{r}$ *is termed* ***k-bounded*** *if the multiplicities of all states w.r.t.* r *are limited to a maximum integer value* k, *i.e.,* $\forall s \in S, \tilde{r}(s) \leq k$.

Definition 10 (Normalization). *Given a multiset* $\tilde{r}$. *The normalization of* $\tilde{r}$ *is defined as the subtraction of the minimal power, i.e.,* $\tilde{r}\downarrow = \tilde{r} - \mathsf{minp}(\tilde{r})$.

Definition 11 (Gradient of a Flow). *Given a transition system* $\mathsf{TS} = \{S, E, F, s_{ini}\}$ *and a multiset* $\tilde{r}$ *defined on the transition system. The gradient of a flow* $f \in F$ *with* $f = (s, e, s')$ *is given as* $\Delta_{\tilde{r}}(f) = \Delta_{\tilde{r}}(s, e, s') = \tilde{r}(s') - \tilde{r}(s)$.

Thus, by Definition 11 for a given transition system TS and a multiset $\tilde{r}$, flows labeled with e can have different gradients. Furthermore, we use $f_e \subseteq F$ to denote the set of flows labeled with event e.

In the context of transition systems, *regions* are a class of special multisets defined as follows:

Definition 12 (Regions and Trivial Regions). *Given a transition system* $\mathsf{TS} = \{S, E, F, s_{ini}\}$, *a multiset* r *derived from* TS *qualifies as a* ***region*** *of* TS *iff. all events* $e \in E$ *maintain a constant gradient across* r, *i.e.,* $\forall e \in E, \Delta_r(e) = const$. *A multiset* r *is a* ***trivial region*** *if all states have uniform multiplicity, i.e.,* $r = \mathbf{0} \ldots \boldsymbol{N}$. *The zero region,* $\mathbf{0}$, *is considered a subset of all regions in* TS.

Throughout this work, we employ the terms *multisets* and $\tilde{r}$ to denote the invalid regions, and for those that are valid, we simply refer to them as *regions* and with r. Since all the flows labeled with e have the same gradient in a region, the gradient of an event e in a region r is denoted by $\Delta_r(e)$. Figure 5 gives a graphical example for regions.

Definition 13 (Minimal Region). *Region r is* ***minimal*** *iff. r has no other subset than $\mathbf{0}$, i.e., if r is a minimal region with $r' \subset r$, then $r' = \mathbf{0}$.*

Definition 14 (Excitation Set and Switching Set). *The* ***excitation set*** *of an event e, denoted by $\mathsf{ES}(e)$, is the set of states in which e is enabled, i.e., $\mathsf{ES}(e) = \{s \mid \exists s', (s, e, s') \in F\}$. Similarly, the* ***switching set*** *of an event e, denoted by $\mathsf{SS}(e)$, is the set of states reachable from states in $\mathsf{ES}(e)$, i.e., $\mathsf{SS}(e) = \{s \mid \exists s', (s', e, s) \in F\}$*

In the literature, the terms *excitation region* and *switching region* are commonly used, as noted in [12]. However, the *region* concept here differs from that defined in Definition 12, a discrepancy highlighted by [5,8]. Despite this, the terminology has persisted. To reduce confusion, this work uses *excitation set* and *switching set* instead. These terms previously lacked precise definitions concerning their multiset representations. Here, we define the excitation set and the switching set by assigning a multiplicity of 1 to active states in $\mathsf{ES}(e)$ and $\mathsf{SS}(e)$, and zero to others, as detailed in Definition 14. For example, in a TS with states $S = \{s_1, s_2, s_3, s_4\}$, and event e is enabled only at state s_2, the excitation set for e is $\mathsf{ES}(e) = \{s_1^0, s_2^1, s_3^0, s_4^0\}$.

Definition 15 (Pre-regions and Post-regions). *A region r is a pre-region of e if $\mathsf{ES}(e) \subseteq r$. A region r is a post-region of e if $\mathsf{SS}(e) \subseteq r$. The sets of pre- and post-regions of an event e are denoted by $^\circ e$ and e° respectively.*

These two relations simply imply how the corresponding places in the PN are related to the event. For example, if a region r is a pre-region of event e, then r is a predecessor of event e. Similarly, a post-region indicates a successor of an event. The weights of the flows in a PN are determined by the following concept:

Definition 16 (Topset, Degree and MAX-K-TOP). *Given an event e and a pre-region r, the multiset $\mathsf{TOP}(r, e)$ is defined as the multiset q, such that $q = \mathcal{T}_d(r)$. It is required that $\mathsf{ES}(e)$ is a subset of $\mathcal{T}_d(r)$ and not a subset of $\mathcal{T}_{d+1}(r)$. Here, the degree d is denoted as $\mathsf{MAX} - \mathsf{K} - \mathsf{TOP}(r, e)$, indicating the maximum level k where $\mathsf{ES}(e)$ fully resides within $\mathcal{T}_d(r)$ but does not extend into $\mathcal{T}_{d+1}(r)$.*

Definition 17 (Enabling Topsets). *The set of smallest enabling topsets of an event e is denoted by $^*e$ and defined as: $^*e = \{q \mid \exists r \in {}^\circ e \wedge q = \mathsf{TOP}(r, e)\}$.*

Given a transition system $\mathsf{TS} = (S, E, F, s_{ini})$, we introduce two specialized sets of regions relative to a given region r and an event $e \in E$, delineated by a gradient constraint g. These sets are designated as $\mathcal{R}_g(r, e)$ and $\mathcal{R}^g(r, e)$. Consider a region $r \neq \mathbf{0}$, the formal definitions of these sets are provided as follows:

$$\mathcal{R}_g(r, e) = \{r' \supseteq r \mid r' \text{ is a region and } \Delta_{r'}(e) \leq g\},$$
$$\mathcal{R}^g(r, e) = \{r' \supseteq r \mid r' \text{ is a region and } \Delta_{r'}(e) \geq g\}.$$

Here, $\mathcal{R}_g(r,e)$ denotes the set of regions that encompass r where the gradient change caused by event e does not exceed g. Conversely, $\mathcal{R}^g(r,e)$ represents the set of regions encompassing r where the gradient change due to e exceeds g.

In the framework of a designated TS, the transformation of a multiset into a valid region requires an expansion process. This process is typically necessitated when certain events, termed *illegal events*, violate the criteria established in Definition 12. The response to these violations is managed incrementally. Specifically, it is critical to identify the minimum necessary augmentation of the multiset to satisfy a particular gradient constraint. This involves the computation of two distinct lower bounds: one for the expansion of the multiset r due to the arcs *exiting* state s, and another due to the arcs *entering* state s.

Definition 18 (Lower Bounds for Multiset Enlargement). *Given a transition system* $\mathsf{TS} = (S, E, F, s_0)$, *a multiset* r, *a state* $s \in S$, *and an event* $e \in E$, *the lower bounds are determined by the following* δ *functions:*

$$\delta_g(r,e,s) = \max(0, \max_{(s,e,s')\in F}(r(s') - r(s) - g)), \tag{1}$$

$$\delta^g(r,e,s) = \max(0, \max_{(s',e,s)\in F}(r(s') - r(s) + g)), \tag{2}$$

where δ_g *represents the lower bound for increasing the value of* $r(s)$ *considering the arcs exiting state* s, *and* δ^g *signifies the lower bound for augmenting* $r(s)$ *in response to the arcs entering state* s.

Definition 19. *Given a multiset* r *and an event* e, *the multisets* $\sqcap_g(r,e)(s)$ *and* $\sqcap^g(r,e)(s)$ *are defined as follows:*

$$\sqcap_g(r,e)(s) = r(s) + \delta_g(r,e,s) \text{ and } \sqcap^g(r,e)(s) = r(s) + \delta^g(r,e,s), \tag{3}$$

where $\sqcap_g(r,e)(s)$ *is a safe move to enlarge* r *in order to obtain all regions* r' *with* $\Delta_{r'} \leq g$. *On the contrast, the growth made by* $\sqcap^g(r,e)(s)$ *is looking for the regions* r'' *with* $\Delta_{r''} \geq g$.

Theorem 1 (Multiset Expansion on Events [5]).

1. *Let* $r \neq \mathbf{0}$ *be a multiset and* e *an event such that there exists some* (s,e,s') *with* $\Delta_r(s,e,s') > g$. *The following holds: 1.* $r \subset \sqcap_g(r,e)$; *2.* $\mathcal{R}_g(r,e) = \mathcal{R}(\sqcap_g(r,e),e)$;
2. *Let* $r \neq \mathbf{0}$ *be a multiset and* e *an event s.t. there exists some* (s,e,s') *with* $\Delta_r(s,e,s') < g$. *The following holds: 1.* $r \subset \sqcap^g(r,e)$; *2.* $\mathcal{R}^g(r,e) = \mathcal{R}^g(\sqcap^g(r,e),e)$.

3.4 Restrictions and Assumptions

Given the extensive theoretical developments in this domain over the past three decades, it is impractical to cover all possible scenarios comprehensively. Therefore, this work formulates the following focused restrictions and assumptions.

Mining of Transition Systems. This work does not explore the methods by which TS are *mined* from event logs, as this is peripheral to the core improvements proposed. However, several established strategies exist for constructing a TS from event logs, notably discussed in [27].

k-Excitation Closed Transition Systems. We focus on the k-excitation closed transition system (k-ECTS) due to its efficacy in ensuring the generation of a PN model. It is well-established that any TS can be transformed into a k-ECTS, making this a practical assumption [5]. The definition of k-ECTS is as follows:

Definition 20 (k-ECTS). *A TS is k-excitation closed (k-ECTS) if it uses minimal k-bounded regions, adhering to these criteria: 1.* ***Event Effectiveness:*** *Each event e must have a non-empty preset, $^{\circ}e \neq \emptyset$; 2.* ***Excitation Closure:*** *For each event e, $\bigcap_{q \in {}^*e} \mathsf{support}(q) = \mathsf{ES}(e)$.*

$^*e$ represents the enabling topsets defined in Definition 17, $\mathsf{support}(q)$ denotes the set of supports of a multiset q as per Definition 9, and $\mathsf{ES}(e)$ refers to the excitation set of event e detailed in Definition 14.

Label Splitting. Due to the limited expressiveness of the synthesis algorithm, label splitting is essential to ensure the algorithm generates a PN that meets specified requirements [12]. As depicted in Fig. 4, with reduced boundedness k, events must undergo multiple splits to replicate the behavior observed in TS_3.

4 Region-Based PN Synthesis

In this section, we first present our innovative algorithms for the generation of minimal regions and multiset expansion in Sect. 4.2 and Sect. 4.1, respectively. Subsequently, we introduce briefly the k-bounded PN synthesis algorithm in Sect. 4.3.

4.1 Multiset Expansion

From Sect. 3.3, we understand that a multiset derived from a transition system (TS) is not always a region if the gradient of event e is not constant. The goal of the multiset expansion process is to adjust the multiset to remove any illegal events, transforming it into a valid region for the TS. This region can then be used to represent a place in the resulting PN model.

For this purpose, we introduce the *Multiset Expansion Algorithm*, designed to effectively transform a multiset into a valid region within the TS. This transformation plays a crucial role in enhancing the efficiency of the *Minimal Region Generation Algorithm* (Algorithm 2). The details of the multiset expansion algorithm are illustrated in Algorithm 1.

In the initial step of this algorithm, the task is to identify illegal events, as specified in line 4 of Algorithm 1. According to Definition 12, a multiset qualifies as a region for a given transition system iff. all events maintain constant gradients throughout the system. Generally, there could be multiple illegal events, necessitating a decision since only one illegal event can be expanded upon at a time. As indicated in line 5 of Algorithm 1, this decision is based on $\overline{g}$, i.e., the floor value of the midrange of the gradients for each illegal event. It is defined mathematically as $\overline{g}_e = \lfloor \frac{g_{e,min}+g_{e,max}}{2} \rfloor$.

In the subsequent step, the multiset $\hat{r}$ is augmented based on the selected illegal event, as defined in Eq. 3. According to [5], if r_1 and r_2 remain as multisets yet are valid candidates, they are both added to the list of candidates for further expansion. This procedure is a primary factor contributing to the high computational costs.

Algorithm 1. Multiset Expansion

Require: k: bound, $\tilde{r}$: multiset, TS: transition system, R: discovered minimal regions, M: explored multiests
Ensure: R: discovered minimal regions, M: explored multiests
1: $\boldsymbol{r} = [\tilde{r}]$, $R = \emptyset$, $M = \emptyset$
2: **while** $\boldsymbol{r}$ is not empty **do**
3: $\quad \hat{r}$ = get_r_with_max_cardinality($\boldsymbol{r}$) ▷ get the element with the max. cardinality
4: $\quad$ **if** $\hat{r}$ in M **then** continue ▷ jump to the next
5: $\quad M$.append($\hat{r}$)
6: $\quad \tilde{e}$ = get_illegal_events($\hat{r}$, TS) ▷ get the list of illegal events
7: $\quad e$ = argmax$_{e \in \tilde{e}}$ ($\overline{g}_e$) ▷ choose illegal event for expansion
8: $\quad r_1 = \sqcap_{\overline{g}_e}(\hat{r}, e)$, $r_2 = \sqcap^{\overline{g}_e+1}(\hat{r}, e)$
9: $\quad$ **for** $r \in [r_1, r_2]$ **do**
10: $\quad\quad$ **if** r in M **then** continue
11: $\quad\quad$ **if** is_valid_candidate(k, r) **then**
12: $\quad\quad\quad$ **if** is$_r$egion(r, ts) **then**
13: $\quad\quad\quad\quad R$.append(r), M.append(r)
14: $\quad\quad\quad\quad$ continue
15: $\quad\quad\quad \boldsymbol{r}$.append($r$)
16: $\quad\quad$ **else**
17: $\quad\quad\quad M$.append(r)
return R, M

The logic from lines 9 to 17 operates as follows. We iterate through the new expansions based on $\hat{r}$. If r exists already in M, i.e., the already explored or seen multisets, then it skips the evaluation and jumps to the next. Otherwise, the validity of being a candidate is checked for r. For the case that r is a valid candidate, there are two possibilities. ① if r is already a region, then we simply append r to R and M to notify that we found a valid region and this instance has been seen. ② r is not a region, then it will be added to the list $\boldsymbol{r}$ for further expansion. Lastly, if r is not a valid candidate, then it will be added to M.

4.2 Generation of Minimal Regions

With the assistance of the multiset expansion algorithm, as depicted in Algorithm 1, we can generate the set of all minimal regions for a given transition system TS. This process is further detailed in Algorithm 2, which outlines the specific steps for the generation of these minimal regions.

Algorithm 2. Minimal Regions Generation

Require: $\mathsf{TS} = \{S, E, F, s_{ini}\}$, k
Ensure: R: discovered minimal regions, M: explored multisets
$R = []$
$M = []$
$P = \{\mathsf{ES}(e) | e \in E\} \cup \{\mathsf{SS}(e) | e \in E\}$ ▷ Candidate multisets for exploration
$P =$ remove_supersets_and_duplicates(P)
while $P \neq \emptyset$ **do**
  $\tilde{r} =$ get_e_with_min_cardinality(P)
  if $\tilde{r} \notin R$ **and** $\tilde{r}$ is region **then**
    R.append($\tilde{r}$)
  else
    $R, M =$ multiset_expansion($k, \tilde{r}, \mathsf{TS}, R, M$) ▷ Multiset expansion algorithm Algo. 1
 return R, M

Note that Algorithm 2 requires an integer k as input to indicate the upper bound, in addition to the transition system TS. In this work, we assume that the value of k is either known or sufficiently large to enable the algorithm to identify all the minimal regions. For cases where k is unknown, a method to determine it has been introduced in [8].

4.3 k-Bounded PN Synthesis Algorithm

In [8], the authors updated the synthesis algorithm for generating k-bounded PN. This approach differs from earlier methods that focused on generating safe PNs by using multisets to represent regions. Earlier definitions of a region, as described in [5,12], typically restricted state multiplicities to either 0 or 1, making them a special case with bound $k = 1$. A detailed explanation of the algorithm's mechanism is available in the cited work.

5 Numerical Results

For comparison and verification, we analyze two literature-based examples. Example 2, reviewed in Sect. 5.1, is discussed in multiple studies [5,18]. Example 3, from Sect. 5.2, originates from [8]. Comparisons are detailed in Sect. 5.3 using these examples. Our algorithms and examples are implemented in Python and available in our GitHub repository.[1]. We do not compare with algorithms from tools like Petrify [11], Genet [7], or ProM [26] plugins, mainly because: ① our focus is on algorithmic enhancements; ② those tools use different data structures, such as Binary Decision Diagrams (BDD) to represent a transition system (TS). In our research, we utilize the TS and Petri net (PN) notions from PM4PY [4] for ease of use.

5.1 Example of Multiset Expansion

We demonstrate the multiset transformation into a region using TS_1 shown in Fig. 6 and multiset $\tilde{r} = \{s_0^1, s_1^0, s_2^2\}$, following Algorithm 1. Observationally, the closest region to $\tilde{r}$ would be $r^* = \{s_0^1, s_1^2, s_2^3\}$ with a constant gradient $\Delta_r(e) = 1$.

[1] https://github.com/Peng-LUH/SIMUTools-2024.git.

The algorithm's first step identifies illegal events; event e is illegal as $\Delta_{\tilde{r}}(e) \neq$ const. For e, the estimated gradients from Sect. 4.1 are $g_{e,\min} = -1$, $g_{e,\max} = 2$, and $\overline{g}_e = 0$. We add a superscript on the left-hand side to $\tilde{r}$ to indicate the number of iterations. The multiset expansion is derived from Eq. 3, where if a state s has no outgoing or incoming flows, its lower bound $\delta_g(r, e, s)$ or $\delta^g(r, e, s)$ is equal to 0. Thus, $\delta_{\overline{g}_e}({}^0\tilde{r}, e, s_2) = 0$ sicne s_2 has no outgoing flows. Specifically, $\delta_{\overline{g}_e}({}^0\tilde{r}, e, s_0) = 0$ and $\delta_{\overline{g}_e}({}^0\tilde{r}, e, s_1) = 2$. Using these bounds, the multiset expansion r_1 for outgoing arcs is ${}^0r_1 = \{s_0^1, s_1^2, s_2^2\}$.

Similarly, for incoming arcs, we obtain ${}^0r_2 = \{s_0^1, s_1^2, s_2^2\}$, identical to ${}^0r_1$, and thus only one is needed for further evaluation. By ${}^1\tilde{r} = \{s_0^1, s_1^2, s_2^2\}$ the subsequent expansions ${}^1r_1 = \{s_0^2, s_1^2, s_2^2\}$ and ${}^1r_2 = \{s_0^1, s_1^2, s_2^3\}$ are derived, with ${}^1r_1$ trivial according to Definition 12 and ${}^1r_2 = r^*$. Notice that $r*$ is not a minimal region since it has a nontrivial subset. By subtracting the minimal power, we obtain the minimal region $r*_{min} = \{s_0^0, s_1^1, s_2^2\}$.

5.2 Cases for Numerical Studies

Case 1. The example transition system, TS_1, depicted in Fig. 5 is taken from the literature, which is used in multiple works such as [5,8]. According to Algorithm 2, four potential candidate multisets can be expanded and converted into valid regions. Here, we take $\tilde{r}_1$ as an example to illustrate how it is expanded into a valid region r_1 given in Fig. 5c.

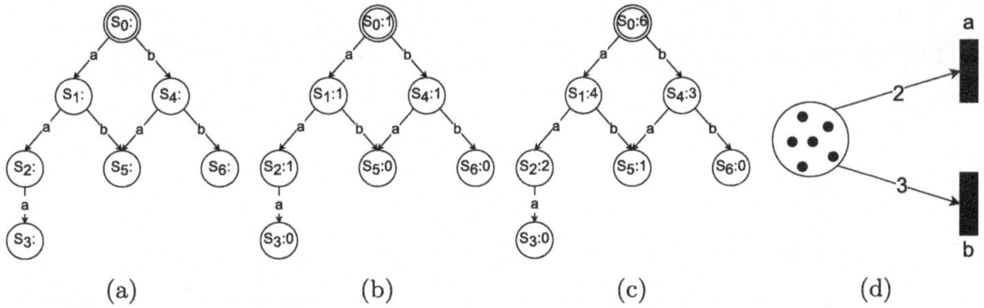

Fig. 5. Case 1 with (a) $\mathsf{TS}_1 = \{S_2, E_2, F_2, s_{ini,2}\}$; (b) Multiset: $\tilde{r}_1 = \{s_0^1, s_1^1, s_2^1, s_3^0, s_4^1, s_5^0, s_6^0\}$; (c) Region: $r_1 = \{s_0^6, s_1^4, s_2^2, s_3^0, s_4^3, s_5^1, s_6^0\}$; (d) PN derived from region r.

Case 2. The transition system TS_2, depicted in Fig. 7, is implemented in a Jupyter notebook titled Example_02.ipynb in the given GitHub repository. Algorithm 2 identified exactly seven minimal regions as stated in [8]. Additionally, the paper illustrates the Petri nets (PNs) derived from each minimal region.

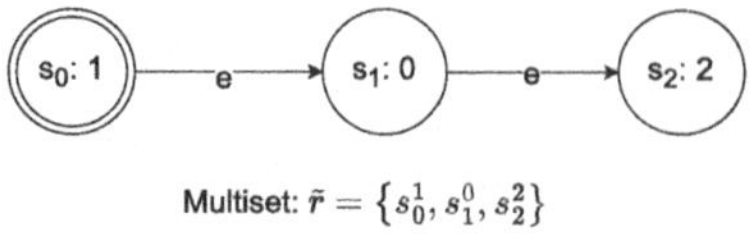

(a) TS_0 with $\tilde{r}$

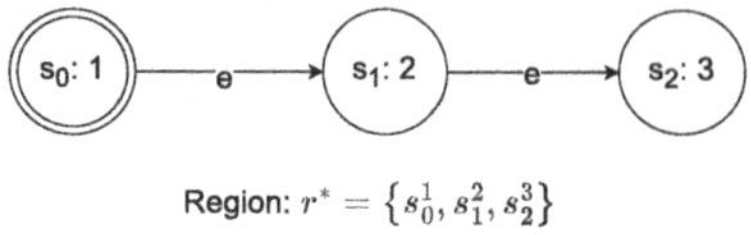

(b) TS_0 with r^*

Fig. 6. Example: TS_0

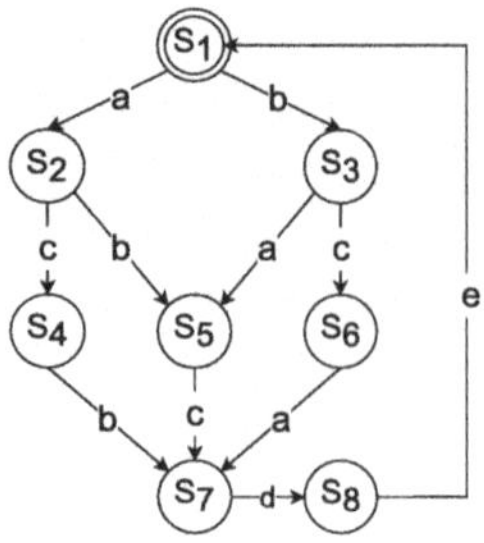

(a) TS_2

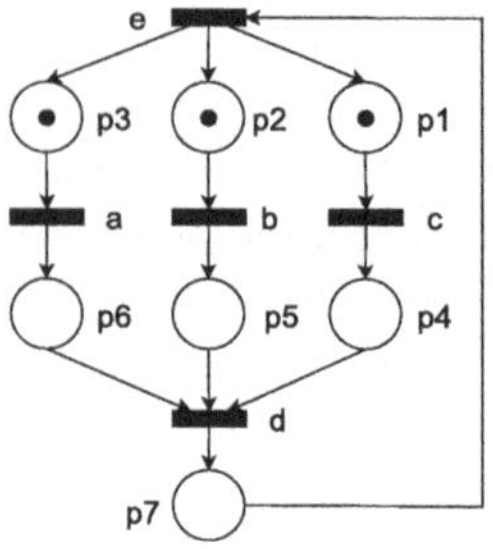

(b) PN_2

Fig. 7. Case 2

Case 3. Another more realistic case was presented in [8]. The event log of the process is given in Fig. 8a and the corresponding transition system is depicted in Fig. 8b. This case study is implemented in a Jupyter notebook titled Case_03.ipynb under the directory cases.

1. r, s, sb, p, ac, ap, c
2. r, sb, em, p, ac, ap, c
3. r, sb, p, em, ac, rj, rs, c
4. r, em, sb, p, ac, ap, c
5. r, sb, s, p, ac, rj, rs, c
6. r, sb, p, s, ac, ap, c
7. r, sb, p, em, ac, ap, c

(a) Event Log

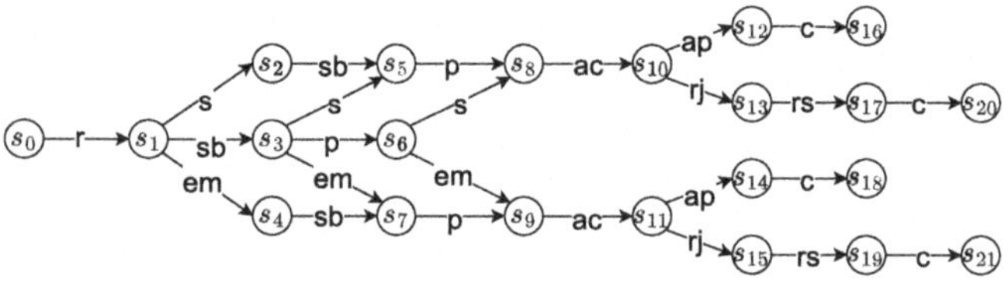

(b) Case 3: TS_3

Fig. 8. Case 03

5.3 Numerical Comparison

Table 1 presents the numerical results for cases 1 to 3 comparing the original approach, CCKKLY08/10, with the approach proposed in this study, MRG_MOD_V1. Generally, MRG_MOD_V1 outperforms its counterpart. First, it finds the identical minimal regions, i.e., it preserves the accuracy and robustness of the original approach. Second, it possesses a smaller search space and requires fewer iterations and less computational time. The advantage of MRG_MOD_V1 is even clearer when the system behavior is complex and the boundedness k is large. Case 3 is notably more complex compared to other cases, making it a useful example to demonstrate how computational efforts escalate as the bound k increases. In terms of the number of explored multisets, i.e., the search space, both MRG_MOD_V1 and CCKKLY08/10 are similar, with CCKKLY08/10 examining slightly more. However, the contrast in the number of iterations, **niter**, and computational time, **t**, is stark. Specifically, for $k = 3$, CCKKLY08/10 requires more than twice as many iterations and computational time as MRG_MOD_V1.

Table 1. Numerical Results

Method	C	k	$\#R$	$\#M$	$niter$	t [s]
CCKKLY08/10	1	6	6	100	144	0.013
MRG_MOD_V1			6	**85**	**63**	**0.011**
CCKKLY08/10	2	2	8	24	47	0.008
MRG_MOD_V1			8	**14**	**15**	**0.003**
CCKKLY08/10	3	1	14	254	341	0.21
MRG_MOD_V1			14	**225**	**148**	**0.17**
CCKKLY08/10		2	14	5434	7381	3.88
MRG_MOD_V1			14	**4362**	**3027**	**2.89**
CCKKLY08/10		3	14	78032	107327	764.47
MRG_MOD_V1			14	**58807**	**42558**	**348.22**

C: Case number; **k**: boundedness; **#R**: number of discovered minimal regions; **#M**: number of explored multisets; **niter**: number of iterations; **t**: computational time in second

6 Conclusion

This paper introduces significant improvements to the region-based PN synthesis algorithm, addressing the computational challenges inherent in existing methodologies. By integrating advanced multiset expansion techniques, the proposed algorithm enhances the generation of minimal regions, thereby accelerating the synthesis process without compromising accuracy or robustness [5]. Our approach has been empirically validated through various numerical experiments, demonstrating its superior performance in terms of speed and scalability when compared to the original algorithm. The enhanced algorithm efficiently handles the synthesis problem for k-bounded PN with complex behaviors, such as concurrency, which are prevalent in process mining.

In summary, this study significantly advances process mining by developing a more efficient and scalable PN synthesis algorithm. This enhanced algorithm is poised to improve the modeling and analysis of complex systems, thereby fostering advancements in process mining applications. Future work will focus on the following: 1). Conducting a detailed analysis of the computational efficiency of the algorithms; 2). Further investigating the algorithm's impact on PN construction and performing extensive numerical experiments with larger datasets; and 3). Comparing its performance with other process discovery algorithms.

Acknowledgments. The authors gratefully acknowledge the financial support by the DFG (German Research Foundation) for the Project "OffshorePlan" (Porject nummer: 411010215).

References

1. Augusto, A., Carmona, J., Verbeek, E.: Advanced process discovery techniques. In: Process Mining Handbook, pp. 76–107. Springer, Cham (2022)
2. Badouel, E., Bernardinello, L., Darondeau, P.: Petri Net Synthesis. Springer, Berlin (2015)
3. Bergenthum, R., Desel, J., Lorenz, R., Mauser, S.: Process mining based on regions of languages. In: Business Process Management, pp. 375–383. Springer, Berlin (2007)
4. Berti, A., Van Zelst, S., Schuster, D.: PM4Py: a process mining library for Python. Softw. Impacts **17**, 100556 (2023)
5. Carmona, J., Cortadella, J., Kishinevsky, M., Kondratyev, A., Lavagno, L., Yakovlev, A.: A symbolic algorithm for the synthesis of bounded petri nets. In: Applications and Theory of Petri Nets, pp. 92–111. Springer, Berlin (2008)
6. Carmona, J., Cortadella, J., Kishinevsky, M.: A region-based algorithm for discovering petri nets from event logs. In: Business Process Management, pp. 358–373. Springer, Berlin (2008)
7. Carmona, J., Cortadella, J., Kishinevsky, M.: Genet: a tool for the synthesis and mining of petri nets. In: 2009 Ninth International Conference on Application of Concurrency to System Design, pp. 181–185. IEEE, Augsburg (2009)
8. Carmona, J., Cortadella, J., Kishinevsky, M.: New region-based algorithms for deriving bounded petri nets. IEEE Trans. Comput. **59**(3), 371–384 (2010)
9. Carmona, J., van Dongen, B., Weidlich, M.: Conformance checking: foundations, milestones and challenges. In: Process Mining Handbook, pp. 155–190. Springer, Cham (2022)
10. Cortadella, J., Kishinevsky, M., Lavagno, L., Yakovlev, A.: Synthesizing Petri nets from state-based models. In: Proceedings of IEEE International Conference on Computer Aided Design, pp. 164–171. IEEE Computer Society Press, San Jose (1995)
11. Cortadella, J., Kishinevsky, M., Kondratyev, A., Lavagno, L., Yakovlev, A., England, N.: Petrify: a tool for manipulating concurrent specifications and synthesis of asynchronous controllers. IEICE Trans. Inf. Syst. **E80-D**(3), 315–325 (1997)
12. Cortadella, J., Kishinevsky, M., Lavagno, L., Yakovlev, A.: Deriving petri nets from finite transition systems. IEEE Trans. Comput. **47**(8), 859–882 (1998)
13. Desel, J., Reisig, W.: The synthesis problem of Petri nets. Acta Informatica **33**(4), 297–315 (1996)
14. Ehrenfeucht, A., Rozenberg, G.: Partial (set) 2-structures: part II: state spaces of concurrent systems. Acta Informatica **27**(4), 343–368 (1990)
15. Faria Junior, E., Neubauer, T., Fantinato, M., Peres, S.: Clustering analysis and frequent pattern mining for process profile analysis: an exploratory study for object-centric event logs. In: Process Mining Workshops, pp. 269–281. Springer, Cham (2023)
16. Murata, T.: Petri nets: properties, analysis and applications. Proc. IEEE **77**(4), 541–580 (1989)
17. Petri, C.A.: Kommunikation mit Automaten (1962)
18. Solé, M., Carmona, J.: Process mining from a basis of state regions. In: Applications and Theory of Petri Nets, pp. 226–245. Springer, Berlin (2010)
19. Solé, M., Carmona, J.: Incremental process discovery. In: Transactions on Petri Nets and Other Models of Concurrency V, pp. 221–242. Springer, Berlin (2012)

20. Teren, V., Cortadella, J., Villa, T.: Generation of synchronizing state machines from a transition system: a region-based approach. Int. J. Appl. Math. Comput. Sci. **33**(1), 133–149 (2023)
21. Teren, V., Cortadella, J., Villa, T.: Seto: a framework for the decomposition of petri nets and transition systems. In: Proceedings of 26th Euromicro Conference On Digital System Design (DSD), pp. 669–677. IEEE, Golem (2023)
22. van der Aalst, W., Weijters, T., Maruster, L.: Workflow mining: discovering process models from event logs. IEEE Trans. Knowl. Data Eng. **16**(9), 1128–1142 (2004)
23. van der Aalst, W., Rubin, V., Verbeek, H., van Dongen, B., Kindler, E., Günther, C.: Process mining: a two-step approach to balance between underfitting and overfitting. Softw. Syst. Model. **9**(1), 87–111 (2010)
24. van der Aalst, W.: Process Mining: Discovery, Conformance and Enhancement of Business Processes. Springer, Berlin (2011)
25. van der Aalst, W., Berti, A.: Discovering object-centric petri nets. Fund. Inform. **175**(1–4), 1–40 (2020)
26. van Dongen, B., De Medeiros, A., Verbeek, H., Weijters, A., van der Aalst, W.: The ProM framework: a new era in process mining tool support. In: Applications and Theory of Petri Nets 2005, pp. 444–454. Springer, Heidelberg (2005)
27. van Dongen, B.F., Busi, N., Pinna, G.M., van der Aalst, W.M.P.: An iterative algorithm for applying the theory of regions in process mining. BETA publicatie: working papers. Research School for Operations Management, Eindhoven (2007)

Cross-Dataset Generalization: Bridging the Gap Between Real and Synthetic LiDAR Data

Martin Strunz[1], Robert Protzmann[2](✉), and Ilja Radusch[3]

[1] Technische Universität Berlin, Ernst-Reuter-Platz 7, 10587 Berlin, Germany
post@mstrunz.de
[2] Fraunhofer FOKUS, Kaiserin Augusta Allee 31, 0589 Berlin, Germany
robert.protzmann@fokus.fraunhofer.de
[3] Daimler Center for Automotive IT Innovations (DCAITI), Ernst-Reuter-Platz 7, 10587 Berlin, Germany
ilja.radusch@dcaiti.com

Abstract. In this paper, we present and evaluate a new synthetic street-view LiDAR dataset for computer vision and object detection in the automated driving domain. The dataset consists of labeled data for 100 scenarios with about 1.1 h of drive time, 40.000 frames and 500.000 bounding boxes and will be publicly available from now. We employed the Eclipse MOSAIC simulation framework in conjunction with the SUMO simulator for routes and traffic densities as well as CARLA for simulation of sophisticated LiDAR sensors and environments. Before generating our own data, we analyzed already existing LiDAR datasets regarding numerous statistics as well as features they contain. As a result, we reproduced key aspects of the analyzed datasets to generate data that will comprise realistic and therefore diverse scenarios. A common challenge is that deep learning models for object detection perform best on test data that are strongly related to the data they were trained on. The comparison in this paper finally shows that our model proved the best cross-dataset performance.

Keywords: Sensor Simulation · LiDAR Dataset · Object Detection

1 Introduction

Object detection based on advanced sensor data like LiDAR or cameras is an important foundation for automated driving technologies, enabling the equipped vehicle to gather information about e.g. other road users, road infrastructure, and obstacles in the local vicinity. The object detection itself is realized by deep learning models, which need to be trained first via annotated datasets with labeled features. For field deployment, cross-dataset generalization is an important aspect, given the fact that deep learning models must cope with scenes, which may not be part of one individual dataset.

Existing LiDAR datasets can be broadly categorized based on the data collection methods: real-world, simulated, or a combination of both.

A. A. Juan et al. (Eds.): SIMUtools 2024, LNICST 603, pp. 202–217, 2025.
https://doi.org/10.1007/978-3-031-87345-4_14

Real-world LiDAR datasets are captured by actual vehicles equipped with genuine sensors, navigating real traffic. Recording and annotating real traffic data is a complex and resource-intensive endeavor and includes various challenges. Fortunately, in the last years, several research groups pursued this work to provide their datasets for the community. The pioneering KITTI dataset [5] is joined by initiatives like nuScenes, Waymo, Lyft, and others. A solution to address data annotation challenges involves generating LiDAR data with simulation, as achieved by PreSIL [8]. Synthetic data, benefiting from the simulator's inherent ground truth knowledge, can be annotated automatically.

However, research also indicates the challenges for model training with simulated compared to real LiDAR data, which ultimately lead to lower detection rates in the case of simulated data [3,20]. The lower performance across datasets clearly underscores the importance of cross-dataset generalization. From our perspective, a better understanding of the scenes and scenarios could bridge the gap between the real and the synthetic data - which leads to our purpose for this paper. We perform a comprehensive analysis of real and synthetic datasets and transfer the results to the generation of our own - the LUCID dataset [15]. Our hypothesis is that data more faithfully based on real, hence diverse, scenarios could improve the performance of an object detection model.

In this paper, we first analyze existing LiDAR datasets in Sect. 2. In Sect. 3, we present the key aspects of our scenario-based dataset generation process and evaluate our own dataset in comparison with KITTI, nuScenes and PreSIL in Sect. 4. Finally, Sect. 5 concludes the paper.

2 Analysis of Existing LiDAR Datasets

Existing street-view LiDAR datasets vary in several ways. For example, they target different usage scenarios, the data is collected in real-world traffic or by simulation, their experimental setup differs, and they might provide object annotations for different classes in different ways like 2D or 3D bounding boxes.

2.1 Existing Datasets

For our analysis, we only consider LiDAR datasets that at least provide 3D bounding boxes for the *Car* class.

Real Datasets: The data of real datasets were recorded by real LiDAR and other sensors in real traffic. One of the first datasets of this kind is KITTI [5]. Being a pioneer, KITTI has limitations. For example, annotations are only available for the front camera in a 90° horizontal FOV. These disadvantages have been addressed by other datasets like ApolloScape [7], nuScenes [1], Woven Planet Perception [10], Audi Autonomous Driving [6], Waymo Open Perception [16], Argoverse2 Sensor [19] as well as the team of KITTI itself: KITTI-360 [12].

Synthetic Datasets: These datasets are computer generated. The authors of PreSIL [8] want to create a dataset comparable to KITTI and therefore imitate its experimental setup. The data were generated with Grand Theft Auto V

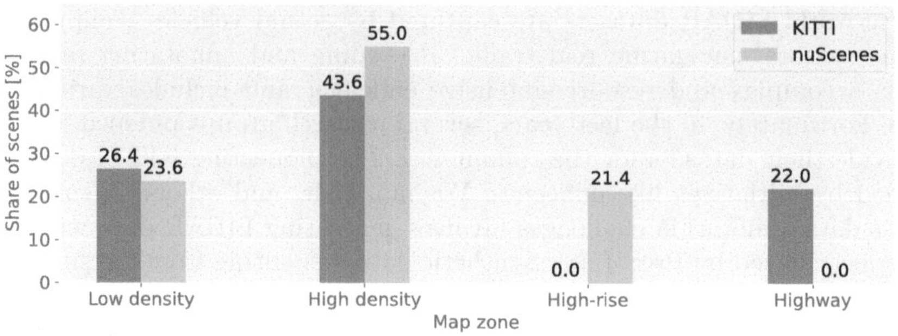

Fig. 1. Share of scenes per map zone of KITTI and nuScenes.

(GTA V). V2X-Sim [11], a rather new dataset, aims at V2X communication. All scenarios are arranged around intersections. SHIFT [17] focuses on domain shifts, e.g. weather changes within the CARLA simulator [2].

2.2 Detailed Analysis

The key facts of LiDAR datasets have been listed many times, e.g. in [12], but a thorough analysis is still missing to the best of our knowledge. As our goal is to define scenes and scenarios based on existing datasets, a more detailed look at them is therefore necessary. To keep this analysis clear and concise, we have to limit it to three datasets. We choose the publicly available KITTI, nuScenes, and PreSIL. KITTI was preferred over the newer KITTI-360, because KITTI is a pioneer and frequently used in object detection experiments. The selected datasets exhibit most citations in literature (KITTI, nuScenes) and include real-world as well as simulated (PreSIL) data. Additionally, the properties of the selected datasets differ as cross-dataset generalization is a key aspect of this work: They cover a wide range of locations (KITTI: Germany, nuScenes: USA and Singapore, PreSIL: GTA V) as well as right-hand (Germany, USA, GTA V) and left-hand traffic (Singapore). Their LiDAR configuration differs also (KITTI, PreSIL: 64 channels, nuScenes: 32 channels).

As KITTI, nuScenes, and PreSIL are multimodal datasets, they contain bounding box annotations for objects that are hit by only a few or no laser beams (but are, e.g. still visible on camera). They do not provide information for our object detection based on LiDAR data. Therefore, we filter out such annotations and will use the filtered datasets from here on.

Map Zones: We expand the classic *rural* and *urban* distinction to a finer gradation and define four map zones: *Low density* (detached houses with gardens), *High density* (city blocks, commercial buildings), *High-rise* (like *High density* but with some skyscrapers), and *Highway* (high speed roads with multiple lanes). The majority of scenes in KITTI and nuScenes take place in *High density* map zones (see Fig. 1). The share of *Low density* map zones is comparable. KITTI, on the one hand, does not provide data collected in a *High-rise* map zone. nuScenes, on the other hand, does not contain any data collected on highways. PreSIL does

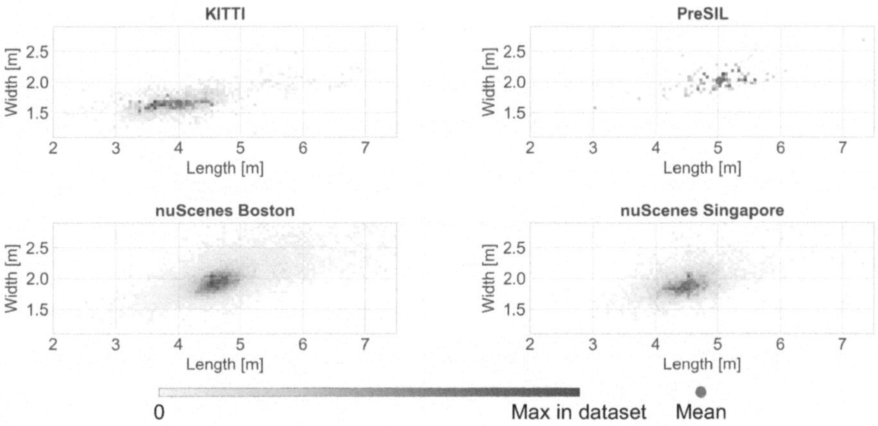

Fig. 2. Histogram of bounding box sizes of *Car* annotations for KITTI, PreSIL, nuScenes Boston, and nuScenes Singapore.

not provide global positioning information of the ego vehicle, which makes such an analysis impossible (yet, GTA V contains all four map zones).

Objects per Scene: PreSIL contains two *Car* objects more on average per scene (5.8) than KITTI (3.8). These numbers are difficult to compare with nuScenes, because KITTI's and PreSIL's objects are annotated in a 90° horizontal FOV while nuScenes utilizes the full 360°.

For simplicity, KITTI's and PreSIL's numbers can be doubled for better comparison. nuScenes then contains a similar number of objects (7.3) as KITTI.

Bounding Box Size: The size of vehicles can differ between continents which makes the bounding box size a key factor for cross-dataset generalization [18]. Cars tend to be smaller in KITTI than in nuScenes (see Fig. 2). The Boston part of nuScenes' dataset offers the widest range of bounding boxes in terms of both length and width. The majority of nuScenes Singapore's bounding boxes tend to be shorter and less wide than in Boston. PreSIL's synthetic bounding box sizes vary also, but are restricted to only a few distinct sizes due to their synthetic origin.

Objects with Respect to LiDAR: The four histograms in Fig. 3 are based on a bird's-eye view and assume the ego vehicle positioned in its center facing north. Each *Car* object is placed according to its relative position to the ego vehicle. The majority of annotated cars in the KITTI dataset appear up to 10 m left of the ego vehicle and up to 5 m right of the ego vehicle. There are almost no annotated cars directly in front of the ego vehicle due to the safety distance. Cars are annotated up to 80 m in front of the vehicle. When reaching the left and right end of the 90° horizontal FOV, this is reduced to about 50 m.

In nuScenes Boston and Singapore the majority of annotated cars is located directly behind the ego vehicle. The Singapore ego vehicle was often following another car, which results in an accumulation of annotations right in front of

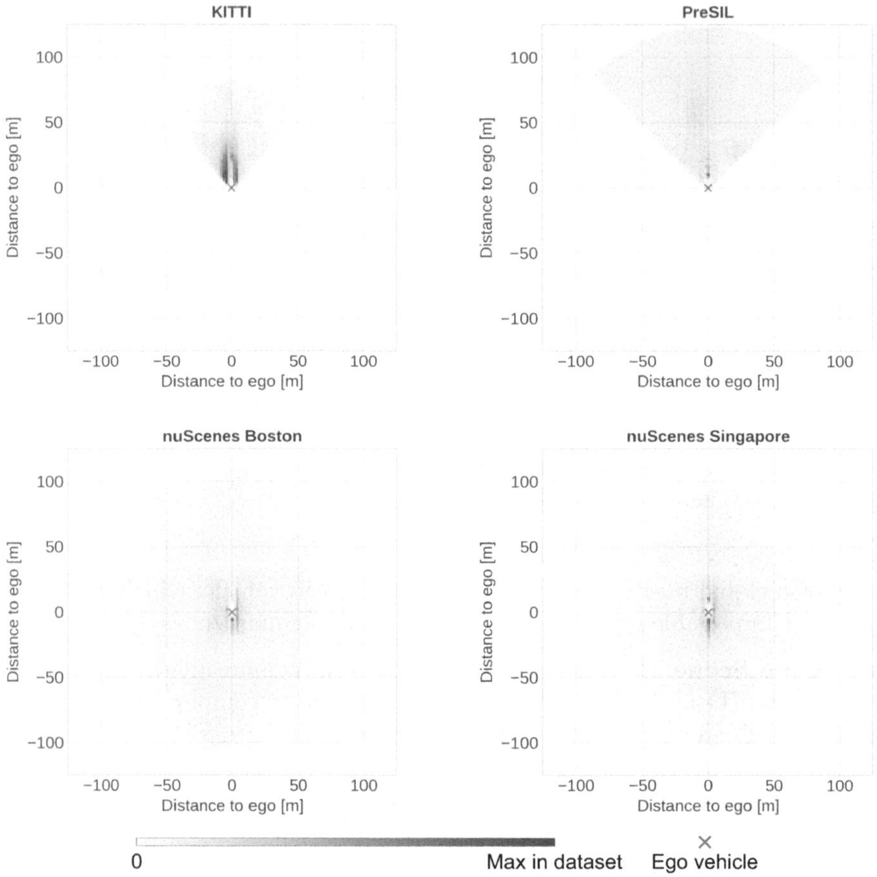

Fig. 3. Histogram of location and frequency of *Car* annotations with respect to the ego vehicle (center of plot, facing north) for KITTI, PreSIL, nuScenes Boston, and nuScenes Singapore.

it. The different traffic rules do not result in very different histograms: More cars are positioned directly right of the ego vehicle than left of it in both cities. Annotations exist more often in ongoing/oncoming direction with respect to the ego vehicle than on its more distant left and right sides. Annotated objects can be further away than KITTI's, stretching out more than 100 m in ongoing/oncoming direction and up to 100 m at the ego vehicle's sides.

PreSIL as the synthetic dataset offers the most distant annotations and a very uniform distribution of objects around the ego vehicle. In addition, PreSIL contains the farthest annotations of the three datasets: They can be as far as 120 m away from the ego vehicle. Regarding the closer vicinity, the already discussed effects can be seen: More annotations occur in ongoing/oncoming direction and an accumulation of annotations right in front of the ego vehicle.

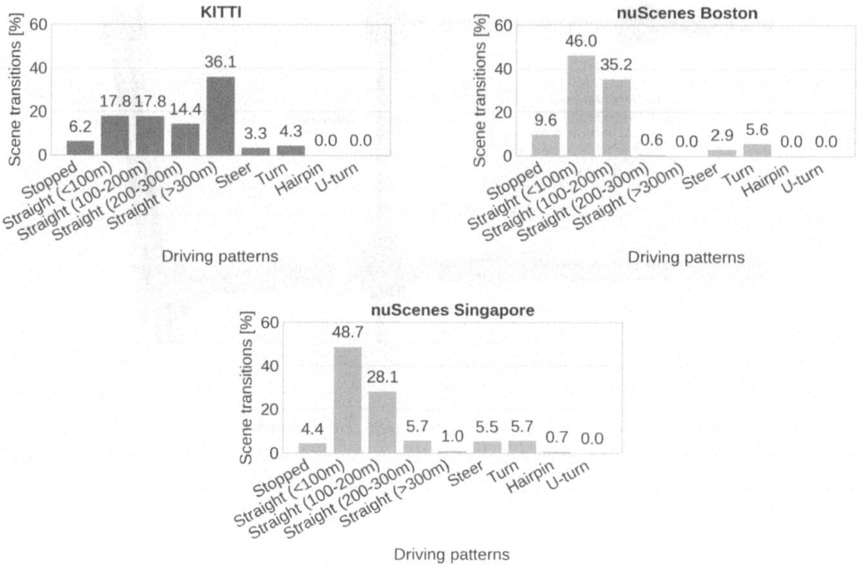

Fig. 4. Driving patterns for KITTI, nuScenes Boston, and nuScenes Singapore.

LiDAR with Respect to Objects: While the previous analysis shows where objects can be found, this analysis depicts the angle from which the objects are scanned by the ego vehicle's LiDAR sensor. Cars in the KITTI dataset are scanned mostly from their front left and rear left side. This is caused by Germany's right-hand traffic. Cars in the nuScenes dataset are most often scanned from their front. Also, in Boston cars are hit by a LiDAR laser beam more often on their left side than on their right side, which is typical for right-hand traffic. However, this effect is almost not visible in Singapore (where it should be on the car's right side). PreSIL again offers a very uniform distribution of LiDAR positions. Cars are scanned from almost every position within the 120 m annotation range, with an accumulation of scans of the cars' back.

Driving Patterns: While we analyzed the objects *within* a scene for the previous metrics, we now focus on the *connection* of scenes: The ego vehicle moves from scene to scene by performing maneuvers, which we aggregate to driving patterns. The results of our driving pattern analysis for KITTI and nuScenes are shown in Fig. 4. *Straight* driving patterns are most dominant with a share of over 80%. KITTI's ego vehicle drives straight ahead for longer distances more often than in the nuScenes dataset. The ego vehicle stops most frequently in the nuScenes Boston dataset. Overall, nuScenes Singapore seems to describe the most agile ego vehicle because it has the lowest share of *Stopped* driving patterns and the highest of *Steer* plus *Turn* patterns. PreSIL does not allow to combine traffic scenes to driving scenarios because this information is missing in the dataset. Therefore, a driving pattern analysis is not possible.

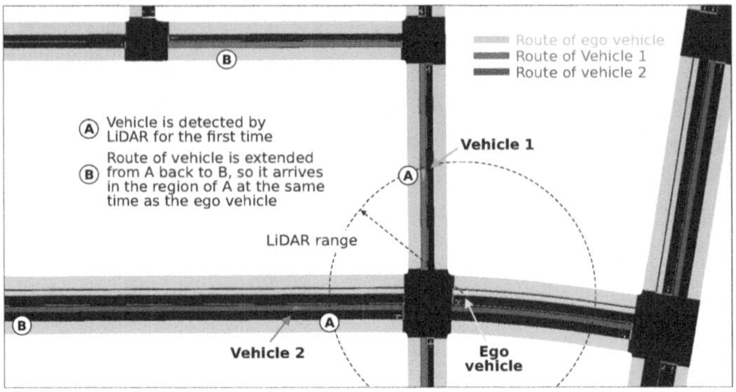

Fig. 5. Example of route extension: Vehicles shall be detected by the LiDAR approximately at point A. The route is extended from A back to B, so that the vehicle arrives in the region of A at about the same time as the ego vehicle.

3 Scenario Based Dataset Generation

From the dataset analysis in the previous section, the aspects of *Map Zones*, *Objects per Scene*, and *Bounding Box Size* directly serve as input to the scenario generation process for our new dataset. The characteristics *Objects with Respect to LiDAR* and *LiDAR with Respect to Objects* are used as guideline for the vehicles' location and orientation, and the *Driving Patterns* describe the transition between consecutive scenes.

Each of our generated and simulated scenarios is based on the analysis results of either KITTI or nuScenes, which form the reference datasets for every individual scenario.

3.1 Random Scenario Generation

The reference dataset serves as a guideline for scenario generation, which is carried out by our own tools. Each scenario is assigned a map zone of the reference dataset and a part of CARLA's 100 km^2 large *Town12* map that covers the selected map zone. The ego vehicle is placed in the map and given a random route through the map's road network. Placement of dynamic objects is key for our scenario generation: We place moving and parked cars, trucks, cyclists, and pedestrians randomly, with their density, locations, and orientations based on the analysis results. In addition, we apply a density scaling factor to compensate for low object class representation in the reference datasets. The moving vehicles are assigned random routes so that they meet the ego vehicle at predefined points (point A in Fig. 5). Static objects from soda cans to bus stops are randomly put in the scenario to add more complexity to the resulting point clouds. We generated a total of 50 scenarios based on KITTI and another 50 based on nuScenes.

Fig. 6. Labeled point cloud example of the LUCID Dataset.

3.2 Scenario Simulation

Eclipse MOSAIC [14] orchestrates CARLA [2] and SUMO [13] to simulate the generated scenarios. Eclipse MOSAIC is also used to export the ground truth as well as the point clouds. Since scenes with little movement can result in similar point clouds, we randomly rotate each moving vehicle about its yaw axis in an interval of $\pm 2^\circ$ in every simulation step. This ensures that the point clouds of two consecutive scenes differ more. The bounding boxes' sizes require some additional attention: In the KITTI data format (which is the format we use for our dataset) they are described in the LiDAR's coordinate frame as upright bounding boxes without pitch and roll. However, CARLA gives the sizes of the boxes in the world coordinate frame which includes pitch and roll. Therefore, both angles have to be factored out. This results in the boxes of identical objects having slightly different sizes, which brings more diversity and is therefore an advantage for us (see Fig. 6 for a labeled point cloud example).

The result is the "LUCID dataset - LIDAR Utilization for Cross-Data Integration and Diversity". It consists of labeled data as outlined in Table 1.

Table 1. Key facts of the LUCID dataset.

Property	Value
Object classes	Car, Truck, Cyclist, Pedestrian
Scenarios	100
Drive time	1.1 h
Point clouds	40.000
Bounding boxes	500.000

Importantly, based on the Creative Commons CC-BY license, we made the new LUCID dataset publicly available to the community[1], providing a valuable resource for scientists who are interested in our contribution [15].

[1] See https://www.dcaiti.com/research/simulation/lucid/.

4 Evaluation

Our experiments consist of two steps: First, deep learning models are trained for each of the four datasets and tested regarding their cross-dataset generalization performance. Second, the models of PreSIL and our dataset are fine-tuned using data from KITTI (fine-tuning the synthetic models using nuScenes produced similar results, so they are not discussed here). The fine-tuned models are retested as in the first step.

The evaluation metrics for our experiments are Average Precision (AP) and Average Recall (AR). For the AP, we use the definition given in the PASCAL Visual Object Classes Challenge [4]. The AR is defined by:

$$AR = \frac{2}{|D|} \sum_{d \in D} \max\left[(IoU(d) - 0.5), 0\right] \tag{1}$$

with D as the set of all detections and $IoU(d)$ as the Intersection over Union (IoU) of detection d.

Our object detection deep learning model utilizes the Occupancy Grid Map method, which discretizes the point clouds and transforms them into a 2D representation from a bird's-eye point of view. The parameters are shown in Table 2. The four datasets have been split into training, validation, and testing subsets.

Table 2. The parameters of our OGM deep learning model.

Parameter	Value
OGM grid size	150 m
OGM grid resolution	0.15 m
OGM image size	1000 × 1000 pixels
Maximum detection range	75 m
Minimum IoU (all classes)	0.5

4.1 Cross-Dataset Performance

A model is trained for each dataset based on its training and evaluation sets. Good performance of a model on its own test set is a prerequisite, but our actual goal is successful object recognition on other, especially real, datasets. The models are therefore tested on all datasets' test sets to assess their cross-dataset generalization capabilities. The results are shown in Fig. 7.

Each test set is handled best by the model of the same dataset. nuScenes' model achieves a higher AP on the KITTI test set (AP 0.51) than the synthetic datasets' models (PreSIL: AP 0.43, LUCID: AP 0.46). The synthetic test sets are handled best by the synthetic models: The LUCID model significantly outperforms the real dataset's models on the PreSIL test set and the PreSIL model on LUCIDs.

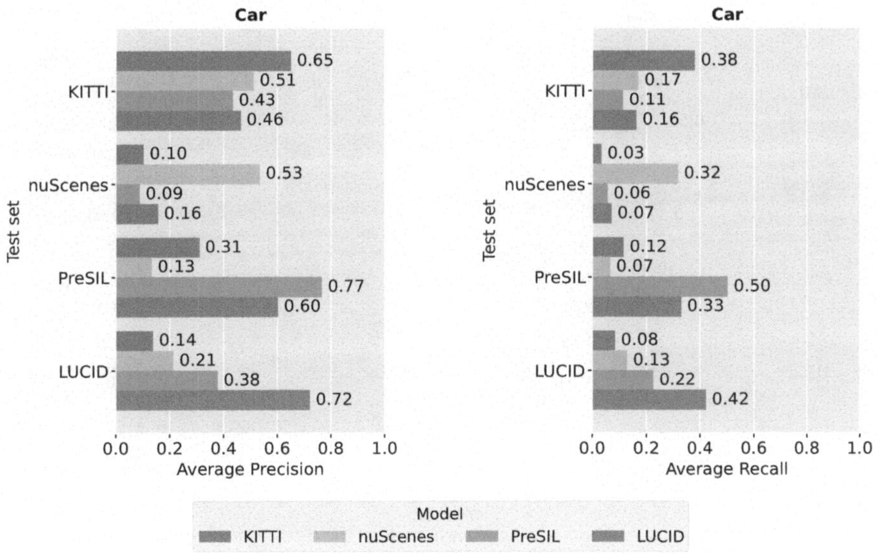

Fig. 7. How each test set is handled by the different models: AP and AR of the dataset's models.

The next step is to quantify each model's cross-dataset generalization performance. For this, we calculate by how much each model's AP and AR differ from the best AP and AR on each test set and compute the mean from that. For a model w, we define the AP Cross-Dataset Performance by:

$$\text{AP-CDP}_w = \frac{1}{|T|} \sum_{t \in T} \left[\text{AP}_{w,t} - \max_{m \in M} \left(\text{AP}_{m,t} \right) \right] \tag{2}$$

with T containing all test sets, M containing all models, and $\text{AP}_{m,t}$ as the AP of model m on test set t. The AR Cross-Dataset Performance is defined accordingly:

$$\text{AR-CDP}_w = \frac{1}{|T|} \sum_{t \in T} \left[\text{AR}_{w,t} - \max_{m \in M} \left(\text{AR}_{m,t} \right) \right] \tag{3}$$

The results are shown in Fig. 8.

The LUCID dataset's model has the best performance (AP-CDP: −0.18, AR-CDP: −0.16), followed by PreSIL (AP-CDP: −0.25, AR-CDP: −0.18). The cross-dataset generalization performance of KITTI's model is worst (AP-CDP: −0.37, AR-CDP: −0.26) due to a low performance on all other test sets. nuScenes' model (AP-CDP: −0.32, AR-CDP: −0.23) is better than KITTI's because of its good AP on the KITTI test set.

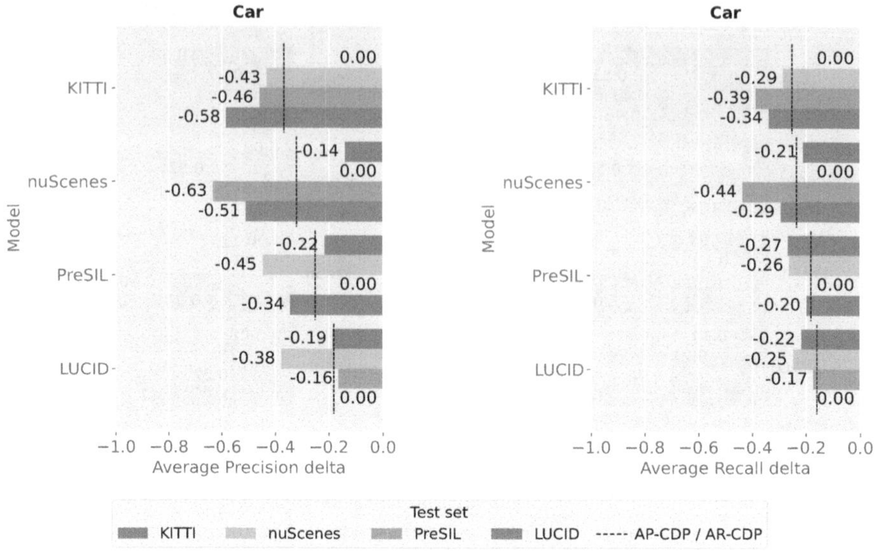

Fig. 8. The model's cross-dataset performance on the test sets: delta of each model's AP (AR) and the AP (AR) of the best model on the test set.

4.2 Fine-Tuning

In order to increase the object recognition performance of the synthetic models on real data, they can be fine-tuned by additionally training them with real data. For this purpose, we randomly select 25% of the training and evaluation sets of KITTI. The resulting dataset is called KITTI-25 and used to train LUCID-KITTI and PreSIL-KITTI models respectively (see Fig. 9).

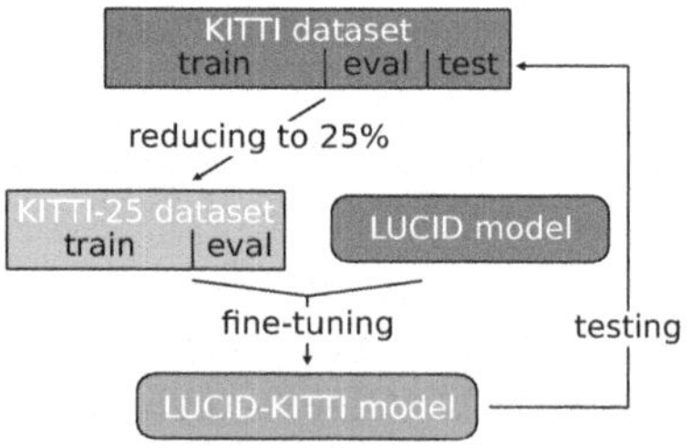

Fig. 9. Schematic concept of fine-tuning our model: The KITTI dataset is reduced to 25% (KITTI-25 dataset). Our trained LUCID model is then fine-tuned with the KITTI-25 train and eval sets. The resulting model LUCID-KITTI is tested on the KITTI test set.

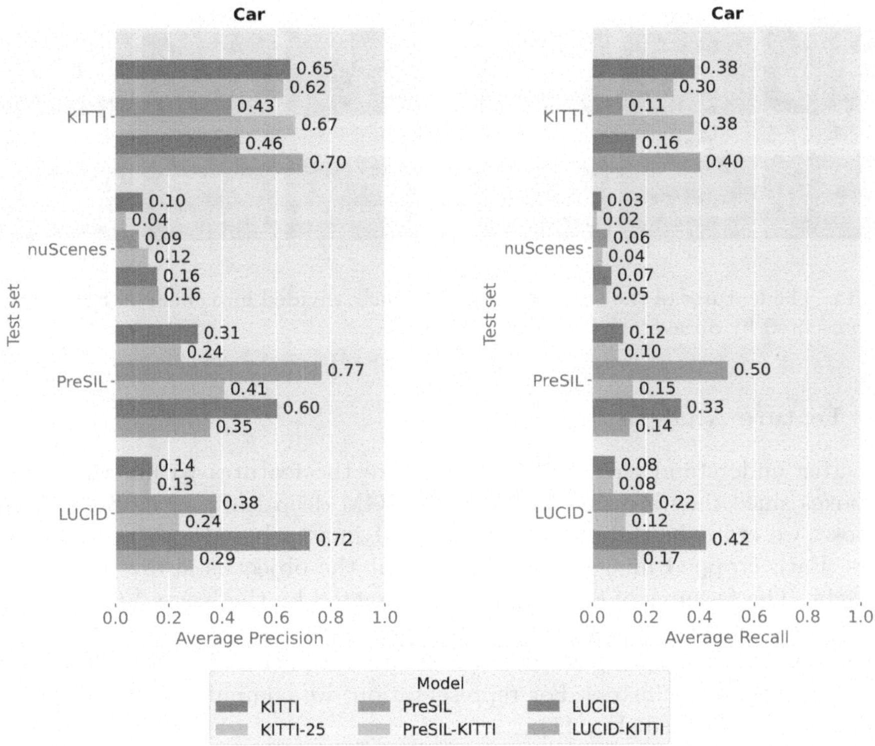

Fig. 10. How each test set is handled by the fine-tuned models: AP and AR for PreSIL-KITTI and LUCID-KITTI. KITTI-25 as well as the original models are shown for reasons of comparison.

In addition, a new model based on KITTI-25 is trained from scratch. This model represents the baseline, because the fine-tuned models must yield higher AP and AR scores on the KITTI test set than the baseline model. If they do not achieve that, fine-tuning the synthetic models would be needless.

The cross-dataset results of the fine-tuned models are shown in Fig. 10 and accompanied by the original models for comparison. Fine-tuning the synthetic models leads to a leap in performance on the KITTI test set. Our fine-tuned model LUCID-KITTI shows the greatest improvements (AP +0.24, AR +0.34). In addition, it outperforms the KITTI and KITTI-25 models and achieves the best result of all models on the KITTI test set.

Fine-tuning aims to achieve good results on the fine-tuned dataset, rather than high cross-dataset performance, which is shown in Fig. 10: For example, fine-tuning reduced PreSIL-KITTI's AP on its own test set from 0.77 to 0.41 (−0.36).

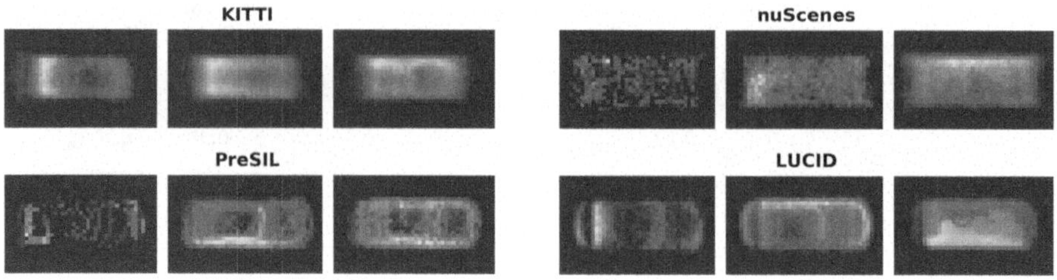

Fig. 11. The features of the four datasets' *Car* class, divided into clusters. Each cluster is represented by an average image of its features.

4.3 Feature Analysis

To better understand the results, we analyze the features within the bounding boxes since they are the basis for our OGM deep learning model. For this purpose, we crop the objects from the OGM images based on their bounding boxes. Each cropped image is rotated so that the object is always oriented to the right. The features of each image are extracted by the Keras VGG16 image classification model [9]. A principal component analysis reduces the number of dimensions in the resulting feature vector and a k-means algorithm divides the feature images into clusters. For representation, we compute an average image within each cluster (see Fig. 11).

The features of each dataset can be divided into three different clusters. First, features that consist of only an accumulation of points (nuScenes, PreSIL) or are I-shaped (KITTI, LUCID). L-shaped or U-shaped features dominate the second cluster. Features that do not form just a contour but an area are common in the third cluster.

The synthetic datasets' features show clearer shapes of the objects: Parts of the vehicles such as the bonnet or the passenger compartment are clearly recognizable. This explains why the synthetic models perform better on synthetic data and the real models on real data. nuScenes' features are the least concise: The first two clusters mostly contain point accumulations and only a few contours, which results in the poor AP and AR scores of all trained models on the nuScenes test set. PreSIL's features in the first cluster are also very sparse. This is probably because the dataset contains many annotated objects that are far away from the ego vehicle and therefore hit less often by the LiDAR due to its limited horizontal and vertical resolution. Our LUCID dataset's features range between the real datasets and PreSIL: Our first cluster is comparable to KITTI's, the second cluster is as clear as PreSIL's, and the third cluster looks more like the real dataset's third cluster than like PreSIL's. In our opinion, this contributes to the LUCID dataset having the best cross-dataset performance.

5 Conclusion

Computer vision and object detection based on deep learning are essential for automated driving. Whereas the performance of the detectors themselves is one important pillar, yet the availability of datasets for training and validation of the detectors is another one. While there could be different sensors utilized for the object detection task, this paper specifically addressed the topic of LiDAR datasets.

In order to train the detection models as comprehensively as possible for use in the field, the datasets must also be as comprehensive as possible and contain a wide variety of scenes. We have therefore analyzed the datasets from KITTI, nuScenes, and PreSIL for their similarities and differences, whereas these datasets come from real measurement campaigns and from simulation. Broad comparisons of these datasets on key statistics have already been made in related work. However, a thorough analysis was still missing to the best of our knowledge.

We identified the following more detailed aspects as central to the analysis. Map zones describe the environment of the recorded data, i.e. the road layout, buildings and vegetation. We identified that the majority of scenes take place in high density environments and only about a quarter covers low density areas. The number of objects in a scene or point cloud characterizes the density of surrounding objects to be detected. In this regard, KITTI's scenes are less dense with on average 2 annotated cars per scene less than PreSIL and 3.5 less than nuScenes. The driving pattern of the ego vehicle can also provide information on the perspective from which the surrounding objects are scanned. Here, KITTI and also nuScenes seem to exhibit an overrepresentation of scenes with straight driving compared to turns. The evaluation of Objects with Respect to LiDAR and LiDAR with Respect to Objects confirms the findings. Finally, there is the size of the bounding boxes: The real-world datasets contain a wide range of sizes compared to PreSIL due to GTA V's limited number of car models.

We do not delve much into details regarding our scenario generation process with Eclipse MOSAIC, CARLA and SUMO in this paper. However, in future work, we plan to elaborate more on the individual steps, as these are interesting enough.

In the Evaluation section of this paper, we compared the four datasets KITTI, nuScenes, PreSIL and our new LUCID in terms of cross-dataset detection performance based on Average Precision and Average Recall, when employed for training and testing with our object detector, which follows an Occupancy Grid Map approach. It does not claim to be the best performing detector. Yet, it can serve as a suitable benchmark. As initial result, we see that the model performs best with the test dataset similar to the training dataset. This is especially true for nuScenes, where differently trained models achieve very low values for AP and AR. A model trained with the LUCID dataset shows respectable results for test on KITTI and PreSIL, and of course on LUCID as well – making it the model with the best cross-dataset performance. Fine-tuning, i.e. additionally training, a model with a small part of another dataset increases detection performance. This fact underscores the importance of cross-dataset generalization. We have done this with models, initially trained on PreSIL and LUCID, and fine-tuned with 25% of KITTI as well as nuScenes data.

In this work, we limited our analysis to three datasets. In future work, additional existing datasets could be examined and the results be incorporated into our scenario generation process. A dataset created on this additional input may show even better cross-dataset performance, which could then also be validated with other detector solutions like Voxel-based ones.

As final conclusion, we could state that synthetically generated LiDAR data are useful. The model based on our proposed LUCID dataset showed the best cross-dataset generalization performance. Fine-tuning it with real data increased its performance on the real datasets even further. This reduced the required amount of real data by 75%, and, at the same time, outperformed the real datasets' models.

Acknowledgment. This work has been performed as part of the "ConnRAD" project (funding number 16KISR031), which is funded by the Federal Ministry of Education and Research (BMBF), Germany.

References

1. Caesar, H., et al.: nuScenes: a multimodal dataset for autonomous driving. In: IEEE/CVF Conference on Computer Vision and Pattern Recognition, pp. 11621–11631 (2020)
2. Dosovitskiy, A., Ros, G., Codevilla, F., Lopez, A., Koltun, V.: CARLA: an open urban driving simulator. In: Conference on Robot Learning, pp. 1–16 (2017)
3. Dworak, D., Ciepiela, F., Derbisz, J., Izzat, I., Komorkiewicz, M., Wójcik, M.: Performance of lidar object detection deep learning architectures based on artificially generated point cloud data from CARLA simulator. In: International Conference on Methods and Models in Automation and Robotics, pp. 600–605 (2019). https://doi.org/10.1109/MMAR.2019.8864642
4. Everingham, M., Van Gool, L., Williams, C.K., Winn, J., Zisserman, A.: The pascal visual object classes (VOC) challenge. Int. J. Comput. Vision **88**, 303–338 (2010)
5. Geiger, A., Lenz, P., Urtasun, R.: Are we ready for autonomous driving? The KITTI vision benchmark suite. In: IEEE Conference on Computer Vision and Pattern Recognition, pp. 3354–3361 (2012)
6. Geyer, J., et al.: A2D2: Audi Autonomous Driving Dataset. arXiv preprint arXiv:2004.06320 (2020). https://www.a2d2.audi
7. Huang, X., et al.: The apolloscape dataset for autonomous driving. In: IEEE Conference on Computer Vision and Pattern Recognition Workshops, pp. 954–960 (2018)
8. Hurl, B., Czarnecki, K., Waslander, S.: Precise synthetic image and lidar (PreSIL) dataset for autonomous vehicle perception. In: IEEE Intelligent Vehicles Symposium, pp. 2522–2529 (2019)
9. Keras VGG16 image classification model. https://keras.io/api/applications/vgg/
10. Kesten, R., et al.: Woven Planet perception dataset 2020 (2019). https://woven.toyota/en/perception-dataset

11. Li, Y., et al.: V2x-sim: multi-agent collaborative perception dataset and benchmark for autonomous driving. IEEE Robot. Autom. Lett. **7**(4), 10914–10921 (2022). https://doi.org/10.1109/LRA.2022.3192802
12. Liao, Y., Xie, J., Geiger, A.: KITTI-360: a novel dataset and benchmarks for urban scene understanding in 2D and 3D. IEEE Trans. Pattern Anal. Mach. Intell. **45**(3), 3292–3310 (2022)
13. Lopez, P.A., et al.: Microscopic traffic simulation using SUMO. In: IEEE International Conference on Intelligent Transportation Systems, pp. 2575–2582 (2018). https://doi.org/10.1109/ITSC.2018.8569938
14. Schrab, K., et al.: Modeling an its management solution for mixed highway traffic with eclipse mosaic. IEEE Trans. Intell. Transp. Syst. (2022)
15. Strunz, M., Protzmann, R., Radusch, I.: Lucid dataset: lidar utilization for cross-data integration and diversity (2024). https://doi.org/10.24406/fordatis/378. https://www.dcaiti.com/research/simulation/lucid/
16. Sun, P., et al.: Scalability in perception for autonomous driving: Waymo open dataset. In: IEEE/CVF Conference on Computer Vision and Pattern Recognition, pp. 2446–2454 (2020)
17. Sun, T., et al.: SHIFT: a synthetic driving dataset for continuous multi-task domain adaptation. In: IEEE/CVF Conference on Computer Vision and Pattern Recognition, pp. 21371–21382 (2022)
18. Wang, Y., et al.: Train in Germany, test in the USA: making 3D object detectors generalize. In: IEEE/CVF Conference on Computer Vision and Pattern Recognition, pp. 11710–11720 (2020). https://doi.org/10.1109/CVPR42600.2020.01173
19. Wilson, B., et al.: Argoverse 2: next generation datasets for self-driving perception and forecasting. In: Conference on Neural Information Processing Systems Datasets and Benchmarks Track (Round 2) (2021). https://openreview.net/forum?id=vKQGe36av4k
20. Yue, X., Wu, B., Seshia, S.A., Keutzer, K., Sangiovanni-Vincentelli, A.L.: A lidar point cloud generator: from a virtual world to autonomous driving. In: ACM International Conference on Multimedia Retrieval, pp. 458–464 (2018). https://doi.org/10.1145/3206025.3206080

Robotics Simulations

On the Simulation of a Neuromorphic Robotic Arm with Dynamic Control for Rapid Trajectories Evaluation

Diógenes Trejos-Hernández(✉), Elena Cerezuela-Escudero, and Alejandro Linares-Barranco

Robotics and Technology of Computers Lab, ETSII-EPS, I3US, SCORE, Universidad de Sevilla, Seville, Spain
diotreher@alum.us.es

Abstract. The development of software simulators for robotic applications involves many advantages such as faster trajectory planning in virtual worlds, savings in energy consumption, reduction in the purchase of real robots, feasibility in collecting datasets for AI model training, etc. Commercial, free-access, open-source simulators for any type of robot can be found on the Internet and in the literature. Some of them allow the implementation of specific or new control models. For a behavior closer to the real world, the following must be taken into account: kinematics and dynamics, gravity, masses, etc. This paper proposes a new simulator for a neuromorphic robotic arm (modified Scorbot ER-VII) whose hardware controllers are based on Field Programmable Logic Arrays (FPGA) to allow the implementation of neuro-inspired motor controllers, such as Spiking Proportional-Integral-Derivative (SPID), to manage each joint of the robot. This simulator is developed in Matlab and Simulink and is available to the public. The simulator allows for the evaluation of different trajectories with two controllers, an Independent Joint Control (IJC) and a Computerized Torque Control (CTC). It has been tested for square and lemniscate trajectories with a small number of internally interpolated points to create reference trajectories with more points. RSME improvements of more than 10x have been measured for CTC over IJC, requiring less than 13 ms per point evaluated for a 3.6 GHz i7 computer and 32 GB RAM.

Keywords: Robot arm simulation · Kinematic · Independent Joint Control · Computed Torque Control · Scorbot

This research was partially supported by the Spanish grants MINDROB (PID2019-105556GB-C33/AEI/10.13039/501100011033), SMALL (PCI2019-111841-2/AEI/10.1309/501100011033), NEKOR (PID2023-149071NB-C54), PAIDI 2020 complementary action (QUAL21 008 USE) from Andalusian Council.

A. A. Juan et al. (Eds.): SIMUtools 2024, LNICST 603, pp. 221–238, 2025.
https://doi.org/10.1007/978-3-031-87345-4_15

1 Introduction

A robotic arm is a mechatronic system designed to simulate the movements of a human arm through its joints. The advantage of using robotic arms in industry is that they can move large loads, have long operating times, reduce production time, etc. A robotic arm is usually made up of a base, which is the robot's pivot point and is generally anchored to the ground or support; then there are the links, which are the rigid moving sections that are connected by joints; the joints are responsible for connecting, supporting, and moving the links, through actuators, transmissions, and reducers, this set of parts makes up the joint. At the end of the chain of links and joints is the End Effector (EE), whose purpose is to manipulate objects, tools, or interact with the environment [8]. The most important component of a robot is the controller. This is the brain of the robot, receiving and processing all the information necessary for the robot to perform the task assigned by the user. In its hardware, the controller has input and output pins. The outputs supply voltages and currents to the actuators in the joints, while the inputs receive measurements from the robot's internal and external sensors. These measurements are fed back to the controller, allowing it to correct faults and make the robot perform its task as accurately as possible.

Nowadays, robotic arms are used in many fields, especially in industry. For this reason, many colleges and universities have included industrial robotics in their curricula to keep up with these technologies. However, the purchase of an industrial robot is very expensive, and instead, 3D simulators are commonly used, which allow the user to comfortably and easily design robotic systems in a graphical environment, with which tests can be performed before a real project is carried out [19]. Developing a robotic application involves tasks such as programming, mechanical design, and mathematical analysis, usually performed in separate software. The advantage of robotic simulators is that they typically allow the user to perform all these tasks together in a single software package. This is not to say that the robot simulator is indispensable, as there will be occasions when other software will need to be used to complement the simulator to implement the project in a robot. Among the simulators, there are those that solve a specific robot problem, such as those related to its movement, and others of general purpose, where it is possible to create a complete industrial station. The most convenient way is to use a robot simulator that contains most of the tools needed to achieve the desired objective.

General-purpose simulators offer the user 3D simulation of systems and offline programming. One of the most widely used is RobotStudio[1]. This software allows using of an extensive library for ABB® robots with their respective design parameters and a wide variety of industrial components (conveyor belts, sensors, etc.); automatically solving the problem of robot motion (Forward Kinematics (FK) and Inverse Kinematics (IK)), which facilitates the generation of trajectories; and exporting the programming performed in the simulator directly to the real-life robot controller [16]. A significant advantage of this simulator is its

[1] https://new.abb.com/products/robotics/robotstudio (Accessed April 5, 2025).

completeness and ease of use; the only disadvantage is that it is not open-source. There are free, open-source simulators, but their problems usually lie in their inability to generate the robot's motion trajectories, so they must be used with other applications. One such simulator is RoboDK[2], which allows users to create, simulate, and generate programs for specific robot arms or robot controllers from different vendors. Another free simulator is CoppeliaSim[3] (Educational license). This simulator is often used with Matlab for robot motion control via its Remote API. An important feature of the CoppeliaSim simulator is its built-in collision detection module, which allows it to check for interference (collisions) between objects [18]. Other simulators, such as Gazebo[4], work like a real-world physics simulator. Usually, the robotic system is implemented in the Gazebo simulation environment and controlled by ROS (Robotic-Operating-System)[5]. However, some preliminary tasks have to be done before implementation, such as describing the robot in a Unified Format (URDF) on an XML file. This XML file format contains all the information about the robot's kinematics, dynamic description, visual representation, and collision model [7]. This is why Gazebo is mostly used in research areas rather than education.

More generalist simulators are commonly used to solve specific problems, such as the motion of a robot. These include Matlab and Simulink, although they are also often used for other general-purpose applications. Matlab is an environment for performing analysis and design tasks using a high-level programming language. Simulink is a Matlab application with a block diagram environment. For robotics applications, within the Simulink environment, we can find "Robotics System Toolbox" (RST) used for kinematic and dynamic analysis of robots and "Simscape Multibody" for modeling physical systems [11]. Both Matlab and Simulink will be essential to the development of this work.

The control of a robotic arm is essential to ensure that it performs a task correctly with a minimum margin of error. In industry, Proportional-Integral-Derivative (PID) control is usually the most widely used due to its versatility and efficiency in the optimization of movement, however, one of the disadvantages of PID control is that it is not sufficient to obtain the desired control results due to the non-linear behavior of the manipulator. Moreover, in addition to this problem, classical robotic systems have many sensors, whose control system requires a high computational and energy cost in the coding and transmission of the information coming from the sensors. This is why neuromorphic (or neuro-inspired) control systems have emerged [3,15]. They emulate the behavior of the neurons of the human nervous system in the way they receive, process, and transmit information, using pulses or spikes [2,17], which allow significant energy savings by processing the data (proprioceptive sensors) only when there are pulses, instead of doing so periodically even if the control set point does not need to be updated, as occurs in classical control.

---

[2] https://robodk.com/ (Accessed April 5, 2025).
[3] https://www.coppeliarobotics.com/ (Accessed April 5, 2025).
[4] https://gazebosim.org/ (Accessed April 5, 2025).
[5] https://www.ros.org/ (Accessed April 5, 2025).

In this work, a robotic arm was simulated using two types of control: Independent Joint Control (IJC) and Computed Torque Control (CTC). These simulations aim to exhaustively compare the two types of dynamic control, checking that the robot's EE can pass through all the points of two reference trajectories.

The main contribution of this work is the development of a simulator in an environment, such as Matlab and Simulink, that allows a complete analysis of the robot. With the amount of tools that these programs have, we can model the robot with its parameters identical to the real robot and make the simulation in many types of realistic industrial scenarios where environmental factors can modify the dynamics of the robot preventing its correct operation. The main advantage of our simulator is that we can design and test different optimization mechanisms (controllers) before investing money in the real robot. In addition, Matlab and Simulink allow an easy implementation in hardware such as Arduino, RaspberryPi, FPGA, etc. admitting the generation of C and C++ code which can be executed in microcontrollers which is what we plan to do in future works. The control designed in this simulator can complement the controllers that already have the motors of the real robotic arm for better trajectory correction.

The next section explains the modeling of the controller and the robot arm. Section 3 describes the materials and methods used to develop a simulator for a concrete robotic arm from our lab and the results for two reference trajectories: square and lemniscate shape paths. Finally, the conclusions are presented in Sect. 4.

2 Materials and Methods

In this section, the different materials used to perform the research around a specific robotic arm simulation are described and then developed methods are presented. It first presents the real hardware infrastructure that our simulator tends to mimic, then several conceptual bases are described. Finally, in the software simulator subsection, we present the developed methods.

2.1 Hardware Infrastructure

ED-Scorbot is a neuromorphic robot composed of a six-degrees-of-freedom (DoF) Scorbot ER-VII educational robotic arm (see Fig. 1) and a set of printed circuit boards, based on a Zynq7100 module, which allows the control of the robot in the spiking domain. The robot is composed of six actuators (DC motors) powered by 12 V direct current that through transmissions produce motion on the axes of its five rotational type joints and to open and close a grip (sixth joint). In addition, each motor is equipped with a double optical encoder to accurately record the motion [2]. Usually, motor actuators drive the motors from digital circuits through the Pulse-Width-Modulation (PWM). In this robot, a more bio-inspired (neuromorphic) solution is adopted, using the Pulse-Frequency-Modulation (PFM) for that purpose. The electronics are fully oriented to support this neuromorphic spiking control in such a way that spike-based PID controllers were developed and included in the control logic [6] for each joint. As any robot would need to command Euclidean space trajectories, FK and IK were proposed for this robot [2].

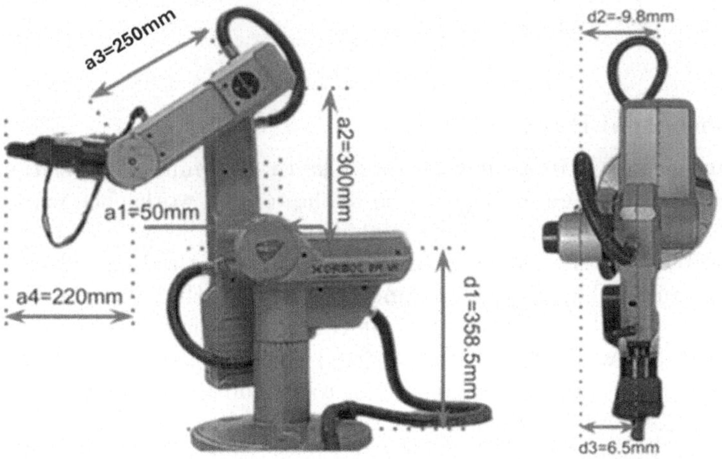

Fig. 1. Scorbot ER-VII robotic diagram. Top view (right). Side view (left).

The kinematic structure of the considered ED-Scorbot includes only four joints J_1, J_2, J_3 and J_4 as shown in Fig. 1. The angle values of each joint are designated $\theta_1, \theta_2, \theta_3$ and θ_4. When we refer to joint coordinates (q) we will consider them q_1, q_2, q_3 and q_4. Although the real robot has five rotational joints we will not make use of the last one, since it is the one in charge of orienting the EE, which we will not take into account in this work because we will only simulate the movement of the robotic arm performing some trajectories. The main goal will be to ensure that the end of the EE passes through all the points of the trajectory regardless of the orientation of the EE. Then in future works where it is desired that the robot performs a specific task with its EE, it will be necessary to take into account the fifth joint to orient it.

Table 1. Denavit-Hartenberg params [2].

Joint	θ_i	d_i(m)	a_i(m)	α_i(Deg)
J_1	q_1	0.3585	0.050	90
J_2	q_2	−0.098	0.300	180
J_3	q_3	0.0650	0.250	0
J_4	q_4	0	0.220	0

Table 2. Upper and lower bounds for joints one through four (taken from [2]).

Joint	Upper (SI)	Lower (SI)	Upper (Deg)	Lower (Deg)
J_1	487	−487	155	−155
J_2	750	−750	85	−85
J_3	383	−383	112.5	−112.5
J_4	1585	−1585	90	−90

2.2 Conceptual Bases

a. Kinematics: FK in a robotic arm seeks to determine the position and orientation of the robot endpoint (or EE) in the robot's workspace with respect to a fixed reference frame from given joint coordinates. So for robots with several degrees of freedom, the Denavit-Hartenberg (DH) method (see Table 1) is often used to obtain the DH parameters and then extract the homogeneous transformation matrix H which contains the information of the position and orientation of the robot EE with respect to the fixed reference frame. The IK allows us to know the joint configuration that the robot must have to place its EE in a specific position and orientation. For the ED-Scorbot, both the FK and the IK are presented in [2].

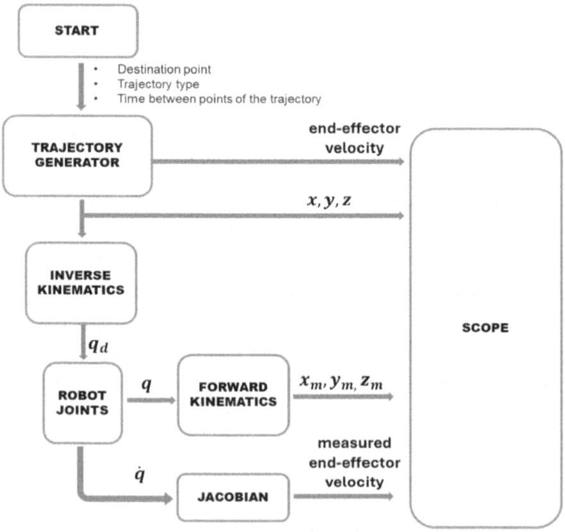

Fig. 2. Kinematic control diagram.

b. Kinematic Control (KC): In the previous sections, it has been shown how through direct and IK one can locate the EE of a robotic arm at a point in its workspace using IK, starting from an initial position. However, to complete this movement from an initial point to a final one, the robot could pass through an infinite number of points within its workspace. This infinite number of points can represent a problem when performing a particular trajectory since the robot can take unwanted joint configurations, which in the worst case will cause the robot to collide with objects (or itself) within its workspace. This problem can be solved by planning trajectories, which will ensure the smoothness of the path without exceeding the maximum allowable velocities and accelerations for each joint in turn, avoiding collisions [14]. In our case, we will make use of kinematic control so that the robot passes through all the points proposed in the workspace by using interpolators included in the trajectory generator (see Fig. 2).

c. Dynamic Model: Dynamics relates the forces acting on a system and the motion that occurs in it. Therefore, the dynamic model of a robotic arm aims to study the relationship that exists between its movement and the forces that generate it. This model is very important in the development of real-time control, for the tracking of a desired trajectory. To establish the dynamic model, it is taken as a starting point for the kinematic analysis of the robot.

With independence of external disturbances, such as friction, the dynamic equation of the n-degree-of-freedom robotic arm is shown in Eq. 1.

$$\tau = M(q)\ddot{q} + C(q, \dot{q}) + G(q) \tag{1}$$

where $\ddot{q}, \dot{q}, q$, denote the angular acceleration, velocity, and joint position vectors $(n \times 1)$, respectively; $M(q), C(q, \dot{q}), G(q)$ are the inertia matrix $(n \times n)$, the Coriolis force matrix $(n \times 1)$ and the gravity force matrix $(n \times 1)$, respectively; τ represents the control torque vector $(n \times 1)$. n if the number of DOF of the robot.

Once the dynamic model of the robot is developed, it is necessary to implement its dynamic control. The main function of dynamic control is to ensure that the trajectories followed by the robot are as close as possible to those proposed by kinematic control.

In this work, two dynamic controllers are included in the proposed simulator and compared in Sect. 3, the PID as independent joint control, and the computed torque control, described in the following epigraphs.

d.1. Independent Joint Control (IJC): There are several types of IJC dynamic control; to choose the right one you must take into account the mechanical characteristics of the robot as dimensions, weight, type of actuators, etc. All of this has a significant influence on the type of control to be used. We implement the PID controller to make the IJC control. The PID is a widely used controller in industrial process control due to its robustness, simple algorithm, easy implementation, and high reliability [20]. Furthermore, it already works with the real ED-Scorbot. To implement the PID on a robotic arm joint, the controller parameters must be integrated with the system dynamics. Mohammet et al. in [13] propose that if actuators are considered as an ideal source of forces and torques, the PID controller would be defined as in Eq. 2,

$$u(t) = K_p \cdot e(t) + K_i \int_0^t e(\xi) d\xi + K_d \cdot \dot{e}(t) \tag{2}$$

where $u = \tau$ is the torque (or force) applied to the joint actuator; K_p, K_i, K_d represent the proportional, integral, and derivative gain arrays, respectively; $e(t) = q_d(t) - q(t)$ denotes the deviation (error) between the desired position (or reference position) $q_d(t)$ and the actual position $q(t)$ in the robot output, and $\dot{e}(t) = \dot{q}_d(t) - \dot{q}(t)$ represents the error between the desired speed and the current speed. "ξ" is an integration variable that represents the cumulative time from 0 to t and $e(\xi)$ is the error at each instant of ξ.

It usually happens that when factors, such as disturbances, act in the system, it is difficult for a conventional PID controller to fulfill its control purpose, due to its fixed parameters. That is why there are techniques for on-line self-tuning of these parameters, thus improving the adaptability of the controller to various disturbances [1,10]. Matlab and Simulink simulation environments have tools to automatically tune the parameters of a PID controller [9]. In [4], El-Khatib et al. propose four 2-DOF PID controllers with the objective of controlling the joint angles of a four-degree-of-freedom robotic arm. This type of PID controller has a better transient response than conventional PIDs. Therefore, we implement a 2-DOF PID controller, aiming to realize IJC (see Fig. 3), in the proposed simulator.

Equation 3 shows the 2-DoF PID formulation.

$$u(t) = K_p \left(b \cdot q_d(t) - q(t)\right) + K_i \int_0^t e(\xi) d\xi + K_d \frac{d}{dt} \left(c \cdot q_d(t) - q(t)\right) \tag{3}$$

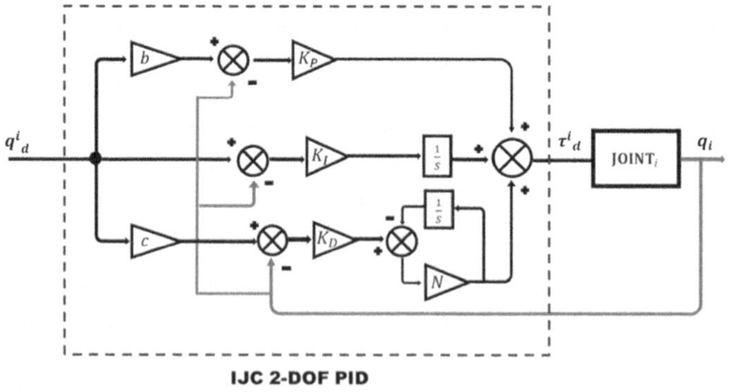

Fig. 3. IJC control scheme using 2-DOF PID; i: number of the Joint; b: proportional setpoint weight; c: derivative setpoint weight; N: filter coefficient.

d.2. Computed Torque Control (CTC): CTC is a classical type of control that is widely used in robotics motion control problems (see Eq. (4)). It is easy to implement and has a low computational cost. However, its response in time varies with the configuration of the robot [12]. This type of control requires an accurate dynamic model of the robot, however, due to the nonlinearity of the robotic arm system, the controller can't perform well. That is why it is usually combined with feedback from a PD controller, since, the PID controller can sometimes lead to instability [5].

Equation 4 shows the formulation for the CTC dynamic control.

$$\tau = M\left(\ddot{q}_d + K_p \cdot e(t) + K_d \cdot \dot{e}(t)\right) + C(q, \dot{q}) + G(q) \tag{4}$$

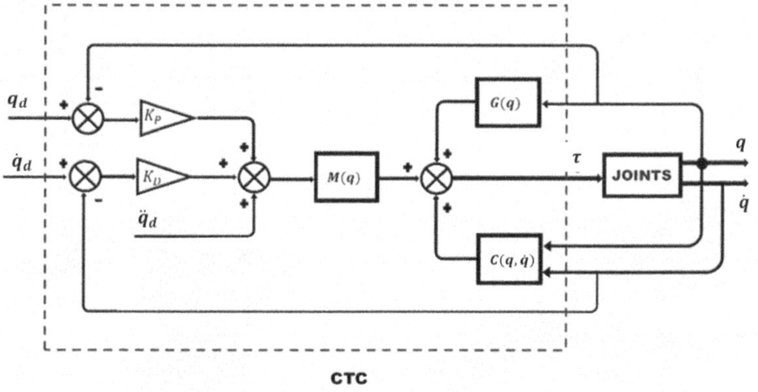

Fig. 4. CTC control scheme.

To quantify the effectiveness of the proposed controllers, two different metrics will be used: the RMSE, which is obtained from the Eq. (6), and the actual time that the simulation takes to run on our computer. These times are obtained with the functions "tic" and "toc" functions in Matlab. To obtain the RMSE, the Euclidean distance between the points of the target and real trajectories is used (see Eq. (5)).

$$d(S_{ref}, S_m) = \sqrt{(x_{ref} - x_m)^2 + (y_{ref} - y_m)^2 + (z_{ref} - z_m)^2} \tag{5}$$

$$RMSE = \sqrt{\frac{1}{n}\sum_{i=1}^{n} d(S_{ref}, S_m)^2} \tag{6}$$

2.3 Software Simulator

The 3D design of the base, the links, the end-effector, the respective lengths, and masses were imported to Simulink/Simscape from a previous model in URDF created from the real robot[6]. This same model complies with all the DH parameters shown in Table 1.

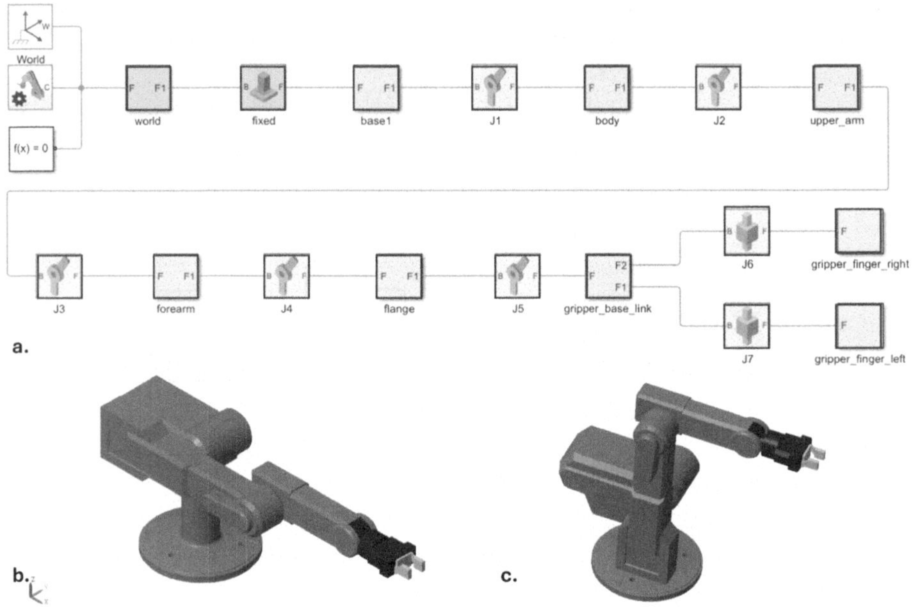

Fig. 5. a. Robot modeling in Simulink/Simscape (red blocks: the origin of the coordinate system and weld joint; orange blocks: links and their coordinate systems; blue blocks: Joints); b. 3D simulation; c. its home position ($x_0 = 0.472$ m, $y_0 = 0.033$ m and $z_0 = 0.6585$ m). (Color figure online)

The rotating joint blocks (J_1, J_2, J_3 and J_4) were adjusted with the values of Table 2, which shows the rotation limits of each joint. In addition, inputs and outputs were enabled for each of these blocks. The inputs of the blocks allow us to supply both joint positions and torques (see Fig. 6). Therefore, we must supply one of these two data to generate joint motion (q or τ).

a. Kinematics Control (KC): Before implementing the two types of dynamic control, we must ensure that our system meets all the necessary requirements for proper operation, so first, we will perform a series of tests based on the

[6] GitHub-RTC: https://github.com/RTC-research-group/ED-Scorbot/ (Accessed April 5, 2025).

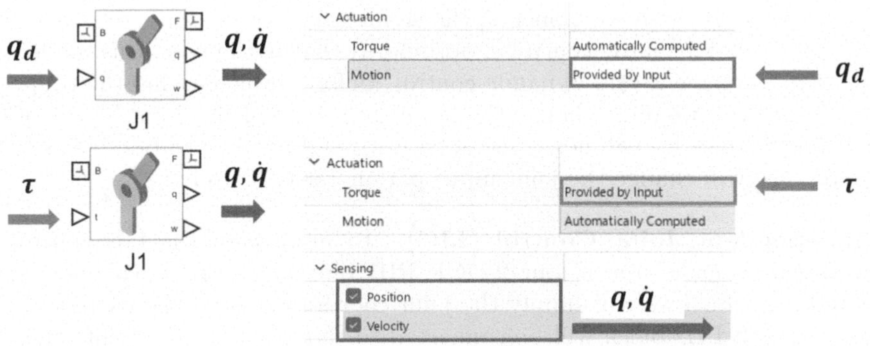

Fig. 6. On the left side: the joint block. On the right: are the input (shaded in red for motion (q) and green for Torque (τ)) and output parameters of the joint (shaded in blue). (Color figure online)

robot's kinematics. To establish the kinematic control we must determine the target points, the type of trajectory, the time in which the trajectory is to be performed, and the start and end points. Therefore, every x, y, z coordinates of the trajectory should be written in an array in Matlab. These start and end points can be at any point in space of the workspace of the robot, including the home position defined by the home sensors of the robot, also known as the rest position (see Fig. 5c). Let's define a matrix S_p with all the points through which we want the robot's EE to pass. Let's test the simulator with two types of trajectories: a square and a lemniscate trajectory.

Within the"Robotics System Toolbox" (RST) it can be found trajectory generator blocks. To these blocks, one can add the S_p matrix. Let's use the "Trapezoidal Velocity Profile Trajectory" and the "Polynomial Trajectory" blocks. These internally have interpolation functions, which will do the task of joining the points of the coordinates S_p and generate a reference trajectory (S_{ref}) for the robot. Depending on the type of trajectory, one will be more convenient than the other. In the output of the trajectory generator block, it will be obtained the Cartesian reference coordinates (x, y, z). The respective Cartesian coordinates will be supplied to the IK stage, composed of the "Get Transform" and "IK" blocks of RST. With this scenario, it can be obtained the reference (or desired) joint coordinates q_{d1}, q_{d2}, q_{d3} and q_{d4}, needed to move the robot.

After supplying the reference joint coordinates to our robot, at the robot outputs, we will obtain the measurements of q_1, q_2, q_3 and q_4 for the joint positions and output joint velocities $\dot{q}_1$, $\dot{q}_2$, $\dot{q}_3$, and $\dot{q}_4$.

To calculate the values of x, y, z corresponding to the trajectory performed by the robot, an FK stage composed of the blocks "FK" and "Get Transform" will be used. Let's designate these values as x_m, y_m, and z_m. As the last block of the simulation chain, the "Scope" block can be used to verify if the measured trajectory at the robot output follows the reference trajectory.

Now, with all these components, the simulation can be done, together with the check if the kinematic control is optimal. If that is the case, this model can be used to implement said dynamic control. Before implementing the proposed dynamic control, we must change the input data type of the Joint blocks of the robot model, since we will now control by force and not by position (see Fig. 6), therefore, we will change the joint input parameter to Torque.

b. Independent Joint Control (IJC): To implement the IJC control, it is proposed to make use of four 2-DOF PID blocks (one for each joint) from Simulink, to which we will supply the joint coordinates from the IK block. The output of each PID block will be connected to the inputs of the joints through the"Simulink-PSConverter" block, which in turn will do the force-to-torque conversion. As this time force control is used, it will be necessary to change the input parameter of the blocks J_1, J_2, J_3, and J_4 (see Fig. 6), since, previously for the kinematic control, the input was the position. Therefore, in this phase, the input to the block will be a force, and from that, the system will do the automatic calculation of position and velocity. Let's use the joint position value measured at the output of each joint as feedback for the PID controllers. To adjust the K_p, K_i, K_d parameters of each 2-DOF PID, the SLTUNER[7] tool is being used. This tool automatically adjusts the parameters of each PID controller. At the output of the IJC model, the torques τ needed to move each joint are obtained.

c. Computed Torque Control (CTC): Based on Eq. 4 we can create in Simulink the dynamic CTC control. To model the inertia matrix M, the Coriolis force matrix C, and the gravity force matrix G, the following RST blocks are being used: "Joint Space Mass Matrix", "Velocity Product Torque" and "Gravity Torque" respectively. The PD controller will be modeled with "Gain" blocks which will represent the gains K_p and K_d. These gains will be multiplied by their respective position and velocity deviations. For more details, see the Fig. 4. The outputs of the CTC model represent the torques τ needed to move each joint. The forces are converted to torque through the "Simulink-PSConverter" blocks.

3 Simulation and Results

The first thing was to perform a series of simulations in Simulink of the KC control model for position control of the robot, as described in the KC section. This series of simulations were done to test the operation of the system components. Once the simulation tests of the KC control were done and observed that the obtained position results at the robot output were equal to the reference ones, we can proceed to implement the dynamic control, with which we will see a more realistic robot behavior. In this case, we can do force control, taking into account the masses of each component of the robot and the gravitational force. These simulation tests of the robotic arm are divided into two different trajectories:

[7] MathWorks: https://es.mathworks.com/help/control/ug/example-focused-on-creation-and-configuration-of-sltuner-interface.html (Accessed April 5, 2025).

one is the simulation of a square trajectory and a lemniscate trajectory. These trajectories were chosen because they allow the movement of all the joints of the robot, so the effectiveness of the IJC control and the CTC can be measured.

It has been used as a computer for executing our model in Simulink for the presented results. The CPU is an i7-12700K at 3.60 GHz, with a GPU from NVIDIA, model GeForce GTX 1660 SUPER, 32.0 GB of DDR memory, a Microsoft Windows 10 OS, a Matlab distro R2024a and Solver ODE23t.

b. Controller Parameters: The 2DOF-PID parameter settings for the IJC control of each joint were made with the SLTUNER tool, while the PD integrated within the CTC control was adjusted manually. All these parameter settings can be viewed in the Table 3.

Table 3. Controller Parameters.

Controller	K_p	K_i	K_d	b	c	N
IJC J_1	4631.79	43723.8	135.87	0.06	0.0045	194294.98
IJC J_2	1428.64	11087.9	62.05	0.20	0.071	267258.55
IJC J_3	128.52	1.4	13.23	1.00	0.011	129942.45
IJC J_4	142.60	1370.1	0.96	1.52	0.115	114556.58
CTC	3500	-	750	-	-	-

c. Square Path: Let's define the coordinate matrix $S_p =$

$$\begin{bmatrix} 0.25 & 0.25 & 0.40 & 0.40 & 0.25 \\ 0.25 & 0.40 & 0.40 & 0.25 & 0.25 \\ 0.30 & 0.30 & 0.30 & 0.30 & 0.30 \end{bmatrix}$$

as the sequence of points that the robot should follow to reproduce a square path.

The proposed time for the robot to complete the trajectory is $t_p = 7.5s$. To make it possible for the robot to follow a straight line between these points, an interpolation method is needed to extract internal points that will be reached by the robot. Since it is a square trajectory, the most convenient is to use a trajectory generator with a trapezoidal interpolator. The Simulink block will be the "Trapezoidal Velocity Profile Trajectory".

d. Lemniscate Path: A lemniscate path is an eight-shaped trajectory. For this trajectory, let us suppose that the whole time to execute the trajectory is $t_p = 10s$.

Unlike the square trajectory, for the lemniscate trajectory, a sequence of 100 points was calculated using the Eq. 7. This sequence of points was enriched with a polynomial trajectory generator.

$$x = 0.05 + \frac{a \cdot \sin(t) \cdot \cos(t)}{1 + \sin^2(t)}; y = 0.033 + \frac{a \cdot \cos(t)}{1 + \sin^2(t)}; z = 0.35 \times ones(size(t)) \quad (7)$$

where the constant a refers to the scale of the lemniscate and t is the time vector.

3.1 Results

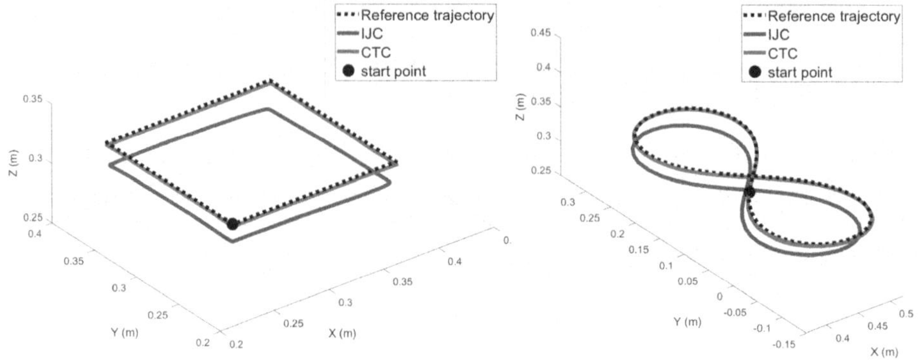

Fig. 7. Square path (left) and Lemniscate path (right).

Figure 7 shows the graphs of the x, y, and z coordinates of the square and lemniscate trajectories generated by the robot with respect to the reference ones (after interpolation), for each kinematic controller. The data for both trajectories are taken from 2 s onwards. This is because the trajectories start at the robot's initial position, so the path the robot takes to reach the starting point of each trajectory is ignored here.

Figure 8 top and bottom correspond to the Euclidean distance in metres between EE of each controller with respect to each reference trajectory for square and lemniscate respectively. Figure 9 top and bottom show the EE evolution of x, y, z of each controller for the two reference trajectories. It should be noted that the x, y, and z coordinates corresponding to the trajectory generated by the CTC control (red line) are very close to the reference x, y, and z coordinates. It can also be seen in Fig. 9 for the IJC control (blue line), that the axis with the greatest deviation with respect to the reference is the z-axis, this is due to the effect of gravity.

Table 4. Simulation Results.

Control	Path	RMSE	$t_p(s)$	No. Ref. points	No. Points gen.	Real time(s)
IJC	Square	0.0219	7.5	5.0	414.0	12.14
	Lemniscate	0.0280	10.0	100.0	383.0	15.05
CTC	Square	0.0020	7.5	5.0	2030.0	76.10
	Lemniscate	0.0028	10.0	100.0	459.0	21.83

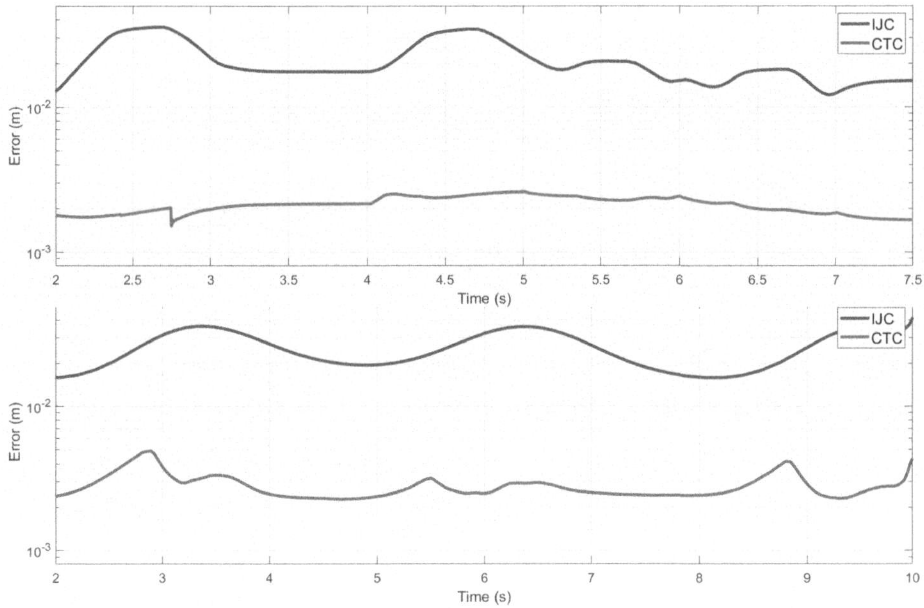

Fig. 8. Square (top) and Lemniscate (bottom) trajectories error. Log scale (y-axis) to highlight CTC smaller error.

From the results shown in Table 4, it can be seen that the CTC controller is more effective than the IJC. This is because the IJC being an independent joint control, by providing a variable trajectory could not generate a torque instantaneously to reject the dynamic effects such as: change of inertia, gravity force, and Coriolis forces generated by the motion of the other links. This means that the trajectory is not corrected. In contrast, the CTC, being a control acting on the complete system, can provide the instantaneous torque necessary to overcome these dynamics effects.

As indicated by the last column of Table 4 (indicates the actual time taken by Simulink to generate and run the simulation), the computational cost of the CTC control is higher for both types of trajectories. This is largely due to the stiffness of the robotic arm, as CTC is a control based on the precise model of the robot dynamics, unlike IJC control, which does not directly depend on these dynamics. Another factor to take into account is the number of reference points given to the trajectory generator (column five of Table 4), because the lemniscate trajectory has more reference points, the generation of the trajectory for the CTC is faster than the generation of the square trajectory. Therefore, for the robot to generate the square trajectory using the CTC, the interpolator must generate a greater number of points. This also added to the complexity of the robot dynamics and increases the computational cost of the CTC.

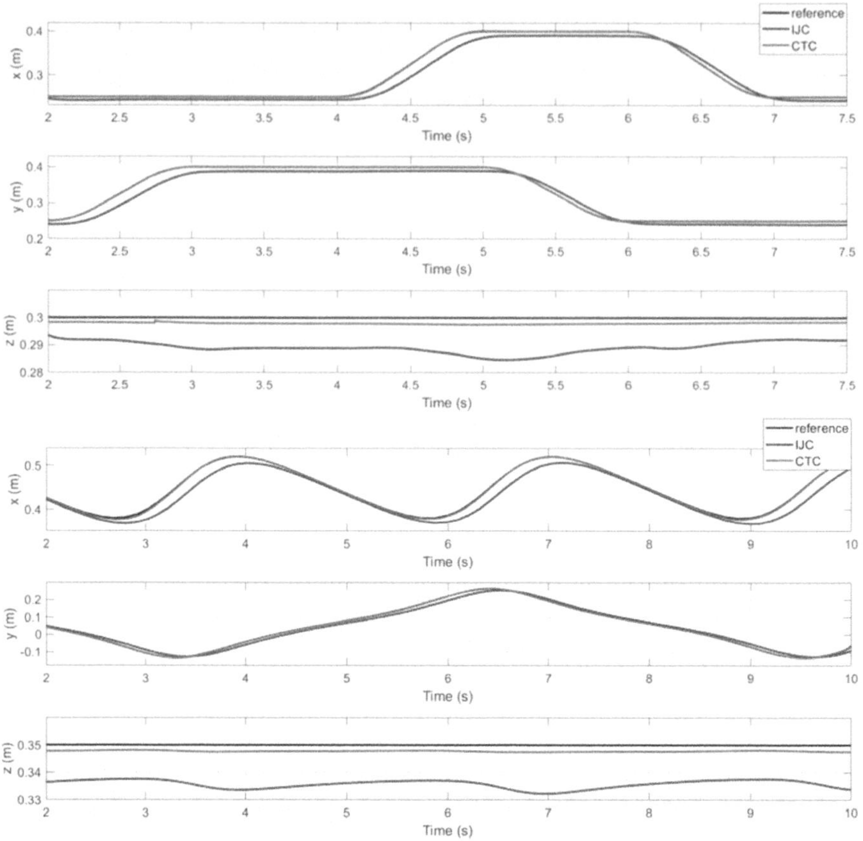

Fig. 9. Deviation of the x, y, z coordinates from the reference coordinates for a Square (top) and Lemniscate trajectory (bottom).

The Simulink and Matlab files corresponding to the generated simulations can be found in the Matlab file repository[8].

4 Conclusion

In this work, a simulator developed in Matlab/Simulink is presented for a neuromorphic robotic arm with neuro-inspired motor controllers. Several mathematical and conceptual robotic foundations are included to facilitate the use of robots in simulated scenarios for more efficient robot research. Two motor controllers (IJC and CTC) have been developed for possible future implementation in the robot FPGA. The results show that the CTC control is more accurate than IJC, in terms of following a reference trajectory, because the CTC control acts

[8] https://github.com/RTC-research-group/ED-Scorbot/ (Accessed April 5, 2025).

on the entire robot system, while IJC controls each joint independently using 2DOF-PID controllers. Therefore, 2DOF-PID does not compensate for inertia changes generated by the motion of the other links, gravity force, and Coriolis force effects. However, the problem with CTC control lies in its computational cost, while IJC is up to 10 times faster. The higher computational cost of the CTC is due to the high rigidity of the system, so the solver takes longer to solve all the mathematical problems related to robot dynamics. Although the IJC control based on 2DOF-PID controllers is less accurate, it can be improved by implementing compensators based on neural networks or similar tools.

Our next work will be to compare the results of these simulations with the trajectories generated by the real robot (ED-Scorbot) and see how the current control of the robot can be improved, taking as a reference the two types of control shown in this work.

References

1. Al-Amin, M., Islam, M.S.: Design of an intelligent temperature controller of furnace system using the fuzzy self-tuning PID controller. In: Proceedings of International Conference on Electronics, Communications and Information Technology, ICECIT 2021 (2021). https://doi.org/10.1109/ICECIT54077.2021.9641467
2. Canas-Moreno, S., et al.: Towards neuromorphic FPGA-based infrastructures for a robotic arm. Auton. Robots **47**(7) (2023)
3. Davies, M., et al.: Advancing neuromorphic computing with loihi: a survey of results and outlook. Proc. IEEE **109**, 911–934 (2021). https://doi.org/10.1109/JPROC.2021.3067593
4. El-Khatib, M.F., Maged, S.A.: Low level position control for 4-DOF arm robot using fuzzy logic controller and 2-DOF PID controller. In: 2021 International Mobile, Intelligent, and Ubiquitous Computing Conference, MIUCC 2021, pp. 258–262 (2021). https://doi.org/10.1109/MIUCC52538.2021.9447617
5. Gabriel, M.T., Din, A.S.E.D.Z.E., Azzam, A.S.: Modeling and fuzzy based computed torque control of a multi-degree of freedom robotic manipulator. In: 2019 21st International Middle East Power Systems Conference, MEPCON 2019 - Proceedings, pp. 902–907 (2019). https://doi.org/10.1109/MEPCON47431.2019.9008021
6. Jimenez-Fernandez, A., et al.: A neuro-inspired spike-based PID motor controller for multi-motor robots with low cost FPGAS. Sensors **12**(4), 3831–3856 (2012). https://doi.org/10.3390/s120403831
7. Jung, H., Kim, M., Chen, Y., Min, H.G., Park, T.: Implementation of a unified simulation for robot arm control with object detection based on ROS and gazebo. In: 2020 17th International Conference on Ubiquitous Robots, UR 2020, pp. 368–372 (2020). https://doi.org/10.1109/UR49135.2020.9144984
8. Kaur, M., Sondhi, S., Yanumula, V.K.: Kinematics analysis and jacobian calculation for six degrees of freedom robotic arm. In: 2020 IEEE 17th India Council International Conference, INDICON 2020 (2020). https://doi.org/10.1109/INDICON49873.2020.9342093
9. Kulkarni, P., Kulkarni, O., Sayyad, J.K.: Tuning of a robotic arm using PID controller for robotics and automation industry. In: 2024 6th International Conference on Energy, Power and Environment (ICEPE), pp. 1–6 (2024). https://doi.org/10.1109/ICEPE63236.2024.10668952. https://ieeexplore.ieee.org/document/10668952/

10. Li, T., Huo, C., Zeng, F., Ding, J., Huang, Y.: Design of PID control algorithm for mechanical arm based on BP neural network model. In: Proceedings - 2023 2nd International Conference on Artificial Intelligence and Autonomous Robot Systems, AIARS 2023, pp. 406–409 (2023). https://doi.org/10.1109/AIARS59518.2023.00088
11. Long, D.T., Binh, T.V., Hoa, R.V., Anh, L.V., Toan, N.V.: Robotic arm simulation by using matlab and robotics toolbox for industry application. Int. J. Electron. Commun. Eng. **7**, 1–4 (2020). https://doi.org/10.14445/23488549/IJECE-V7I10P101. https://www.internationaljournalssrg.org/IJECE/paper-details?Id=364
12. Mhiri, S.A., Romdhane, N.M.B., Damak, T.: Comparison of two techniques for controlling the parallel robot par4: CTC and SMC. In: 2018 15th International Multi-Conference on Systems, Signals and Devices, SSD 2018, pp. 1007–1011 (2018). https://doi.org/10.1109/SSD.2018.8570474
13. Mohammed, A.A., Eltayeb, A.: Dynamics and control of a two-link manipulator using PID and sliding mode control. In: 2018 International Conference on Computer, Control, Electrical, and Electronics Engineering, ICCCEEE 2018 (2018). https://doi.org/10.1109/ICCCEEE.2018.8515795
14. Qin, W.: Simulation of path planning model of manipulator based on artificial intelligence algorithm. In: 2023 International Conference on Telecommunications, Electronics and Informatics (ICTEI), pp. 191–196 (2023). https://doi.org/10.1109/ICTEI60496.2023.00159
15. Sandamirskaya, Y., Kaboli, M., Conradt, J., Celikel, T.: Neuromorphic computing hardware and neural architectures for robotics. Sci. Robot. **7** (2022). https://doi.org/10.1126/SCIROBOTICS.ABL8419/ASSET/6E58F7A5-F159-4CB7-9FA6-53FF65FFC435/ASSETS/IMAGES/LARGE/SCIROBOTICS.ABL8419-F2.JPG. https://www.science.org/doi/10.1126/scirobotics.abl8419
16. Shen, W.: Research on virtual simulation design of ABB robot welding operation based on robotstudio. In: Proceedings of 2020 IEEE International Conference on Artificial Intelligence and Computer Applications, ICAICA 2020, pp. 894–897 (2020). https://doi.org/10.1109/ICAICA50127.2020.9182551
17. Stagsted, R.K., Vitale, A., Renner, A., Larsen, L.B., Christensen, A.L., Sandamirskaya, Y.: Event-based PID controller fully realized in neuromorphic hardware: a one DOF study. In: IEEE International Conference on Intelligent Robots and Systems, pp. 10939–10944 (2020). https://doi.org/10.1109/IROS45743.2020.9340861
18. Tursynbek, I., Shintemirov, A.: Modeling and simulation of spherical parallel manipulators in coppeliasim (v-rep) robot simulator software. In: 2020 International Conference Nonlinearity, Information and Robotics, NIR 2020 (2020). https://doi.org/10.1109/NIR50484.2020.9290227
19. Zhang, X., Luo, B.: Simulation of industrial robot and automatic production conveyor based on robotstudio. In: 2022 IEEE 2nd International Conference on Data Science and Computer Application, ICDSCA 2022, pp. 1222–1226 (2022). https://doi.org/10.1109/ICDSCA56264.2022.9987762
20. Zhang, Y., Sun, L., Zhang, Y.: Research on algorithm of humanoid robot arm control system based on fuzzy PID control. In: Proceedings - 2022 International Conference on Artificial Intelligence and Autonomous Robot Systems, AIARS 2022, pp. 337–341 (2022). https://doi.org/10.1109/AIARS57204.2022.00082

On Implementing the Sparse Events Closed-Loop Control Theory for the CartPoleSimulation

Santiago Díaz-Romero[1(✉)], Marcin Paluch[2], Alejandro Linares-Barranco[1], and Antonio Rios-Navarro[1]

[1] Robotics and Technology of Computers Lab. ETSII-EPS, I3US, SCORE, Universidad de Sevilla, Seville, Spain
sdiaz5@us.es

[2] Institute of NeuroInformatics, UZH-ETHZ, Zurich, Switzerland

Abstract. Event-based or neuro-inspired motor control systems communicate information through pulses, instantaneous bursts of electrical current that encode information very efficiently, as occurs in biological organisms. This work proposes a software implementation for sparse events closed-loop neuromorphic motor control theory (SECLOC) in a software tool. The control algorithm has been included in a simulator developed in Python, and publicly available, of a robotic cart controlling an inverted pendulum. The proposed implementations can be easily ported to any FPGA or microcontroller-based board and allow control of the real robotic cart. We have tested and verified the functionality using the algorithm to generate control events for proportional-integral-derivative (PID) and linear-quadratic-regulator (LQR) controllers and obtained the parameters equivalent to the proportionality, integrative, and derivative constants for these pulsing controllers. The empirical results demonstrate the validity of both the theory in simulation and its test in an actual robot in the pulsed domain. In the simulation, for angle control using a PID, with a minimum reaction time of 1 ms from the controller, the pendulum remains in equilibrium along the cart pole travel for more than 5 min, registering the 0-degree passage more than 2800 times. For the real pendulum used, the LQR controller, and the optimal control constants, with a minimum reaction time of 6 ms of the controller, the pendulum remains in equilibrium along the carriage path, as well as under slight and moderate perturbations without dropping during all experiments performed over a simulated period of almost 3.5 days.

Keywords: Neuromorphic engineering · Motor control · Neuromorphic controller · Event based control · Simulation · Python

---

Smart Computers Systems Research and Engineering (SCORE). University of Seville.

A. A. Juan et al. (Eds.): SIMUtools 2024, LNICST 603, pp. 239–254, 2025.
https://doi.org/10.1007/978-3-031-87345-4_16

1 Introduction

Traditionally, the control of power electronic systems has been dominated by analog controllers. Digital controllers have been steadily improving in terms of cost and ease of use over the past decades, making these types of controllers more attractive to replace analog controllers in many devices [12]. The implementation of digital controllers includes potential advantages such as significantly improved flexibility, reduced design time, programmability, elimination of discrete tuning components, increased reliability, easier integration, and the ability to include a variety of performance features [13].

In digital controllers, one of the main aspects is the sampling frequency of the signal, which allows discretization. The choice of a suitable sampling frequency depends on the dynamics of open-loop systems and on the desired dynamics of the controlled system. A system with fast dynamics needs a high sampling frequency to ensure the stability of the controlled system, at the cost of higher computational power. Furthermore, the controlled input of a dynamic system is traditionally updated at each time step independently of the error amplitude, i.e. periodically. When a controlled system is at a stable set point, there is obviously no need to sample the data, update the controller, and actuator. In fact, doing it so is energy-inefficient.

This lack of efficiency, coupled with lower computational capability, is the starting point for event-driven control systems [5,15]. These systems are very interesting for many reasons. One of them is the fact that they are very similar to the way a biological nervous system behaves as a controller, such as that of the human one. The human motor control system is based on events or impulses rather than periodic commands [11]. A new control action is taken only when the measurement signal has deviated sufficiently from the desired set point. Another interesting reason is resource utilization. An embedded controller is usually implemented with a real-time operating system that supports concurrent scheduling. CPU resources are shared among the cores/threads in such a way that it appears as if each task is running independently. Therefore, using CPU resources to perform control calculations when nothing significant has occurred in the process is clearly an unnecessary waste of resources. We can also apply this idea to communication resources. The communication bandwidth available in a distributed system is limited. Using it to send data in a timed fashion is clearly a waste of bandwidth. The last reason is that these types of system are excellent candidates for low-power, low-latency computing, since the power consumption is lower than in similar systems, and their latency is also much lower, just as it is in biological systems.

In event-based control systems, an event is sent whenever the sampled signal increases or decreases by a certain threshold. When the signal does not change, intrinsically, there are no further updates. These control systems also have drawbacks. For example, when transmitting the value of the signal within an event, as it limits the dynamic range of the system, in other words, the relationship between the largest and smallest value that can assume a signal within a control system. This is because the data transfer must have the same representation as the system data. Thus, if you want to control a system with high accuracy over a wide range of values, such a control system would need a network with a high bandwidth to transmit the signal values [8]. Using simulators such as CartPoleSimulation to work with real-time systems such as the inverted pendulum can have numerous advantages:

- It is possible to accelerate the calculations by performing the simulation at a speed much faster than the real time.
- It allows setting up the environment and setting the initial conditions of the experiment in a faster and easier way.
- It is usually much easier to recreate the experiments performed.
- It allows easy modification of the experiment parameters.
- It is easier to isolate potential failures and eliminate random noise.
- Allows the import and export of data generated during the simulation.
- The training of learning-based algorithms is more feasible thanks to said properties.

In this paper, we present an implementation of the event-driven algorithm proposed in [4] (hereafter SECLOC) for CartPoleSimulation software[1], developed by the Institute of Neuroinformatics at the University of Zurich, used in [6]. This algorithm proposes a non-linear discretization method based on the duration between events, demonstrating that the method achieves arbitrary accuracy regardless of the set point amplitude without increasing the data transmission bandwidth of the network. The method decreases the total number of samples required to estimate the states of a dynamic system and the update rate of an actuator, making it more energy efficient. The implementation proposed in this paper and all the simulations performed concern the particularization of the algorithm by using a discretization based on logarithmic events with base 1.05. This basis was selected because it was shown in the original article to provide good results. Throughout this paper, we present a software implementation of the SECLOC algorithm, as well as its inverted pendulum simulation and real inverted pendulum implementation. The remainder of the article is organized as follows. Section 2 provides a brief explanation of the SECLOC theory. Section 3 describes the various implementations developed for the simulator. Section 4 describes the inverted pendulum experiment. In Sect. 5 the conclusions are presented.

2 SECLOC Algorithm

A large number of dynamic systems use discrete controllers. The choice of sampling time is fundamental in the design of these controllers. A very low sampling time increases the accuracy at the cost of higher computational and energy costs. Conversely, very low sampling times can reduce power consumption, but also reduce the region where the control is stable, and therefore the usefulness of

[1] https://github.com/SensorsINI/CartPoleSimulation.

the control may be diminished or even nullified for a particular application. In addition, the use of a fixed sampling time causes resources to be consumed even when the set point value has been reached, making it energy-inefficient. In the SECLOC algorithm, the discretization is performed non-linearly. In nonlinear discretization (as opposed to linear discretization), the step required to generate events decreases as the control signal approaches the set point. That is, the number of events generated tends to infinity as the absolute error approaches 0. Therefore, it becomes necessary to stop the generation of events when the absolute error is less than a set threshold value by adding a refractory or rest period. Figure 1 shows first a non-linear event-based discretization. It is also possible to observe how the number of events increases (the green lines are closer to each other) as the error approaches 0.

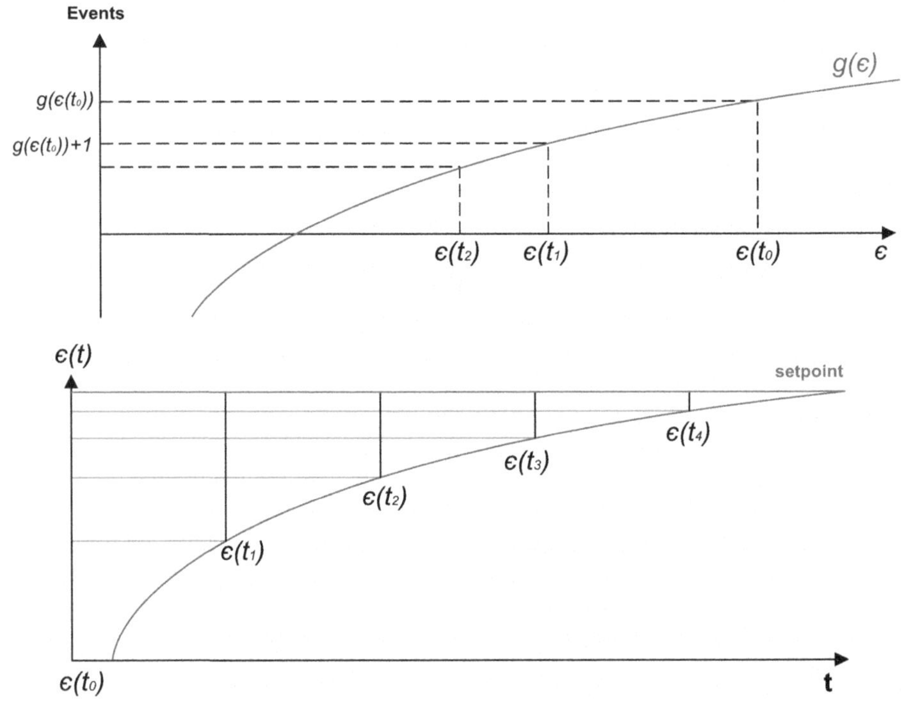

Fig. 1. Nonlinear discretization based on logarithmic events and temporal evolution of the system. (Color figure online)

A candidate discretization function g must satisfy three conditions:

1. $g : \mathbb{R}^{+,*} \to \mathbb{R}$
   $x \mapsto g(x)$
2. g must be continuous and strictly monotonic in $\mathbb{R}^{+,*}$.

3. $\lim_{x \to 0} g(x) = \begin{cases} -\infty \text{ if dg/dx} > 0 \\ +\infty \text{ if dg/dx} < 0 \end{cases}$

A logarithmic function of base b of $\epsilon(t)$ for g and satisfying the above requirements has been selected:

$$\forall b \in \mathbb{R}^+, b \neq 1$$

$$g(\epsilon) = \frac{\ln|\epsilon|}{\ln b} = log_b|\epsilon| \tag{1}$$

In this way, it is possible to generate a time series such as:

$$\forall b \in \mathbb{R}^+, b \neq 1, i \in \mathbb{N}^+$$

$$\left\{ ti| \quad |\frac{\ln|\epsilon(t_i)|}{\ln b} - \frac{\ln|\epsilon(t_{i-1})|}{\ln b}| = 1 \right\} \tag{2}$$

To indicate whether the error has increased or decreased between two consecutive events, polarity information is added to the equation:

$b > 1$

$$(t_i, p_i = +1)| \left| \frac{\epsilon(t_i)}{\epsilon(t_{i-1})} \right| = b \tag{3}$$

$$(t_i, p_i = -1)| \left| \frac{\epsilon(t_{i-1})}{\epsilon(t_i)} \right| = b \tag{4}$$

It should be noted that it has been defined in this way because of the choice made for the basis (1.05). Modifications to the equation can be made to take a basis $0 < b < 1$ [4].

Thus, the error over time is defined as: $b > 1$

$$\epsilon(t) = \epsilon(t_0) + (-1)^{s_N} \sum_{i=1}^{N} (b^{p_i} - 1)\epsilon(t_{i-1})H(t - t_i)) \tag{5}$$

where $H(x)$ is the Heaviside step function.

By subtracting from (3), the error value of the function at time t_i can be written using geometric recursion.

$$\epsilon(t_i) = \frac{\epsilon(t_0)}{b^i} \tag{6}$$

So for any finite value of $\epsilon(t_i)$:

$$\lim_{n \to +\infty} \epsilon(t_i) = 0$$

This shows that it is possible to achieve arbitrary precision by means of the described logarithmic discretization. Arbitrary precision is necessary to ensure that the control system achieves an error value that can be considered to be zero (point at which the set point is reached, Fig. 1).

As discussed previously, it is necessary to include a refractory period, since once ϵ is 0, the time between events decreases to 0 as well. That is, the number of events would (theoretically) be ∞. Thus, the refractory period is defined as the minimum time between two events that the system is able to generate. This term arises in neuroscience as a property of neuronal activity [7]. It must be taken into account that the ratio between the past and the current error may have changed several times during the refractory period. For this reason, a last parameter is added, which represents the number of times the set value is exceeded between two r_n events:

$$\begin{aligned} r_i &= \left\lfloor \frac{\ln\left(\epsilon(t_{i-1})/\epsilon(t_i)\right)}{\ln b} \right\rceil \quad if \;\; p_i = -1 \\ r_i &= \left\lfloor \frac{\ln\left(\epsilon(t_i)/\epsilon(t_{i-1})\right)}{\ln b} \right\rceil \quad if \;\; p_i = +1 \end{aligned} \tag{7}$$

Finally, the equation including r_n can be written as:
$b > 1$

$$\epsilon(t) = \epsilon(t_0) + (-1)^{s_N} \sum_{i=1}^{N} (b^{-p_i r_i} - 1)\epsilon(t_{i-1})H(t - t_i) \tag{8}$$

This discretization makes it possible to benefit from an event-based representation in the context of system control. Moreover, it allows to apply, when these events arise, the desired control algorithm. In this work, we use a PID (Proportional, Integral and Derivative) controller to maintain the pendulum in a minimum oscillation range of its equilibrium position and an LQR (Linear-Quadratic Regulator) [9] controller to control the system in both desired angle and position.

3 Implementation

The software used during the experiments was the aforementioned CartPoleSimulation, which was developed in Python language by the Institute for Neuroinformatics at the University of Zurich. It allows the simulation of different preprogrammed control strategies such as PID, LQR, MPC, etc. Additionally, the simulator allows to add custom control algorithms programmed in Python. This last option has been used for the implementation of the SECLOC algorithm. The interface of the simulator can be seen in the Fig. 2. This software implements the dynamic equations of the robot and allows programming any type of control and testing its performance in the simulator. In addition, it can use a hardware module, based on a microcontroller, which acts as a bridge between the software and a physical cart (Fig. 3).

CartPoleSimulation allows to modify the initial parameters of the simulation. It is possible to alter the starting angle and the initial position of the carriage, add random noise, and control signal delay, as well as exert a lateral force on the pendulum that disturbs its operation. Additionally, it is possible to slow down or speed up (if the available computing hardware allows it) the simulation speed as well as the frequency of the control signal update and simulation drawing. At the end of the simulation it is also possible to visualize graphs of position of the carriage, angle of the pendulum and force exerted by the motor throughout the simulation time (Figs. 5, 6 and 7).

Finally, the simulator offers the possibility to export the detailed data of the simulation such as time, position, velocity, acceleration, exerted force, etc. in comma-separated-values (CSV) format. This detailed data allows replicating the results of a specific simulation (which the simulator also allows). Moreover, this data is very useful to feed a neural network in order to train it to learn how to perform the cart pole control. The simulation and data export mode can be performed without the continuous update of the graphical interface, or without it, which increases the simulation speed even more than with the graphical interface.

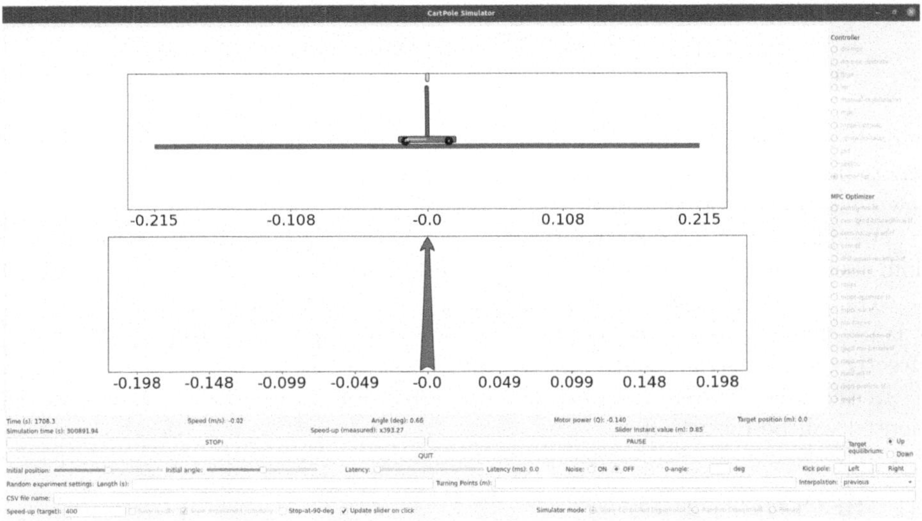

Fig. 2. CartPoleSimulation software GUI.

The software has been developed on the basis of a specific physical cart pole model (Fig. 3), which allows the results obtained to be used directly on the cart pole without the need to re-find the control parameters. It can also be configured to emulate the behavior of a carriage with user-defined characteristics.

The software implementation of SECLOC controller in the CartPoleSimulation can be divided into two main parts: the generation of events using the SECLOC algorithm itself, and the generation of the control signal for the motor controller applied to a discrete signal in time.

A basic rendition of the event generation implementation is illustrated in Algorithm 1. Initially, a determination is made about whether the error surpasses the dead band. Subsequently, it is verified if the refractory period has elapsed, thus permitting the emission of an event. Under these circumstances, the current

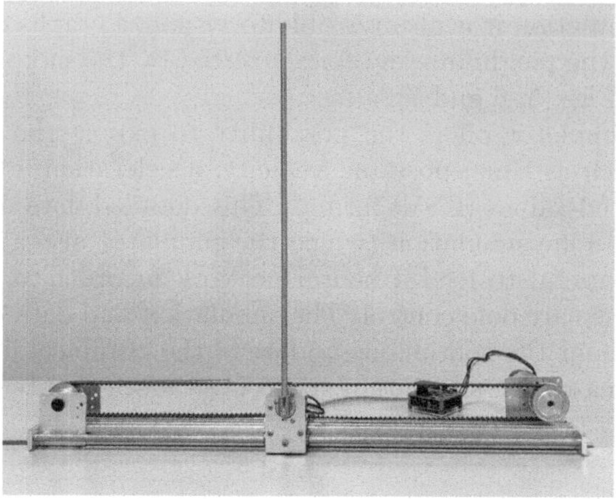

Fig. 3. Physical cart pole and STM32-based controlboard.

error is compared against the error recorded at the issuance of the preceding event. If the ratio between these errors exceeds the predetermined threshold, a new control event is generated.

For SECLOC's and control theories (PID and LQR) hardware implementation, there is a microcontroller-based control board that can function as a bridge between the simulation software and the physical cart pole (Fig. 3). In this way, it is possible to use the controller that has been implemented in the simulator directly on the carriage without any additional coding.

In the following subsections, the different motor controller variants implemented will be discussed.

3.1 SECLOC + PID

PID or proportional-integral-derivative controller is a feedback-based control loop mechanism commonly used in industrial control systems [10]. Although it dates back to 1910, more than 90% of industrial controllers are still implemented based on PID algorithms mainly because they offer high simplicity, clear functionality, applicability, and ease of use [1].

This phase has allowed us to explore different ranges of the PID constants needed to tune SECLOC for optimal pendulum control behavior.

The PID control signal for the proposed event-based logarithmic discretization can be written as:

$$u(t_k) = K_p \epsilon(t_k) + K_i I(t_k) + K_d \frac{d\epsilon(t_k)}{dt} \tag{9}$$

where each of the terms associated with the errors can be calculated as:

$$\epsilon(t_k) = (-1)^{S_k}(\epsilon(t_{k-1}) + (b^{p_k} - 1)) \tag{10}$$

Algorithm 1. SECLOC event generator

```
error ← set_point − position
if |error| > dead_band then
    if time ≥ period_ref then
        if prev_error = 0 then
            aum_ratio ← base
            sign_ratio ← sign(error)
        end if
        if (error ≠ 0 & prev_error ≠ 0) then
            aum_ratio ← |error/prev_error|
            red_ratio ← 1/aum_ratio
            sign_ratio ← sign(aum_ratio)
        end if
        if aum_ratio ≥ log_base then
            change_sign ← sign_ratio
            prev_error ← error
            polarity ← 1
            emit_event()
        else if red_ratio ≥ log_base then
            change_sign ← sign_ratio
            prev_error ← error
            polarity ← −1
            emit_event()
        end if
    end if
end if
```

$$\frac{d\epsilon(t_k)}{dt} \approx \epsilon(t_{k-1})\frac{(-1)^{S_k}(b^{p_k}-1)}{t_k - t_{k-1}} \tag{11}$$

$$I(t_k) = \int_0^{t_k} \epsilon(\sigma)d\sigma \quad \approx I(t_{k-1}) + \epsilon(t_{k-1})\frac{2+(-1)^{s_k}(b_k^p - 1)}{2(t_k - t_{k-1})} \tag{12}$$

The software implementation of this control signal is a direct conversion of Eqs. (9) to (12).

It can be seen that a dead band has been added where the controller does not act. This has been done to help filter out sensor noise, as this can greatly distort the behavior of the filter.

Subsequently, to mitigate these effects, an LQR controller has been implemented in the simulator using the event generation proposed by the SECLOC algorithm and the same base, refractory period and dead band as in the PID controller

3.2 SECLOC + LQR

The LQR controller is usually more effective in nonlinear systems than PID, such as an inverted pendulum. The major drawback with respect to PID is that the LQR controller requires a model of the system. For this reason, use has been made of the analytical expressions derived from the Euler-Lagrange equations. The descriptions of these, as well as of the operation of the LQR controller, have been obtained from [2] and [3].

LQR or Linear Quadratic Regulator is an optimal control law of full state feedback, probably the most important and influential [14]. In LQR control inputs $u = -Kx$ need to minimize a quadratic cost function to regulate the control system. The cost function depends on system states (x) and mentioned control inputs (u):

$$J(U) = \sum_{\tau=0}^{N-1} (x_\tau^T Q x_\tau + u_\tau^T R u_\tau) + x_N^T Q_f x_N \tag{13}$$

where $U = (u_0, ..., u_{N-1})$ and $U = Q^T \geq 0 \quad Q_f = Q_f^T \geq 0 \quad R = R^T > 0$ are given state cost, final state cost, and input cost matrices. In summary, in LQR controllers, the cost matrices Q and R (instead of the constants K_p, K_i and K_d) must be parameterized.

The LQR solution implemented in the simulator, first calculate Jacobian around equilibrium set point around which the Jacobian should be linearized and uses the cost matrices Q (relative weights of state deviation) and R (relative weights of input usage) for LQR controller. Then, tries to solve the Riccati equation to get the system state and obtains the optimal gain K. Once K have been obtained $u = -Kx$ is calculated every time a control event occurs. For this purpose, the SECLOC algorithm has been used to trigger every time the pendulum or carriage deviates from the set angle or position and the other SECLOC conditions have been met.

4 Inverted Pendulum Experiments

First of all, the results obtained in the simulator are presented and then the performance of the constants obtained by the simulation on the hardware is checked.

4.1 Results in the Simulator

CarPoleSimulation has been used to speed up the workflow and find the necessary parameters to satisfy the control conditions of the inverted pendulum. The main features with which the CartPoleSimulation software is configured by default correspond to the aforementioned physical cart (Fig. 3). These can be found in the Table 1:

First, we have tried to control the inverted pendulum using SECLOC and the PID controller described in Subsect. 3.1. Due to the characteristics of the proposed event generation, it has not been possible to use any classical method for parameter tuning of a PID controller, such as the Ziegler-Nichols [16] or Cohen-Coon methods [1].

Table 1. Cartpole characteristics.

Property	Value
Usable track length	220 mm
Pole length	395 mm
Carriage length	44 mm
Pole mass	87 g
Carriage mass	230 g
Maximum motor force	2.62 N

To facilitate the task of obtaining the PID constants, the possibility of performing loop simulations has been added to the simulator's GUI. In this mode, the simulator starts performing the simulation with the PID constants that are defined in a configuration file. It counts the number of times the pendulum angle changes sign and therefore passes through 0° (equilibrium position) and stops the simulation when the pendulum falls below the horizontal. When the simulation is finished, it displays the number of times the pendulum has passed through 0° and indicates the current PID constants. It then increments one of the constants and restarts the simulation until all possible combinations in the indicated range have been tested. The increment size of the PID constants, as well as the upper and lower limits of each, are individually configurable.

Using this tool, the controller has been configured so that the search for constants is defined with the parameters shown in the Table 2. In all experiments, the starting angle *theta* has been set to 0.10 rad (5.73°) to help initiate the motion. On the other hand, the refractory period has been set to 1 ms and the dead band to 0.001 rad (this parameter does not influence the simulation, only its actual application).

Table 2. Search configuration of PID constants.

Parameter	min	max	step
K_p	0	100	10
K_i	0	1	0.1
K_d	0	100	10

The complete distribution of the results obtained for the $11^3 = 1331$ experiments performed by the simulator. Figure 4 shows the number of times each of the PID controller constants tested in the simulator has passed through 0. Despite the high number of tests performed, it is possible to observe how some results stand out from the rest; these results are the ones that have been presented by means of a label, the best result being the one that can be seen highlighted in green.

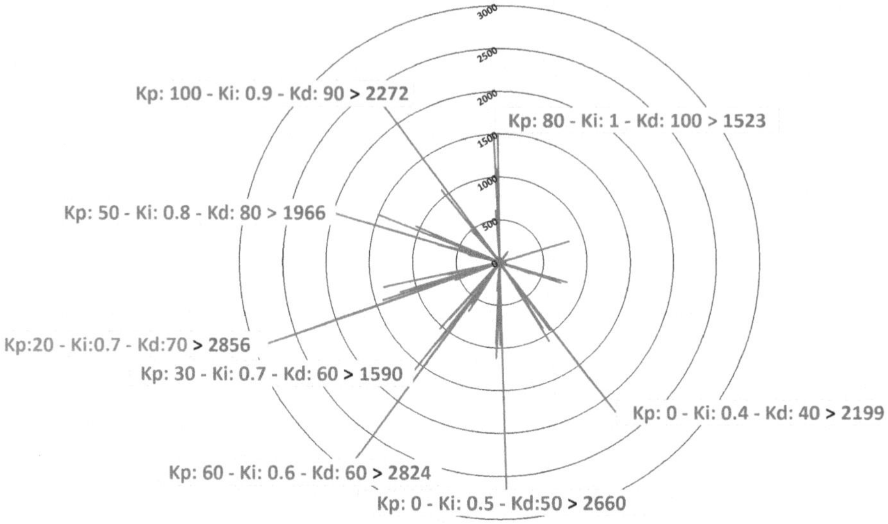

Fig. 4. PID constants search results. (Color figure online)

It can be seen how the controller with constants $K_p = 20$, $K_i = 0.7$ and $K_d = 70$ obtains the best result with a total of 2856 steps per 0. Subsequently, a simulation with these constants has been performed to check the result in detail. This has been translated into 340 s of control before reaching one of the ends of the carriage and falling as a consequence of the collision, the results of this simulation can be seen in Fig. 5 where the evolution of the pendulum angle (0 represents the equilibrium position), the cart position, the motor force and the desired position of the cart at each time instant are shown.

Although with this parameterization, during the simulation, the pendulum maintains verticality for the indicated time, analyzing the simulation results in detail, the system seems to tend to instability. For this reason it was decided to repeat the experimentation ignoring completely the error in the carriage position and relying only on the stability of the angle since this is really the variable to be controlled. Among all the options $K_p = 750$, $K_i = 0$ and $K_d = 0$ was the one that produced the best results, being able to balance and maintain the pendulum position for approximately 2 s, showing a stable behaviour as can be seen in the first row of the Fig. 6. Although, as expected, the cart pole quickly hits the limit and falls as shown in the second row of the Fig. 6, the same behaviour can be observed both in the simulation and in the real pendulum.

Since a PID controller has not been sufficient to effectively control the cart pole in both angle and position, it has been decided to perform a simulation using a LQR controller together with the SECLOC algorithm to try to achieve an effective control in angle and position.

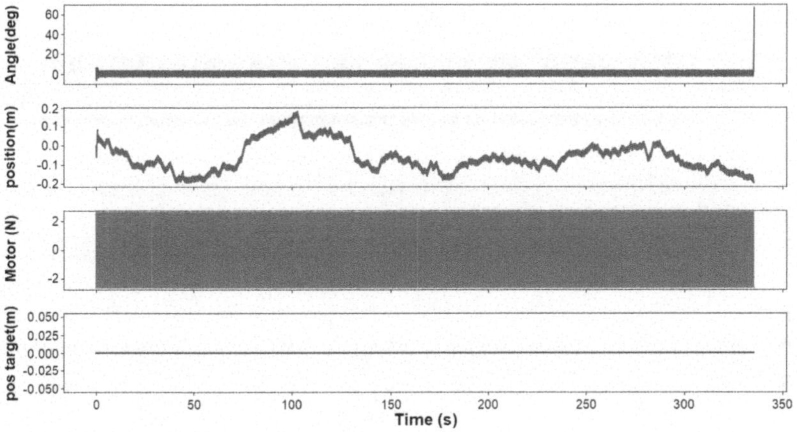

Fig. 5. PID simulation results with $K_p = 20$, $K_i = 0,7$ y $K_d = 70$.

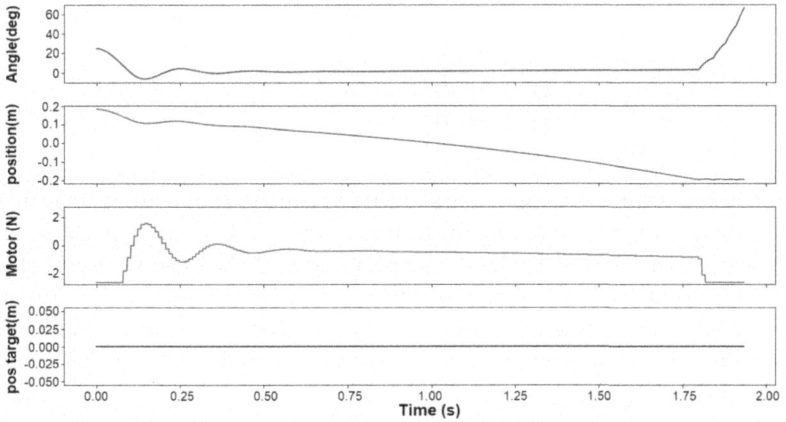

Fig. 6. PID simulation results with $K_p = 750$, $K_i = 0$ y $K_d = 0$.

As with the PID controller, the choice of the necessary parameters is usually left to the designer. Again, due to the nonlinear characteristics of SECLOC the required Q and R values have been found on a trial-and-error basis.

In this case, no systematic testing has been necessary, as good results have been obtained very quickly. Priority has been given to maintaining balance over maintaining the position of the carriage, and the following values of Q and R have been selected:

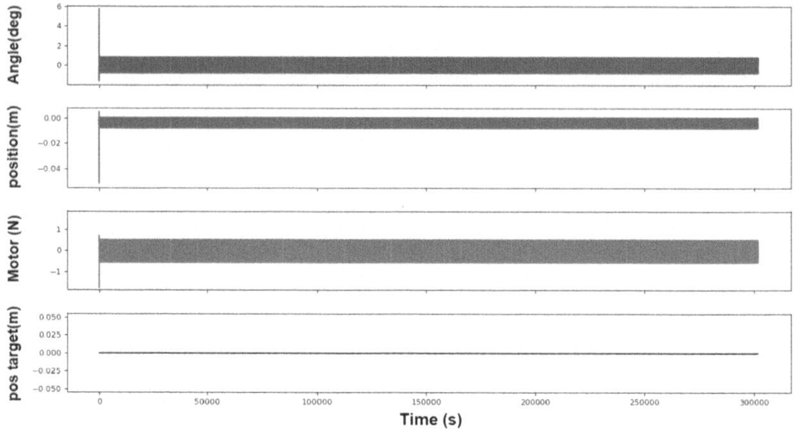

Fig. 7. LQR simulation results

$$Q = \begin{bmatrix} 1 & 0 & 0 & 0 \\ 0 & 0 & 0 & 0 \\ 0 & 0 & 100 & 0 \\ 0 & 0 & 0 & 0 \end{bmatrix} \qquad \textit{and} \qquad R = 1$$

With these parameters, the results obtained during the simulation were excellent, stabilizing the pendulum in both angle and position and maintaining stability against disturbances. It should be remembered that the values of the diagonal of Q represent the cost of the deviation from the optimal values of the cart position (center of the track in this case), cart speed, pendulum angle (in this case 0 has been taken as the equilibrium point) and the angular velocity of the pendulum, respectively.

In order to verify that the SECLOC+LQR combination effectively controls the cart pole, an extensive simulation was carried out over an extended period of time. For this purpose, the acceleration feature included in CartPoleSimulation was used and a desired simulation speed of 400x was set. The time between evaluation of control events was set to 1ms and the time between visible frames was set to 10 ms. The simulation was performed for a period of time slightly over 300,000 s (almost 3.5 days) which took an actual time of approximately 1700 s (slightly over 28 min), resulting in an average acceleration of roughly 176x over real time.

Figure 7 shows the results obtained after the simulation. It is possible to observe how the angle of the pendulum does not deviate more than 1° from the equilibrium position, whilst the cart never deviates more than 80 mm from the desired position (the center of the track).

4.2 Results on the Actual Cartpole

Due to the good results obtained by the LQR controller in the simulator, it has been tested with the real cart pole. For its implementation, it has been necessary to make some changes, since the system has some limitations to the maximum frequency at which it can work. For this reason, the refractory period has been increased to 6 ms and a dead band of 0.01 rad has been added to ignore the noise generated by the sensors.

Despite the increased refractory period and the inclusion of a dead band, the pendulum has been effectively controlled in angle and position.

It should be taken into account that since good results have been obtained with these values, they have been used without additional tests, so it is possible that there are other values that offer the same or better control results.

5 Conclusions

The simulation through CartPoleSimulation has improved research time by speeding up the workflow, which allows not only to work with simulations well above 170x real time but also to recreate reliably the characteristics of a physical inverted pendulum and the initial conditions of the experiment. In addition, the fact that it is written in Python helps to make changes or additions easily in case it is necessary to implement some particular functionality, as in our case, the need of restarting the experiment by modifying the controller parameters every time the pendulum falls below a certain angle. In addition, CartPoleSimulation uses the actual dynamic equations of the robot and therefore can collect data that can be used for analysis or used in control algorithms or other types of algorithms. It should be noted that although the average acceleration achieved over real time has been notorious, we have always worked with the GUI activated and on an average computer[2] on CPU. In principle, with CartPoleSimulation it would be possible to achieve even higher simulation speeds without the graphics and using GPU acceleration.

Two different controllers based on the SECLOC algorithm have been implemented and simulated to control an inverted pendulum, one based on a PID controller and the other on an LQR controller. The algorithm has demonstrated its functionality with both controllers, although the PID controller has not been able to control the inverted pendulum in angle and position. This is due to a limitation of the PID controllers, not of the SECLOC event generation algorithm.

On the other hand, the implementation of the LQR controller has been able to control both the angle and the position of the carriage, yielding excellent results both in its deployment on the simulator and on the physical carriage, despite the limitations imposed on the latter.

These good results leave the door open to a future hardware implementation of the algorithm on a Field Programmable Gate Array (FPGA). This would make it possible to eliminate the physical limitations imposed by the current

[2] Intel Core i7-12700H/16GB with Ubuntu 20.04.1.

system and use it to control a real system. It is also possible to study if this method of event generation can be applied to other more sophisticated control algorithms that allow a more optimal control of the system or the control of more complex systems.

References

1. Ang, K.H., Chong, G., Li, Y.: PID control system analysis, design, and technology. IEEE Trans. Control Syst. Technol. **13**(4), 559–576 (2005). https://doi.org/10.1109/TCST.2005.847331
2. Brunton, S.L., Kutz, J.N.: Data-Driven Science and Engineering. Cambridge University Press, Cambridge (2019)
3. Corriou, J.P.: Process Control. Springer, London (2004)
4. Daye, P., Ieng, S.H., Benosman, R.: A theory for sparse event-based closed loop control. Front. Neurosci. **13**, 827 (2019)
5. Dorf, R., Farren, M., Phillips, C.: Adaptive sampling frequency for sampled-data control systems. IRE Trans. Autom. Control **7**(1), 38–47 (1962)
6. Heetmeyer, F., et al.: RPGD: a small-batch parallel gradient descent optimizer with explorative resampling for nonlinear model predictive control. In: 2023 IEEE International Conference on Robotics and Automation (ICRA), pp. 3218–3224 (2023). https://doi.org/10.1109/ICRA48891.2023.10161233
7. Heiss, H.W.: Human physiology. Edited by Robert F. Schmidt and Gerhard Thews. Springer-verlag, Berlin-Heidelberg-New York (1983) 725 pages, 569 figures, approx. $39.20 ISBN: 3-540-11669-9. Clin. Cardiol. **6**(9), A43–A44 (1983). https://doi.org/10.1002/clc.4960060912. https://onlinelibrary.wiley.com/doi/abs/10.1002/clc.4960060912
8. Hetel, L., et al.: Recent developments on the stability of systems with aperiodic sampling: an overview. Automatica **76**, 309–335 (2017)
9. Kwakernaak, H., Sivan, R.: Linear Optimal Control Systems. Wiley, Nashville (1972)
10. Levine, W.S.: PID Control in the Control Handbook. CRC Press (1996)
11. Mead, C., Ismail, M.: Analog VLSI implementation of neural systems, vol. 80. Springer (1989)
12. Murphy, P., et al.: Study of digital vs analog control. In: Power Electronics Seminar Proceedings (CPES Center for Power Electronics Systems), pp. 203–206. Citeseer (2002)
13. Prodic, A., Maksimovic, D.: Digital PWM controller and current estimator for a low-power switching converter. In: COMPEL 2000. 7th Workshop on Computers in Power Electronics. Proceedings (Cat. No. 00TH8535), pp. 123–128. IEEE (2000)
14. Tedrake, R.: Underactuated Robotics (2023). https://underactuated.csail.mit.edu
15. Tomovic, R., Bekey, G.: Adaptive sampling based on amplitude sensitivity. IEEE Trans. Autom. Control **11**(2), 282–284 (1966)
16. Ziegler, J.G., Nichols, N.B.: Optimum settings for automatic controllers. Trans. Am. Soc. Mech. Eng. **64**(8), 759–765 (2022). https://doi.org/10.1115/1.4019264

Simulation and Operation of 6DoF Robotic Arms: a Microservices Approach

Tomas Munoz-Gonzalez[1(✉)], Adalberto Farias[2], Enrique Piñero-Fuentes[1], Antonio Rios-Navarro[1], Sergio Segura-Ramos[1], and Alejandro Linares-Barranco[1]

[1] Smart Computer Engineering Research Lab, I3US, Universidad de Sevilla, Seville, Spain
tmunoz1@us.es

[2] Systems and Computing Department, Federal University of Campina Grande, Campina Grande, Brazil

Abstract. The use of robotic arms in industrial and academic settings has grown exponentially, however, the process of simulating and operating these systems continues to be a significant challenge, particularly for users without prior experience. The learning curve is steep due to the technical complexity associated with programming, calibrating and controlling precise movements, which can be daunting. Robotic devices are usually controlled using proprietary software or ad-hoc low-level programs, hindering their shared use and integration with other applications. This work presents a software application for robotic arm trajectory simulation, with a remote service for allowing access control and arbitration in the use of robots as a shared service. This software allows the design of trajectories in robot and Cartesian coordinate spaces in a simple and convenient way for the user. The service allows the execution of said trajectories whenever the robot is available. Robotic arms ED-RobotAnno and ROS-RobotAnno are presented as use cases for this service. Concepts such as closed-loop motor control or direct robot kinematics are abstracted from the user, allowing the creation of unsupervised learning iterations of closed-loop trajectories or the creation of datasets for supervised training. Moreover, the servitization is based on a heterogeneous ecosystem composed of microservices that use different platforms/languages to provide a novel Web experience to users, while still being flexible to allow easy addition of new robotic arms.

Keywords: Robotic · Servitization · Simulation · Neuromorphic

---

This work is supported by grant NASAI (PDC2023-145841-C33), NEKOR (PID2023-149071NB-C54) and SMALL (PCI2019-111841-2) funded by MICIU/AEI /10.13039/501100011033, by "ERDF A way of making Europe" and by the European Union NextGenerationEU/PRTR. E. P.-F. was supported by a "Formación de Profesorado Universitario" Scholarship from the Spanish Ministry of Science, Innovation and Universities.

A. A. Juan et al. (Eds.): SIMUtools 2024, LNICST 603, pp. 255–267, 2025.
https://doi.org/10.1007/978-3-031-87345-4_17

1 Introduction

The use of robots is more common nowadays than ever. They are used in most activities, providing benefits such as efficiency, precision, and cost. New trends, such as neuromorphic engineering, focus their efforts on reducing the power consumption of robot components [4,8]. Neuromorphic takes inspiration from biological nervous systems for developing engineering solutions [11]. Nevertheless, they usually require specialized hardware and software controllers [9,12,20] only available at research labs. Remote interaction is not always possible and this restricts other researchers to explore the benefits of these robots and controllers.

In this context, servitization has been viewed as an inflection point, affecting the business model and bringing significant productivity gains [19], as it provides a general, intuitive, independent, portable, and (usually) scalable way of offering functionalities. Simulation tools improve considerable development times in the deployment of the best trajectories for particular tasks of the robot [18] or a set of robots [13]. This work focuses on the integration effort by providing a solution that represents a service context in which a robotic arm can be easily integrated and used under simulation or with a real robot, both locally and remotely [2,6,15]. The adopted robotic arm – ED-Robotanno[1]– is already used as a service. However, it requires extra knowledge for remotely controlling the arm, such as establishing a direct connection via SSH with the authorised machine, sending commands to the robot by using low-level tools (scripts and programs), applying specific data conversions, and sometimes handling low-level parameters of the arm motor controllers. The demand to evolve this scenario to a new service model has inspired our solution.

The servitization ecosystem proposed in this work makes the ED-Robotanno available as a web application to users who need to know only basic details about the arm (business information). In this sense, our solution pushes the arm's service to a richer and more up-to-date model: Software as a Service [7] (SaaS). As the provided user interface is specific for this kind of robot, it is applicable to robotic arms of the same family (or characteristics), whose movement information is based on the notion of joint coordinates (a list of values for each joint). SaaS has influenced the rise of an effective opportunity to change the focus from deploying and supporting applications to managing the services provided by applications. A common materialization of SaaS is the microservice architectural style [10], which is an approach to develop an application as a suite of small services, each running in its own process and available through some communication mechanism (often an HTTP resource API[2]).

The main contribution of this work is to provide an ecosystem based on the microservices architectural pattern that allows simulated, local or remote control of a robotic arm hosted at the University of Seville. The solution, over most of the existing ones in the literature, promotes the abstraction of details about

[1] https://www.robotanno.com/en/commercial-robotic-arm/602-robotic-arm.html (accessed April 5, 2025).

[2] API: Application Programming Interface.

the arm, allows easy addition of new robotic arms (neuromorphic or not), and provides an intuitive, scalable, and portable tool to control the arm (a Web-based user interface).

The next section provides the background of our work for the ED-Robotanno and the microservices. Section 3 is focused on servitization and tests. Then, Sect. 4 presents some experiments. Finally, Sect. 5 concludes the paper.

2 Materials

This section describes the different materials needed in this work, such as the neuromorphic robotic arm ED-Robotanno, its ROS controller and a set of microservices to make the framework accessible for remote users.

2.1 ED-Robotanno Robotic Arm

ED-RobotAnno is an Event-Driven robot consisting of a modification of the light industrial robot RobotAnno Q602. The ED-RobotAnno is a six degrees of freedom (DoF) robotic arm whose joints are controlled by servo motors that are driven by pulse frequency modulation (PFM), making it suitable for event-driven control. The controller that came by default with the initial robot, based on an STM32 microcontroller, has been replaced by the Zynq-7100 FPGA platform where the new neuro-inspired spike-based motor controllers have been implemented to control the robotic arm. Each motor is powered at 24 V and has a four-signal control interface (P+, P−, D+, D−) where P signals are used to move the motor a particular rotation at a particular speed, while the D signals are used to indicate the direction of motor rotation. The P signals are square signals complementary to each other, similar to motor neuron spike bursts controlling agonist and antagonist muscles [5] of any articulation in mammals, for example. To move the RobotAnno motor, a square signal must be generated where each pulse of the signal is equivalent to a small rotation of the motor, and depending on the time between when these pulses are received the speed will be controlled. This behavior is similar to that of the stepper motors, however, even though it seems a similar behavior, the open-loop control of the ED-RobotAnno motors is performed by the number and frequency of pulses of the square signal introduced by the P signals. On the other hand, the D signals encode the direction of rotation, being clockwise with D+ on high and D- on low and counterclockwise with D+ on low and D- on high.

To drive each of the joints of the robotic arm, one controller per joint has been implemented in the FPGA. To move the motor of a particular joint of the robot, the controller of that joint is provided with the number of pulses to be generated, the desired rotation and speed. To know the current position of each of the joints of the robot each controller implements a counter that accumulates the number of commanded pulses to the joint. This counter is a signed number where the positive values indicate positions on the right and the negative values

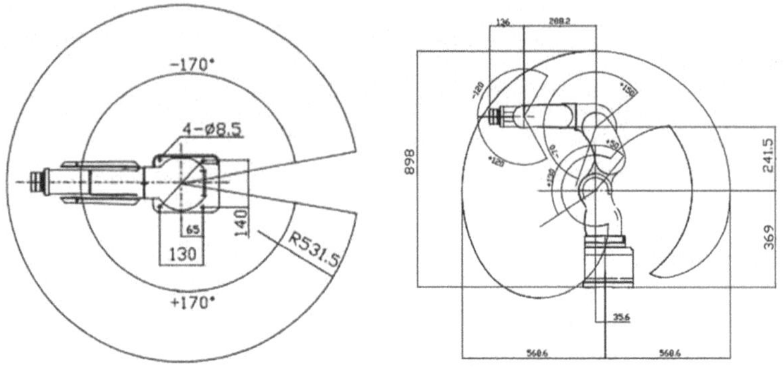

Fig. 1. ED-RobotAnno Operating Range.

indicate positions on the left of the home position of the joint. In Fig. 1 a diagram of the robot DoF with their operation ranges and the segment lengths is shown.

A picture of the ED-RobotAnno and the neuromorphic controller infrastructure is shown in Fig. 2. All joint controllers are hosted at the Zynq platform, which is connected to the internet through the ARM-based embedded computer.

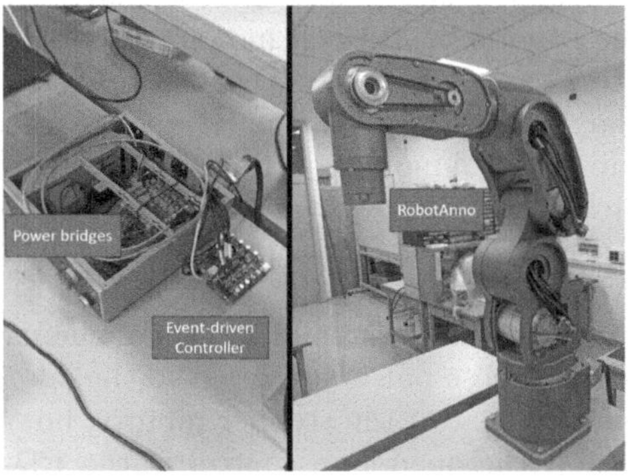

Fig. 2. ED-RobotAnno lab picture.

2.2 ROS-Robotanno Robotic Arm

For comparison purposes, a second, not modified robot RobotAnno Q602 was acquired. This one has the same characteristics as ED-RobotAnno, with the exception being the way it's supposed to operate. This model offers a hardware controller based on a multiprocessor system on chip (MPSoC) running an Ubuntu Linux OS, that acts as a ROS node that can be communicated with by a properly set up ROS environment or its dedicated desktop application. Its joints are encoded so that the instantaneous joint position can be read by its controller.

2.3 Microservices

Regarding basic functioning requirements, the ED-Robotanno arm controller presents the following items:

- It has a cyclic behavior to be available and responsive to new interactions from client applications via asynchronous messages.
- It is able to inform clients about its ERROR state and current owner all the time.
- Only one user can be the owner at a time.
- Only the owner can request to move the arm (point or trajectory), cancel a trajectory execution or disconnect from the arm.
- After accepting a new owner, the arm must be moved to its home position. During this procedure, the arm cannot execute other functions.

In terms of the state machine, Fig. 3 represents the behavior of the controller microservice.

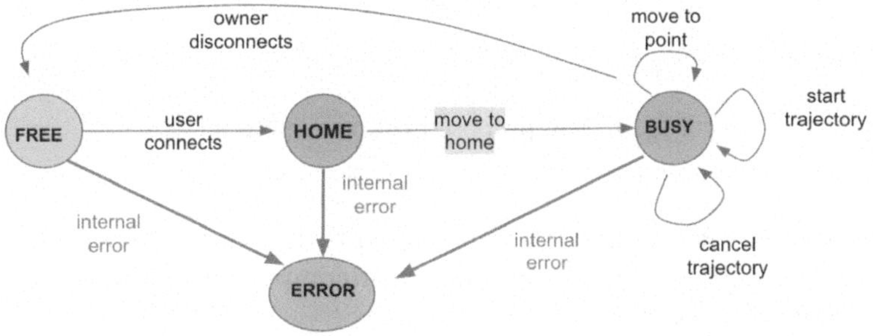

Fig. 3. The basic state machine of ED-Robotanno.

Upon initialization, the controller becomes available for the Web service only after the physical arm or its simulation counterpart is working properly. If a user requests to connect to the arm and the arm is FREE, it accepts the user as the current owner and changes to state HOME. After that, the controller automatically moves the arm to its home position, changes the internal state to BUSY, and accepts requests from the owner to move to a point, apply a trajectory, cancel trajectory execution, or disconnect from the arm. Only the latter functionality changes the robotic arm state to FREE again.

As the controller is associated with a physical device, it can go to an ERROR state if some internal problem occurs. This is abstractly represented by the red arrows leading to the ERROR state where the controller cannot execute all functions that forward commands to the arm and requires human intervention (to restart the services or the physical arm).

3 Servitization

To provide a more sophisticated control for the ED-Robotanno arm both in simulation or remotely, an ecosystem (illustrated by Fig. 4) composed of independent microservices where each service has a well-defined role (high cohesion) and adheres to a contract established by API specifications (low coupling) is used.

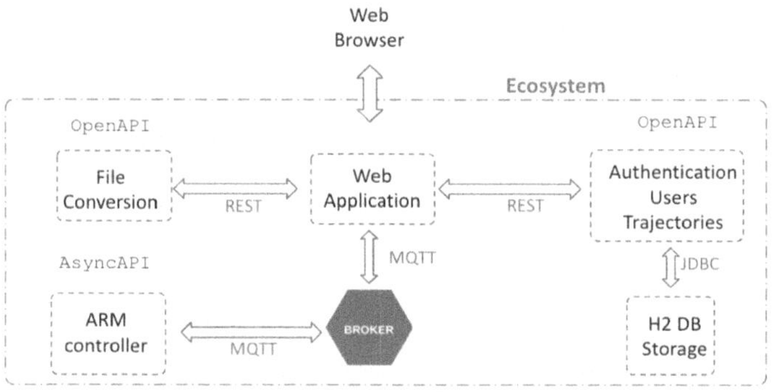

Fig. 4. The proposed robot ecosystem.

The Browser is at the user level and executes the Web application provided by the corresponding service. Internally, each component of the ecosystem has its role explained as follows:

- **Broker** - the asynchronous communication middleware responsible for handling all messages over the MQTT protocol. Eclipse Mosquitto broker [14] was adopted for this solution.
- **ARM Controller** - the service responsible for controlling the arm, implementing all features related to configuration, fault tolerance, error recovery, and business logic. Broadly, it receives requests, performs all validations, executes commands in the physical arm using underlying tools (platform-dependent executables and scripts), and sends responses associated with the requests. It has been implemented as an asynchronous C/C++ service.
- **Authentication, Users and Trajectories** - a compound microservice with features for storing data in H2 database [3], authentication, users management and trajectories manipulation. Java Spring Boot framework [16] is used to implement it as a synchronous RESTful [17] service.

- **File conversions** - a microservice providing features for applying conversions between binary and JSON/TSV format that are accepted by the user interface. These binary files contain trajectory data manipulated by the Numpy library and need to be converted prior to their use in our tool. This service has been implemented in Flask/Python.
- **Web Application** - the top-level microservice that provides the graphical user interface. It interacts with all other services (synchronous and asynchronous) to offer remote control of the arm as a Web application. Angular [1] framework is used here to implement this microservice that will interact with the others.

3.1 Implemented Microservices

All microservices of our ecosystem have been implemented using different technologies and are available as independent projects at Github, with detailed instructions about compiling, installing and running.

The microservice related to authentication, users, and trajectories[3] has been implemented in Java. The functionalities described by the specification are implemented as routes that are available over HTTP.

The microservice related to file conversions~[4] is implemented in Python and is available over HTTP.

The microservice implementation for the arm controller[5,6] uses auxiliary libraries such as Mosquitto[7] and Niels Lohmann[8] to interact with the Mosquitto MQTT broker and to convert objects into JSON (and vice-versa), respectively. It is, indeed, an implementation of a simulated robotic arm, proposed as a basic implementation to be evolved to any target platform. This effort involves modifying the code to interact with the physical arm and embedding the microservice directly into the arm's infrastructure.

The Web application[9] has been implemented in Angular and is the top-level service of the ecosystem, providing a new user experience for controlling any arm. The interaction with other services was implemented using design patterns to reach transparency about the internal structure of the ecosystem and low coupling between application modules that depend on the interaction with other microservices. This minimizes the effort to adjust the user interface when any API specification changes.

---

[3] https://github.com/adalbertocajueiro/edscorbot-java.
[4] https://github.com/adalbertocajueiro/edscorbot-py.
[5] https://github.com/TomasMu97/ED-Robotanno.
[6] https://github.com/TomasMu97/ROS-Robotanno.
[7] https://mosquitto.org/.
[8] https://github.com/nlohmann/json.
[9] https://github.com/adalbertocajueiro/edscorbot-angular.

4 Experiments and Results

Once having detailed the servitization ecosystem, a robot model can be put to work. By declaring a new robot and assigning a Denavit-Hartenberg (DH) matrix to it in the web application microservice, a new robot can be represented in the 3D viewer while working with it. In this section, a trajectory affecting the three first joints will be sent to the simulation and both the event-driven and ROS-driven robotic arms. The rest of the joints are not included since they are normally used for setting the orientation of the end-effector. Upon reaching a new position, the joint values are read and analyzed for positional errors.

4.1 Simulating a Robotic Arm

In this section, a model of Robotanno Q602 is simulated. Our ecosystem includes the direct and inverse kinematics of the robot with the inclusion of the DH matrix in the code.

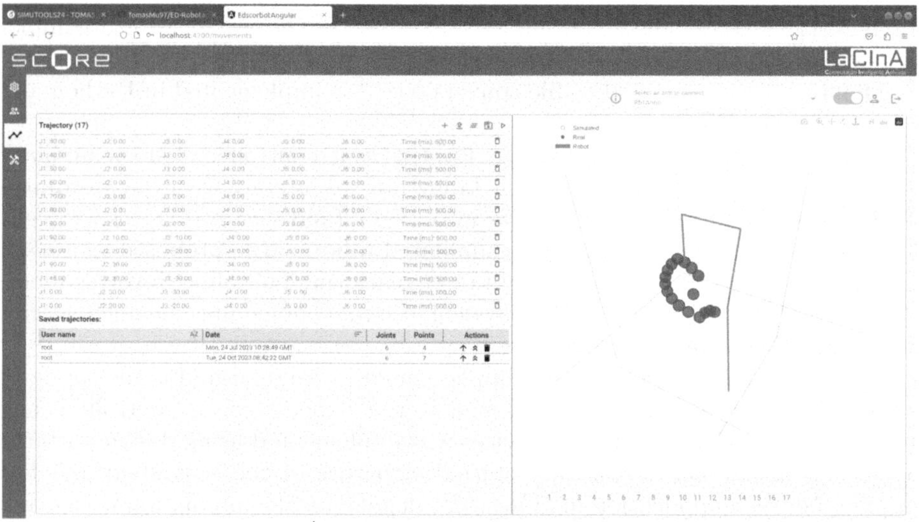

Fig. 5. ED-Robotanno simulation.

In Fig. 5 the web application environment can be appreciated. A 3D plot of the simulated robot shows a blue circumference for every reference point in Table 1 and a blue circle for every reached point. Given that the figure presents a simulated trajectory with an ideal version of the robot, circumferences and circles coincide and no error is read. When the web application is used with a real robot, some errors are expected.

Table 1. Reference values.

	J1	J2	J3	J4	J5	J6
1	10	0	0	0	0	0
2	20	0	0	0	0	0
3	30	0	0	0	0	0
4	40	0	0	0	0	0
5	50	0	0	0	0	0
6	60	0	0	0	0	0
7	70	0	0	0	0	0
8	80	0	0	0	0	0
9	90	0	0	0	0	0
10	90	10	−10	0	0	0
11	90	20	−20	0	0	0
12	90	30	−30	0	0	0
13	45	30	−30	0	0	0
14	0	30	−30	0	0	0
15	0	20	−20	0	0	0
16	0	10	−10	0	0	0

4.2 ED-Robotanno

The event-driven Robotanno stores its relative joint values in an accessible file from which they are read later on as an absolute value (see Sect. 2.1). Having the web application operate this robot and feeding it the same trajectory that was used earlier provided these results:

The difference between these values can be analyzed by the Root-mean-square deviation method (1).

$$RMSE = \sqrt{\frac{1}{n}\sum_{i=1}^{n} d(S_{ref}, S_m)^2} \tag{1}$$

The RMSE values have been obtained using the joint values from Table 2. They are quite low, as shown in Table 3. This makes sense, as the control of this robot is not actually a closed-loop control, so this could mean the difference between these values comes from the servo motors step resolution. ROS-Robotanno does come with a closed-loop PID controller, so a similar experiment operating it is in order.

4.3 ROS-Robotanno

ROS-Robotanno is operated by its dedicated controller, which acts as a ROS node in our environment. For a proper communication between our MQTT nodes

Table 2. ED-Robotanno joint values.

	J1	J2	J3	J4	J5	J6
1	9,99997408577866	0	0	0	0	0
2	19,9999481715573	0	0	0	0	0
3	29,9999222573359	0	0	0	0	0
4	39,9998963431146	0	0	0	0	0
5	49,9998704288933	0	0	0	0	0
6	59,9998445146719	0	0	0	0	0
7	70,00014253	0	0	0	0	0
8	80,00011661	0	0	0	0	0
9	90,0000907	0	0	0	0	0
10	90,0000907	9,999849316	−9,999954261	0	0	0
11	90,0000907	19,99969863	−19,99990852	0	0	0
12	90,0000907	29,99987552	−29,99986278	0	0	0
13	45,00004535	29,99987552	−29,99986278	0	0	0
14	0	29,99987552	−29,99986278	0	0	0
15	0	19,99969863	−19,99990852	0	0	0
16	0	9,999849316	−9,999954261	0	0	0

Table 3. ED-Robotanno root-mean-square difference (in degrees).

J1	J2	J3	J4	J5	J6
9,0134E−05	0,000130753	6,95553E−05	0	0	0

and this controller, the arm controller microservice has been modified to act as a bridge between ROS and MQTT. It will translate the information into a ROS-comprehensible format and send it through the controller topics. Following the same steps that those of the former sections, the same reference values were sent to ROS-Robotanno and it gave the results shown in Table 4.

The RMSE for each joint in this case is shown in Table 5.

Unsurprisingly, there is positional error in every joint now. An error value different from 0 is common in closed-loop control as it is a continuous process in nature. The fact that it is higher than the error registered in ED-Robotanno is an interesting fact. It could very well be due to internal tolerances in the controllers PID, given that although they are higher, the RMSE is still around 1/20 of a degree.

Table 4. ROS-Robotanno joint values.

	J1	J2	J3	J4	J5	J6
1	9,998462074	0	−0,038051467	0,04570312699	−0,042187501	0,02109375
2	19,93891535	0,0210938	0,039705881	0,040429687	−0,02109375	−0,024609375
3	30,04152842	−0,017138714	−0,041360294	0,026367188	0,056250003	−0,045703127
4	40,03603496	−0,027685613	0,04797794	0,028125001	0,017578126	−0,02109375
5	50,04372377	0,022412164	−0,04963235	0,045703127	−0,05449219	0,038671877
6	60,03163917	0,026367252	−0,011580882	−0,04746094	−0,05449219	−0,024609375
7	70,05119202	−0,05141614	0,033088234	−0,017578126	0,045703127	0
8	79,95341587	−0,032959065	0,008272059	0,045703127	0,010546875	−0,003515625
9	90,02306816	−0,048779414	−0,008272059	0,003515625	0,028125001	0,014062501
10	90,05075774	9,964183916	−10,03566099	0,036914064	0,02109375	0,035156251
11	90,05734888	19,98901308	−19,95055058	−0,008789063	0,04921875	0,052734377
12	90,02306816	30,00593289	−29,95643109	−0,010546875	0,031640625	0,04921875
13	45,03526557	30,03757374	−29,97628645	−0,022851563	0,04746094	0
14	0,018457075	30,00988757	−30,01102821	0,038671877	0,028125001	0,045703127
15	−0,040869241	19,95869046	−19,97371175	0,029882815	0,050976563	0,014062501
16	−0,0105469	9,973413209	−10,03235262	0,029882815	0,035156251	0,035156251

Table 5. ROS-Robotanno root-mean-square difference (in degrees).

J1	J2	J3	J4	J5	J6
0,064233576	0,053157912	0,056129492	0,053721237	0,065031146	0,051409131

5 Conclusions

In this paper, concepts like Software as a Service are introduced to elaborate a novel servitization model for the ED-RobotAnno robotic arm, with the aim of enabling the use of a specific neuromorphic robot in simulated and real scenarios, both local or remote, easily. The robot can now be used in-the-loop of higher-level neuromorphic algorithms from international research groups, as it is done in the SMALL EU project. The solution is based on an ecosystem composed of heterogeneous and independent microservices that provide all functionalities to be offered in the entire system.

A low coupling of components was achieved by using the concept of API specifications (synchronous and asynchronous) to be followed by the microservices. At the same time, the microservices have high cohesion as each of them deals with a specific aspect/functionality. The first microservice provides support for authentication, user and trajectory manipulation, and persistence for the entire ecosystem. The second microservice provides facilities to handle trajectory files written in other formats that need to be converted before being used. The third microservice represents an implementation of a simulated robotic arm and is intended to be a *baseline* to be evolved and embedded in the arm's platform. Implementation was evolved, simplified, embedded into the ED-RobotAnno platform, and used it in the proposed ecosystem. Finally, the fourth microservice is the top-level service that communicates with all others to provide a high-level web application as a modern user interface for remotely controlling robotic arms, providing an abstraction layer for users that simplifies all the neuro-inspired components deployed in the real robot.

By using API specifications, design patterns, and moderns resources of web development, our solution is scalable in the sense that any new arm will be automatically available in the ecosystem as long as they are adherent to the asynchronous API specification, publishes its metainformation at startup and its conversions and kinematics functions are informed to the conversion and the web application microservices.

References

1. Angular Framework. https://angular.io
2. Aer neuro-inspired interface to anthropomorphic robotic hand. In: The 2006 IEEE International Joint Conference on Neural Network Proceedings, pp. 1497–1504. IEEE (2006)
3. H2 database engine (2022). https://www.h2database.com/
4. Blum, H., Dietmüller, A., Milde, M., Conradt, J., Indiveri, G., Sandamirskaya, Y.: A neuromorphic controller for a robotic vehicle equipped with a dynamic vision sensor. In: Robotics Science and Systems, RSS 2017 (2017)
5. Bullock, D., Grossberg, S.: Chapter 11 vite and flete: neural modules for trajectory formation and postural control. In: Hershberger, W.A. (ed.) Volitional Action, Advances in Psychology, vol. 62, pp. 253–297. North-Holland (1989). https://doi.org/10.1016/S0166-4115(08)61915-9, https://www.sciencedirect.com/science/article/pii/S0166411508619159
6. Canas-Moreno, S., et al.: Towards spike-based motor control FPGA integration for neuromorphic robotic arms for learning applications through remote access. Submitted to Springer Autonomous Robots (2021)
7. Carraro, G., Chong, F.: Software as a service: an enterprise perspective (2006)
8. Casanueva-Morato, D., Lopez-Osorio, P., Piñero-Fuentes, E., Dominguez-Morales, J.P., Perez-Peña, F., Linares-Barranco, A.: Integrating a hippocampus memory model into a neuromorphic robotic-arm for trajectory navigation. In: 2024 IEEE International Symposium on Circuits and Systems (ISCAS), pp. 1–5. IEEE (2024)
9. Donati, E., Perez-Peña, F., Bartolozzi, C., Indiveri, G., Chicca, E.: Open-loop neuromorphic controller implemented on VLSI devices. In: 2018 7th IEEE International Conference on Biomedical Robotics and Biomechatronics (Biorob), pp. 827–832. IEEE (2018)
10. Fowler, M., Lewis, J.: Microservices (2014)
11. Indiveri, G., Liu, S., Delbruck, T., Douglas, R.: Neuromorphic systems
12. Jimenez-Fernandez, A., Jimenez-Moreno, G., Linares-Barranco, A., Dominguez-Morales, M.J., Paz-Vicente, R., Civit-Balcells, A.: A neuro-inspired spike-based PID motor controller for multi-motor robots with low cost FPGAs. Sensors **12**(4), 3831–3856 (2012). https://doi.org/10.3390/s120403831, https://www.mdpi.com/1424-8220/12/4/3831

13. Kudelski, M., Gambardella, L.M., Di Caro, G.A.: RoboNetSim: an integrated framework for multi-robot and network simulation. Robot. Auton. Syst. **61**(5), 483–496 (2013)
14. Light, R.A.: Mosquitto: server and client implementation of the MQTT protocol. J. Open Sour. Softw. **2**(13), 265 (2017). https://doi.org/10.21105/joss.00265
15. Linares-Barranco, A., Perez-Peña, F., Jimenez-Fernandez, A., Chicca, E.: ED-BioRob: a neuromorphic robotic arm with FPGA-based infrastructure for bio-inspired spiking motor controllers. Front. Neurorobot. **14**, 96 (2020). https://doi.org/10.3389/fnbot.2020.590163, https://www.frontiersin.org/article/10.3389/fnbot.2020.590163
16. Webb, P., Syer, D., et al.: Spring boot reference documentation. https://docs.spring.io/spring-boot/docs/current/reference/html/
17. Przybilski, M.: Rest - representational state transfer. Technical report. http://www.cs.helsinki.fi/u/chande/courses/cs/MWS/reports/MichaelPrzybilski_REST.pdf
18. Rohmer, E., Singh, S.P., Freese, M.: V-REP: a versatile and scalable robot simulation framework. In: 2013 IEEE/RSJ International Conference on Intelligent Robots and Systems, pp. 1321–1326. IEEE (2013)
19. Wirtz, J., et al.: Brave new world: service robots in the frontline (2018). https://doi.org/10.1108/JOSM-04-2018-0119
20. Wu, C., Zhao, J., Zendrikov, D., Indiveri, G., et al.: Towards hardware implementation of WTA for CPG-based control of a spiking robotic arm. In: 2022 IEEE International Symposium on Circuits and Systems (ISCAS), pp. 1057–1061. IEEE (2022)

Flexible Visualization for Modular Autonomy Cores of Autonomous Robot Swarms

Alexander Puzicha(✉)

Chair of Modelling and Simulation, TU Dortmund University, Dortmund, Germany
alexander.puzicha@cs.tu-dortmund.de

Abstract. In the realm of autonomous robotics, particularly in disaster response scenarios, the ability to efficiently visualize swarm behaviors and decision-making processes is crucial for development, testing, and real-time operation. This paper delves into the autonomy core system developed for combined virtual and real robot swarms, emphasizing the modular architecture that allows for seamless integration of different visualization methods without necessitating significant code alterations. We explore the autonomy system's design, its benefits for flexibility in visualization, and potential applications across various domains of robotics.

Keywords: Autonomous Robots · Modular Autonomy · Real-Time Simulation · Flexible Visualization

1 Introduction

The deployment of autonomous robot swarms in disaster areas presents a myriad of challenges, from unpredictable environments to limited communication infrastructure. Visualization plays a vital role in understanding and optimizing these swarms' behaviors, both during development and in operational scenarios. Traditional approaches often tie specific visualization techniques to the underlying codebase, resulting in rigid systems that are difficult to adapt to new visualization needs [4]. Those needs can be different usecases or trainings for different levels of rescue responders from first hand directly in the vicinity of the robots to the overall coordinator with a top down perspective [9].

This paper discusses the autonomy core's modular architecture, which supports a wide range of visualization tools, making it a versatile solution for different scenarios. The system's design allows developers and researchers to integrate or switch visualizations without altering the code base of the software. This adaptability is crucial for rapid prototyping, simulation, and real-world applications where diverse visualization needs may arise.

Our autonomy core system [14,16] is designed to manage large-scale autonomous robot swarms with more than 70 decentralized planning ermgent

A. A. Juan et al. (Eds.): SIMUtools 2024, LNICST 603, pp. 268–282, 2025.
https://doi.org/10.1007/978-3-031-87345-4_18

agents. It integrates a model predictive controller tailored for mobile robotics and provides functionalities for tasks such as reconnaissance, convoy escorting, transportation, localization, teaming, and network setup in disaster areas. The system's key feature is its modular tree-like architecture, which separates core functionalities from peripheral systems, including visualization.

This separation ensures that changes in one module, such as visualization, do not require modifications to other parts of the system and allows for different application builds from real-time ARM architecture version up to large VR simulations on x64 architectures. It is designed with respect to the software metrics of weak coupling and strong cohesion as well as a strict separation between components and their data. Hence, a strict read-and-write order and read-only accesses improve performance and adaptability. This implies the benefits of Interoperability, Scalability, Flexibility, and Maintainability. But it costs a more planned, sophisticated, and complex architecture.

Related Work: Various simulators exist for mobile robots, robot swarms [3,8,10–13], and for networks such as OMNet++ or ns-3 [17]. However, these simulators typically either simulate hardware and its dynamics or overly abstract the processes. The issue with direct physical simulation is that only a very limited number of agents can be simulated simultaneously. Conversely, highly abstracted simulations simplify control or operate in grid-based environments like the multi-agent path finding (MAPF) problems [2,18,19]. Additionally, autonomous mission management is often not covered, and communication is handled via ideal connections or external programs not designed for real-time applications. This work aims to address this gap with the proposed approach. Each agent operates a fully independent unit of the Autonomy Core, which can also function independently of the simulation. Data within a core can be shared across processes, with each core generating its own instances, such as for obstacle objects. Communication occurs through a real-time capable virtual communication network with physical propagation, which can be connected to real networks. While no friction or physical interaction is enabled, physical dynamic models are used as control systems. This allows for the simulation of a large number of agents without abstracting away significant physical constraints due to kinematics or data transmission.

Contribution of this Paper: In this paper we present new modular visualization techniques for a large-scale autonomous robot swarm autonomy system. Therefore we dive into the structure and architectural design of the autonomy system to connect this in a flexible and modular way to different visualizations for different usescases and evaluate the overall simulation performance and possibilities.

Structure of the Paper: In the following section we describe the basic structure and architectural design of the autonomy core for dezentralized autonomous robot swarms and its interfaces to middelware systems. Section 3 elaborates on the different visualization levels, their action possibilities, and their main purpose. In Sect. 4 some visualization examples and short performance visualizations are given. The paper ends with a conclusion and some topics for future research in Sect. 5.

2 Autonomy Core and Interfaces

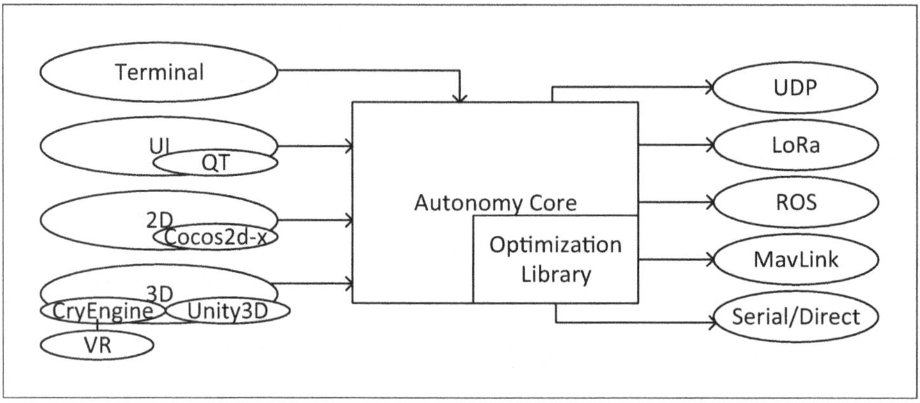

Fig. 1. Visualization possibilities and interface graph of the autonomy core.

This section provides an in-depth description of the structure and concepts behind the developed control program, referred to as the "Autonomy Core", designed for autonomous agents. The foundation of this program is based on the simulation developed in [15]. This simulation allows for easy testing of missions and straightforward extraction of data from agents and the environment, as all components are linked to a parent scenario object. Additionally, this scenario object has references to every existing object within it, enabling direct reading and manipulation of states and environmental influences, which is typical for simulations. Some simulations may also integrate pre-recorded real-world data. However, these approaches cannot facilitate real-time integration with real agents, as real agents cannot possess a scenario object-this would represent the entire real world. Moreover, the sharing of obstacle objects in memory is not feasible. Thus, a new system was developed from scratch, adopting only some of the visualization functions.

The overall architecture and its subordinate components were developed with the aim of achieving high modularity and encapsulation while maintaining runtime efficiency (see Fig. 1). This approach enhances the reusability, adaptability, and exportability of individual components, allowing them to be used both in real agents and within simulations. To achieve this, the core controller and the mathematical solution for model predictive control are outsourced to an independent program library referred to as the optimization library. The agents'

Autonomy Core is built on this library but can also utilize alternative controllers and optimization libraries. An implemented alternative is the pagmo2 optimization library [1], which is used for performance comparisons. The entire program is set up using the CMake build system for the C++ programming language, enabling modular and platform-independent compilation, thus supporting Microsoft® Windows™ and Ubuntu Linux operating systems on X86, X64, and ARM processor architectures.

2.1 Optimization Library

The optimization library includes the *Control Particle Belief Propagation* (CPBP) source code associated with the publication by [5] as well as the extended version *Advanced Control Particle Belief Propagation* (ACPBP) [16]. ACPBP is implemented as a C++ template to facilitate maximum compiler optimization. The template defines the dimensionality of control variables, state dimensions, the number of random walks, and time steps. Consequently, most loops have a fixed iteration count, and matrix operations have fixed dimensions, allowing memory allocation to occur during initialization. The template also allows for the specification of data types, thus determining the precision of the calculations. The result of this source code optimization is a consistent runtime with significantly increased computational complexity for the optimizer [14]. The fixed dimensions also enable some matrix operations to be computed on the GPU using the CUDA framework. However, GPU usage is primarily suitable for large matrix operations where memory has been pre-allocated; otherwise, the delay from memory allocation and copying data from the CPU's direct access memory to the GPU's memory can prolong the operation beyond what would be possible without GPU support. Initial investigations into parallel optimization on GPUs were undertaken. The optimization library has only one dependency on the "Eigen3" library [7], which provides functions and data types for linear algebra.

2.2 Simulation and Control Core

The objective of this work is to develop and analyze behaviors and solution strategies for autonomous robot swarms. This can be achieved through experiments with real robot swarms or by using simulation models tailored for analysis purposes. To expedite development by simplifying error isolation and analysis and due to the costs associated with real robot swarms, simulations are initially used, followed by adaptations to real systems.

2.3 Structure of the Autonomy Core

The structure and internal dependencies of the Autonomy Core are illustrated in Fig. 2. It is noteworthy that the graph structure is acyclic, forming almost a tree. This allows for modular integration of only the components needed for different

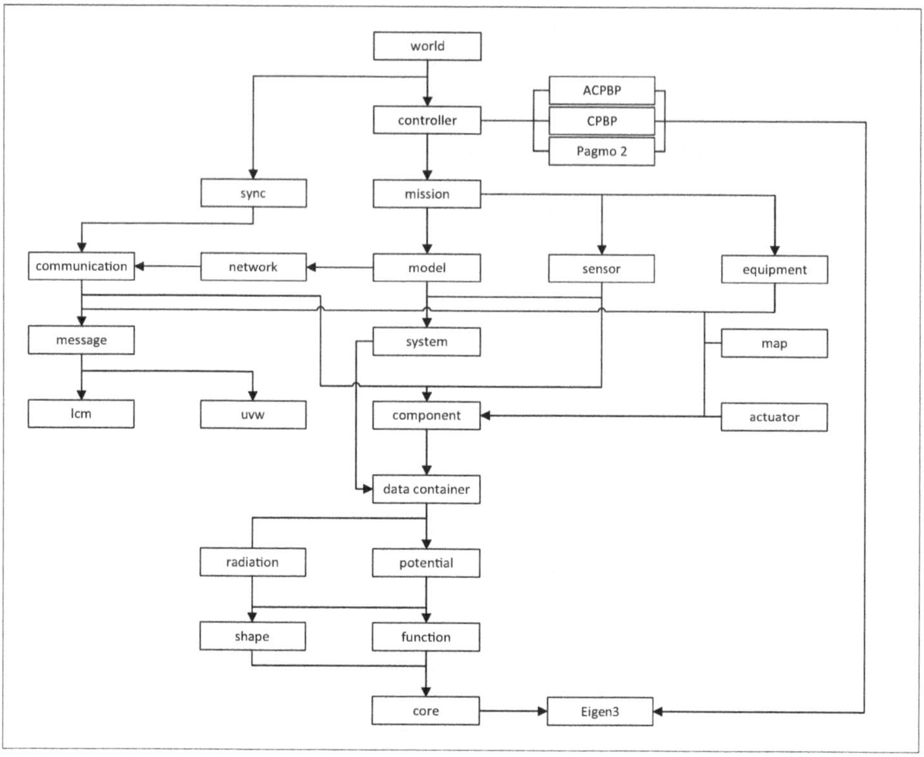

Fig. 2. Acyclic module structure of the autonomy core.

requirements, ranging from small, constrained real systems to large simulations. This results in minimal memory and build time consumption while achieving high modularity and reusability. This is accomplished through strict adherence to software construction metrics, emphasizing low coupling between modules and high cohesion within modules. Each module constitutes a static C++ library. While static libraries increase build time and program size in memory, they offer significantly faster runtime performance.

The autonomy core's structure and internal dependencies are visualized in an acyclic, nearly tree-like configuration. This design enables modular inclusion of only the necessary components, accommodating both small, resource-constrained systems and large-scale simulations. The architecture ensures minimal memory usage and build-time while maximizing modularity and reusability by adhering to software design principles such as low coupling between modules and high cohesion within modules. Each module is implemented as a static C++ library, which, despite increasing build time and memory footprint, significantly enhances runtime performance.

The core module includes base classes and utility functions for console output and basic graph generation using Gnuplot. It also employs a semaphore implementation to manage subprocesses effectively, preventing active waiting. Two key files, Macros and Factory, are used for automatic source code generation, standardizing access functions, variable names, and component functions. The Factory design pattern creates objects at runtime based on class names, extended with an additional layer called Machine to reduce memory footprint and allow more flexible object instantiation.

The function module encompasses various functions for generating potential fields used in mission planning and obstacle modeling. The shape module manages basic and complex polygon shapes, while the potential module combines cost-generating elements to compute costs based on the robot state. To store robot states and other shared information, data containers are used with strict read-and-write orders, reducing the number of locks and waiting processes, thereby enhancing reaction speed and conserving resources. Each system component shares the same execution procedures and system states, allowing different robots, radio stations, and rescue operators to be defined by combining different sets of components, forming a plug-and-play system.

The actuation of a robot is managed by an interface, which reads planned control inputs from a time-based component pointing to a data container containing planned controls and sends them to the system at a specified rate. The map module includes a map analysis component that handles various obstacle and information sets, while the local planner reduces computational effort by generating a list of nearby obstacles using methods like distance filters, mipmapping, and level-of-detail approaches. The module also supports generating polygon-based obstacles from OpenStreetMap data for real-world scenarios. The equipment module manages smart extensions like cargo boxes, arms, and lights.

The message module handles highly compressed byte streams using the LCM Library and libuv [6]. It leverages mathematical system definitions of the robot's kinematics for compression, facilitating control value transmission and restoring omitted model states, with current support for car-like robots, tracked vehicles, and ships. A point cloud-based obstacle detector generates continuous map shapes like lines, polygons, and circles, rather than using traditional occupancy grids.

The communication, network, and message modules build virtual or real robotic long-range networks, supporting bandwidth and connection quality forecasts. The network feeds into the model set for each robot, enabling forward planning within the mission module and model predictive controller. The sync module maintains synchronization across mobile ad hoc networks using a specialized Lamport clock and update mechanism.

The mission management module supports standard, prioritized, and timed missions, employing cost functions that allow discontinuities. These are optimized using a variety of predictive controllers and optimization libraries, such as pagmo2, CPBP, and ACPBP. Data export is achieved through recursive calls, leveraging the recursive structure of components and data containers to save and load data in YAML format. The world module assembles predefined robots and radio stations from these components.

In a co-simulation the autonomy core integrates with *Robot Operating System* (ROS) and ROS2 frameworks, enabling multi-level simulation with Gazebo for a single agent. This involves creating communication channels from the autonomy core to ROS and implementing realizations for key sensor interfaces. These realizations form reloadable libraries based on the ROS framework's presence, highlighting the system's modularity and flexibility in working with various simulators.

To ensure high-quality implementation, unit tests have been introduced for each component. The "GoogleTest" framework is used for this purpose. After each change or extension, the source code is compiled and each test is executed before a new version is deployed to the agents.

3 Visualization and Interaction

The autonomy core has been shortly described. However, to enable the rapid and intuitive development of new missions and functions for the agents, and to share and adjust the swarm's computed solutions with rescue teams, effective visualization and interaction capabilities are essential. Various visualization and interaction methods have been developed, which can be deployed based on the available resources and real-time requirements.

3.1 Methods and Design

The overall design idea of the visualizations is to represent different components of the core by writing a wrapper for each demanded component. This wrapper accesses the corresponding data containers of the autonomy core components in a read-only access to prevent syncronization issues and enlarged runtimes of the real-time core. Changes are made via callbacks and function calls of the components. Different visualizations only require different data containers. All wrappers of the same component type are stored in one a layer for easier management. In addition, each logic layer can be directly used as rendering layer for 2D simulations. It is even useful for 3D as well.

3.2 Console and QT Framework

The simplest method of interacting with the agents is via a console window, where agents can be configured and data can be retrieved. However, this approach requires manual input, making it particularly suitable for embedded systems in real robots, where conserving computational resources is crucial. These resources can then be allocated to the autonomy core. A slightly enhanced representation of individual agents' information is facilitated through an interface implemented within the QT framework, which allows for simple user interface visualizations even on embedded systems.

3.3 2D Graphics

The most commonly used visualization method is the two-dimensional representation of the entire scenario. This is implemented using the Cocos2d-X game engine framework (see Fig. 3). We extended its support for ARM based Linux systems to run on Windows and Linux, x86, x64, and ARM architectures. The visualization has been extended to include missing objects such as radio stations, packages, drop-off locations, and charging stations. Additionally, data sources have been redirected to data containers. Different display menus for agents and stations have been added, and a help menu that showcases most available functions has been realized alongside an overview map. In a real-world integration, only a reduced data set from the agents can be displayed, as only a limited amount of data is stored in the models and message bridges. In contrast, nearly all data from the simulated agents can be displayed. This includes position, control inputs, the Lamport clocks of the network, and the list of active missions. The advantage of this visualization is that it requires very few resources, can operate nearly in real-time, and still offers a clear, user-friendly visualization and interaction.

3.4 3D Graphics

The data container approach also enables the integration of the autonomy core into significantly more powerful visualizations without modifying the core software. The integration into the CryEngine and Unity is described as an example.

CryEngine version 5.6 is a highly efficient game engine, written in C++, that uses the same build system, CMake, making integration straightforward. The advantage of the three-dimensional representation is that simulated objects can also be overlaid with the agent's model view (see Fig. 4). This allows for the clear identification of network delays and the earlier detection of implementation or mission planning errors. Additionally, the use of *Virtual Reality* (VR) support provides an immersive experience. This allows rescue and emergency personnel to train their interaction with robot swarms. The Oculus Quest VR headset is used as the hardware for this purpose.

Integration into other non C++ based game engines can be achieved by generating a dynamic library that encapsulates the static libraries of the autonomy core. The *Dynamic Linked Library* (DLL) or *Shared Object* (so) can then be loaded by other programming languages. For example, the Unity Engine integrates the DLL as an extension written in C#.

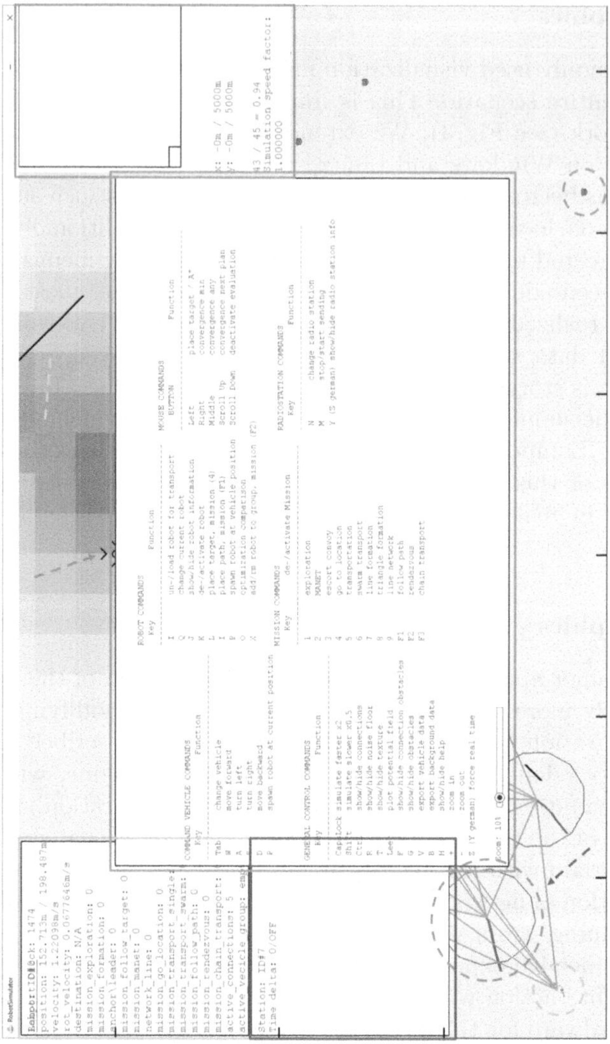

Fig. 3. The new two-dimensional user interface is structured as follows: The yellow box displays the data of the currently selected agent, including its position, size, missions, mission objectives, and network data. The blue box contains information about the radio station, outlined in yellow dashes, which can initiate network transactions. The orange box shows a map, the current map section, and time information. The green box lists the available keyboard commands and the current scaling level. A green dashed circle indicates a package to be picked up by an agent, who is outlined in orange dashes. This agent is located at the center and displays a red trajectory for the next 30 s. A blue dashed arrow points to a high-quality network connection, which changes color from green to red to black. The yellow dashed arrow points to a static obstacle line, while the orange dashed arrow indicates a potential drop-off location for the package. The different shades of gray in the background represent the ground conditions. The black scale on the bottom and left edges marks 100 m per division. (Color figure online)

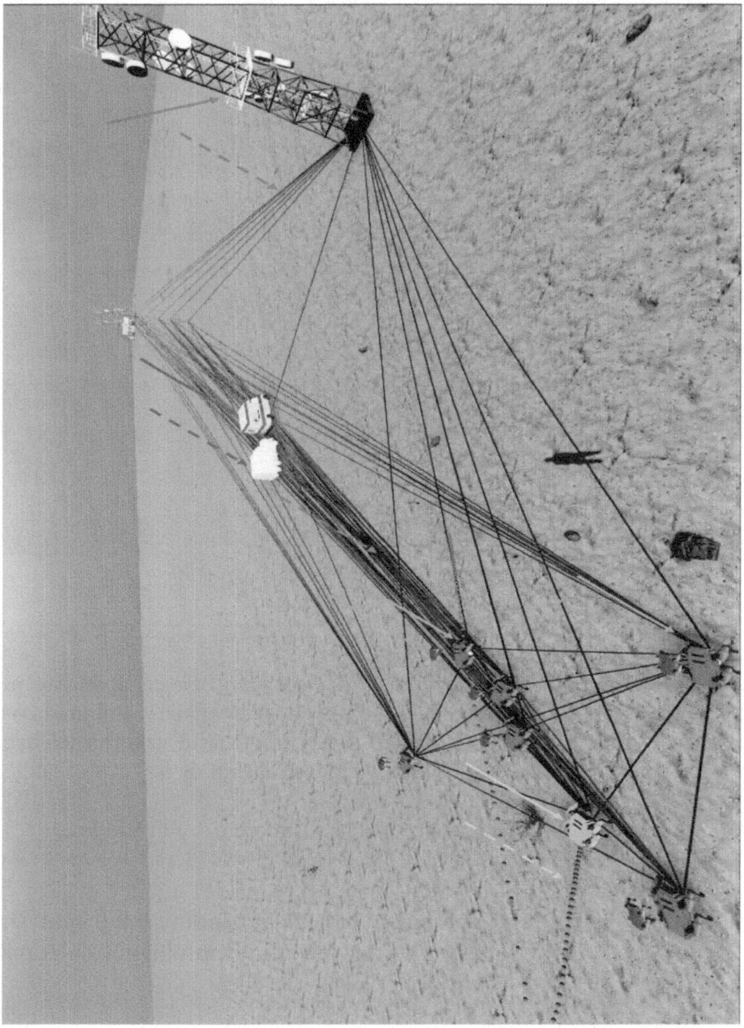

Fig. 4. Representation of the three-dimensional view: The yellow arrow points to the currently selected green agent, whose perspective is being displayed. The dashed yellow arrow shows its planned trajectory for the next 30 s, represented by pins. The green arrows point to other agents, whose models are visualized in blue from the perspective of the selected agent and are highlighted by green dashed arrows. The blue arrow points to a command or rescue vehicle, whose model, indicated by the dashed arrow, is slightly behind the vehicle due to network latency. The orange arrows point to a network station and the blue visualized network connections. The ground conditions are not shown in grayscale but are visualized through texture. (Color figure online)

4 Experiements and Examples

In this section we are conducting one experiment to show the performance of the implemntation. In addition, we show how to connect to other simulations via common middelware to add additional features and use different visualizations.

4.1 Experiment

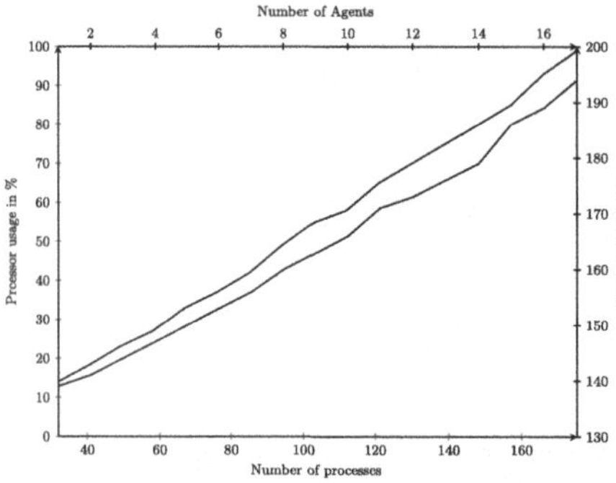

(a) Resource usage of debug mode of a fully decentralized combined hybrid mobile robot swarm, where each agent is calculated on its own.

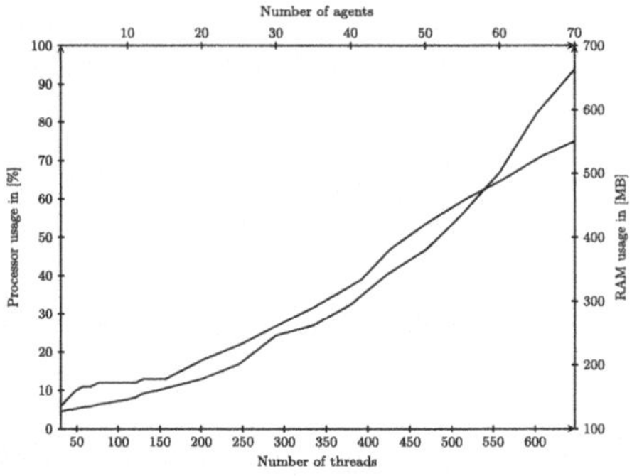

(b) Resource usage of release mode of a fully decentralized combined hybrid mobile robot swarm, where each agent is calculated on its own.

Fig. 5. Performance comparison of different build modes.

The memory efficiency and parallelism of the autonomy core and the entire scenario simulation were examined by measuring main memory consumption and CPU utilization.

Experiment. Start a scenario with one simulated agent, three message bridges, a communication vehicle, and an obstacle within the two-dimensional visualization. Gradually add more simulated agents until the processor is fully utilized. During the 30-minute experiment, measure the main memory usage, thread count, and CPU utilization.

The Experiment was conducted in both "Debug" and "Release" modes to assess the effect of the code design aimed at compile-time optimization, alongside the performance limits. The experiments run on a PC that has an Intel Core i9-9900k CPU, NVidia RTX2080Ti GPU, 32GB RAM, and a SSD installed. From Fig. 5, it is evident that in the unoptimized case, there is an almost linear increase in CPU usage and memory consumption relative to the number of agents, and thus the number of processes. Each new agent generates nine processes. The base scenario, including the visualization, consists of 31 processes.

The memory consumption is about 3 MB per additional agent. Full CPU utilization is reached with 17 agents. These agents do not execute complex missions but manage models for the agents, the vehicle, and the message bridges while predicting their behavior. This number is quite low for a swarm and mission simulator, even though many optimization problems are solved.

However, when the code is optimized at compile-time, up to 70 agents can be simulated simultaneously on one computer. The limiting factor is no longer CPU usage but the rendering pipeline of the visualization. The visualization cannot draw the lines fast enough because each agent has a connection line to every other agent, the vehicle, and the bridges. Additionally, the state trajectory of each agent is drawn with 60 lines, corresponding to 60 time steps. This results in 6,905 lines that need to be continuously updated with 70 agents. For larger simulations, a more powerful 2D game engine should be used, or visualization should be entirely omitted. This would free up the remaining CPU capacity to run more complex scenarios with many obstacles and intricate missions.

Despite this limitation, the new approach has significantly surpassed the performance of the previous simulation, which supported up to 60 agents. Additionally, it was observed that in "Debug" mode, the memory requirement seemingly increases linearly with the number of agents and the models generated per agent. However, this increase is actually quadratic because each agent maintains a model for every other agent in memory. Nevertheless, the main memory consumption remains very low, making it suitable for embedded and resource-constrained systems.

4.2 Link to ROS2 and Gazebo

Another way of interacting with the autonomy core is the optional integration and data bridge to ROS 1 and ROS 2 including precise physical simulations of friction for single agents. This can be extended to a multi-level co-simulation for different purposes in analysis. The data is broadcasted via messages and the autonomy core converts received actions, data, and sensor data to its internal data container format for faster processing and real-time capabilities. All visualizations can run simultaneously showing the same data from different perspectives as shown in Fig. 6.

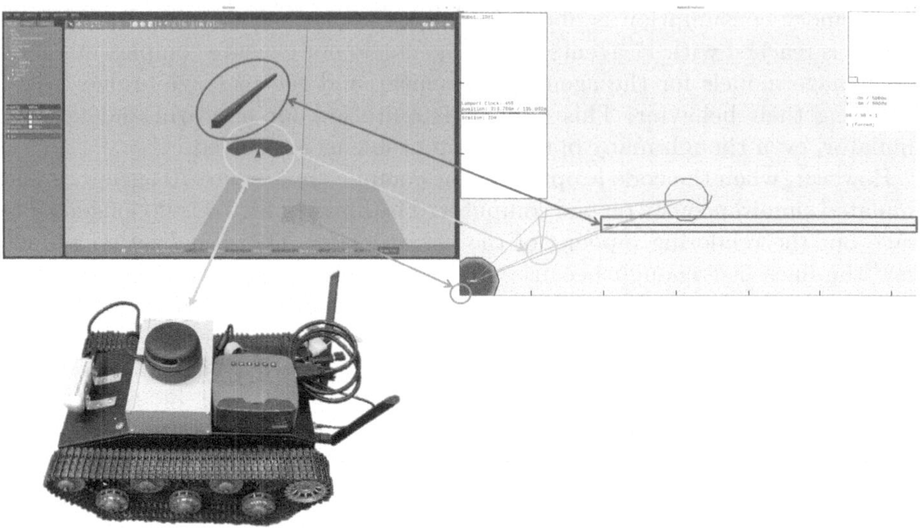

Fig. 6. Multi-level emulation, co-simulation, and co-visualization approach where one agent is a real prototype or physically simulated in Gazebo and linked to the swarm presented in the 2D visualization.

5 Conclusion

The autonomy core system's modular architecture is a powerful enabler for flexible visualization in autonomous robotics. By decoupling the core functionalities from the visualization tools, the system supports a wide range of visualization methods, allowing developers to adapt to new challenges without altering the underlying code. This flexibility not only improves the efficiency of development and testing but also enhances real-world operations, making the system highly versatile across different application domains.

The work presented in this paper highlights the significant advantages of modular software design in autonomous robotics and suggests a path forward for further innovation in the field. The flexibility offered by the modular architecture opens up various potential applications, beyond disaster response. For instance, in urban planning by visualizing the deployment of autonomous vehicles in urban settings, in agriculture by monitoring and managing autonomous farming equipment, in military operations by coordinating and visualizing unmanned vehicles in complex terrains, and in environmental monitoring by real-time visualization of autonomous drones in environmental monitoring tasks.

As the next step, we improve the rendering issues for Cocos2d-X, because most game engines can handle much more line drawings per frame without crashing. In addition, we strongly extend the support of the CryEngine and Unity Engine and dive deep into the performance analysis of the autonomy core on its own without visualizations. With this information, we can identify the visualization interaction impact on the modular software architecture, due to its access to all data containers. The best combination will be the default for open-source publication of the code, but we will keep the high and cross-platform interoperability to many visualizations as one of our key features. Finally, the tool aims to become a major contribution to planning, developing, supervising, and evaluating robot swarm behavior algorithms and controllers on a larger decentralized scale.

References

1. Biscani, F., Izzo, D.I.: A parallel global multiobjective framework for optimization: pagmo. J. Open Sour. Softw. **5**(53), 2338 (2020). https://doi.org/10.21105/joss.02338
2. Bogatarkan, A., Erdem, E., Kleiner, A., Patoglu, V.: Multi-modal multi-agent path finding with optimal resource utilization. In: Wang, L., Majstorovic, V.D., Mourtzis, D., Carpanzano, E., Moroni, G., Galantucci, L.M. (eds.) Proceedings of 5th International Conference on the Industry 4.0 Model for Advanced Manufacturing, pp. 313–324. Springer, Cham (2020)
3. Carpin, S., Lewis, M., Wang, J., Balakirsky, S., Scrapper, C.: USARSim: a robot simulator for research and education. In: Proceedings 2007 IEEE International Conference on Robotics and Automation, pp. 1400–1405. IEEE (2007). https://doi.org/10.1109/ROBOT.2007.363180
4. Chen, J., Li, S., Liu, D., Li, X.: AiRobSim: simulating a multisensor aerial robot for urban search and rescue operation and training. Sensors **20**(18) (2020). https://doi.org/10.3390/s20185223, https://www.mdpi.com/1424-8220/20/18/5223
5. Hämäläinen, P., Rajamäki, J., Liu, C.K.: Online control of simulated humanoids using particle belief propagation. In: Proceedings of the SIGGRAPH 2015. ACM, New York (2015)
6. Huang, A.S., Olson, E., Moore, D.C.: LCM: lightweight communications and marshalling. In: 2010 IEEE/RSJ International Conference on Intelligent Robots and Systems, pp. 4057–4062. IEEE (2010). https://doi.org/10.1109/IROS.2010.5649358
7. Jacob, B.: Eigen. Website. http://eigen.tuxfamily.org/index.php?title=Main_Page
8. Koenig, N., Howard, A.: Design and use paradigms for gazebo, an open-source multi-robot simulator. In: IEEE/RSJ International Conference on Intelligent Robots and Systems, Sendai, Japan, pp. 2149–2154 (2004)
9. Kruijff-Korbayová, I., et al.: German rescue robotics center (DRZ): a holistic approach for robotic systems assisting in emergency response. In: 2021 IEEE International Symposium on Safety, Security, and Rescue Robotics (SSRR), pp. 138–145 (2021). https://doi.org/10.1109/SSRR53300.2021.9597869
10. Lächele, J., Franchi, A., Bülthoff, H.H., Robuffo Giordano, P.: SwarmSimX: real-time simulation environment for multi-robot systems. In: Noda, I., Ando, N., Brugali, D., Kuffner, J.J. (eds.) SIMPAR 2012. LNCS (LNAI), vol. 7628, pp. 375–387. Springer, Heidelberg (2012). https://doi.org/10.1007/978-3-642-34327-8_34
11. Michel, O.: Webots: professional mobile robot simulation. J. Adv. Robot. Syst. **1**(1), 39–42 (2004)
12. Pinciroli, C., et al.: ARGoS: a modular, parallel, multi-engine simulator for multi-robot systems. Swarm Intell. **6**(4), 271–295 (2012). https://doi.org/10.1007/s11721-012-0072-5

13. Pitonakova, L., Giuliani, M., Pipe, A., Winfield, A.: Feature and performance comparison of the V-REP, Gazebo and ARGoS robot simulators. In: Giuliani, M., Assaf, T., Giannaccini, M.E. (eds.) Towards Autonomous Robotic Systems, pp. 357–368. Springer, Cham (2018)
14. Puzicha, A.: Modellbasierte regelung dezentraler systeme in unbekannten umgebungen. TU Dortmund (2023). https://doi.org/10.17877/DE290R-24139, https://eldorado.tu-dortmund.de/handle/2003/42302
15. Puzicha, A., Buchholz, P.: A simulation environment for autonomous robot swarms with limited communication skills. In: Song, H., Jiang, D. (eds.) SIMUtools 2020. LNICST, vol. 370, pp. 206–226. Springer, Cham (2021). https://doi.org/10.1007/978-3-030-72795-6_17
16. Puzicha, A., Buchholz, P.: Mission-based autonomy core for decentralized mobile UGV swarms. In: ISR Europe 2022; 54th International Symposium on Robotics, pp. 1–8 (2022)
17. Riley, G.F., Henderson, T.R.: The ns-3 network simulator. In: Wehrle, K., Güneş, M., Gross, J. (eds.) Modeling and Tools for Network Simulation, pp. 15–34. Springer, Heidelberg (2010). https://doi.org/10.1007/978-3-642-12331-3_2
18. Wang, L., Majstorovic, V.D., Mourtzis, D., Carpanzano, E., Moroni, G., Galantucci, L.M. (eds.): Proceedings of 5th International Conference on the Industry 4.0 Model for Advanced Manufacturing. Springer, Cham (2020)
19. Yakovlev, K.S., Andreychuk, A.A., Skrynnik, A.A., Panov, A.I.: Planning and learning in multi-agent path finding. Dokl. Math. **106**(1), S79–S84 (2022). https://doi.org/10.1134/S1064562422060229

Applications of Simulations

A653MSim: An ARINC 653 Multicore Simulator

Jean-Baptiste Lefoul[1](✉), Felipe Gohring de Magalhães[1], Brandon Bhatnagar[2], and Gabriela Nicolescu[1]

[1] Polytechnique Montréal, Montreal, QC, Canada
{jean-baptiste.lefoul,felipe.gohring-de-magalhaes, gabriela.nicolescu}@polymtl.ca
[2] Mannarino Systems & Software Inc., Montreal, Canada

Abstract. The ARINC 653 standard imposes stringent timing and behavioral requirements on avionic software applications. As multicore systems gain interest in aerospace applications, there is a growing need for tools to aid in their design and implementation. To address this challenge, we propose *A653MSim*, a simulation solution that enables the validation of multicore ARINC 653-compliant system functionality. Our validation demonstrates that *A653MSim* not only ensures functional compliance with the ARINC 653 standard but also exhibits linear scalability as the number of simulated cores increases.

Keywords: ARINC 653 · avionics · Simulation · Multicore · SystemC

1 Introduction

Failures in avionic systems can have catastrophic consequences, including potential fatalities. Traditionally, aircraft functions were managed by separate computers working together in a federated architecture. Nowadays, the integrated modular avionics (IMA) architecture is the trend. It consists of having multiple applications running on the same computer. The ARINC 653 standard [2] gives some guidelines on how these systems must behave and what API the applications must use to interface with it. The current trend in aerospace systems is a shift from single-core to multicore systems. These parallel systems introduce new challenges, particularly in meeting the strict regulations and certification requirements for real-time architecture design and software development [1]. Recently, ARINC 653 was updated with guidelines specific to multicore architectures software development.

In the development cycle of an ARINC 653 system, a critical challenge is validating that the software applications function correctly according to their specifications. There are two main approaches to validate the software against specifications: the simulation-based approach and the approach using the target hardware. While the most accurate execution is on the target hardware, sometimes this approach is more difficult to adopt because the hardware is not

A. A. Juan et al. (Eds.): SIMUtools 2024, LNICST 603, pp. 285–304, 2025.
https://doi.org/10.1007/978-3-031-87345-4_19

available or some low level decisions or implementations are not yet finalized. Simulation remains a very interesting approach for the early stages of validation. There are several challenges in simulating avionics multicore systems. These challenges are directly related to standards compliance, determinism, scheduling policies, parallelism and related phenomena in multicores. In this paper we propose *A653MSim*, a system-level simulator enabling the fast validation of applications to be deployed on multicore avionic architectures. In order to take into account the ARINC 653 standard and the multicore execution specificity, we propose an extension of SystemC [16], a library used for system-level simulation of architectures that are not subject of standard compliance and real-time constraints. We validate the proposed extension by analysing the efficiency and the scalability of the simulator using a set of applications and multicore architectures. The rest of the paper is organized as follows. Section 2 presents the background of the proposed contribution. Section 3 reviews relevant work related to our research. Section 4 discusses the proposed simulation approach. Section 5 gives the results and discusses the simulator's efficiency. Section 6 concludes the paper.

2 Background

2.1 ARINC 653 Standard

ARINC 653 is a standard for Real-Time Operating System (RTOS) supporting avionics applications. It introduces a standard separating applications into partitions and how they should interact with each other and the OS. An ARINC 653 compliant RTOS should implement the following main elements.

Time and Space Partitioning
The CPU time is divided into several time windows. Each time window is allocated to an ARINC 653 partition. During one of its time windows, a partition is the only one executing on a CPU. All partitions are allocated time windows within a period of time called major time frame, as seen in Fig. 1. The schedule is then repeated every major time frame.

An ARINC 653 partition is comprised of several ARINC 653 processes that share the partition's memory space. Each partition is isolated regarding hardware usage, such as memory space: each partition has a set of addresses in memory and it is the only one having the rights to access them.

Intra and Interpartition Communication
The ARINC 653 standard outlines a variety of communication mechanisms tailored to support both interpartition and intrapartition interactions. Interpartition communication facilitates message exchange between processes in different partitions, ensuring strict temporal and spatial isolation as required in safety-critical systems. Intrapartition communication, on the other hand, provides mechanisms for processes within the same partition to share data and synchronize their execution, while adhering to the standard's defined rules for resource management and process coordination.

APplication EXecutive (APEX) API
The standard also specifies services that should be provided by the RTOS. These services are called APEX services and are detailed in part 1 of the standard [2]. The services offered by this API are the ones responsible for creating the ARINC 653 partitions and of the potential communications between them.

Health Monitoring
The health monitoring component in ARINC 653 plays a critical role in ensuring system reliability and safety by continuously detecting faults, errors, and anomalies during runtime. When such issues are identified, the health monitor is responsible for taking predefined corrective actions, such as isolating faulty components, resetting partitions, or triggering fail-safe mechanisms. This proactive monitoring ensures that the system can maintain its operational integrity even in the presence of unforeseen errors.

2.2 Simulation

In the domain of systems simulation, it is crucial to distinguish between simulators and emulators, as each serves different purposes with varying degrees of complexity and resource demands. Emulators aim to replicate the exact behavior and timing of a system with high fidelity, offering an accurate portrayal of how the system would operate in a real-world scenario [9]. However, this accuracy comes at a significant cost: emulators often require extensive computational resources, including high memory and CPU usage, and they tend to have long execution times due to the detailed level of simulation they perform.

On the other hand, simulators allow for a certain degree of abstraction, which enables faster execution and reduced resource consumption while still providing valuable insights into system behavior. This abstraction is particularly advantageous for exploring complex, multi-threaded applications within multicore configurations. It makes the simulation process more manageable and feasible.

Our study employs a discrete-event simulator, a type of simulator that advances the system state at discrete points in time based on the occurrence of specific events [11]. This approach allows us to efficiently model the interaction and timing of events in a multi-threaded environment without the prohibitive overhead associated with full emulation. By leveraging this level of abstraction, the simulator can provide meaningful performance analysis and insights while maintaining practical execution times and resource requirements.

2.3 SystemC

SystemC [16] is a powerful and versatile system-level modeling (SLM) language that extends C++ to support the design and simulation of complex hardware and embedded systems. SystemC enables the creation of abstract models of hardware components, facilitating the early design exploration, performance analysis, and verification of systems before committing to physical implementation. While SystemC is traditionally used for simulating hardware components, its robust simulation environment also lends itself effectively to modeling and simulating multicore, multi-threaded applications, offering valuable insights into their performance and behavior, such as done in [12].

SystemC models are built using modules (`sc_module`), which encapsulate functionality, and processes (`sc_process`), defining system behavior over time. Modules communicate via ports (`sc_port`), interfaces (`sc_interface`), and channels (`sc_channel`), effectively separating communication logic from implementation. Events (`sc_event`) and sensitivity lists control the dynamic execution of processes, enabling precise event-driven simulation. The simulation kernel manages time, ensuring accurate synchronization across processes. Moreover, Transaction-Level Modeling (TLM) allows higher abstraction for communication, speeding up simulation and aiding in early architectural exploration.

3 Related Works

Recent advancements in simulator development have provided essential tools for a variety of applications. System simulators [4], enable engineers to model, simulate, and analyze complex systems, facilitating the optimization of multiphysics systems and the acceleration of engineering decisions. Additionally, virtualization-based solutions, create virtual environments that simulate physical computers, enhancing compatibility and resource management. Despite these advancements, there remains a critical need for simulators specifically tailored to ARINC 653 systems, which are crucial for safety-critical avionics real-time operating systems. This paper focuses on the development and implementation of a simulator designed specifically for ARINC 653 systems, addressing the unique requirements and challenges associated with this standard.

In [15], a simulator named AMOBA is presented, which aims to provide a multi-platform, modular ARINC 653 simulation environment for the development and verification of safety-critical space applications. While it supports a wide range of platforms and modular configurations, the simulator may not fully emulate the performance characteristics of the final hardware and is limited to the ARINC 653 API and POSIX-compliant systems. Additionally, significant customization may be required to accurately emulate specific hardware configurations. Expanding on this, [17] introduces IMADE, a development environment for prototyping, testing, and analyzing ARINC 653-based on-board applications. It offers time and space partitioning and real-time behavior on Linux, making it particularly useful for developers working within Linux-based systems. However, it is limited to Linux-based development environments, which may not fully replicate the timing and behavior of the final target platform, potentially affecting the accuracy of system validation. Developers also need to be familiar with both Linux and ARINC 653 APIs, which could limit its utilisation.

In [7], the use of virtualization to implement ARINC 653 partitions is explored, allowing legacy software to run unmodified on various virtual machine monitors (VMMs). The main advantage is the ability to run legacy software without modification. However, there is a performance overhead associated with full virtualization, and compatibility depends on specific VMMs. Maintaining real-time performance and low latency in virtualized environments can also be challenging. Further, [8] discusses the implementation of ARINC 653 partitioning at the kernel level in Linux, which can reduce computational overhead and scheduling jitter in real-time avionics applications. This approach is beneficial for systems running the Linux kernel. However, it is limited to Linux systems, which may not be suitable for all avionics applications. There may also be compatibility issues with existing Linux distributions and kernel versions, and modifications to the Linux kernel could impact system stability and security.

In [10], a portable and configurable implementation of ARINC 653 temporal partitioning for small civilian UAVs is presented. This ARINC 653 hypervisor aims to provide a virtualized environment for running multiple ARINC 653 partitions on a single hardware platform, supporting robust partitioning and real-time scheduling. The main advantage is the ability to manage multiple partitions on a single platform. However, there is a performance overhead from hypervisor-based virtualization, and managing multiple partitions can be complex. There are also potential security and isolation concerns if hypervisor vulnerabilities are exploited. Moreover, [5] introduces a virtual simulation platform designed to simulate ARINC 653 systems using virtual experiment technology, focusing on partition management, communication, and health monitoring. The platform's strength lies in its comprehensive simulation capabilities. However, there may be performance overhead due to the use of general-purpose operating systems, and limitations in accurately simulating real-time behavior under heavy loads. Ensuring stable communication and partition scheduling as the system scales up can also be challenging.

Finally, [12] presents a modular SystemC RTOS model for uncertainty analysis, providing a virtual ARINC 653 environment for developing and verifying integrated modular avionics (IMA) systems. It supports time and space partitioning and robust communication. However, there are performance limitations when simulating large, complex avionics systems, and achieving precise time and space partitioning for highly time-sensitive applications can be difficult. The accuracy of the underlying operating system's scheduling and resource management is also a dependency.

For all aforementioned contributions, one important limitation is the single-core architecture they simulate. In contrast to the aforementioned contributions, this paper introduces *A653MSim*, a novel methodology for simulating both the functional and performance behaviors of applications designed to operate on an ARINC 653-compliant multicore system. Substantiated by the findings presented in [12], SystemC was selected as the foundational tool for the simulator description, easing the evaluation and prediction of performance metrics such as execution time.

Table 1 summarizes the state-of-the-art revision, positioning each contribution and highlighting main aspects of each: simulation *type*, *Abstraction level*, whether the simulator supports *multicore* architectures simulation or not and if it provides any level of *hardware emulation*. The simulation *type* dictates if the simulator simulates the entire system (e.g., hardware-software dependencies), if it virtualizes the target, if it operates as a hypervisor (i.e., translating the simulated environment to the host environment) or if it adds a layer to the host operating system directly. The *abstraction level* tells the level of description it uses. For instance, it can use only the application to simulate, or it needs more details to operate. *Multicore* defines if the simulator is able to simulate the multicore architectures (e.g., at the target level, not host). In other words, it identifies if a simulator is able to simulate parallel, concurrent applications or not. Finally, *Hardware Emulation* presents the simulator capability of handling different target hardware specifications. For instance, the ability to change a target (e.g., from a PowerPC based target to an ARM based target) and observe the different metrics of the application on both.

Table 1. Comparison of Simulators for Avionics Applications with ARINC 653 Compliance.

Reference	Type	Abstraction Level	Multicore	Hardware Emulation
[15]	Simulator	Application	No	Yes
[17]	Simulator	Application	No	No
[7]	Virtualization	Virtual Machine	No	Limited
[8]	Layer	Application	No	Target
[10]	Layer	Hypervised	No	Target
[5]	Simulator	Virtual Machine	No	NA
[12]	Simulator	System	No	Limited
A653MSim	**Simulator**	**Application**	**Yes**	**Yes**

As the table shows, *A653MSim* is the only solution that provides full application simulation with minimal intrusion of the applications' source code. Further, *A653MSim* enables different targets hardware emulation, enriching the design-space exploration, not being limited to only target. *A653MSim* stands out as the only solution that fully supports multicore simulation and hardware emulation, providing a comprehensive tool for the design and validation of ARINC 653-compliant systems.

4 ARINC 653 Multicore Simulation with *A653MSim*

In this section, we explore the key aspects of A653MSim's design, including the primary design considerations and the implementation choices that shaped its development.

4.1 Simulator Overview

A653MSim aims to provide a robust platform for comprehensive analysis and optimization of ARINC 653-compliant applications in multicore environments.

Functional Specifications
In Fig. 1, we can see the different inputs and outputs expected from the simulator. The simulator's inputs can be categorized into two groups: ARINC 653-related inputs and simulator commands. As discussed in Sect. 2, three elements are required to correctly define an ARINC 653 system: the partition source code (with minimal modifications), the partition time window allocations and the partition communication configuration. Simulator commands can be used to control execution either by providing a predefined set of commands or through direct interaction via a console.

During the execution of the simulation, the simulator gather information and presents various reports available during and after simulation:

- Execution times of the partitions' time windows;
- Functional behavior of the simulated applications, and;
- Logs of different events with the timestamps of the occured events.

Additionally, an external tool, not covered in this paper, provides timing annotations necessary for accurately simulating execution time. The tool can use the generated data from the simulator to compute the execution time.

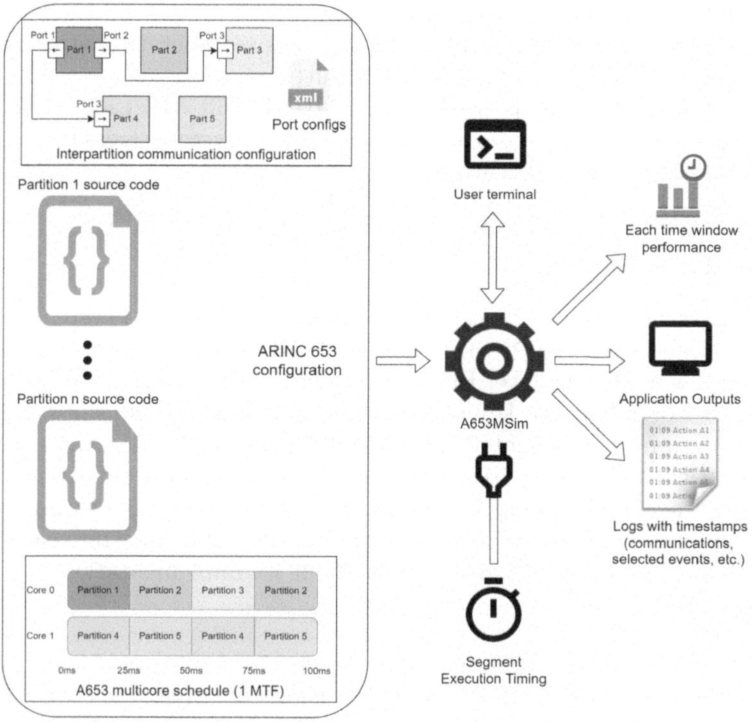

Fig. 1. Simulator's inputs and outputs

Behavioral and Timing Specifications
Given the simulator's focus on real-time applications, stringent behavioral and timing requirements are imperative. Importantly, the simulator must accurately simulate application execution times and ensure the correct sequence of events.

Restriction and Assumptions
Several assumptions were made regarding the inputs and simulated environment to simplify implementation and ensure feasibility. These assumptions are intended to streamline the simulation process while maintaining the accuracy of the results:

- Each partition is restricted to a single core, a common practice in the aerospace industry to simplify certification and adhere to safety standards, as emphasized in CAST-32A's guidance on managing the complexities of multi-core processors [1];
- Communications can only be done using ARINC 653 communication mechanics for strict ARINC 653 compliance;
- The applications' source codes are written using C/C++ programming language;
- The applications' source codes are standalone and do not use any other libraries than the ARINC 653 API;
- There are no external interrupts, which makes segmentation of uninterruptible portions of code possible (discussed further), and;
- There are no infinite loops without an ARINC 653 API call, as such loops would serve no functional purpose unless used for system stress testing, which is beyond the scope of this study.

4.2 Simulator Modelling

Drawing inspiration from [12], *A653MSim* models ARINC 653 system execution using several abstractions: A653 processes, A653 partitions, core modules, and the simulator's main interface. Figure 2 illustrates the hierarchical structure of the simulator, detailing the key components and their relationships. Each core in the simulation is represented by a CoreModule, which manages partitions through PartitionScheduler objects. Within each partition, the PartitionModule coordinates process scheduling, communication, and health monitoring, ensuring a faithful simulation of ARINC 653 systems. Next, we will delve into each module composing the simulator and give details about its implementation.

Process
The A653 process is the container that holds the application logic and thus makes all the calls to the APEX API. We chose to directly use the SystemC class *SC_THREAD* for the A653 processes. The execution can be stopped by a call to `sc_core::wait()` and can be resumed by notifying an event it is sensitive to. These calls are done in the APEX functions, which will be presented with more details next.

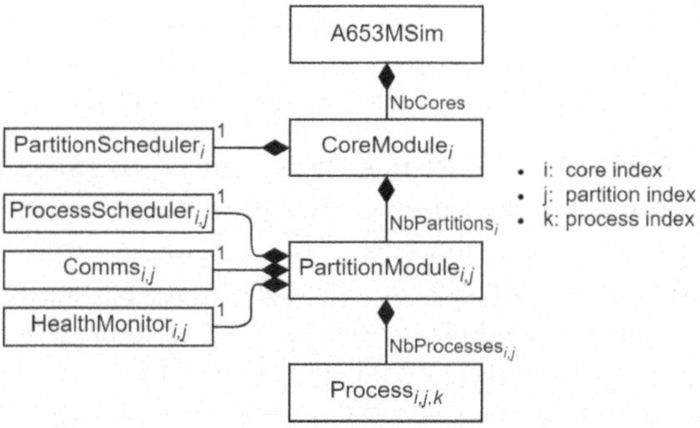

Fig. 2. Simulator's main objects diagram

Partition Module
The partition module represents the A653 partition. The role of this class is to schedule the partition's processes, manage the communication between its processes as well as with processes of other partitions and monitor errors through a health monitor. We use a derived class of the SystemC class *SC_MODULE* to implement the partition module. This is a natural choice, since *SC_THREAD* objects are the processes of an *SC_MODULE* and are created using SystemC's `sc_core::sc_spawn`. Each partition has one scheduling thread of type *SC_THREAD* sensitive to an event that occurs either at process switch or to schedule the partition for a new time window.

Core Module
The core module is a container for the partitions scheduled on a core. Its role is similar to the partition module, but instead of processes it schedules the partitions. A *SC_MODULE* derived class is therefore used to implement the core module. The scheduling thread is sensitive to an event that occurs at the end of a partition's time window.

A653MSim
The *A653MSim* class is the main interface for the user with the ARINC 653 simulation. There is only one instance of this class. Its role is to set up the simulation, by parsing the configuration, then instantiate all the objects of the classes described previously, execute the commands inputted and log the various events occurred during the simulation. More details of the interaction are given in Sect. 4.6.

4.3 ARINC 653 Application Specification and Simulation

Segmentation of Partition Code
In this work, we concentrate on architectures that exclude external interrupts, allowing us to focus solely on deterministic events that can interrupt the execution of a partition's process:

- the end of the time window (e.g., a deadline miss);
- the preemption of the process from a higher priority process, and;
- a system call when using a function from the ARINC 653 API.

Each call to the ARINC 653 API has the potential to cause the ARINC 653 process to be interrupted. We use these events to segment the process execution. Figure 3 illustrates the segmentation using the typical example of two tasks, one producer and one consumer (with higher priority). At the beginning of the time window, process 1, with the highest priority, is scheduled. Then when it reads in the empty message queue, it is blocked waiting for a message, hence it is rescheduled and process 0 takes over. When process 0 writes in the message queue, it preempted by process 1 that can resume its execution. Once process 1 ends its periodic execution, process 0 is rescheduled and can finish its own execution. We can clearly see the potential preemption points are located at the ARINC 653 API calls.

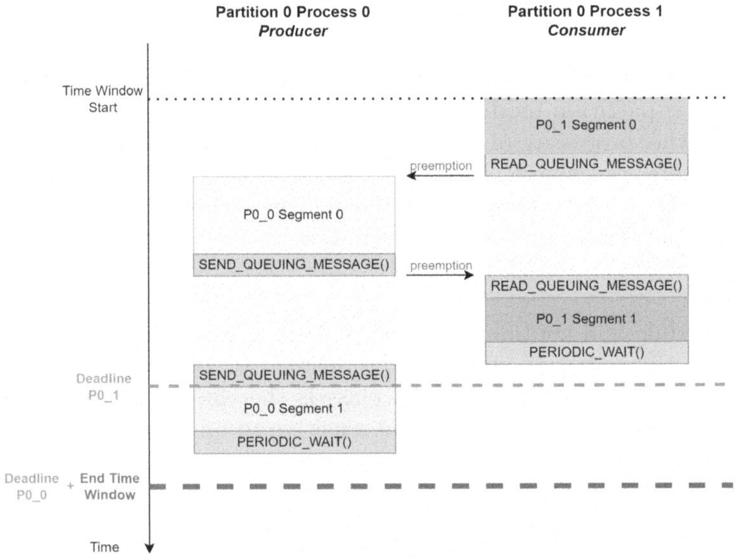

Fig. 3. Segmentation of typical Consumer/Producer tasks communicating via ARINC 653 message queues

Time Estimation of Segments

Each segment corresponds to a continuous execution of an ARINC 653 process on a core without any interruption. The duration of these segments, which is crucial for accurately simulating the behavior of the multi-threaded application, is provided in this work, as part of the simulation input in the form of annotations.

These annotations encapsulate the execution time required for each segment and are used directly by the simulator to determine the timing and order of operations within the simulated environment. It is important to note that the methodology for obtaining these execution time annotations is beyond the scope of this paper. However, it is assumed that these annotations are accurate representations of the actual execution times, ensuring the fidelity of the simulation outcomes.

By utilizing these predefined or dynamically computed annotations, the simulator can focus on the precise timing and interaction of threads across multiple cores, providing a detailed and accurate simulation of the multi-threaded application's performance in a multicore system.

APEX API Implementation
As discussed previously, all interactions initiated by a process with the system happen through APEX API calls. There are three main steps done in the implementation of each API function:

1. Stop trace gathering, estimate the segment's execution time and advance simulation clock using `sc_core::wait(execTime)`. If the execution time is longer than the remaining time to the end of the time window, the simulator advances to the end of the time window, calls for a partition switch, then resumes next time it is scheduled. Preempt and reschedule the process if required.
2. Carry out all operations required and described by the ARINC 653 standard Part 1 [2](some of which may also require rescheduling)
3. Restart trace gathering and execute next segment.

4.4 Simulation Scheduling

This sections presents the scheduling of the process segments and the partitions using SystemC. Here are important and invariable rules in the simulation:

1. There can only be one SystemC event notified per core: this ensures that there can be only one thread scheduled by the SystemC scheduler for each core at any time.
2. There is only one sensitive *SC_THREAD* per event: this guarantees that when an event is notified only one thread can be scheduled
3. Each call to notify an event is immediately followed by a `sc_core::wait()`: this releases the running thread, proceeds to the rescheduling and guarantees rule 1

Figure 4 shows the different states of the SystemC *SC_THREAD* and the transitions between them. By default, once a thread is created, it is ready to be selected by SystemC's scheduler. However to meet the ARINC 653 requirements and control the scheduling, we removed this transition. As for preemption, since we can have only one SystemC thread ready per core (per rule 1 given above), only threads from different cores can preempt each other. Since the Ready state is truly a transitory state in our implementation, all but the transition *schedule* from the Ready state is never used.

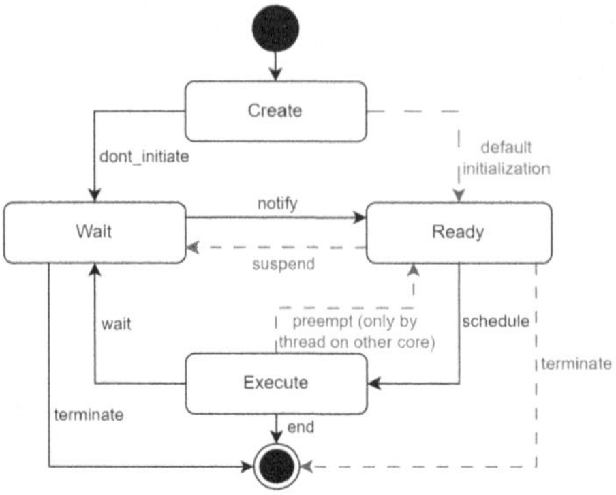

Fig. 4. SystemC thread state diagram (in dotted blue what is removed in our implementation to meet ARINC 653 requirements) (Color figure online)

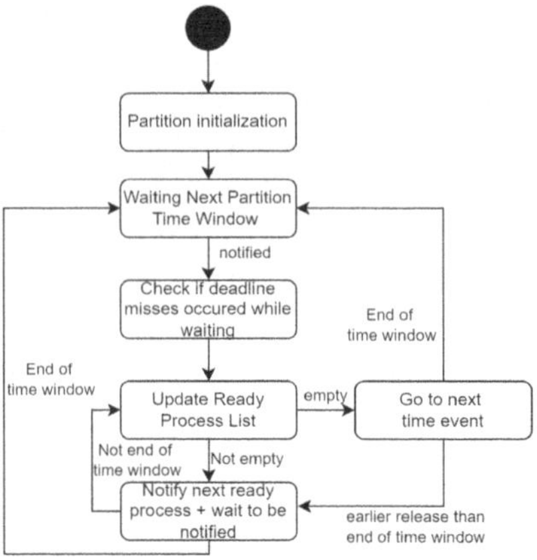

Fig. 5. Process scheduling flow diagram

Simulation Time Step of Segment Executions
If an event, such as the end of the time window, should occur within the estimated elapsed time, the simulator advances to that event and updates the remaining elapse time by deducting the time step. Once the event is resolved with potential rescheduling and the process is back to running, we do the same check of potential events until there is no longer any remaining time to simulate. The SystemC function `sc_core::wait(time)` is used to advance the simulation time. Since no other *SC_THREAD* on the same core is ready, nothing happens for that core which simulates the execution of the process for the given amount of time.

Process Scheduling
As introduced in Sect. 4.2, each partition has a scheduling thread, which is an *SC_THREAD* and is sensitive to an event (*partitionEvent*). Figure 5 shows the flow of execution of the process scheduler of each partition. There are several causes when the scheduler is called and can be separated into three groups: at the beginning of a partition time window, when a process gives back control through an API call, and when a process should be preempted by an event during a segment execution. The selection of the ready process to run is done using a priority preemptive algorithm described in the ARINC 653 standard. Once the next process to run is selected, its SystemC event is notified and the scheduling thread calls the function `sc_core::wait()` waiting to be notified again to restart the scheduling loop. If no process is ready to run, the scheduling thread calls `sc_core::wait(time)` to advance simulation time, either to the time a process is waiting to be released or to the end of the partition's current time window, whichever is the closest. Once the end of the time window is reached,

the scheduling thread calls for a partition switch, which is done by notifying the SystemC event of the core module that releases the partition scheduler followed by a call to `sc_core::wait()`.

Partition Scheduler
Since the scheduling of partitions is static, the scheduling thread has to release the partition as described in the configuration and repeat the major frame scheme. The scheduling thread has a list of release points for the partitions (there can be more than one for a given partition). Similarly to what is done in the process scheduler, the scheduling thread goes to the next release point with `sc_core::wait(time)`, then notifies the *partitionEvent* of the concerned partition followed by a call to `sc_core::wait()`. Once a partition has finished its time window, it initiates a partition switch. This resumes the core scheduling thread and moves to the next time window release point to release it.

4.5 APEX Communication Mechanism

Interpartition Communication
The ARINC 653 standard provides detailed guidelines for implementing interpartition communication, primarily through the use of communication channels with defined source and destination ports. In *A653MSim*, these communication mechanisms are faithfully modeled by creating objects that represent the channels, source ports, and destination ports. When communication is initiated between partitions, the simulator adheres to the standard's specifications, passing the message through the appropriate objects. This simulation handles various scenarios, including rescheduling when a partition attempts to read from an empty message queue, ensuring compliance with ARINC 653 requirements. The behavior of these communication operations is closely aligned with the ARINC 653 standard, ensuring that the simulator accurately reflects the timing and control flow expected in a real system.

Intrapartition Communication
For intrapartition communication, the ARINC 653 standard clearly defines the behavior for each supported communication method, such as Blackboard, Mutexes, Semaphores, Buffers and Events. *A653MSim* implements these communication methods by creating corresponding objects that simulate their behavior. Whenever an API call is made using one of these methods, the simulator executes the operations as described in the standard, modifying the state of the relevant object to reflect the interaction. For example, in the case of a Blackboard, the simulator manages the posting and reading of messages, ensuring that only one message is stored at any given time, as per the standard. The simulator also handles the scenarios such as notifying waiting processes when a message is posted. This object-oriented approach allows the simulator to precisely emulate the standard's communication mechanisms, ensuring that the simulated system behaves consistently with the expectations for real-world ARINC 653-compliant systems.

4.6 Simulator Integration (Input/Outputs)

ARINC 653 Configuration
The simulator accepts configuration files in ARINC 653 XML format, defining system partitioning and scheduling parameters. These XML files are parsed by the simulator, allowing it to accurately incorporate the specified configurations into the simulation process, ensuring compliance with ARINC 653 standards.

Source Code Instrumentation
To simulate the execution of ARINC 653 applications, the simulator requires the source code to be provided as input. The simulator offers specific macros that must be used to instrument the source code with minimal intrusion. Each partition within the application needs to be wrapped with these one-liner macros, one placed before and one after the partition's execution code. This lightweight instrumentation ensures accurate simulation of the application's behavior while maintaining the integrity of the original code structure.

Tracing with TraceCompass
The simulator is equipped to output traces in the Common Trace Format (CTF) [3], ensuring seamless integration with Trace Compass for in-depth analysis and visualization. This feature enables users to leverage Trace Compass's powerful tools to explore and debug the behavior of simulated multi-threaded applications with high precision [14].

Live Interaction (Console)
The event-based nature of the simulator allows for flexible control through commands issued via a terminal interface. Users can start or advance the simulation by a specified amount of time using commands such as `start`, which leverages the underlying SystemC engine. Additionally, the simulator provides commands to control tracing, enabling users to specify elements for tracing and decide when to dump trace data for analysis. It also offers the ability to query the state of partitions and their processes, retrieve details on interpartition and intrapartition communication elements, and efficiently manage the simulation flow, including terminating it when desired. For automation purposes, these commands can also be sent as a script, allowing for streamlined and repeatable simulation tasks.

Debugging Capabilities
In addition to utilizing commands and trace outputs to gather execution data, the simulator fully supports debugging with any standard C++ debugger, such as gdb, allowing for in-depth analysis of applications running within the simulation environment. This compatibility also extends to graphical debuggers like ddd, providing developers with familiar and powerful tools to step through code, inspect variables, and troubleshoot issues directly within the simulator. This integration ensures a seamless debugging experience, enhancing the ability to diagnose and resolve complex problems effectively.

5 Evaluation and Discussion

This sections seeks to evaluate the two main features of *A653MSim*: its compliance to the A653 standard and its performance compared to hardware executions.

5.1 Hardware and Environment Used for Validation

The reference target system is configured with a QorIQ T2080-RDB2 PowerPC E6500 processor, featuring 4 cores (x2 with multithreading) operating at 1.8 GHz. It runs a proprietary ARINC 653 operating system.

The host system for executing the simulator is an Intel Core i7-5500U with 4 cores operating at 2.40GHz, running Ubuntu 18.04.6 LTS. However, because the SystemC engine operates in a single thread, the simulator's process was constrained to a single core on the host system. These test could have also been done using another operating system such as Windows.

5.2 ARINC 653 Functional Validation

First, we evaluate *A653MSim*'s functional compliance with the ARINC 653 standard.

Selected Benchmark
We use the publicly available applications from the benchmark SFPBench proposed in [13] to evaluate the functional behavior of the simulator with respect to the ARINC 653 standard. The benchmark includes applications that utilize various functions from the APEX API, covering a range of ARINC 653 standard functionalities. To validate the multicore feature of the simulator, we create a configuration scheduling multiple tests from the benchmark on a dual core configuration. We arbitrarily set a major time frame of 100 ms on both cores. An illustration of the configuration can be seen in Fig. 6. The configurations used to compare the simulator execution with the target execution are given in Table 2.

Validation Method
The goal here is to determine whether the simulator has the same functional behavior as the system running on the hardware system. We use the CTF traces generated for each core by both, the simulator and the proprietary RTOS, and compare them to verify that they are sequentially identical and in the same order. These traces include partition switch, partition mode change, process switch, process status change and all APEX API calls.

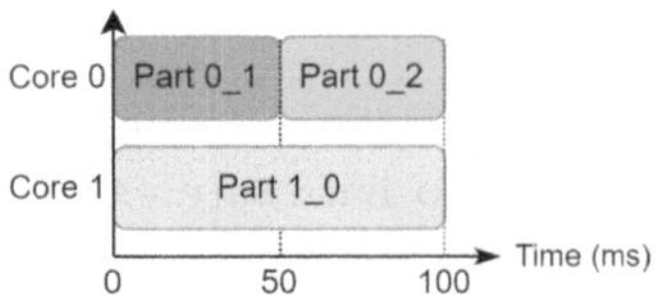

Fig. 6. ARINC 653 benchmark configuration

Table 2. Mapping of SFPBench Applications to ARINC 653 Partitions.

Test Configuration	Core 0		Core 1
	Partition 1	Partition 2	Partition 1
1	App 7	App 1	App 15
2	App 8	App 12	App 16
3	App 17	App 9	App 10

Observed Results

In Fig. 7, we can see the execution traces on TraceCompass of the first test configuration, more precisely at the beginning of the first time window of partition 2 on core 0. We can see that the sequences of task scheduling from both the simulator and the target are identical.

A validation tool is used to automate the comparison of traces. Figure 8 shows the tool going through the traces and comparing the various events and their sequence. The events compared here are those occuring when an ARINC 653 process created and started. When created, the state of the process is set to DORMANT and once the call to the START API is done, the state is changed to WAITING, as shown in the Figure.

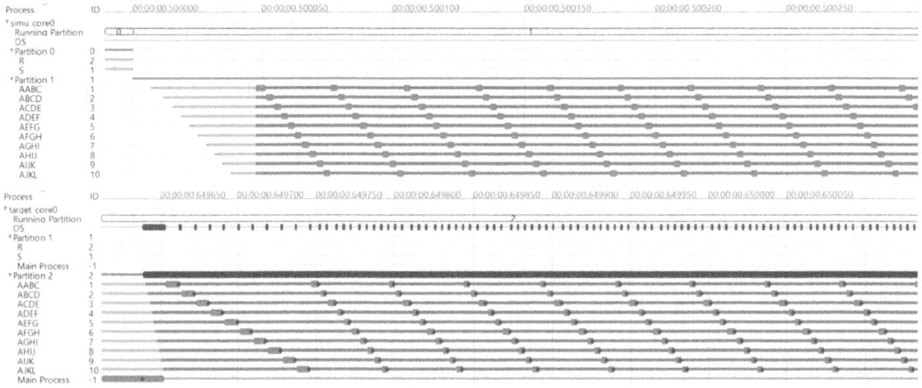

Fig. 7. Comparison of Task Execution and Scheduling between *A653MSim* (top) and Target System (bottom) using Trace Compass

Table 3 shows the results from the described functional validation experiments. The results shows a 100% equivalence between the traces from the simulator and the target. The traces from core 1 in the third configuration could not be compared due to the application generating a large number of rescheduling events, which caused the on-board memory allocated for the trace buffer to overflow, resulting in a hardware limitation.

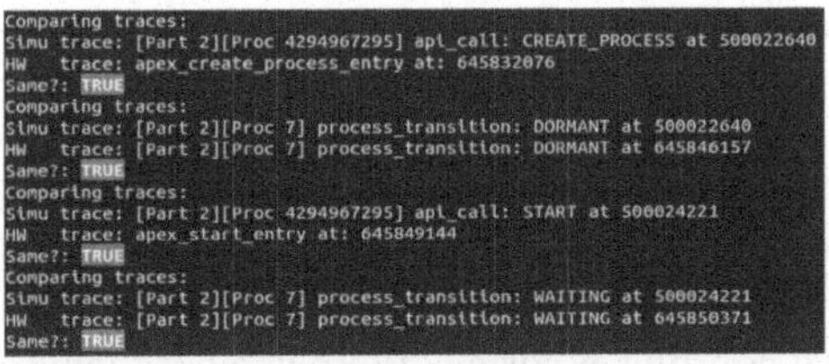

Fig. 8. Trace validation example: sequence of creating and starting an ARINC 653 process

Table 3. Number of compared traces per core per configuration and percentage of similitude.

Test Configuration	Core 0	Core 1
1	20083 (100%)	25 (100%)
2	12086 (100%)	25 (100%)
3	868 (100%)	NA

Discussion
The experiments done here show *A653MSim* can execute applications from an ARINC 653 benchmark and can accurately simulate its behavior on a multicore configuration. In these tests, the execution time annotations only include the segments' execution times and not the time spent by the Real-Time Operating System. This explains why in Fig. 8, we can see the processes of the partition executing faster on the simulator than on the target.

5.3 Performance Assessment of *A653MSim*

This section assesses the performance of *A653MSim*, focusing on two key aspects: simulation overhead and scalability concerning the number of cores in the simulated system. These metrics provide a comprehensive understanding of the simulator's efficiency and serve as a benchmark for future developments.

Selected Benchmark
The TACLeBench benchmark suite [6] is commonly used in embedded systems research for timing analysis. One advantage of the benchmark is that the applications are standalone, they do not have any dependencies. We selected the following applications: Dijkstra, FFT, and Epic. Each application is embedded in an ARINC 653 partition as a process and are looped over several times to increase execution time. We set the period of the partition to 100ms, enough time to complete the loop at each period. The execution time of each loop is measured for a total of 100 major time frames. As the applications from the benchmark are not designed to be ran several times, the initialisation function of the applications are modified to reset the values of the variables used.

Performance Overhead
To validate the performance of *A653MSim*, we conduct a series of tests comparing the simulator's execution time with that of the actual hardware. One key aspect of *A653MSim* is its ability to outperform the real hardware in terms of execution speed. This is primarily due to the simulator's design, which is not an emulator and can bypass certain time-consuming aspects inherent to the physical system.

In the typical ARINC 653 environment, periodic processes within a partition execute their tasks and then enter an idle state, waiting for the next period to begin. On real hardware, this waiting time is inevitable, resulting in periods of inactivity that consume real-time. *A653MSim*, however, can skip these idle times, thereby significantly reducing the overall execution time of the simulated processes.

To quantify the performance gain, we conduct a series of experiments where identical workloads were run both on the simulator and on the actual hardware:

- Dijkstra: 1.40 s
- FFT: 0.69 s
- Epic: 0.07 s

In comparison, the target system took 10.1 s for each test, since in runs in real-time the 100 time windows of the 100ms periodic partition, plus one for the initialization. The results demonstrate that the simulator consistently completed tasks faster than the hardware, primarily due to its ability to bypass idle times during execution.

Scalability
The scalability of our multicore ARINC 653 simulator is a critical aspect, especially given that the simulator runs on a single physical core, while the simulated system can have any number of cores. To assess the performance and scalability of the simulator, we conducted a series of experiments by scaling up the number of cores in the simulated ARINC 653 systems.

In our validation experiments, we ran the same Dijkstra partition with multiple instances on each additional simulated core. This approach allowed us to observe how the simulator handles an increasing number of cores and to measure the corresponding execution times. The results can be seen in Table 4.

Table 4. Execution Time and Scalability of *A653MSim* Across Different Core Configurations

Number of Cores	Execution Time (s)	Speedup
1	1.32	1.000
2	2.64	0.500
4	5.30	0.249
8	10.62	0.124
16	21.24	0.062

Our experiments reveals that the execution time of the simulator increases linearly with the number of cores simulated. This linear relationship indicates that the simulator efficiently manages the additional workload introduced by each new core. The linear increase in execution time suggests that the overhead introduced by simulating additional cores is proportional to the number of cores, rather than exponential or otherwise disproportionately large.

The linear scalability observed can be attributed to the simulator's architecture, which is designed to handle multicore simulations effectively on a single physical core. Each simulated core's processes and interactions are managed within the simulator's framework, ensuring that the addition of more cores does not introduce significant complexity or inefficiency.

Discussion
The performance validation of the multicore ARINC 653 simulator, *A653MSim*, highlights its efficiency and scalability. The simulator not only reduces execution times by eliminating idle periods but also maintains minimal overhead, ensuring accurate process simulations. Moreover, its linear scalability in handling an increasing number of simulated cores underscores its robust architecture, allowing it to effectively manage larger, more complex systems on a single physical core. These validations confirm that *A653MSim* is a robust tool for developing and testing ARINC 653-partitioned systems, offering both speed and scalability without compromising accuracy.

6 Conclusion

ARINC 653 is widely adopted in avionic systems as a standard for application deployment, ensuring safety and correctness in these critical environments. However, simulating ARINC 653-compliant systems presents challenges due to the complexity of accurately modeling real-time behavior and ensuring compliance with stringent standards. Additionally, current ARINC 653 simulators lack support for most state-of-the-art architectures based on multicore processors. This paper introduces *A653MSim*, the first simulator capable of accurately modeling multicore architectures in ARINC 653 systems, providing a valuable abstraction for the deployment and validation of ARINC 653 applications. Our results demonstrate that *A653MSim* can accurately replicate event sequences across different targets, validating its effectiveness in capturing precise execution traces. Additionally, by abstracting the hardware layer, *A653MSim* facilitates the simulation of various target configurations, thus broadening the scope of design-space exploration for future ARINC 653 applications. A653MSim represents a significant advancement in the simulation of ARINC 653 multicore systems, offering a powerful tool for developers and researchers to ensure the safety and reliability of next-generation avionics.

References

1. Position paper cast-32a - multi-core processors. Technical report CAST-32A, Certification Authorities Software Team (2016)
2. ARINC 653 avionics application software standard interface, part 0: Overview of ARINC 653 and part 1: Required services (2021)
3. Common trace format (2024). https://diamon.org/ctf/v1.8.3/
4. Binkert, N., et al.: The gem5 simulator. SIGARCH Comput. Archit. News **39**(2), 1–7 (2011). https://doi.org/10.1145/2024716.2024718
5. Chen, K., Du, C., Chen, J., Gu, Q.: Design of virtual simulation experiment platform based on ARINC 653 specification. In: 2020 IEEE 4th Information Technology, Networking, Electronic and Automation Control Conference (ITNEC), vol. 1, pp. 963–967 (2020). https://doi.org/10.1109/ITNEC48623.2020.9084836
6. Falk, H., et al.: TACLeBench: a benchmark collection to support worst-case execution time research. In: Schoeberl, M. (ed.) 16th International Workshop on Worst-Case Execution Time Analysis (WCET 2016). Open Access Series in Informatics (OASIcs), vol. 55, pp. 2:1–2:10. Schloss Dagstuhl – Leibniz-Zentrum für Informatik, Dagstuhl (2016). https://doi.org/10.4230/OASIcs.WCET.2016.2, https://drops.dagstuhl.de/entities/document/10.4230/OASIcs.WCET.2016.2
7. Han, S., Jin, H.W.: Full virtualization based ARINC 653 partitioning. In: 2011 IEEE/AIAA 30th Digital Avionics Systems Conference, pp. 7E1-1–7E1-11 (2011). https://doi.org/10.1109/DASC.2011.6096132
8. Han, S., Jin, H.W.: Kernel-level ARINC 653 partitioning for Linux. In: Proceedings of the 27th Annual ACM Symposium on Applied Computing, SAC 2012, pp. 1632–1637. Association for Computing Machinery, New York (2012). https://doi.org/10.1145/2245276.2232037
9. Hennessy, J.L., Patterson, D.A.: Computer Architecture, Sixth Edition: A Quantitative Approach, 6th edn. Morgan Kaufmann Publishers Inc., San Francisco (2017)
10. Jo, H.C., Park, J.K., Jin, H.W., Yoon, H.S., Lee, S.H.: Portable and configurable implementation of ARINC-653 temporal partitioning for small civilian UAVs. IEEE Access **7**, 142478–142487 (2019). https://doi.org/10.1109/ACCESS.2019.2944662
11. Law, A.M.: Simulation Modeling & Analysis, 5th edn. McGraw-Hill, New York (2015)
12. Lazzara, L., Mancuso, G., Cremona, F., Ulisse, A.: A modular SystemC RTOS model for uncertainty analysis. In: Chamberlain, R., Edin Grimheden, M., Taha, W. (eds.) CyPhy WESE 2019. LNCS, vol. 11971, pp. 3–27. Springer, Cham (2020). https://doi.org/10.1007/978-3-030-41131-2_1
13. de Magalhaes, F.G., Dugo, A.T.A., Lefoul, J.B., Nicolescu, G.: On the benchmarking of partitioned real-time systems (2020)
14. Nadeau, D., Ezzati-Jivan, N., Dagenais, M.R.: Efficient large-scale heterogeneous debugging using dynamic tracing. J. Syst. Architect. **98**, 346–360 (2019)
15. Pascoal, E., Rufino, J., Schoofs, T., Windsor, J., Portugal, S., Jõ, A.: AMOBA-ARINC 653 simulator for modular based space applications (2008)
16. Schlebusch, H.J.: SystemC based hardware synthesis becomes reality. In: Proceedings of the 26th Euromicro Conference. EUROMICRO 2000. Informatics: Inventing the Future, vol. 1, pp. 434 (2000). https://doi.org/10.1109/EURMIC.2000.874663
17. Schoofs, T., Santos, S., Tatibana, C., Anjos, J.: An integrated modular avionics development environment. In: 2009 IEEE/AIAA 28th Digital Avionics Systems Conference, pp. 1.A.2-1–1.A.2-9 (2009). https://doi.org/10.1109/DASC.2009.5347582

Docker-Based Web Service to Aid Prostate Cancer Diagnosis Using Deep-Learning Techniques

Antonio M. Pérez-Peña(✉), Luis Muñoz-Saavedra, José Manuel Marrón-Esquivel, Lourdes Durán-López, J. P. Dominguez-Morales, Saturnino Vicente-Díaz, and Alejandro Linares-Barranco

Smart Computers Systems Research and Engineering (SCORE), Escuela Técnica Superior de Ingeniería Informática (ETSII), Escuela Politécnica Superior (EPS), Robotics and Computer Technology Lab (RTC), Universidad de Sevilla, Seville, Spain
aperez7@us.es

Abstract. Artificial intelligence and deep learning are increasingly developed and better integrated into the medical environment to facilitate and assist in the most routine and time-consuming tasks for doctors. Image classification with convolutional neural networks has demonstrated a high degree of maturity and very high effectiveness rates. In this work, we present a solution for doctors to use these techniques in an efficient and simple way. Focusing on the detection of prostate cancer by classifying biopsied tissue as cancerous or not, and providing the stage of the disease according to the Gleason scale, the work focuses on the creation of a web-based service that executes the requested algorithm on a machine specifically configured to minimize execution times. This machine uses containers to facilitate replication of the solution to new machines, or replicas of it and uses a Django database manager to manage users, images to be analyzed and diagnostics obtained. So that users can consult these solutions when required. These results are displayed as heat maps overlaid on the original image using the open-source QuPath tool. Our solution, which also includes execution on a hardware system specifically designed to optimize system performance, can be used not only by experienced medical pathologists, but also by junior doctors who are in the process of learning the subject.

Keywords: Servitization · deep learning · prostate cancer · computational pathology

1 Introduction

Prostate cancer is one of the types of cancer with the highest detection rate at present, becoming the second most detected type of cancer in men and the fifth leading cause of death worldwide [18].

A. A. Juan et al. (Eds.): SIMUtools 2024, LNICST 603, pp. 305–317, 2025.
https://doi.org/10.1007/978-3-031-87345-4_20

One of the most important factors in determining the degree of survival of the disease is its early detection, thus allowing us to apply the most appropriate treatments for each case. For this purpose, we have a series of methods with which to take samples from the patient in non-invasive ways, such as computerized tomography or magnetic resonance imaging [9], and in more invasive ways, such as the extraction of tissue samples by means of biopsies. The latter method allows us to know in a more detailed way the cellular morphology of the extracted tissue, making it possible to digitize these samples utilizing specialized scanners in order to subsequently be able to work on the sample with different computational methods.

The different screening tests mentioned above need to be reviewed and analyzed by a group of professionals in order to detect possible signs of cancer cells in the tissue. In many cases, this task involves a heavy workload and time for the personnel dedicated to the analysis of these samples, slowing down in some cases the study of patients and sometimes resulting in a late detection of the pathology. Therefore, in recent years, the development of tools for the analysis and detection of pathologies has been increasing, looking for a solution to provide the necessary support when analyzing and detecting pathologies in different histopathological samples.

An approach that is demonstrating a high rate of success and improvement is the use of artificial intelligence algorithms focused on the detection and classification of histopathological images [3,11,12,19], achieving prostate cancer detection results with a 99.98% success rate when using the PROMETEO neural network [6]. With these data, we can see the advantage of this type of technology in the field of pathology, both in the educational field, serving as a tool for students and pathologists, and in the professional field, helping to speed up the analysis of medical samples and serving as a decision-making mechanism when diagnosing those cases that generate certain doubts in professionals.

Focusing on neural networks as a support tool for students and specialists in pathology, we can say that the analyses performed by the latter are exposed to the bias of each pathologist, which leads to a certain level of discrepancy in the decision taken when diagnosing a case analyzed by several pathologists. In some cases, the level of discrepancy can be somewhat high, for example, for a set of prostate cancer samples of different Gleason grades, a discrepancy of 47% is reached in the selection of the area noted as an area with the presence of cancer cells [14]. This discrepancy is reduced if we use an appropriately trained network where, not only does the selection of the affected area improve, but also the accuracy in determining the Gleason grade present in the sample [14]. With this type of tool, doctors who are learning to diagnose will reduce this indicated bias.

As previously mentioned, histopathological image analysis models have proven to be of great help to pathologists and pathology students, but most of the time making use of tools that include cancer cell detection algorithms is not an easy task, since advanced knowledge of the use of technologies is necessary to install and operate such algorithms. For this reason, it is necessary to develop tools that extend and facilitate the use of these technologies to contribute to the analysis of different types of pathologies, as is the case of the web application developed in this work.

The developed web application proposed in this work focuses on allowing the analysis of histopathological images of prostate biopsies, with the aim of offering the user a heat map with the different cellular regions with the presence of tumor tissue and offering its classification in Gleason scale. All this, seeking a high level of efficiency and scalability of the application itself, using containers based on docker technology to enhance portability and applying advanced web development technologies to facilitate its use.

The main contributions of this work are the following:

- Extending histopathological analysis using artificial intelligence.
- An easily scalable tool.
- Usable by pathologists for routine tasks or by trainees in a university or residency setting.

The rest of the paper is structured as follows: in Sect. 1 we find the introduction to this work where the problem to be addressed and the given solution are presented. In Sect. 2 the information on the artificial intelligence algorithms used for the analysis of the tissue images is reviewed. Section 3 discusses the architecture of the developed application, as well as the data flow of the developed application. In the Sect. 4 several tests are performed on the developed application and the characteristics of the server used are analyzed. Finally, in Sect. 5 the conclusions obtained with the development of this work are reviewed.

2 Deep Learning as an Aid to Diagnosis

Tissue samples obtained after a biopsy are processed in a laboratory using a technique called Hematoxylin-Eosin (H&E) staining, which improves contrast and highlights some cellular structures of the tissue [4]. This staining process is not standardized, so it varies between preparations. This, coupled with the fact that each scanner used to digitize the samples influences aspects such as color, saturation and brightness of the image, means that the whole process results in a great heterogeneity between scanned samples. This variability between samples, coupled with the fact that there is a limited amount of publicly available data, makes the development of a universal intelligent system for detecting malignancy in histological images a task yet to be solved.

In the current analysis process, tissue samples that have been processed and digitized result in very high-resolution images, which will be referred to as WSI or TMA depending on how they were acquired [7,8]. These images are analyzed by pathologists, who evaluate the tissue and assign a Gleason scale score [15] based on the two Gleason patterns with the highest presence on the image. The higher the aggressiveness of the cancer, the higher the value of the Gleason pattern identified (which has a range between 1 and 5). The two most predominant patterns are added together, giving rise to the Gleason scale value of the complete image. Several studies have reported the large interobserver variability among expert pathologists in assigning the corresponding scale value [1,13,14,16]. This is why the rise of artificial intelligence and Deep Learning have been of interest to minimize this variability and serve as a second opinion when making a decision in the analysis.

Digitized WSI have a very high resolution (around 200k × 200k pixels per image). With current hardware, it becomes impossible to work with images of such a high size as input to a convolution neural network. Therefore, it is necessary to partition the images into smaller subimages, commonly called *patches*, which can be processed by neural networks.

In order to train a system based on convolution neural networks for the purpose of detecting benign or malignant tissue and its corresponding Gleason pattern, different training methods can be applied. In this case, we will focus on supervised training methods, which are the most present in the literature. In order to train a neural network by this method, the images used must be labeled. In our case, this would correspond to each *patch* having a class assigned to it (benign, Gleason pattern 3, 4 or 5). In order to do this, a team of pathologists has previously had to specifically annotate each of the WSI to be considered in the study, indicating which regions of the tissue correspond to each of the designated classes, which is very laborious and time-consuming. Because of this, there are few public datasets in which each image has been specifically labeled, which is why there is a tendency to study other training methods that do not depend on them.

In our case, we started from three private datasets obtained from the Virgen de Valme (Seville, Spain), Clínic (Barcelona, Spain) and Puerta del Mar (Cadiz, Spain) hospitals, which were labeled by pathologists from these centers. In total, 938 WSI were obtained from Virgen de Valme from 199 different patients, 221 WSI from Clínic from 43 different patients, and 144 WSI from Puerta del Mar from 18 different patients. It should be noted that, due to the reasons discussed above, not all of them were labeled by the pathologists. In particular, 70 labeled specimens were obtained from Virgen de Valme and 80 from Clínic. For the rest, those corresponding to healthy patients were used to obtain benign *patches*. In total, about 30000 Virgen de Valme, 17600 from Clínic and another similar volume of benign patches from Puerta del Mar, of size 750 pixels at 40x magnification, were obtained.

With this, two tasks were performed. On the one hand, a network was designed, trained and validated to differentiate between malignant and benign patches. This network was built with response time optimization in mind, so the design was proprietary and contained a total of 9 processing layers. The results obtained from this system can be seen in detail in the work published by Durán-López et al. [5,6]. On the other hand, a system based on DenseNet121 [10] was trained and evaluated for the classification of *patches* between Gleason 3, 4 and 5 patterns, which are those corresponding to malignant tissue. The results obtained from this system can be seen in detail in the work published by Marrón-Esquivel et al. [14].

Each of the previously mentioned algorithms is used to automatically process complete WSI images, from which all the tissue *patches* they contain are first extracted densely (without overlap). These *patches* are used as input to the models, which generate a heat map, indicating those malignant areas of the image and the Gleason pattern detected in each malignant tissue area. This heat map is generated in CSV format, which can be displayed in the desired environment.

In our case, we make use of QuPath to represent such heat maps. QuPath [2] is an open-source tool that allows you to open large histological images and navigate through them, as well as perform some processing on them. At the same time, it has a system of annotations that can be created and exported (a tool used by Clínic pathologists to report the labeled areas of malignant lesions) as well as represented. In this sense, QuPath has an editor and launcher of *scripts* in Groovy programming language, with which a code fragment has been developed to load the CSV heat maps generated by the trained models and represent them on top of the corresponding WSI image. In this way, we have a complete visual of the image with a layer on top that can be activated/deactivated and whose opacity can be modified, in order to see the result of the developed algorithms.

3 Servitization

In order to carry out the development of the application, we have taken into account the approach it should have, oriented towards an agile and simplified functionality. Firstly, the user must have his own work profile. Secondly, a section was required where the user could have a series of histopathological images associated with his profile and work with them. In addition, it offers the possibility of applying different algorithms depending on the desired result when performing the analysis. In the Subsect. 3.1 the different technologies used for the development of the system are described. On the other hand, in the Subsect. 3.2, the operation flow of the complete system is detailed based on the technologies presented in the previous section.

3.1 Technologies Employed

The technology used in the development of the web application is divided into frontend and backend. In the first one, the Django framework has been used to offer a simple and dynamic operation and, in the second one, a development based on container technology has been carried out to favor the portability and scalability of the developed application. This allows us to move the application from one machine to another without taking into account the dependencies of installed libraries, thus enabling rapid deployment of the complete system on new equipment for new centers (see Fig. 1).

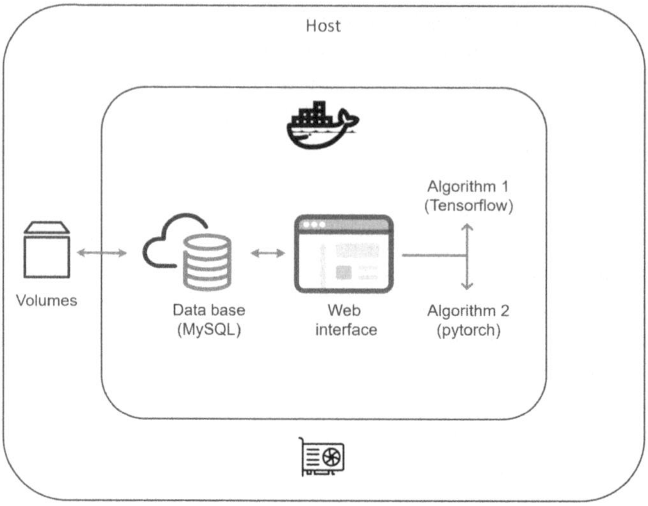

Fig. 1. General diagram of the PROMETEO WEB service.

On the other hand, the development based on the use of containers implies adding a layer of abstraction between the machine and the whole system that composes the application, making communication between the web application that executes the different AI algorithms to analyze images and the hardware devices, such as the graphics card, which allow acceleration in the execution of the implemented algorithms, more difficult. For this reason, the development has been based on optimized containers to favor the communication between the application and the server hardware, favoring an efficient execution of the web application.

Container-based development brings another very important advantage compared to traditional application development. It is the scalability of the application. This concept refers to the possibility of increasing the processing capacity of the web application in the case of a growing demand, avoiding the possible saturation of the system. Another advantage of the developed application is the possibility of running in cloud container services, increasing the computational capacity and, thus, accelerating the execution of the analysis algorithms included in the application. For this reason, container-based development has been carried out using files that automate the startup and installation of all dependencies, separating the image used to create the container and the applications that run in it.

When using container technology, we find that they provide several advantages, as discussed above. But their use also brings some disadvantages, such as the loss of all the data present in the container if it stops. For this reason, the development of the web application has been focused on keeping on the server all the files that need persistence, such as the user database, histopathological images, analysis results, etc. With this measure, we keep all the data stored on the server, avoiding losses. However, this raises the problem of synchronization between the data stored on the server and the data in the container. To avoid this problem, volumes have been used, a technology that allows a hierarchy of files and folders to be dynamically shared between the container and the server, synchronizing any changes made to the data.

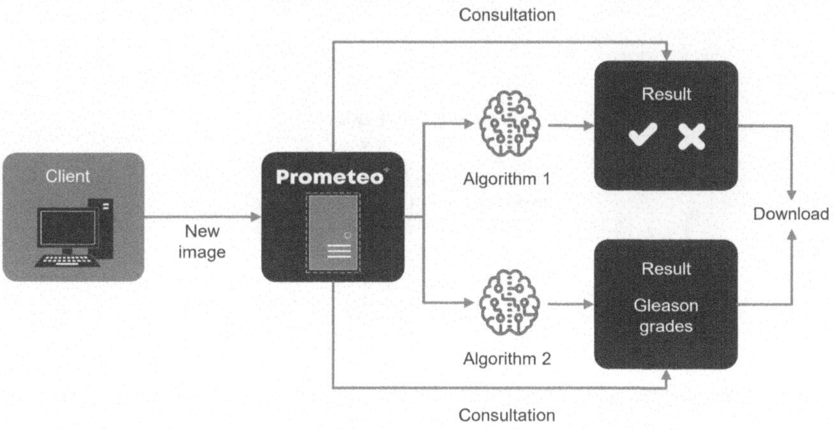

Fig. 2. Operation flow of the PROMETEO WEB application.

3.2 System Operating Flow

Once we have seen the more technical part of the development, we can focus on the user-level operation of the PROMETEO WEB application (see Fig. 2). We start with a user accessing the web application, who must register or login depending on whether it is his first access to the system. After this, the user has the possibility to upload a new image to analyze or access the section of his images to consult the result of the analysis performed, being able to restart the analysis with another algorithm if he needs a second result or download the resulting heat map to load it in the histopathological image viewer of the user's choice.

When uploading a new image, the user is given the option of selecting which algorithm will be used to perform the analysis (see Fig. 3), and can choose a fast algorithm that offers a map with two classes (indicating whether or not there is cancerous tissue and which areas are affected), but with a somewhat lower percentage of accuracy; or an algorithm with a longer inference time and that offers a map with the Gleason patterns identified, but with a higher percentage of accuracy than mentioned above. By offering two different analysis options, the aim is to give versatility to the application, providing a lighter option for rapid detection and another somewhat heavier option for more in-depth analysis.

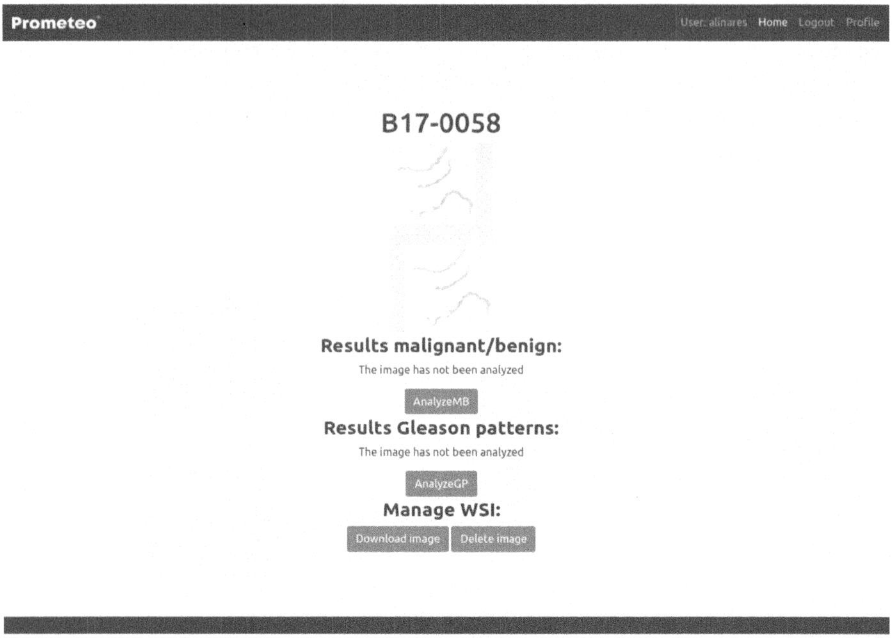

Fig. 3. Algorithm selection in PROMETEO WEB.

Once the different analyses have been carried out, the application provides a list of the images analyzed and whether or not it has found cancerous tissue in the sample, allowing the user to access each histopathological image separately and enabling the download of the heat map resulting from the analysis (in CSV format). With this heat map, the user can locate the areas of the tissue where the algorithm has found the presence of cancer cells, providing valuable information for a pathologist in his daily work (or a pathology student).

In order to visualize the heat map mentioned above, it is necessary to have a viewer prepared to load histopathological images and their respective heat map to delimit the affected areas. This is not a simple task and most of the viewers currently available are private and have a high economic cost. It is for this reason that together with the result of the analysis we provide a script of the free open-source tool QuPath[1] [2], with which we can automatically select the heat map and the analyzed image (see Fig. 4). This allows the user to study in a comfortable and simplified way the results of the analysis performed in the PROMETEO WEB application[2], visualizing the image and the result at different resolutions.

[1] https://qupath.github.io/. Accessed on April 5, 2025.
[2] https://prometeo.t-cober.es/. Accessed on April 5, 2025.

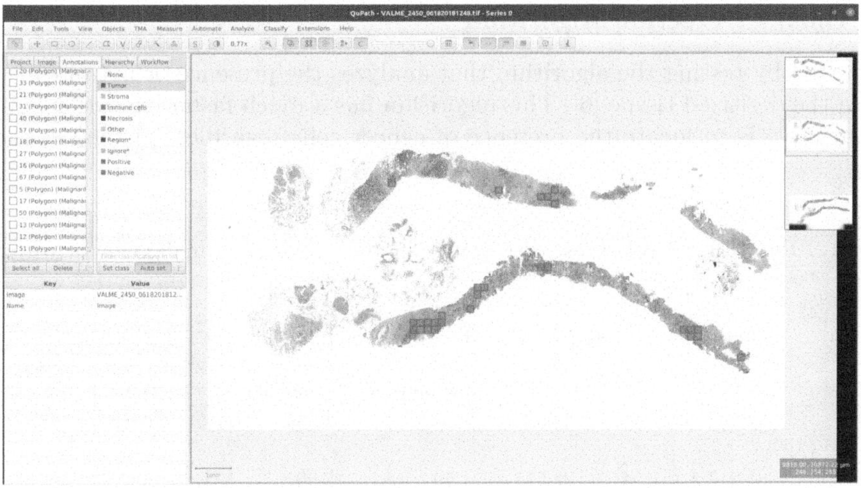

Fig. 4. Result display in the QuPath application [2].

4 Experimental Results

Once we have seen the system architecture, we are ready to present a series of tests on the developed tool to test its behavior at different load levels.

Before starting with the tests, we need to briefly analyze the architecture of the system on which the developed application runs. This system has not been selected randomly, but a series of tests have been carried out on different computers and, finally, a system with an AMD Ryzen 5 5600x processor and an NVIDIA GeForce GTX 1660 graphics card has been selected as the best candidate [5].

On the other hand, it is necessary to give a brief introduction to the different phases that an image goes through when it is analyzed. First of all, the image goes through a preprocessing phase, where the image is traversed by regions of pixels called *patches*, while the presence of tissue in the selected pixels is analyzed and filtering is applied to this set of pixels. Subsequently, the inference is made with the neural network of those *patches* that contain a high percentage of tissue.

For the tests, a set of WSI-type images of different sizes is going to be used on the two artificial intelligence algorithms currently available in the web application. These tests are intended to evaluate the following metrics:

- **Analysis time:** calculation of the time required to analyze an image, divided into preprocessing time and neural network inference time.
- **Percentage of resource use:** percentage analysis of processor, RAM and graphics card usage during the analysis of different images.

4.1 Binary Detection Algorithm

We started by testing the algorithm that analyzes the presence or not of cancer cells in the digitized tissue [6]. This algorithm has a much faster execution since the objective is to locate the presence of cancer cells regardless of the Gleason grade.

Table 1. PROMETEO WEB test with binary analysis algorithm (malignant vs. benign tissue).

	Dimensions (Pixels)	Patch number	Preprocessing time (seconds)	Inference time (seconds)	% CPU usage	% RAM usage	% GPU usage
Image 1 675,7 MB (.tif)	84.752 × 159.456	24.025	2,50	12,50	17%	67,4%	16%
Image 2 553,1 MB (.tif)	81.217 × 151.547	22.578	1,50	7,60	17%	68,5%	18%
Image 3 1,5 GB (.bif)	84.400 × 150.480	21.881	37	40	17%	69,5%	18%
Image 4 1,1 GB (.tif)	73.648 × 186.976	24.480	6,90	32	17%	68,5%	19%

After testing different images, we can see that the consumption of system resources is low (see Table 1), except for the load on RAM, which reaches 69% of occupied capacity in some tests.

For these tests, 4 images of different sizes and formats have been analyzed, obtaining very varied temporal measurements. The influence of the image format can be highlighted since, if we look at the Table 1, we find "Image 3", which has very similar dimensions to the rest of the images, but its inference and preprocessing time is higher compared to the rest of the images. This is mainly due to the resulting format at the time of digitizing the biopsy, in addition to the possibility of a higher concentration of tissue per *patch* in this image.

4.2 Algorithm for Detection of Gleason Grades

After analyzing the performance of 4 images on the PROMETEO algorithm for the detection of malignant tissue [6], we proceed to the second part of the experimentation, where we evaluate the performance when analyzing the same images as in the previous case, but with the algorithm that detects cancerous regions by determining the Gleason grade of the same (see Table 2).

As can be seen in Table 2, there is a reduction in CPU and GPU usage when compared to the results obtained when evaluating the PROMETEO algorithm (1), increasing RAM consumption with the execution of the second algorithm.

On the other hand, it can be observed that the preprocessing times for each image have increased due to the complexity of the processing for the analysis of

Table 2. PROMETEO WEB test with Gleason pattern identification algorithm.

	Dimensions (Pixels)	Patch number	Preprocessing time (seconds)	Inference time (seconds)	% CPU usage	% RAM usage	% GPU usage
Image 1 675,7 MB (.tif)	84.752 × 159.456	24.025	116	9,1	13%	75,6%	10%
Image 2 553,1 MB (.tif)	81.217 × 151.547	22.578	84,5	7,6	14%	76%	12%
Image 3 1,5 GB (.bif)	84.400 × 150.480	21.881	1408,9	68,5	15%	75%	10%
Image 4 1,1 GB (.tif)	73.648 × 186.976	24.480	319,3	23,2	14%	75,5%	13%

the Gleason grades. However, the inference time is similar between both neural networks, being the time spent in preprocessing what makes the time difference between the two available analysis options.

As in the analysis performed on the binary detection algorithm(1), we found a direct relationship between the type of image compression and the analysis time, highlighting "Image 3" which has a preprocessing time 3 times longer than the rest of the images analyzed.

Once the results of the analysis of the two algorithms are presented, it can be known that the consumption of hardware resources is reduced in both cases, demonstrating the ability of the system to run on computers with few computing resources. On the other hand, it has been demonstrated the great importance of the type of compression used when digitizing the images to be analyzed, assuming in some cases, a significant increase in the analysis time.

5 Conclusions

This paper presents a web-based service to support the diagnosis of prostate cancer in histological images. The system has been implemented using a Django database manager, which is responsible for managing everything related to user access control, uploading and allowing access to images with their corresponding permissions, in addition to the management of diagnostic requests. The web service integrates two convolution neural network models, which allow analyzing the images and report results of both malignant tissue areas and the information related to the aggressiveness of cancer in that tissue (distinguishing between Gleason grades 3, 4 and 5).

The reported diagnostic result is stored in comma-separated value (CSV) files, which can be downloaded from the website itself, along with the necessary software (QuPath) and a tutorial to visualize the heat map overlaid on the original image. The entire system has been validated and numerous tests and experiments have been carried out to demonstrate its operation. The system presented provides a complete workflow, from the reception of the scanned image to its analysis, being very useful as a diagnostic tool due to its high percentage of accuracy and as a second opinion to the pathologist, helping him in particularly complex cases and as a triage mechanism in the clinic.

The tool developed, as discussed throughout this work, not only focuses on supporting professional pathologists in the task of detecting cancerous tissue, but also seeks to serve as a simulator of histopathological analysis results so that pathology students can analyze and compare results in a quick and simplified way, without having to rely on a professional already trained in the area of pathology.

Although the developed application has a functionality that facilitates and simplifies the analysis of images with biopsy tissue, there are still some lines of improvement for this application. Some of the pending improvements are the deployment of the system on a specialized server for the task, the addition of new algorithms focused on the early detection of different types of cancer or the deployment of a histopathological image visualization and annotation service within the Prometeo Web application itself.

Acknowledgments. This work has been partially funded by the project I+D+i FEDER Andalucía 2014–2020 DAFNE (US-1381619), with support from the European Regional Development Fund, and by the MINDROB project (PID2019-105556GB-C33) funded by MCIN/AEI/10.13039/501100011033.

References

1. Arvaniti, E., et al.: Automated Gleason grading of prostate cancer tissue microarrays via deep learning. Sci. Rep. **8**(1), 1–11 (2018)
2. Bankhead, P., et al.: QuPath: open source software for digital pathology image analysis. Sci. Rep. **7**(1), 1–7 (2017)
3. Campanella, G., et al.: Clinical-grade computational pathology using weakly supervised deep learning on whole slide images. Nat. Med. **25**(8), 1301–1309 (2019)
4. Chan, J.K.: The wonderful colors of the hematoxylin-eosin stain in diagnostic surgical pathology. Int. J. Surg. Pathol. **22**(1), 12–32 (2014)
5. Duran-Lopez, L., et al.: Performance evaluation of deep learning-based prostate cancer screening methods in histopathological images: measuring the impact of the model's complexity on its processing speed. Sensors **21**(4) (2021). https://doi.org/10.3390/s21041122
6. Duran-Lopez, L., Dominguez-Morales, J.P., Conde-Martin, A., Vicente Díaz, S., Linares-Barranco, A.: Prometeo: a CNN-based computer-aided diagnosis system for WSI prostate cancer detection. IEEE Access 1 (2020). https://doi.org/10.1109/ACCESS.2020.3008868
7. Eskaros, A.R., Egloff, S., Boyd, K.L., Richardson, J.E., Hyndman, M.E., Zijlstra, A.: Larger core size has superior technical and analytical accuracy in bladder tissue microarray. Lab. Invest. **97**(3), 335–342 (2017)
8. Farahani, N., Parwani, A.V., Pantanowitz, L., et al.: Whole slide imaging in pathology: advantages, limitations, and emerging perspectives. Pathol. Lab. Med. Int. **7**(23–33), 4321 (2015)
9. Fitzgerald, R.C., Antoniou, A.C., Fruk, L., Rosenfeld, N.: The future of early cancer detection. Nat. Med. **28**(4), 666–677 (2022)

10. Huang, G., Liu, Z., Van Der Maaten, L., Weinberger, K.Q.: Densely connected convolutional networks. In: Proceedings of the IEEE Conference on Computer Vision and Pattern Recognition, pp. 4700–4708 (2017)
11. Iizuka, O., Kanavati, F., Kato, K., Rambeau, M., Arihiro, K., Tsuneki, M.: Deep learning models for histopathological classification of gastric and colonic epithelial tumours. Sci. Rep. **10**(1), 1504 (2020)
12. Kuntz, S., et al.: Gastrointestinal cancer classification and prognostication from histology using deep learning: systematic review. Eur. J. Cancer **155**, 200–215 (2021)
13. Lessells, A.M., et al.: Observer variability in the histopathological reporting of needle biopsy specimens of the prostate. Hum. Pathol. **28**(6), 646–649 (1997)
14. Marrón-Esquivel, J.M., Duran-Lopez, L., Linares-Barranco, A., Dominguez-Morales, J.P.: A comparative study of the inter-observer variability on Gleason grading against deep learning-based approaches for prostate cancer. Comput. Biol. Med. **159**, 106856 (2023). https://doi.org/10.1016/j.compbiomed.2023.106856
15. Matoso, A., Epstein, J.I.: Grading of prostate cancer: past, present, and future. Curr. Urol. Rep. **17**(3), 1–6 (2016)
16. McLean, M., Srigley, J., Banerjee, D., Warde, P., Hao, Y.: Interobserver variation in prostate cancer Gleason scoring: are there implications for the design of clinical trials and treatment strategies? Clin. Oncol. **9**(4), 222–225 (1997)
17. P., R.: Epidemiology of prostate cancer. World J. Oncol. (2019)
18. Sung, H., et al.: Global cancer statistics 2020: GLOBOCAN estimates of incidence and mortality worldwide for 36 cancers in 185 countries. CA: Cancer J. Clin. **71**(3), 209–249 (2021)
19. Wang, Y., et al.: Improved breast cancer histological grading using deep learning. Ann. Oncol. **33**(1), 89–98 (2022)

Seamless Data Persistence in Simulation Models: A Metaprogramming Approach in Julia

Piet Van Der Paelt[1,2(✉)], Ben Lauwens[1], and Beat Signer[2]

[1] Royal Military Academy, Renaissancelaan 30, Brussels, Belgium
{ben.lauwens,piet.vanderpaelt}@mil.be

[2] Web and Information Systems Engineering Lab, Vrije Universiteit Brussel, Pleinlaan 2, Brussels, Belgium
bsigner@vub.be

Abstract. Simulation software addresses complex problems that are difficult to solve analytically. Due to probabilistic elements, simulations often require multiple runs, generating critical decision-making data. However, many users are unfamiliar with the necessary persistence technologies to store and access this data, hindering effective utilisation. We propose a transparent data persistence architecture integrated into the ConcurrentSim package for the Julia programming language. By leveraging Julia's metaprogramming capabilities, we dynamically generate an object-relational mapping (ORM) model, automating data storage without requiring user expertise in persistence technologies. We provide two solutions for accessing the data, including a web-based interface for immediate access and a REST API for broader integration with external frameworks. The REST API allows for seamless incorporation of simulation data into diverse workflows, offering flexibility and ease of use. Our contribution improves the usability of the ConcurrentSim ecosystem and demonstrates the power of macro expansion in Julia for creating dynamic ORM configurations. Thereby, we simplify data persistence and enhance user productivity by removing most of the technical overhead, enabling users to focus on analysis.

Keywords: Discrete Event Simulation · Persistence · ConcurrentSim · Object-Relational Mapping · ResumableFunctions · Metaprogramming · Julia

1 Introduction and Motivation

The rationale behind simulation is to collect data on systems or processes that are more likely to be described by a model which can be evaluated numerically rather than being subject to exact mathematical methods which produce an analytic solution [15]. Therefore, the goal is to generate data by means of simulation, which, in turn, allows for conclusions to be drawn about the system from which the model originated.

A. A. Juan et al. (Eds.): SIMUtools 2024, LNICST 603, pp. 318–337, 2025.
https://doi.org/10.1007/978-3-031-87345-4_21

We focus on the ConcurrentSim [12,14] Discrete Event Simulation (DES) framework implemented in the Julia programming language [3]. This framework has been inspired by SimPy [11] and DISCO [8], which is a SIMULA [5] class for combined continuous and discrete simulation. The framework has been adopted in diverse research projects situated in several domains, including the medical [6], human resources [2], ballistics [9] and network dynamics modelling[1] domains.

Abar et al. [1] presented an extensive list of Agent-based Modelling and Simulation (ABMS) tools, both open-source and proprietary, with a categorisation based on the model development effort. Furthermore, Abar et al. stated that "An ideal simulation system should require minimal learning effort as well as provide flexible support to creating models and running robustly on any type of computing machine" and we share that thought. Moreover, since ConcurrentSim is a process-oriented framework where a simulated entity can be seen as an independently coded agent, ConcurrentSim deserves its place amongst other ABMS tools.

We think that Abar et al.'s statement can be extended to monitoring and persistence. To the best of our knowledge, none of the open-source frameworks provides an easy-to-implement data storage mechanism. Monitoring creates an additional burden for an end user due to the required knowledge of persistence technology and how to interact with it from within the simulation model, regardless of the chosen programming language or implementation. Our goal is to lower that burden by removing this requirement. Currently, ConcurrentSim lacks the functionality to transparently store state variables characterising the evolution of a running DES model. To mitigate this shortcoming, we extended both the `ConcurrentSim.jl` [12,14] and `ResumableFunctions.jl` [13] packages by implementing a transparent probing and data persistence architecture, making use of Julia's metaprogramming functionality [18,19]. The high-level architecture of our solution is outlined in Fig. 1.

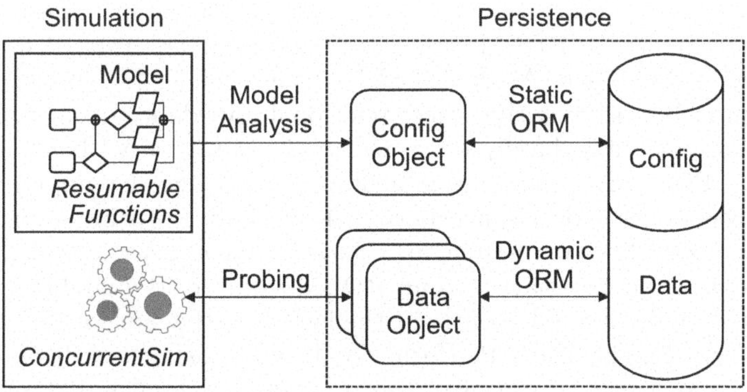

Fig. 1. High-level persistence architecture

[1] https://qs.quantumsavory.org.

At a high level, we distinguish a static phase, during which model analysis and metadata extraction takes place via a modification of `ResumableFunctions.jl`, from a dynamic phase, where a simulated system is probed to retrieve generated data by employing an added callback function in the `ConcurrentSim.jl` package. To store the model metadata (represented by config objects) and simulation-generated data (represented by data objects), both phases make use of the Object-Relational Mapping (ORM) concept [16] offered by the `PostgresORM.jl` package[2], supported by the PostgreSQL Relational Database Management Systems (RDBMS)[3]. Transparency for end users is achieved through metaprogramming, which drives the dynamic phase by using the config data extracted in the static phase.

We start by providing an overview of related work and presenting the three main packages playing a central role in our work. This is followed by the presentation of our architecture for probing and persistence in `ConcurrentSim.jl` simulations. The technical evaluation describes use cases and recorded outcomes. The subsequent discussion section explains the rationale behind some of our important decisions and choices. Finally, we conclude with the improvements acquired through our new persistence architecture.

2 Related Work

Booth et al. categorise persistent data as data that outlives the application, both in time and space [4]. Once data is generated in an object-oriented model, it must remain available in a data container for later use. In existing applications, this data container is often an RDBMS. Ireland et al. describe the *impedance mismatch problem*, particularly for the object-relational case, and mention ORM as a technique to address this problem [10]. The impedance mismatch problem refers to the challenges that arise when implementing a software artefact that relies on distinctive technologies using different data representation and storage paradigms that were not designed to work together in the first place.

An alternative to an RDBMS used as data containers were db4o and other object-oriented databases. As described by Hauser et al. [7], db4o represented another approach to solving the object-relational impedance mismatch problem. Object classes can immediately be stored in the database without any further intervention. Primarily conceived as a library for a one-tier approach, db4o's main goal was to provide applications with a small footprint data container. Despite the possibility of running in a two-tier client-server mode, db4o was not to be seen as an alternative to an RDBMS due to its inability to run in a high-available mode in a data centre or the lack of native authorisation support.

The Jakarta Persistence API (formerly Java Persistence API or JPA) provides a well-maintained alternative. Saeed et al. [17] discussed the three main aspects that make up the API. *Data modelling* concerns the annotations necessary to transform Plain Old Java Objects into entities. *Data persistence* treats

[2] https://juliapostgresorm.github.io/PostgresORM.jl/.

[3] https://www.postgresql.org.

how instances of these entities can be stored in the underlying RDBMS. Finally, *data querying* is about retrieval of the persisted objects using a dedicated query language. Closely related is the Hibernate ORM[4]. Despite being a native implementation, Hibernate also implements the JPA specification.

When moving towards Julia, we turn our attention to `DataFrames.jl`[5], which is the preferred method of working with tabular data in Julia, and `JuliaDB.jl`[6], a persisted tabular data package based on CSV files. The latter shares many of `DataFrames.jl`'s properties. However, these two solutions do not solve the object-relational impedance mismatch problem since they do not provide any means to persist simulation data in an RDBMS. Therefore, these two solutions are inappropriate for our purpose.

A promising alternative is `SearchLight.jl`, representing an ORM backend for the `Genie.jl` package for Model-View-Controller (MVC) web applications in Julia. Both are part of the Genie framework[7]. SearchLight disposes of several implementation libraries integrating MySQL, PostgreSQL and SQLite databases. However, in practice, SearchLight is tightly coupled to Genie. The segregation of the domain object definitions and persistence API is implemented, but each separate type needs its own module for both the object definition and persistence API.

The impedance mismatch problem between object-oriented data models implemented in Julia applications and the PostgreSQL RDBMS has been addressed by Laugier et al. in the `PostgresORM.jl` package. As stated by Russell [16], PostgresORM relies on a Julia module providing the object classes and another module providing the persistence API. Lauwens et al. have developed the `ResumableFunctions.jl` [13] and `ConcurrentSim.jl` [12,14] Julia packages on which the simulation applications we target rely on.

We believe there is a gap to be filled regarding the persistence of data generated by simulation applications. ConcurrentSim and ResumableFunctions are advanced, as proven by their adoption in other simulation research projects [2,6,9]. The choice to pursue transparent data persistence in a simulation environment provided by the Julia ecosystem appears legitimate, given that Julia solves the two-language problem. The two-language problem concerns the paradox between fast programming languages, such as C and Fortran, and high-productivity but slower languages, such as Python, MATLAB and R. Julia's main reason of existence is its capability to solve this paradox to a large extent. PostgresORM could provide a statically configured persistence interface for an RDBMS. However, in such a scenario, Abar et al.'s concerns about learning effort and model creation [1], which we extended to the monitoring and persistence aspect, remain valid. Therefore, we decided to implement a transparent architecture where the issue is mitigated through an automated probing and persistence mechanism.

[4] https://hibernate.org.
[5] https://dataframes.juliadata.org.
[6] https://juliadb.juliadata.org.
[7] https://qs.quantumsavory.org.

The novelty of our work is primarily at the level of this transparency and how it is achieved. The simulation model's metadata, extracted without any user intervention, is used to create the necessary structures to persist the simulation data. To store the live simulation data, object definitions must be foreseen and related to the tables where they will be stored. This requirement is typically fulfilled by an ORM "handcrafted" for specific needs. Our solution employs Julia's metaprogramming support to drive code generation at compile time for each ORM related to distinctive simulation models. Lastly, when the model runs, it is probed at each step through an extension of the simulation library with an automated probing mechanism. In this way, we achieved complete transparency for end users about data persistence.

In the remainder of this section, we present the three most relevant Julia packages before presenting our solution.

2.1 ResumableFunctions.jl

`ResumableFunctions.jl` contains the `@resumable` and `@yield` macros, transforming plain Julia functions into functions which can be interrupted during evaluation with the possibility to be resumed afterwards. The argument of the `@resumable` macro is a function definition, which, in the context of this work, represents a process we want to simulate. Several internal functions rewrite the argument function's body. The resumable character is realised by substituting the `@yield` macro with a return statement, followed by a label the iterator can jump to when resuming the execution. This new body constitutes the definition of a finite state machine. Using `MacroTools.jl`[8], it is integrated into a function which, when called, results in the Finite State Machine Interface (FSMI). The FSMI is subsequently assigned to a field in a callable mutable struct, which also contains the variables included in the FSMI, and a field which holds the FSMI's current state. Finally, a function definition is generated, bearing the same signature as the original argument function.

2.2 ConcurrentSim.jl

Previously known as `SimJulia.jl`, `ConcurrentSim.jl` is the event-driven simulation framework that we extended with automated persistence features. A simulated system consists of processes defined as (nested) resumable functions and a simulation environment. The latter holds the data structures necessary to run the simulation. The simulation environment is a mandatory argument for each of the resumable functions.

The top-level process is initialised through an instantiation of its corresponding callable mutable struct as an argument to the `@process` macro in the global scope. Other processes can be nested in functions as well by means of the `@process` macro in a local function scope. Having defined the simulation

[8] https://fluxml.ai/MacroTools.jl/.

model and the environment, the simulation can be run through a call to the `run` function with the simulation environment as an argument.

When evaluating the top-level process, the `@process` macro causes an event to get scheduled on the heap of the simulation environment. This heap is a priority queue provided by the `DataStructures.jl` package[9]. The event has an array of callback functions that get appended functions to be executed once the event occurs.

Finally, the `run()` function runs the simulation in a stepwise manner. The first event in the priority queue is dequeued and its corresponding array of callback functions gets executed. All events that are scheduled on the simulation heap occur in this way. Nested functions cause events to get scheduled as well, albeit with a different priority. This approach allows for the chaining of events that cycle through the states of the different processes such that the execution of the simulation corresponds to the model which defined it.

2.3 PostgresORM.jl

`PosrgresORM.jl` provides an object-relational mapping between a Julia application and a PostgreSQL database. Data lives in an application and needs to move back and forth between the database and the application itself. Standard SQL could provide a bidirectional interface between both, but this comes with the downside that a programmer needs to master the technology.

The package provides several functions which map directly to the Create, Read, Update and Delete (CRUD) operations. All of these functions take an object as an argument. Depending on the nature of the function it was passed to, the object is persisted or used as a filter object in the context of an SQL `WHERE` clause. The object possesses uniquely identifying attributes, which translate into primary key attributes in the relation.

3 Probing and Persistence Architecture

Our architecture's main design principle is to probe a running simulation model for the values of its current state variables and to persistently store this information for later exploitation. The array of callback functions gets executed after the occurrence of each event and is therefore suitable for invoking the probing function as illustrated in Fig. 2. After an event e_i gets executed, the array of n callback functions c_j gets executed, where c_n is the probing function itself.

Since active processes switch back and forth, the probe might collect a different set of variables after the occurrence of each event. For this reason, the probe needs to be aware of the kind of active process. The latter implies a need to pass the FSMI as an argument to the probing function, resulting in the correct set of state variables. This set gives rise to an object which includes the necessary fields for every process and must be persisted in the database.

[9] https://juliacollections.github.io/DataStructures.jl/.

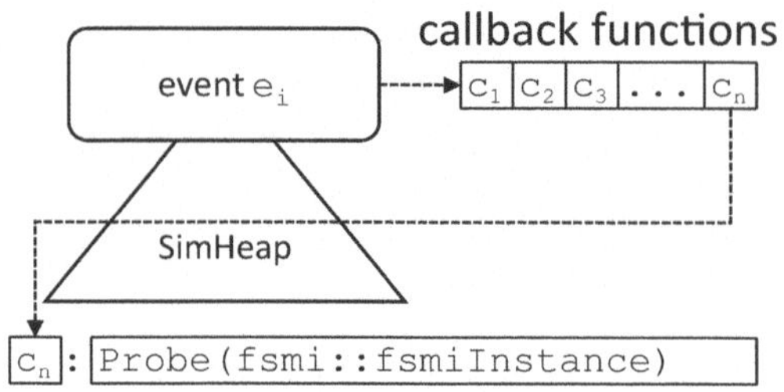

Fig. 2. Event callback functions and probing

This is closely related to the definition of an ORM, the technique of choice to persist data. Often, ORMs have a static configuration to determine which objects can exist and to which relations and attributes they map. PostgresORM applies the same approach, using modules to achieve it. In our implementation, macro expansion is applied to generate these modules dynamically at compile time. The corresponding macros take the ORM configuration as input and produce the PostgresORM-compatible modules. As such, a dynamic ORM is realised. The probing function selects a suitable object instantiator function and persists the object in the correct relation due to the mapping module. Note that multiple simulation runs can benefit from the same macro expansion.

To retrieve the necessary input driving these macros, we must analyse the corresponding model. However, it is not necessary to execute the analysis before each simulation run. If the simulation model remains unchanged, the data model and hence the state variables that need to be persisted remain stable as well.

`ResumableFunctions.jl` performs such an analysis at compile time via the `@resumable` macro. Our architecture benefits from this implementation to retrieve and store the simulation model's metadata. The model metadata is stable and needs to remain available throughout several simulation runs and must therefore be persisted separately. Thus, a classic use of a static ORM is suitable in this case.

Figure 3 shows the implementation of our novel architecture, which executes in three phases, along with the main Julia modules and functions. Each of these phases requires specific infrastructure:

1. In a first phase, the simulation model is analysed. Static programming logic and infrastructure are used to retrieve and store model metadata for internal exploitation.
2. In a second phase, the dynamic ORM is realised through macro expansion, driven by the metadata gathered in the first phase. To persist data, dynamic infrastructure, dependent on the model under consideration is created and used to persist data.
3. In a third phase, data is made externally available using the data model created in the previous phase. A REST API and a `Vue.js`-based data interface are provided.

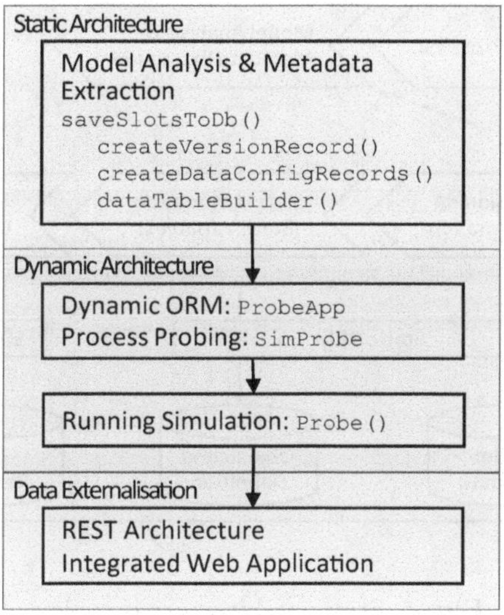

Fig. 3. Three-phased approach

In the following sections, we explain how these three phases have been realised in terms of programming logic and database configuration.

3.1 Static Architecture

The starting point for each simulation is the definition of the model as resumable functions. We benefit from this macro expansion step to store the extracted information about the state variables (slots) present in the function. For this purpose, we extended `ResumableFunctions.jl` in two ways: (1) the macro now additionally saves metadata about the model itself and the slots present in each process and (2) it takes a second boolean argument to persist or not persist the evolution on the state variables.

The `@resumable` macro internally depends on the existing `get_slots()` function. We introduced our new `saveSlotsToDb()` function, which (1) saves information about the model version through the function `createVersionRecord()`, (2) saves the configuration of these slots to the database by making use of the `createDataConfigRecords()` function and (3) creates the relations that will hold the data for the function/process under consideration through the `dataTableBuilder()` function. Figure 4 highlights the subordinate function calls of a call to `saveSlotsToDb()` and the respective database parts that are affected.

The function `createVersionRecord()` only creates a *modelmetadata* record in a dedicated relation if the model did not exist before. Otherwise, the corresponding record gets updated. The primary key for such a process (and therefore also of a *modelmetadata* record) is the function name (that was initially passed to the `@resumable` macro), along with a hash of the slots. The relation holding information about the process under consideration includes the attribute names,

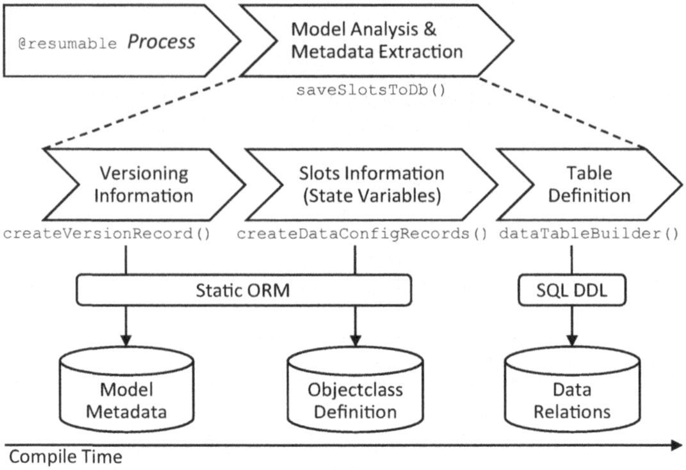

Fig. 4. Static architecture overview

a hash of the slots, a UUID, a model creation timestamp and a last used timestamp. To store the data, a static ORM was defined and is used to query the relation for the primary key of the process under consideration. Should the key exist, then the last used timestamp gets updated, otherwise a record is created.

After having saved the metadata concerning the current process, more fine-grained metadata concerning the process's specific slots is saved through the `createDataConfigRecords()` function. This function provides the necessary information to the macros that create the dynamic ORM. In the dedicated *objectclassdefinition* relation, each slot's metadata is stored, including the object and relation name, the object's field name, the data type, the mapping attribute and information whether the field forms part of a primary key. This is realised through two static ORM definitions pointing to the same relation.

Both of the relations we have considered so far are statically defined. The attributes are known upfront, which allows for a static ORM and a non-changing SQL DDL statement. The relation necessary to persist the slots of a process during the simulation is different since the attributes may vary depending on the slots present in the process. Therefore, a dynamic SQL DDL statement must be established and executed for each new process. This is the task of the `dataTableBuilder()` function, which builds and executes the SQL DDL for each process. We benefit from the SQL `IF NOT EXISTS` constraint to skip the creation of tables that already exist due to prior simulations of a certain process with the same set of slots.

The architecture requires a PostgreSQL database instance running with a dedicated schema. The schema must contain both statically defined relations, *modelmetadata* and *objectclassdefinition*. Access must be granted to a specific user for connections from static and dynamic ORM definitions. The schema holds the dynamically defined relations as well.

3.2 Dynamic Architecture

Given the availability of model and process metadata, the probing and persistence of a running simulation model is possible by using that metadata in the dynamic part of our architecture. The starting point is the `@runPersisted` macro that has been added to `ConcurrentSim.jl`, which must be used to start a simulation rather than the `run()` function. The newly added macro fulfils two functions: (1) it includes the `ProbeApp` module, which is a dynamically created module depending on the gathered metadata and (2) it designates which provided dynamic ORM object instantiator functions are used to probe which processes.

ProbeApp Module

`ProbeApp` is the module implementing the internal `Model` and `ORM` modules that make up a standard PostgresORM configuration. Figure 5 depicts the point in time when the `ProbeApp` module is loaded due to the call to the `@runPersisted` macro, which in turn results in the subsequent macro calls to `@makeObjectDefModule` and `@makeOrmDefModule`. Both of these macros are responsible for model (Object Classes) and ORM (Persistence API) creation at the same place where one would configure PostgresORM statically. These macros share the design principle that they both exploit metadata collected in the static part of the architecture described in Sect. 3.1, which alters the standard static approach of PostgresORM to the novel dynamic behaviour.

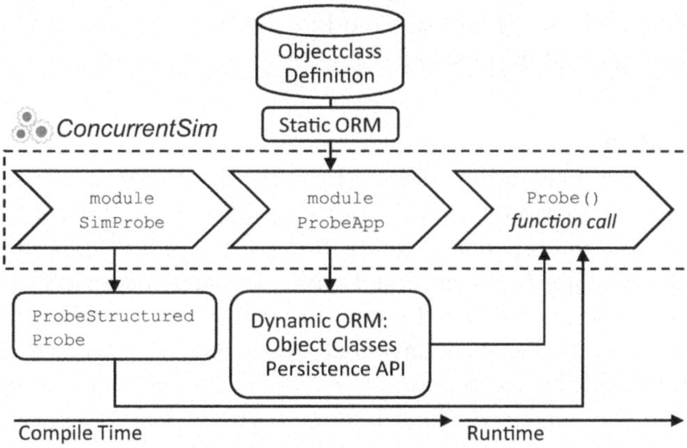

Fig. 5. Dynamic architecture overview

The makeObjectDefModule Macro

The aim of `@makeObjectDefModule` is to build a PostgresORM-compliant module containing object definitions synthesised from the records available in the objectclassdefinition table. The task is accomplished by building an expression that evaluates to the `Model` module which configures PostgresORM. The object definitions included in this expression are created through mapping the `objToObjDef()` function over an array of metadata objects which originated from the table. Only the attributes of interest are retained in the record for metadata-object translation. The same static ORM we used previously to store data in the concerned table is now used to query it. A secondary task of the macro is to identify the current model's instantiator functions since the probe will later use only these. These are added to an array that becomes available in the global scope after evaluation of the macro.

The `objToObjDef()` function realises individual struct definitions. It does so for what is concerned with the fields of the struct using string interpolation in a quoted expression. Further, the function also uses `MacroTools.jl`'s `combinedef()` to generate both of the necessary positional and keyword constructor functions to comply with `PostgresORM.jl`'s requirements. As such, `objToObjDef()` is an aggregating function on the metadata objects.

The makeOrmDefModule Macro

The inner working of `@makeOrmDefModule` is similar to `@makeObjectDefModule`. The macro evaluates to an `ORM` module which is internal to PostgresORM and works in tandem with the object definition created through the evaluation of the `@makeObjectDefModule` discussed earlier. Each object definition requires the corresponding ORM.

Metadata objects resulting from the *objectclassdefinition* table serve as input to the `createOrmsFromDB()` function that dynamically generates the ORM modules on a per-object basis. The final module body is generated through string interpolation in a quoted expression.

SimProbe Module

Probing and persistence are realised through the `SimProbe` module, which exports the probing function and acts upon the different (sub)processes. Figure 5 shows the point in time when the probe becomes available. As illustrated earlier in Fig. 2, the probing function is activated through inclusion in the array of callback functions getting executed when an event occurs. Only after the object classes and the persistence API have become available through the inclusion of the `ProbeApp` module, as explained in Sect. 3.2, the corresponding probing function calls can be executed. This is due to the object instantiator selection mechanism, which only works when the object classes are known in the global simulation environment.

Probe Implementation

The `SimProbe` module implements the `probeStructured()` probing function with the FSMI instance as an argument. To comply with `ConcurrentSim.jl`, a `probe()` wrapper function exists as well. A mapping dictionary available at the main simulation environment struct provides information on whether the

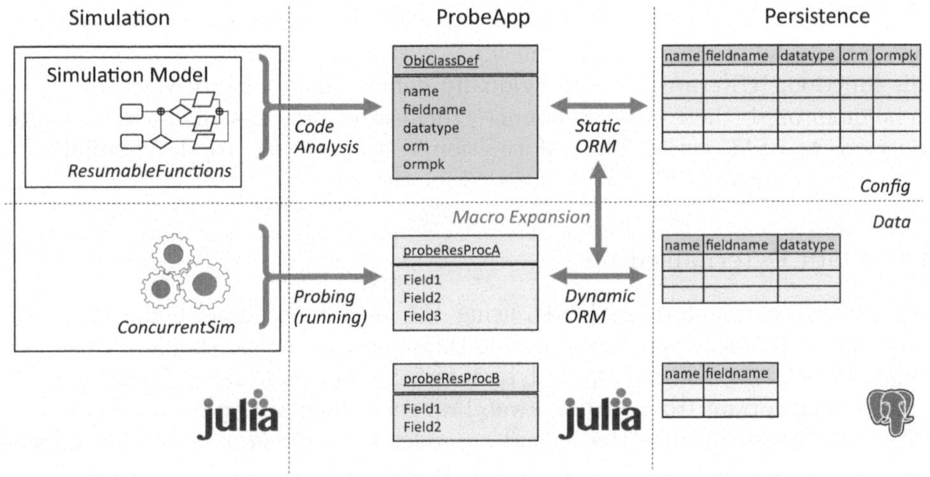

Fig. 6. Detailed persistence architecture

FSMI instance under consideration is truly a monitored process through the presence of the corresponding object instantiator function. The probing function transfers the variables present in the FSMI to a corresponding struct with the latter being persisted in the database. This mechanism relies entirely on the availability of the dynamic ORM which is available in the global scope through macro expansion from within the `ProbeApp` module, and on the coupling of FSMI types to the correct instantiators.

Probe Activation

The `probe()` function is activated using the array of callback functions. The evolution of the variables in a running simulation maps to the evolution of the state variables in the corresponding state machine. The latter represents a (sub)process contained in the simulation model. To capture state variables, the full array of callback functions must be executed first. Only then can a state machine make a transition from one state to another, or in other words, proceed to the next event.

Finally, the probing aspect and the dynamic ORM aspect are joined by coupling the type of FSMI to the correct instantiator. This is only possible when the static phase has terminated and the dynamic phase is beyond the evaluation of the `SimProbe` module. At this stage, the information on which functions must be monitored and how their ORMs should look is available. Furthermore, through the dynamic phase, the necessary ORMs are in place. The ORMs are available to the `SimProbe` module to create and store shadow objects for each monitored process. A detailed overview is provided in Fig. 6, showing the static architecture which extracts and stores model metadata through an ORM definition known upfront and then dynamically generates the ORMs based on that metadata. Object definitions and a persistence API are now available on a per-process basis.

The coupling of the type of the FSMI to the instantiator is executed just before the simulation starts. The newly added `@runPersisted` macro performs this function. It iterates over the globally defined array of processes that need to be monitored (those who "announce" themselves) and designates instantiator functions to FSMI types. This information is stored at the top-level simulation environment struct, which was extended for this purpose.

3.3 Data Externalisation

To externalise the data gathered using the techniques described earlier, we devised two distinct approaches sharing the same goal: a user should have access to all persisted data, either through an interface implementing an open standard or in tabular format from within a web browser. The first approach consists of a REST architecture, while the second approach is an integrated solution including a web application running in a single thread, mainly based on the `VueJS.jl` package.

REST Architecture

The REST architecture consists of a Julia implementation of the REST API using the `HTTP.jl` package. A HTTP server listens at a given port for a request for a virtual directory. The required table, which maps to a monitored process, is then passed to the server as a virtual directory in the requested URL and extracted using the positional pattern matching features provided by the `HTTP.jl` package. Due to the `HTTP GET` method, the server knows that the request is a READ operation on a particular table.

The base implementation is inspired by the Cross-Origin Resource Sharing (CORS) example from the `HTTP.jl` documentation[10]. However, in our implementation, a request arriving at the server invokes a `getTableContent()` service function to request the data from the back-end database. Since the `ProbeApp` module is imported in the global scope where the HTTP server runs, and the required table was passed as a positional parameter (virtual directory) in the URL, we can instantiate the correct filter object for the required table and pass it to the ORM's `retrieve_entity()` function. The resultset is then transformed to the correct JSON format using the `JSONMiddleware()` and `CorsMiddleware()` functions provided by the documentation. These two functions implement the CORS-oriented aspects as well. We refer to the documentation for the inner workings of the two latter functions.

Integrated Web Application

A router is defined in a global scope and several routes are registered on the router. Such a route combines a requested virtual directory and one of the HTTP request modes. When an HTTP client sends a request, a route invokes a function which returns a well-formatted HTML page.

[10] https://github.com/JuliaWeb/HTTP.jl/.

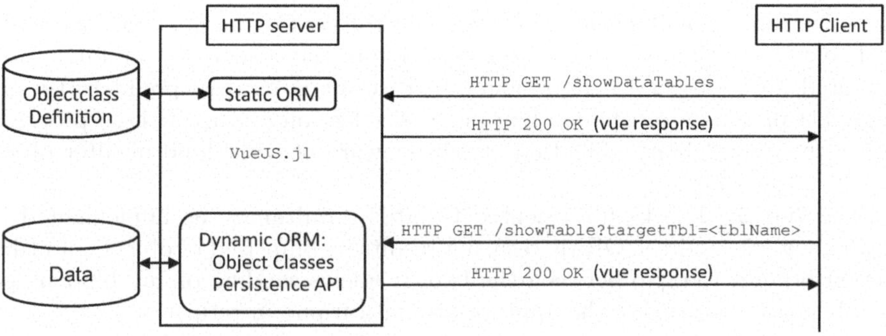

Fig. 7. Integrated web application architecture

The `VueJS.jl` package intervenes in the local scope of such a function (which is called through the request to the router), exposing several HTML elements enriched by the original `Vue.js` framework. Apart from some static definitions, our application is centred around two functions that implement the dynamic approach. Figure 7 shows the web application architecture and its intended use. The `showDataTables()` function is invoked by the `GET` request for the corresponding virtual directory `/showDataTables` and implements the landing page showing a list of all processes ever persisted in the connected schema. Figure 8 shows an example of the landing page for the simulation model used throughout this text. Upon selection of a process, a request for the `/showTable` virtual directory is sent to the HTTP server invoking the corresponding `showTable()` function, which composes the process-specific HTML page showing the requested data table.

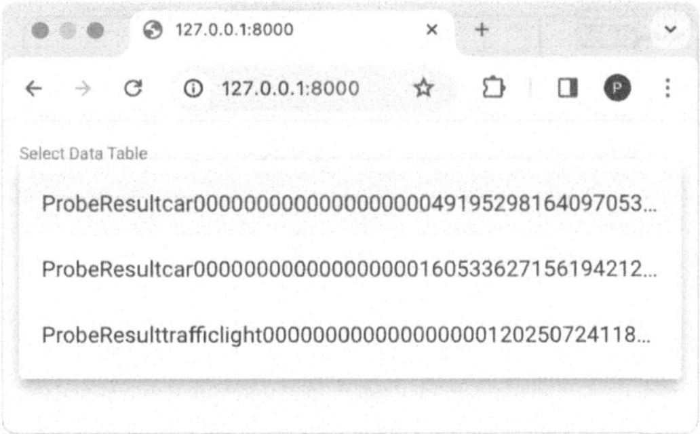

Fig. 8. Integrated web application landing page

The two functions integrate our earlier presented statically and dynamically defined ORMs. Whereas these ORMs have the role of data persistence, they are now employed in data retrieval. The `ProbeApp` module is imported into an application's global scope. The `showDataTables()` function uses the static ORM to retrieve the list of processes available in the schema by sending a non-configured filter object to the schema. The result is used to populate the list of possible processes on the landing page. A selection of one of these processes invokes the `showTable()` function which is aware of what kind of filter object to send to the schema.

Since `VueJS.jl` is highly oriented towards dataframes, as implemented by `DataFrames.jl`, and the ORMs return a resultset comprised of objects, a utility function bridges the gap between the two. It allows sending of any filter object to a schema and receiving the appropriate data frame in return.

4 Technical Evaluation

The implementation of our architecture[11] was validated using several scenarios reflecting the intended use during simulations. We used a MacBook Pro, equipped with an Intel Core i5-5257U processor with 8 GB RAM. We further used VSCode v1.84 with Julia v1.8.5 and `PostgresORM.jl` v0.5.0. The changes to `ResumableFunctions.jl` were implemented starting from version v0.6.3 and for `ConcurrentSim.jl` we used version v0.8.1. Further, the used RDBMS is PostgreSQL v13.13. Our test cases simulated a car that parks, waits for some time and then starts driving[12]. The car then encounters a traffic light, needs to stop and wait before resuming driving as illustrated in Fig. 9. The simulation is stopped after an arbitrarily chosen amount of units of time or can run indefinitely. Both the car and the traffic light are implemented as functions passed on to the `@resumable` macro.

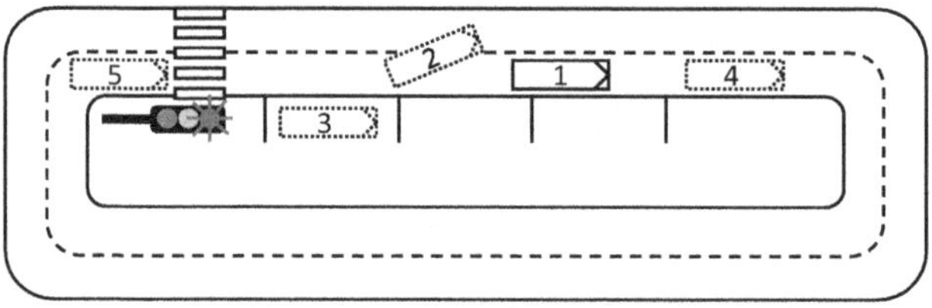

Fig. 9. Car simulation model

4.1 Inital Run

The first group of scenarios cover metadata generation and initial simulation runs. We ran the simulation model with both the `car` and `trafficlight` processes unmonitored, which resulted in alterations in the modelmetadata and

[11] https://github.com/vanderpp/SimJuliaPersistence.git.
[12] https://github.com/vanderpp/SimJuliaPersistence/blob/main/test_SimProbe.jl.

objectclassdefinition tables. In the modelmetadata table, records are added which indicate the same model "creationtime" and "lastused" timestamp. The object metadata to feed the dynamic ORM creation macro's is present in the second table. As expected, no data was recorded and a subsequent run of the model altered the "lastused" timestamp. We conclude that these scenarios led to the expected outcome.

Having run the scenarios directed towards metadata generation, a subsequent series of scenarios directed towards data generation was run. The preconditions for these scenarios were either none or having run the metadata scenarios. For this purpose, the `car` and `trafficlight` processes were set to "monitored", which, upon evaluation of the model, resulted in the creation and population of the corresponding data tables. All possible variations on which process was monitored during simulation were explored, with conclusive results.

4.2 Successive Runs

Starting from a model that had run previously, we devised a scenario where successive runs of the same, non-altered model were evaluated. In the metadata tables, the "lastused" timestamps were updated with every run. The corresponding data tables got appended newly generated data, distinguishable from earlier runs through the "simulation start time" attribute.

Next, an existing simulated model with persisted data was altered to evaluate the detection of the alteration and to observe the creation of new metadata records. Furthermore, we expect new data tables to accommodate the modified model data. The result for this scenario was positive. Continuing with this scenario, we reverted to the pre-existing scenario, resulting in the already existing data tables getting appended to the new data generated by the reverted model.

4.3 Data Externalisation

The starting condition for this scenario is to have a simulation that has run and data was recorded. The REST endpoint is queried using an `HTTP GET` request to the URL `http://127.0.0.1:8001/api/tablecontent/<tableName>` where `<tableName>` must be replaced with the real table name containing the data.

The integrated web application is reachable via the IP address on which HTTP server was started on. A drop-down list on the landing page was filled dynamically from the available metadata. Such a landing page example is depicted in Fig. 8, allowing for selecting any of the available processes' data.

4.4 Performance Comparison

Using the `@time` macro, we recorded the elapsed time for simulations started with the new `@runPersisted` macro. To compare performance, a series of twenty measurements were taken for each of the following configurations: non-persisted configuration (nn) and persisted configuration (np). We also took measurements using the prior method to start simulations using the `run` function (on). All of these scenarios are based on our standard simulation.

This lead to the following mean elapsed times: $\bar{t}_{nn} = 0.0342$ s, $\bar{t}_{np} = 7.2781$ s and $\bar{t}_{on} = 0.276$ s. We observed a difference in means using ANOVA ($\alpha = 0.05$, $p < 0.001$). Multiple comparisons (Fisher LSD with Bonferroni) revealed a homogeneous group amongst t_{nn} and t_{on}. When used in the persisted configuration (np), our architecture is significantly ($p < 0.001$) slower than the non-persisted configuration (nn).

5 Discussion

The starting point for our architecture was the absence of a persistence architecture in `ConcurrentSim.jl` and the underlying `ResumableFunctions.jl` packages. Currently, we rely on a user's knowledge of persistence technology to implement this aspect. From our experience, we know that the presence of such knowledge is a strong assumption, which is not valid in many cases. Therefore, our goal was to integrate a fully automated and transparent solution for persistence in `ConcurrentSim.jl` and `ResumableFunctions.jl` with minimal user intervention. We identified two distinctive parts of the problem that our architecture is addressing. First, the data needs to be extracted from the running simulation and second, this data must be persisted for later use. Further, a solution should require a minimal configuration and little additional infrastructure.

For what concerns the data extraction, we must decide when the probing function should be executed. It seems obvious that the right time is the moment prior to the transition from one state to the next state. In ConcurrentSim, this is after the execution of an event which is the trigger to execute the callback functions. Therefore, ConcurrentSim's `execute()` function was altered to schedule a callback Probing function.

The probing function is exported by the `SimProbe` module, which is imported into ConcurrentSim. `SimProbe` imports the `ProbeApp` which is, in fact, the encompassing ORM module including the domain objects and the persistence API. Both are generated dynamically using macro expansion, driven by the metadata collected while evaluating the ResumableFunctions macros.

Due to the approach we took to extract metadata to drive the macros which generate the ORM modules and the requirement to hide the model analysis phase from the running simulation phase, which is probed in the background, we introduced the risk of a potential problem. This risk occurs when we want to load the module which provides the probing function with the object instantiators to persist data using the dynamic ORM. This can only be done after the model analysis has taken place. So, in the simulation application, one would need to include the `using SimProbe` statement after the model declaration and just before the `run()` function call. We decided to hide that as well using a `@runPersisted` macro to load the probing module when model metadata is available and before the probing function is scheduled as a callback.

The newly introduced architecture comes with some performance costs. Our analysis of the elapsed times for both persisted and non-persisted scenarios revealed the introduction of a non-negligible delay in the simulation process due to some I/O processes. Improvements can be made at that level by introducing some buffering mechanisms. `PostgresORM.jl` allows to flush an array of objects to the database. That approach was not explored but seems promising. Another possibility would be to run the database in memory to reduce the I/O overhead.

With regards to the decision when to consider a process as "altered" from the previous version during successive simulations, we took the approach in which the name of the function that describes the process together with a hash of the array containing the local variables of such a process determines the unicity of a process. As a consequence, when the semantic meaning of a process changes, this is not recorded in the persistence tier of our architecture. However, this can be circumvented by annotating the process using a variable. This approach is exploited to associate the proper object instantiator in the global context of the simulation application with a version of a process. When the probing function is invoked, it uses this information to decide which object to create and persist.

We investigated several approaches before integrating `PostgresORM.jl` in our architecture. The most noteworthy alternatives were `SearchLight.jl` or using a proper ORM. `SearchLight.jl` has the advantage of being an established package with a large user community. However, we believe it is too tightly coupled to Genie. The way it is implemented (using separate modules for each object and the concept of migrations to create the tables) resulted in a preference for `PostgresORM.jl`. The approach of making our own ORM was explored profoundly and led to the conclusion to cease that approach due to development time and the typical quality of code realised in such approaches. `PostgresORM.jl` gained the preference due to its straightforward approach with the domain objects module and the persistence API. We saw an ideal combination in the capabilities of Julia's macro expansions and the `MacroTools.jl` package, driven by external metadata to dynamically generate the modules at compile time.

Our implemented REST API allows processing and analysing the generated data using an external (web) application. During the implementation, we encountered the need to implement the Cross-Origin Resource Sharing solution since such an application is not guaranteed to run at the same location as the REST API. A simple REST implementation would suffice if only retrieving the JSON file would be of interest. However, our version supports both the basic and richer approach. A shortcoming of the REST API is that a user needs to know upfront the rendezvous point. A page summarising the possible rendezvous points could easily be implemented based on the available metadata.

To provide the user with an immediately available web interface to explore the stored data, we devised an architecture using Vue.js, based on the dynamically generated ORM. In this scenario, there is a landing page on which the user can select amongst the tables existing in the database, hence the simulated processes that have been persisted. The user is taken to the corresponding table, where data is available for further exploration.

A known limitation of our solution is the absence of the possibility to make certain variables non-persistent. This is a consequence of our decision to streamline the integration of the analysis and simulation phases. Should we desire to implement more fine-grained probing, the decision of what to include in the "shadow-object" used for persistence would have to be taken between these phases—after the generation of the metadata driving the dynamic ORM generation, but before the creation of the corresponding relations.

6 Conclusion and Future Work

Starting from the observed shortcomings of ConcurrentSim in its ability to easily persist simulation data and the requirement to provide such features without imposing additional knowledge requirements on the end users, we devised an architecture capable of persisting simulation data. The infrastructure and configuration requirements for using the presented architecture are minimal. The `ConcurrentSim.js` and `ResumableFunctions.js` packages were extended with modules that implement probing of a running simulation and persist it through a mechanism using a dynamically generated ORM. A running PostgreSQL instance is necessary, but the required configuration of that database schema is also minimal. As such, we were able to implement and evaluate a solution based on the presented architecture. Further, we developed two data interfaces: a REST API enabling external applications to process and explore the data and a Vue.js application supporting immediate data exploration via a web interface.

The remaining challenges for end users could be further reduced or even entirely removed by incorporating our architecture into a web application that accommodates the packages and architecture in an enclosed environment. Such an environment could facilitate model expression through a web interface. The same web application might provide easy data access after running the simulations. In that way, the remaining technical details could be hidden from end users who could focus solely on the simulation task.

References

1. Abar, S., Theodoropoulos, G.K., Lemarinier, P., O'Hare, G.M.: Agent based modelling and simulation tools: a review of the state-of-art software. Comput. Sci. Rev. **24** (2017). https://doi.org/10.1016/j.cosrev.2017.03.001
2. Abdessameud, O.M., Van Kerckhoven, J., Van Utterbeeck, F., Guerry, M.A.: Manpower planning using simulation and heuristic optimization. In: Proceedings of ISC 2019, International Industrial Simulation Conference, Lisbon, Portugal (2019)
3. Bezanson, J., Edelman, A., Karpinski, S., Shah, V.B.: Julia: a fresh approach to numerical computing. SIAM Rev. **59**(1) (2017). https://doi.org/10.1137/141000671
4. Booch, G., Maksimchuk, R.A., Engle, M.W., Young, B.J., Connallen, J., Houston, K.A.: Object-oriented analysis and design with applications. SIGSOFT Softw. Eng. Notes **33**(5) (2008). https://doi.org/10.1145/1402521.1413138

5. Dahl, O.J., Nygaard, K.: SIMULA: an ALGOL-based simulation language. Commun. ACM **9**(9) (1966). https://doi.org/10.1145/365813.365819
6. De Rouck, R., Debacker, M., Hubloue, I., Koghee, S., Van Utterbeeck, F., Dhondt, E.: Simedis 2.0: on the road toward a comprehensive mass casualty incident medical management simulator. In: Proceedings of WSC 2018, Winter Simulation Conference. Gothenburg, Sweden (2018). https://doi.org/10.1109/WSC.2018.8632369
7. Hauser, P.: Review of db4o from db4objects. University of Applied Sciences Rapperswil, Switzerland (2011). https://cis.bentley.edu/lwaguespack/CS630_Site/Downloads_files/OODBMS-db4o-Review.pdf
8. Helsgaun, K.: DISCO-a SIMULA-based language for continuous combined and discrete simulation: simulation software. Simulation **35**(1) (1980). https://doi.org/10.1177/003754978003500102
9. Hermosilla, I.: Simulating a stochastic differential equation model by exact sampling. In: Proceedings of MCM 2017, International Conference on Monte Carlo Methods and Applications, Montréal, Canada (2017)
10. Ireland, C., Bowers, D., Newton, M., Waugh, K.: A classification of object-relational impedance mismatch. In: Proceedings of DBKDA 2009, International Conference on Advances in Databases, Knowledge, and Data Applications, Gosier, France (2009). https://doi.org/10.1109/DBKDA.2009.11
11. Müller, K., Tony Vignaux, S.S., Lünsdorf, O.: SimPy, a process-based discrete-event simulation framework based on standard python (2020). https://simpy.readthedocs.io/en/latest/
12. Lauwens, B.: Monte Carlo simulation using SimJulia. In: Proceedings of MCM 2017, International Conference on Monte Carlo Methods and Applications, Montréal, Canada (2017)
13. Lauwens, B.: ResumableFunctions: C# sharp style generators for Julia. J. Open Sour. Softw. **2**(18) (2017). https://doi.org/10.21105/joss.00400
14. Lauwens, B.: SimJulia: discrete event process oriented simulation framework written in Julia (2017). https://simjuliajl.readthedocs.io/en/stable/welcome.html
15. Law, A.M., Kelton, W.D.: Simulation Modeling and Analysis, vol. 3. McGraw-Hill, New York (2007)
16. Russell, C.: Bridging the object-relational divide: ORM technologies can simplify data access, but be aware of the challenges that come with introducing this new layer of abstraction. Queue **6**(3) (2008). https://doi.org/10.1145/1394127.1394139
17. Saeed, L., Abdallah, G.: Persistence with Jakarta EE persistence. In: Pro Cloud Native Java EE Apps: DevOps with MicroProfile, Jakarta EE 10 APIs, and Kubernetes. Apress (2022). https://doi.org/10.1007/978-1-4842-8900-6
18. Van Der Paelt, P., Lauwens, B., Signer, B.: A data persistence architecture for the SimJulia framework. In: JuliaCon 2023 (Extended Abstract), Cambridge, USA (2023)
19. Van Der Paelt, P., Lauwens, B., Signer, B.: Model-driven data storage using dynamic object-relational mapping. In: SIMULTECH 2023, 13th International Conference on Simulation and Modeling Methodologies, Technologies and Applications (Abstract), Rome, Italy (2023)

Network Simulations

Positioning of a Next Generation Mobile Cell to Maximise Aggregate Network Capacity

Paulo Furtado Correia(✉), André Coelho, and Manuel Ricardo

INESC TEC and Faculdade de Engenharia, Universidade do Porto, Porto, Portugal
{paulo.j.correia,andre.f.coelho,manuel.ricardo}@inesctec.pt

Abstract. In wireless communications, the need to cover operation areas, such as seaports, is at the forefront of discussion, especially regarding network capacity provisioning. Radio network planning typically involves determining the number of fixed cells, considering link budgets and deploying them geometrically centered across targeted areas. This paper proposes a solution to determine the optimal position for a mobile cell, considering 3GPP pathloss models. The obtained position for the mobile cell maximises the aggregate network capacity offered to a set of User Equipments (UEs), with gains up to 187% compared to the positioning of the mobile cell at the UEs' geometrical center. The proposed solution can be used by network planners and integrated into network optimisation tools. This has the potential to reduce costs associated with the radio access network planning by enhancing flexibility for on-demand deployments.

Keywords: 5G/6G network capacity · Mobile cell positioning · ns-3 performance evaluation · Radio planning optimisation

1 Introduction

Industrial environments should provide seamless wireless connectivity throughout operational areas, enabling communications among various devices, diverse machinery, and personnel. This paper studies the added value of a Next Generation Mobile Cell (NGMC) in a seaport container yard, where ground and sea operations are bustling with variable demand for wireless connectivity. Facilities are typically used for storage, handling and maintenance of shipping containers, where ships, mobile cranes and trucks operate. NGMCs have the unique ability to move within seaport areas, carried by automated guided vehicles or Unmanned Aerial Vehicles (UAVs), offering enhanced capacity and improved coverage for UEs. The complex and dynamic environment and the variable traffic demand within the port, including tractor boats and mobile cranes or trucks taking and stacking containers, require on-demand wireless connectivity. In order to address these challenges, tailored network planning and further deployment approaches are crucial to provide communications with adequate Quality of Service. Optimising NGMC positioning includes multiple factors to consider, including container stacking areas, truck movement patterns, and key operational zones. Radio coverage should ensure network capacity maximisation to improve communications performance and enhance the

A. A. Juan et al. (Eds.): SIMUtools 2024, LNICST 603, pp. 341–356, 2025.
https://doi.org/10.1007/978-3-031-87345-4_22

overall productivity of port operations' services within smart ports [1]. Moreover, legacy networks can coexist with NGMCs operating in different frequency bands, such as Frequency Range 1 (FR1) and Frequency Range 2. This paper focuses on FR1 and provides the following original contributions:

1. An optimisation problem formulation to obtain the 3D positions for NGMCs, maximising the aggregate network capacity over an outdoor area with multiple UEs. 3GPP recommends an error model to compute the block error rate and manage hybrid automatic repeat request (HARQ) retransmissions. It does this based on Signal-to-Interference-plus-Noise Ratios (SINRs) per resource block (RB) historical data. Developed according to standard link-to-system mapping techniques, this model is an exponential effective signal-to-noise ratio mapping (EESM), originally created for single-antenna transmissions. We have simplified this 3GPP error model using a heuristic that provides a spectral efficiency regression line as a function of SINR, while maintaining the link-level performance accuracy;
2. A network performance evaluation study conducted using MATLAB and the ns-3 network simulator, employing the proposed optimisation problem and considering randomly generated scenarios. The performance evaluation study considers a specific seaport configuration, as a representative example. However, the contributions are applicable to any other outdoor scenario.

The remainder of this paper is structured as follows. Section 2 provides a literature review, presenting the related work on the positioning of NGMCs across outdoor areas such as seaports. Section 3 introduces the system model, including a description of the main constraints, methodology, and performance metrics employed. Section 4 presents the performance evaluation for diverse scenarios, including an analysis of the results obtained. Finally, Sect. 5 summarises the key findings and identifies directions for future work.

2 Related Work

NGMCs have been proposed in the literature since 2015, enabling multiple Heterogeneous Networks to improve network throughput, extend wireless coverage, and offload network traffic in multiple use cases [14]. Typical radio and network planning optimisation best practices, conducted by Mobile Network Operators (MNOs) or subcontracted entities, are based on link budgets and the number of fixed cells to deploy, geometrically referenced to the center of each coverage area. This procedure is described in [20, 21], focusing on optimising data rates by leveraging Carrier Aggregation with radio planning. However, optimal cell positioning is not addressed. [12] explores the optimal UAV 3D position carrying a 28 GHz cell. The study was improved to a 3D case based upon [13], incorporating actual, fine-grained terrain data and accounting for location-dependent line-of-sight (LoS) conditions measured on the fly, resulting in higher gains by avoiding non-line-of-sight (NLoS) conditions and considering UAV heights. However, it does not present simulation results and does not consider 3GPP-compliant pathloss models. Integrating visual information and obstacle avoidance mechanisms, alongside mathematical analyses of capacity bounds, have enriched connectivity solutions [2–4].

[2] proposes an obstacle-aware wireless connectivity for 5G UEs, leveraging a novel on-demand mobility management function, which enables the remote positioning of a communications mobile robotic platform by using visual information from on-board video cameras. [3] studies network capacity bounds expressed as the maximum number of users. It considers cell interference and limited uplink transmission power, while assessing the performance of 5G links in different propagation environments using the extended COST-231 Hata model. [3] and [4] leverage context information related to user positions, using a combined Control/User-plane split to improve the directional cell discovery process through information gathered over time. Moreover, considerations for different backhaul link types and user-centric approaches, rather than network-centric, have been explored to optimise served UEs and backhaul sum rates. However, no placement accuracy and capacities are detailed [5]. In Integrated Access and Backhaul (IAB) deployments, studies have optimised precoder designs, UE-Base Station (BS) associations, and UAV hovering locations to maximise network sum rates or spectral efficiencies [6–8]. In city centers, IAB solutions positioned in buses or trains can improve passengers' connections in terms of throughput and latency on uplink and downlink [11]. However, IAB still lacks further standardisation and existing studies do not consider network capacities. [9] focuses on ultra-reliable low latency communications users, optimising drone base station locations, user associations, and backhaul bandwidth allocations for delay-sensitive applications while maximising sum rates. Wireless backhaul optimisation between fixed small cells and UAV cells, adaptive modulation and coding (AMC) techniques, and traffic-aware UAV placement algorithms have been proposed to maximise system throughput and facilitate controlled topology and backhaul communications paths [17–19]. [17] proposes the optimal placement for a UAV, in order to maximise the sum rates of the whole network, consisting of UAV cells and terrestrial small cells. However, the work focuses on wireless backhaul. In contrast, [18] formulates the problem of maximising the number of covered UEs, subject to bit rate requirements, for a certain capacity limit while mentioning the absence of capacity maximisation studies in the literature. [19] focuses on uplink throughput maximisation using a reinforcement learning multi-agent proportional fair scheduling in the reward function. In [10], communications strategies for Sidelink are studied to convert NLoS to LoS conditions to improve outage probability in smart factory indoor environments; however, this can also apply to smart ports. Sidelink refers to a communications mode where devices in close proximity to each other establish a direct wireless connection. Flying networks, consisting of access points or cellular BSs, can also leverage traffic-aware UAV placement algorithms to enable controlled topology and backhaul communications paths with sufficient capacity. Within this context, [15] and [16] address the placement of a single UAV using Wi-Fi.

Overall, through multiple works spanning NGMCs, urban simulations, UAV deployments, optimisation techniques, and smart factory environments, the literature addresses network access and backhaul sum rates optimisation with micro or macro cell positioning, including network performance evaluations. Additionally, combined factors, such as resource allocation, interference, transmission power and obstacles' interposition are also shown how they can impact results. However, the existing works do not focus on aggregate capacity, as addressed in this paper, but mostly on sum rates.

3 System Model

Let us consider a three-dimensional networking scenario where NGMCs must be placed to provide wireless connectivity to multiple UEs. The problem involves positioning these NGMCs and determining their associations with UEs. In order to obtain the Euclidean coordinates for placing them (x_m^M, y_m^M, z_m^M) and respective user associations ($S_{j,m}^M$) offered to the UEs, an optimisation problem is formulated herein.

3.1 Problem Formulation

The problem is formulated as a Mixed-Integer Nonlinear Programming problem, with the objective function given by (1). It maximises the sum of the network capacities offered to the UEs with single user associations, ensured by (2), and whose 2D distances (3) and respective applicable spectral efficiencies (4) align with [22–24]. Although this paper considers only a single NGMC, the problem formulation is generic and can be applied to M NGMCs. Table 1 lists the main notations used in the problem formulation.

$$\underset{x_m^M,\, y_m^M,\, z_m^M,\, S_{u,m}^M}{\text{maximise}} \quad \sum\nolimits_{u\in U} \sum\nolimits_{m\in M} \left(C_{u,m}^M S_{u,m}^M\right) \tag{1}$$

Subject to:

$$\sum\nolimits_m S_{u,m}^M = 1,\ \forall \mathrm{u} \in [1, U] \tag{2}$$

$$10 \le d_{2Du,m}^M \le 5000, \forall \mathrm{u} \in [1, U], \forall \mathrm{m} \in [1, M] \tag{3}$$

$$0 \le SE_{u,m}^M \le 6.4,\ \forall \mathrm{u} \in [1, U],\ \forall \mathrm{m} \in [1, M] \tag{4}$$

The capacity of the RNTI between UE_u and $NGMC_m$ is introduced in (5).

$$C_{u,m}^M = \frac{B \Delta fr1 \eta_{u,m}^M}{U_m} \tag{5}$$

It depends on the spectral efficiency defined in (6), which is always positive. It also considers the SCS of the FR1 frequency band, as defined in (7), the number of RBs, and the number of user associations to the same NGMC, as presented in (8). The bandwidth used per RNTI, representing the direct wireless link between UE_u and $NGMC_m$, is given by (9).

$$\eta_{u,m}^M = \begin{cases} SE_{u,m}^M, & SE_{u,m}^M \ge 0 \\ 0, & SE_{u,m}^M < 0 \end{cases} \tag{6}$$

$$\Delta fr_1 = 2^{\mu_{fr1}}.15\,\text{kHz} \tag{7}$$

$$U_m = \sum\nolimits_{u\in U} S_{u,m}^M \tag{8}$$

Table 1. List of the main notations used in the problem formulation.

Notation	Definition
u, m	Symbols representing UE and NGMC in volume V
$NGMC_m$	NGMC m, out of M
UE_u	User equipment u, out of U
V	Volume of coverage defined by 3D Cartesian coordinates between minimum (−1000 m) and maximum (1000 m) values
$C^M_{u,m}$	Capacity provided by $NGMC_m$ to the UE_u, in bits per second (bit/s)
B	Number of RBs used per numerology
Δfr_1	Subcarrier spacing (SCS) for FR1, in Hz
U_m	Number of UEs associated to $NGMC_m$
$S^M_{u,m}$	Binary variables indicating user association of UE_u to $NGMC_m$, where '1' means associated and '0' otherwise
$Bw^M_{u,m}$	Bandwidth of the channel between UE_u and $NGMC_m$, in Hz
$SINR^M_{u,m}$	SINR of the channel between UE_u and $NGMC_m$, in dB
$R^M_{u,m}$	Reference Signal Received Power (RSRP) of UE_u with respect to $NGMC_m$, in dB
N_{fr1}	Thermal noise power for FR1, in dB
G_t, G_r	Transmitter and receiver antenna gains, in dBi
P_t	Transmission power, in dBm
c	Speed of light in vacuum (3×10^8 m/s)
f^M_m	Carrier frequency, in GHz
x^M_m, y^M_m, z^M_m	Euclidean coordinates of $NGMC_m$, in m
x^U_u, y^U_u, z^U_u	Euclidean coordinates of UE_u, in m
h_{BS}, h_{UT}	Heights of $NGMC_m$ and UE_u, in meters. $h_{BS} = 25$ m; $h_{UT} = 1.5$ m, as defined in Table 7.4.1–1 of [23] for 3GPP Urban Macro (UMa) scenario
$d^M_{2Du,m}$, $d^M_{3Du,m}$	Euclidean 2D and 3D distances between UE_u and $NGMC_m$, in meters
$d^M_{BPu,m}$	Euclidean 2D Breakpoint distances between UE_u and $NGMC_m$, in meters
μ_{fr1}	Numerology used for FR1
$\eta^M_{u,m}$	Spectral efficiency of the established downlink Radio Network Temporary Identifier (RNTI) between UE_u and $NGMC_m$ in bit/s/Hz
$SE^M_{u,m}$	Obtained regression for spectral efficiency of the established downlink RNTI between UE_u and $NGMC_m$, as a linear function of the $SINR^M_{u,m}$, in bit/s/Hz
$PL^M_{UMa\_LOSu,m}$	Pathloss for UMa scenarios considered for wireless link between UE_u and $NGMC_m$

$$Bw_{u,m}^{M} = \frac{B\Delta fr1}{U_m} \tag{9}$$

Equation (10) represents the spectral efficiency as a linear regression obtained as a function of $SINR_{u,m}^{M}$ (dB), as shown in Fig. 1.

$$SE_{u,m}^{M} = 0.23\ SINR_{u,m}^{M} - 0.21 \tag{10}$$

The SINR intervals, ranging from minimum to maximum values, for each Modulation and Coding Scheme (MCS), form the basis of the EESM error model used in next generation radio communications. According to the MCS index Table 2 in [22] for PDSCH, the MCS index is related with modulation order, target code rate and respective spectral efficiency. [24] also discusses these SINR intervals for both NR PHY LDPC base graph types 1 and 2, for different code block sizes.

The spectral efficiency chart, presented in Fig. 1, which is a function of SINR in dB, consists of a set of values and a linear regression. These values represent the middle points of the SINR intervals for each MCS, each associated with a corresponding spectral efficiency. The linear regression in (10) is also depicted in Fig. 1. It was obtained to simplify the abstraction model and approximate the spectral efficiency using a least squares method. When (10) is applied in (6), it provides the spectral efficiency $\eta_{u,m}^{M}$. Heuristic 1 describes the process of transitioning from the set of SINR intervals to the regression line represented by (10). The SINR per RNTI, in the absence of interference, is given by (11).

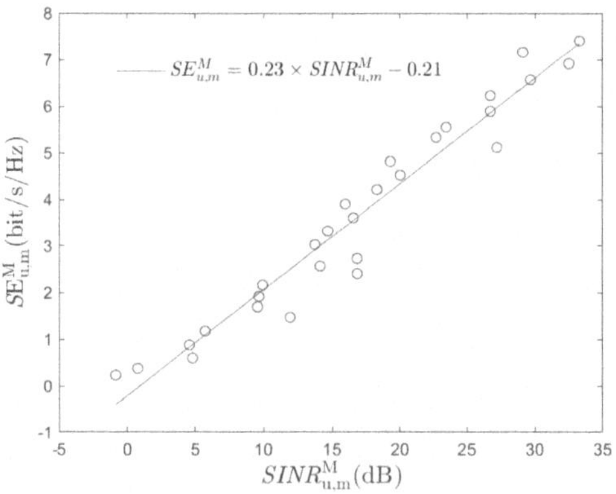

Fig. 1. Linear regression of the interpolated points for $SE_{u,m}^{M}$ versus $SINR_{u,m}^{M}$ as per (10).

$$SINR_{u,m}^{M} = 10\ log_{10}\left(\frac{R_{u,m}^{M}}{Nfr1}\right) \tag{11}$$

The received power and thermal noise power for each RNTI are given by (12) and (13), respectively.

$$R_{u,m}^{M} = \frac{10^{\left(\frac{Pt-30}{10}\right)}}{U_m PL_{UMa\_LOSu,m}^{M}} \tag{12}$$

$$N_{fr1} = 10^{[-19.9+\log_{10}(B\Delta fr1)]} \tag{13}$$

The RSRP defined in (12) is based on 3GPP path loss model for an UMa scenario, whose cells are positioned at a height of 25 m, according to [23]. This configuration simplifies the problem to a 2D optimisation, considering the plane $z_m^M = h_{BS} = 25$ m, for all the M cells.

The pathloss is modeled as a two-branch function by (14) with a non-linearity point at a 2D breakpoint distance between the UEs and cells.

$$PL_{UMa\_LOSu,m}^{M} = \begin{cases} PL_{1u,m}^{M}, & 10\,m \leq d_{2Du,m}^{M} \leq d_{BPu,m}^{M} \\ PL_{2u,m}^{M}, & d_{BPu,m}^{M} \leq d_{2Du,m}^{M} \leq 5\,km \end{cases} \tag{14}$$

In UMa scenarios, this 2D breakpoint distance depends on the antenna heights, the probability of LoS, the effective environment height (h_E) and the carrier frequency. hE is set to 1 m, with a LoS probability of $1/(1 + C\,(d_{2Du,m}^{M}, h_{UT}))$, which is 1 for user heights (h_{UT}) up to 13 m. According to the definition in [23], $PL_{UMa\_LOSu,m}^{M}$ is represented by $PL_{1u,m}^{M}$ for 2D distances below the breakpoint distance and takes the values of $PL_{2u,m}^{M}$ for 2D distances above that point, as presented in (15) and (16).

Heuristic 1 – SE vs SINR linear regression leading to (10). *(Comments in gray refer to the lines below)*

```
/* Access the structured information containing the 28 SINR intervals, for each
/* MCS, in [22] and [24]
SINR_min(0 to 27) = read structure of min SINR values
SINR_max(0 to 27) = read structure of max SINR values
/* Convert the SINR values from dB to linear scale
for MCS = 0 to 27
  SINR_min (MCS) = 10^(SINR_min (MCS)/10)
  SINR_max (MCS) = 10^(SINR_max (MCS)/10)
  /* For each SINR interval, calculate the average SINR and convert it back to
  /* dB
  SINR_avg (MCS) = 10log10[(SINR_max (MCS) – SINR_min (MCS))/2 +
  SINR_min (MCS)]
  /* Each MCS corresponds to a specific spectral efficiency value by 3GPP
  /* definition, as in [22]
  get spect_eff (MCS) value from [22]
/* Calculate the slope and intercept of the regression line that best fits the 28
/* (SINR; Spectral Efficiency) points in Fig. 1
compute slope, intercept from SINR_avg and spect_eff
```

$$PL_{1u,m}^{M} = 10^{2.8} {d_{3Du,m}^{M}}^{2.2} {f_m^{M}}^{2} \tag{15}$$

$$PL_{2u,m}^{M} = 10^{2.8} \frac{d_{3Du,m}^{M} \,^{4} f_{m}^{M\,2}}{(d_{BPu,m}^{M}\,^{2} + (hBS - hUT)^{2})^{0.9}} \tag{16}$$

The model excludes pathloss values for 2D distances above 5000 m, as these are beyond the range considered for V, and below 10 m, which is ensured by the optimisation constraint (3). The distances $d_{3Du,m}^{M}$, $d_{2Du,m}^{M}$, and $d_{BPu,m}^{M}$ are given by (17), (18) and (19), respectively.

$$d_{3Du,m}^{M} = \sqrt{\left(x_m^M - x_u^U\right)^2 + \left(y_m^M - y_u^U\right)^2 + \left(z_m^M - z_u^U\right)^2} \tag{17}$$

$$d_{2Du,m}^{M} = \sqrt{\left(x_m^M - x_u^U\right)^2 + \left(y_m^M - y_u^U\right)^2} \tag{18}$$

$$d_{BPu,m}^{M} = \frac{4(h_{BS} - h_E)(h_{UT} - h_E) f_m^M \, 10^9}{c} \tag{19}$$

In 5G NR, the SCS for FR1, as referred to in (7), and the typical numerology μ_{fr1} $= 0$, result in a bandwidth equal to 15 kHz per RB. With 9 sub-carriers per RB used for data (the remaining 3 are used for control) and 266 RBs per slot, the total bandwidth available for data transmission is equal to $266 \times 9 \times 15$ kHz $= 35.9$ MHz.

The user association binary variable $S_{u,m}^{M}$, as defined in constraint (2), ensures that each UE_u is associated with a single NGMC. The constraint in (3) establishes the lower bound of 10 m for the 2D distance between each UE_u and the NGMC, ensuring the applicability of the 3GPP pathloss PL1 range, as described in [23]. Constraint (4) sets the upper limit for the spectral efficiency according to the definition in [24], considering Table 2 of EESM 5G NR error model type, with chase combining. In the frequency domain, we have considered 9 sub-carriers per RB instead of 12; in the time domain, we have also considered 12 OFDM symbols per slot rather than 14, to account for overhead. Therefore, the spectral efficiency's upper bound is 6.4000 bit/s/Hz compared to the typical 7.4063 bit/s/Hz for an MCS index of 27 and modulation order of 8, as stated in [22].

3.2 Solving the Problem

The optimisation problem requires solving the 3D Euclidean coordinates of the NGMCs (x_m^M, y_m^M, z_m^M) and the set of Boolean user associations $S_{u,m}^{M}$ for each pair UE_u and $NGMC_m$. In order to solve this optimisation problem, we have initialised the optimisation variables and used a state-of-the-art solver to iteratively converge to a solution. The Genetic Algorithm (GA), implemented in MATLAB, was employed to determine solutions for the various scenarios considered. GA is an optimisation solver inspired by the principles of natural selection and genetics [18]. It is widely used to solve complex optimisation problems where traditional mathematical approaches may be inefficient or impractical. However, the problem formulation is independent of the solver used; exploring different types of solvers is beyond the scope of this work and is recommended for future research.

4 Performance Evaluation

In this section, we introduce a network performance evaluation based on a series of process steps, detailed in Fig. 3, for each of the scenarios. The study focuses on Terminal XXI of Sines seaport, a future smart port with high wireless connectivity. We consider an environment with different sets of UEs, their centroid points or Geo-Means, and the maximum pairwise distance or diameter between them. For example, the NGMC's obtained position that best serves the UEs is shown in Fig. 2.

Fig. 2. Example of NGMC deployment at Terminal XXI of the Sines seaport, compared with the commonly used Geo-mean or Centroid position of the five UEs considered.

First, we obtained the NGMC position, user associations, and aggregate capacity using the optimisation problem in (1); this was developed with a maximum of 5000 generations and a tolerance of 10^{-30} for fast convergence and higher accuracy of the fitness function. Then, we simulated each scenario in ns-3, considering the parameters presented in Table 2, to obtain the aggregate throughput and delay. For each networking scenario, we calculated the mean geographical location of the UEs, their diameter and the respective aggregate capacity with the Calculator (MATLAB), as shown in Fig. 3. This process was repeated in ns-3 to establish a baseline to compare aggregate capacity with throughput. Along the performance evaluation, we used a set of metrics and indicators, including:

- Aggregate capacity – sum of the U RNTI capacities provided by an NGMC to all associated UE_u within V. This value is calculated by both the solver and the calculator;

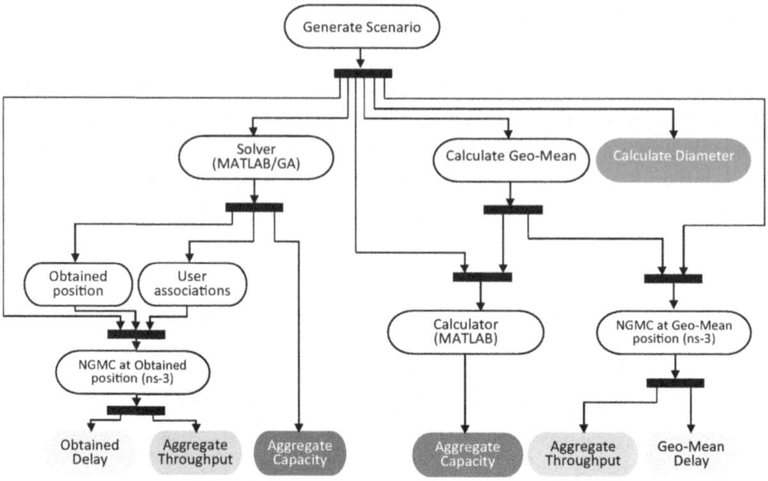

Fig. 3. Performance evaluation methodology for each scenario.

- Aggregate throughput – sum of the average throughput measured by the ns-3 *flow monitor* module on each RNTI's downlink packet flow. This output is obtained from each ns-3 simulation;
- Maximum pairwise distance – also called diameter, it measures the distance between the two most distant UEs;
- Delay – average delay across all U RNTI downlink packet flows, measured by *flow monitor*. Each RNTI's downlink packet flow is provided by the NGMC and is an ns-3 simulation output for each scenario;
- Obtained position – NGMC's Euclidean position determined by the solver to optimise the aggregate capacity;
- Geo-mean position – NGMC's Euclidean position based on the geographical average of all considered UE_u in a scenario. This was used as input to the calculator to obtain the baseline aggregate capacity.

In order to compare the results from the solver and the calculator with those from the ns-3 network simulator, we analysed a first scenario with two UEs at 1 km 2D distance from each other, as depicted in Fig. 4.

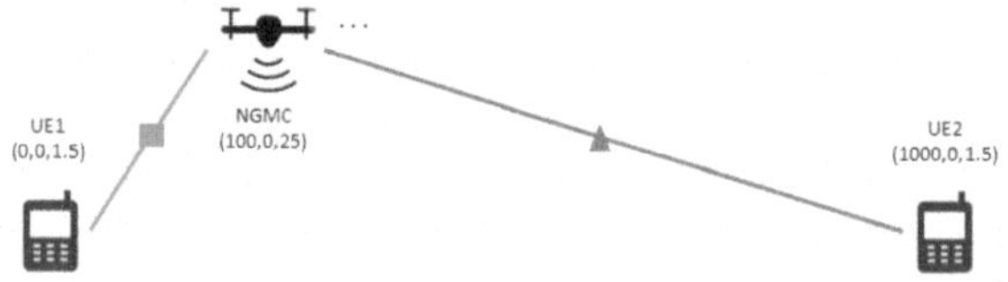

Fig. 4. First scenario with 2 UEs and an NGMC.

The solver output is confirmed at the extreme points of the scenario - (100, 0, 25) and (900, 0, 25) - as obtained positions with the highest aggregate capacity values. This is shown in Fig. 5, with step point coordinates depicted at the x-axis and respective results on y-axis. For each point, between a 100 m distance from UE1 to a 100 m distance from UE2, the aggregate capacity and aggregate throughput were obtained using the calculator and then validated in ns-3, with evaluations conducted at every 100 m step. The results show significant similarities between capacities and throughputs. The lines with round markers in Fig. 5 represent the sum of the flows below them. The upper blue continuous line represents the aggregate throughput of the two corresponding flows below, with 95% confidence intervals. Analysing the trajectory lines reveals that the aggregate throughput and capacity values at the geo-mean position (500, 0, 25) are lower compared to the obtained positions at the extremes. This is because the flows are not linear; they follow an exponential pattern.

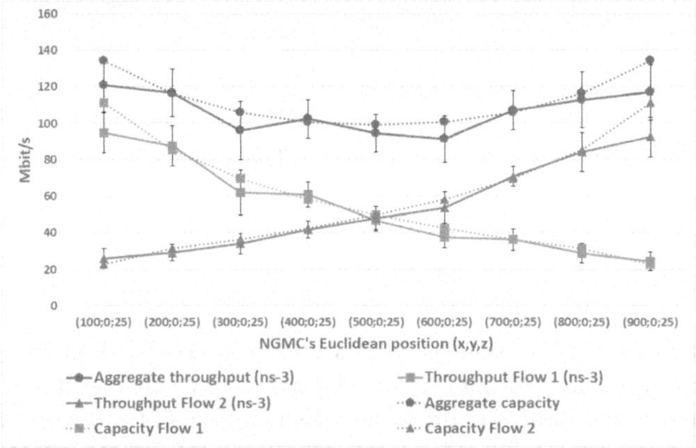

Fig. 5. Aggregate capacity, aggregate throughput and average results for each flow. (Color figure online)

This paper studies several scenarios and uses the set of parameters presented in Table 2, which were applied to the solver, the calculator and the ns-3 simulator. As a preliminary study, this paper does not consider obstacle shadowing or any backhaul capacity limits. It uses an FR1 macro scenario with the simplest numerology and corresponding SCS, taking advantage of the maximum number of RBs in frequency per slot (266); however, some subcarriers are not considered for data (3), as they are assumed to be used for control or reference signals. Additionally, AMC technique in EESM error model was chosen to be simpler for HARQ processes with Chase Combining (NrEesmCcT2), rather than the more complex Incremental Redundancy (NrEesmIrT2) option. A detailed study of the NGMC for every point along the trajectory between the two UEs was made only for the first scenario. Since the results in Fig. 5 show significant similarities, we continued with additional scenarios, following these calibration tests, which validate our initial findings.

Figure 6 presents results starting from first scenario, labeled as "Set 0". The other scenarios on the x-axis of Fig. 6 were studied with different sets of UEs, randomly generated and distributed across the plane at z = h_{BS} of V. The maximum pairwise

Table 2. Parameters used in the solver and ns-3 simulations.

Parameter	Value
3GPP Scenario	UMa
Number of NGMCs (M)	1
Number of UEs (N)	From 2 to 5
Carrier frequency (FR1)	5 GHz
Numerology (μ_{fr1})	0
SCS (Δfr_1)	15 kHz
gNB and UE antenna model	Isotropic (SISO)
Transmission power	24 dBm
Required data rate	100 Mbit/s
Traffic direction	Downlink
Error Model	AMC with NrEesmCcT2
NR MAC Scheduler Type	OFDMA Round Robin
Number of RBs	266
Number of Subcarriers per RB	9

distances for each scenario are plotted on the rightmost y-axis showing an increase from Set 1 to Set 5. For each scenario, we followed the threads of process described in Fig. 3, leading to the metrics presented in the same colours in Fig. 6. Each ns-3 simulation was repeated ten times, each one considering 1000 subframes, 12000 OFDM symbols and 266000 RBs for numerology 0, allowing for significant variability. Results are presented in Fig. 6 with 95% confidence intervals.

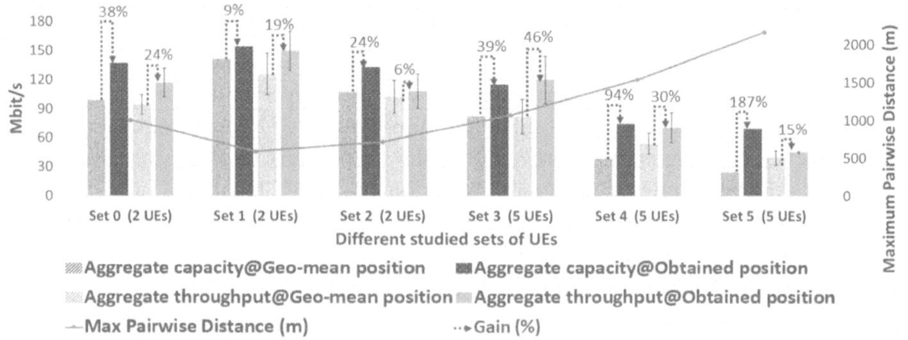

Fig. 6. Aggregate capacities and respective throughputs from ns-3 for obtained positions and geo-mean positions. (Color figure online)

When considering the dark and light blue bars (second and fourth in each set) for the obtained position of the NGMC, we observe aggregate capacity values similar to the respective aggregate throughputs. Conversely, comparing the dark and light green bars (first and third in each set) for the geo-mean position of the NGMC, they are generally below the first two, although similar for each set. The blue bars consistently exceed the green, indicating that placing the NGMC at the obtained positions with the solver, allows for better results than at geo-mean positions. It is also worth mentioning that the bar heights decrease as the diameter increases, which means lower throughputs and capacities for UE sets with greater maximum pairwise distances.

Delay is not considered in the formulation of our problem. As such, optimising delay is outside the scope of this work; however, the ns-3 network simulator results for delay are presented in Fig. 7. These results, plotted alongside the scenarios' maximum pairwise distance, follow the process outlined in Fig. 3 that end up in delay measurements. Overall, delays increase with greater diameter distances, but delays corresponding to the obtained positions by the solver are consistently lower than those for the cells positioned at geo-mean locations.

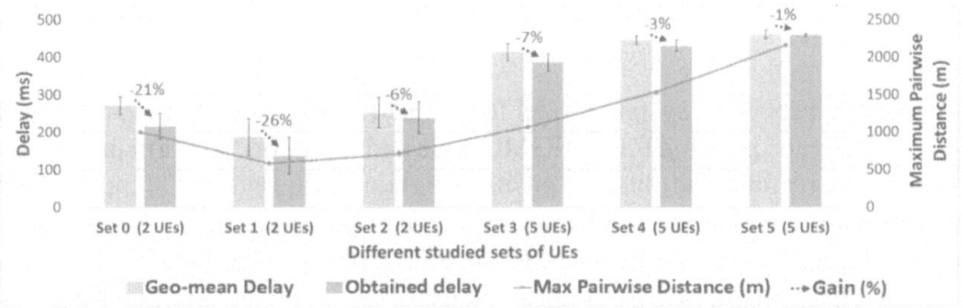

Fig. 7. Delays obtained on ns-3 for the obtained positions and geo-mean positions.

The gains in capacity, throughput and delay obtained by positioning the NGMC at obtained locations, when compared with geo-mean positions, are highlighted by red dotted arrows in Fig. 6 and Fig. 7. The gains reach up to 187% for capacity with obtained positioning (Set 5 in Fig. 6) when compared to geo-mean positioning: up to 46% for throughput (Set 3 in Fig. 6) and up to a 26% reduction for delay (Set 1 in Fig. 7). For scenarios with larger diameters, capacity gains are significantly higher, despite lower throughput and delay gains due to increased HARQ retransmissions.

Figure 8 depicts the Cumulative Distribution Function (CDF) of the delays obtained from ns-3 simulations, which were conducted 10 times for each position. For each set of UEs studied, there are two CDFs: one for the obtained position of the NGMC (continuous lines) and the other for the geo-mean position (dotted lines). Scenarios with larger diameters present steeper delay distributions, while scenarios with smaller diameters present more dispersed distributions, indicating greater variability in delays. For the 90th percentile, delay reductions reach up to 30%, as depicted in Fig. 8 for Set 1.

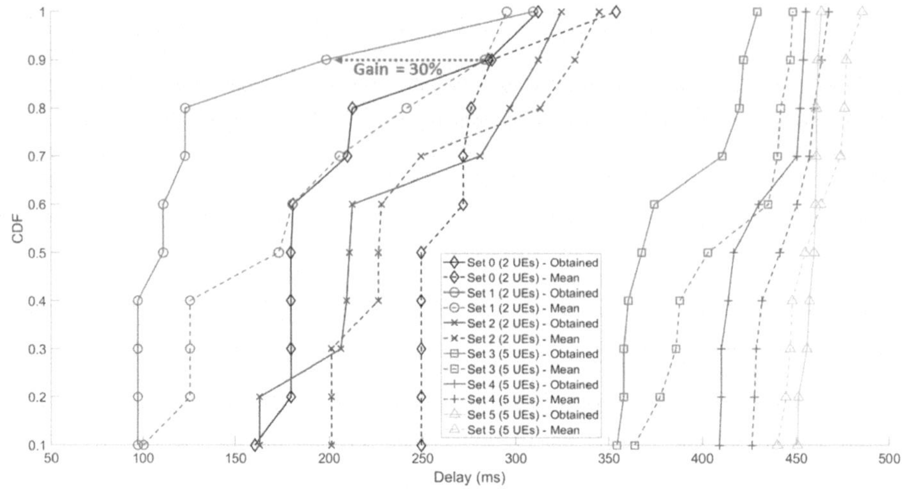

Fig. 8. CDF of the delays from the simulations.

5 Conclusions

In this paper, we propose a system model formulated as an optimisation problem with a heuristic to obtain the position for an NGMC node and a network performance evaluation study to compare results. The obtained position maximises the aggregate capacity for a set of UEs. The proposed system model and solver consistently determine obtained positions for the NGMC, achieving significant gains, including delay reductions. With this paper's contributions, we pave the way for improving dynamic radio network planning tasks for MNOs in next-generation outdoor environments, such as seaports with multiple UEs. This approach allows MNOs to optimise their investments in radio planning by focusing on performance rather than merely covering areas with geometrically distributed fixed cells.

As future work, we aim at addressing scenarios with a larger number of UEs and consider the blockage effect caused by obstacles, such as containers in seaports, which can limit signal propagation and reduce network capacity and throughput. Moreover, we aim at considering multiple mobile and fixed backhaul cells and explore different types of scheduling over available RBs with appropriate numerologies.

Acknowledgements. This work is co-financed by Component 5 - Capitalization and Business Innovation, integrated in the Resilience Dimension of the Recovery and Resilience Plan within the scope of the Recovery and Resilience Mechanism (MRR) of the European Union (EU), framed in the Next Generation EU, for the period 2021 - 2026, within project NEXUS, with reference 53.

References

1. Gizelis, C.-A., Mavroeidakos, T., Marinakis, A., Litke, A., Moulos, V.: Towards a smart port: the role of the telecom industry. In: Maglogiannis, I., Iliadis, L., Pimenidis, E. (eds.) AIAI

2020. IAICT, vol. 585, pp. 128–139. Springer, Cham (2020). https://doi.org/10.1007/978-3-030-49190-1_12
2. Maia, D., Coelho, A., Ricardo, M.: Obstacle-aware on-demand 5G network using a mobile robotic platform. In: 18th International Conference on Wireless and Mobile Computing, Networking and Communications (WiMob), Thessaloniki, Greece (2022)
3. Zreikat, A.: Capacity bounds analysis of 5G networks in different propagation environment. College of Engineering and Technology, American University of the Middle East, Kuwait (2023)
4. Filippini, I., et al.: Fast Cell Discovery in mm-Wave 5G Networks with Context Information. Politecnico di Milano, Dipartimento di Elettronica, Informazione e Bioingegneria, Piazza L. da Vinci, 32, Milan 20133, Italy and NEC Europe Ltd., Heidelberg HA4 6QE (2017)
5. Kalantari, E., et al.: Backhaul-aware robust 3D drone placement in 5G+ wireless networks. In: ICC 2017: WS07-Workshop on Flexible Networks (FlexNets) (2017)
6. Fouda, A., et al.: UAV-Based in-band Integrated Access and Backhaul for 5G Communications. Department of Electrical and Computer Engineering, Florida International University, Miami, Department of Electrical and Computer Engineering, North Carolina State University, Raleigh, NC, Department of Computer Science, University of Chicago, Chicago, IL (2018)
7. Fouda, A., et al.: Interference Management in UAV-Assisted Integrated Access and Backhaul Cellular Networks. Department of Electrical and Computer Engineering, Florida International University, Miami, FL, Department of Electrical and Computer Engineering, North Carolina State University, Raleigh, NC, Department of Computer Science, University of Chicago, Chicago, IL, IEEE Access (2019)
8. Qiu, C., et al.: Joint Resource Allocation, Placement and User Association of Multiple UAV-Mounted Base Stations with In-Band Wireless Backhaul. Key Laboratory of Universal Wireless Communications, Ministry of Education, Beijing University of Posts and Telecommunications, Beijing 100876, China (2019)
9. Kalantari, E., et al.: User association and bandwidth allocation for terrestrial and aerial base stations with backhaul considerations. In: 2017 IEEE 28th Annual International Symposium on Personal, Indoor, and Mobile Radio Communications (PIMRC) (2017)
10. Kubota, A., et al.: A study on conversion of NLoS to LoS conditions using Sidelink in smart factory environments. In: 2021 IEEE VTS 17th Asia Pacific Wireless Communications Symposium (APWCS), Osaka, Japan (2021)
11. Monteiro, V., et al.: Paving the way toward mobile IAB: problems, solutions and challenges. IEEE Open J. Commun. Soc. **3** (2022)
12. Chen, J., et al.: 3D urban UAV relay placement: linear complexity algorithm and analysis. IEEE Trans. Wirel. Commun. **20**(8) (2021)
13. Chen, J., et al.: Efficient local map search algorithms for the placement of flying relays. IEEE Trans. Wirel. Commun. **19**(2) (2020)
14. Lee, C.-H., et al.: Mobile small cells for further enhanced 5G heterogeneous networks. ETRI J. **37**(5) (2015)
15. Coelho, A., et al.: Traffic-aware gateway placement for high-capacity flying networks. In: 2021 IEEE 93rd Vehicular Technology Conference, VTC2021-Spring (2021)
16. Almeida, E., et al.: Joint traffic-aware UAV placement and predictive routing for aerial networks. Ad Hoc Netw. **118**, 102525 (2021)
17. Shehzad, M., et al.: Backhaul-aware intelligent positioning of UAVs and association of terrestrial base stations for fronthaul connectivity. IEEE Trans. Netw. Sci. Eng. **8**(4) (2021)
18. Zhong, X., et al.: QoS-compliant 3-D deployment optimization strategy for UAV base stations. IEEE Syst. J. **15**(2) (2021)
19. Huang, Y., et al.: Joint AMC and resource allocation for mobile wireless networks based on distributed MARL. In: 2022 IEEE International Conference on Communications Workshops (ICC Workshops), Seul, South Korea (2022)

20. Karo, F., et al.: 5G New Radio (NR) Network planning at frequency of 2.6 GHz in golden triangle of Jakarta. In: 3rd International Seminar on Research of Information Technology and Intelligent Systems (ISRITI) (2020)
21. Agelliza, V., et al.: Analysis of the implementing inter band carrier aggregation (ca) on the 5G new radio (NR) networks. J. Inf. Technol. Utilization **6**(1) (2023)
22. 3GPP TS 38.214 V16.5.0, Table 5.1.3.1-2
23. 3GPP TR 38.901 version 17.0.0 Rel. 17, Table 7.4.1-1
24. Lagen, S., et al.: New Radio Physical Layer Abstraction for System-Level Simulations of 5G Networks. CTTC, Interdigital

Dynamic Data Radio Bearer Management for O-RAN Slicing in 5G Standalone Networks

Pedro Silva[1], Ricardo Dinis[2], André Coelho[1(✉)], and Manuel Ricardo[1]

[1] INESC TEC, Faculdade de Engenharia, Universidade do Porto, Porto, Portugal
up201905678@edu.fe.up.pt, {andre.f.coelho,manuel.ricardo}@inesctec.pt
[2] NOS SGPS, S.A., Lisbon, Portugal
ricardo.dinis@nos.pt

Abstract. The rapid growth of data traffic and evolving service demands are driving a shift from traditional network architectures to advanced solutions. While 5G networks provide reduced latency and higher availability, they still face limitations due to reliance on integrated hardware, leading to configuration and interoperability challenges. The emerging Open Radio Access Network (O-RAN) paradigm addresses these issues by enabling remote configuration and management of virtualized components through open interfaces, promoting cost-effective, multi-vendor interoperability. Network slicing, a key 5G enabler, allows for tailored network configurations to meet heterogeneous performance requirements. The main contribution of this paper is a private Standalone 5G network based on O-RAN, featuring a dynamic Data Radio Bearer Management xApp (xDRBM) for real-time metric collection and traffic prioritization. xDRBM optimizes resource usage and ensures performance guarantees for specific applications. Validation was conducted in an emulated environment representative of real-world scenarios.

Keywords: 5G · Data Radio Bearer · Network Slicing · O-RAN · xApp

1 Introduction

The telecommunications field is rapidly evolving, driven by increasing user demands and technological improvements. In order to meet these demands, telecom operators are adopting new networking paradigms for emerging applications, including industry use cases, requiring adaptable network capabilities to ensure targeted Quality of Service (QoS) levels, including low latency, high availability, and enhanced reliability.

Traditional mobile networks, often deployed on monolithic hardware, face challenges such as vendor lock-in, proprietary configurations, and interoperability issues. These challenges have led to a shift towards more flexible, interoperable, and sustainable mobile network solutions.

A. A. Juan et al. (Eds.): SIMUtools 2024, LNICST 603, pp. 357–366, 2025.
https://doi.org/10.1007/978-3-031-87345-4_23

The emerging Open Radio Access Network (O-RAN) paradigm, initiated by the O-RAN Alliance [1], aims at replacing traditional all-in-one radio units with modular, open software-based solutions. O-RAN enables resilient, manageable, and reconfigurable networks, improving flexibility while reducing environmental impact and costs. O-RAN architecture supports the development of software applications (rApps and xApps) tailored to specific network performance needs.

Telecom operators should plan and deploy networks that meet user requirements. Network slices – virtualized, independent networks sharing physical resources – can be configured to meet specific demands. Industry use cases, such as industrial automation, often have orthogonal requirements, requiring the on-demand creation and configuration of multiple virtual networks. The dynamic nature of radio signal propagation and environmental interference adds to the complexity of network management.

The main contribution of this paper is a private Standalone (SA) 5G Network based on the O-RAN architecture, which enables the provisioning of network slices through dynamic Data Radio Bearer (DRB) management. The proposed solution includes a DRB Management xApp (xDRBM), which collects Radio Access Network (RAN) metrics and executes an original algorithm that manages DRB creation/release and assigns traffic to appropriate DRBs. xDRBM reduces latency by prioritizing traffic while ensuring a good utilization of the network's resources.

This paper is organized as follows. Section 2 reviews related work. Section 3 describes the proposed solution. Section 4 details the implementation. Section 5 presents the performance evaluation and main results. Finally, Sect. 6 points out the main conclusions and directions for future work.

2 Related Work

Several works in the literature explore the implementation of private 5G SA networks and network slicing techniques in O-RAN-based 5G networks. In [2], the authors propose a latency-aware RAN slice descriptor to improve RAN slicing's ability to manage the deterministic periodic traffic demands common in Industry 4.0. Similarly, [3] presents a framework using configuration descriptors to define RAN slices, outlining the traits, policies, and resources needed across the radio protocol layers of next-generation RAN nodes. O-M^3, a real-time scheduler for O-RAN networks introduced in [4], optimizes beamforming, resource block allocation, and modulation across multiple cells to meet stringent timing requirements. While this work shows the potential for real-time RAN optimizations, it does not specifically address network slicing challenges.

Deep Reinforcement Learning (DRL) agents as xApps have been explored to optimize performance metrics across network slices, focusing on real-time RAN optimization through data-driven closed-control loops using large-scale experimental testbeds [5]. ColO-RAN [6] is a reference testbed for large-scale O-RAN-based solutions, while [7] introduced UnionLabs, a platform for remote access and sharing of Over-The-Air testbeds, supporting xApp development within O-RAN environments. Most network slicing research using community testbeds focuses on O-RAN's near real-time RAN Intelligent Controller (RIC). However, RAN experimentation using alternative solutions like OpenAirInterface (OAI) and FlexRIC presents additional challenges.

At the OAI Osaka Conference [8], the integration of OAI with FlexRIC [9] was presented, focusing on monitoring network delay and establishing new DRBs when predefined latency thresholds are exceeded, enhancing Quality of Experience (QoE) during high latency periods triggered by iPerf3 sessions. ProSLICE [10], an open-source platform designed to implement the complete O-RAN specification, improves RAN slicing with a detailed taxonomy covering design principles, enablers, and security aspects. It also introduces novel xApps for RAN slice creation, statistics computation, and a GUI for configuration and visualization. However, despite its open-source design, ProSLICE is not yet publicly available.

Currently available solutions either do not implement RAN slicing or lack openness. This paper advances the state of the art by developing a private 5G SA network using only open-source software, implementing network slicing techniques that dynamically adapt to heterogeneous traffic demands and radio channel conditions.

3 DRB Management xApp

DRB management allows the allocation of specific traffic types to DRBs with distinct 5QI values, enabling Quality of Service (QoS) management at the bearer level. This method arises from the absence of RAN slicing functionality in open-source 5G implementations available. The utilization of additional DRBs allows us to customize traffic handling according to the requirements of different applications. For instance, latency-sensitive applications can be supported by low-latency 5QI DRBs, while high-throughput applications can utilize DRBs with higher bandwidth allocation. The dynamic creation and release of DRBs enable the network to adapt in real time to varying traffic conditions, leading to optimized resource usage and improved performance. It is worth noting that managing several DRBs introduces potential challenges in signaling and additional overhead and might not guarantee the same level of isolation and predictability as sub-band allocation. Despite these concerns, dynamic DRB management and configuration represent a feasible approach for implementing a proof of concept for network slicing.

Emerging wireless networks should simultaneously meet high throughput and low latency requirements. Network slicing enables the sharing of physical infrastructure to meet heterogeneous QoS levels through different virtual networks, called network slices. In order to accomplish the network slicing technique in O-RAN, we propose the dynamic configuration and management of DRBs.

We developed a novel DRB Management xApp (xDRBM) capable of creating and releasing DRBs. xDRBM operates by collecting RAN metrics through the Near-RT RIC and employs a novel algorithm for DRB configuration and management. O-RAN enables the acquisition of various metrics from the 5G New Radio (NR) protocol stack, including Key Performance Metrics (KPMs), which transverse the entire network. xDRBM focuses on downlink (DL) throughput and the delay packets experience at the Radio Link Control (RLC) layer, including possible retransmissions – referred to as sojourn time. Table 1 outlines the variables in the proposed algorithm, detailed in Algorithm 1, which was executed as an xApp.

Table 1. Definition of the variables used by Algorithm 1.

Variable	Definition
$Throughput_{average}$	The running average of the network's throughput over time.
$Throughput_{threshold}$	The target throughput level that the network aims to maintain on average.
$SojournTime_{average}$	The running average of packet sojourn time within the network.
$SojournTime_{max-threshold}$	The maximum allowable sojourn time. Exceeding this threshold indicates severe network delays.
$SojournTime_{high-threshold}$	An intermediate alert threshold for rising network delays, but still below the maximum threshold.
$SojournTime_{min-threshold}$	The minimum sojourn time, indicating optimal network conditions with minimal delay.
$SojournTime_{low-threshold}$	An intermediate alert threshold for decreasing network delays, but still above the minimum threshold.
$control\_period$	The predefined period after which network adjustments may be implemented.
t_{create_DRB}	The timestamp recorded when an additional DRB is created, used for managing the network's resource lifecycle.
t_{delete_DRB}	The timestamp recorded when a DRB is deleted.
$t_{current}$	The current time, used for determining the timing of network operations.

In Algorithm 1, several conditions are considered for creating and deleting a DRB. The first *if* clause evaluates whether the average sojourn time of the last N measurements exceeds the maximum threshold, as well as if the sojourn time, while not critically high, is associated with a low average throughput. This indicates network congestion and may lead to QoS degradation. Conversely, the *else if* clause assesses whether the average sojourn time falls below the minimum threshold or whether the sojourn time, while not critically low, is associated with a high average throughput. These conditions indicate that the network is not congested and QoS degradation is not severe, thus avoiding the need of an additional DRB. This reduces the time and overhead required to map incoming traffic between two DRBs. Both clauses in Algorithm 1 ensure that a certain

Algorithm 1. DRB Management xApp - xDRBM

if ($SojournTime_{average}$ > $SojournTime_{max-threshold}$ **OR** ($SojournTime_{average}$ > $SojournTime_{high-threshold}$ **AND** $Throughput_{average}$ < $Throughput_{threshold}$)) **AND** $t_{current}$ - t_{delete_DRB} > $control\_period$ **then**
  $t_{create\_DRB} \leftarrow t_{current}$
  Create new DRB ▷ Function that creates a DRB
else if ($SojournTime_{average}$ < $SojournTime_{min-threshold}$ **OR** ($SojournTime_{average}$ < $SojournTime_{low-threshold}$ **AND** $Throughput_{average}$ > $Throughput_{threshold}$)) **AND** $t_{current}$ - t_{create_DRB} > $control\_period$ **then**
  $t_{delete\_DRB} \leftarrow t_{current}$
  Delete DRB ▷ Function that releases a DRB
end if

time period has elapsed since the last network adjustment, whether it involved creating or deleting a DRB. This interval allows the RAN sufficient time to reconfigure itself and associate traffic to the suitable DRB.

When the RAN is triggered to create and configure a new DRB, it must map the traffic to the adequate DRB. This mapping process considers various criteria, including the type of traffic - such as Transmission Control Protocol (TCP), User Datagram Protocol (UDP), or Internet Control Message Protocol (ICMP) - and the destination port numbers, found in the packets' Internet Protocol (IP) headers. Additionally, the QoS levels associated with each DRB must also be taken into account. This solution allows to prioritize latency-sensitive applications' traffic during periods of high traffic demands. Upon the creation of a DRB, it is assigned a 5G QoS Identifier (5QI), which defines several parameters, including different priorities for the scheduling of packets. These are used for the network's traffic mapping approach. The creation of a new DRB with different QoS levels requires that this network condition is shared within the network and across all layers of the 5G NR stack, managing RAN resources accordingly.

4 Implementation

The developed slicing-aware 5G O-RAN comprises three main components: the Core Network (CN), the Radio Access Network (RAN) - which includes a disaggregated gNB and User Equipments (UEs) - and the Near-RT RIC. The architecture of the proposed solution is illustrated in Fig. 1.

Regarding the hardware setup, all components were deployed on a single Asus VivoBook F512D computer. Using a single machine simplifies the implementation and testing, while also facilitating a more straightforward approach to troubleshooting and debugging. The OpenAirInterface (OAI) software package was used to implement the CN and the RAN. OAI supports proof-of-concept development for thorough validation and improvement. The Near-RT RIC was implemented with Mosaic5G's FlexRIC, an open-source package enabling metric extraction from different 5G NR protocol stack layers in the RAN and enabling control actions for RAN reconfiguration.

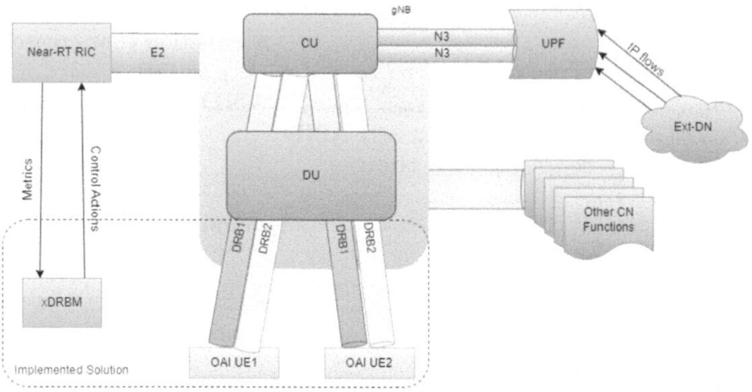

Fig. 1. Slicing-aware 5G O-RAN architecture [11]. The proposed xApp, xDRBM, for dynamic DRB management, collects RAN metrics and sends control actions for RAN reconfiguration via the Near-RT RIC.

5 Performance Evaluation

To evaluate the performance achieved when using the proposed solution, we conducted two tests. In the first test, a single UE triggered the xDRBM to assess the solution functionality and network performance. The second test considered the xDRBM triggered by two UEs. We employed ping and iPerf3 tools for network performance evaluation, with the iPerf3 configured to generate TCP traffic.

5.1 Single UE Test Scenario

In the first test scenario, we launched a ping from the external network (cf. Ext-DN, in Fig. 1) to the UE along with an iPerf3 session. This significantly increased the traffic being exchanged through the default DRB, increasing the throughput and sojourn time beyond values the thresholds defined in xDRBM. This is depicted in Fig. 2 by the red and blue lines between event index 0 and 290.

To improve network performance, xDRBM created a new DRB, assigning a 5QI value of 3. This value is associated with high-priority guaranteed bit rate flows, which are suitable for latency-sensitive applications. The ICMP packets were forwarded through this second DRB, while keeping the iPerf3 traffic on the default DRB. As shown in Fig. 3, this network reconfiguration led to a network performance improvement. The Round-Trip Time (RTT) for ICMP

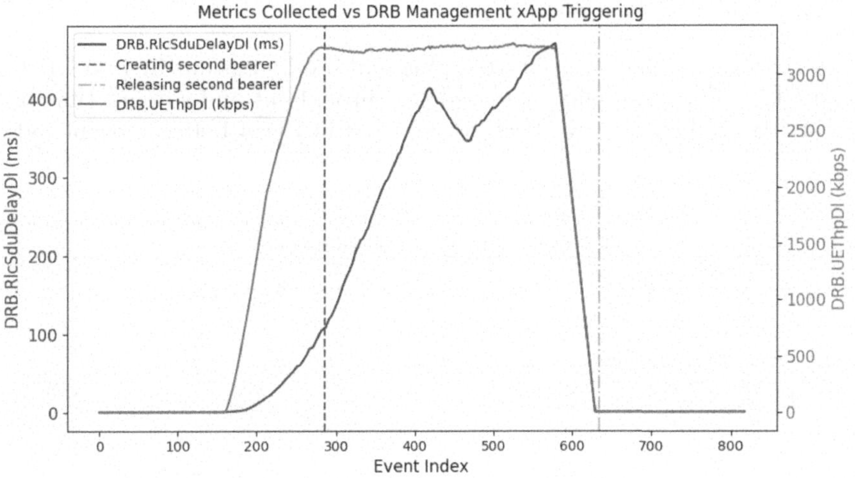

Fig. 2. Evolution of throughput (red line), in kbit/s, and sojourn time (blue line), in ms, for the default DRB used by UE 1. (Color figure online)

packets, which had been severely delayed due to network congestion to approximately 270 ms with only one DRB, was reduced to an acceptable RTT value of 60 ms after the second DRB was created (cf. dashed red line in Fig. 3).

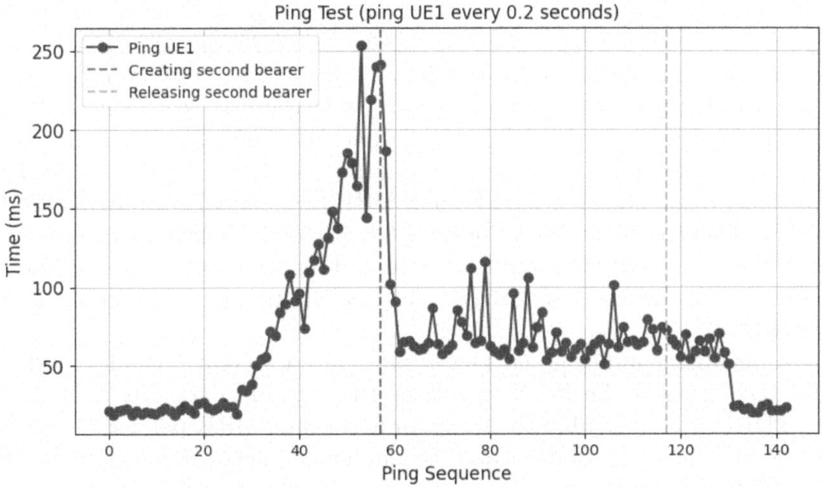

Fig. 3. Evolution of RTT for UE 1 (blue line), in ms, when it triggers the xDRBM to create a second DRB (dashed red line). (Color figure online)

5.2 Multiple UE Test Scenario

In the second test scenario, we started ping and iPerf3 sessions first on UE 1 and then on UE 2. This gradually increased the throughput and sojourn time in the default DRB used by the two UEs, as depicted in Fig. 4 between event index 0 and 1020.

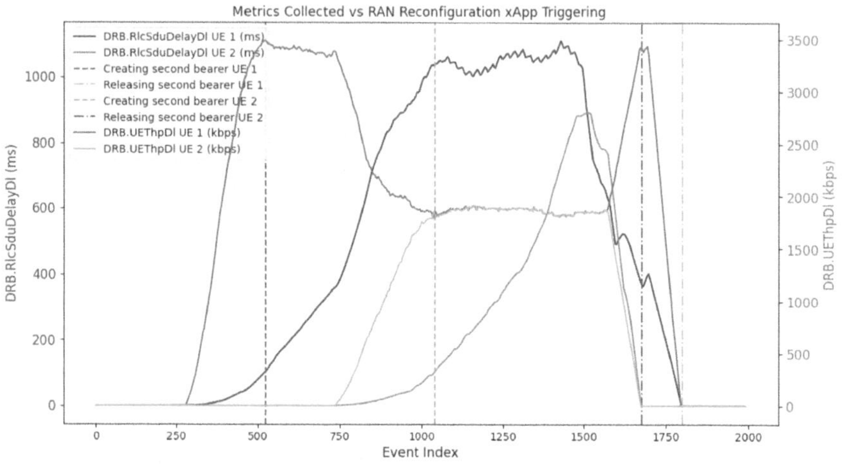

Fig. 4. Evolution of throughput, in kbit/s and sojourn time, in ms in the default DRB for UE 1 and UE 2 when both trigger the xDRBM.

Once the parameters exceeded the defined thresholds, xDRBM created a new DRB. For UE 1, the 5QI value was set to 3, as in the first test scenario. For UE 2, the 5QI value was set to 9. The ICMP packets were forwarded through the newly created second DRB, while maintaining the iPerf3 traffic on the default DRB for both UEs. The creation of a new DRB for both UEs improved the RTT of ICMP packets to acceptable values: for UE 1, the RTT decreased from 270 ms to 60 ms; for UE 2, the RTT reduced from 450 ms to about 70 ms, as shown in Fig. 5. This confirms the RAN allows to meet the targeted requirements when using xDRBM.

When network conditions no longer motivate a second DRB for both UEs, xDRBM reconfigured the RAN to release the second DRB. Due to OAI limitations, xDRBM is only able to create an additional DRB per UE. It serves as a proof-of-concept of a solution able to implement network slices in the RAN through DRB management.

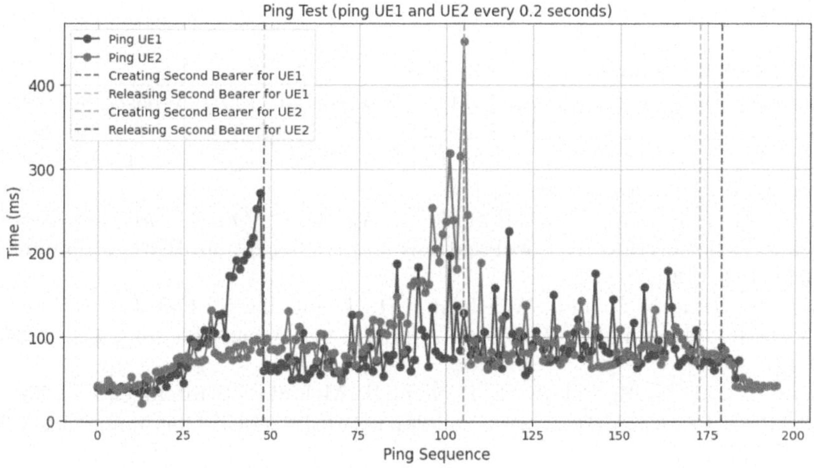

Fig. 5. Evolution of RTT, in ms, for UE 1 (blue line) and UE 2 (red line) when both trigger xDRBM to create a second DRB for each (dashed green lines). (Color figure online)

6 Conclusion

We proposed a private 5G SA network that enables the creation of O-RAN slices by dynamically managing DRB configurations via a novel xApp, xDRBM. xDRBM collects RAN metrics to configure new DRBs during network congestion and releases them when congestion disappears. Our experimental validation demonstrates the effectiveness of xDRBM in triggering RAN reconfigurations, successfully establishing and releasing DRBs as needed. The results show that our solution is able to manage multiple traffic flows, prioritizing latency-sensitive applications during high traffic demand.

For future work, we plan to evolve the solution for handling multiple QoS flows, enabling the Service Data Adaptation Protocol (SDAP) layer to map these flows to DRBs rather than IP streams, as currently supported by OAI. Additionally, incorporating more 5QI parameters will allow for a broader evaluation and potentially improve communications performance.

Acknowledgments. This work is co-financed by Component 5 - Capitalization and Business Innovation, integrated in the Resilience Dimension of the Recovery and Resilience Plan within the scope of the Recovery and Resilience Mechanism (MRR) of the European Union (EU), framed in the Next Generation EU, for the period 2021–2026, within project Produtech-R3, with reference 60.

References

1. O-RAN Alliance. https://www.o-ran.org/
2. García-Morales, J., Lucas-Estañ, M.C., Gozalvez, J.: Latency-based 5G RAN slicing descriptor to support deterministic industry 4.0 applications. In: 2019 24th IEEE International Conference on Emerging Technologies and Factory Automation (ETFA), pp. 1359–1362 (2019)
3. Ferrus, R., Sallent, O., Perez-Romero, J., Agusti, R.: On 5G radio access network slicing: radio interface protocol features and configuration. IEEE Commun. Mag. **56**(5), 184–192 (2018)
4. Chen, Y., Hou, Y.T., Lou, W., Reed, J.H., Kompella, S.: O-M3: real-time multi-cell MIMO scheduling in 5G O-RAN. IEEE J. Sel. Areas Commun. **42**(2), 339–355 (2024)
5. Bonati, L., D'Oro, S., Polese, M., Basagni, S., Melodia, T.: Intelligence and learning in O-RAN for data-driven nextg cellular networks. IEEE Commun. Mag. **59**(10), 21–27 (2021)
6. Polese, M., Bonati, L., D'Oro, S., Basagni, S., Melodia, T.: Colo-ran: developing machine learning-based xapps for open ran closed-loop control on programmable experimental platforms. IEEE Trans. Mob. Comput. **22**(10), 5787–5800 (2023)
7. McManus, M., et al.: Demo abstract: unionlabs: AWS-based remote access and sharing of nextg and IoT testbeds. In: Proceedings of the IEEE International Conference on Computer Communications (INFOCOM), Vancouver, Canada (2024)
8. Schmidt, R.: 2023-06 O-RAN F2F Osaka. https://wiki.o-ran-sc.org/display/EV/2023-06+O-RAN+F2F+Osaka
9. FlexRIC. https://gitlab.eurecom.fr/mosaic5g/flexric/-/wikis/home
10. Kak, A., Pham, V.-Q., Thieu, H.-T., Choi, N.: ProSLICE: an open RAN-based approach to programmable RAN slicing. In: 2022 IEEE Global Communications Conference, GLOBECOM 2022, pp. 197–202 (2022)
11. Silva, P.: Dynamic data radio bearer management for O-RAN slicing in 5G standalone networks. M.Sc. thesis, Faculdade de Engenharia, Universidade do Porto, Portugal (2024)

CyReal: A Unified Framework for Continuous Evaluation of Simulations, Emulations, and Real Systems

Toshiyuki Miyachi[1,2](✉), Yota Ishida[1], Shinichi Miyakawa[1,2], Masahiro Takagi[1], Satoshi Uda[1,2], Shinsuke Miwa[1,2], Fumihide Kojima[1], Hiroaki Harai[1,2], Yasuo Tan[1,2], and Yoichi Shinoda[1,2]

[1] National Institute of Information and Communications Technology, Tokyo, Japan
miyachi@nict.go.jp

[2] Japan Advanced Institute of Science and Technology, Ishikawa, Japan

Abstract. The development of new network services often involves separate evaluation and implementation stages, leading to inconsistencies and delays. To address these challenges, we propose CyReal, a continuous development framework that integrates simulations, emulations, and real systems into a cohesive testbed environment. CyReal facilitates seamless transitions between different levels of abstraction, enabling comprehensive and consistent evaluation throughout the network lifecycle.

To implement CyReal, we developed TENTOU, a middleware system that manages this integrated environment, ensuring efficient resource allocation, unified experiment execution, and seamless integration of user-defined facilities. We validated TENTOU through a wireless emulation case study in a smart office, demonstrating its ability to improve accuracy, reduce costs, and streamline the development process.

Validation confirmed that CyReal effectively integrates simulations, emulations, and real systems into a cohesive evaluation environment, offering greater flexibility and depth of analysis than traditional methods. Our validation also indicates that further study is needed to enhance time synchronization and develop more generalized data exchange mechanisms, which are essential for maximizing the effectiveness of CyReal in complex, real-world applications.

Keywords: Network testbed · Simulation · Emulation · Evaluation · Digital Twin · CyReal · TENTOU

1 Introduction

The rapid evolution of network technologies, necessitates advanced testing and evaluation environments. Traditional approaches often rely on distinct methodologies across different stages of development, from initial conceptualization using simulations to real-world deployment. This fragmented process leads to

A. A. Juan et al. (Eds.): SIMUtools 2024, LNICST 603, pp. 367–382, 2025.
https://doi.org/10.1007/978-3-031-87345-4_24

inconsistencies in evaluation results, complicating the identification of issues and delaying the development cycle.

Digital twin frameworks have emerged as a powerful tool for simulating and analyzing network systems. However, these frameworks typically operate solely in the simulation domain, limiting their applicability to theoretical analysis without seamless integration into real-world environments. Similarly, network testbeds and emulators, such as GENI [5] and Mininet [10], provide robust platforms for specific stages of testing but do not offer a unified environment that bridges simulation, emulation, and real systems.

To address these challenges, we introduce CyReal, an innovative framework designed to provide a continuous abstraction environment that integrates simulations, emulations, and real systems into a cohesive testbed. CyReal enables the seamless transition between different levels of abstraction, allowing for consistent and comprehensive evaluation throughout the entire development lifecycle. By facilitating the integration of digital twins with real systems, CyReal offers a versatile and scalable solution for network testing, capable of adapting to the evolving demands of modern network technologies.

In this paper, we present the CyReal concept and TENTOU: the middleware for building CyReal environment, highlighting its unique contributions to network testing. We demonstrate the practical application of CyReal through a case study in wireless network emulation, showcasing its potential to improve accuracy, reduce costs, and streamline the development process from simulation to real-world deployment.

2 Concept of CyReal

This section outlines the CyReal framework, which integrates real systems, simulators, and emulators into a continuous evaluation environment. CyReal provides a versatile and scalable platform that enables seamless transitions between different levels of abstraction, supporting ongoing evaluation throughout the network development lifecycle.

2.1 Description of Real System, Simulator, and Emulator

In this section, we first clarify the definitions of real system, simulator and emulator as addressed in this paper.

Real System. In the context of CyReal, a real system refers to actual hardware or software components that are operational in real-world environments. These systems function with real-time performance and interact with other systems through well-defined protocols and APIs. The primary advantage of using real systems is the ability to observe true behavior and performance under realistic conditions. However, setting up and managing real systems can be resource-intensive and complex, particularly in large-scale network environments.

Simulator. A simulator in CyReal is a software tool that models network behavior and physical phenomena using mathematical representations. Simulators are invaluable for early-stage development and conceptual validation, as they often allow researchers to explore various scenarios and configurations without the need for powerful physical resources. However, simulators operate in a highly abstracted environment, which can sometimes lead to discrepancies between simulated results and real-world performance or behaviors.

Emulator. Emulators bridge the gap between simulators and real systems by mimicking the behavior of a real system or its components while interacting with other systems using real-world interfaces. Emulators provide a more realistic testing environment than pure simulations but are more flexible and less resource-intensive than real systems.

2.2 Concept of CyReal Continuous Evaluation Environment

CyReal is designed as a continuous evaluation environment that allows for seamless transitions between different levels of abstraction. This environment supports the entire lifecycle of network development, from initial simulations to real-world operations. The framework is organized into three primary configurations: as a simulator, as a testbed, and as an operational system. The conceptual overview of CyReal is shown in Fig. 1.

The provided diagram illustrates the conceptual framework of CyReal, demonstrating its operation across three distinct modes: as a Simulator, as a Testbed, and as an Operational Environment.

CyReal as a Simulator. On the left side of the diagram, CyReal is depicted in its simulation mode, where multiple simulators collaborate to create a comprehensive simulation environment. This mode is primarily used for early-stage development, allowing researchers to test and validate algorithms in a controlled, abstracted environment. The diagram shows how simulators are interconnected through a collaboration platform, enabling the integration of various simulation modules to reproduce complex network behaviors.

CyReal as a Testbed. In the middle of the diagram, CyReal is shown in its testbed configuration, where simulators, emulators, and real systems are combined. This mode allows for more detailed and realistic testing by introducing emulated components that mimic real system behavior. The diagram highlights the flexible transition between different levels of abstraction, enabling researchers to gradually introduce real-world elements into the simulation, facilitating a more accurate evaluation of network algorithms and systems.

CyReal as an Operational Environment. On the right side, CyReal is depicted in its most concrete form, where the environment consists entirely of real systems. This mode represents the final stage of network development, where

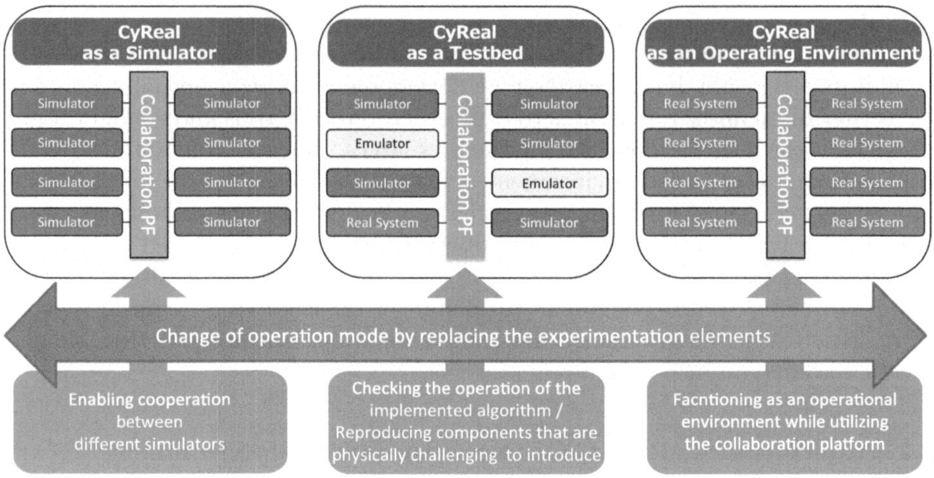

Fig. 1. Conceptual Overview of CyReal Evaluation Environment. The environment on the left side operates as a simulator, the middle section as a testbed, and the right side as a real system.

all elements operate as they would in a live deployment. The diagram illustrates how CyReal evolves from a purely simulated environment to a fully operational system, ensuring that the transition from development to deployment is smooth and well-tested.

The Collaboration Platform (PF) serves as the backbone for integrating and managing the interactions between simulators, emulators, and real systems. It ensures that data flows seamlessly across different modes, maintaining consistency and coherence throughout the development process.

The leftmost CyReal environment as a simulator is a digital twin [6] of the rightmost CyReal environment as a real system. Digital twins built in cyberspace are entirely based on simulators and have traditionally been used for simulating physical phenomena. We apply and extend this idea to the verification of ICT systems, proposing CyReal as an environment where verification can be performed while changing the abstraction level of each verification element. CyReal continuously connects the digital twin and the real environment with a gradual change in the level of abstraction.

From an evaluation point of view, some network simulators like ns-3 [3] allow the capture of real-world program code. However, it is necessary to create a program in a form linked with an existing program, and the program is generated as a single binary. Since our purpose is to sparsely connect programs with different functions and replace them with elements at different abstraction levels that have the same function, the original purpose is different.

As examples of experiments conducted using CyReal, there are wireless emulation scenarios [9] and simulations of disaster situations [7,8].

3 Related Works

CyReal is a conceptual framework that envisions a continuous evaluation environment where simulators, emulators, and real systems function as distinct yet interconnected components. Unlike traditional frameworks that segregate these elements into separate layers, CyReal promotes their integration and interaction, enabling a more flexible and holistic approach to network testing. This section reviews related works and discusses how they can be integrated within the CyReal environment.

Digital Twin Frameworks. Digital twins create detailed simulations of both physical and cyber-physical systems, allowing for comprehensive modeling and analysis of system behaviors. These frameworks are not limited to physical systems; they also encompass virtual and computational elements, making them versatile tools for a wide range of applications. However, digital twins often operate in isolation from real systems and emulators, which can limit their ability to interact with live components in real-time scenarios. Within the CyReal framework, digital twins are integrated as independent simulation components that actively interact with emulators and real systems. This integration enables a dynamic exchange between the simulated environment and real-world data, allowing the digital twin to both influence and be influenced by real-time operations, thereby enhancing the fidelity and relevance of the simulation outcomes.

ns-3 Network Simulator. ns-3 is a discrete-event network simulator widely used for modeling network protocols. It excels at creating controlled, reproducible simulation environments but operates independently of emulators and real systems. In CyReal, ns-3 can act as an autonomous simulation component that exchanges data with emulators and real systems, facilitating continuous testing and validation as the system evolves from simulation to real-world deployment.

OMNeT++. OMNeT++ [13] is a modular simulation framework designed for network modeling. It operates effectively as a simulation tool but traditionally remains isolated from real-world systems. In CyReal, OMNeT++ can function as a discrete simulation component that communicates with emulators and real systems. This integration enables OMNeT++ models to be continuously updated and validated against real-world data, ensuring that simulation results remain relevant throughout the development lifecycle.

Mininet. Mininet is a network emulator that allows users to create and test virtual networks on a single machine. It is particularly valuable for rapidly prototyping and testing software-defined networks (SDNs) by simulating a full network topology with hosts, switches, and controllers. Mininet provides a controlled environment where network behaviors can be tested and observed in real-time, making it an excellent tool for early-stage development and educational purposes. However, while Mininet is effective for emulation on a small scale, it operates independently from real systems and lacks the ability to integrate seamlessly with larger, more complex environments that include real-world network elements and advanced simulations.

PlanetLab. PlanetLab [12] is a global research network that provides a platform for deploying and testing distributed systems and network applications at scale. It allows researchers to conduct experiments on a geographically distributed set of nodes, offering real-world insights that are difficult to achieve with isolated simulation environments. While PlanetLab is highly effective for large-scale distributed experiments, it traditionally functions independently of other testing environments like simulators or emulators. In CyReal, PlanetLab could be integrated as a real system component, interacting with simulators and emulators to create a more comprehensive and continuous evaluation environment.

GENI Testbed. GENI [5] is a large-scale infrastructure that supports network and distributed systems research, offering both virtual and physical resources. GENI typically functions independently as a testbed platform. Within the CyReal framework, GENI can be incorporated as an emulation component that interacts with other simulators and real systems. This interaction allows GENI's experimental results to be continuously refined and validated against real-world conditions, enhancing the robustness of network testing.

FABRIC Testbed. FABRIC [1] is a next-generation research platform that provides programmable networking, compute, and storage resources for advanced network experiments. Building on GENI's foundation, FABRIC offers enhanced flexibility and programmability, enabling complex network topologies and diverse computational integrations. However, unlike CyReal, which integrates simulations, emulations, and real systems into a continuous evaluation environment, FABRIC operates as an independent platform focused on isolated, sophisticated experiments. CyReal's strength lies in its ability to dynamically combine and interact with different components, offering a more flexible and comprehensive approach to network testing across the entire development lifecycle.

StarBED Testbed. StarBED [11] provides a large-scale environment for network emulation, simulating complex network topologies using physical and virtual nodes. Traditionally, StarBED operates as an isolated emulation platform. However, in CyReal, StarBED can serve as a separate emulation component that interacts with simulators and real systems. This setup allows for a more dynamic evaluation process, where emulation results can be directly influenced by real-world data and adjusted in real-time.

Hardware-in-the-Loop (HIL) Simulation. HIL integrates real hardware with simulation models, making it a specialized tool for validating control systems. While HIL typically functions as an independent validation tool, within the CyReal framework, it can be utilized as a real system component. HIL interacts with simulators and emulators, providing real-world feedback that helps refine and validate simulation models, ensuring that they accurately represent actual system behavior.

CyReal is a conceptual framework that envisions simulators, emulators, and real systems as distinct yet interacting components within a continuous evaluation environment. This approach enhances the utility of existing tools by

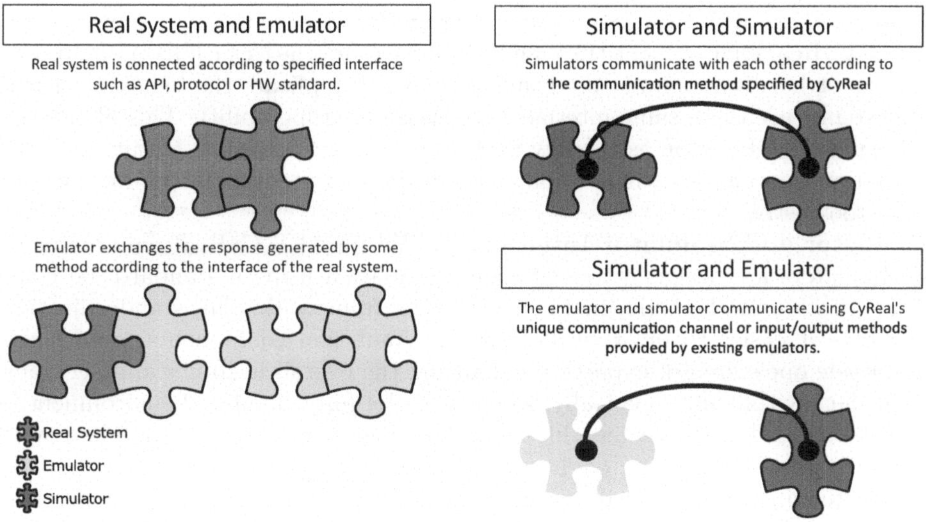

Fig. 2. Concept of how experimental elements are connected in the CyReal environment. The simulator does not directly interface with the real system; instead, it communicates with emulators through a specialized channel. The emulator, in turn, interfaces with the real system using standard interfaces.

enabling them to operate in concert, allowing for dynamic adjustments and continuous validation across the network development lifecycle. By integrating these elements within the CyReal environment, researchers can achieve a more comprehensive and consistent approach to network testing, from initial simulation to real-world deployment.

4 Fundamental Techniques for Building the CyReal Continuous Evaluation Environment

This section outlines the core concepts and techniques for realizing the CyReal environment, focusing on how real systems, simulators, and emulators connect and interact to support continuous evaluation throughout the network development lifecycle.

4.1 Integration of Real Systems, Simulators, and Emulators

The CyReal environment is designed to connect real systems, simulators, and emulators in a cohesive and flexible manner. Unlike traditional environments where these components operate independently or within isolated layers, CyReal allows them to interact as distinct but interconnected elements. This approach ensures that each component can contribute to a continuous and iterative evaluation process.

Real System and Emulator Interaction. Real systems are connected to the CyReal environment through well-defined interfaces such as APIs, protocols, or hardware standards. Emulators, which replicate the behavior of real systems, use these same interfaces to ensure interoperability. This allows the emulator to function as a proxy for the real system, enabling testing and validation in scenarios where deploying a full real system might be impractical or too costly.

Simulator and Simulator Interaction. Within the CyReal environment, simulators are designed to exchange information using a standardized communication method specified by the CyReal framework. This standardization makes it easier to incorporate existing simulation components, even those outside one's area of expertise, enhancing the overall usability and accuracy of the environment. Typically, when part of a fully simulated environment is implemented in the real world, the API changes can require a complete overhaul of the surrounding environment. However, CyReal is designed to allow selective integration, enabling changes to only specific parts of the environment without disrupting the entire system. This flexibility ensures that simulations remain coordinated and their outputs compatible, contributing to a more effective and cohesive evaluation process.

Simulator and Emulator Interaction. The APIs of simulators and emulators differ, requiring data format conversion for seamless communication. As previously mentioned, designing and implementing a generalized communication channel would expand CyReal's capabilities, enabling more versatile and integrated interactions between simulators and emulators.

Figure 2 illustrates the concept of how these experimental elements are connected within the CyReal environment.

4.2 Ensuring Real-Time Operation and Time Synchronization

Time management is a critical factor when integrating real systems, simulators, and emulators. Real systems inherently operate in real-time, while simulators and emulators may not. This discrepancy can lead to challenges in ensuring that all components operate synchronously, particularly when real-time performance is required.

Real-Time Considerations. When real systems are part of the evaluation environment, it is essential that simulators and emulators can produce outputs at speeds that match real-time requirements. This may involve optimizing the computational processes within simulators or precomputing certain elements to reduce the time needed during live interactions. For network systems, maintaining real-time performance is crucial, as delays can lead to inaccurate results or system instability.

Time Synchronization. In scenarios where strict time synchronization is necessary, such as in the evaluation of network performance metrics, CyReal implements synchronization techniques that ensure the progress of time is

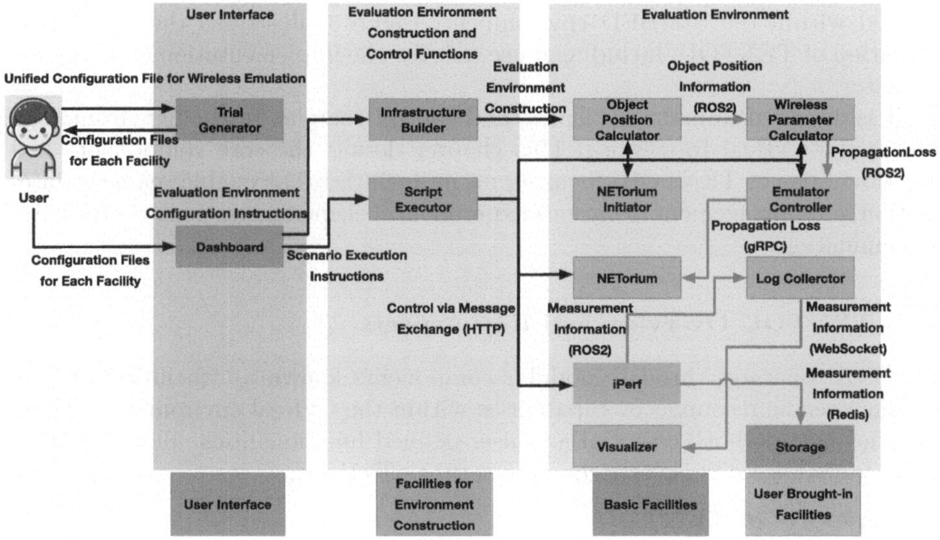

Fig. 3. Architecture of Wireless Emulation Using TENTOU. The diagram illustrates the integration of TENTOU facilities in managing and executing a wireless emulation environment.

unified across all components. This might involve aligning the clocks of simulators and emulators with the real system or employing methods to simulate time in a way that is consistent with real-world operations.

Handling Asynchronous Operations. In some cases, simulators or emulators may operate asynchronously, processing data at different rates. CyReal may address this by allowing for asynchronous communication channels, where the progress of time in one component does not need to directly match that of another. This approach could be particularly useful in scenarios where high computational complexity in simulations might otherwise slow down real-time operations. In such cases, precomputed data or approximation methods could be used to maintain the overall flow of the evaluation process.

By implementing these techniques, CyReal should be able to ensure that the integration of real systems, simulators, and emulators is not only feasible but also effective in maintaining the continuity and accuracy of the evaluation process across different stages of network development.

5 TENTOU: Middleware for Managing CyReal Environments and The Use Case for Building Wireless Emulator

TENTOU, which stands for Toolkits for Empowering Network Testbed Operation and Utilization, is a middleware solution that we have developed and implemented within the StarBED environment. Figure 3 illustrates the conceptual operation of TENTOU, including a use case for the implementation of a wireless emulator.

It is designed to manage, deploy, and control complex testbed environments within the CyReal framework. This chapter details the core components and functionalities of TENTOU, focusing on its facilities that enable seamless integration and management of various experimental elements, particularly for wireless emulation.

5.1 TENTOU Overview and Key Aspects

TENTOU operates through modular components known as "facilities", representing specific resources or capabilities within the CyReal environment. These facilities include both essential and user-defined functionalities, allowing TENTOU to manage diverse experimental setups effectively.

Key Aspects of TENTOU

1. **Modularity.** Facilities in TENTOU are highly modular, allowing easy addition, removal, or reconfiguration without disrupting the overall environment. This flexibility is crucial for accommodating the dynamic needs of large-scale testbeds.
2. **Consistent Environment Construction and Scenario Execution.** TENTOU ensures the consistent construction of the testbed environment and the seamless execution of scenarios, integrating various components into a unified framework that supports complex experiments.
3. **API Provisioning at Various Levels.** TENTOU provides APIs at multiple levels, allowing users to interact with the environment in a way that best suits their experimental needs. These APIs facilitate fine-grained control over the environment, from high-level orchestration to low-level configuration.

5.2 Basic Facilities of TENTOU

TENTOU provides several core facilities that are integral to the operation and management of the CyReal environment. These basic facilities form the foundation of TENTOU's functionality, enabling comprehensive control over the testbed environment.

Infrastructure Builder (I.B.). The Infrastructure Builder is responsible for setting up the physical and virtual infrastructure of the testbed. It configures physical nodes, virtual machines, and network devices according to the specifications of the experiment, ensuring that all components are properly initialized and interconnected. The IB automates tasks such as OS and application installation and network topology setup, significantly reducing the need for manual intervention.

Script Executor (S.E.). The Script Executor manages the execution of experimental scenarios by controlling the sequence of operations across different facilities. It uses predefined scripts to trigger actions, adjust parameters, and manage the experiment's flow, ensuring that scenarios progress as planned and adapt to real-time changes.

Dashboard. The Dashboard is a user interface that provides an overview of the entire testbed environment. It allows users to monitor and control experiments in real-time, offering insights into the status of various facilities and the overall progress of scenarios. The Dashboard also serves as a centralized point for managing experiments, adjusting configurations, and visualizing results. The dashboard is implemented as a service running on a bastion host, rather than as a facility.

Other Basic Functions. In addition to the core facilities, TENTOU includes integrated Storage and Database facilities as examples of the many generic facilities available. These are used for storing experimental data, logs, and configuration files, ensuring that all necessary information is preserved for analysis and future reference. The Database facility also supports the retrieval and management of data, facilitating complex queries and data-driven decision-making during experiments.

TENTOU's architecture allows for the inclusion of other generic facilities, providing users with a wide range of tools to support various aspects of their experiments.

5.3 User-Defined Facilities

TENTOU also supports the integration of user-defined facilities, which can be added to complement the basic ones provided by the system. These facilities allow users to introduce custom tools, specialized simulators, or other unique components that are tailored to their specific experimental needs. User-defined facilities are not limited to any single application and can be utilized across a wide range of environments managed by TENTOU, enhancing the flexibility and extensibility of the CyReal framework. TENTOU ensures that these additional facilities are seamlessly integrated into the environment, functioning alongside basic facilities like the Infrastructure Builder and Script Executor to create a cohesive testbed.

6 Case Study: Wireless Emulation in a Smart Office Environment

To validate the operation of TENTOU, we conducted a wireless emulation in a smart office environment. This case study focuses on evaluating network performance and behavior under realistic conditions, demonstrating TENTOU's capabilities in managing complex experimental setups.

6.1 Environment Overview

The smart office environment used in this case study includes 58 wireless devices operating on the IEEE 802.11g standard. These devices consist of access points (APs) and stations (STAs), with some STAs are mounted on mobile objects that move throughout the office. The environment is modeled using a map provided in Drawing Exchange Format (DXF), which is imported into TENTOU to set up the simulation.

6.2 Wireless Emulation Setup

The wireless emulation is carried out using NETorium [4], with iPerf [2] serving as the traffic generator. By implementing iPerf as a facility within TENTOU, the system is capable of controlling any application that runs on Linux where NETorium is operational. The traffic generation is precisely timed and managed by TENTOU's scenario control feature, ensuring that the flow of traffic is synchronized with the movement of devices and changes in the environment.

A simplified simulation model is initially used to calculate path loss between wireless devices. However, TENTOU allows for the model to be switched to a more detailed one if higher simulation accuracy is required. The path loss calculations are typically performed in a full-mesh configuration, meaning every device's connection to every other device is considered. To reduce computational load, the simulation can be segmented by channels, and the calculations may focus solely on AP-STA pairs.

6.3 Wireless Emulation with TENTOU

TENTOU's modular facilities are instrumental in implementing wireless emulation environments.

NETorium is a high-fidelity wireless network emulator designed to replicate the behavior of wireless communication systems within a controlled environment. It operates within the Linux Kernel, where it encapsulates wireless frames and transmits them over an Ethernet network. NETorium simulates wireless conditions such as signal propagation loss, interference, and frame collisions by applying these parameters to the emulation. Additionally, by applying simulation results directly on edge nodes where NETorium operates, it enhances scalability, allowing researchers to test and validate wireless technologies without the need for actual radio frequency transmissions. This makes NETorium particularly useful for large-scale and complex network evaluations.

Through the integration of these facilities, TENTOU enables the creation of realistic wireless networks that simulate real-world conditions, including signal interference, propagation loss, and dynamic network topology changes.

To implement wireless emulation, we developed the following user-defined facilities:

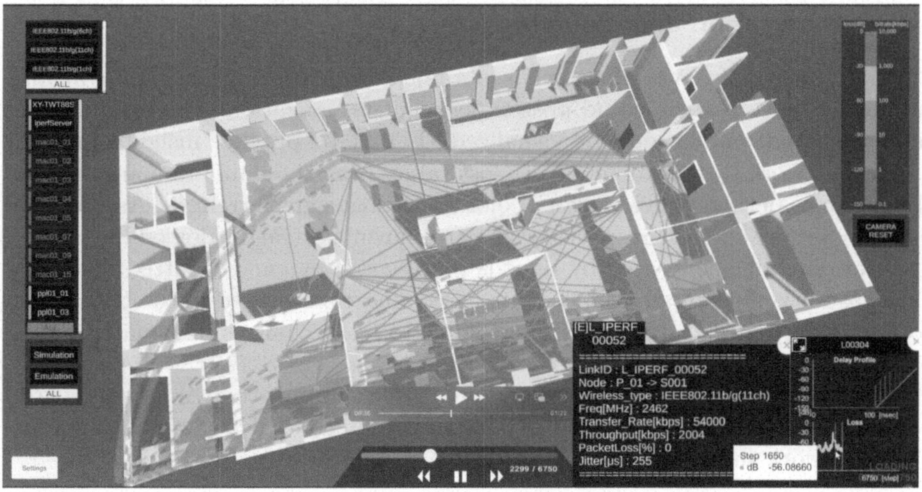

Fig. 4. An example of visualizing the radio wave conditions in a smart office. It shows the physical layout of the space, the path loss values calculated through simulation based on that layout, and the results of the emulation execution.

Object Position Calculator. Calculates wireless node positions at each experimental step, ensuring accurate simulation of movement and distance effects.

Wireless Parameter Calculator. Computes path loss by considering node positions and environmental data. Users can switch between simpler models for faster calculations or more complex models for higher accuracy, depending on the experiment's needs.

NETorium Initiator. Configures each NETorium node with its specific settings, tailoring them to their roles in the emulation.

Wireless Emulator Controller. Dynamically sends configuration updates to each NETorium node during the experiment, ensuring that settings are adjusted in real-time to maintain realistic conditions.

NETorium. Deployed as embedded code in the virtual machine's disk image, rather than as a separate facility.

iPerf and Log Collection. Manages network traffic generation and collects performance data for comprehensive analysis.

While additional user-defined facilities may require separate configuration files, we developed the Trial Generator (T.G.) to unify these settings. T.G. simplifies the configuration process by generating consistent, integrated files from a single input, ensuring that all basic and additional facilities are correctly configured for the experiment. This is particularly important in complex scenarios involving multiple parameters across different facilities.

6.4 Visualization and Analysis

The information for visualization is obtained from the log collection facility, supporting both real-time and post-experiment visualization. The results of the simulation and emulation are visualized (Fig. 4) to provide insights into the wireless network's performance. Path loss values from the simulation are depicted as solid lines between devices, with color indicating signal strength. Associations between STAs and their respective APs are shown as straight dotted lines, while application traffic generated by iPerf is represented by curved dotted lines. The office layout is illustrated with the internet connection located in the bottom left corner. Time-series graphs are also available to track changes in signal strength, bandwidth, and other parameters over time.

These visualizations provide a comprehensive view of the wireless network's performance within the smart office, enabling detailed analysis and optimization of the network setup.

6.5 Key Outcomes

This case study demonstrated the effectiveness of the TENTOU framework in managing the entire process from resource allocation to experiment execution, ensuring consistent and reliable results. It also highlighted TENTOU's flexibility in integrating user-defined facilities, such as the Object Position Calculator, and maintaining unified control, which allowed for smooth operation and accurate simulation.

7 Conclusion

In this paper, we introduced the CyReal concept, a framework that seamlessly integrates simulations, emulations, and real systems into a continuous evaluation environment. To support the implementation of the CyReal Evaluation Environment, we developed TENTOU, a middleware system designed to manage and control the various components involved. Through a case study of wireless emulation in a smart office environment, we validated TENTOU's functionality as a control system, demonstrating its capability to handle resource allocation, experiment execution, and the integration of user-defined facilities within a unified control framework.

While our work has confirmed the effectiveness of TENTOU in managing the CyReal environment, several areas for future improvement have been identified. A critical area is the development of a more generalized and robust mechanism for information exchange between simulators, emulators, and real systems. Enhancing this capability will ensure better interoperability and data consistency across different components.

In the current wireless emulation example, step instructions were sent from a user-defined facility. However, it is crucial to develop multiple types of facilities for general time synchronization, allowing users to select the most appropriate option for their specific needs. This will be essential for ensuring that all nodes operate in full synchronization, particularly in complex and time-sensitive network scenarios.

In conclusion, CyReal, supported by TENTOU, represents a significant advancement in the continuous evaluation of network systems. However, ongoing research and development are necessary to further enhance the system's interoperability, synchronization accuracy, and overall robustness in managing integrated network environments.

Acknowledgement. Part of this research has been conducted under the contract "R&D for the advancement of radio wave simulation system technology in virtual space" (JPJ000254) made with the Ministry of Internal Affairs and Communications of Japan.

References

1. FABRIC: A National Research Infrastructure. https://fabric-testbed.net. Accessed 16 Aug 2024
2. iPerf - The ultimate speed test tool for TCP, UDP and SCTP. https://iperf.fr/. Accessed 22 Aug 2024
3. ns-3 Network Simulator. https://www.nsnam.org. Accessed 16 Aug 2024
4. Akashi, K., Inoue, T., Yasuda, S., Takano, Y., Shinoda, Y.: Netorium: high-fidelity scalable wireless network emulator. In: 12th Asian Internet Engineering Conference (AINTEC), pp. 25–32 (2016)
5. Berman, M., et al.: Geni: a federated testbed for innovative network experiments. Comput. Netw. **61**, 5–23 (2014). https://doi.org/10.1016/j.bjp.2013.12.037. Special issue on Future Internet Testbeds - Part I
6. Fuller, A., Fan, Z., Day, C., Barlow, C.: Digital twin: enabling technologies, challenges and open research. IEEE Access **8**, 108952–108971 (2020). https://doi.org/10.1109/ACCESS.2020.2998358
7. Hiroi, K., Kohiga, A., Shinoda, Y.: Performance evaluation of a cyreal sensor system. Int. J. Inform. Soc. (IJIS) **14**(2), 75–84 (2022)
8. Hiroi, K., Nakagawa, S., Takahashi, R., Kohiga, A., Fukaya, S., Shinoda, Y.: Demo: flood damage cyrealization with an orchestrator framework. In: The 22nd International Conference on Pervasive Computing and Communications (PerCom 2024) [Demo Session], pp. 1–4 (2024)
9. Kojima, F., Miyachi, T., Matsumura, T., Sawada, H., Harai, H., Harada, H.: A large-scale wireless emulation environment with interaction between physical and virtual radio nodes for beyond 5g systems. In: IEEE 33rd Annual International Symposium on Personal, Indoor and Mobile Radio Communications (PIMRC), pp. 42–47 (2022)
10. Lantz, B., Heller, B., McKeown, N.: A network in a laptop: rapid prototyping for software-defined networks. In: Proceedings of the 9th ACM SIGCOMM Workshop on Hot Topics in Networks, pp. 1–6 (2010). https://doi.org/10.1145/1868447.186846
11. Miyachi, T., Nakagawa, T., Chinen, K.I., Miwa, S., Shinoda, Y.: Starbed and springos architectures and their performance. In: 7th International ICST Conference on Testbeds and Research Infrastructures for the Development of Networks and Communities (TridentCom) (2011)

12. Peterson, L., Anderson, T., Culler, D., Roscoe, T.: A blueprint for introducing disruptive technology into the Internet. In: HotNets-I 2002 (2002)
13. Varga, A., Hornig, R.: An overview of the OMNeT++ simulation environment. In: Proceedings of the 1st International Conference on Simulation Tools and Techniques for Communications, Networks and Systems & Workshops (SIMUTools 2008) (2008)

JASPER: An Agent-Based Simulation Tool for Test and Evaluation of Jammer-Angle Allocation Algorithms

Ahmet Burak Baraklı[1,3](✉), Okan Topçu[2], and Halit Oğuztüzün[1]

[1] Middle East Technical University, Ankara, Türkiye
ahmet.barakli@metu.edu.tr
[2] Middle East Technical University, Northern Cyprus Campus, 99738 Kalkanlı, Güzelyurt, Mersin 10, Türkiye
[3] Aselsan Inc., Ankara, Türkiye

Abstract. As a result of the increasing use of unmanned aerial vehicles in modern warfare, advanced anti-drone systems have been developed, making it more important to analyze threat assessment and jammer-angle allocation algorithms. We introduce JASPER, an agent-based simulation tool that allows testing and evaluating these algorithms in customizable environments. JASPER's modular design allows users to integrate various algorithms, define their test cases, and measure key performance indicators related to their analysis. This paper also includes a case study demonstrating how an algorithm can be evaluated using JASPER. Scaling and sensitivity analyses demonstrate JASPER's robustness in handling a large number of entities and provide insights into algorithm performance under varying conditions.

Keywords: Simulation-based test and evaluation · Agent-based simulation · Jammer allocation algorithms · Threat evaluation and weapon allocation · Anti-drone systems

1 Introduction

With the development of technology in today's world, unmanned aerial vehicles (UAVs) are extensively used as weaponry, which has triggered the development of countermeasures. Anti-drone systems play an important role in protecting critical areas and facilities. These systems provide functions such as detecting, tracking, identifying, interfering, and assessing threats specifically against UAVs, usually in addition to traditional air defense systems [24,27].

Detection and tracking of UAVs is accomplished through various sensors such as radars and camera systems. The detection phase is the primary step to ensure the effectiveness of anti-drone systems because preventive measures cannot be taken against undetected UAVs. Then detected trace is identified and a threat importance is assigned. As a result of this assignment, if it is deemed that the

A. A. Juan et al. (Eds.): SIMUtools 2024, LNICST 603, pp. 383–396, 2025.
https://doi.org/10.1007/978-3-031-87345-4_25

trace is dangerous and countermeasure is required, then the interfering starts. The ways to interfere with UAVs can be divided into two: hard kill and soft kill. Hard kill methods, such as laser weapons or missile systems, aim to physically destroy UAVs. In contrast, soft kill methods focus on neutralizing UAV activities without physical destruction, using techniques like signal jamming and frequency jamming. Jammers, a popular soft kill approach, disrupt the control of UAVs by interfering with their communication signals, effectively rendering them inoperable. Omni-directional jammers are commonly used for this purpose; however, in scenarios where surrounding signals (e.g., those used for daily communication) must not be disrupted, directional jammers that target specific angles are preferred [28]. Anti-drone systems can operate either under human supervision or autonomously. In autonomous mode, algorithms analyze and track information from sensors, calculate threat priorities, and execute necessary actions through jammers. This decision-making process needs to be completed rapidly because the acceptable response time against incoming threats is generally restricted to a few seconds [10,17].

Given the increasing complexity and speed of UAV threats, developing effective algorithms for threat evaluation and weapon allocation is crucial. Various algorithms have been proposed, each with its strengths and weaknesses in terms of prioritization, computational efficiency, and adaptability to different types of threats and environments. To determine the most effective algorithms and tune their parameters, comprehensive testing under a wide range of scenarios is essential. However, real-world testing of these algorithms is costly and hard to reproduce. Thus, a simulation environment that can test and evaluate jammer-angle allocation algorithms to simulate different test scenarios and obtain the necessary metrics is needed. In response to this need, this study proposes a simulation tool named JASPER (Jammer Allocation Simulation Platform for Evaluation and Reporting). JASPER is a modular, agent-based environment for testing and evaluating the performance of various jammer-angle allocation algorithms, and it is based on the MASON framework [20]. It offers a customizable simulation for analysts and planners to analyze different key performance indicators (KPIs) and refine algorithmic strategies.

The primary contribution of JASPER is its modularity and adaptability, which let users customize the simulation environment to fit their unique requirements and scenarios. Through the integration of multiple algorithms, test cases, and reporting modules, JASPER offers an adaptable environment for the examination and comparison of different jammer-angle allocation techniques. This adaptability is especially useful for research and development contexts, where it allows for the quick prototyping, testing, and optimization of new algorithms against a variety of UAV threat scenarios. Furthermore, JASPER's capability to integrate different reporter modules that record various KPIs, like coverage percentages, algorithm run times, and angle adjustments, enables the evaluation of various results, supporting analysts and planners in determining the advantages and disadvantages of each strategy.

2 Related Work

2.1 Simulation for Test and Evaluation

Simulation is an important tool for testing and evaluating systems, particularly in fields like defense, where physical testing can be expensive and risky. By developing computer models that replicate various conditions, threats, and scenarios, simulations help identify vulnerabilities and optimize system performance in a safe, controlled, and cost-effective environment [4,12]. There are three commonly used simulation strategies: activity scanning, process interaction, and event scheduling [11]. However, object-oriented simulation provides a more comprehensive approach by modeling entities (such as algorithms, people, or machines) as objects with unique characteristics and behaviors, facilitating understanding and development of the model [26].

The success of a simulation depends on several key factors, including realism, accuracy, consistency, adaptability, and efficiency [4]. Simulations allow analysts and planners to study the impact of these algorithms under various scenarios [12]. As a result, simulations are applied in diverse areas such as autonomous robots [25], wireless communication [9], cooperative intelligent transport systems [2], and autonomous vehicles [1].

2.2 Threat Evaluation and Weapon Allocation

The Threat Evaluation and Weapon Allocation (TEWA) problem is a critical optimization challenge in defense systems, where the goal is to minimize the expected value of surviving threats by prioritizing and assigning the most suitable countermeasures [14]. TEWA is commonly studied within command and control (C2) systems, where various methods such as neural networks, genetic algorithms, simulated annealing, and taboo search are used to solve the problem [3,8]. Threat evaluation involves determining the priority of threats based on factors like proximity, capability, and intent, which help in deciding the appropriate action against each threat [16].

Weapon allocation is about efficiently assigning available defense systems to respond to threats. This problem is classified as NP-Hard, meaning that the computational time for any ideal solution increases exponentially with problem size [15,18]. In practice, meta-heuristic approaches are preferred due to the complexity of finding exact solutions. In specific applications, such as assigning jammers to angles rather than directly to targets, unique algorithms are required because a jammer can impact multiple targets within a given angle. These specialized algorithms vary based on the characteristics of the anti-drone system and potential types of attacks, necessitating a tailored approach for each scenario [5,13].

2.3 Agent Based Simulation

Agent-based simulation (ABS) provides a flexible and dynamic method for modeling complex systems by allowing individual agents to act independently and interact with one another, capturing the system's collective behavior and outcomes [7]. Unlike traditional simulations that rely on fixed rules or equations, ABS is well-suited for representing real-world uncertainties and complexities, as agents evolve over time, delay actions, and decide when to take initiative. This approach is particularly advantageous for modeling complex systems because it allows for modular structures, where agents' behavior rules can be easily modified to test different scenarios [21].

ABS has gained popularity in UAV simulations and defense applications because it facilitates coordination and cooperation among units, allowing dynamic and adaptive solutions to complex problems like TEWA [19,22]. In TEWA problems, ABS can simulate the strategic decisions of weapons and targets under varying conditions, providing a framework to develop robust defense strategies. Various frameworks such as MASON [20], JADE [6], and Repast Simphony [23] are used for ABS, each offering unique advantages depending on the specific requirements of the simulation. In this study, MASON was chosen due to its open-source nature, documentation, and level of control over simulation.

3 JASPER Modeling and Design

JASPER is a specialized simulation platform designed to evaluate jammer allocation algorithms in anti-drone systems. Built on the agent-based simulation framework MASON, JASPER facilitates detailed modeling of interactions between UAVs and jammers, providing a controlled environment for testing and refining these algorithms.

A key feature of JASPER is its modular design, which allows users to integrate different algorithms and reporting agents seamlessly. The platform focuses on executing these integrated components, enabling analysts and planners to observe the behavior of jammer algorithms under various scenarios. The performance metrics, such as coverage percentages and response times, are generated by user-defined reporter agents, which can be customized and incorporated into JASPER. This modularity ensures that the core simulation environment remains flexible and adaptable to different research requirements.

3.1 Assumptions

Modeling a real-world anti-drone system with all its complexity can be an overwhelming task. To make the problem easier to handle and focus on the crucial elements of the jammer allocation methods, the following simplifications and assumptions were made:

- **2D Aerial View Model**: To simplify the environment's representation, an aerial view model was used in the simulation's design. This method focuses on the interactions between the jammer and the UAV while simplifying the visualization and coverage tasks. The algorithms intended to be tested also work in this kind of modeling. In simplifying, certain land features, such as topography plant cover, and atmospheric conditions are also ignored.

- **Grid System**: Dealing with real-world coordinates introduces a huge overhead for computations. Thus, a continuous grid system was used to keep the locations of the jammers and tracks. This simplification makes it more straightforward to create test scenarios and to use the algorithms by enabling simple computations of angles and distances.
- **Radar Range**: It was assumed that the radar would detect only in a circular, static manner. The assumption assures consistent behavior across every scenario. Typically, geography, meteorological conditions, speed, and frame of the detected object can all affect radar detection ranges. However, these complications are reduced to allow for a more straightforward and predictable implementation by assuming a static and circular range.
- **Track Movement**: Track movements can often be varied and can be affected by a variety of factors, including its mission, environmental conditions, random deviations, and obstacles. These difficulties are avoided by assuming that tracks moved uniformly, following predetermined way-points in designated simulation time. Because of this assumption, track behavior is less variable, enabling more planned and easily replicated experiments.
- **Jammer Coverage**: Jammers' coverage areas were represented as idealized segments with set angles. This simplification concentrates on the angular optimization component of the algorithms, avoiding the complications of signal transmission and interference. Usually, jammers do not cover a set angular range; their jamming signals might spread into adjacent locations. Jammers also operate on specific frequencies, which might alter their coverage and efficacy. However, we excluded frequency information from our assumption, further simplifying the model to focus on angular optimization.

These simplifications and assumptions were determined to balance realism with computational efficiency. They ensure that the simulation stays focused on the essence of jammer allocation while remaining controllable and extensible.

3.2 Agents

Track. Track agents represent the data from radar, which can be UAV, suspected UAV, and other unimportant tracks. Suspected UAVs are threats that cannot be identified as UAVs with certainty but are classified as being closest to the UAV in terms of probability. Each track agent has several properties:

- Location: The track's current position, as represented by a Double2D object.
- Waypoints: A list of waypoints that the track will follow, each with a specific arrival time.
- Velocity: The speed and direction of the track's movement.
- Type: The type of track (UAV, suspected UAV, or other).
- Distance to Closest Jammer: Used to calculate the track's proximity to the nearest jammer.

Track agents' position changes depending on their velocity and waypoints, and it calculates the distance to the nearest jammer to determine if the track is coming closer or farther away. Tracks are constructed once for each scenario and traverse on their own.

Jammer. Jammer agents reflect the simulation's jamming devices. Jammer agents have the following attributes:

- Location: The jammer's fixed position.
- Directed At Angle: The current angle from which the jammer is directed.
- Angle Swivel From Previous Step: The angle swivel from the previous step.

Jammer agents do not change the angle on their own. Instead, they alter orientation according to the algorithm agent's assignments.

Algorithm. The algorithm agent is responsible for calculating the optimal angles for the jammers based on the current state of the tracks and jammers. At each step, the algorithm agent processes the simulation state, which includes all tracks' positions and jammer statuses. It then determines the new optimal angles for the jammers to meet its set objectives. These new angles can be assigned through the interface provided by the jammer class.

Users can give different algorithms to be used without the simulation needing to know their implementation as long as they implement the interface IAlgorithmAgent given by JASPER.

Reporter. The reporter agent is responsible for calculating and reporting KPIs at each time step of the simulation. At each step, the reporter agent accesses the simulation state to acquire data and calculates its set KPIs, they may include but are not limited to coverage percentages, angle swivels, and algorithm execution times. The reporter agent then processes these KPIs in accordance with its design.

Like the algorithm agent, users can give different reporter agents. Thus, different reporter agents can be used to calculate and report different sets of KPIs, giving control over what metrics the user monitors and how the user handles them. Depending on the user's needs, the reporter agent can write the KPIs to a file, display the KPIs on the screen, or even send the KPIs over a network for remote analysis. The simulation framework does not need to know the specifics of each reporter's actions, as long as they implement the interface IReporterAgent given by JASPER.

3.3 Integration of Components

Algorithm Agent. To integrate an algorithm agent, the user provides a file that includes the algorithm. As both MASON and JASPER are in Java, the given file should be a JAR file. Additionally, users give where JASPER can find the algorithm in this file as a path. The user's algorithm agent must implement JASPER's IAlgorithmAgent interface to ensure compatibility with the simulation environment. With this approach, it is easier to switch out and test various algorithms without having to change the JASPER code.

Reporter Agent. To integrate a reporter agent, similar to the algorithm agent, the user provides a file containing the agent itself. For the same reason as the algorithm agent, the file must be a JAR file and the user also specifies the path within this file where JASPER can locate the reporter agent. The user's reporter agent needs to implement the IReporterAgent interface provided by JASPER to be compatible with the simulation environment. To carry out the required computations, the reporter agent receives the simulation state. Different reporter agents can use the state to measure different metrics.

Test Cases. The test cases include information regarding jammers and tracks used in the simulation.

For jammers, the input specifies the number of jammers, along with details such as their positions (X and Y coordinates) and their initial orientation. These parameters define the setup for each jammer within the simulation.

For tracks, the input contains the number of tracks, the total time steps in the simulation, and the type of each track. Additionally, it provides data on the number of waypoints for each track. A waypoint refers to a specific location track is expected to reach during the simulation. For each waypoint, the input also specifies the corresponding simulation time step at which the track is at that location. The sequence of these waypoints and their associated times is used to determine the movement pattern and timing of the track throughout the simulation.

Users can create several test scenarios to try different kinds of attacks. Thus, it is possible to simulate distinct attack methods and enable the users to see the way many variables interact under different scenarios. This variation in scenario design helps to discover possible weaknesses in algorithms and test them in a controlled, repeatable way, in addition to improving the realism of the simulations.

4 Case Study

In this section, a use case to demonstrate how the JASPER simulation environment can be used to evaluate a jammer allocation algorithm is presented. In the test case, an analyst who wants to evaluate how the algorithm presented in [5] behaves in an attack in which some UAVs are detected as suspected UAVs.

In real-life usage, frequent device rotations in a short time may increase maintenance requirements, or slower assignments relative to track updates might require speeding up the algorithm's decision-making time, even if it means sacrificing performance. To analyze these trade-offs, the analyst creates a reporter agent that records coverage percentages, angle swivel, and algorithm execution time, using these KPIs to decide if adjustments are necessary. The analyst also creates a test scenario in which, there are two jammers, four UAVs, two suspected UAVs, and eleven unimportant tracks. In the scenario, paths for UAVs and suspected UAVs are hand-crafted considering the initial positions, speeds, and movement patterns of the UAVs and suspected UAVs. The representation of initial assignments of jammers in JASPER can be seen in Fig. 1.

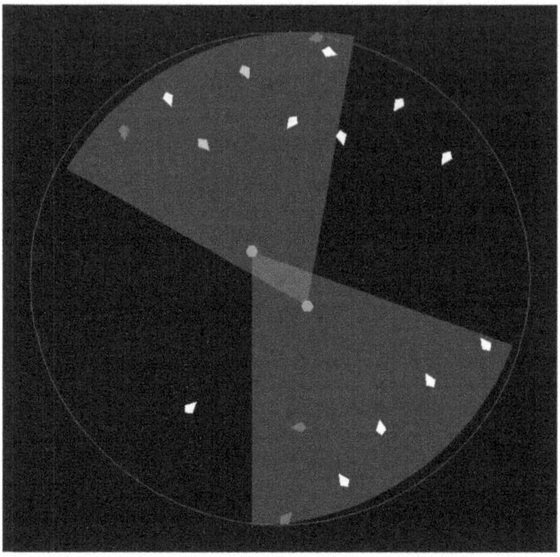

Fig. 1. Simulation state after the initial assignment has been made.

During the simulation, coverage percentages can be visualized in a chart. The algorithm's performance was evaluated using the UAVs' coverage percentages, suspected UAVs' coverage percentages, and overall coverage percentages.

The algorithm often produced high UAV coverage percentages throughout the experiment, decreasing only to 75% under circumstances where all UAVs could not be covered. Figure 2 represents a real-time visualization generated by JASPER during the simulation process, showcasing coverage percentages over simulation time. It demonstrates the algorithm's performance and variations in coverage percentages during the test scenario.

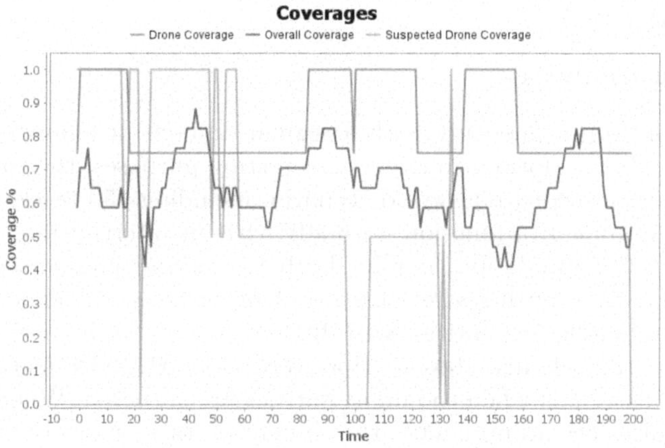

Fig. 2. Coverage percentages of the algorithm in the case study. (1.0 corresponds to 100%.)

While coverage performance is important, an algorithm needs to take a reasonable time to calculate angles. Otherwise, it cannot be used in real-world applications. For that reason, the time taken by the algorithm to compute new angle assignments at each step was recorded. This metric indicates how long the algorithm took to make new angle assignments at each step. In this case, the reporter agent selected includes this metric and the graph of the time taken for the algorithm to calculate can be seen in Fig. 3 obtained from the JASPER.

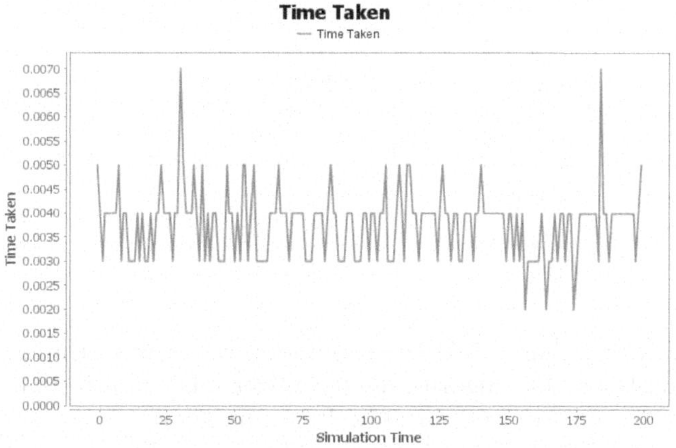

Fig. 3. The time taken for the algorithm to calculate the jammer-angle assignments, in seconds.

5 Evaluations

5.1 Scaling Analysis

The simulation works smoothly with a regular amount of jammers and tracks, with no noticeable performance issues. For testing purposes, the simulation was run with a more crowded real-world scenario, including 150 tracks and 10 jammers, and it continued to function normally without interruption.

Given that the simulation handles both tracks and jammers equally, they are treated the same during stress testing. During tests, it was found that the simulation can handle 512 entities with little to no lag, while performance may vary based on the settings chosen. However, some MASON features, such as inspectors, can struggle when too many entities are gathered. When the number of entities approaches around 4000, the simulation takes more time to calculate the next state. Despite the additional computing load, it continues to function successfully. The largest number of entities tested was 16384, and while it had some slowdown, the simulation performed successfully. To see the effect of the visualization, the simulation was run on the console under the same conditions. Although there was some speedup, there was not much gain compared to the visualized version. Results of the scaling analysis can be seen in Table 1. Tests were conducted on a computer with an AMD Ryzen 5 7600 processor and 32GB of RAM. For each test, the tested scenario took 100 steps to complete and only execution time is recorded (i.e. no contribution from the algorithm or reporter).

Table 1. Execution Time for Various Entity Counts and Visualization Modes

Entity Count	Execution Time (in seconds)	Execution Time without visualization (in seconds)
2	3.752	3.567
16	3.885	3.632
512	3.923	3.749
1024	4.159	3.893
4096	4.968	4.013
16384	11.106	6.515

It's worth noting that, while the simulation scales well, the algorithm used may have limitations. The algorithm's optimizer might reach limits in terms of the amount of formulations or variables it can handle.

Furthermore, real-time viewing of all trails drastically degrades performance. Even with as few as 30 tracks, displaying all trails can make the simulation incredibly slow and practically unusable. For that reason, the simulation only shows the trail of the selected track, one at a time.

5.2 Sensitivity Analysis

Validation in simulation for testing and evaluation is important to ensure the accuracy and reliability of the model. Without proper validation, the results produced by the simulation may not reflect the true behavior of the system, leading to incorrect conclusions or decisions.

Ideally, validation would involve direct comparison with real-world data. This method provides the highest level of accuracy, as it directly correlates the simulation results with actual observations. However, such comparisons are often expensive and challenging due to the difficulty of obtaining accurate and comprehensive real-world data. Given these challenges, in this study, sensitivity analysis is employed as a practical alternative for validation. This approach examines how variations in input parameters affect the model's output, allowing for an assessment of the simulation's robustness.

In this study, sensitivity analysis was conducted by running the jammer assignment algorithm at different intervals within the simulation. Using the same test scenario from Sect. 4, instead of executing the algorithm at every time step, it was tested at intervals of every 2, 3, 4, and 10 time steps. This variation showed the impact of reduced frequency on KPIs.

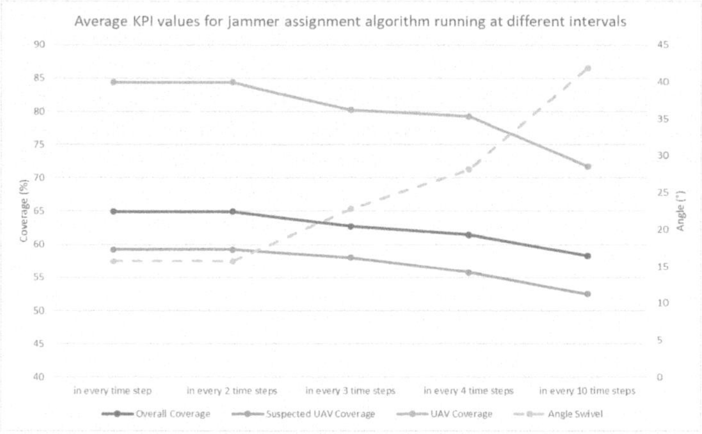

Fig. 4. Average KPI values for jammer assignment algorithm running at different intervals.

The results of this analysis are illustrated in Fig. 4. As the interval between algorithm executions increased, there was a slight decrease in coverage percentages, UAV coverage being the one that fell the most. Additionally, the angle swivel showed a significant increase. In addition to this figure, it is worth noting that the execution time of the algorithm remained constant across all intervals.

The sensitivity analysis revealed that as the algorithm was executed at larger intervals, corresponding declines in performance metrics were observed. This indicates that changes in the frequency of algorithm execution directly impact the simulation outcomes.

6 Conclusion

In this study, JASPER, a modular, agent-based simulation testbed was developed to evaluate jammer-angle allocation algorithms for anti-drone systems. JASPER simulation environment, built using the MASON framework, supports the integration and comparison of different algorithms across various scenarios. Key features include a configurable reporter agent and the ability to create diverse test cases. For observing how variations in input parameters affect the model's output, a sensitivity analysis is performed to JASPER. Moreover, for observing the performance under different numbers of jammers and tracks, a scaling analysis is also performed. Simplifications like ideal jammer coverage and a 2D aerial view were made to focus on essential elements, though these also introduced some limitations. These simplifications were deliberately chosen to minimize their impact on its application to real-world scenarios. If the real-world modeling of the algorithm to be tested, significantly differs from these assumptions, this tool may not be suitable for testing such algorithms.

Future improvements to the simulation environment could address several limitations and enhance its realism. For instance, evaluating the effects of multiple jammers' interference and supporting different jammer coverage patterns could provide a more accurate assessment of jammer effectiveness. Additionally, future research could incorporate frequency-specific jamming capabilities, reflecting the diverse operating frequencies of different UAV types. Moreover, developing a tool for automatic test case generation could make the simulation more user-friendly. Such improvements would give analysts and planners in the field of anti-drone systems a more complete tool for the evaluation of jammer allocation methods.

References

1. Alghodhaifi, H., Lakshmanan, S.: Autonomous vehicle evaluation: a comprehensive survey on modeling and simulation approaches. IEEE Access **9**, 151531–151566 (2021)
2. Aramrattana, M., Larsson, T., Jansson, J., Nåbo, A.: A simulation framework for cooperative intelligent transport systems testing and evaluation. Transport. Res. F: Traffic Psychol. Behav. **61**, 268–280 (2019)
3. Athans, M.: Command and control (C2) theory: a challenge to control science. IEEE Trans. Autom. Control **32**(4), 286–293 (1987)
4. Balci, O.: Principles and techniques of simulation validation, verification, and testing. In: Proceedings of the 27th Conference on Winter Simulation, pp. 147–154 (1995)
5. Baraklı, A.B., Semiz, F., Atasoy, E.: The specialized threat evaluation and weapon target assignment problem: genetic algorithm optimization and ILP model solution. In: International Conference on the Applications of Evolutionary Computation (Part of EvoStar), pp. 19–34. Springer, Cham (2023)

6. Bellifemine, F., Poggi, A., Rimassa, G.: JADE–a FIPA-compliant agent framework. In: Proceedings of PAAM, vol. 99, p. 33. London (1999)
7. Borshchev, A., Filippov, A.: From system dynamics and discrete event to practical agent based modeling: reasons, techniques, tools. In: Proceedings of the 22nd International Conference of the System Dynamics Society, vol. 22, pp. 25–29. Oxford, England (2004)
8. Cai, H., Liu, J., Chen, Y., Wang, H.: Survey of the research on dynamic weapon-target assignment problem. J. Syst. Eng. Electron. **17**(3), 559–565 (2006)
9. Cai, W., Song, X., Liu, C., Jiang, D., Huo, L.: An adaptive and efficient network traffic measurement method based on SDN in IoT. In: International Conference on Simulation Tools and Techniques, pp. 64–74. Springer, Cham (2021)
10. Carling, R.L.: A knowledge-base system for the threat evaluation and weapon assignment process. Nav. Eng. J. **105**(1), 31–41 (1993)
11. Carson, J.S.: Introduction to modeling and simulation. In: Proceedings of the Winter Simulation Conference, pp. 8–pp. IEEE (2005)
12. Choi, S.Y., Park, K., Yang, J.H., Kang, H.I.: Application of agent-based multi-method simulation approach to the simulation testbed prototype for the concept exploration and requirement analysis of UGV. In: ECMS, pp. 57–63 (2015)
13. Gül, K.: Model and procedures for the jammer and target allocation problem. Master's thesis, Middle East Technical University (2018)
14. Hosein, P.A.: A class of dynamic nonlinear resource allocation problems. Ph.D. thesis, Massachusetts institute of technology (1989)
15. Hosein, P.A., Athans, M., et al.: Some analytical results for the dynamic weapon-target allocation problem (1990)
16. Johansson, F., Falkman, G.: A Bayesian network approach to threat evaluation with application to an air defense scenario. In: 2008 11th International Conference on Information Fusion, pp. 1–7. IEEE (2008)
17. Karasakal, O.: Air defense missile-target allocation models for a naval task group. Comput. Oper. Res. **35**(6), 1759–1770 (2008)
18. Lloyd, S.P., Witsenhausen, H.S.: Weapons allocation is NP-complete. In: 1986 Summer Computer Simulation Conference, pp. 1054–1058 (1986)
19. Lorig, F., Dammenhayn, N., Müller, D.-J., Timm, I.J.: Measuring and comparing scalability of agent-based simulation frameworks. In: Müller, J.P., Ketter, W., Kaminka, G., Wagner, G., Bulling, N. (eds.) MATES 2015. LNCS (LNAI), vol. 9433, pp. 42–60. Springer, Cham (2015). https://doi.org/10.1007/978-3-319-27343-3_3
20. Luke, S., Cioffi-Revilla, C., Panait, L., Sullivan, K., Balan, G.: Mason: a multiagent simulation environment. Simulation **81**(7), 517–527 (2005)
21. Macal, C., North, M.: Introductory tutorial: agent-based modeling and simulation. In: Proceedings of the Winter Simulation Conference 2014, pp. 6–20. IEEE (2014)
22. Mualla, Y., Bai, W., Galland, S., Nicolle, C.: Comparison of agent-based simulation frameworks for unmanned aerial transportation applications. Procedia Comput. Sci. **130**, 791–796 (2018)
23. North, M.J., et al.: Complex adaptive systems modeling with repast simphony. Complex Adaptive Syst. Model. **1**, 1–26 (2013)
24. Park, S., Kim, H.T., Lee, S., Joo, H., Kim, H.: Survey on anti-drone systems: components, designs, and challenges. IEEE Access **9**, 42635–42659 (2021)
25. Puzicha, A., Buchholz, P.: A simulation environment for autonomous robot swarms with limited communication skills. In: Simulation Tools and Techniques: 12th EAI International Conference, SIMUtools 2020, Guiyang, China, 28–29 August 2020, Proceedings, Part II 12, pp. 206–226. Springer, Cham (2021)

26. Rothenberg, J.: Object-oriented simulation: where do we go from here? In: Proceedings of the 18th Conference on Winter Simulation, pp. 464–469 (1986)
27. Shi, X., Yang, C., Xie, W., Liang, C., Shi, Z., Chen, J.: Anti-drone system with multiple surveillance technologies: architecture, implementation, and challenges. IEEE Commun. Mag. **56**(4), 68–74 (2018)
28. Tyurin, V., Martyniuk, O., Mirnenko, V., Open'ko, P., Korenivska, I.: General approach to counter unmanned aerial vehicles. In: 2019 IEEE 5th International Conference Actual Problems of Unmanned Aerial Vehicles Developments (APUAVD), pp. 75–78. IEEE (2019)

Barriers and Challenges of Network Simulation Tools: A Case Study on CORE/EMANE

Manal Ghanem[1(✉)], Nicholas Micallef[1], Sara Correia-Hopkins[1], and Jonathan-Lee Jones[2]

[1] Swansea University, Swansea, UK
{2200761,nicholas.micallef,s.correia}@swansea.ac.uk
[2] ITSUS Consulting, Cardiff, UK
jonlj@itsusconsulting.com

Abstract. Network simulation tools provide advanced simulation solutions. These tools reduce costs and simplify the testing of scenarios to mitigate risks before deployment. However, many of these tools still possess shortcomings that hinder their usability and widespread adoption. Notably, many tools cannot accommodate dynamic scenarios, thus limiting the scale and complexity of simulations they can support. Our study explores professionals' experiences with network simulation tools, with a focus on CORE/EMANE, aiming to understand their shortcomings and future potential. While existing research highlights technical drawbacks, our mixed-methods approach, uses a questionnaire to gather perspectives on network simulators and a design workshop to explore both technical and usability barriers associated with CORE/EMANE from an industry perspective. Our research highlights critical technical and usability barriers and challenges as perceived by industry professionals who frequently use these tools. Our work improves the understanding of the technical and usability requirements of network simulation tools. More importantly, we provide features that are grounded in participants' feedback, aiming to streamline user interfaces and align tools capabilities with the evolving network simulation landscape for improved project outcomes. These insights are key for informing future development, emphasising the need for tools that address technical requirements while ensuring user-friendliness.

Keywords: Network Simulation Tools · CORE/EMANE · User Experience · GUI Design · Interface Design

1 Introduction

A wide range of network simulation tools, including NS-2 [2], NS-3 [22], OPNET Modeler [3], QualNet [15], and OMNet++ [43] have enabled the modelling of various types of networks, ranging from local area networks (LANs) to wide area

A. A. Juan et al. (Eds.): SIMUtools 2024, LNICST 603, pp. 397–417, 2025.
https://doi.org/10.1007/978-3-031-87345-4_26

networks (WANs). These tools play a pivotal role in developing and evaluating modern communication systems, allowing controlled testing and optimisation of networks without extensive physical setups. Real-time simulation, replicating the timing behaviour of real-world targets, is significant in this field, enabling cost-effective experimentation.

As wired and wireless networks continue to grow, the importance of evaluating network performance through simulation becomes more essential [4,17]. While network simulation tools offer a cost-effective alternative for performance evaluation, the increasing reliance on them raises concerns about accuracy and validation issues, including technical and usability aspects. Despite the emphasis on developing high-performance network simulation tools, there are significant challenges in accurately representing real-time networks. The precision of wireless network simulations is crucial for both accuracy and scalability [25,35]. The limitations often arise from the inherent constraints of the simulator supplied with the operating system, directly impacting the accuracy of results. Additionally, the abundance of choice further complicates the selection of the most suitable simulation tool [37]. Many tools rely on abstract simulation models, which, though useful for specific analyses, may not fully capture the intricate behaviour and performance of wireless networks, resulting in less accurate outcomes compared to real-world implementations [27].

To the best of our knowledge, no prior research has undertaken a comprehensive examination of the usability of network simulation tools from a user's perspective. Our research builds upon the existing body of comparative reviews and technical evaluations of network simulation tools, expanding the scope to study user experiences with CORE/EMANE. This research, conducted in collaboration with ITSUS Consulting, a technology solutions provider specialising in ICT solutions for critical communication systems, aims to understand how network simulation tools are used, with the ultimate goal of designing solutions that could address current limitations of these tools. The study focuses on technical and usability challenges faced by users, aiming to enhance the tools' effectiveness and efficiency by compiling a list of requirements that can be used by the wider community to improve the development of next-generation network simulation tools. The research contributes to improving network infrastructure design and deployment processes. Our research is guided by the following research questions:

[RQ1] What are the key features of network simulation tools according to professionals?
[RQ2] What are the strengths/weaknesses of network simulation tools according to professionals?
[RQ3] How would professionals who use these tools like to see them evolve in the future?

To answer our research questions, we employed a mixed-methods approach, utilising a questionnaire for an overview followed by a design workshop focused on one tool, CORE/EMANE, involving six professionals in each activity. Our findings reveal technical and usability issues associated with network simulation tools, emphasising the importance of considering specific operational contexts when selecting, designing or upgrading these tools.

In the rest of the paper, we begin by presenting related work in Sect. 2. Section 3 details the methods employed for the research. The results of the study are presented and discussed in Sects. 4 and 5. Finally, Sect. 6 offers our concluding remarks and avenues for future research.

2 Related Work

Network simulators, emulators, and testbeds are three distinct tools and approaches used in network evaluation and experimentation [16]. Each approach offers unique strengths and limitations. In this research, the term *'simulation'* refers to the use of any of the tools discussed; specific tool categories are mentioned as necessary. Simulation tools' development serves as an indispensable resource in the research community, enabling the development and evaluation of new protocols, and facilitating comparisons between novel and existing protocols. Many of the comparative reviews shed light on the technical aspects and performance metrics of these tools [9,12,24,26,37,39,42]; however, they rarely focus on the user experience and usability challenges encountered by day-to-day users and non-experts.

In the subsequent sections, we explore the design and usability issues by investigating research in data processing and decision-making, human-computer interaction design, and the usability of network management tools, and introducing the benefits and drawbacks of CORE/EMANE the tool used in our design workshop. By exploring these areas, we aim to shed light on the usability challenges and opportunities within network simulation tools, ultimately contributing to the development of more effective and user-centric solutions.

2.1 Data and Decision-Making

Modern network implementation facilitates the collection of a vast and growing volume of data. Leveraging simulation tools to make informed decisions about the appropriateness of a particular implementation or protocol heavily relies on utilising this data. Schroder et al. indicated that the quality of decision-making improves with the increasing volume of data available [36]. However, the potential to make better decisions through the processing of huge datasets comes with challenges. Cognitive overload may arise if the proper processing and display of the data are not well-suited for the task at hand [28]. Ensuring the data is presented in a meaningful and easily comprehensible manner is crucial to avoid overwhelming users with information.

Falschlunger et al. demonstrated that the relationship between task complexity and decision-making outcomes is mediated by information overload [18]. The researchers found that when faced with complex tasks, individuals may experience information overload, which can negatively impact their decision-making abilities. This highlights the importance of managing information effectively in decision-making processes. The study reaffirmed Gettinger et al. conclusions that well-implemented visualisations serve as an effective aid in the comprehension of large amounts of information, suggesting an improved ability to detect trends and patterns, ultimately leading to better decision-making [19]. Given the critical role of data in modern network implementation and decision-making, the efficiency and effectiveness of decision-making using simulation tools heavily depends on the tools' ability to handle data in a user-friendly manner, reducing cognitive load, and facilitating informed choices based on data-driven insights. Therefore, improving the way network simulation tools present and process data can increase the tools' efficiency. Our research aims to create an actionable list of features to facilitate decision-making.

2.2 Human-Computer Interaction for Data Visualisation in Network Tools

Human-Computer Interaction (HCI) research, recognising the potential of visualisation and usability resources in advancing user interfaces for network management applications, is the most relevant to our research [8,18,21,34]. These resources offer benefits to both non-specialists and experts, enhancing productivity in daily monitoring tasks [21]. Consequently, recent initiatives have proposed HCI-based usability guidelines, or heuristics, to aid in the design of user interfaces for network management tools [44]. Researchers developed guidelines for network monitoring tools through experimental studies involving network administrators [38,44]. They introduced "guidelines for usability design in network monitoring tools" [38,44]. However, these guidelines have yet to be evaluated by network management tool developers to assess their usability benefits and potential need for refinement.

Graphical representations can provide a visual and intuitive understanding of the simulated network environment and alleviate the cognitive load [14]. The limited visualisation in many of these tools can make simulating complex network topologies and scenarios challenging for users to understand the interactions between nodes, links, and traffic [33]. Inadequate or complicated visualisations may lead to difficulty in identifying potential issues, bottlenecks, or inefficiencies in the network design. This in return makes debugging network simulations a specialised task that requires expert users. It also would lead many users to identify errors or anomalies in the simulated network using log files and textual outputs, which can be cumbersome and time-consuming.

Pretorius et al. utilised Eye Tracking as an evaluation method, to highlight significant challenges in the usability of the implemented graphics. Their results revealed issues in data visualisation legibility, user preferences for graphical representations, and issues of presented visualisation in some parts of the screen [33]. Based on these findings, it is evident that poorly designed graphical interfaces can significantly hinder the user experience. Users may find it challenging to create, modify, and manage network configurations. Limited customisation options can present another issue, restricting users from tailoring the visualisation according to their specific needs. This can be directly linked to simulation tools, especially when trying to analyse and evaluate the impact of various protocols or network settings on the simulated environment. Our research explores user-centred design of network simulation tools to enhance their usability.

2.3 Usability of the Tools

Yang et al. found that usability issues in network monitoring and management tools for both network administrators and non-expert users are related to technical knowledge requirements and lack of visualisations for the tools [45]. Inconsistent user interfaces were also identified due to the absence of guidelines, leading to variations among suppliers, devices, and operating systems [45]. Similar issues were discussed in recent research [42], where researchers surveyed six simulation tools to be used by students in classrooms. The tools had issues with their interfaces and ease of use [42]. Issues with time investment to learn and use the tools were also discussed [42].

While specific literature that directly addresses the usability challenges of network simulation tools was not identified, our review of related studies has provided valuable insights into the design and usability issues common to network management tools. These findings can be extrapolated to potentially impact network simulation tools as well. The usability research has highlighted various aspects, such as the importance of catering to different user profiles [45], effectively handling collected data for generating meaningful insights [28], mitigating cognitive loads associated with learning and comprehending these tools [18,45], and addressing issues concerning poor interfaces [45].

Utilising the insights from these studies, we devised a comprehensive approach to further probe and directly understand changes that need to be implemented while working with users of these tools. This involved the development of a questionnaire and a design workshop. These methods were employed to collaboratively engage with end-users, allowing us to gain a more nuanced understanding of the necessary enhancements to be integrated into these tools. Through this approach, we aimed to bridge the gap between the challenges identified in the literature and the practical implementation of upgrades, ensuring that the proposed upgrades would meet the requirements and usability expectations of current users.

2.4 CORE/EMANE

In the literature on network simulation tools, the Common Open Research Emulator (CORE) is often highlighted for its open-source framework and capability to emulate networks across multiple machines, including integration with live networks [5,6,20,41]. CORE provides a graphical interface to manage network topologies and offers Python bindings for scripting, enhancing its adaptability for various research needs. It visually represents wireless connections with antennas and green lines, which helps in effectively demonstrating the layout of wireless networks.

Similarly, the Extendable Mobile Ad-hoc Network Emulator (EMANE) is noted for its modular MAC and PHY layer architecture that supports varied network emulation [1,6]. EMANE allows for the development of different radio interface models through its Network Emulation Modules (NEMs), facilitating real-time, distributed network emulations when used in conjunction with CORE, thus enhancing the realism and scope of network simulations.

According to comparative studies comparing various simulation tools [20,41], CORE/EMANE has limitations, particularly in detailed event execution and the lack of support for capturing wireless packets, including complex packet exchanges. This limitation restricts the tool's efficacy in studying real-world wireless networking scenarios. Additionally, CORE's focus on the physical and data link layers without built-in support for wireless security protocols poses significant restrictions, especially when deploying comprehensive system configurations without manual adjustments.

The real-time emulation feature of CORE allows for observing protocol and application behaviours in a temporally accurate environment. It also offers pre-built network models that researchers can adapt and expand to construct intricate network topologies [5]. However, the necessity for elaborate configuration scripts and the high computational demands for running extensive network scenarios make CORE less accessible for many researchers and increase the complexity and learning curves for new users [29]. In our work, we use CORE/EMANE as a case study because it is the most popular tool among our participants.

3 Methods

We employed a mixed-methods approach, utilising a questionnaire and a design workshop, to address our RQs. The mixed-methods approach was used to gain a more nuanced understanding of the use of these tools. The questionnaire offered a broad perspective, which was subsequently refined during the design workshop to extract more in-depth qualitative data focused on CORE/EMANE to design the features required to improve such tools. All study procedures were approved by our University's Institutional Review Board (IRB). The online questionnaire targeted ITSUS Consulting employees who regularly use or have previous experience with simulation tools. A convenience volunteer sampling technique, facilitated by contacts at ITSUS Consulting, invited participants meeting our inclusion criteria, specifically individuals working directly with simulation tools, leading projects that use simulation tools, or working with clients' projects utilising simulation tools. Participants' backgrounds included expertise in software engineering, cybersecurity, and data science, along with educational backgrounds in computer science, cybersecurity, physics, and astrophysics.

To better understand tool usage patterns, client requirements, and visualisation preferences, the questionnaire was designed with open-ended questions to allow participants to provide detailed, qualitative insights. The questionnaire contained 24 questions, organised into three main sections to align with the study's research questions and typically required about 30 min to be completed.

The first section collected general information on the tools participants used, including their experience levels, common features, and tool limitations. This section aimed to address RQ1 by identifying the core functionalities that professionals consider essential, as well as any client requirements that current tools do not meet. The second section focused on clients' perceptions, common pain points, and usability challenges, exploring how these tools are used in various scenarios. Aligned with RQ2, this section provided insights into the strengths and weaknesses of these tools, capturing client expectations and highlighting areas for improvement in usability and functionality.

The final section investigated visualisation needs and preferences, exploring current limitations and future expectations for visualisation components in network simulation tools. This section was aligned with RQ3 and examined participants' views on emerging trends, necessary enhancements, and the importance of visualisation for effective decision-making.

The questionnaire analysis informed the design of the subsequent workshop. Participants recruitment for the design workshop used a purposive sampling technique, facilitated by our project partners. Since participants were recruited from the same partners, some participants have participated in both studies because participants of the design workshop reported expertise similar to the ones who participated in the initial questionnaire. Besides exploring CORE/EMANE's usage experiences and challenges, the design workshop, conducted in an open and collaborative environment, involved two design activities: (1) listing interface additions to improve CORE/EMANE; and (2) suggesting important data visualisations to incorporate into the tool to aid analysis and decision-making. Two researchers moderated discussions to maintain focus and ensure productivity. The design workshop lasted for two hours.

For both activities, we recruited six participants in total, with the possibility of some overlap among participants. The questionnaire participants reported a collective experience ranging from 1 to 20 years, indicating a mix of experienced and novice professionals. Similarly, the design workshop included participants with experience ranging from 1 to 5 years, enriching discussions on the challenges and opportunities in this domain.

3.1 Data Analysis

Data analysis of the qualitative information gathered from both the questionnaire and the design workshop followed an inductive thematic analysis approach, as outlined by Braun and Clarke [10,11]. This analysis consisted of two primary stages: open coding and axial coding. During the open coding phase, the data was carefully reviewed multiple times by the lead author. This iterative process allowed the researcher to form initial impressions of the data and identify distinct ideas, which were then coded. A second researcher went through these codes and in most instances confirmed the impressions of the lead researcher. There were only a few cases in which the second researcher suggested different codes. Conflicts were resolved through discussion to arrive at a consensus between coders.

Subsequently, in axial coding, these codes were organised and grouped based on their connections and relationships.

3.2 Limitations

While the study aimed to provide insights into the use of simulation tools among ITSUS Consulting employees, certain limitations were acknowledged. Reliance on self-reported data might lead to recall bias or subjective interpretations. An overall small sample ($N \approx 9$) of ITSUS Consulting employees limits the generalisability to other organisations. However, as the findings of this research are intended as exploratory, they lay the groundwork for future research. Expanding the sample in future studies to include a more diverse group of participants across industries—such as telecommunications, defense, academia, and commercial IT—would ensure generalisability of the results.

To enhance the robustness of future studies, larger-scale quantitative approaches, such as online surveys distributed across industry networks and professional organisations, could be employed to validate the observed patterns and trends statistically. Additionally, a longitudinal approach could provide insights into how user needs evolve as new technologies, like 5G, 6G, and AI-driven automation, become more integrated into network simulation tools. Despite the constraints of a smaller sample, the richness of the collected data is evidence that we managed to extract meaningful insights. Ethical considerations, a mixed-methods approach, and expert review enhanced the study's rigour. The small sample size suggests the list of strengths and shortcomings may not be exhaustive, but can still be relevant for end-users who use network simulation tools.

4 Results

In this section, we present results from the questionnaire and the design workshop, aiming to understand participants' perspectives on network simulation tools. The questionnaire results provided initial answers to our research questions, while the design workshop provided a more nuanced understanding of the identified themes. A summary of key findings from the questionnaire and the design workshop is listed in Table 1.

4.1 Questionnaire Results

Participants' responses shed light on the technical and usability needs in their work, addressing clients, projects, and colleagues.

Key Features, Needs, and Challenges. CORE/EMANE was the most frequently used tool among participants, followed by other tools like OPNET Modeler, Cisco CML, and GNS3. In terms of selection criteria, the answers included testability (3/6), open-source options (1/6), and managerial preferences (1/6).

Table 1. Key Findings from Questionnaire and Design Workshop

Category	Questionnaire Findings	Design Workshop Findings
Requirements	Need for better performance and scalability to handle large, complex simulations. Importance of accurate radio propagation modeling for wireless signal behaviour. Essential need for an improved, user-friendly interface for efficient simulation.	Clear and effective data visualisation is crucial, with CORE/EMANE's GUI needing more parameter representations. Open-source development affects data quality, with inconsistent dataset contributions impacting usability.
Challenges	Technical limitations include scalability issues, compatibility challenges, and limited software configurability. Usability challenges such as a steep learning curve, leading to ineffective use and fewer conducted tests. Frequent reliance on workarounds due to limited configurability and complex setup.	Challenges in client engagement, especially during ad hoc, command-line-based demos. Weak visualization in mobility scenarios, with difficulties in real-time parameter adjustments. Development challenges including complex GUI, steep learning curve, and limited documentation. Fragmentation due to reliance on multiple tools across projects.
Tools Evolvement	Anticipated evolution to include advanced technologies like 5G and improved scalability. Suggestions for a user-centered design approach to improve initial user experience, reduce complexity, and enhance configurability. Interest in future enhancements like virtual reality integration, dynamic routing, and mesh networks.	Recommendation for intuitive data visualisation and dynamic user profiles. Increased customisability, including easier configuration and enhanced visual tools for data interpretation. A unified simulation tool with features that reduce reliance on workarounds and multiple tools.

Our Participants identified essential features for effective simulation, addressing our first research question. These features include the ability to replicate scenarios, isolation from operating systems, noise introduction, and dynamic manipulation of parameters. They stressed that for clients, the capability of these tools to mirror real-world scenarios and measure essential network metrics is fundamental. Additionally, the need for virtual topologies, modular architecture, scalability, and effective integration was highlighted.

"Common key features would include generic network would be bandwidth, packet loss (and distributions), Latency and Jitter." - (QP1)

Participants expressed a need for better performance and scalability in simulation tools to handle larger, intricate simulations while maintaining optimal performance. They emphasised the significance of accurately modelling radio propagation to represent wireless signal behaviour in varied environments. The anticipation of tool evolution in line with upcoming technologies like 5G was noted, pointing to the need for continuous adaptation. Additionally, the importance of an improved user interface was stressed to make the simulation process more streamlined and user-friendly.

"We need greater performance/scalability, more accurate/realistic radio propagation, more diverse mobility models, 5G and beyond, and improved user interface." - (QP6)

Participants expressed concerns about the tools, providing insights that addressed our second research question. They highlighted technical limitations, scalability issues, and compatibility problems. The focus was more on technical aspects than usability, with a need for enhanced software configurability, better interfaces, and advancements in radio propagation modelling, mobility models, and real-time adaptability. The importance of scalability in line with emerging technologies was also reported.

User Experience and Usability. Participants' perceptions of client experiences varied, emphasising the impact of individual backgrounds. The diversity of viewpoints underscores the complexity of this domain and its intersection with the evolving landscape of technology. A common theme among the responses was the acknowledgement of the uniqueness of each tool and the influence of individual backgrounds in shaping their experiences.

Several participants reported the difficulties encountered while using these tools, requiring workarounds to navigate through them (2/6). Participants also pointed out that tools with poor usability could lead to fewer people being able to use them effectively, ultimately leading to fewer tests being conducted (2/6), this also can be linked to another answer describing the steep learning curve associated with these tools, noting that users might focus on learning a single feature that they perceive as essential, missing out on other valuable functionalities due to usability issues.

"Complex and frustrating tools lead to avoidance or limited usage, with users often mastering only essential features due to a steep learning curve, leading to missed opportunities to explore and benefit from other valuable features." - (QP5)

Usability and user experience of the visualisation component of wireless network simulation tools were considered highly important. When asked about how the current visualisation is perceived by their clients, our participants reported that their perception of visualisation features varied. While some clients find the visualisations acceptable but not exceptional (3/6), others feel the visualisation is not very good, lacks clarity, and may not effectively convey important information (3/6).

"The user experience of these tools is not great. It's a hard thing to get across as the spectrum may not always be visualised." - (QP1)

All participants agreed about the importance of well-implemented visualisation. They highlighted the need for aids for configuration, ease of understanding, efficient analysis, faster decision-making, and higher adoption rates.

"Visualisations that are well-utilised are important for ease of understanding, efficient analysis, faster decision making, higher adoption, training and a competitive advantage." - (QP6)

Emerging Trends and Next Steps for Design. Participants recommended a user-centred design approach, focusing on improving initial user experiences, reducing complexity, and enhancing configurability. Integration of virtual reality, dynamic routing, and mesh networks were suggested for future enhancements. Simultaneously, they also emphasised the importance of improving initial user experiences, reducing complexity, and enhancing configurability to make the tools more accessible to a broader user base.

"users needs should be at the centre of experience, not technology." - (QP1)

4.2 Design Workshop Results

Informed by the questionnaire results, the design workshop discussions were focused on participant-client collaboration using network simulation tools, exploring both positive and negative aspects. Discussions unveiled development challenges in meeting clients' demands. Afterwards, to answer our third research question, two design activities were conducted using CORE/EMANE as a case study, to compile feature lists addressing usability and reducing complexity. Participants emphasised that a human-centric approach to enhance usability and realise the tool's potential is crucial.

Challenges of Simulation Tools. Starting the discussion, participants shared challenges and frustrations in utilising simulation tools, particularly focusing on CORE/EMANE, the primary tool used by our participants. Challenges highlighted in clients' engagement when using simulation tools include simulation demonstrations that often appear to be ad hoc and unprofessional, leading to difficulties in conveying information to clients. Participants expressed difficulties when urgent changes are requested by clients during demos which can be time-consuming and involve command-line operations, disrupting the workflow and coming back with results that cannot be verified.

"It always looks ad hoc and unprofessional ... Stakeholders may ask for changes to the simulation, which can take 15 min of fiddling around with command-line commands. It may or may not work, and even when it does, because the tool does not provide visual outputs, it can be difficult to understand what is happening." - (WP3)

The tool's visualisations were criticised for their lack of clarity. Participants emphasised that the tool sometimes leaves stakeholders to interpret data independently. Mobility-related scenarios, which involve the dynamic movement or changing locations of entities within a network, were identified as particularly problematic, causing crashes and difficulties in altering parameters on the fly.

Open-Source and APIs. A strong theme that emerged from the design workshop was the impact of open-source development on data quality and library usability, with tool choices influencing dataset quality. CORE/EMANE, while recognised for extensive datasets, posed challenges due to varying quality dependent on contributors' efforts. Participants expressed concerns about datasets ranging from well-structured to hastily created ones, emphasising the impact on project outcomes.

"Some tools may look better but have limitations, focusing on specific aspects like Cisco. CORE/EMANE tends to have more comprehensive data. The quality of datasets can vary, ranging from well-done ones to incomplete ones crafted for specific projects." - (WP3)

Development Challenges. The challenges discussed while working with clients transitioned into development challenges, particularly concerning the graphical user interface (GUI) limitations in exposing essential parameters for network conditions. While the GUI was praised for user-friendliness in node representation, manipulating critical parameters remained obscure, requiring a balance between flexibility and usability. Additionally, beginners face a steep learning curve and insufficient documentation. To address this challenge, the development team has resorted to collaboratively developing internal documentation. This has helped to improve the documentation, but some challenges still remain.

"The CORE/EMANE GUI is visually straightforward, depicting node types and network topology. However, crucial parameters for network conditions are obscured, especially in complex radio models with numerous tweakable parameters. Balancing flexibility with simplicity poses challenges for developers, as more parameters enhance flexibility but make explanation and consistency more difficult." - (WP1)

Participants noted that while standard routing algorithms were easy to use, customising the tool to meet specific clients' requests was a challenge. Customisation can be difficult and time-consuming, as it requires substantial research efforts by developers to identify the appropriate parameters and learn about the many parameters available in CORE/EMANE. Some parameters are not intuitive, and it can be difficult to understand their impact on the simulation.

While simulations present numerous advantages, they aren't without challenges, including integration complexities, manual setup steps, data sharing limitations, and adapting to future requirements. Many projects involve multiple tools, leading to fragmentation. Participants acknowledged these challenges but noted the difficulty in creating a single tool with all features. They prefer to develop workarounds for diverse projects until a unified tool becomes available.

"Many of these projects are proof-of-concept, aiming to demonstrate an idea's feasibility. As a result, it is not always important if it is a kludge or a quick/dirty solution. This approach can result in a patchwork of kludges. Each project caters to specific client needs, making a comprehensive system challenging without anticipating all customer requirements. Quick solutions remain essential." - (WP1)

Data Visualisation. During the discussion, CORE/EMANE's GUI design was praised for its ease of use but deemed in need of new features. However, the absence of visual representations for many parameters was noted. Addressing data visualisation challenges, a participant stressed the importance of clear and visually appealing visuals, crucial for conveying complex simulation results to non-technical stakeholders. Participants emphasised the significance of clear data visualisation and the challenges posed by raw, unprocessed data in complex simulations. Emphasis was placed on user-friendly interfaces for intuitive data interpretation, aligning with the questionnaire results advocating for dynamic user profiles. CORE/EMANE lacks built-in visualisations for various data types, prompting users to rely on third-party tools for desired visualisations.

"My role involves speaking to customers and ensuring they can easily interpret and visualise the data. The data must be presented in a clear and visually appealing way... This can be challenging when dealing with non-technical customers who simply want to know if something will work in a given situation. So, presenting data in an easily understandable way is a priority for us." - (WP5) Following the initial discussions, participants engaged in two design activities to propose enhancements for simulation tools, addressing our third research question. The subsequent subsections will detail these activities and the list of features our participants recommended to improve CORE/EMANE and other simulation tools.

Activity 1: Designing the GUI Interface. In the first design activity, participants were presented with a screenshot of the CORE/EMANE interface, shown in Fig. 1, and asked to identify positive features. Our participants highlighted several positive features, including the clear and user-friendly design, emphasising the ease of dragging nodes and customising the interface for improved usability. Icons were considered representative enough for users to quickly understand their functions, even with minimal prior knowledge. The interface effectively distinguished wireless nodes with a small antenna icon, facilitating easy identification. Moreover, the editing capabilities, such as modifying connections, adjusting bandwidth, adding labels, and managing properties, were acknowledged for providing users with convenient and flexible options.

Afterwards, participants were given the task of designing the added features and functions they would like to see added to the tool's interface. Participants were given the choice to jot down on the printed interface or use blank papers

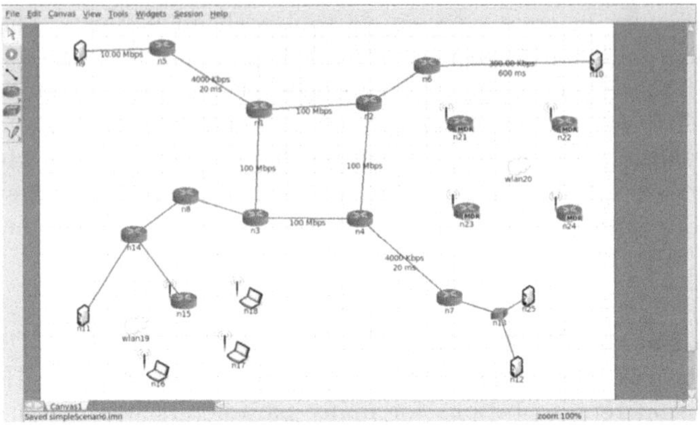

Fig. 1. CORE/EMANE interface used in activity 1.

to complete the task. One of these designs is displayed in Figs. 2. Following are the features our participants suggested to be added to the interface:

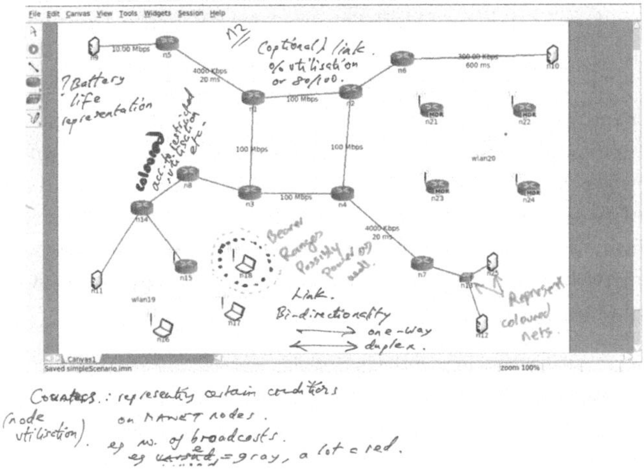

Fig. 2. Participants added features in activity 1.

- Toggle visual indicators for identification of network conditions like congestion or bottlenecks.
- Switch between full and simplified network topology views.
- Show areas of overlap between wireless nodes to identify potential interference or connectivity issues.
- Quickly identify nodes connected to a WLAN.

- Colour coding to visualise network connectivity, segments, & vulnerabilities.
- Display battery life of network devices or nodes.
- Provide alternative data transmission paths to increase network reliability.
- Add sliders to adjust and visualise different parameters.
- Select and display specific properties or details of nodes.
- Assign different icons to nodes to distinguish their types.
- Add controls to simulate network events, as traffic changes.
- Set performance thresholds for varying conditions.

Activity 2: Required Visualisation and Data Types. After the first activity, the participants were asked to draw visualisations they would like to see in the tool. One of these designs is displayed in Fig. 3. After the activity, our participants discussed their visualisation and agreed that the following features should be added to enhance the visualisations of network simulation tools:

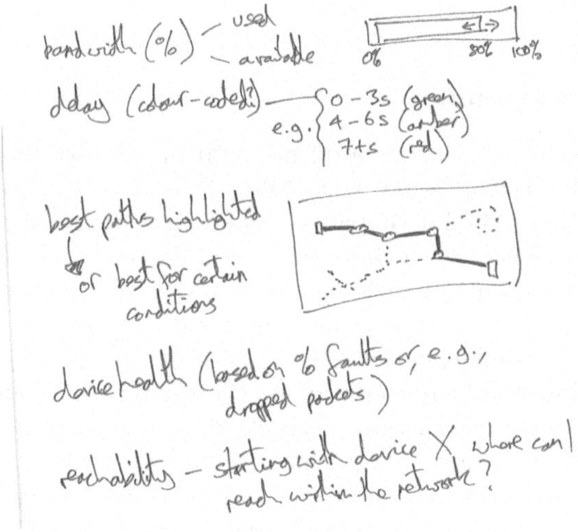

Fig. 3. Example of the designed visualisations.

- Show available and utilised bandwidth on network links, identifying potential bottlenecks.
- Use colours to represent link delays for better optimisation.
- Represent different network paths graphically, including the best path to a destination.
- Provide a visual indicator of network devices' health status, identifying potential faults.

- Use colours to show network reachability and connectivity.
- Display frequency of node transmissions, identifying traffic bottlenecks or security risks.
- Show link between network traffic and throughput over time.
- Highlight areas with poor connectivity on a map, pinpointing areas needing improvement.
- Show bandwidth utilisation over time, with moving average.
- Visualise significant network events using a bar chart.
- Generate interactive graphs to visualise network data.
- Enable personalised dashboards and reports, with configurable widgets and content.

5 Discussion

Participants' insights, gathered through the questionnaire and the design workshop have provided an understanding of both technical and usability requirements and challenges in network simulation tools. The following section will discuss the key findings of our research.

5.1 Usability Shortcomings

Our findings, in alignment with related research in network management tools research, explore the crucial issue of usability faced by users and clients when implementing projects [34]. Participants' experiences reveal diverse client perceptions of user experiences with these tools, emphasising the complexity of this domain amid technological advancements. Non-technical end-users commonly struggle with interfaces to comprehend numerical outputs, requesting simpler means to manipulate simulation scenarios. These sentiments align with the conclusions that handling significant data for decision-making is challenging without tailored processing and presentation methods [28].

Our findings reveal a common agreement among participants about the integral connection between user-friendliness and the effectiveness of tool usage, emphasising the pivotal role of usability in determining the efficacy and impact of network simulation tools. The potential hindrance of usability issues resonates with findings from usability research indicating that perceived ease of use and output quality were associated with perceived usefulness [13,31].

The challenges highlighted in our study emphasise the significance of the GUI in these tools. While the GUI in CORE/EMANE was commended for simplicity and user-friendly clarity, participants observed that essential parameters controlling network conditions are not easily accessible. This lack of customisation makes manipulation and visualisation of these parameters challenging through the GUI, resulting in a steep learning curve and limiting accessibility for users with varying technical proficiency [34].

5.2 Fragmentation and Multi-tool Utilisation

Our findings reveal persistent challenges in network simulation tools like CORE/EMANE, originally developed for a military context, reflecting shortcomings common in general-purpose network simulation tools. Our findings align with prior research highlighting the persistence of challenges across various simulation platforms when used for specific domains and industries [46]. The identified fragmentation issues hinder project consistency, causing disjointed simulations and requiring substantial time and effort. Incompatibility can lead to time-consuming workarounds and may even require custom development to bridge the gaps between tools. It is not uncommon for simulations to produce outputs that are incompatible with each other, making analysis and interpretation difficult.

In addition to compatibility challenges, the increased learning curve associated with multiple tools can slow down project progress. Team members must invest time in learning how to use each tool effectively. This complexity may result in a knowledge gap within the team, where some members are proficient in one tool while others are experts in another, further complicating collaboration. As projects grow in complexity or scale, the challenges associated with using multiple tools become more pronounced. Scalability becomes an issue when juggling multiple tools, data sharing and results across multiple tools can be cumbersome; this can lead to data loss, errors, and additional manual work.

5.3 Open-Source Nature of the Tools

Unlike commercial simulators, open-source projects often suffer from insufficient resources and contributions dedicated to documentation [7]. As a result, understanding and tracing codes across different versions can become challenging, hindering efficient development and troubleshooting. This aligns with prior work conclusions that although these tools benefit from openness and community contributions, they are affected by the lack of proper documentation [32,37]. With a broader range of contributors, maintaining systematic and complete documentation becomes more difficult, leading to potential gaps in understanding and utilising the tools.

Another related shortcoming is the lack of robust version control support and API integration. As open-source simulation tools evolve with new features and updates, the lack of version control can make it hard to manage changes and ensure backward compatibility [23,30]. Users may find it challenging to migrate from older versions to newer ones, impacting the longevity and applicability of open-source simulation tools.

5.4 Emerging Technologies Integration

Integrating emerging technologies like AI, 5G, and 6G into CORE/EMANE presents significant opportunities for enhancing the tool's adaptability and scalability. For instance, incorporating AI could enable real-time automation of network parameters, making simulations more responsive to dynamic conditions.

This approach has already been explored in other tools, such as NS-3, where ns3-ai toolkit enhances data transmission speeds and supports complex AI-driven tasks, such as Channel Quality Indicator (CQI) prediction [47]. This setup lays the groundwork for the potential use of applications to optimise network parameters and resource allocation, thereby improving the responsiveness and efficiency of network simulations. Additionally, support for advanced network standards like 5G could expand CORE/EMANE's utility in simulating ultra-low latency and high-throughput environments, aligning it with the capabilities found in simulators like NetSim [40]. Incorporating these technologies into CORE/EMANE, alongside user-centered design improvements such as interactive visualisations, could enhance user experience and streamline the simulation process, meeting the needs of both novice and experienced users.

6 Conclusion

Addressing the growing demand for network simulations, our research offers key insights into professionals' needs, challenges, and opportunities when working with these tools. Addressing technical and usability issues is crucial, necessitating the integration of new technical capabilities alongside enhanced usability considerations. Our mixed-methods approach, involving both a questionnaire and a design workshop, addressed three key research questions regarding the essential features, strengths and weaknesses, and future expectations for network simulation tools. The findings provide insights into the shortcomings and future potential of these tools, particularly from a user-centered perspective.

In response to RQ1, professionals highlighted essential capabilities such as real-time adaptability, scalability, and accurate modeling of network scenarios. CORE/EMANE's strengths in offering open-source, flexibility, and extensive customisation were valued. However, limitations in usability and GUI design, as well as challenges with radio propagation modeling, restricted its applicability.

Subsequently, RQ2 addressed the strengths and weaknesses of network simulation tools. While CORE/EMANE was praised for its adaptability, the study revealed significant weaknesses in terms of steep learning curves, fragmented tool functionality, and the lack of robust visualisation features. These limitations make it challenging for both novice and experienced users to fully leverage the tool's potential, often resulting in workarounds or dependence on additional tools to meet specific needs.

Finally, RQ3 focused on how professionals envision the evolution of these tools. Participants expressed a clear need for the integration of emerging technologies to improve both usability and scalability. Suggestions for future improvements included user-friendly interfaces, enhanced visualisation capabilities for real-time tracking, and automation features that reduce manual configuration time. A more intuitive, customisable interface and dynamic visualisations were highlighted as priorities for addressing both technical requirements and enhancing the user experience.

Our study highlights the need for network simulation tools that not only meet technical demands but also prioritise usability. By addressing the challenges identified and incorporating user-centered design principles, future developments can improve accessibility and efficiency, making tools like CORE/EMANE more adaptable to evolving professional needs.

References

1. EMANE Integration - CORE Network Emulator. https://coreemu.github.io/core/emane.html. Accessed 15 Apr 2024
2. The network simulator. https://www.isi.edu/nsnam/ns/. Accessed 20 July 2023
3. Riverbed Support: OPNET Modeler. https://support.riverbed.com/content/support//software/opnet-model/modeler.html. Accessed 14 Feb 2025
4. Huawei 6G Research Team: 6G - the next horizon (2021). https://www.huawei.com/en/huaweitech/future-technologies/6g-the-next-horizon. Accessed 03 Jan 2024
5. Ahrenholz, J., Danilov, C., Henderson, T.R., Kim, J.H.: Core: a real-time network emulator. In: MILCOM 2008-2008 IEEE Military Communications Conference, pp. 1–7. IEEE (2008)
6. Ahrenholz, J., Goff, T., Adamson, B.: Integration of the core and emane network emulators. In: 2011-MILCOM 2011 Military Communications Conference, pp. 1870–1875. IEEE (2011)
7. Ayala, C., Hauge, Ø., Conradi, R., Franch, X., Li, J., Velle, K.S.: Challenges of the open source component marketplace in the industry. In: Boldyreff, C., Crowston, K., Lundell, B., Wasserman, A.I. (eds.) OSS 2009. IAICT, vol. 299, pp. 213–224. Springer, Heidelberg (2009). https://doi.org/10.1007/978-3-642-02032-2_19
8. Bajpai, V., Schönwälder, J.: A survey on internet performance measurement platforms and related standardization efforts. IEEE Commun. Surv. Tutor. **17**(3), 1313–1341 (2015)
9. Bilalb, S.M., Othmana, M., et al.: A performance comparison of network simulators for wireless networks. arXiv preprint arXiv:1307.4129 (2013)
10. Braun, V., Clarke, V.: Using thematic analysis in psychology. Qual. Res. Psychol. **3**(2), 77–101 (2006)
11. Braun, V., Clarke, V.: Can I use TA? Should I use TA? Should I not use TA? Comparing reflexive thematic analysis and other pattern-based qualitative analytic approaches. Couns. Psychother. Res. **21**(1), 37–47 (2021)
12. Chéour, R., Jmal, M.W., Lay-Ekuakille, A., Derbel, F., Kanoun, O., Abid, M.: Choice of efficient simulator tool for wireless sensor networks. In: 2013 IEEE International Workshop on Measurements & Networking (M&N), pp. 210–213. IEEE (2013)
13. Davis, F.D.: Perceived usefulness, perceived ease of use, and user acceptance of information technology. MIS Q. 319–340 (1989)
14. Dilla, W., Janvrin, D.J., Raschke, R.: Interactive data visualization: new directions for accounting information systems research. J. Inf. Syst. **24**(2), 1–37 (2010)
15. Dinesh, S., Sonal, G.: Qualnet simulator. Int. J. Inf. Comput. Technol. (2014). ISSN 0974-2239
16. El-Mouaffak, A., El Alaoui, A.E.B.: Considering the environment's characteristics in wireless networks simulations and emulations: case of popular simulators and WSN. In: Proceedings of the 3rd International Conference on Networking, Information Systems & Security, pp. 1–4 (2020)

17. Ericsson: 6G - follow the journey to the next generation networks - Ericsson (n.d.). https://www.ericsson.com/en/6g. Accessed 03 Jan 2024
18. Falschlunger, L., Lehner, O., Treiblmaier, H.: Infovis: the impact of information overload on decision making outcome in high complexity settings. In: SIGHCI 2016 Proceedings (2016). https://aisel.aisnet.org/sighci2016/3, paper 3
19. Gettinger, J., Koeszegi, S.T., Schoop, M.: Shall we dance?-the effect of information presentations on negotiation processes and outcomes. Decis. Support Syst. **53**(1), 161–174 (2012)
20. Gökarslan, K.: Menes: towards a generic, fully-automated test and validation platform for wireless networks. arXiv preprint arXiv:2006.02270 (2020)
21. Guimaraes, V.T., Freitas, C., Sadre, R., Tarouco, L., Granville, L.Z.: A survey on information visualization for network and service management. IEEE Commun. Surv. Tutor. **18**(1), 285–323 (2015)
22. Henderson, T.R., Roy, S., Floyd, S., Riley, G.F.: ns-3 project goals. In: Proceedings of the 2006 Workshop on ns-3, pp. 13–es (2006)
23. Jaaksi, A.: Experiences on product development with open source software. In: IFIP International Conference on Open Source Systems, pp. 85–96. Springer, Cham (2007)
24. Khan, A.R., Bilal, S.M., Othman, M.: A performance comparison of open source network simulators for wireless networks. In: 2012 IEEE International Conference on Control System, Computing and Engineering, pp. 34–38. IEEE (2012)
25. Kojo, M., Gurtov, A.V., Manner, J., Sarolahti, P., Alanko, T.O., Raatikainen, K.E.: Seawind: a wireless network emulator. In: MMB, pp. 151–166 (2001)
26. Kumar, A., Kaushik, S.K., Sharma, R., Raj, P.: Simulators for wireless networks: a comparative study. In: 2012 International Conference on Computing Sciences, pp. 338–342. IEEE (2012)
27. Lessmann, J., Janacik, P., Lachev, L., Orfanus, D.: Comparative study of wireless network simulators. In: Seventh International Conference on Networking (ICN 2008), pp. 517–523. IEEE (2008)
28. Lurie, N.H., Mason, C.H.: Visual representation: implications for decision making. J. Mark. **71**(1), 160–177 (2007)
29. Mahajan, R., Wetherall, D., Anderson, T.: Understanding BGP misconfiguration. ACM SIGCOMM Comput. Commun. Rev. **32**(4), 3–16 (2002)
30. Merilinna, J., Matinlassi, M.: State of the art and practice of opensource component integration. In: 32nd EUROMICRO Conference on Software Engineering and Advanced Applications (EUROMICRO 2006), pp. 170–177. IEEE (2006)
31. Mlekus, L., Bentler, D., Paruzel, A., Kato-Beiderwieden, A.L., Maier, G.W.: How to raise technology acceptance: user experience characteristics as technologyinherent determinants. Gruppe. Interaktion. Organisation. Zeitschrift für Angewandte Organisationspsychologie (GIO) **51**(3), 273–283 (2020)
32. Pan, J., Jain, R.: A survey of network simulation tools: current status and future developments. Email: jp10@ cse. wustl. edu **2**(4), 45 (2008)
33. Pretorius, M.C., Calitz, A.P., van Greunen, D.: The added value of eye tracking in the usability evaluation of a network management tool. In: ACM International Conference Proceeding Series, vol. 150, pp. 1–10 (2005)
34. Quiñones, D., Rusu, C.: How to develop usability heuristics: a systematic literature review. Comput. Stand. Interfaces **53**, 89–122 (2017)
35. Riliskis, L., Osipov, E.: Maestro: an orchestration framework for large-scale WSN simulations. Sensors **14**(3), 5392–5414 (2014)
36. Schroder, H.M., Driver, M.J., Streufert, S.: Human information processing: individuals and groups functioning in complex social situations (1967)

37. Sethi, A., Saini, J., Bisht, M.: Wireless adhoc network simulators: analysis of characterstic features, scalability, effectiveness and limitations. Int. J. Appl. Inf. Syst. (IJAIS) **5**(9) (2012)
38. Silveira, S.A., Zaina, L.A., Sampaio, L.N., Verdi, F.L.: On the evaluation of usability design guidelines for improving network monitoring tools interfaces. J. Syst. Softw. **187**, 111223 (2022)
39. Sundani, H., Li, H., Devabhaktuni, V., Alam, M., Bhattacharya, P.: Wireless sensor network simulators a survey and comparisons. Int. J. Comput. Netw. **2**(5), 249–265 (2011)
40. TETCOS: 5G network simulator for R&D and academics (2024). https://tetcos.com/5g.html. Accessed 02 Nov 2024
41. Toor, A.S., Jain, A.: A survey on wireless network simulators. Bull. Electr. Eng. Inform. **6**(1), 62–69 (2017)
42. Richards V, T.A., Gamess, E., Thornton, D.: A survey of wireless network simulation and/or emulation software for use in higher education. In: ACM Southeast Conference, pp. 63–70 (2021)
43. Varga, A.: Omnet++. In: Modeling and Tools for Network Simulation, pp. 35–59. Springer, Cham (2010)
44. Verdi, F.L., de Oliveira, H.T., Sampaio, L.N., Zaina, L.A.: Usability matters: a human-computer interaction study on network management tools. IEEE Trans. Netw. Serv. Manag. **17**(3), 1865–1878 (2020)
45. Yang, J., Edwards, W.K.: A study on network management tools of householders. In: Proceedings of the 2010 ACM SIGCOMM Workshop on Home Networks, pp. 1–6 (2010)
46. Yao, F., Liang, Q., Xu, R., Tong, L.: Some key issues on modeling and simulation of military communication network. In: 2012 International Conference on Computer Science and Electronics Engineering, vol. 1, pp. 532–535. IEEE (2012)
47. Yin, H., et al.: ns3-AI: fostering artificial intelligence algorithms for networking research. In: Proceedings of the 2020 Workshop on ns-3, pp. 57–64 (2020)

Author Index

A. A. Juan et al. (Eds.): SIMUtools 2024, LNICST 603, pp. 419–420, 2025.
https://doi.org/10.1007/978-3-031-87345-4

The manufacturer's authorised representative in the EU is Springer Nature Customer Service Centre GmbH, Europaplatz 3, 69115 Heidelberg, Germany. If you have any concerns regarding our products, please contact ProductSafety@springernature.com

Printed and bound by CPI Group (UK) Ltd, Croydon, CR0 4YY
01/10/2026
02225951-0019